# TALES OF SANAWAR

# TALES OF SANAWAR

Curated by

## PANKAJ SAPRU

PENGUIN
ENTERPRISE

An imprint of Penguin Random House

PENGUIN ENTERPRISE

USA | Canada | UK | Ireland | Australia
New Zealand | India | South Africa | China

Penguin Enterprise is part of the Penguin Random House group of companies
whose addresses can be found at global.penguinrandomhouse.com

Published by Penguin Random House India Pvt. Ltd
4th Floor, Capital Tower 1, MG Road,
Gurugram 122 002, Haryana, India

First published in Penguin Enterprise by Penguin Random House India 2022

ISBN 9780670097227

Typeset in Adobe Caslon Pro
Printed at Thomson Press India Ltd, New Delhi

www.penguin.co.in

*To all those who have kept the spirit of Sanawar alive*

# Contents

# Disclaimer

This book is an effort to bring together the experiences and stories of Sanawarians in their own words, based on their own imperfect recollections of events that have long since transpired. While all efforts have been made to accurately and fairly depict the events and experiences, the publisher and the author(s) do not take any responsibility for errors, inaccuracies, omissions, or any other inconsistencies herein, and hereby disclaim any liability to any party for loss, damage or disruption caused by the same.

The disciplinary methods referred to in this book may have been applied on occasion in the period in question and were in keeping with the values and customs of the time. However, it is clarified that corporal punishment was not employed at the school and none of the authors endorse or support corporal punishment.

The authors' sentiments towards their school, teachers and other students are characterized by deep affection and nostalgia. The intention of this book is not to hurt anyone's sentiments or be biased in favour of or against any particular person, community, profession, region, linguistic identity, caste, religion or gender.

# Foreword

One of the best ways of getting to know a school, its ethos and the education imparted there is to listen to its students' stories. Commemorating the 175th anniversary of Sanawar with a compendium of stories of memories of former students is an ideal way of conveying the essence of a school. Anecdotes about escapades, teachers, great sporting wins or losses, of peaks climbed and even of the porridge at breakfast, of dorms and baths, of Founders' and Trooping of Colours. All these are what makes a school a living, vibrant institution and remain in our memory long after the school becomes a distant marker in the story of one's life.

The learning at Sanawar is so much more than studies, homework, the passing of exams and the drudgery of the syllabus. Indeed, the tyranny imposed by the syllabus completely obfuscates the learning and so many schools fall prey to it. Not Sanawar. Learning goes on for several hours outside the classroom as well—in dorms, on treks, on playing fields, in the art room, the library or the CDH. And what memories! The wonderful moments of sharing joy and happiness, and the sadder moments of weeping on a friend's shoulder, all coalesce into one and remain as punctuations in the story of life. A full stop here, a comma there and paragraphs waiting to be recalled: at a reunion, when a mother or father point their offspring to a name board in the library, or at the cannons where they met their future partners or their memories of marching down to Chapel. These things liberated and saved the Sanawarian from becoming a robot, regurgitating in parrot fashion the books that one carried up the hill to Birdwood.

The stories here reflect the common thread that weaves its way down the ages for every student who walked the campus. I thoroughly enjoyed reading these stories which brought to life the undying love of generations of students for their alma mater. Several moving pieces struck me as they showed the impact that the beauty of the campus had on its denizens, while others that described the deep relationships formed between student and teacher, and all that they learnt from them. The ones that stood out for me

include 'The March of Time', 'Frames Etched in My Mind', 'Bandy Room and the Bhuttas', 'Ode to My Teachers' and 'To Sir with Love'. The trek to Ozark is recounted in another piece that must bring back memories to countless Sanawarians. How could one not remember climbing the Chapel steeple or firing the cannon? The walking-out pass and the bunsums in Kasauli, too, remain a part of the fond memories of schooldays.

Sanawar had on its campus a myriad characters. The rough and tough hero, the sensitive artist or the poet, the jolly boisterous 'jack in the box' who couldn't be suppressed, or the nerd who did well in academics no matter the hurdles, or indeed, the beautiful graceful dancer mesmerizing the audience at a Founders' show. The actor, the sportsman, the artist, the con guy, the math wizard and the 'chamcha', all lived on the magical campus and drew inspiration from it. The stories in this compendium reflect all this and more. You might think the students remember only their friends and teachers. Read how while marching down to Chapel, some noticed the wisteria cascading down the wall or the view of Kasauli's twinkling lights as they contemplated a *bhutta* raid.

The seasons changed and so did the mood. One remembers the cold winter's morning when the blue sky was brighter than bright and the Dhauladhar was glistening with icy peaks; walking on Short Back, how one lingered a moment to soak in that spiritual experience. One remembers, too, the sunshine holidays which, after days of drenching under gloomy dark clouds, brought such joy and excitement. Watching the wispy cottonwool clouds that floated up the valley to wrap the campus in mist and mystery, and made dreamers of every one. These were the indelible footprints in the sands of time.

A century from now, the campus may have transformed yet again, as it has so many times—who can predict the future? But the magic and exhilaration experienced will remain as it has, for the past 175 years.

My prayers and good wishes for a great future for the 'best school of all'.

**Shomie Ranjan Das**
Headmaster 1974–1988

# Acknowledgement

Subsequent to my seven years of schooling, my visits to the hilltop became frequent and extended between 1989 to 1996, when my brother, Dhiraj (H-1985) taught in Prep School. The aura of Sanawar, although forever alive within, was rekindled to become even more vivid and I, for the first time, began contemplating on writing my enthralling recollections of those sunshine years. However, being predisposed to staying true to fact and not fictionalizing the narrative, my scripts remained anecdotal and episodic. Failing to string them together into a 'complete' story, 'my book' remained an unexpressed and unfulfilled dream.

And then in September 2020, while ideating at an OSS executive meeting on what all we could do to commemorate our school's 175th foundation year, that latent desire of bringing alive those memories took centre stage, clearly a *eureka* moment came about: 175 years = 175 stories! Without giving it a second thought, I settled for a working title – which, as it turns out, could not have been more appropriate – and thus was born *Tales of Sanawar*!

The Book would have continued to be an unspoken aspiration but for numerous aficionados who converged, as if ordained by the forces of the universe, to make it happen. And it is my cardinal duty to give credit where it is due.

At the outset, I am deeply obliged to both, Maj. Gen. Kulpreet Singh, under whose presidency the first seed of the project was sown, and the current President, OSS Maj. Sanjeev Sharma, for entrusting me with this first-of-its-kind project; reassuring me at every step from the start to the finish line—from the conceptualization, content creation, design, typesetting, publication, to the pre-ordering of the book.

The first mammoth task of scouting for 175 stories turned out to be the most enriching experience of this momentous journey. Reaching out to the fraternity through batch and chapter coordinators presented me with the enviable opportunity to associate with, without exaggeration, hundreds of

Old Sanawarians of all vintages. Although it is impossible to name all 141 authors who played an eloquent part in the making of *Tales of Sanawar*, I would like to applaud a select few extraordinary endeavours.

I salute the Super Seniors for their concerted, dogged determination to stay true to the course—Vikram Soni (V-1952), Timothy Carter (H-1953), Dewan Ramesh Chand (S-1953), Nanda K.C. Cariappa (V-1954), Col. H.S. 'Billy' Sodhi (H-1954), James L.C. Coombes (H-1954), Lt. Gen. Tajinder 'Maun' Shergill (V-1958), Sarabjit Arjan Singh (V-1958), Harjit Kochhar (N-1958), Lila Kak Bhan (S-1958), Col. Rupinder Brar (S-1959), Aroon Gidwani Shivdasani (N-1961), Jai Singh Gill (H-1961), Navin B. Chawla (H-1961), Arjun Batra (V-1964), Champa Banerjee (N-1964), Dr Harbans Nagpal (N-1964), Tonsing 'Vunga' Vunglallian (N-1967), Preminda Batra Langer (V-1970), Vivek Mehra (H-1971) and Gen. Gaurav S.J.B. Rana (H-1972). Some other Super Seniors find mention under a different category.

I am grateful to the Published Writers, who took time out from their flourishing literary careers to contribute to this venture: Maj. Gen. AJS 'Abdo' Sandhu (V-1962), Aditya Raj Kapoor (S-1972), Dr Mininder Kaur (N-1975), Rohit Brijnath (H-1981), Mohyna Khurana Srinivasan (N-1981), Himmat Dhillon (V-1989), Pooja Bedi (S-1989), Omar Abdullah (V-1989), Chirag Jain (S-1995), Rajika Bhandari (H-1988), Rahat Mahajan (S-2004) and Sagat Shaunik (N-2009). Many of them went the extra mile to obtain copyright clearances from their erstwhile or present publishers.

A special word of appreciation for the Pacesetters, for fast-tracking this creative co-creation expedition by giving me the permission to select stories from their year book(s) which were brought out to commemorate their batch's golden jubilee: Ashok Bhatia (1953), Gita Bery Bhatia (1954), Sanjaya Varma (1964) and Kalpana Johri Saran (1969).

I respect the True Leaders for lighting a fire under their batchmates and pushing them to meet the timelines: Vinay Chopra Tuli (1961), Anjali 'Thappo' Khosla (1984), Col. Nirmaljit S Pannu (1964), Bhupi Aggarwal and Aruna Mongia (1967), Tarun Sawney (1979), Neville Wadia (1986) and Shubh Mangal (1996).

I acknowledge the industriousness of the Busy Bees, who did not stop at one story and continued to stride forward, submitting *two*: Vinay Chopra Tuli (S-1961), Vivek Umesh Mundkur (S-1961), Siddharth Kak (V-1963), Zafarullah Khan (S-1965), DIG Dilbagh S. Sidhu (H-1969), Dr Vasant Dhar (N-1972), Tarun Sawney (V-1979), Sajan Sethi

(H-1981), Sanjeet Bajwa (V-1982), Anjali 'Thappo' Khosla (N-1984), Anuradha Varma Bhatt (N-1984), Jaimal S. Shergill (V-1985), Himmat S. Dhillon (V-1989), Col. H.P.S. Sidhu (N-1989), Maneet Singh (N-2001) and Aradhye Ackshatt (H-2003). Some others went a step further to submit *three*: Lt. Gen. Tajinder 'Maun' Shergill (V-1958), Rakesh Sood (V-1965), Dr Mininder Kaur (N-1975) and Chiraj Jain (S-1995). Ravinder Raizada (S-1969) and Harjaspreet Gill (S-1979) sent in *four*. I, myself, dear reader, surrendered to temptation and eventually wrote *eight*!

A special thank you to Mr Vinay Pande (Headmaster 2016–19) for taking the time to author 'The Ghosts of Sanawar'.

Eighteen months! 190 tales in all!

It would not have been humanly possible to edit the 2,46,078-word manuscript on my own. I stand in recognition of the devotion and diligence of Lalit Varma (V-1964), Sanjaya Varma (V-1964), Zafarullah Khan (S-1965), Harveen Sachdeva Mann (H-1973), Vivek Ahluwalia (N-1975), Mrinalini Dhadha Watson (H-1976), Mohyna Khurana Srinivasan (N-1981), Samyukta Kumari (H-1987), Mahima Mehta Anand (H-1997) and Aradhye Ackshatt (H-2003). These ten burned the midnight oil, way beyond 'lights-out' to help me organize the manuscript for publication.

I cannot thank Derek Boddington (Roberts-1947) enough. The 190 tales spanned across the period from 1948 to the present day, and therefore, *Tales of Sanawar* remained incomplete, with more than 100-odd years of Sanawar's journey still remaining unreported. I reached out to Derek, our very own historian, who willingly consented to unrestricted access and reproduction from his well-researched, archival treasure 'The Lawrence Royal Military School SANAWAR' (https://freepages. rootsweb.com/~derekboddington/school-alumni/index.html).

I have included twenty-seven chronicles that take the reader back in time, from the founding of the Lawrence Royal Military Asylum in 1847 to the Independence of India in 1947.

A thank you is also in order to the current headmaster, Mr Himmat Dhillon (V-1989) for his generosity in granting permission to reproduce thirty-six commentaries that provide a vivid description of the post-Independence years, which I extracted from various editions of the school's annual magazine, *The Sanawarian*. Authors featured include William Gaskell, T.A.C. Kemp, E.G. Carter, V.W. Carter, William H. 'Bill' Colledge, Bhupinder Singh, Romola Chattterji, Major R. Som Dutt, Maneka Anand Gandhi, U.A. Mundkur, Gulshan Ewing and Manjari Khan.

Other members of the staff whose articles were submitted from other sources, include Mrs Joy Coombes, Mr Rathin Mitra, Mrs Gomti Vyas, Mr M.V. Gore and Dr D.C. Gupta.

I would like to place on record the efforts of Maneet Singh (N-2001) in acquiring the copyrights to make available six enchanting short stories from the published collection of middles, *Of Cabbages and Kings*, authored by the late Dr Harishpal Dhillon. I would like to mention here that other than these six middles, the book also contains other stories written by him in different avatars, as Harishpal, the OS (N-1957); U.D., the English teacher and Housemaster (1971–1986); and Dr Dhillon, the Headmaster (1995–1999).

I must give credit to Vasant Dhar (N-1972), who dived into his Sanawarnet archives to unearth five masterpieces written by George Browne (Havelock 1937), which transports the reader back to the Sanawar of the 1930s.

I sincerely applaud the stunning sketches rendered by Mr Rathin Mitra, Art Master 1950–53, who remains among India's most celebrated visual essayists; Birinder Malhans (V-1955), Illoosh Judge (H-1979), Ina Mehta, the current Art Teacher in school, and eleven of her most gifted OS students: Georgina Maddox (V-1994), Rajdeep Ranawat (S-1997), Bhavya Grover (H-2014), Kudrat Kashyap (H-2014), Karyna Thapa (N-2016), Aveeva Palta Dhillon (S-2016), Navrup Kaur (H-2017), Jasmine Chauhan (H-2019), Jivika Sachdev (S-2020), Vashima Mansukhani (S-2020) and Kripang Kashyap (H-2021). I had envisioned that *Tales of Sanawar* would end up as a collector's piece—a classic in its purest state. From the start, I was unwavering with regard to its aesthetics—no photographs, not even in black-and-white, but solely pencil line sketches that would be interwoven with the tales, to complete the Sanawar experience. The eighty-eight sketches herein bring the pristine 139-acre campus to life.

I'm forever indebted to 'Heady' Mr Shomie Ranjan Das, who has the unique distinction of being Headmaster, Mayo College, Ajmer (1968–1974), The Lawrence School, Sanawar (1974–88) and The Doon School, Dehradun (1988–1996), for consenting to write the foreword to *Tales of Sanawar*. He asked me to mail him some forty-five-odd tales, which he read before penning his thoughts on Sanawar; what it takes to become a Sanawarian; and a personal account of the fourteen years that he lived on the hilltop—his longest stint as Headmaster.

After eighteen months, the first-cut edit of the manuscript was finally in the bag. I then began my search for a recognized, reputed publisher as I was convinced from day one that readers do not take self-published authors seriously. In my master plan, the target audience of *Tales of Sanawar* was not confined to the Sanawarians—old, not-so-old or young. The book was curated to be an unputdownable read for anyone who has experienced the ups and downs of life in a boarding school or would like to do so.

My deepest gratitude to Archana Pratap Shankar (H-1980) for encouraging me to aim for the best and directing me to Penguin Random House India.

I would like to commend Gursharan 'Gugi' Sandhu (Batch Coordinator 1988) for introducing me to his batchmate, Gaurav Shrinagesh (H-1988), now CEO, Penguin Random House India and South East Asia. At the end of our fifteen-minute conversation, Gaurav had decided to put his money on the winning horse.

And finally, a big thank you to Gaurav and his brilliant team at Penguin, without whom *Tales of Sanawar* could not have seen the light of day.

Gaurav put me in touch with Milee Ashwarya, Publisher, Ebury and Vintage Publishing. Milee and her team read the manuscript in its entirety, and were favourably disposed to it. She opined that the custom publishing route was better suited and suggested I explore the same with Penguin Enterprise.

With this in view, Gaurav introduced me to Sameer Mahale, Associate VP – Sales (eCommerce and North), who in turn introduced me to Ankit Juneja, DGM – Special Projects. Over the next seven months, Ankit and I, with valuable inputs from Sanjeev and Sameer, worked on every detail of the publication. Sumer Brar, Member OSS Executive ironed out the commercial contract between the OSS and PRH India.

In conclusion, I would like to say that although bringing the *Tales of Sanawar* to life was challenging, it has been far more rewarding and gratifying than I could ever have imagined. It would not have been possible without the unconditional support of each and every person involved . . .

Last but not the least, I would like to acknowledge and express my loving gratitude to Mridula, my wife. She has been an integral part of this two-year journey, standing by me through thick and thin, encouraging and pushing me every step of the way to realize my dream: *Tales of Sanawar*.

Happy Reading!

**Pankaj Sapru**
Vice President
The Old Sanawarian Society

# The Lawrence School, Sanawar (Simla Hills)

Past the War Memorial, the ante porch of the School Chapel reads: 'In memory of the Founder by Col. Herbert Edwards 1858'. The elegant, neat little Chapel is perhaps the oldest of the surviving buildings and within its sombre and stately interior, is a niche with the bust of the Founder, Sir Henry Lawrence, gazing out into eternity. The clean-cut features, the determined list of the chin and a kindly but firm mouth bespeak of a man of lofty vision, great ideals and a humane approach. To those who have read passages from the biography of Sir Henry Lawrence, a vision emerges of a man – a great man – whose humanity transgressed the narrow limits of race, creed or nationality. And it is indeed a proud privilege of The Lawrence School, Sanawar, that it should have been the fruit of the vision of this man.

Established in 1847 as an asylum for the children of the British other ranks from the squalid barrack-room conditions, the school made a start in April or May 1847, with about fourteen children of both sexes; the task of building being entrusted to Hodson of Hodson's Horse fame, the first bursar of the school. And throughout the remaining spans of their respective existence, it remained the personal responsibility of Sir Henry and his wife Honoria.

Parker, the first principal of the school, must have passed through a haranguing period as he struggled to give 'infant' Sanawar its identity—an identity which steadily but surely established itself as Sanawar moved from strength to strength. It must have indeed been a day amongst days when the notification appeared in the *Gazette of India* dated 16 October 1920 that His Majesty King George V was pleased to approve of the institution being designated as 'The Lawrence Royal Military School, Sanawar'. And amidst the varying sentiments of the OS, the universal emotion may best be summed up in what H.C.B. Whitly had to say when he wrote back, 'This is indeed a great honour conferred on the Old School, which it has truly earned and is well-deserving of, and I write to congratulate the teachers and pupils heartily on the honour conferred.'

Amongst the stalwarts who laboured and struggled for the school, no name stands out as prominently as that of Barnes, during whose tenure of office emerged the 'Modern Sanawar'. He instituted the House system, organized the prefectorial system, placed games on an organized basis and introduced educational innovations and reforms which placed Sanawar amongst the premier educational institutions within the country. His death in 1954 was mourned by Sanawarians the world over.

Sanawar of yesteryears, as of today, came to acquire a distinct soul of its own. It became a living, breathing and pulsating entity, with a body of honoured and cherished traditions—traditions woven into an intricate pattern binding Old Sanawarians, scattered across the four corners of the globe, into close ties of brotherhood and camaraderie. If not here, then where would one find the living example of integration—not only national but international?

And the motto 'Never Give In' was not conceived in vain. Sanawar and Sanawarians have weathered many a storm, keeping that motto in view. 1947, the centenary year, though presided over by Lord Mountbatten with a special message from the King, was yet indeed a bleak year for Sanawar, as it saw the mass exodus of the British children. The fate of the school was in doldrums. The first term of 1948 commenced with only forty-eight children. One mistress had only one pupil, George Wake, in her form. A dreary future! The Ministry of Defence passed on the baby to the Ministry of Education. It was decided that it would be run as a public school. On 1 January 1953, the school subsequently passed on into the hands of an autonomous Board of Governors. Lean years and thin years! But the school emerged triumphant and today, it has flowered into a major public school with a definite contribution to the life of the country, continuing to send out men and women into the world, who in keeping with the best traditions of the public school, will fit in and adjust themselves in any walk of public life.

'The tremendous thing about Sanawar is that children learn to do everything the hard way', remarked a distinguished visiting headmaster of a well-known public school as he watched children moving downhill and uphill, from games to hobbies, swimming to House dramatics, to fall-in for meals and march up to 'The silent hour'—the evening prep. Everything done to split-second timing. A hard day ahead? Not for a Sanawarian. The early morning reveille, even though it be in the chill of a late November morning, finds both boys and girls jumping out of bed, going through their morning physical jerks and then following the whole gamut of the day's chores—classes, games and a host of co-curricular activities. For the boys: carpentry, crafts, gymnastics, music/band, and after a vigorous exchange in the boxing ring, he sits down complacently to study for the next day's biology test. Rudyard Kipling would be proud – God bless his soul – that the adage from his *Kim*, 'send him to Sanawar and make a man of him' continues to hold good. With due apologies to Kipling from Elizabeth Lincoln Otis in *An If For Girls* which, for years, has occupied a place of honour in the 'cloisters':

> 'If you can ply a saw and use a hammer
> can do a man's work when the need occurs'.

The Sanawar girl is an example of sheer perseverance. Whether it be the feminine grace at dancing, the delicate touch at embroidery, the feeling note on the piano; the soulful engrossment on the veena, *israj*, sitar, violin or the *jaltarang*—all belie the mettle of the Sanawar girl when she marches shoulder-to-shoulder with the Sanawar boy. She holds her own when they meet on the common field of debating and dramatics. In Sanawar, there is not a moment to sit and stare and R.L. Stevenson's prayer, read out in turn at Assembly: 'The day returns and brings us the usual round of duties and concerns, help us to perform what we have to do with smiling faces; let cheerfulness abound with industry; give us to go blithely on our business all the day and bring us to our resting beds, weary and content and un-dishonoured, and grant us in the end the gift of sleep', was perhaps, essentially, meant as a compliment for Sanawar.

October heralds the Founders' week; 'the eternal lure of Founder's. Sanawar . . . the vast expanse of Barnes thrills to Athletics . . . a rather lively coffee session. And let me go on record to say that the staff of Sanawar are truly the staff of Sanawar—harried, hard-pressed, overworked and imposed upon, they are a valiant and ever-smiling corps of dedicated men and women, to whom I would like to convey admiration and gratitude on behalf of all the visiting parents. The staff play—hilarious. The Prep School concert, always the most charming. And then the torchlight Tattoo, preceded by a grand PT display, enthralling acrobatics and the marvellous bugle band. The Trooping of the Colour was always the most inspiring item at Founders'. The sombre occasion of speeches; the main school concert; but not without mention of the art, crafts and needlework exhibition, were first-class; the very enjoyable Fete with its usual motto: 'Fleece the Parents. And so another Founders' is over', coined by Gulshan Ewing. A parent remarked, 'It is incredible that you achieve what you do, after all this, by way of results.'

Then comes the sombre atmosphere of studies and final examinations—the day dips to dusk and the last post is sounded. 'Never Give In' is our motto . . . and we live in that motto's powers till the last bugle call'. The school song is sung. Somewhere in Shakargarh area, the last post was sounded—Arun Khetarpal stuck to his guns. He stood at his post 'like a boy from Sanawar' (Rudyard Kipling's *Stalky & Co.*).

**Bhupinder Singh**
Staff | Deputy Headmaster 1970–1993

**Source and Acknowledgement:** *Souvenir Brochure 1847–1972*

# Message from the King to the Lawrence Royal Military School Sanawar, on the occasion of its centenary celebration.

BUCKINGHAM PALACE

Many great events have happened in India during 1947 and not least of them is the celebration of your famous school of its centenary.

As you all know, the school was originally for the sons and daughters of the British soldiers. Recently it has entered a new phase of its life, and it is now open to both Indian and British alike. Your school is therefore marching along with the times.

It is in the school and on the playing fields where bonds of friendship are formed. You children who come from different parts of the world therefore have a unique opportunity to form close bonds of friendship which will not be broken as you grow up.

By building up faith and trust in each other and with other people of the world you will do a great service to mankind.

The Queen and I wish you and your school every success in the future.

23rd September 1947                                             GEORGE R.

# Founders' Day Parade 1947

Despite the significance of the occasion, Founder's Day Parade and Trooping of the Colour for the centenary celebrations in October 1947 was a lean, austere and very simple affair compared to former times. The new date for India's Independence had been announced earlier in the year and the partition of the subcontinent had become imminent sooner than expected. Parents anxious for the safety of their children began to withdraw them from school and department strengths diminished daily throughout the early part of the year.

For this hugely important parade, the school only just managed to field three guards, each about fifteen-strong. The band, which in former times could boast the same number of musicians as any Regimental band in India, was reduced to a few bugles and drums. The second band Master had already left some months earlier and the direction of the band fell to the senior bugler. The Chief Instructor WOI (RSM) Davies who formerly ruled the parade ground with a rod of iron, did not return for the '47 school term. His place was taken by WOII 'Jock' Watt APTC. Jock was an exceptionally good physical training instructor but knew little or nothing about foot drill and parade ground protocols. So for this important parade, we were drilled and knocked into some semblance of order by Sgt. Willis, the weapons and drill instructor! We also relied to some extent on the 'corporate' knowledge of the senior boys, who had been through the parade routines and protocols many times before.

The School 'dharzis' (tailors), all three of them Muslims, had left for the newly settled border with the rest of their brethren, the previous month, so on this of all occasions, we paraded in our everyday barrack dress and not the usual full Service Parade uniforms. The parade format was also radically revised and simplified. The Advance in Review Order was conducted solely by the colours, colour guard and parade commander, and the three guards marched past the saluting base just once in the column of route and not (as usual) for a second time in slow time and line abreast.

The band, bless them, gave us all the familiar bugle marches but could not, of course, manage the school song march. However, somehow or other, we managed to put on a performance to honour the occasion and do justice to the visit of the viceroy, the CinC and the Indian Government ministers who attended the ceremony.

- Parade Commander: K. Wagstaff, Nicholson [Head Boy]
- No.1 Guard Commander: R. Jones, Outram
- No.2 Guard Commander: J. Rogers, Herbert-Edwardes
- No.3 Guard Commander: P. Edwards, Lawrence
- School Colour Bearer: J. Winton, Havelock
- King's Colour Bearer: D. Boddington, Roberts
- Parade Right Marker: R. Bailey, Nicholson
- Band Leader/Senior Bugler: R. Brodie, Lawrence

**D.V. Boddington**
LRMS Sanawar 1942–1947
March 2005

# School Nicknames

The subject of school nicknames could be a rich field of study in itself. School nicknames can be of many kinds. They could originate in physical attributes. For instance, a huge fat boy could be called 'Katta' and a bald-headed teacher could be called 'Eggie'. They could originate from the individual's attitude towards life. For instance, an individual who is very cocky could be called 'gassy' and, as an extreme example, one who exhibits great lassitude could well end up being called 'dead'.

Nicknames can also be contractions of real names. For example, when a child says 'Ahloo and Gobi came to dinner at my parents' place,' he is not talking about the vegetables at all but about two individuals with the names 'Ahluwalia' and 'Gobind'.

School nicknames also tend to be generic. For example, a girl who had buck teeth was called 'Tusky' and when her younger siblings joined school, they in turn were called 'Tusky' and 'Chut Tusky'. Incidentally, there was also a 'Katti' who was sister of 'Katta' and yes, a 'Chut Dead'! This generic trend is not necessarily limited to blood relatives. There was a time when all boys with the surname 'Gupta' were called 'Chappu', only because there had once been a boy named Gupta who had earned that nickname.

The wonderful thing about school nicknames is that they may have originated with derogatory connotations but with frequent use, all negativity is worn out and sometimes replaced by very deep and warm affection. When I was in school, we had a very young, new history teacher who had a huge, walrus moustache. He was immediately given the nickname 'Mucchoo' and there was a tinge of amusement in this christening. Over the years, he rose to be the deputy headmaster and one of the most enduring legends in the school's history. Today, when former students refer to him as 'Mucchoo', they do so with tremendous respect and love.

In my own case, I was nicknamed UD. I was told that it was because when I initialled the pupils' notebooks my 'H' looked like a 'U'. I didn't believe this—my handwriting was bad but not so bad. Then I wrote a letter to someone in Solan, HP. After months of travelling around and a long stint in the dead letter office, the letter came back to me. It had travelled to a host of places like Sitapur, Shajahanpur and Ballia—all in UP. I had to finally admit that my 'H' did read like a 'U'.

I know that my nickname, too, originates in a faint contempt for my inability to write legibly. But with long and frequent usage, this contempt has been worn away. Almost thirty years after I taught him, one of my former students, who runs a chain of educational institutions, sent me a corporate new year gift—a personalized year planner, only it did not have my name 'Harish Dhillon' stamped on the cover but instead, carried the initials 'UD'.

**Dr. Harishpal S. Dhillon**
UD | Nilagiri 1957 | 1949–1957
STAFF 1971–1986 | HOD English | Housemaster | Headmaster 1995–1999 | Headmaster YPS Patiala 1986–1995 | YPS Mohali 1999–2010

OS Sibling – Sister – Yogindra (Dhillon) | Nilagiri 1956 | 1951–1956

OS Children –  Daughter – Priya Dhillon | Himalaya 1988 | 1979–1988
Daughter – Naina Dhillon | Himalaya 1988 | 1979–1988
Son – Jai Singh Dhillon | Nilagiri 1991 | 1982–1989

OS Grandchildren –  Granddaughter – Mannat Tipnis | Himalaya 2013 | 2006–2013
Grandson – Abhay Tipnis | Himalaya 2017 | 2009–2011
Granddaughter – Inaaya Kumar | Himalaya | 2018–To Date
Grandson – Rehaan Kumar | Himalaya | 2020–To Date

**Source and Acknowledgements:**
Published as a Middle in *The Tribune* on 11 December 2006 and reproduced in *Of Cabbages and Kings – A Book of Middles* (New Delhi: Picus Books, Hay House Publishers India, 2014).

# The Bandy Room and Bhuttas

It was decided by fate that I, Taji, would have a bed adjoining the door; Granny Bedi to my right and SAS on the next bed; CK had his bed across the aisle. It was also kismet that Granny's elder siblings were buglers and natch, Granny was too, and so, all of us bugled, apart from SAS, who took to drumming. We were not the best tootlers; the best was the mad scientist Vinod (Nair), who played the trumpet too. He wasn't part of the 'four' because he was always muttering to himself and scribbling complicated diagrams in a thick, well-thumbed notebook that he hoped would be printed in a popular science magazine—*MAD Magazine*, we thought.

We went for music practice to Bandy's House, below the dormitory that housed the low-life Siwalikans—all Houses other than Vindhya were low-life, natch. Our Bandy was Master Warrant Officer Hancock, recently retired band Master from the Armoured Corps Centre and School, Ahmednagar. Hancock is an English surname derived from the name Johan combined with the suffix 'cok', which came into fashion in the thirteenth century, used to refer to 'a young lad who strutted proudly like a cock'.

MWO Hancock was not what we had expected. He stood at five feet four inches tall, he was not tubby, but beer, spirits and beef had pronounced his midriff; he looked old—anybody over twenty looked old to us. He had a drumstick twitching in his hand and the look in his eyes spelt trouble. In these days of wokeness and political correctness, if one calls somebody white or black, one can get cancelled, but the writer has to describe the whole picture, so here goes: amongst us browns, he was the deepest shade of brown. Mrs Hancock was shorter, broader and had a softness of face that shouted, 'if he gets after you, come to me'. We felt somewhat safe and breathed easier around her. What foxed us was we could not count how many little Hancocks there were in the House as they ran in and out constantly—four . . . eight? We gave up counting and agreed that 'many' would do nicely.

Bandy lined us up by height; Granny had the biggest top-knot I had ever seen, that gave him an additional four inches, so he was at the extreme right; next was SAS with a two-inch top knot, then me a few inches lower, and finally CK. This order changed when we had grown up after school, but CK remained where he was and is still there. Bandy taught us many things and not all of them music; our army slang and cursing acquired a certain polish. He made it clear that he had served in the 'British' Indian Army and not the Indian Army—but he had learnt the choicest abuses in both in his career. We once saw Mrs Bandy polishing his medals and concluded he must have fought both the Germans and Japanese, but he never let on how many he had killed; if we asked, his drumstick would twitch and so it was better left to our imagination. The British Indian Army was part of him like fish and chips, even while teaching us to play the review order march of fourteen rapid quick steps. To make it easy for us to remember when to start and stop, he had set the march to a ditty that he must have learnt as a young drummer. Fourteen steps at the rifle brigade, quick march at 140 paces to the minute—'Review order march!' It went like this:

'I stuck my head
In a billy goat's bum
And the stink was
Enough to blind me.
When I looked around
Guess who I found—
It was the girl
I'd left behind me.'

After a couple of music sessions, we discovered a strange fact with all kinds of possibilities—Bandy enfamille had occupied only half the House. Granny, trailed by SAS, had discovered that the empty rooms were not bolted shut and at the rear was a small room with a fireplace and a window that gave out to a drain and a high retaining wall; the tin eaves of the roof were a foot or so away from the wall and if a lad dropped down from the wall, he could prize open an unbolted window unnoticed. The nimblest of us, CK (not for nothing did Jagga Daku call him 'macchhar' (mosquito), during boxing training), was sent to test this secret entry while the mad scientist was asked to play the trumpet to drown any noise that CK might make. CK returned with knees muddy but beaming from success!

Summer was upon us and cuckoos were calling as we walked towards our dorm bubbling with excitement at what we would do in our secret Bandy Room equipped with a fireplace. 'Let's collect pinecones for the fireplace'; 'good idea—pine needles have fallen and we can glissade down the khuds sitting on our raincoats'; 'we can ask Mrs Sehgal at the kitchen for bread to toast in the fireplace!' Ah, the aroma of toasting bread that we never got at meals! 'Yayyy beans on toast!' A tin of Crosse and Blackwell baked beans was 14 annas in the Tuck Shop (a princely sum; pocket money was one rupee a week and there were 16 annas in the rupee and 12 pice to an anna). 'What about Oxford Sausages too, heated in an empty biscuit tin together with the toast and beans?' (At 1 rupee 3 annas, more than a princely sum). 'When the brain-fever bird begins calling "beej beejo, beej beejo" (sow your seeds, sow your seeds) the monsoon will be here and there will be bhuttas for the plucking in the khuds below!' Oh, the smell of roasting bhuttas! Stomachs growling and juices churning, though not in eager anticipation of the horrible grub in the dining room that evening, the four of us, shying stones at pine trees, reached the dorm.

Lugging two pillowcases each full of pinecones gathered from the khuds in summer, was sweaty business. Bruised knees and hands, hook thorns that had to be prized out of socks and clothing, stinging nettles – *bichu buti*, that left one scratching like a monkey with fleas – were no hardship. To attain the vision of a blazing fire on a cold evening while rain lashed on the windowpanes, the aroma of toasting bread thick in the air overpowering that of grungy socks; beans, sausages, condensed milk at hand and us four at their ease in our secret Bandy Room.

After the game at Barne's, the four would hang as high as possible on the wire netting that prevented balls from being kicked into the khud— although Ginger, who could kick like a donkey, invariably kicked the balls over; no wonder he was called 'Khota' (Punjabi for 'donkey'). The four were lucky not to have been given nicknames from the animal and insect kingdoms—family pet names were a no, no. Hanging like limpets on the wire, the four looked into the khud, assessing how high corn had grown in the fields. Our sleuth, Granny, had struck up a conversation with Ruldu, the head sweeper and said 'in Punjab the corn ripens in July (actually he had no idea), what about in the hills?' Ruldu looked at him, knowing at once that this lad had something else in mind, and frowning, said, 'end of August.' Well, it was the end of August already! Ruldu's frown had us worried; what if he repeated this conversation to our Housemaster? Or worse, if he mentioned it to our elder siblings, who were a nuisance, prying into our lives and getting us into trouble? A short while ago, the elders had cut carpentry class so all siblings were summoned to the music room by Mr Sam Cowell; his fat, black cocker spaniel, Wendy, in attendance. All of us were made to stand in a circle while he cut at the air swishing his cane murderously this way and that. The eldest of all siblings was then told to bend and Mr Cowell's cane descended with a whack! So, round and round we went six times, with Mr Cowell slashing away merrily and many of us bleating, 'sir, sir, I didn't do anything!' Mr Cowell perspiring and replying 'you might, you might!' Then it was over, bottoms stinging, we swore never to trust our elder siblings, ever. Baths would be an ordeal too, with sneaky giggling spectators walking past our shower stalls to see the stripes on our buttocks as we bathed.

Munching black daal and chips in the Bandy Room that day, we knew the time had come for us to forage for bhuttas. Hanging on the wires at Barnes, we had seen the wet green leaves of corn sparkling in the sunlight. SAS swore he could see the ears of corn too, 'rubbish!' cried the other three! 'There is a lot at stake', said SAS, 'what if we were caught?' 'Would we be expelled?' asked CK. 'For our siblings cutting carpentry classes, we had got two of six of the best, and this would be worse, no?' Queried Taji and added, 'if it's raining, dark and cloudy, maybe we have a chance.' Granny came up with, 'we have to be brave, no?' We had all read 'Westerns', and six-gun shootouts and outsmarting 'Injuns' were freely enacted from the books by Max Brand, Zane Grey, Louis Lamour and James Fenimore Cooper. Recently, we had all seen the film *High Noon* starring Gary Cooper and Grace Kelly, and we practised walking like him: nonchalant, deliberate, grave, no fear on his face and . . . sigh . . . Grace Kelly! The four of us practised walking on the pavement, deliberate, slow, purposeful steps, a slight swing of the shoulders with each step, hand nowhere near the six gun, eyes crimped into crow's feet (though we were too little to have them) and an attempt to sing the ballad:

'Do not forsake me, oh, my darlin'
On this, our weddin' day
Do not forsake me, oh, my darlin'
Wait, wait along

I do not know what fate awaits me
I only know I must be brave

And I must face a man who hates me
Or lie a coward, a craven coward
Or lie a coward in my grave.'

Gary Cooper and *High Noon* did it for us (Grace Kelly, too) and one Sunday
afternoon, when clouds had blotted out the sun and rain hammered on
roofs as it can only drum on tin roofs, the four of us began our fearless
descent down the khud. We were clad in shorts, shirts, canvas PT shoes
(no Nikes existed then) and raincoats—Macs and Duckbacks of different
sizes, colours and parentages. Granny's Mac had a belt that he claimed
would help hold a record number of ears of corn. To cover his large top-
knot, he had a conical khaki rain cap with ear flaps that drooped down and
made him look like a Lama of the khaki hat sect, in close competition with
the yellow and red of the Dalai and Panchen Lamas. SAS with top-knot
secured in a handkerchief, was wearing what seemed to be a translucent
plastic shower cap; the rain beat a relentless tattoo on the cap that could
be heard up at Birdwood Hall; so much for a stealthy and silent approach
to the fields below. CK and Taji had their heads unadorned and already,
streams of rain were running down their necks and they were soaked,
through and through.

The first field was reached without incident, other than pauses if one or the other dislodged a stone that, with cracks and crashes – our hearts in our mouths – rolled down the hill. Granny stared into the green mass of corn stalks then cocked his head to the left then right, like a falcon searching for prey and whispered, 'The next one!' Like Tom stalking Jerry in cartoons, we tip-toed forward and reached bhutta heaven. Stripping ears of corn from the stalks was easy but for a soft crack and rustle; one bhutta for each of the two shorts pockets and one more each for the two raincoat pockets and we were ready to go. A whisper went around 'let's go!' Granny did his falcon bit again and whispered excitedly—'no, the next one!' Three of us looked at each other, shaking our heads as we were fully stocked up; any more bhuttas and we might stumble going uphill. Granny took one look at us and shuffled off into the green mass that soon enveloped him. We had noticed that he seemed to have blown up like a balloon above his waist. There was more rustling from the depths of the of the corn field— some popping of bhuttas stalks then suddenly, a clattering, snapping and crashing of stalks, and voices screaming '*pakro saalon ko!*'

Mindful that Bandy had told us that drill had to be embedded into our skulls so that we played and marched without the need to think, we had practised our getaway drill. In a terrific film, Robin Hood had got away from the Sherriff of Nottingham and so had Ivanhoe from the evil King John—although Ivanhoe was an ass settling for Rowena-Joan Fontaine, rather than Rebecca-Elizabeth Taylor . . . sigh. Our drill was simple: face uphill and scramble like langurs with their tails on fire. CK and Taji followed the drill to perfection but SAS had his mental compass point in the wrong direction and went due west, plunging into a nullah with a crash that was followed by silence; the fox had gone to earth. Hearts pumping, the former duo was up the hill like rockets on Diwali. Choice curses in vernacular followed them, though not of the quality and artistry they had heard at Bandy's feet. There was a cry from below in vernacular, 'those monkeys are too fast'; followed by 'leave them, we have the big one'. The big one was our Khakhi Lama.

CK and Taji stopped to take stock. Downhill, about 200 yards away, was a large black rock. A further 100 yards down was a larger rock with small bushes around it. Fifteen yards below that was a bush and beneath that was an empty field; in the field, Granny stood surrounded by triumphant and screaming villagers, not unlike a cowboy surrounded by red Injuns with skinning knives at the ready to take a scalp—Granny's would have made a trophy. Abuses were wafting up to us and many were directed our way. Startled, we heard a crackling in the bush behind us and fortunately, it was not a posse of villagers but SAS; and then we were three. There was only one big question—how do we get Granny back? There was another question related to the first one—if we don't get Granny back, what do we tell our Housemaster Mr Vyas? He was a frightfully nice chap but his niceness would melt, quick as a frozen custard ice cream at Alasia, once he learnt what we had been up to. Slowly, a plan emerged: Taji would descend to the lowest rock to plead with the villagers that we were after all only little boys and willing to make restitution. CK would go down to the upper rock to keep an eye on any attempt by the villagers to outflank Taji and nab him. SAS would remain at the spot and await developments.

For Taji, this indeed was *High Noon* and so a four foot tall Gary Cooper descended the hill. There was screaming form the villagers, 'come here, you badmash' and much worse vulgarities, yes, but they didn't have the virtuosity and subtlety of the slang lexicon of Bandy. Reaching a safe perch, Taji looked down at the tableau of Granny and his captors. The captors were old, neither too short nor tall; Granny was shorter than most but his conical cap stood out like a lighthouse. There he was, belted tightly around the waist, swollen with bhuttas like the Michelin tyre humanoid; Jayne Mansfield also came to mind. Two ears of corn stuck out from his neck, their silken tassels below his nose like a moustache; Khaki Lama and Genghis Khan rolled into one! 'God forgive me Granny,' said Taji to himself, 'I whose bed was next to yours since 1951; together we had learnt Newton's laws of gravity from prefects Kulbhushan and Kalyana—held aloft by our ears and slaps counted as we were dropped and here I am, safe behind a rock and cannot help laughing at you!'

Taji stood up to plead with the villagers a smile still lingering on his face—'the badmash is laughing!' screamed the motley company below. Looking immediately grave – the Gary Cooper look – Taji said, 'I was smiling seeing so many surrounding a little boy'. There was more vulgar vituperation at this, however, a few who were looking at Granny, seemed to be suppressing their laughter too. There was some hope there. Taji asked 'what can we do for you?' and a wag replied, 'Come here, you badmash, and we will tell you!' Not a successful ploy by Taji, so his soulful pleas continued; Granny who was groveling his best (the situation demanded it) seemed to have turned the tables and gradually, tempers cooled. After a lot of to and fro, Taji asked the question, 'what do you want for the bhuttas?'

There was some debate amongst the villagers and reply came, 'soap, two cakes of Lux soap; but not one bhutta from those this badmash has stolen.'

Taji searched his pockets and found two pice. 'CK, you have money?' 'No,' replied CK. SAS spoke up 'I do.' With that, SAS charged up the hill for the Tuck Shop – a sure candidate for the Hodson Run – while CK and Taji held grimly onto their positions. On the field below, Granny was being divested of his plunder with great merriment and counting, 'One, two, three, four . . . nine, ten, eleven,' and there was cheering from the gathering! With each bhutta removed, his figure shrank, like a hay-stuffed scarecrow whose hay was being pulled out and eaten by a cow. It took time waiting for the cavalry, but at last, SAS was seen loping downhill carrying a brown paper package. He handed the package to CK, who brought it down to Taji. 'Let him go!' screamed Taji and CK. 'Soap first,' came the reply. In a few minutes, the handover protocol was hammered out. First, a single soap would be lobbed over the bush and Granny could simultaneously climb up ten yards; second soap over and he could scramble up to safety. The second soap soared into the sky and Granny took off like hare chased by hounds aided by cries of 'pakkar lo phir se' (catch him again), loud laughter and whistles.

The four did not pause for breath till Barnes, where they lay under a water tap drinking lukewarm water nonstop. These bedraggled four climbed through the window into Bandy Room. Raincoats and caps were peeled off and the pinecone accountant, SAS, asked, 'How many?' The count was twelve, as shared by SAS, CK and Taji, but our falcon-eyed Khakhi Lama had understandably drawn a blank. 'So that's three each,' said SAS; 'Should I light the fire?' Soon, the delicious aroma of roasting bhuttas filled the room; the four looked at each other, smiled and munched on the bhuttas. Our Khakhi Lama's ego had been mightily bruised; Taji wondered if he should ask him, 'does it hurt?' Granny, like the Bwana explorer tied to a stake, transfixed with spears and asked the same question, might have replied, 'only when I laugh!'

Dramatis Personae (Vindhya, BD, 1958)

- Ambassador Gurdip Singh 'Granny' Bedi (Sonny); U-IV; age twelve.
  Indian Foreign Service | Served as Ambassador to a number of countries

- Sarabjit Arjan 'SAS' Singh; U-IV; age eleven.
Indian Railways | Wounded in the spine by militants when heading the Railway Coach Factory, Kapurthala, in June 1989 and confined to a wheelchair | Member of the Central Administration Tribunal, Principal Bench, Delhi
- Chander Krishan 'CK' Mahajan; L-IV; age ten.
Hon'ble Justice Delhi High Court
- Lieutenant General Tajindar 'Taji' Singh Shergill (Maun); U-IV; age eleven.
Mention in Dispatches 1965 | PVSM 2002 | Authored *Counter Insurgency Support to a Host Nation* (Lancers Publishers, 1987) | Co-authored with Capt. Amarinder Singh, *The Monsoon War – 1965 India Pakistan War* (Rolli Books, 2015)

**Lt. Gen. Tajinder S. Shergill PVSM**
Taji and Maun | Vindhya 1958 | 1951–1958

OS Sibling – Brother – Lt. Gen. M.S. Shergill PVSM, AVSM, VrC | Vindhya 1957 | 1951–1957

OS Children – Son – Jaimal Inder Singh Shergill | Jami | Vindhya 1985 | 1977–1985

# Creating Electricity

While Science was simply mind-boggling for me, Physics, in particular, was my arch nemesis. So when I somehow reached U-VI, I had only a vague idea about what was expected of both, the teacher as well as myself. Mr Uma Prasad Mukherji, aka Mukhoo, could be found chewing on his smoking pipe; shoving his specs into his ear to scoop out the wax; pulling at some prehistoric springs to demonstrate some imaginary horizontal waves; lifting metal bobs. He took up the impossible challenge to teach me Physics. As the year progressed, we (yes, I wasn't alone) saw the situation go from bad to worse—so bad that when asked a question, our standard reply became 'Sir, pass'.

Dhyan learnt a new way to beat the heat, requesting to be excused at least thrice in the 40-minute 'school'. On 1 December 1982, Mukhoo did a quick quantitative analysis and declared, 'fourteen of you, eleven are surely failures. Only God can help you . . . heeeaaaah, even he won't baaa-dar.' He wrote home a three-sword end-of-term report saying, 'Will surely FAIL'. My dad stared at it for a long time before comprehending the true meaning of this verdict. When he asked me, 'Why the hell did you take up Physics?', I explained that Sangha, Surdy, Bugsy, Amolak, Dhyan, Khalsa, Kaul, Chadha, Sharma, and Lup Up had all done so. He was stunned by the well-researched nature of my argument.

Talking of Lup Up, otherwise christened Maheshwar Prasad Srivastava, during a particular class test, once, he braved the odds and kept asking, 'Sir, sheet' every three-and-a-half minutes. Sensing the stunned, utter disbelief written over all our faces, he grinned and explained, 'Today, I got up half an hour earlier (read 0330 instead of 0400 hours) and skipped my training to study properly'. A Black Belt in Taekwondo, he would go down to Barnes at 0400 hours each morning, come rain or shine, and relentlessly practiced his art. 100 push-ups on each thumb, 500 stomach crunches, his each flying kick accompanied by an ear-piercing roar. Eggy, the privileged recipient of the bellowing, would be terrified out of his slumber and initially took the sound to be the donkeys of dhobi-ghat being in heat, only to eventually learn that it was Lup Up, warming up. Anyway, coming back to the class test, all of us were suitably impressed except Mukhoo, who was getting increasingly irritated at every instance of 'Sir, sheet' as he probably visualized himself going through the crap that Lup Up was churning out at lightning speed. Nevertheless, it was truly a gallant effort, filling up thirty-four fullscape sheets in all. Only, the result left everyone, including Lup Up, speechless: 0/50. Mukhoo, visibly exhausted and tortured by trying to make sense of the scribble, had added a remark to his signature, 'Waste of Ink and Paper'.

Finally, that dreadful day arrived—board practicals. Given the constraints of resources and faculty, I had adopted an exceedingly selective learning strategy, giving a miss to Optics, Thermodynamics and other 'confusing' topics. I was hoping to secure the 'swinging metal bob – simple harmonic motion' practical. For the second assignment, I had made up my mind to use my eyes and ears and our ever-obliging lab ass, Subhash Gupta's brains and hands. Given my extremely tidy hand, the external invigilator from Solan, examining my impeccable practical book, was convinced that he was in conversation with one of the toppers. He smiled and made a generous offer—'choose any two'. I smiled back and played along, suggesting 'it didn't really matter'. He misunderstood the whole thing and said, '*theek hai bete, ek electricity wala kar lo aur doosra metal bob diameter wala*. Best of luck'. The first thought to cross my mind was that I was destined to lose some of my best friends thanks to my sudden good fortune. I immediately summoned Subash, who looked at the idling equipment, understood, put pen to paper, drew out the circuit and left. I once again put my best paw forward and neatly fudged the rest of the crap. The invigilator complimented himself for having an eye for 'talent'. I struggled through the maze of wires, rheostat, ammeter, galvanometer and what have you. OK, done! Now what? Surdy (Harinder Singh) was on the lab station in front of me, figuring out some slightly different contraption. I whispered to him, 'Surdy, now?' Surdy whispered back, 'keep setting the rheostat at different positions, note down the readings and put them down in the table'. I almost shouted, 'which table?' Silence. I rephrased, and when I'd got close enough to him, asked softly, 'what table?' He knew his beans, at least on this one, and passed on the chit of paper. I looked at it, recognizing the table immediately, and said, 'Oh, that one.'

The external invigilator, in the meantime, had decided to leave the 'toppers' alone, not wanting to come in the way of our concentration and disrupt our sense of purpose, and turned his vigil towards Mukhoo's Favourite Four, who looked fidgety and suspicious. The reason for their apprehensive and leery glances at us was that these four were being bombarded by the eleven of us with dim-witted queries which were getting louder and more frantic as the clock ticked.

Dhyan was finding it impossible to tie the string around the metal bob and wished he hadn't have to keep going to the loo every twelve minutes, all round the year; Amolak was offended, to put it mildly, and wanted to bash the invigilator for handing him a caliper, which he mistook for a shaving razor. After being explained that the purpose of the experiment was to gauge the diameter of the bob, he still couldn't figure out as to what use the caliper could be put to; Chadha was intrigued by the prism and was reflecting on the refraction. Dhyan finally managed to strangulate the metal bob, only to be told that he had secured the wrong end. Witnessing all this from close quarters, the invigilator was engulfed in self-doubt, promising (to himself) to enroll in a refresher course for his subject upon his return to Solan. He couldn't help but marvel, in a way, at the ingenuity and out-of-the-box creativity of these budding geniuses. 'No wonder.' He must have thought to himself, 'This isn't the 'best school of all' for nothing . . .'

Undistracted by the circus unfolding around me, I was living my own nightmare. Giving a gentle thrust to the clamp on the rheostat, I stared at the needle of the galvanometer, which refused to budge. 'Warming up, probably', I told myself. Another three minutes of pushing and shoving, but the damn needle remained adamant. I was now pulling at the strings (so to speak) with raging ferocity, but the needle, also well-versed with the school motto, continued to misbehave. I was convinced that it was a technical snag, and with time running out, threw caution to the wind and summoned Mukhoo, who had just entered the lab.

'What is it now, you eeeediath?'

'Sir, there's something wrong with this galvanometer.'

'You must have connected the circuit wrongly,' he concluded. I almost told him that that was impossible since Subash had intervened. Mukhoo took his specs off his ear and put them on his eyes instead. He checked and was shocked to discover that everything was alright. Seeing his expression change from irritation to shock to doubt, mine quickly moved from embarrassment to confidence, 'Sir, I told you, this galvanometer doesn't work'.

He cut me short, 'Wait, you eeeediath', rechecked all the connections and trailed the lead wire to the plug point. It was unplugged, dangling freely from the edge of the table.

Mukhoo was relieved that his equipment had not been faulty and barked at me, 'EEEEDIATH, are you trying to create ELECTRICITY?!'

**Pankaj Sapru**
Himalaya 1983 | 1976–1983
Senior Management – Petroleum Downstream sector | Travel & Street Photographer | Member – OSS Executive Committee 2019–21 | Vice President – OSS 2021–23

OS Sibling – Brother – Dhiraj Sapru | Himalaya 1985 | 1977–1985

# Awesome Excursions into Nature

The resumption of school in 1995 (after the scare of the 1994 plague had receded), brought with it the prospect of annual camping (Hikes Week). Being at the lowermost rung of Prep School, we went in large supervised groups to Sadhupul (near Chail – famous for the highest cricket ground in the world) for a week in April. I experienced staying in tents for the first time – and despite the cliché about first times, it really was special.

The next years' hikes took us to Dehradun and Mussoorie, exploring the pristine surroundings of these hill stations. Ellora's in Dehradun was a must-visit for us, just as it had been for generations of hiking Sanawarians. Kempty Falls, Robber's Cave and Sahastradhara spring (literally, sahastra meaning thousand or infinite; dhara meaning stream or spring) come to mind. Sahastradhara has amazing therapeutic sulphur-water springs.

Spirals, both serendipitous and truly random, pervade our universe. I would visit Sahastradhara again, as part of a much smaller delegation hosted by Welham's School for the Round Square Conference, a few years later. The theme of the annual conference was environmental conservation, and upon my revisit to Sahastradhara, we observed solar cookers in the locals' homes and tested the pH levels of the springs. Undoubtedly, the seed of nature conservation was sown in my mind during this trip. The degradation of nature is reprehensible, no matter how much it is excused in the name of development and progress.

In keeping with my newly awakened awareness on the fragility of nature, I was picked to go to Simla as part of a student-led pollution control initiative, but that turned out to be only a token visit to the officials without much real effect—at least none that I became aware of at any time. Still, the feeling of being part of a positive movement remains a highlight, even so many years down the line. It is the inherent hope in young minds that should be nurtured, and I'm glad that mine was.

Once we reached Senior School, we went to Dakpathar and Paonta Sahib for our annual Hikes Week. I recall playing tennis-ball cricket at the Gurudwara, and helping out at the langar. We went parasailing, which entailed being strung up to a parachute behind a jeep and landing at a run. A few unlucky girls did not follow instructions and hit the ground without treading the air, and unfortunately scraped their knees.

I cannot place the exact time I learnt treading water or swimming, but it was at some time during these years during a stay at some resort or the other. My most prominent memory is of a swimming pool beside a rushing river. The swimming pool was pretty crowded and Marco Polo became the first water sport I learned. We had swum in the solar-heated swimming pool back in school, but that had been regimented, routinized, scheduled—not too fun-conducive. Unsupervised moments were rare, and we made the most of them.

Until I went on the trek to Rohtang Pass during Hikes Week the following year, I had never imagined that the light reflecting off the snow could hurt our eyes. To make our way safely up the frozen snow, we were taught how to place our feet sideways and, so, form a flat and firm footing to reduce the chances of slipping and smacking our faces into the snow. We had Army personnel helping us, and for most of the trek, we subsisted on Maggi and aloo poori. Bags of glucose candies were passed around frequently, to keep our energy levels up, but I distinctly remember the views of completely snowed-under mountains pumping up my adrenaline like no food could have. The valley we had ascended through stretched into the distance till it was blanketed by clouds. That was indeed a top-of-the-world moment for me.

In the years prior to such gruelling outings that required trudging through packed snow, we went to Narkanda for a rock-climbing course. Mastering the tying of knots was a time-consuming affair, as is everything that needs practice. Bowlines and thumb knots, figure-of-8s, reefs and hitches—all these made me appreciate how heavily human lives depended on practical knowledge. When the actual activities started, rappelling was easily my favourite. I didn't mind waiting for the climbers, too, and it helped that the karabiners and harnesses were top-notch. The essence of quality in life—especially the crucial things—became clearer to me, but not in so many words.

When I read about the Everest expedition undertaken by the Sanawar boys a few years later, I felt even more proud of the rigorous training that made those youngsters, and their mentors, stand literally on top of the world.

These experiences, at the best school of all, have proved crucial in shaping my identity. After all, what is the point of existence if not to assimilate all our experiences into our unique identities?

NEVER GIVE IN . . .

**Aradhye Ackshatt**
Himalaya 2003 | 1994–2001
DCE and FMS, Delhi University | Author, A Life Afloat (2020)

# The Greatest Holiday on Planet Earth

As we regroup again in October this year, to savour the nostalgia yet again, I feel thankful to each and every member of the group for their love and friendship on that incredible and memorable journey, which can best be described in retrospect as the Greatest Holiday on Planet Earth. We knew no caste or creed. No social or economic backgrounds. We just accepted each other for who we were. And so, as a consequence, some of us are now celebrating sixty-eight years of a wonderful fun-filled bond of friendship. It's one of the finest gifts of life. And it feels like it happened just the other day. Each time we meet, we still behave like kids on a holiday, much to the chagrin of some others. But that's what makes life so much more beautiful. Our unusual holiday gave us the opportunity to live life to the fullest, in a good, clean and joyous atmosphere. Sure, there were upsetting moments now and again. But, clearly, life is only what you make of it, or rather, how you choose to look at it.

And, most pertinently, I would like to express sincere love and gratitude for those who made it happen. To those highly qualified and professional men and women of calibre, ethos and stature, who took us by the hand into this fairytale adventure of a holiday, and nurtured us through it, and to those who took over the baton from them over the years to carry on that glorious tradition. We salute you!

Insulated and secluded in these pristine and salubrious hill-top surroundings, living in a world of its own, Sanawar was home to a mix of about 500 'holidaying' boys and girls aged between eight to eighteen years. Being split up into four groups, or Houses, induced a sense of competition between everyone that lasted a lifetime.

The best part about this holiday was that your parents paid for it. You joined the holiday as a child and left as an adult. There was never a dull moment, and it actually grew on you over the years. An array of sports, crafts and hobbies kept us blissfully occupied for the better part of our days.

The traditional cross-country race called the Hodson Run and the competition there was unique as, theoretically, a particular House could win even if it didn't have any champions, because each child who took part and qualified gave a point towards the tally of his or her House. A significant life lesson on the power of team work, and on how one could be a winner just by participating. You don't need to be a champion to win.

Each April, we went camping, with tents pitched close to a mountain stream, where swimming and fishing were our favourite pastimes. We were always enamoured by the manner in which the locals could catch live fish with their bare hands out of the gushing streams.

On weekends, hiking to distant peaks around Sanawar and trekking to closer spots were a regular pastime. A hot favourite used to be spending a day in Kasauli town. With the grand sum of one rupee in our pockets, we were able to paint the town red with just enough to buy a movie ticket, a coke and a bun samosa. But it made for a real fun outing, regardless.

On campus, there were a couple of really exciting games, that one would find difficult to replicate anywhere else. We used to play one called Rescue, over an area of about five acres, on three levels, comprising of considerable open spaces amidst large colonial double-storey dormitory buildings, a huge gymnasium, a bath House, a boiler room, and a set of elevated midsized water tanks which formed the Jail House. The game was about jail House cops catching escaped prisoners who had the run of the five acre outdoors, whilst the escaped prisoners could simultaneously attempt to rescue captured inmates. It could go on for hours but was often cut short by a lunch or dinner bugle, much to the dismay of the players.

Another game, King, was played in a literal hole in the ground, the size and shape of a squash court. This was an unused and uncovered water tank, with a sloping floor. Two teams would jump into this concrete tank to play. Each, in turn, had to eliminate the other by hitting every player of the other team with a ball made out of rolled up handkerchiefs. Extremely fast moving, it normally lasted about forty minutes. The real tough part came after that. The only way out of the tank was to run up and scale its vertical walls, which at their lowest point, were over ten feet high. Some of us often scaled the highest point at around fourteen feet, by first catching hold of a water outlet hole, some way short of the top.

Other fun activities included pine cone fires during the cold winter evenings. We would run down into the valleys with empty jute sacks, to gather pinecones. The smell and crackling of burning pine in our dormitory fireplaces and radiant warmth of the cone fire itself, were just unbeatable.

The sound of monsoon rain on a huge dormitory tin roof, when one had just slipped into bed for the night, had to be amongst the best stress busters of all time, as the heavy patter lulled one into a different world of no mind, and a floaty, heavenly sensation coursing through the body.

Anytime we felt like getting lost to the world, we would head into the large hollows of the gymnasium roof. This spot offered the very best of sun-soaking experiences on sunny winter days. Another good sun-soaking spot was the ledge on the east side of the Vindhya House dormitory, if you could keep your balance getting there.

The size, location and layout of the campus offered numerous spots to explore and discover, and also good scope for a few adventurous activities of a somewhat unauthorized nature. These mostly ranged from having midnight feasts to breaking of campus bounds after darkness fell. Quite harmless, really, unless you got caught. But that risk was often worth the sense of bravado that followed a successful attempt.

Every year, at the beginning of October, you got to invite your parents to share a small piece of the holiday with you for a few days during the Founders' Day celebrations.

And the fun didn't just stop there. Fifty years on and you realize that it just keeps getting better and better. The holiday never really stops. You can go back to it whenever you want. Alas, for just a few days at a time.

And no matter how much you try and give back, Sanawar just keeps giving you more. You will remain forever in its debt . . .

**Arjun Batra**
Vindhya 1964 | 1955–1964
OSS President 1985–1987

OS Siblings –   Sister – Kumkum (Batra) Kapur | Vindhya 1958 | 1953–58
             Brother – Late Ashok Batra | Vindhya 1962 |1953–62
OS Children – Son – Aman Batra | Bata | Nilagiri 1991 | 1983–91
             Daughter – Amba Batra | Nilagiri 1998 | 1996–98
             Daughter – Avni Batra | Vindhya 1999 | 1997–99

# Mr G.E. Foster

He recognized me after a lapse of eighteen years as we both stepped to the gangway of *H.M.T. Lancashire* when the troopship docked at Bombay en route to the far East. I saluted, regulations required that a NCO should so greet a commissioned officer, in this case Captain G.E. Foster. His acknowledgement came in the form of a firm handshake but the press of the crowd forced us down the gangway to the dock. 'I'm getting off here', he said, 'going to Dehra Dun after a course in Blighty. And you?' 'Active service in Shanghai,' I replied. 'Oh! Making a career of it? Good, perhaps it won't be long before I'm saluting you!' His batman indicated that '*bistra*' and '*saman*' were ready and GEF left for Dehra.

He recognized me again after another lapse of twenty-two years. He did as he had prophesied—sprang to attention and saluted me. He had heard that I had attained my Majority. His home in Fareham near Portsmouth was shared with Mrs Foster. He introduced me as 'One of my boys'. There was a distinct note of pride in his voice as he said it. I could barely mutter, 'Everything I have, sir, I owe to you.' He turned away quietly. So did I. We both feared emotion. Mrs Foster said, 'I'll get some tea,' and left us, diplomatically. Tea helped us to recall and relive Sanawar for hours.

My next visit was made a few years later and I was accompanied by a 'new' OS Subhash Malhotra. Mrs Foster had passed on and GEF found that living alone with the memories of the hilltop hardly sufficed to fill the gap. The spring had gone from his step, there was an intense longing for the peace and tranquillity of the blessed hills (he was a true 'pahari'), but we relived the past with a vividity that shook the years and cares from his shoulders. It was with no surprise that I learned from his sister that GEF had also passed away, 'Full of Sanawar!'

He came to us as a warrant officer, II North Staffordshire Regiment. He was neat and dapper in a well-fitting khaki uniform. He had a distinct advantage over his compatriot instructors—he was an Old Sanawarian. We were drawn up on the 'pavement' in front of the BD dining room by companies, viz., 'A' Coy, 'B' Coy, 'C' Coy and 'D' Coy. Somehow we guessed what he was thinking as he viewed the ranks of blue-coated, blue velvet-shorted, 'Kar-pooh-tar-lars!' his favourite expression with the emphasis on the 'pooh'. 'I'm going to change this.' He did.

'Padar' Ricks had left us some weeks earlier. His tenure of office had left most of us smarting—we were 'Jahnnies' to him and he maintained discipline rigidly in accordance with the general idea of what a Sanawar boy should look like; not very inspiring.

The changes came thick and fast with a new interest kindled in the boys, firstly with a change in appearance. Blue gave way to Khaki, there was a new pride in what we did, 'Clothes do make the man!' Next, the parade ground took on a new spirit of adventure, musketry improved beyond all recognition, 'Companies' gave way to 'Houses', the raucous, '"A" Company has to turn up' was replaced by a recognizable bugle call, one for each House. Route marches, complete with full band, roused the garrison in Kasauli as dawn broke, field days with Sanawar boys opposing battalions of the regular army night attacks. 'Get a puttee off and wrap it round your middle!' and thus he stopped night colic with a kindly thought for 'his boys' as we scaled the height above Garkhal.

GEF saw 'his boys' attain heights that have never been equalled. He walked feet in the air when he commanded the escort to the Ashburton Shield as it was conveyed from Dharampore to the School. 'His boys' had beaten the cream of the Empire's marksmen. His normally firm set of the lips set even firmer when he took up past the Prince of Wales as right-hand man after the presentation of the Colours at Dehra Dun. 'His boys' were now part of the Lawrence ROYAL Military School and was he not an Old Boy himself?

No one would have thought that of him for very long. GEF was a boy at heart. He revelled in our boyish pranks, pranks that were traditional and part of his own make-up when he found relaxation after supper on Saturdays in his time. It was refreshing to find GEF taking his place at our disorganized games, he would call 'Kala-guchi' as loud as any of us when playing 'goolie-dunda' and we were grateful that payment for broken windows came from his pocket. He joined us on our sapping pursuits after the nighttime moths. The crime was 'being caught'. Even now, village headmen recall the fairness that 'Farster sahib' meted out to them when one would appear with a miscreant's hat in return for the 'bhuttas' that had been purloined. Yes, he'd get them back, except for one. That would be tied round the miscreant's neck for the rest of the day, part of the punishment for getting caught.

GEF took command of the annual Easter Camp at Dagroo. Problems that were never encountered in the school campus made appearances all too suddenly but never was camp cancelled or curtailed. He found solutions. He showed that he had pride in everything we did; we, in turn, lived in a sort of reflected glory in his own accomplishments, viz., long-distance running, and for years, he held the championship of the British Army. His lithe figure clad in the light garb of the athlete, took as its practice run the tedious miles from the Lawrence Arch to the refreshment room at Kalka Railway Station; then back again. He led us by paths known only to him to Gurkha fort and got us back in time for supper. He played no mean cornet in the band and we looked eagerly for the Sunday evening programme from the Staff tennis court to contain 'The Echo'. GEF would disappear quietly during the preceding item and lodge himself in the Chapel belfry. As the time came during the playing of 'The Echo' for the actual echo, we were never disappointed, GEF fulfilled.

What is my most vivid recollection? There are many 'mosts'. Taking the theme of this short description of the man that was a boy, perhaps I must return to Dagroo. It was a glorious evening and the many separate 'gangs' had given up their peculiar activities and gathered round the large campfire. There were soloists, instrumental as well as vocal, some of the 'pat' yarns at the time seemed censorable, they were innocent, recitations bore no resemblance to the schoolroom promptings but GEF wound up the proceedings with a rendering of 'When I Leave the World Behind'. It was a plaintive song. 'I haven't any gold to leave when I grow old, somehow it's passed me by,' he sang. That was definitely true. 'I leave the night time to the dreamers,' he continued. 'I leave the songbirds to the blind; I leave the moon above to those in love . . . and to the old folks, I leave a memory . . .'

He did just that. A memory, a very dear one, of a man who gave everything for an ideal, an ideal that found fruition in the Sanawar of the Barne era and that in itself was achievement unparalleled. His 'kapoothalas' in turn—do remember.

**William H. 'Bill' Colledge (Bilkul)**
Old Sanawarian (Roberts 1917–1927)

**Source and Acknowledgement:** *The Sanawarian* (December 1972)

# Interview – Mr Stewart Mclean (OS 1942–1946)

Q 1. How long have you been away from India and what did you feel coming back to Sanawar—just nostalgia?

Mr McLean: I've been away for almost thirty-two years. And yet, coming back to Sanawar was like coming home.

Q 2. What was Sanawar like in your time – academically; sports-wise; attitudes of the teachers and students and their relationship; relationship between the boys and girls?

Mr McLean: Academically, I think it was good. I made teaching chemistry my profession – my life's work – and the chemistry I learnt here from Mr Kemp served me till I got to university. I didn't have to do it again. I feel Chemistry here was begun significantly before it did in North America.

Ah! Sport-wise—very strong in most ways. There was a lot of emphasis on competitive sport. The big game of the year was with BCS. They were our biggest rivals. But between the Houses too, there was keen competition! As far as attitudes and relationship are concerned, we were probably closer in the last years. The relationships were much more formal than they are today—I'm not a scholar here any longer to judge but from what I see, I suspect they're much easier now. The academic staff were responsible for us almost entirely in school. Each House has Housemaster but very few of them paid a day-to-day interest about what went on in the Houses. Mostly, the Houses met their Housemaster only on Saturday; a period used to be given to House meetings at the end of classes, when we used to write letters, the letter-writing period. The important difference was that the military staff were responsible for the discipline outside the classroom and the discipline was very strict, indeed! Sergeants from the regular army were seconded to the school. For each House, we had one Sergeant Major and a staff of three sergeants.

About the relationship with the girls—well, we were at the same school but we saw girls from a distance. We never had classes together. During Church in the mornings, the girls sat on the left side of the Chapel and the boys on the right – we'd sneak-peek at them! They used to wear very pretty uniforms. In the summer, they would wear uniforms of a pretty print and in winter, gym tunics sort of things. They wore hats as well. We almost never spoke to them. I had a sister and those of us who had sisters were allowed on Sundays, after Church, to go to Peacestead to meet them, I remember this was called 'sisters boys'.

For classes, the girls had half of Birdwood and we occupied the other half. Some (very few) of the forward ones would sneakily see some girls at the cannons—that was considered the heights of dare and boldness. During the time I was here, towards my senior years, 'sister boys' became more liberal. Above a certain class, we could go to meet girls who were not your sisters—but only remained confined to Peacestead. I don't remember all the details but mostly we used to admire the girls from a distance.

Q 3. What was the routine and the extracurricular activities then?

Mr McLean: Well! There was very much less than you have now—there was so little time to do anything other than the usual organized work. School went on till 4.00 p.m. and prep was from 7 o'clock till 9 o'clock. Between 4 o'clock and supper we had organized sports. We had military organization for almost everything.

There were a few things people were engaged in. One was the Dramatics Society. Another, the Debating Society on Sunday evenings. There were relatively few other things.

The things we looked forward to were the 'roaming holidays', when we could break bounds and go for walks and hikes. We had three ten-day holidays in the year—the main one of course being Founders' Holidays.

Every morning, we'd be up as soon as it was light and then have some activity depending on what section we were in—maybe PT or Drill till breakfast.

Our term started in the beginning of March till the middle of December with the Founders' vacations as a break. But boys whose journey home would take more than two days were not permitted to go home.

Our routine was an extremely strict one.

Q 4. What were classes like?

Mr McLean: Strict! We had to be quiet and speak only when spoken to. Occasionally, we had a little fun but mostly we had to put in a lot of hard work. I suspect a lot of difference now! We would be given mostly instruction during classes and most of the work and problem-solving would be done at prep.

Q 5. What were the Socials, House parties and House shows like? Did you enjoy them?

Mr McLean: Well, as I said, we had very little time for such things. We never used to have any House parties or House shows. The only time for fun and games was Saturday evenings. It depended on the time, actually. Near Home Day, we had more relaxed fun.

Organized social events were rare. We maybe had one school dance a year. I remember one school dance which was a big farce because no boy had the courage to go and ask the girls for a dance. Most of the boys were up on the balcony peering down at the shy girls and various devices had be tried to try and get the boys down.

Founders' celebrations were our main social event. We would have a big parade, display of exhibitions, PT, Gymnastics and the A.D.S. I remember there was sort of a Gymkhana, where you had to play foolish games and the like.

Did I enjoy the Socials? I think people enjoy them though no one would admit it but he wished he had the courage to get into the swing of things. But he was too shy—we were not very socially advanced.

Q 6. What differences and changes have you found now? Are they positive or merely on outcome of the changing times?

Mr McLean: The changes I have seen are vastly weighed against the things that remain the same. The changes I have observed, so far, have all probably been for the better.

The very strict military organization was most probably a good thing for us but that time has passed. The atmosphere now is more relaxed but I think it's more possible now for young people to develop good work habits and attitudes from inspiration and as something from within, and these are probably of more permanent value than if they are forced upon or dictated to you.

I must say that one of the changes that I suspect that you people may find hard to believe is that the food is considerably better—much better. If we had food like this, we'd consider we were living in a first-class hotel. The food we had was in small quantities and generally inedible.

Q 7. Is there any change which is specially confined to the school?

Mr McLean: I see the world and society changing around me. But I feel the important things about Sanawar stay constant.

Q 8. What do you think about the atmosphere in Sanawar today?

Mr McLean: Well, I've been here two days and I find it a very fine and happy atmosphere. People seem to be enthusiastic about what they're doing and I don't think I'm looking through rose-coloured spectacles but we still have the same school spirit.

Q 9. What did Sanawar do for you?

Mr McLean: I think Sanawar moulded me. I was here during my formative years and whatever I have developed into, for good or bad, is strongly influenced by every year of my life at Sanawar.

I feel I'm a better person having been at Sanawar.

Q 10. If given a choice, would you prefer studying at Sanawar now or back in your times?

Mr McLean: This is one of the question that is so hypothetical because I'll have to be young now. And nowadays I would certainly like to be in the Sanawar of today. That's the best I can say but I suspect at present, you are more close to what I consider an ideal than we were then. By that, I mean I sense that you have much more individual responsibility to develop your own self than we had. The very strict discipline we had was probably good for us but in the modern times, we feel that you should develop individually rather than have something forced upon you.

But I liked studying here. I sometimes try to see—to understand and to appreciate what we were going through then and if you'd asked any of us then, at any given time, we'd have said, 'life is dreadful' but we would have also said, 'we wouldn't like to be anywhere else'. Only when we had moved away did we realize how much we had enjoyed our times here—we certainly lived to the full.

**Anu Bedi U-VI A**
Old Sanawarian (Vindhya 1979)

**Source and Acknowledgement:** *The Sanwarian* (December 1977)

# The Path

Life used to be so simple, or so it seems.

Prep School sat on a small hill, accessible via a path that meandered up and ended in a flat rectangular playing field paved over with concrete. A long stone building with the iconic red roof ran across the other length of the field. This structure housed and fed us all: boys' dormitories to the left, girls' dormitories to the right with a dining room and kitchen in the middle. Curiously, I don't recall ever going behind that building.

On weekdays, after breakfast, we descended down well-worn stone stairs to our school rooms. I recall a large bell; wooden desks with names of kids scratched into the wood; glass pots full of ink resting in a hole in the corner of each desk, and blotters that slurped up inky globs; learning how to enunciate English words by holding tiny mirrors close to my mouth to see where the tongue hit the palate; and the shame of my classmates standing atop chairs because they had upset the teacher, but not much else. It was a confusing time. Within days, I had learned it was dangerous to cry. Girls who cried made us all uncomfortable and we avoided them. I didn't want to be one of them. It was best to just follow orders and soldier through.

Prep School was a self-contained universe. On those rare occasions when you visited the outside world, you had to walk down that path until you came to Mrs Rudra's (the Prep School headmistress) charming little House. It sat behind a small well-tended garden, to your right. I can still see her face clearly; dark frizzy hair caught in a low bun, deep voice and kind eyes behind thick-lensed glasses. They crinkled at the edges when she smiled. There was something both comforting and intimidating about her. Continue past her House and the texture of the road changed from tar to cobblestone. You were now in Senior School territory.

Turn left at Mrs Rudra's House and the path lead you past homes of teachers nestled behind clumps of trees on the right (a no-go-zone), and a steep hill on the left. Keep going, pass the Hospital, and you eventually end up in a dishevelled old cemetery just past the school limits. I discovered it

on a biology field trip. A fascinating place. Our biology teacher, I forget his name now, instructed us to collect flora and fauna and look for insects and toads. But I was more interested in grave markers. I had never seen a Christian graveyard outside the books I had read. The grave stones looked lonely and in need of love and attention. Like forgotten sentinels, a few stood upright but most lay on their backs; toppled by time and circumstance. Round splotches of green, yellow, and gray moss bloomed across their stone surfaces and grasses sprouted out from their crevices. If you brushed away the weeds, you could just barely decipher English names like Mary and Ruth etched into the stone. I wondered who these people were. How did they end up in this forgotten place? What were their lives like? My lifelong fascination for cemeteries and love of biology was born there.

I type out these words from an armchair in Kansas, USA, with my computer propped on my lap. What have I forgotten or missed? I don't know or care. It is only the remembering that matters now.

A few years ago, I reconnected with three Prep School friends. For old times' sake, we decided to meet in Colorado, USA and attend the Jaipur festival together. We are old now but forever tethered by memory. We checked into our rooms and talked well into the night.

During a lull in the conversation, I absentmindedly asked my friend if she remembered the day her father walked up the path to Prep School?

I recall two things clearly about that day: a sinking feeling in my stomach and the look on her father's face; a curious mix of joy and something else I cannot describe but never forgot.

It was a glorious Sunday. We were playing in the sun. A red ball was involved. The sky was blue. There was much laughter and merriment. I saw him before she did; a tall, slender man in a brown tweed suit and neat brown shoes. I learned later that he was a physician at the TB sanatorium in Kasauli. She squealed with joy when she saw him and ran to meet him. The rest of us stopped what we were doing and watched, a little jealous. He opened his arms and swung her around in the air before bringing her close to his chest. My heart dropped to my stomach. I felt queasy. My father used to do that. And for the first time since my father had died on the battlefield, a year earlier, it dawned on me that he would never hold me again.

Did she remember that day? Without missing a beat, she said, 'Of course, I know exactly what day you are talking about. I will never forget it. My mother had been sick for a while. That's the reason my brother and I were sent to school in the first place. That day, he had come to tell me that she had died.' We sat on the bed, holding hands and bearing witness to each other's suffering in silence. Nothing more needed to be said.

Over the past 175 years, thousands like us have walked into Prep School, carrying trunks that weighed more than we did. Those trunks held more than our stuff; they held our stories. We have unpacked and contributed to the story of Sanawar. Children with English names walked down the same paths we did. And that Sanawarian story belongs to all of us and we belong to it.

What more can we ask of that school of paths, buildings and red-roofed wonderment?

**Dr Mininder Kaur**
Mini | Nilagiri 1975 | 1966–1975
King George's Medical College, Lucknow | PG Internal Medicine | Practicing Zen Buddhist | Trained Soto Zen Chaplain | WHO Community Health & Development volunteer – Haiti, S Africa, Zimbabwe

OS Siblings – Sister – Rupinder Kaur | Pedro | Nilagiri 1968 | 1966–1968
Sister – Navneet Kaur | Neeti | Nilagiri 1977 | 1968–1977

# 1960s – The Defining Decade

**Tanks:** As kids, we would hang around the tailor for hours to get an empty thread spool. Needless to say, there was intense competition for the spools. The tailor was a fair man and managed the distribution process well, never favouring anyone. The spools were painstakingly ground, cut and assembled into deadly fighting/racing tanks. Additional components included a pencil and a rubber band. The pencil was used to wind up the rubber band. The unwinding rubber band released tension and propelled the tank. The spool edges were notched for better traction that allowed the tank to traverse rough terrain and even climb over the opponent's tank.

**Paper Airplanes:** On a good day, if the wind currents were just right and you had assembled a 'good' airplane, you could set it airborne from behind the Siwalik House dorms towards Monkey's Point and watch it fly over Barnes and on forever, or at least until it disappeared from sight.

**Crystal Radios:** There was a craze to construct crystal radio sets that operated without a power source. One could pick a strong radio signal on ear pieces, especially on a cold, clear night. One Himalayan, who shall remain unnamed, constructed the crystal sets inside an expensive library book by carving out the inside of the book. The crystal set looked like a book. Mr Kemp got wise to this and the parents paid handsomely for the destroyed hardcover classic.

**Pine Bark Boats:** A favourite hobby was to build a miniature boat and sail it after a good rain. The starting material was pine bark. Having good quality pine tree bark, of the right size and thickness, was critical. After all, you couldn't make a silk purse from a sow's ear. The bark was shaped into a boat by rubbing it on the hard, rough concrete pavement. More elaborate models had a mast and a sail.

**Gallery Cricket:** Sunday mornings, there were cricket matches in the narrow alley by Siwalik House. There was a natural wicket—one only had to make sure they did not step into the drain that ran through the alley. Many a test match was played in that alley bordered by the Siwalik dorms on one side and the twenty-foot-high stone wall leading to the BD pavement on the other. All one needed was a cricket bat and a tennis ball. There was never a shortage of cricketers.

**Hide-and-Seek:** 'Prep' for L-III was one period shorter than for the rest of the school. The extra time was well-spent playing hide-and-seek around the Boys' Dining Hall. A favourite hiding place was in the khud above and behind the Dining Hall. The steep slope and narrow dark alley were scary places to be by yourself in and many lacked the courage to wander around in the dark.

**Wall Climbing:** A competitive challenge was climbing walls. It was usually the athletics types who participated in this. The walls of primary interest were by the BD Quad near Gaskell Hall; the walls of the empty water reservoir on the other side of Gaskell Hall and the midpoint of the stairs leading up to the BD pavement from the Siwalik House dorms. The process involved getting a good run-up to allow your momentum to reach as far up the wall as feasible and then pulling yourself up the rest of the way.

**Siwalik–Vindhya Firecracker Wars:** Being so close created a special rivalry between the Vindhyans and the Siwalikians, that reached new heights during Diwali. The entire House could participate in the battle that ensued. All one needed was a few exploding firecrackers. These little bombs would explode when they came in contact with a hard surface. The target was the torso, however, the bombs usually missed their mark and exploded everywhere, sometimes even on some unfortunate's head. Catapults were also deployed to make matters worse. It was just plain dumb luck that no one was seriously hurt.

**Charlie's Mithai:** Charlie's sweets were definitely out of this world and one of the highlights of life in Sanawar. Charlie got tired of having sweets pilfered out of his basket. The poor man tried unsuccessfully to manage the security and sales of the mithai. Frustrated, he finally constructed a kiosk to House and sell his sweets through. It was a small structure with a backdoor and a small window in front from which he conducted business. One Rupiya went a long way, as the most expensive items were two annas, whereas everything else was one anna. Items included *daal-moth*, peanuts, barfi, samosa, gulab jamun, rasgulla, and of course, everyone's favourite – Charlie's palang-tod. I am a palang-tod connoisseur, having eaten it everywhere I can find it – unfortunately no one makes it quite like Charlie – no one!

**Ice Cream Sundays:** Mrs Sehgal had an ice cream machine installed in the BD kitchen. On Sundays, the whole school walked over to the BD Kitchen to get their cup of the most delicious ice cream. We had the multiple choice of vanilla, vanilla or vanilla, but it was truly appreciated. Almost as good as the ice cream was seeing the girls as they came over to the BD Kitchen looking for them.

**The School Dance:** The school social was the only time to meet a girl one fancied. The juniors learned and practised dance for days before the event, leaning on the more experienced seniors for tutorials. At the social, boys and girls usually stayed on opposite sides of the dance floor. On occasion, a boy would pull himself together and walk towards the girl's side, while the rest of the boys watched in anticipation. The most difficult part was the long walk back after a girl had turned him down. The ones who didn't even make a move were always there to snigger and laugh. Still, that did not deter the bold who saw this as an opportunity to make their feelings known to the opposite sex.

### Zafarullah Khan
Zafar | Siwalik 1965 | 1957–1965
Landed in the US (BS Chemical Engineering, University of Nevada; MBA, Washington University) with $200 and a semester's fees | Brought parents to the US for mom's successful open-heart surgery | Worked for forty years in positions of increasing responsibility in Africa, Asia, Australia, Europe, North and South America for Monsanto and Coca-Cola | Served as President IFN | Chairman of the Board ECIC | Board of Directors, Amana Academy | Semi-retired | Consultant.

# Baptism by (Forest) Fires

Character is definitely the single most important factor in determining the destiny of a person. Of course, there is the never-ending debate around whether it is heredity or the environment that is the determining factor in shaping one's character. While I believe genetic inheritance does play a critical role in how a child turns out, the environment during their formative years also plays a very important role in shaping the child's dispositions. However, there is no doubt at all that, as propounded by Heraclitus in ancient times, 'Character is destiny'.

The end of the winter and the flowering of the lemon yellow flowers of the Banksia creeper would lead to the best weather ever when cool breezes would make everyday a pleasure and it would be sheer bliss to be alive. However, this wonderful weather was the precursor to the seasonal forest fires. The pleasant spell would lead to an abundance of bright sunshine that ushered in dry weather, in which the pine needles would fall and carpet the steep slopes. Suddenly, the slopes would be tussocks of strawberry blonde softness and you could slide down the steepest of rocky slopes with no broken bones.

It was an unwritten rule of life in boarding school that once we were back in the dormitories post dinner, there was no venturing out. After the lights-out bugle had been sounded, the expectation was that one was in bed and asleep.

On certain rarest of rare nights, when it was unbearably warm, we were allowed to take our bedding onto the narrow balcony of our dorm, from where we watched the odd vehicle as its lights zigzagged along the road to the plains. Then the seasonal forest fires started—flailing tongues of tangerine and gold against the velvet darkness. They seemed alive as they blazed, illuminating the very ridges they so hungrily devoured as they danced in the forests of the night and raced at will up and down the hills, destroying all that stood in their way.

And then there were the nights when we were summoned to battle these very flames as they came too close for comfort—Lower Barnes . . .

Garden City . . . Leisure . . . below Squire Hall and on the steep slopes around Stone View . . .

The same Chir pine needles that formed luxurious beds on the slopes and were a pleasure underfoot, became prone to becoming the perfect fuel to feed the blazing forest fires.

It is in the introductory portion of basic fire-fighting training that one is educated on the role that arson plays in the breaking out of a fire and, later in life, dear friends from the Forest Department confirmed the same—that most forest fires are caused by humans. Some out of carelessness, and some by design.

We actually had khud-cleaning prefects appointed by the school, who were most active during the summers. Interestingly, there were boys with an uncanny ability to sense the presence of forest fires almost before they erupted, especially during classes.

The fire-fighting that occurred on the hilltop will remain etched forever in our collective memories. At the end of a tiring day, barely would our eyes close for what seemed like a mere few seconds in blissful sleep, that the bells would ring frantically and the entire dormitory was flooded by the bright lights of the overhead tubelight and the shouts of 'Fire! Fire!' ringing in our ears . . .

Almost magically, we would then find ourselves hundreds of feet below our dormitories, facing a line of fire that was moving, and moving fast. Did the school bell ring? Did we change into our games kit? Who asked us to go? Were we at risk? There was no time for any of the above. Fight the fire we must and we were not bidden to do so, but it was as if by reflex—we did it out of sheer drive of instinct.

Darkness visible all around and live flames in a spectrum of hues that blazed as the they hissed and leapt as if alive. All we had to fight it was the odd branch broken off from some hapless tree to kill the flames . . . And we did! The trick was to tackle the flames from downhill. If one was uphill and the breeze started to blow up the hill, there was no way that a human being could outrun the fire. Many a times, the smoke was so thick that we were unable to make out who was fighting the fire beside us; the smoke would be choking and the fire seemed like a wild serpent whose orange tongue singed as it came closer.

One woke up as usual to the rouser bell at 5.45 a.m. for PT the next morning; scorched hair and all. We would go about our daily routine in spite of the headache caused by a combination of smoke inhalation and a disturbed night's rest. There was no preferential treatment whatsoever, just because you had fought a fire in the wee hours the night before. In fact, it was just another fact of daily life that one took for granted and no one talked about. It was never about bravery and certainly not about that glorious thing called courage. Perhaps, somewhere, it was about a thing called duty. It was also about choosing to do the harder right as opposed to the easier wrong.

As I reflect, I realize how these tenets form the bedrock of one's character and that they must never be neglected in life.

**Himmat S. Dhillon**
Vindhya 1989 | 1984–1989
Principal, The Gandhi School, Jakarta, Indonesia | Principal/CEO, GEMS Our Own English High School, Fujairah, U.A.E | Executive Principal, GEMS Modern Academy, Gurgaon | Headmaster, The Lawrence School, Sanawar

OS Siblings –   Sister – Diviya Dhillon | Vindhya 1997 | 1987–1995
OS Children –   Daughter – Aafreen Tara Dhillon | Himalaya 2022 |
                2020– 2022

# Then and Now

I write this as Germany, where I live, endures another Covid-19 lockdown. It's been a year now, give or take, punctuated by periods of almost-normalcy. While it's never been as strenuous (or stressful) a lockdown as some have experienced, it still bites.

When lockdown was first announced, the first people I reached out to were my school friends. Not the way I did when we were on our hols, all those years ago; we weren't writing letters to each other, detailing meals, trips, and haircuts (as applicable). Now, with digital communication being cheap and ubiquitous, I could be with a friend in Singapore; in New York; in New Delhi; in Karnal. It was immediate and healing, not least because the questions were known and had been dealt with, decades before.

Could we slime out of it? If not, how best to bear it? And wouldn't we all feel better if we could just jam someone else's scene into the bargain? It helped that being locked down is something all Sanawarians are used to. We know what it means, at an instinctive, granular level. This is the essence of boarding school life, after all. Once there, you don't leave. In my time, that was pretty much non-negotiable, aside from the one SOP per term, and whatever break the crowd at Peacestead could extort from the chief guest at Founders'.

But that wasn't true either, as we remembered while we spun yarns at each other, miles and years melting away. Because when you scratched the surface, there were literally tons of ways for an inmate of Sanawar to get out into the outside world. Charging off was the most basic, of course, and one guy in my class (let's leave him unnamed) took off twice before milk break. On the same day. But there were legal ways, and I treasured them all.

Mr Batish was liberal with Walking-Out Passes, and we were in Kasauli at least one weekend a month, spending our contraband cash on Frooti and the like. The sports-minded had trips to other schools to look forward to, that we graded on the basis of their food—Punjab Public School, Nabha

48

sat proudly atop the pile. The intellectual elite had quizzes, debates and other mysterious matters to attend to, in places as far-flung as Gwalior and Delhi. Even the abjectly unsporting and under-brained had teeth that needed work from real dentists. Those of us without braces would watch with sullen envy, as Dr P.P. Sahni's party trooped out of CDH, wired faces agleam, licking their lips at the prospect of home food while we looked despondently at our weekday *tori*.

When lockdown began, it was almost thirty years to the day that I'd left school. Legally. Permanently. A last drive down Tilley's that, for the first time ever, I didn't want to end. I spent that first lockdown walking in the forest with my dog – thank god for Germany's almost cultish regard for its shared open spaces – thinking about other places I could be. I'm not sure I have ever wanted to be back in school again. But I've thought often of the places I've been in since, with friends I made up there.

So many of my cherished memories are of trips made since school with my OS friends. I went all over the USA when I was an undergraduate there, seeking out classmates and contemporaries. Later, birthdays took us to Portugal and Vietnam; visits to Thailand, Singapore and Indonesia; a classmate's wedding in Croatia. (I knew King's Landing looked familiar when I saw *Game of Thrones*: I'd already been there, when it was still plain old Dubrovnik.) We performed Dance Exercise (with change, naturally) in a church there, to the bemusement of the locals. I can't remember if there was a hand-stand.

I rewound to all those places in my head and heart as I walked in the forest behind my home with my dog. Being confined to one place will do that to you. I had seen that movie before; sitting in Dr D.C. Gupta's class, for example, chastely acerbic Hindi washing over me as I thought of home; my parents; meals in distant schools where a bowl of meat and veg sat in front of each group of hungry students.

I can still see the faces of those others around me, in my mind's eye, equally adrift on the tides of their own thoughts as Chappu droned on. I don't see them as they are now. I see them as they were then. Some with clear faces, others conspicuously pimpled; braces, spectacles, hair worn in plaits; today's poised women foreshadowed in those distant gawky adolescents curling their hair around their fingers. Next to me, Fifi Contractor biting the end of a pencil as he struggled to make sense of a language he clearly didn't understand.

When I am like that, the face in the mirror comes as a surprise. This man with a mostly white beard and lines on his face, his son asleep in his room—the same age, almost, as his father had been when he went up to the school for the first time.

That first day, driving through the Gaskell Hall passage as the rain pelted down. Two boys, clearly cutting class, watching my father and I exiting the car. One is in Jammu now, and the other in Singapore. Both Siwalikans. They are with me, still.

**Avtar Singh**
Chajju | Siwalik 1990 | 1986 – 1990

Author, *The Beauty of These Present Things* (2000); *Necropolis* (2014) | Founding Editor, *Time Out Delhi* | Managing Editor, *The Indian Quarterly*

# Our Founder

Sir Henry Montgomery Lawrence KCB (1806–1857)
A Biographical Synopsis

- Born in Matara, Sri Lanka, of Anglo-Irish and Scottish descent, the fourth son of Colonel Alexander Lawrence and Catherine Letitia Knox, on 28 June 1806.
- Educated at Foyle College, Derry, the Rev. James Gough's school at College Green, Bristol and the East India Company's Addiscombe College near Croydon.
- Commissioned 2nd Lieutenant Bengal Artillery after passing out of Addiscombe in May 1822.
- Sailed for India in February 1823, joining his battery in Dum Dum, near Calcutta.
- Served in the first Burma war and took part in the capture of Arakan.
- Appointed adjutant of artillery, southeast division, April 1826.
- Contracted malaria in Burma and sent home on sick leave, August 1826.
- During his convalescence, met and courted his future wife Honoria Marshall of Fahan, Co. Donegal, Ireland.
- Joined the trigonometrical survey in Ireland.
- Returned to India in 1829 accompanied by his sister Honoria and younger brother John, arriving Calcutta in February 1830.
- Posted to a Foot Artillery battery in Karnal (Sindh Ed.) on the northwest frontier.
- Lived with his elder brother, George, and intensively studied his profession and Indian languages with the intention of obtaining future civil employment.
- Qualified in Urdu, Persian and Hindi languages, 1832.

- With the help of George, appointed assistant revenue surveyor in the North Western Provinces, assuming his duties at Moradabad in 1833.
- Elevated to the rank of full surveyor in 1835.
- Promoted Captain of Artillery, 1837.
- Married Honoria Lawrence at St. John's Church, Calcutta on 21 August 1837.
- Accompanied by his wife, returned immediately to Gorakhpur to continue with his survey duties. His wife accompanied him on most of his field trips during his work for the revenue survey.
- While at Gorakhpur, became involved in a dispute with a Captain McNaughton over a memoir of General Sir John Adams that he had adversely reviewed, and was dissuaded by his friends from fighting a duel.
- Rejoined his battery upon the outbreak of First Anglo-Afghan war and asked to be placed at the disposal of the C-in-C but following the reduction in the armies of the Indus, his services were not required by 1838.
- Birth of first child, son Alexander Hutchinson ('Alick') in Allahabad, 1838.
- Appointed officiating assistant to George Clerk, the Governor-General's Agent, (AGG), for the North West Frontier Provinces and the Punjab.
- Took charge of civil administration of Ferozepur District, 1839.
- Oversaw the rebuilding of Ferozepore, built a fort, improved roads, drainage, settled boundaries and, with his wife's help, found time to write a series of articles for the *Delhi Gazette*.
- Confirmed in his appointment as assistant and deputy to the AGG, North West Frontier Provinces and the Punjab, March 1840.
- Feeling now settled and secure in his first administrative appointment, built a House in Ferozepore, and at the same time, built and furnished a small cottage for the summer months in the Simla hills at Kasauli, 1840–41.
- Birth of second child, Letitia Catherine ('Lettice'), Ferozepore, 11 November 1840.
- Death of his daughter Letitia Catherine at Subathu, August 1841.
- Following the disastrous British retreat from Kabul, sent to Peshawar to assist the senior political officer, December 1841.

- Went with Pollock's 'Army of Retribution' into Afghanistan and up to Kabul, having joined the expedition at Jalalabad, August 1842.
- In command of the Sikh contingent, took part in the advance on Kabul and saw action at the battles of Tezin and Haft Kotal.
- Returned to India in October 1842.
- Promoted Brevet-Major but disappointed at not being made a CB.
- Mistakenly appointed superintendent of Dehra Dun and Mussooree, a covenanted Civil Service post for which he was not legally qualified.
- After three months in Dehra Dun, transferred to Ambala as assistant to the envoy at Lahore.
- Adroitly and peacefully settled the state of Kaithal, bringing it under British rule after the Raja died without a successor, 1843.
- Promoted to the important post of Resident at the court of Nepal, 1843.
- Lived in Katmandu with his wife – the first white woman in Nepal – from 1843 to 1845.
- Promoted to Major Bengal Artillery.
- Wrote articles for *The Calcutta Review* and first conceived the notion, and advocated the establishment of asylums (schools) in the hills for children of European soldiers.
- Wrote and published Volume 1 of his first book, *Adventures of an Officer in the Service of Ranjit Singh*, Henry Colburn, 1845.
- Birth of third child, son Henry Waldemar ('Harry') in Kathmandu, 24 January 1845.
- Accompanied his wife to Calcutta at the end of 1845, when it became clear that for her health and that of their two children, they needed to return to England.
- Ordered to join the army of the Sutlej following the start of the First Anglo-Sikh War, 1846.
- Appointed AGG for foreign affairs and for the affairs of the Punjab by Lord Ellenborough, Governor-General.
- Present at the battle of Sobraon and later, the occupation of Lahore, February 1846.
- Assisted in negotiating the treaties of Kasuri and Amritsar.
- Strongly opposed the annexation of the Punjab, preferring to leave the Sikh state intact as a potential source of support for the British. Lawrence was firmly opposed in principle to the 'annexation policy' of the British in India in general.

- Promoted to Brevet Lieutenant-Colonel for his services at Sobroan, June 1846.
- Appointed Resident at Lahore, January 1847.
- Founded the first school (asylum) for children and orphans of European soldiers at Sanawar in the Simla hills, near Kasauli, 15 April 1847.
- His arduous duties as Resident caused his health to fail and he proceeded on sick leave to England, November 1847.
- Feted on arrival in England and on the recommendation of Hardinge, the retiring Governor-General, was made KCB in 1848.
- Returned to India with his wife and son Harry in November 1848, landing at Bombay, a month later.
- Leaving his family to follow at their own pace, he proceeded immediately by ship to Karachi and then up the Indus by steamer to Multan and finally overland to Lahore, joining the army in the field in early 1849.
- Compelled the surrender of Kashmir to Gulab Singh.
- Present at the siege of Multan and witness to the bloody battle of Chilianwala, January 1849.
- Resumed his duties as resident at Lahore, 1 February 1849.
- Resigned his post following the annexation of the Punjab to British India, which he had always strongly opposed.
- Eventually persuaded to withdraw his resignation by Lord Dalhousie and appointed President of the new Board of Administration for the affairs of the Punjab, along with his brother John and Charles Greville Mansell, April 1849.
- Persuaded to accept the appointment of AGG for the Punjab. After its annexation (despite his former opposition) in April 1849.
- Birth of fourth child, daughter Honoria Letitia ('Honey'), Lahore 26 April 1850.
- Following disputes on matters of policy between himself and his brother, John, he resigned his post as president and the Board of Administration was abolished.
- Bitterly disappointed that he was not given charge of the Punjab which went instead to his younger brother, John.
- Was offered and accepted the AGG in Rajputana (Rajasthan) with the same salary as in the Punjab, 1853.

- Declined Lord Dalhousie's offer of the residency in Hyderabad (Central Provinces), on the grounds of his wife's ill health, July 1853.
- Death of his wife Honoria, who had been in bad health for several months, 14 January 1854.
- Appointed ADC to Queen Victoria and promoted to Colonel in the Army 19 June 1854.
- Established the second of the Lawrence Asylums in the Aravalli hills at Mt. Abu in 1856, and mooted the possibility of a third at 'Utakamund' in the Nilgiri Hills of southern India. The asylums at Sanawar and Mt. Abu were supported at considerable self-sacrifice by him throughout his life.
- Wrote to Lord Canning, the new Governor-General, to set himself right on points which he believed he had been misjudged, 29 February 1856.
- Promoted to (Regimental) Lieutenant Colonel of the Artillery.
- Prepared to return to England with his daughter Honoria Letitia 'Honey' in order to restore his own health, which was again failing.
- Was offered and accepted the post of Chief Commissioner and AGG in Oudh from 21 March 1857 which he regarded as rightful compensation for the loss of the Punjab to his brother John, and as public recognition of his services.
- Sent his daughter Honey home and despite his own ill health, took up his new post at Lucknow, March 1857.
- Upon receiving news of the outbreak of the Indian 'mutiny' in Meerut and Delhi, prepared, with great skill and foresight, for the defence of Lucknow, May 1857.
- Promoted to Major General and given command of all troops stationed in Oudh, 1857.
- After the disastrous engagement at Chinhut, on 30 June, fell back on, and limited the defence to the Residency.
- Mortally wounded during the siege while resting in his room, by a piece of shrapnel from an exploding shell on 2 July.
- Despite his wounds and severe pain, gave detailed instructions about the conduct of the defence of the Residency, and ordered them never to surrender.
- Died at about 8 a.m. on 4 July, having earlier stated that his epitaph was simply to be 'Here lies Henry Lawrence, who tried to do his duty'.

- Buried in the Residency churchyard at Lucknow on the same day, 4 July 1857.

Ironically, before news of his death reached England, the Directors of the East India Company had convened to appoint him provisional Governor-General of India, should any accident have befallen Lord Canning during those troubled times. Henry Montgomery Lawrence, soldier, statesman and administrator, was commemorated by a statue erected to his memory in St. Paul's Cathedral, London, and with memorial tablets in St. Paul's Cathedral, Calcutta and the church in Lucknow. His eldest son Alexander was made a Baronet in recognition of his services.

During his time in India, he wrote several essays and books on Indian subjects, and had considerable literary merits. But he is best remembered for his administrative ability, his energy, his sympathies with the native aristocracy and consideration for the ordinary people, his high character and of course, his tragic death. Perhaps his most important and lasting legacy will be the military asylums (latterly schools) which he set up initially for the children and orphans of British soldiers, which bear his name to this day. Two more Lawrence asylums were opened as memorials to him after his death, one (as he had wished) at Lovedale, Ootacamund in the Nilgiri Hills in 1859, and the other at Ghora Gali in the Murree Hills in 1860. Certainly, there can be little chance of Henry Lawrence's name being forgotten among the many generations of children, whose lives and characters have been forged in one or other of these four hill schools.

**D.V. Boddington**
LRMS Sanawar, 1942–1947
June 2011 (Revised 15 September 2020)

**Bibliography:**

- *Sir Henry Montgomery Lawrence*, T.R. Moreman.
- *Life of Sir Henry Lawrence*, Sir Herbert Benjamin Edwardes, Herman Merivale
- *Lawrence of Lucknow 1806–1857*, J.L. Morison
- *Lives of Indian Officers*, Volume 2, J.W. Kaye
- *Journals of Honoria Lawrence – India Observed 1837–1854*, J. Lawrence, A. Woodwiss

# Tarzan of the Khuds

How they screened *Tarzan the Ape Man* for us, I don't know, but there we were in Barne Hall, goggle-eyed and giggling at Bo Derek displaying almost all. Ashish Bhatia, our Head Boy roared 'keep quiet' and so we did, but nevertheless giggle fits travelled up and down the hall. Miles O'Keeffe was an ersatz Tarzan like the gymming six packs of today, not like Johnny Weissmuller as Tarzan, who had been an Olympic swimming champ. Johnny used to wear a leopard skin breechclout to cover his dingle-dangles, whereas O'Keeffe wore a nondescript, saggy leather piece that looked like something from our Mochi's; and I bet he had a Victor Y Front underneath and not a version of the good old Indian '*langot*'. Growing up on highly prized dog-eared copies of Tarzan and Phantom comics, we had come to consider the jungle as the ultimate adventure. We fancied being either one of the superheroes, swinging deftly from vines and giving the bad guys hell. Luckily for us, we had our own real-life school Tarzan too—Parry.

Even though wall-climbing was invented as a sport in 1964, our adventurous seniors had handed it down to us well before that. This was evidenced by the fact that all of us participated in 'edging', which was using just the toes and outside edges of the foot to power climbing moves. At every opportunity, boys were busy edging along walls holding onto protruding masonry, brick and lightning rods, betting on who could edge the longest route. Without the additional skill of exceptional shoe polishing to hide the scuffs, edging could also cost you a serious hiding, so it was a high-risk sport.

Parry, ably supported by AP (aka Dollar), were one of the best exponents in our batch. Being natural adventurers with the attendant traits of tenacity, curiosity and ingenuity, Parry had the added advantage of being one of the longest residents of Sanawar; without having repeated a class. His full twelve years in school had given him ample opportunity to scale every manmade wall and explore each moss-lined open drain in school. After surveying all the open drains, ably guided by AP and Bala (aka Manni), he added the peculiar speciality of potholing storm drains that criss-crossed the 139-acre campus, that too, without the aid of a torch, which in those days was quite a luxury. This yet-to-be-declared-sport needed additional qualities of patience and calm while the rhodopsin in the eyes adapted to the dark. An even stronger mind was needed while navigating sticky spider webs, crawling insects and scurrying rats.

To the outsider, this skill may seem pointless, but it was superbly handy in helping us duck class, games, unpleasant seniors, teachers doing their rounds and most importantly, eating grub without it being 'grabboed'. It was on one of these marathon spelunking expeditions that Parry was discharged from a storm drain under CDH and into the steep Khud behind. The rapid trajectory of his descent was arrested by a large pine tree that he found was draped with a stout Tinospora Cordifolia vine. The plant prefers to grow on steep khuds and develops a forearm like thick vine and entices novices towards it's bright red berries, which once eaten, act as an alarmingly effective purgative, having one throw up the very precious 'grub'. Juniors have also reported foraging for these berries on the ground and unknowingly brushing against 'bichu buti' or stinging nettle, and scratching ferociously like the grey langur monkeys atop CDH.

Parry looked down; Long Back was seventy feet below and the crown of the tree leant well over the road. In a flash, Parry connected the dots between Tarzan, tree, vine and swing; but what he needed now was an axe. Undaunted, he set to fashion a Palaeolithic stone axe to start hacking at the vine with gusto. It took him a few days of secret endeavour and then we were called to witness the Tarzan Swing. Starting from up slope, Parry holding the end of the vine slipped and scrambled downhill building momentum and launched himself as Tarzan into the air crying 'aaaaeee . . . aaaaa . . . eee . . . aaaa!' Parry the screeching bob of a giant pendulum swung out; at equilibrium position he was fifty feet above the road and at massive point, well beyond it. The return trajectory brought Parry, twisting like a tornado, showering leaves and vine stems in every direction back to the khud side with a shin-splintering crash! Parry was all smiles and perspiration, despite his raked shins and bleeding palms, and looked around for someone to hand the vine to for a go. There were no ready takers after this terrifying, hair-raising exhibition, even though we risked being called 'funky', as it was a fair description of the terror kicking at the pits of our stomach, knowing one was next. However gradually, funk backed down and one by one, we pushed the bile deep into our bowels and swung out on this jungle trapeze.

It was then a matter of practice with ripped shirts, open unshorn hair and bleeding body parts, that allowed for the perfect time to launch into the passage of the familiar green and yellow Himachal Roadways bus below and swing over it with all boys screaming Tarzan's call in a deep Punjabi accent. Startled passengers of the bus, sitting on the roof, hair parted and flattened by the wind, like Rhesus monkeys, bewildered eyes streaming tears, would snap their necks upwards and see this large shape resembling a wild, Stone Age Neanderthal swing past them. With the rest of the boys screaming and jumping on the hillside, looking very much like a supporting troupe of cavemen. There was one downside—if the vine broke, the swinger would find himself on the top of the bus along with baskets of poultry, inquisitive goats and bewildered passengers headed to Dharampur or Garkhal.

Note: *Tarzan of the Apes* came out in 1981. Johnny Weissmuller had starred in the Tarzan pictures all through the late 30s to late 60s.

**Jaimal Inder Singh Shergill**
Jami | Vindhya 1985 | 1977–1985

OS Parent – Father – Tajindar Singh Shergill | Taji | Vindhya 1958 | 1951–1958

# Where Are They All Now?

In August 1950, I was in transit from one school to another. And, it must be some kind of record that between 1945 and 1950, I had been to two prestigious boarding schools, Welham and Doon, before joining the third, Sanawar. After Welham, I attended St. Thomas' Convent in Dehra Dun, followed by Delhi Public School in its various named avatars.

My Aunt had taken my sister and me to Kasauli to spend a night with the Maharani of Kashmir before dropping us off at Sanawar, the following day. On arrival, we were taken directly to the Sick Bay, as the Infirmary was then called, to be kept in quarantine. This was done because we had come up from the plains and to ensure we did not carry any infection that could be transmitted to the others. Our Resident Medical Officer was Dr Soin and the Resident Nurse was Mrs Paige, whose husband taught history. In those years, children were not permitted to go down to the plains during the longer mid-term breaks. As such, a child either spent those periods in school, or, if fortunate, would have parents/guardians come up to visit them in the mountains.

The first few days were traumatic for my sister, who for the first time in her seven years, had come away from the warmth of home life. I was, of course, by now a seasoned veteran. After three days or so, we were moved to join the rest of the children. She to PD, and I to 'Blue' House in BD. My first prefect was the short, stocky (obviously Scotsman) Donald Mackintosh. His preferred form of dealing with any infraction was painful knocks on the head using his knuckles. The other House at the time was 'Yellows'. In 1951, the House names were changed to Nilagiri (obviously blue), and Himalaya (yellow). In due course, the two Houses were further divided, with two additions. Vindhya had its boys drawn from Nilagiri's with red as its House colour, and Siwalik was allotted green as its colour.

My Housemaster was the tall, slim, affable Virendra Vyas, a bachelor who then married a few months into the year. His great friends and colleagues were the inimitable, handsome, debonair Salim Khan, who taught history and looked after the cricket team; Rathin Mitra, the arts master, was responsible for the soccer team; and the genial Bhupinder Singh who did not teach my class—they comprised the four Musketeers. An occasional addition was N.K.S. Rao, who taught biology. Of course, there were the 'femme fatales' who were wooed and pursued from time to time. Also, among the distaff element was the wonderful Piloo Rudra, whose choreography, especially her production of *Shakuntala*, with Sita Bhai in the lead role, is unforgettable.

Other icons etched in memory are Trevor Kemp, he of the unerring aim with pieces of chalk, who taught chemistry; the dour 'Chicky' Evans and dapper EA Cuzens taught physics and English respectively. The latter also coached us in cricket till Salim Khan took on that responsibility. Boss Carter once gave me 'six of the best' because of an 'act of commission' that deserved punishment. Mrs Carter taught math to the Sixth-formers, and Mrs Coombes taught geography. Her son James (Jasper) was my classmate, who attended the sixty-fifth reunion of our class in October 2019, having flown in from UK. There was Headmaster Sam Cowell, a martinet, if ever there was one, who ensured discipline in the Boys' School. Who can forget Subedar Major Jagdish Ram, who taught boxing and was responsible for the drilling and turnout of NCC cadets? Among other

characters who were very much part of our lives, were Nappi, the wizened four-foot pahadi barber, and the indispensable Charlie Bootlace, whose barfis were considered legal tender for any bets that were wagered and lost.

I recall with nostalgia, trips to Simla in the school bus that was called Shakabpa, named after a former student from Tibet or wherever. Teams would go to play against BCS to reciprocate their visit to Sanawar. One memorable visit was by our sister school Lovedale, who brought their wonderful marching band under the baton of a student, Denzil Prince. They also performed at the end of Founder's Social, where they were a great hit among all the girls, much to our disgust. And, talking of Socials, the greatly looked-forward-to event in Barne Hall where the girls were arrayed on one side of the Hall, and the boys on the other. We learned to do the foxtrot to 'Sugar bush, I love you so' and the waltz to the lilting notes of 'The Blue Danube'.

Other memories come flooding back. In my first term—or was it in '51—that I created some kind of record by swimming non-stop twenty laps? I don't think anyone had done something like that before! Our Dagroo picnics were always looked forward to with great anticipation. On one occasion, we, in the senior class, were able to get bicycles to ride to Subathu. I don't recall how far it was from Dharampur but the excursion was great fun. We were back in time for lunch.

Then there were the most memorable NCC camps in Delhi's winter in 1952, and in the more amenable weather of Poona, a year later. In the first, the Camp Commandant was Major W.A.G. Pinto of the Guards Brigade, who went on to become Lieutenant General. His standard advice to all cadets is still imprinted in my mind:

'You can fool some of the people some of the time,
You can fool some of the people all the time but,
You cannot fool all the people all the time.'

It was the first camp we attended. My Dad was then Commander-in-Chief Army and had come to visit the camp. I was accordingly detailed at the Quarter Guard to be inspected by him. And, typical of him, he stopped in front of me and asked my name!

The Poona camp was particularly remarkable because we had put up a strong cross-country team of six. Apart from me, the others were Shoki Bhatia, Ramesh Chand, Brijinder Bala, Ravi Bhatia and Aditya Nehru.

Sanawar did brilliantly with all of us finishing among the first seventeen of 102 runners!

I went into Sixth Form in 1954, and a few months later, left school to join the 12th Course at the Joint Services Wing, Dehra Dun. Among my predecessors who joined the 10th Course, were Pritam Singh, Vinod Raj Kumar, Pardaman Singh, and Sowarnjit Dhillon. I had many illustrious classmates and some from junior classes, too. There was M.V.K. Sharma who Sam Cowell dubbed 'Archie'. He went on to become Navy Chief. And there was a string of outstanding polo players who achieved international fame and recognition. Where are they all now?

**Air Marshal K.C. Cariappa VSM PVSM**
Nanda | Vindhya 1954 | 1950–1954

Qualified Flying Instructor | 1965 War – shot down / taken PoW on 22 Sep; repatriated on 22 Jan '66 | ADC to Air Chief Marshal Arjan Singh | 1971 War – commanded a Helicopter Unit on the Eastern Front; Vayu Sena Medal for gallantry | Commanded 3 fighter stations | AOC-in-C, South Western Air Command | Avid Trekker – Ladakh, Uttarakhand and Nepal – Annapurna Half-Circuit (2018) 18,500ft. | Forest and Wildlife Conservationist

OS Sibling – Sister – Nalini Cariappa | Vindhya 1959 | 1950–1952

OS Children – Daughter – Gayatri Cariappa | Vindhya 1994 | 1987–1994
Son-in-Law – Saurabh Gupta | Nilagiri 1990 | 1985–1990

# The Prompter

One of the most looked-forward-to events in my last school was the staff play at Founders'. In spite of my own secret theatrical ambitions, I had to be content to play the prompter. I had my work cut out for me. Many of the actors just could not learn their lines, the most incorrigible being two senior teachers who had been my teachers when I was in school. One year, they had a rather extended scene between them. The scene opened to a complete and deadly silence. I threw them a line with no response. I threw it again. But all they did was smile—first at each other, then at the audience. Then one of them turned his back to the audience, and through the side of his mouth, muttered, 'Babu it's your line'. Then he turned back to the audience and smiled. After a pause, the other actor repeated this performance and said, 'No, Babu, it's your line'.

For the rest of the scene, my prompting took the form of: 'Mr G. Sir, your line "- - - - - - -'. 'Mr B. Sir, your line " - - - - - -"'.

At the traditional greenroom party, a member of the Board of Governors asked me, 'Were you in the play too? I don't remember seeing you on stage.'

'I was the prompter,' I said with the right touch of modest pride.

'Oh!' he said. 'You did your job very well. We were up in the gallery, and we could hear every single word you said, throughout the play.'

Another time, a teacher had a walk-on part in the third act as the butler. All through rehearsals, he would stand close to me, muttering for hours on end. It destroyed my concentration and one day, I snapped at him, 'Look, you don't come on till the third act—what are you muttering away for already?'

'I need to learn my cues, don't I?' he said and went on with his muttering.

On the final day, his cue came and he was nowhere to be seen. He had to bring in a pie and for the next ten minutes, the dialogue was centered around this pie. In despair, the director called out to the actor on the stage:

'Just pretend to eat the damn pie.' The actor tucked his serviette under his chin, sawed at the tablecloth with his fork and knife and pretended to eat the pie. A crisis was averted. Later in the act, the young lovers settled down to play out their famous love scene. Just then, the butler appeared behind them, carrying his tray, and announced in a deep sepulchral voice, 'Here is the pie.'

Once, the director gave me a small role. I had a love scene. Everything went well till the dress rehearsal, when there was a loud scream from my little son, who was sitting in the audience: 'Wait till I get home. I am going to tell Mummy what a dirty man you are.'

After this, I stayed firmly behind the curtains and limited my role to that of the prompter.

**Dr Harishpal S. Dhillon**
UD | Nilagiri 1957 | 1949–1957
STAFF 1971–1986 | HOD English | Housemaster | Headmaster 1995–1999 | Headmaster YPS Patiala 1986–1995 | YPS Mohali 1999–2010

OS Sibling – Sister – Yogindra (Dhillon) | Nilagiri 1956 | 1951–1956

OS Children – Daughter – Priya Dhillon | Himalaya 1988 | 1979–1988
    Daughter – Naina Dhillon | Himalaya 1988 | 1979–1988
    Son – Jai Singh Dhillon | Nilagiri 1991 | 1982–1989

OS Grandchildren – Granddaughter – Mannat Tipnis | Himalaya 2013 | 2006–2013
    Grandson – Abhay Tipnis | Himalaya 2017 | 2009–2011
    Granddaughter – Inaaya Kumar | Himalaya | 2018–To Date
    Grandson – Rehaan Kumar | Himalaya | 2020–To Date

**Source and Acknowledgements:**
Published as a Middle in *The Tribune* on 11 December 2006 and reproduced in *Of Cabbages and Kings – A Book of Middles*, (New Delhi: Picus Books, Hay House Publishers India, 2014).

# Sanawar through the Eyes of a Young Bride

Starting a new life – life after marriage – comes with excitement and apprehension for any young girl. Add to that a distant and remote residential school tucked away in the hills and the trepidation can assume dizzying heights.

On 8 March 1953, I boarded the Kalka Mail from Delhi along with my late husband Virendra Vyas, who was the first Housemaster of Vindhya House at Sanawar. We were part of a school party returning to school after winter vacation. Travelling in the train, pondering upon what the days ahead would hold, I had 'curious little visitors' coming in to see me under some or the other pretext—young boys and girls who had been wondering what Mrs Vyas looked like. We reached Kalka the next morning and had our very own personalized limo waiting for us—the school's official vehicle, a military truck driven by the driver, Hans Raj.

We were allotted a beautiful Cottage—the one just below the Tuck Shop. It was heavenly and peaceful—except when some of the cheekier students passing by would abruptly develop a loud cough. The more daring ones would pelt stones on the roof, just to frighten me. That was a nice introduction. Better still were groups of kids singing 'Jago Mohan Pyare'. After a while, I actually had to step out and request them to change the song, to which they obliged and switched to 'Ichak dana, beechak dana'.

I was amazed by the schedule the boys and girls (and teaching staff) followed. People seemed forever to be on the go. Classes, games, drill, prep, extracurricular activities or PT—all done in quick succession to the sound of a bugle. Uniformity and super-consistency seemed to be the order of the day. Even the appearance of students seemed so much alike—what with their haircuts and crisp uniforms. While the students and staff were welcoming, the food in the Dining Hall certainly wasn't. Stews of various sorts and bread pudding it was, on most days.

The other thing that struck me most about Sanawar was its location. Henry Lawrence had truly chosen a very special place. The cool, crisp air, the lovely walks fringed by tall pine trees, the view of surrounding hill stations, made it all look fairytale-like. Kasauli and Dagshai at a distance, looked like pieces of cake. Every spot gave one the feeling of being on top of the world. Sometimes, the silence and quiet were almost disturbing. At times, you could hear the sound of your own breathing and of dew falling on dry leaves. The numerous ghost stories about the place added to the discomfiture.

Rathin Mitra, Saleem Khan, Bhuppi (Mr B. Singh to most) among many others, soon became close family friends with whom we spent memorable times, chatting over tea sessions and get-togethers, going for countless walks; the constant leg-pulling, laughing at silly jokes and just having fun. Once, we went to Saleem's House for dinner and he offered us coffee afterwards. Everyone was served coffee in elegant-looking cups except Saleem Khan himself, who drank out of a glass. Bhuppi started to explain that I should not mind as he likes to drink his coffee that way, while he winked at the others and they all giggled. The giggles soon turned into uncontrollable laughter—it turned out that Saleem had just four cups in his House.

When I had just reached Sanawar, on the first day, the DHM Mr Cowell hosted a lunch—a rather lavish affair, where I met many friends with whom we were to build wonderful associations. Just after lunch, I asked Bhuppi inquisitively, 'I don't see Mrs Cowell'. With a serious face, Bhuppi whispered back in my ear, 'Mr Cowell does not have a wife—he has a dog instead.'

A bit trying as the period may have seemed – today, decades after leaving it – Sanawar is a second home to me. As my late husband Virender joined the IAS in 1957 and we moved on in life, Sanawar never really left us. We made life-long bonds with some of the most wonderful people I have known, and we constantly looked for reasons to revisit the hilltop. Sanawar is a place like that—its magical spell affects you for life.

**Mrs Gomti Vyas**
Wife of Late Mr Virendra Vyas | Teacher 1952–1957 | First Housemaster – Vindhya

OS Children – Son – Subir Vyas | Vindhya 1980 | 1975–1980

# In My Mind's Eye

My first memory of Sanawar is from when I was still in Col. Brown in Dehra Dun. My father had heard of Sanawar and so thought it would be a good idea to break the train journey at Dharampur, on our family annual holiday to Simla, to go and have a look. I think we took a bus to Garkhal and a tonga up to Sanawar. We both liked the place and I joined in March 1951—to start what turned out to be the happiest three years of my childhood. Even today, seventy years later, I feel nostalgic about Sanawar and some of my closest friends are from my relatively short stay there.

There were only two houses in 1951. I was in the Blue House and when that became Nilagiri, I was shifted to a new Green House, Siwalik. I cannot forget that during a morning inspection soon after I had joined, I got a hard knock on my head with Macintosh's knuckles. He had instructed me gruffly the previous day to get a haircut, so off I went that evening to the barber, but it turned out that it just wasn't cut short enough to satisfy the Head Boy.

The food that first year was practically inedible—and to think that one of the major reasons for my leaving Col. Brown was the lousy food there. We would get a lump of cold congealed 'green' dal with four slices of unbuttered bread for dinner every night. And once a month, the occasional pudding at night would have an opening dose. There would then be a mad rush for the 'bogs' around 3 a.m., summer or winter. Charlie's barfis, gulab jamuns and samosas were our sustenance and our luxuries. Our miserable pocket money of Rs 10 per month did not only have to buy our toiletries, but afford us our luxuries too. Some of the boys would receive regular food parcels from home, particularly Pradeep (affectionately called Pussy) Khanna, whose parents owned Britannia Biscuits and Exchange Stores in Delhi. He had to have his arm gently twisted to share his tuck. But things changed dramatically when Mrs Nanda joined as the matron in the Boys' Department. We even started to get tandoori rotis and chicken for Sunday lunches. And so, naturally, she was very popular. We would look forward to the night tutorials in Sammy Cowell's House for poetry, as Mrs Cowell would bring us cups of steaming hot chocolate.

There were treks to Gurkha Fort and Monkey Point, picnics on the hillside and in the cemetery, and the annual picnic at Dagroo. One of the very enjoyable outings that I vividly remember, happened in the week when we went to Narkanda and beyond with the Three Musketeers – Virendra Vyas, Salim Khan and Rathin Mitra. Vyas Sahib was a keen photographer and inculcated this love in quite a few of us. It was during this time that Gomti came as a young bride and we spent many enjoyable hours in the Vyas household, food being an integral part of those good times.

I can never forget the first time I saw 'stars'. I had never boxed in my life and on my first entry into the ring, Subedar Major Sahib sent me in to fight Raj Sondhi. I had hardly stepped back after shaking hands when Raj landed an almighty knock on my face. I collapsed and saw stars. A few seconds later, I tottered up shakily and had hardly taken my guard when Raj landed another mighty knock and I collapsed again. This happened a couple more times before the Subedar Major felt that my initiation was complete. I got the Best Loser's Medal that year as I was declared the pluckiest (or was it for the most bashed up?) boxer.

A number of parents would drive up from Delhi over long weekends and the term breaks to take their children and wards to Kasauli and neighbouring places. My parents never came up in the three years that I was in school, but I was adopted by Vinod's father. He would take Vinod and me to Kasauli and we would stay at the MES Inspection Bungalow. I first tasted Indian Chinese food in Kas. Walking through the bazaars, having a coffee at Alasia and going to the Club were our favourite pastimes, while making sure to avoid all the stray dogs. I was petrified of them. We would sometimes bump into the Bhatias, Berys and Nehrus at the Kasauli Club and be invited to join them for lunch.

There was always music at the morning Assembly before the Principal, Mr Carter, walked in. I can't remember anybody telling us about the music. It was therefore a very pleasant surprise when I heard the familiar music many years later at London's Covent Garden, where I had gone to see *Swan Lake*. There would be singing at Assembly and I remember Sammy Cowell often came and reminded Gurdip, Vikram and I that we could only mouth the words and that not a sound should come out from us. One of the most memorable assemblies I can recall was when we were in Sixth Form, in fact, during the last few months of our stay in school. After

Assembly, Mr Carter asked the Sixth Form to stay back and we were given a real shelling. The previous evening at Prep, when we should all have been supervising the younger students, we were in our class having a chalk fight, while Shoki Bhatia played 'La Paloma' on the mouth organ. Mr Cowell had walked in just then and a chalk had hit him. 'La Paloma' then became our class anthem.

We learnt so many interesting things at school and some are still so fresh in my mind. Mr Cuzens taught us a ditty – Willy, Willy, Henry, Ste, Henry Dick John Henry 3, Teds 1,2,3, Dick, Henry 4,5,6 – for us to remember the names of kings of England from 1066 to 1485. He also taught us three short stanzas to remember the causes, wars and the results of the Hundred Years' War. Mr Kemp taught us a ditty to remember the atomic weights of the elements in descending order – Pot, So, Cal etc. – and Mrs Carter taught us Mathematics; to this day, I can hear her words 'Tangent comes from tango; I touch!' Mrs Coombs taught us Geography, Mr Cowell English, Mr Evans Physics and Mr Vyas Hindi—all so very dedicatedly.

The memories are so many—like a kaleidoscope. The secret clubs that we formed – Spider's Web of four boys and four girls – marching to school, dances, movies and plays in Barne Hall; the *pagal* Gymkhanas and swimming galas; the punishments to run down to Barnes and back several times (was it 100 steps?); shining our shoes so that the prefect was able to see his face in it; the daily M.I. room with Mastu dispensing Soda Sal and Mendel's throat paint as sinecures for most ailments, and boys walking in with a limp pretending that they had sprained their foot to avoid taking part in some sport; Miss Chatterji catching me sleeping in the front row of a class of only eight people; and the gorgeous Miss Ahuja supervising us at Prep . . . I could go on and on . . .

The Annual Public School NCC camps were started in 1952. The first camp was in Delhi Cantonment. Ranjit Bhatia was our ace long-distance runner. Ravi Bhatia and I were also in the cross-country team and heard clapping as we came in. Imagine our surprise when we realized that we were not the last to come in but amongst the first, as Ranjit had led the fast pack into Connaught Place. The second one was in Pune in 1953. My most vivid memory of that is that once again, I was pushed into the boxing ring and received the worst thrashing of my life. I had been training for distance running but our 'boxer' pretended that he had the 'runs' as the opponents were the tough boys from Jabalpur (then Jubbalpore). Unfortunately for me, I happened to be in the same weight category and wasn't given a choice, and had to box for the school.

Founders' was always very special—so much preparation went into it. I remember the President Dr Rajendra Prasad coming for my first one in 1951, and the Maharaja of Patiala for the last one in 1953, when out of the blue, I was awarded the President's Medal. Shoki Bhatia was the front runner for it, but he was caught gadding at night. We had no girl in our class, so Sita Bhai from the Class of '54 got it that year.

A number of people from our class left early, either to do their Matriculation examination or join the National Defence Academy or the Dufferin. This meant that there were only seven of us doing our Senior Cambridge. In those 'good days', we did not have a moment's doubt that after Sanawar, we would not be accepted at St. Stephens College. Mrs Sircar was the head of the Prep Department and her husband, Mr Sircar was a senior member of the college faculty (he went on to become the Principal, a few years later). Vikram Soni (Class of '52) and I were the two Sanawarians who were in residence and our rooms were the meeting place for all the Sanawarians who were day scholars, including Ranjit Bhatia (who went on to become the College and University Athletics' Captain and later, ran for India at the Rome Olympics), Shoki Bhatia, Ashok Nehru and Raj Sondhi.

The School Motto and the school song left a deep impression on most of us. 'Never Give In' gave us the determination and the tenacity during the difficult moments of our lives, though my wife always insists that my stubbornness comes from there. Although moral or religious instruction was never part of the curriculum, the environment provided by the staff certainly inculcated in us a sense of fair play and uprightness, which have been great pillars in our lives. The staff in those days was so sincere and dedicated, and their lives and actions made them excellent role models for us. There has never been a day since that I have felt ashamed of my actions; other than that, I should probably have been less forthright and more diplomatic at times. There was no ragging or bullying that I can remember in those days and the thought of the sadistic ragging that goes on nowadays in most educational institutions is abhorrent to the alumni from our times. I am proud to say that I do not recollect any of the vices of most public schools that exist today, existing then.

Many years later, we sent our two girls, Sandhya and Aarti, to Sanawar. I was very keen that they go there but my wife wanted to keep them at home. However, the choice was out of our hands when I was transferred from Bombay to Delhi, and we could not get them admitted to a local school. I think that the girls had a happy and fulfilling time there. Sandhya went on to be the Head Girl, while Aarti had to leave in L-V as we had, by then, moved to Hong Kong. I remember Aarti writing to me to explain that she had slipped down in the Mark Reading as a number of girls had cheated. She asked for my advice. I was taken back to my first term in school, when I topped the Mark Reading. Until then, Tup Carter had always stood first and so everybody thought that I must have cheated. I took that up as a challenge and never slipped down from the first position in my three years at the school. Now here I was, being asked by my daughter what she should do. After much thought, I wrote and told her that she would have to take the decision herself and then be responsible for it and live with her conscience and the consequences of her actions. I am proud that both our girls learnt to be responsible for their own decisions throughout their lives. While the girls were in Sanawar, I had the honour to be invited to be part of the school's Board of Governors for six years. The girls have proudly taken their spouses to Sanawar for a 'pilgrimage' but unfortunately, their children will not be able to enjoy Sanawar as they live abroad.

**Dewan Ramesh Chand**
Nilagiri/Siwalik 1953 | 1951–1953

OS Children – Daughter - Sandhya Chand | Siwalik | 1977 – 1982
Daughter - Aarti Chand | Siwalik | 1977 – 1982

# Life in Prep School

I had made one visit to see the school before joining. The only thing I remember was that the shorts the girls wore for games were shorter than any mini-skirts I had seen in my life. I don't know if that was a deciding factor, but it must have meant something if that's the only thing I remember. At the age of nine, I joined the school.

Getting to school involved quite a journey if you lived in Calcutta. From Howrah station, we caught the Kalka Mail that took thirty-six hours to get to Kalka station, from where we had to take a ninety-minute bus ride up to school. In later years, it was the overnight Rajdhani Express and the Himalayan Queen that got us to Kalka. The Calcutta School Party had children not only from Calcutta but also from the north-eastern states. So we'd have an entire train compartment dedicated to fifty to seventy children, along with the unfortunate staff members assigned to manage the lot. Farewells could be emotional, but thirty minutes into the train journey, multiple conversations would kick off and homesickness would quickly be pushed to the back of our minds. We were too busy trying to find out who'd had the most fun in the holidays and what tuck was being carried back to school.

I seem to have it in my mind (possibly having brainwashed myself) that I was never homesick, always loved school, and was very macho and brave. On one occasion, when my parents dropped me to the station, I asked them to leave before the train departed. When they didn't, I asked them again. I wanted to show that I was tough and not the clingy type who would cry and miss his parents. My mother told me that they were going to stay on anyway and chat with the other parents and if I didn't want to hang out with them, I was welcome to go to my berth and spend time with my friends. Of course, her take on this now is that I wanted to cry and didn't want them to see me do so. As tough as I would like to think I was, I'm 100 per cent sure that my mother's version is the truth. Till date, if I'm troubled by something, I tend to not share it with my parents. Not because I'm not close to them or feel uncomfortable sharing, but because I don't want them to stress over it. I'd rather have a crack at fixing it myself first. It's only when options within my capabilities have been exhausted that I reach out for help. This is a trait I've definitely picked up from my father. In all these years, I'm yet to hear him complain about anything.

For a boy who hadn't left home until the age of nine, I settled into boarding school quite well. With boarding schools, you either fit in or you don't. There's rarely a middle ground. Luckily for me, I fitted in.

Classes in Prep School were from Monday to Saturday. The last class on Saturday was 'letter writing'. Back then, letters were really the only form of communication and oh, what joy it was to receive a handwritten letter. There was an entire ceremony that took place before the letter was read. You'd first try and guess who it was from by the handwriting on the envelope. Then you'd hold the envelope against the light to ensure no part was torn while opening it. Your heart would beat with even more excitement when the envelope had 'DO NOT BEND. PHOTOGRAPHS ENCLOSED' written on it. That, of course, presented a delicious dilemma when you opened it—should you read the letter first or look at the photograph? And even when you had the photograph in your hand, should you look at the image first or at what was written behind it? The entire process was like eating a meal—some eat their favourite dish first while others save it for the end, for the taste to linger on.

In the early days, I was diligent about writing and my father still has a file that contains all the letters I wrote from school. I'd like to say that my early diligence was because I wanted to ensure communication between my parents and their only child was regular, transparent and filled with love so that the wonderful connection I had with them would remain eternally beautiful. However, the fact was that we received our weekly pocket money only after we submitted our letters, and so it had to be done! By the time I got to Senior School, with no letter-writing class, my parents would give me pre-addressed, stamped envelopes and tell me to post one every week so they knew I was alive.

The food we got from home never lasted. If you didn't share it, the others would soon enough, break into your trunk or your locker and steal it. A 'system' of 'sharing partners' was in place. You and one other person (could be more) decided to share the food that each brought from home. You were obliged to share half of what you had. The duration of this contract was one school term, during which, like canvassing talent for a sports league, you looked around to see what kind of tuck others had got, so you could find a more lucrative sharing partner the following term.

Food was a rare commodity and we were starving all the time. Not only would we eat absolutely anything, we also invented rules that allowed us to do so. The most famous was the 'forty-second' rule. According to this, if any edible item fell on the ground, 'science' reliably said that it would be forty seconds before it became unfit for human consumption. As long as you picked it up within that time, you could put it in your mouth. There were times when someone was eating say, a chocolate, and you asked him for a piece. He would pretend not to hear and put the whole thing in his mouth. Then he would take it out and say, 'Sorry brother, I already put it in my mouth'. More than once I've replied, 'No problem, brother' and broken off a piece of saliva-soaked chocolate and put it in my mouth. Desperate circumstances called for such desperate measures. Then there were those who really did not want to share their food. If it was too big for them to down in one go, they would spit all over it. The appropriate response, if they were not bigger built than you were, was to pull the said food item in your direction and sprinkle it with your own share of saliva.

Of the tuck we could buy in school, my favourite was a little orange sweet. We got ten for one rupee. A packet of glucose biscuits also cost one rupee. Sometimes a bunch of us pooled in and bought a tin of condensed milk, into which we would dip our glucose biscuits. Or we'd just eat it plain. Milk powder was something else we ate plain. Just dry milk powder, poured onto palms that we would lick clean. In the later years, we could afford chocolates and packets of crisps. Of course, Maggi noodles were the most popular even then. If we had the luxury of an immersion rod, it would be 'cooked' in a plastic mug. If not, it would be soaked in cold water. More often than not, it was just crushed and eaten uncooked.

Bedtime was 8 p.m., but on Saturdays, 'lights-out' was at 9 p.m. On Saturdays, we were also allowed to dance with the girls in the Common Room. I remember the floor of the Common Room was tiled and as ten- and eleven-year-olds we would count how many tiles close we could get to the girls we were dancing with. Advait liked Gaurika, but rumour was that she had a preference for me. Advait was a giant in those days—56 kgs at the age of ten. I was skinny and scrawny. One Saturday night, he grabbed me by the collar and dragged me to the staircase below the girls' dormitory, which was just above the Common Room. He then put his foot just past the tile below the staircase that boys were not supposed to cross.

With me still held by the collar, he shouted up towards the girls' dormitory in the most booming voice a ten-year-old could possess, 'Gaurika Gupta! Who do you want to dance with, him or me?' This was followed by the whispering of four or five girls at the top of the staircase, after which a squeaky voice answered, 'She wants to dance with him'. Advait's face was hit by a wrecking ball of shock and he instantly burst into tears and ran to the dormitory. I was not as pleased about the young lady's preference as I was about the fact that Goliath had chosen not to crush David that night.

**Papa CJ**
Chirag Jain | Siwalik 1995 | 1986–1995
Stand-up Comedian | Author | Executive Coach

*Excerpt from Papa CJ's autobiography titled* Naked.

# It's Not Rocket Science

I had dreamt of joining the Indian Air Force ever since I saw Hawker Hunter jet fighters from Ambala Airbase piloted by Old Sanawarians, soar in the skies above Sanawar, do aerobatics and break the sound barrier. Sometimes, they would come very low and show off. Major Som Dutt, [the] headmaster, suggested that I go for the selection. But unfortunately, I could not pass the strict medical examination. It was a huge disappointment.

Eventually I joined the Army Corps of Engineers and decided to follow through my dream of flying, by building a hang glider and learning to fly it. I did not realize how difficult and dangerous that experiment was. The years in Sanawar had given me the confidence to achieve a seemingly impossible feat. I had the chance to tinker with tools and machinery in the Arts and Crafts Department at School, and the stamina and agility built on the school's playing fields stood me in good stead.

On 31 August 1976, as I prepared for my first flight from a 500 ft hill, I wondered whether I would survive. A whole lot of things could go wrong. To begin with, my hang glider was not built out of aircraft-grade materials, as specified in the drawings received from Freeflight USA. Instead, I had used local substitutes, whatever I could find in the hardware shops around Pune—aluminum tubes of doubtful origin instead of 6061-T6 alloy tubes; white plastic tarpaulin fabric instead of Dacron. Many hang gliding pioneers, who had built their own wings and learnt to fly, had perished. It was not recommended even in the construction plans that I had got hold of.

My initial idea was to make a full-scale non-flying model and see what it really looked like and then find a sponsor to help me import a professionally built hang glider from USA, UK or Germany, where the new sport of hang-gliding was becoming popular. I did not have the means to either import a hang glider or train at a hang-gliding school abroad. And nobody in their right mind could have imagined that a locally built hang glider with untested materials could be flown in our country, and that too without any training. A couple of experienced sailplane pilots in India had tried and failed. They cautioned me not to 'challenge' the law of gravity. The odds were stacked heavily against the success of my experiment. If I succeeded, it would be the first in India. My efforts to get some advice from the Government Gliding Centre in Pune were also of no use. They cautioned me that I would be breaking rules if I tried to build and fly without permission from the civil aviation authority.

With no sponsor in sight, I was getting impatient. I joked with friends from the paratrooper regiment to try out my hang glider. No volunteers came forward. My contraption looked too crude—nothing like a sleek hang glider should look. People were beginning to laugh and dared me to fly it. The two-page 'Flight Instruction' attached with the construction plans cautioned, 'DO NOT ATTEMPT TO FLY WITHOUT THE HELP OF A QUALIFIED INSTRUCTOR'.

I decided to do a simple test. Check whether my hang glider would withstand wind pressure and lift me a few feet off the ground. 'DO NOT FLY HIGHER THAN YOU ARE WILLING TO FALL', warned another guideline that came with the drawings. Expecting the hang glider to collapse any moment, I ran with it on level ground for a few days and learnt to handle it, while it bucked like a wild horse in gusty winds.

It was time for a small flight, no higher than three to five feet above the ground. I figured that I could manage to handle a fall from the low height. I identified a suitable wind-facing slope, at Dighi Hills, not far from my House, north of Pune City. The slope was strewn with rocks. In hang-gliding schools abroad, initial training is conducted on sand dunes or smooth grass slopes to minimize injury in case of a heavy landing. It took several days to clear the rocks and make the slope safe for running without tripping.

Now this is where my skill at running downhill came in handy. I had acquired the ability run downhill while collecting pinecones in Sanawar. Walking up and down on rocky slopes was easy for me.

For my first low-level flight, I chose a perfect morning with the wind blowing steadily from the west on to the hill. I lifted the 20 kgs hang glider, faced directly towards the wind and ran a few steps down this slope and to my utter surprise, got lifted a couple of feet off the ground. The flight lasted only about five seconds. And as I neared the ground, I pushed the control bar forward to stall the wing a few inches off the ground. I realized how the Wright Brothers and other aviation pioneers must have felt like and got hooked to flying. It was the most exciting moment of my life. I had succeeded in building and flying my very own hang glider, the first in India. Luckily, I managed to get support from General H.K. Kapoor and General S.N. Sharma, and they sent me off to do an instructor course in the UK and bring back the latest equipment. I was tasked to start a Hang Gliding School for the Army at the College of Military Engineering in Pune.

Our school motto has sustained me through the years, from that first flight in 1976 till today, I have continued to fly. I have had more than my share of hard landings and crashes, but repaired and recuperated both body and equipment each time, to soar higher the next day . . . and continue to fly to this day, at seventy-seven.

## NEVER GIVE IN!

**Lt. Col. Vivek Umesh Mundkur**
Siwalik 1961 | 1957–1961
Army Engineers, Innovator – built and flew India's first hang glider in 1976 (Limca Book of Records) | Built a Hovercraft; designed a portable Solar Pump for small farmers to win Greenpeace Innovation Challenge 2013 | Installed windmill at Komic Monastery at 4582 m, the highest in the world.
Adventure fanatic in Aero sports and Water sports.

Parents – Father – Umesh Anand Mundkur | STAFF 1956–1981 |
       Biology Teacher | Cricket and Athletics Coach | Housemaster
       Mother – Kumud Mundkur | STAFF 1957–1981 | Matron

OS Sibling – Sister – Aruna (Mundkur) Kodical | Siwalik 1964 | 1957–1964

# Interview – Dr H.P.S. Dhillon

Q.1. Who is a Sanawarian? How long does it take to become one?

Ans. A Sanawarian is anyone who can look upon this hilltop as a sort of second home and who, when he's away from here, regards Sanawar as a sort of emotional anchor. As far as time is concerned, I don't think it is possible to lay down any specific time—though, of course, it would have to be some length of time to be able to think of Sanawar as a second home.

Q.2. What is your opinion of the students, their attitude towards the school, the teachers, one another and towards the opposite sex?

Ans. Well! I find that by and large, they're very lovable—they're a little confused in their minds about how they feel towards the school. Their attitude towards teachers – let's say in the last three years – has gone through a change. Before, they were obviously respectful and yet didn't really seem to know the teachers, now they are more familiar with the teachers and there seems to be more of a sense of friendship than before. Towards each other, I find they tend to get into groups and all their affections and loyalties are centred only on these groups.

Q.3. What is your attitude to a boy–girl relationship? For example what would you do if you caught a girl and boy holding hands behind the Art Room?

Ans. I'd ask myself: why behind the Art Room? Surely, if it was a harmless thing like holding hands, they wouldn't need to go behind the Art Room to do it. Well, I feel since it's a co-ed school, there must be a greater coming together of boys and girls and yet the times—the world is very promiscuous today and we owe it to ourselves and to our children to give them some measure of protection from the instincts which could lead them astray.

Q.4. Has being an OS helped you as a teacher?

Ans. It's a difficult question. It's as if the Sanawar that I knew as a student was different and the Sanawar that I know as a teacher is a different entity altogether. But yes, in problems arising in dorm life, I suppose, my own experience has helped. But this would have been true even if I had been educated in any other public school.

Q.5. Do you approve of the words of the school song?

Ans. Yes, I do! Only if we believe we are the best will we strive to achieve perfection because there'd be a standard that we have to maintain and of course, for me, it's the only school that I've really known and so I just accept the words.

Q.6. Do you enjoy teaching the boys as much as the girls? Who has been or is your favourite student?

Ans. I've taught different batches from year to year. I found, generally speaking, that girls are more responsive, more sensitive and especially when you are teaching literature, you can feel an immediate communication develop with the girls. Of course there have been boys with whom I've been able to achieve this and there have been girls who've yawned in the middle of an explanation of Keats' 'Ode to a Nightingale' but what I say is an overall generalization. It's difficult to single out one student but I can say that the 1972 group has been my favourite group – Maneka Anand, Jyostna Jamwal, Rohini Arora, Harsimiran Grewal, Gayatri Sondhi, Vasant Dhar, Neeraj Madhok, Sonali Parmar, Mala Khosla – they all came together in one group and were all very alive, very responsive, very challenging. I liked them because side by side, with the classroom teaching, there seemed to be some personal give and take. I feel I did the most with this group. I was totally involved with them and was truly a teacher.

Q.7. You're obviously a very popular teacher. How much of a lift does it give you? Can a teacher function without being popular? How much of a handicap can it be?

Ans. Yes, I do feel flattered by this popularity thing. This may be a sign of my mental immaturity but that's the way I am. I feel a certain amount of popularity does help, especially in your dealing with the children outside the classroom—performing an unpalatable task like meting out punishment becomes easier because you know the children will accept these in the right spirit and harbour no grudges and resentment towards you afterwards. In the same way, I suppose the unpopular teacher's task becomes so much more difficult. Of course, as I've discovered, popularity and unpopularity have little to do with playing down to the children. I've known teachers who have constantly tried to curry favour with their students and still been very unpopular and I've known teachers who were strict to the point of harshness and yet were fairly popular.

Q.8. Can you recall your own English teacher? Do say something about her.

Ans. Actually, I had a series of English teachers but I suppose the person you want me to talk about is Miss Chatterji. I remember the first day she came to teach us in U-III. The term had started and we were without an English teacher. Just after the Milk Break, Jaideep Singh came running into the class shouting at the top of his voice, 'Yaar, she's come—she's fab'; we didn't use the word 'Jaaz' then. Of course what he was referring to was her appearance, because she always used to be so elegantly dressed. In fact, she was fastidious about everything. What I remember most about her was the painstaking way in which she corrected all our written work. I look back with regret now and think that if I had done my correction work properly, my English would have been much better than what it is.

Q.9. That was lovely, Sir, but what is your relationship with her now, both of you being English teachers at Sanawar?

Ans. I am still in awe of her, still a little frightened of her – nothing to do with the person she is – and yet in spite of this, we do have a cordial, friendly relationship.

Q.10. You have been heard to say that you'll happily spend the rest of your life teaching at Sanawar. For Heaven's sake, Sir, do you mean it?

Ans. Yes, I mean it. There are times when you feel resentful of this splendid isolation, when you feel that all the staff here are very inbred, but I myself get into a terrible rut. I resent the lack of intellectual stimulus and sometimes for weeks together, I would not have had an intelligent conversation with another adult and then I go into class and teach and find that my teaching is getting across to the children and I experience such an upsurge of feeling, a sense almost of intoxication, and at that time, nothing else seems to matter. And of course, outside of class, I've been able to achieve such a satisfying relationship with the children that it gives me great fulfilment to teach. For these things, there is no substitute and this is why I say so happily that I am willing to spend the rest of my life at Sanawar.

Q.11. Then, Sir, what's happened to your ambition as writer—the ambition of your salad days?

Ans. It's question which always bugs the rest of my family as well. I remember five years ago, my sister said something along similar lines and the words she used were, 'Oh God! It makes me sick to see your contentment, your smug satisfaction. You're like a pig wallowing in the muck and the mire, with no desire to improve.'

Yes, I do have ambitions. I want to be a recognized writer and to this end, I do write a fairly great deal. It's just that I am not the sort of person with drive and push. All these years, I just haven't known how to cross the bridge between finishing a piece of writing and getting it published. Now that my first novel has finally been published, I am more than ever convinced that I can further my ambition just as well being here at Sanawar as anywhere else.

Q.12. Do you find material for your novels, stories here? Intellectual stimulation among the staff, students? Do you find it all amusing, i.e., the people and situations?

Ans. Not so far. Till now, I've been drawing on my experiences before I came here but just this last year, an idea has come to my mind for a story and I'm just letting it grow. It's about a boy from a low-income, rural background who wins a scholarship to come and study in a school like ours and I'd like to be able to write about the conflicts and tensions in his mind, the almost grim experience of being brought up with children who are from a very different background. I don't know—it's still an idea but I feel if I ever get down to it, it has great potential. What I find amusing is the earnest seriousness which is brought to the most trivial matter. Sort of things being blown out of proportion and a sense of balance, a sense of perspective getting lost and this is true not only of the students but the teachers as well. Often, it becomes difficult to keep a straight face when you see people getting all worked up about whether a decision in a cricket match was correct or not.

Q13. Would you clearly make out in your stories that it is Sanawar you write about?

Ans. Whatever it was, I wouldn't specify in my stories that it was Sanawar. It would obviously be Sanawar. I would use material from here and project it against a more general background.

Q.14. What is your reaction to rudeness—is it violent or merely indifferent? What is it that you hate most in the attitude of the students/staff?

Ans. As a person, I react very strongly to rudeness but I also feel that sometimes it is not intentional. For instance, when I'm walking down the road and there are a group of students sitting on the wall deep in conversation, I wouldn't regard it as rudeness if they didn't jump up like jack in the boxes to wish me. The sort of rudeness which really bugs me is when you're trying to give a child a talking to and the child puts on a pose of annoyance and indifference. With the staff, I think it is the sort of cynicism, the ability that some of them have, to mock everything, everyone and to criticize. I feel if they do not believe even in themselves or in what they are doing, they are just throwing away their lives.

Q.15. Do you find the staff narrow-minded—the younger or the older? Do you think it has something to do with age?

Ans. By and large, I don't think the staff are really narrow-minded here. I feel as a group, they are friendly, enterprising and fairly outward going. The problem, as I think I said before, is our location. We're forced always, even against our choice, to interact only with members of the school community. If there some frequent contact with others, even if it were only with the army in Kasauli or Subathu, we'd always have some yardstick for comparison and it would be easier to understand each other, easier to accept things without giving them an exaggerated importance. In Sanawar, at least, I feel age has little to do with the sort of person one is.

Q.16. What would involve conforming to a place like Sanawar? Do you consider yourself a conformist?

Ans. I feel a conformist in Sanawar, at least among the teachers, would be a person who is willing to answer any calls that may be made upon his time or his mind, even beyond what we normally regard as our job or as our working hours. In this regard, I think most of us are conformists. I, as an individual, do sometimes tend to grumble when I have to do a little extra bit but I don't really mean it. So I suppose I am a conformist.

Q.17. Do you find anything lacking in Sanawar?

Ans. It's something you can see right away—the isolation. Of course, the physical isolation, we can't do anything about—we're just on a hilltop and we can't do anything about that, but on the mental and emotional plane, we must try and let the world in. I feel our children are so very sheltered and protected that when they find themselves suddenly confronted with an absolutely different kind of world, most of them would be at a loss as to how to make a place for themselves in this new world. I wish somehow, that at least in the last two years in school, we could do something so that our children, when they go out, don't feel so lost and so completely at sea.

Q.18. Can you honestly say that you're satisfied with the life you're leading?

Ans. In one particular respect, I'm not. I feel I'm not qualified enough to teach English Language. My MA was in English Literature. Of course, I have evolved some sort of a method and my teaching does bring fairly satisfactory results but I'm not entirely satisfied with it. I wish I could do a course in the teaching of English Language and then I would feel better equipped for my job. But when I'm teaching Literature and also outside the class, in my dealings with the children and the staff, I'm completely satisfied. Quite apart from anything else, this place is so beautiful that life passes happily and quickly and that brings personal satisfaction.

**Anu Bedi U-VI**
Old Sanawarian (Vindhya 1979)

**Source and Acknowledgement:** *The Sanwarian* **(December 1977)**

# ODE (Owed) to Sanawar

These lines we pen true to our love
that rests upon a hill.
We walked these cloisters morn and eve
and truly we were loath to leave—
our hearts are here now still.

Our steps were faltering in PD—
We were homesick almost through.
By and by, we played and learnt,
Sometimes with our fingers burnt—
Our childhood we soon outgrew.

Were up at dawn before the lark
to fall in for PT
A man in spotless white there stood—
the run and exercise were good
with dog biscuits and tea.

Breakfast was all gobble, gabble:
bread and eggs and jam.
Fatty would eat eight bread slice;
the worms in porridge were quite nice
with love from Matron Ma'am.

While marching up the Tuck Shop slope,
we dug our heels in so loud.
'Chin up! Chest out!' did Jagga shout,
'Look left!' Memorial, without doubt—
We were far above the crowd.

Many sung in splendid voices
though some were mostly hoarse.
The morning prayer and song did touch
our hearts and heads and souls so much
to banish all that's coarse.

Birdwood classes were a breeze:
Lowers, Uppers, and Sixth Form.
The tests did keep us on our toes
but these brought much more fun than woes—
our home was in the Dorm.

Our teachers were endearing, quite:
Devotedly supreme.
'I'll come down like a ton of bricks!'
While others had some other tricks
to bolster academe.

'My lad!' said one in a baritone
so deep that all did scare;
and those who'd fidget night and day
had 'ants in pants', another'd say—
their illness to repair.

On Sunday hikes, we ventured far
or near, explored around;
Drinkies, Jabli, Eagles' Nest,
Kachhra, Lover's Pond for rest,
or places newly found.
Ozark and Gurkha Fort did call
all champion hikers' footfall.

Childhood fancies were the norm
and Socials a delight,
but those equipped with two left feet
would spend their evenings glued to seat;
could not improve their plight.

Others spruced up really smart
and practised how to dance.
While Barne Hall reeked of perfume too,
They sought their heartthrob now to woo,
and never missed a chance.

The hint of winter chill would send
us all to scour the hills.
Our raincoats served as gunny bags;
our vim or vigour never flags:
with pinecones these it fills.

The freeze of winter frost we'd shun
with crackling pinecone fires
that warmed the dorms, our hearts and bone;
such snugness we have never known
that sated all desires.

O Lord! If we must children be,
do hearken this, our only plea:
Admit us all back on this hill
that we our hearts with joy may fill.

Forever let Thy bounties shower
To let our alma mater flower!
O Lord! Do shower down all your power
to help our school grow every hour!

**Harisimran Singh Sandhu**
Sam | Vindhya 1970 | 1964–1970
PG – English Literature | Inspired by Major R. Som Dutt, joined the
Army Educational Corps 1980–2011 | Poet and Writer | Trekker

OS Sibling – Brother – Manavjit Singh Sandhu | Chut Sam | Vindhya
1976 | 1969–1976

# Lady Honoria Lawrence
## (née Marshall) – (1808–1854)

Honoria Lawrence was born on 25 December 1808 in Cardonagh, Donegal, the twelfth of fifteen children of the Revd. George Marshall and his wife, Elizabeth. She was brought up by her uncle Admiral Heath, who lived nearby, and was educated in a devoutly protestant environment; her literary tastes and love of nature were both encouraged. She first met her future husband, Henry Montgomery Lawrence (1806–1857), who was a cousin, on his return from India in 1827. Despite their mutual attraction, he was deterred from proposing by his lack of prospects; they finally married in Calcutta on 21 August 1837. She bore four children, of whom two sons and one daughter survived.

Lady Honoria was slight and lithe, with fair hair and blue eyes, but her attraction lay in more than her looks: 'She was not beautiful in the ordinary sense of the term; but harmony, fervour and intelligence breathed in her expression, emanating from a loving heart and cultured mind' (Diver, 78).

Honoria Lawrence's maturity, independence, flexibility, and sense of humour helped her face the demands of her husband's career as a soldier–administrator. She was always on the move in northwestern India and was the first European woman to live in several areas, including Kashmir and the independent state of Nepal. The difficulties of life in these remote areas were considerable, particularly with regard to the birth and upbringing of children. She recorded her life with perception and enthusiasm in voluminous letters and journals, including those written for her two young sons at school in England, selections from which were subsequently published. In these, she also reflects her ever-deepening appreciation and love for India.

However, while Honoria Lawrence later became known as a writer, contemporaries singled out her invaluable role in supporting her husband in his career and other activities. Her view of marriage and of the role

of women marked her life in India. She was deeply romantic, quoting Coleridge's view that an individual found his or her completion only in another being. Nevertheless, as she wrote in an article in *The Calcutta Review* in 1845, she believed that a husband played the dominant role: 'a wife is useful and happy just in proportion as she can . . . identify herself with her husband . . . He has a profession as well as a family; her profession is that of being a wife' (Lawrence, 'English women in Hindustan', 100–01). She carried out her precepts with dedication and enthusiasm. In the early months of their marriage, she revelled in Henry Lawrence's camp life as a surveyor, and assisted him in his work. When he was placed in civil charge of Ferozepore, she spent long hours helping run the post office, while in 1849–50, she threw herself wholeheartedly into the professional demands of his life in Lahore, where he was president of the Board of Administration for the Punjab. The Lawrences shared a deep commitment to philanthropy and Mrs Lawrence played a valuable part in helping establish near Simla, the Lawrence Asylum for the children of soldiers, to provide them with a boarding education in a healthy hill climate.

Writing became an important medium for the expression of Henry Lawrence's views on Indian affairs, and here, too, Honoria Lawrence played an essential collaborative role. She edited many of his articles on military and political matters for the *Delhi Gazette*, which paper also published in instalments *The Adventurer in the Punjaub*, a novel which she helped write, composing some of the romantic sections, including poetry. More influential were the articles Henry Lawrence contributed from 1844 to the newly formed *Calcutta Review*; these his wife edited, and in some cases co-authored. Though she published little independently, several of her own articles dealing with the female 'profession' of marriage and motherhood appeared anonymously in the *Calcutta Review* and the *Friend of India*. She was sceptical about the performance of British women in India and was critical of their lack of concern for Indians and the wives and children of British soldiers. Her success in fulfilling her own role was attested by many. Her friend Lady Login commented: 'I have never met a woman quite like Honoria, never a wife who more entirely shared in, and helped, her husband in his work, yet without in any way bringing that fact to the knowledge of the world at large.' (Login, 63)

She became Lady Lawrence when her husband was knighted in 1848, following the First Anglo-Sikh War. She died at Mount Abu in Rajputana on 15 January 1854 and was buried there, two days later.

*Rosemary Cargill Raza*

**D.V. Boddington**
(LRMS Sanawar 1942–1947)
23 April 2002

**With acknowledgements to:** © Oxford University Press 2004–13. All rights reserved. Rosemary Cargill Raza, 'Lawrence, Honoria, Lady Lawrence (1808–1854)', *Oxford Dictionary of National Biography*, Oxford University Press, 2004. Available at: http://www.oxforddnb.com/view/article/47680. Accessed 14 Sept 2013. 'Honoria Lawrence (1808–1854)', doi:10.1093/ref:odnb/47680.

# Letitie Catherine Lawrence – An Elegy

We gathered many a fragrant flower
To deck our pleasant bridal bower,
And life and joy their sunshine shed,
When first my love and I were wed.

Time passed—the bridal flowers might fade,
Sickness and care our brows might shade,
But then the olive branches sprung
To bid our hearts feel fresh and young,
And banish, with their joyous bloom,
Each passing breath of fear and gloom.

The thunderbolt of judgement flew—
And, where our tender nursling grew,
What rests to us, my husband, now?
A narrow grave—a cypress bough!

Hush, hush, my heart, such deep complaint!
Forbid oh Lord! my soul to faint!
Befits me more a thankful lay
To Him who gave and took away.
Withdrew our darling from our eye,
To shrine her with Himself on high,
And gives, while we watch her dust,
The humble faith, whose steadfast trust,
Can change the cypress bough of death
Into an amaranthine wreath!

And thou of one sweet bud bereft,
Yet ye, our firstborn hope, is left,

And, had our sky been cloudless blue,
Could we have loved, as now we do?
The storms have made us cling for rest,
More closely to each other's breast.

**Honoria Lawrence**
21 August 1841
Kasauli

# Cupid's Arrow

In our day, the girls wore sky blue summer frocks and white ankle socks (I think). I was always looking the other way. During lessons, they sat on the other side of the classroom and were a cause for humiliation when they proved cleverer than a boy, or of irritation and discomfort by just being there. This new concept of co-education introduced by Headmaster Evans was not at all popular. I don't know if the girls liked it, but none of the boys I knew did, except for a few oily Romeos, but none of the decent chaps did. I can tell you of the times when it was downright embarrassing. But I'll keep that for another day.

Generally speaking, girls were an alien species to be avoided. For instance, their sudden and pointless fits of giggling, which appeared infectious and inane, affecting groups of them at a time, could be upsetting to a chap if he happened to be passing when the cackling burst out. I know I felt serious discomfort when they giggled and pointed at me as I passed. I must admit I often glanced down to see if my fly was open.

However, I'll confess that my interest in girls, after a nerve-shattering experience on Lovers' Hill, did not end. It kind of submerged like a submarine. On one occasion, when the periscope went up, I saw a sight that affected me so deeply that it caused a huge change in my perception of one of the chaps, fortunately in Lawrence House and not Havelock, in particular, and made a profound change in my efforts on the sports field in general.

What I saw was a blue-eyed, flaxen-haired girl of exceptionally pleasing proportions and facial beauty, sitting on one of the cannons outside Birdwood, with her shapely legs dangling in the air. The sight shot with unerring accuracy, a Cupid's arrow through my heart. I was staggered but as I was about to lose consciousness, the memory of my bleeding lip, Joan brushing the grass off her skirt, restored me, like cold water being thrown in my face, to my senses and normality.

The submarine submerged, but the arrow stayed embedded, like a fish hook, permanently. The chap in Lawrence House, I got to hear, was squaring the vision of heavenly beauty whose dart remained in my heart. He never learned of my smitten state and that the object of my desire was the girl he was squaring. That secret, I kept locked in my breast and few have been told of it until now.

He had won the girl, but I wanted him and her to know that he was always second best to me. I had to beat him on the Long Hodson. That was why I came second. He was third. I had to get my school colours in all the first elevens. He wasn't in any of them. And then, fate gave me an unexpected but perfect opportunity I could never have conjured up in a month of Sundays.

Sgt. Flagg, our PT and boxing instructor, was making the final selections of the team to fight against BCS. The Lawrence House chap and I were the same weight. Flagg suggested we spar to see who should represent the school. How delightful, I thought. I smashed his nose. As the blood spouted from it, a strange thing happened: the arrow in my heart fell out. I thought how foolish I had been. I was really very sorry for what I had done.

If you think squaring was an easy thing to do, think again. In 1936, the Head Boy was expelled. In 1927, George Barne publicly flogged six aspiring Romeos and expelled them. He imposed draconian measures, cancelled the spring camping holiday, Founders' Week and curtailed privileges. Between these two dates, boys were flogged and expelled for doing no more that I had done on Lovers' Hill. The difference was, they got caught.

School days, my mother always told me, are your happiest days. I think she was right, don't you?

**George Browne**
Havelock 1937 | 1930–1937

# The Teacher of English

She came to us when I was in U-III or Class Six. The elegance of her attire, the whiff of delicate perfume that preceded and followed her as she clip-clopped down the cloisters, and her flawless enunciation, earned her instant admiration.

She was an excellent teacher but there was a streak of arrogance, a looking down upon her pupils, that precluded any endearment. She would walk into class, turn immediately to the blackboard, and, raising herself on her toes – she was petite – she would, in her beautiful, immaculate handwriting, write across the top of the board: 'Pin Drop Silence'.

While she did this, I would pull out a pin from my turban, hold it up for the class to see and drop it to the floor, raising much laughter. Inevitably, I was caught.

'And pray, what may you be doing?' she asked.

'I was only testing the silence ma'am.'

'Out, you uncouth villager, get out of my class.'

Thus began a running battle between us. I loved the subject and worked diligently at it but the years she taught me, I never scored higher than 44. In our final year, a lady from the British Council came up to our school and was asked to mark our half-yearly papers. You can imagine my excitement when my essay paper was returned with a big, red '89' across the top. I compared my marks with the others—yes, I had scored the highest. She waited for me to return to my desk.

'Across the top right-hand corner, in bold, red pencil is the mark that some upstart English woman thinks you deserve. In the top left-hand corner, in small red ink, is the mark that you have scored.' I looked closely at my paper. Yes, there it was – '44'.

I returned to school fourteen years later as an English teacher, and was given two sections of U-V or Class Ten. I worked very hard and produced an excellent result. My English teacher, now my head of department, came down to the staff club in the evening. I was playing tennis and she called out to me.

'Harishpal, I want a word with you.'

I abandoned my game and went up to her. She handed me two chocolates, one for each of my results.

'I always knew you had great potential,' she said.

'You had a strange way of showing it, ma'am. You never gave me more than forty-four.'

'That was for your own good, to make you work harder. Without it you would not have got firsts in your graduation and postgraduation—you would not have produced such excellent results today.'

I knew she was waffling, but it did not matter. She had been meticulous with her correction work, adamant that we do all our corrections and whatever merit I have achieved as a teacher or as a writer, is all because of the work I did in her class.

**Dr Harishpal S. Dhillon**
UD | Nilagiri 1957 | 1949–1957
STAFF 1971–1986 | HOD English | Housemaster | Headmaster 1995–1999 | Headmaster YPS Patiala 1986–1995 | YPS Mohali 1999–2010

OS Sibling – Sister – Yogindra (Dhillon) | Nilagiri 1956 | 1951–1956

OS Children –  Daughter – Priya Dhillon | Himalaya 1988 | 1979–1988
                Daughter – Naina Dhillon | Himalaya 1988 | 1979–1988
                Son – Jai Singh Dhillon | Nilagiri 1991 | 1982–1989

OS Grandchildren –  Granddaughter – Mannat Tipnis | Himalaya 2013 | 2006–2013
                    Grandson – Abhay Tipnis | Himalaya 2017 | 2009–2011
                    Granddaughter – Inaaya Kumar | Himalaya | 2018–To Date
                    Grandson – Rehaan Kumar | Himalaya | 2020–To Date

**Source and Acknowledgements:**
Published as a Middle in *The Tribune* on 11 December 2006 and reproduced in *Of Cabbages and Kings – A Book of Middles*, (New Delhi: Picus Books, Hay House Publishers India, 2014).

# Chapel Steeple Wind Cock

The Chapel steeple was roofed with tin. A lighting conductor, three inches wide, ran down it, and adorning the spire was a wind cock. The lightning conductor was useful in climbing up to the steeple on a dare but touching the wind cock atop that slippery tin sheet was too risky to attempt. So there it stood, turning languorously this way and that in a feeble breeze or with alacrity with a sharp turn of wind; in a gale, it seemed to nod and hum, too. The wind cock watched us every morning as we marched up to Birdwood Hall for Assembly. In the early years at school, around the winter, we wore battle dress like those in the army; a patch pocket on one thigh and one each on the left and right breast. It was a nice feeling like being a little soldier and that added a spring to the step.

We would 'eyes left' at the stone cross, the memorial to long-forgotten school boys who had gone out to fight during World War I and laid down their lives. The names of the fallen were engraved on the stone base of the cross. We had no connection with those names but they were always a source of wonder—how had they been killed? Had it been a heroic end? Their ranks were mentioned and the names seemed to have a number of initials and then the surname. All English, Irish and Scottish surnames, but they must have once answered to given names that were silent as the stone now. The Houses at school had then been named after the heroes of the 'Indian Mutiny of 1857', amongst them the school founder, Sir Henry Lawrence and some of his 'Punjaub Men'—Nicholson, Edwardes and Hodson. The 'Mutiny' is now known as the 'First War of Independence'; the Sikhs had fought the East India Company buttressed with Crown troops to a standstill in 1845–46 and in 1949.

After the memorial, the road switched back and up towards the school office and short of it to the right, were the steps up the Golden Staircase. At the top of this staircase on either side, there stood a pair of Turkish cannons and two small oak trees, almost opposite the Upper- and Lower-IV classrooms where 'the four' came to study.

The four used to meet often at the 'guns' (the aforementioned Turkish cannons) when they were not down at Bandy Room, to ruminate over some new project other than collecting pinecones or food to satisfy their hunger. The guns were a fascination for the four as all their parents fancied themselves shikaris. Shikar was then considered a manly hobby that got people into the open air and for exercise; the feathered and quadruped community felt otherwise. The Tara Chand Library supplied information on the differences between cannons, howitzers and mortars; also on calibre, bore, muzzle and breach. The third verse of Lord Alfred Tennyson's 'The Charge of the Light Brigade' was often recited with gusto and SAS, the drummer, would beat the 'Review order March' on the gun trail:

> 'Cannon to right of them,
> Cannon to left of them,
> Cannon in front of them
> Volleyed and thundered;
> Stormed at with shot and shell,
> Boldly they rode and well,
> Into the jaws of Death,
> Into the mouth of hell
> Rode the six hundred.'

The film of the charge had been shown to us in Barne Hall with Trevor Howard, John Gielgud and David Hemmings as the dashing Captain Louis Nolan; Vanessa Redgrave was the female lead—too old and horsy for us. Of great interest to us was that the Victoria Cross medal was struck from Russian guns captured in that Crimean campaign. We asked ourselves the question: what metal was used to cast the Param Vir Chakra? Could it have been from some cousin of these Turkish guns'? Guns to the right of them, Guns to the left of them . . .' belching shell and shot, and here were two guns, eternally silent. The greater question was, could we get one of these guns to fire? This called for further study in the library and a detailed inspection of the guns. The inspection revealed that the breach blocks of both guns were missing; the elevation and traverse hand wheels were jammed. The four would have to fashion a breach block at carpentry and hope that some diesel begged for from the power House, would get the wheels to move. A divider and scale from a geometry box answered the size of the rifled bore: three and a half inches. We would need Diwali atom bombs for explosives; a ramrod; and a hockey stick to keep the breach block in place. CK was told to get the diesel and fashion a shot; Taji to get the atom bombs and ramrod; SAS and Granny to make the breach block.

The four chose a Sunday to fire the cannon. For Taji, sourcing the atom bombs from Moti's Corner had been easy, so also the ramrod—a broomstick kept in the lavatory behind Birdwood Hall; CK had wrapped paper over a tennis ball that seemed fairly snug in the bore; the diesel had helped to free the elevating gear but not so the traverse—we would have to lift the trail to align the gun; the wooden breach block was not thick enough, so a brick was added and all would be kept in place with a hockey stick. The target selected was the wind cock on the Chapel steeple. All four lifted the trail and aligned the gun and Granny using the elevating gear, felt that the gun was 'bang on target!' The ball was rammed down but the rifling of the bore compressed the paper, leaving gaps. Taji placed three atom bombs with joined fuses in the breach with Granny, CK and SAS standing by, ready to push the breach block shut with the hockey stick. Taji lit the fuse, the breach block was shut with a crack and the four waited for the bang and when it came, it was more like that of a tonga horse farting! The ball, leaving its wrapping behind, was coughed out of the muzzle, and it plop-plopped down the Golden Staircase!

The tennis ball had not fit tightly enough in the bore, failing Mukho's 'equal and opposite reaction' test so well learnt in physics; gaps in the wadding had led gas to escape and the ball dribbled out of the muzzle to the accompaniment of the noise from equine rectal evacuation. A better projectile had to be found. Coming back to the dorm, CK and Taji discovered that the new shiny aluminium glasses that all the boys had were three and half inches at the mouth and might just be the answer! The glass however, needed a bit of weight at the base so a prized collection of lead slugs dug from the firing range butt came handy. The glass with some slugs was taken down to the boiler room. Ruldu gave us permission and the boiler door was opened and using tongs, the glass was inserted; very soon, the slugs melted to a silver liquid; the glass was then removed and allowed to cool. We now had a lead-bottomed, heavy super projectile.

Come Sunday, the four went excitedly through a well-practised aiming and arming drill. The new projectile mouth first, was put in the cannon muzzle and rammed down the barrel, its edges settling nicely in the rifling; atom bombs were placed in the breach; the fuse was lit and breach block quickly clapped shut. There was a boom and the glass, glinting in the sun, rose in an arched trajectory for the steeple! The projectile hit the tin sheeting of the steeple below the wind cock with a loud clang, bounced off, clattered on to the Chapel tin roof, bounced and rattled again, then a final metallic thud and silence! The four cheered and laughed!

There was much back-thumping; the congratulatory air was thick with pride of achievement as the four sat on the gun, however, Granny, jumping up and down, repeatedly chanted, 'did you see the aim . . . did you see the aim?' A thunderous voice emanating from the hollow of the Golden Staircase answered, 'Yes I did!' The startled four looked around. Seeing nobody at first but then emerging from the staircase, they saw a hat, followed by tie, shirt, tweed coat, corduroy trousers, burgundy-coloured suede shoes and all of Mr Salim Khan, a lit pipe in his hand: 'Which stupid blighters fired that bomb?' He roared! There was no defence the four could mount; evidence lay scattered about and the best they could do was lower their heads and look at their dirty PT shoes in silence. 'You could have killed somebody!' Shouted Mr Salim Khan, well-known for his sartorial elegance and graceful wielding of the willow. His residence abutted the Chapel and the 'bomb' had landed close to him while he was engaged in reading the morning papers in the sun. 'Now repeat thirty times: I will never, ever, fire the cannon again!' Thirty unsynchronised warblings of the four later, Mr Salim Khan said, 'put the cannon back in place and disappear!' Just before the four decamped, a breeze rustled the leaves of the oak trees; the wind cock languidly turned, stopped and looked down upon them.

## Dramatis Personae (Vindhya, BD, 1958)

- Ambassador Gurdip Singh 'Granny' Bedi (Sonny); U-IV; age twelve
  Indian Foreign Service | Served as Ambassador to a number of countries
- Sarabjit Arjan 'SAS' Singh; U-IV; age eleven;
  Indian Railways | Wounded in the spine by militants when heading the Railway Coach Factory, Kapurthala, in June 1989 and confined to a wheelchair | Member of the Central Administration Tribunal, Principal Bench, Delhi.
- Chander Krishan 'CK' Mahajan; L-IV; age ten
  Hon'ble Justice Delhi High Court
- Lieutenant General Tajindar 'Taji' Singh Shergill (Maun); U-IV; age eleven
  Mention in Dispatches 1965 | PVSM 2002 | Authored *Counter Insurgency Support to a Host Nation* (Lancers Publishers, 1987) | Co-authored with Capt. Amarinder Singh, *The Monsoon War – 1965 India Pakistan War* (Rolli Books, 2015)

**Lt. Gen. Tajinder S. Shergill PVSM**
Taji and Maun | Vindhya 1958 | 1951–1958

OS Sibling – Brother – Lt. Gen. M.S. Shergill PVSM, AVSM, VrC | Vindhya 1957 | 1951–1957

OS Children – Son – Jaimal Inder Singh Shergill | Jami | Vindhya 1985 | 1977–1985

# Some (Manek)Shaw-isms

'Never Give In? Oh, don't like that motto for girls!'

To General Dev (Member, Lovedale Board): 'you mean you've been living in Ooty since last year and haven't looked me up? You couldn't have been thirsty, then.'

Sitting in the middle of a circle of girls in the garden of [the] headmaster's House, the Field Marshal was admonished by a lady guest: 'Sam, you're only talking to the girls—what about boys?' 'What do you think I've come here for?' Then turning in the direction of the boys: 'And what are the boys doing there? They should be here, talking to the girls!'

'Oh, I don't like this modern dancing. I am dancing in one place and my partner is way over across the floor and then some other lady comes in between, and I don't know what's happening.'

'I used to smoke 100 cigarettes a day. I gave up overnight. Not for any moral or ethical or health grounds, but simply because they are damned expensive. Oh, but was a bad-tempered fellow for a fortnight—so much so that my colleagues used to tell my wife: "for God's sake, give the blighter some cigarettes!"' And how do you feel now, after having given up smoking? 'Just virtuous that's all!'

To the girls (at lunch): 'You are all so pretty, why must you wear these long skirts? Can't you get your headmaster to allow a higher hemline? Just a little higher up . . .'

When told that one of the girls in the Ballet was excited about having a moustache painted on: 'Oh, it can't be as nice as mine!'

When he expressed disappointment over the fact that, at the Parade, all the Marches were played except 'Sam Bahadur', Mrs Das almost tearfully said: 'Oh, We didn't know about that.' 'And how would you know,' commiserated the FM, 'after all, you're a mere civilian.'

**Mrs Gulshan Ewing**
Parent | Former Editor, *Eve's Weekly*; *Star & Style*; *Femina*

**Source and Acknowledgement:** *The Sanawarian*, 1975

# Dhobi Ka Gadha

10 February 1975 was when I set eyes on the magical hilltop, in all its magnificence, as I trudged up from Garkhal with my lifelong mate Raman Seth. The absence of horses made it less magical, though. I had been around horses since age two, riding ponies that hauled manufactured CTC tea from our family-owned garden factory at Salmari Tea Estate, to the nearest railway station. This was way back in the '60s in the glorious Assam. It was no wonder that by the age of twelve, I was the proud owner of a saddle-hardened butt.

Come Sanawar, these buttocks withstood the dreaded 'bend-over' and 'take your hockey stick like a man' (a parody of Kipling's *Kim* by the ranking prefect perfecting his hockey swing). However, the lack of signs of pain madly infuriated the prefect, blemishing his till-then perfect record of howling juniors. It became more of a friend than enemy (the hockey stick, that is, not the perfect prefect).

Ditto for the Six of the Best – Heady's canes – the loving strokes of his TLC (Tender Loving Care) for erring children. Consolation was that HRH the Prince of Wales, Charles, at Gordonstoun, must have also been a deserving recipient (Heady was his tutor master), later making HRH a Polo-mad royal, who captured the heart of the exquisite Lady Diana Spencer. Another part common aspect was that I was nicknamed 'Prince of Wales' by the Anglo-Indian/Irish/Welsh Army Nursing Corps girls at Shillong Military Hospice, being the only boy born in the Officer's Family Maternity Ward for weeks, making me the perfect prospective student for the co-ed Sanawar; although there wasn't a Lady Diana in my story, I did follow her brother, Mark Shand's adventures of riding elephants through India and attended his UK-/NY-based foundation's 'Human Elephant Conflict Meet' at Guwahati, under the aegis of the Eastern Himalayan Naturenomics Forum by the Balipara Foundation, many years later (as riding, unlike humans, never distinguishes the animal!).

The absence of horses proved no real hardship, though, once the splendid donkeys of Dhobi Ghat were discovered. Delivering bundles of

washed linen/clothing to NBD led to a lasting friendship between the
dhobi, his donkey and me. Frequent visits were made to Dhobi Ghat;
pocket-sized flat grounds were found, where during the all-important
'bunking' sessions with a hockey stick and 'marrowed' cricket ball, we
engaged in many hours of happy practice at bare-backed *dhobi ka gadha
ka pulu*. In later years, when people commented that Sanawar didn't have
horses but a large number of illustrious polo players, one wondered if the
secrets of 'dhobhi ka gadha ka pulu' were like a Masonic Lodge's secret pledge.

Sanawar meant the late Pheroza Das's lovely garden, her dogs and
delectable kitchen treats, supplemented the hearty Sanawar cuisine served
in the CDH; the grace before meals, in Sanskrit, leading to silently
muttering *'Om Sahenu Bhunaktu, Saheveriam Karva Vahahi, Om Shanti
Shanti'* along with 'Ruba ruba dub, thanks for the grub'. Later in life,
when one rode reluctant horses elsewhere, it was found that the said grace
actually worked in calming down the quadruped's appetite for bolting.
Sanawar thus, triumphed again.

The Rouser leading to Chota Hazri is still integral to my life as the
Raj Bhawan in Guwahati has the guard blow the bugle at 5.30 a.m. sharp,
while my morning cuppa and Bakery-baked Doggies are munched at the
stables on most days. In the evening, the stand-down by the R.B. bugler
reminds me to have my soup at 7.45 p.m. and the earlier dinner call 'Boys,
come to the kitchen door'.

The 'Grabbo' at Milk Break ensured equitable distribution of available
resources by the serving staff, making for a fair and just character later
in life. Sonya Bhandari, Bani Duggal and Simrat Virk were positive
influences on moi, not just for feeding me Cadbury's chocolate and Verka-
flavoured milk at Tuck Shop often enough, though I was a nipper in U-IV
and they in Sixth Form. The Gore sisters, the Mukherjis' and Nita Roy's
bungalows provided additional 'hogging' on Sundays and holidays (being
in close proximity to our old friend Charlie). We would watch romantics
stroll down Leisure's in pairs and wondered at them. The Last Bend was
reserved for our supporters from GD to cheer us on to finish our Hodson
heats and finals. To our minds, what a waste by the romantics on those
Sundays when we were not 'fagging' as ball boys for the tennis players
at Staff Courts. Of course, it was the Longman–Attri combination that
created a lifelong passion for raising chickens and growing mushrooms,
which meant we were Sanawar-certified to survive life, instead of being
dependent on others.

Friendships with Manju Khan, Paul Symonds, (late) Prithviraj Mishra, Brij Bhardawaj, (late) C.B. Abraham, gave one the core required to deal with the older boys and to receive unstinted support in one's career as a lawyer. Open access to OS's family homes meant that Sanawar was sort of an extended family—Rohit and Shiraz Das's (along with aforementioned late Pheroza Das's lovely garden and dogs), Gautam Shaunik, Kabir, Radhika and Chetan Bhandari (their Doberman, Atticus, took nine bites out of me before sleeping on my chest and insisting on being hand-fed by me), Sudershan Bansal, Subir Vyas, Sanjay Thakran, Jassi Bakshi, Raman Seth, Manoj Mohanka, Mona Bhandari, Nixy and her lovely sisters, Khushu Gill's parents (if I'd listened to his dad, then undergoing the NDC course, I'd have been inducted as a JAGS officer. But civvie life beckoned me with more adventures); Ketaki Banerji, Ambika Anand's mother, Sukhbir Badal, Manjit and Hardip Singh, Chetan Gupta's movie hall (in Patiala), Mohanbir's Hot Millions, Harjit Kochhar's Giggles, Devichand's (in Simla and Connaught Place), Lalit Suri's, and last but not the least, P. Khanna, a classmate and scion of the upmarket Claridges Hotel, ensured we had many a Saturday swimming pool rendezvous, leading to much mirth with fellow OS in our reminiscent glorious schooldays of gaddar and khup. Today, the interactions continue on Nilagirian Khup and Sgt. Tilley's WA groups.

It would be remiss not to mention Vivek Sondhi, our dashing IAF pilot, for introducing me to his Vir-Chakra-awardee superior (who led the IAF raid on Pak's Sargodha air base) and his wonderful daughters. He also showed us the vintage car collection of HH Gaj Singh of Jodhpur at Umaid Bhavan; got us a swim in the underground pool, and helped me when I was evicted for attempting post-swim shower opera in a high falsetto, followed by a slap-up dinner at Terrace Café while watching his helicopter unit airborne stallions doing their night exercises. Ajai Singh, now a Lt. Gen., who as a Capt. 81 Armoured, allowed me to bash around in his iron steed T-72 tank in the unit training grounds; taught me the value of lining one's stomach with Amul Butter pre-prandial libation in steel glasses followed by his Sqn. Promotion 'Bara-khana' consisting of stacks of roti, chunks of mutton in a sea of gravy with *piyaz*; as Piper made me deliver frequent bouquets of flowers to his amour (now lovely wife), while he sweated in his black dungarees in the Thar Desert during OP Brass-tacks. His admonition to me of not crossing her threshold was broken by his future MIL, who treated me to tea and savouries. On his strict intructions, I focused on the feast and as a good classmate, ignored the lovely Mushran ladies.

The core physical fitness levels at Sanawar stood us in good stead when we were kicked later in life, either by humans or horses, which led to cellulitis of the soft tissue in the left fore-shin with three weeks in AIIMS (Delhi); double-back kick full in the chest (in Assam); punctured lung with dislocated clavicle from a violent throw by a startled horse from a coughing leopard (in Assam); and a pulled muscle from vaulting off a horse to pull the riding (late) Ustad Umed Khan from floating down the Brahmaputra after falling off his horse during water obstacle training (Assam). The fast recoveries stumped the medical professionals, who were explained that these were a result of a youth spent in clean living, high thinking at Sanawar (which most did not know of) and its rigorous regimen that afforded a robust outlook on life.

While pushing for a fledgling career as a Family Disputes Law Expert (never learnt at Sanawar), Brazilians Andrea and Ana appreciated my dancing skills learnt at school Socials and House parties with the pop music of the day at the Barne Hall Paper dances with Bali Sohi, Thangminglian Tonsing and others, leading later to appreciative leg-shaking at various disco hotspots in Delhi, where my Lambada was the then talk of the town. The muscles needed for dancing were developed by lifting the towing-eye of the cannons at school. The de-horsed artillery regiment should be grateful that I didn't enlist.

Having decided that I wanted to meet a larger section of society and enlarge my network, the English Literature Department of a top North Campus college (Delhi University) gave me the opportunity to have fellow OS girls (considered to be the prettiest in Delhi back then and highly sought-after, whom we considered merely close buddies, thereby confirming that OS guys didn't know the jewels in their crowns, being solely followers of Kipling alone) popping in to the hostel (where I was an illegal guest), with delicious homecooked food packed in tiffins. My fellow college-mates were in awe that I came from an aristocratic public school, and so was entrusted with escorting their female guests (one of whom was Devina, Dev Anand's daughter, whose fellow alumnus from Woodstock, Mussoorie was also in the hostel and who often had a craving for 'golgappas' at Kamla Market). She was of the opinion that my school comrades such as Parikshit Sahni, Sanjay Dutt and other Bollywood glitterati, were responsible for my stiff upper lip.

The strenuous running while at school ensured that no University Special was left unclimbed, as the ability to chase the creaking, groaning DTC bus from one U–Stop to another, enhanced the Sanawarian legend. The smell of luncheon meat, baked beans, condensed milk, coffee (Nikhil Sawhney's contraption – a eraser held between two razor blades attached to bare electric wires – for his in-House Vindhya coffee nostalgia), seasonal gooseberry collection and bhutta raids, bring nostalgic memories when one goes to country markets in Guwahati and spots, these serve as reminders of those ever-youthful days.

Leading fashion models OS Vandana Sarin and fellow stage actor (in C.B. Abraham's English House plays) Firoze Ewari enhanced my public estimation at Pragati Maidan, when at the end of the runway, having met them in the green room, they placed me in the front row along with leading supermodel Nandini Sen's minor son. They surprised the audience as they twirled one extra time to smile at him, but Delhi thought the smile was for me.

Friendship with late Oona Mansingh (NGD), whose father as the then president of the EFI, sped the wheels to form the Equestrian Federation of Assam in 1992, leading to the highly popular National and International Endurance in the scenic and salubrious tea garden country of Upper Assam. The noble Equus was reintroduced to the erstwhile Polo-playing (Silchar Polo Club, the oldest registered polo club in the world) within the British-era tea culture as well as keeping of the younger generation enjoined to riding in Assam Valley School (where Iftikar Hassan and Sonya Ghandy were the Sanawar connection). From time to time, other OS have popped into the northeast, either for mountain car rallies, armed services postings or tea estate jobs to augment the local OS population. It would not be out of place to mention a fellow Nilagirian, Manmegh Singh, who organized a memorable OS get-together, floating on a mid-Brahmaputra cruise on a river ship, otherwise used for carrying military equipment. We picnicked under supply parachutes decorated with camouflage arty nets by the MES Inspection Bungalow.

As a lawyer representing Ashok Chakra, Sena Medal and other Gallantry Award holders, I was reminded of my classmate Dushyant's father, Brig. Hoshiar Singh, PVC and many other (schoolmates) war heroes and Gallantry Awardees, while tackling the Commission of Enquiry criminal cases filed against serving military personnel, performing IS duties in OP Rhino, Bajarang I and II in Assam, Nagaland and Manipur. I was given respect and esteem far higher than deserved, more so in view of the Sanawar legacy supplemented by the legal knowledge applied where ballistics learned on the Sanawar Rifle Range were concerned, and long conversations with the In-Charge Armourer of the Kot while cleaning the weapons ranging from WWI Lee Enfield's, .22 on RAT and culminating in Sig Sauer and Glocks on the NSG Maneswar Range. The hard physical activity at school also allowed for increased stamina during the preparation for intricacies required to prevent the cognizance, convictions or sentencing of those taught to defend the country, all of which fitted into my vision of the parameters of 'Never Give In' credo.

Lt. Gen. Mao Shergill as GOC 3 Corps bestowed upon me great prestige by inviting me to be the chief guest in a hot insurgency-prone village in Phek District, Nagaland. The villagers, for the first time in their lives, saw a helicopter, which brought Mao at close range. The speech by the village Gau Bura (headman) was memorable as he said that the smart General and the discipline of the 1st Assam Rifle troopers had ensured stability in the region, and the villagers no longer feared the army. Mao Shergill, fearless of militant attacks, played local Manipuri Polo. This legend emboldened me to appear at will or whenever needed in the Imphal Valley, including during the Sanjita Death Enquiry, Manorama Death Enquiry, Chitranjan Immolation Enquiry, Justice (Retd.) Santosh Higra Supreme Court Enquiry Commissions (1,528 extrajudicial killings).

During this sojourn, I was proud to meet Vungalian and Mungpi in their Sanawar-modelled 'Foundation School' in insurgency-wracked Churachandpur, where S.N. Albert's family opened their home and hearts to me and Dilbagh Sidhu (then Comdt. BSF Trg. Centre CCpur, who had the privilege of having 300 ex-Bodo militants leave his camp during post-surrender Para Military Forces absorption training.

The strict stoic discipline I maintain ensures that my kids appreciate a Sanawar they've never seen, though they have met many of my OS friends. They often wonder why there is a lighter step and spring in my walk, and how I revert to being a happy twelve- to seventeen-year-old when in company of OS, regardless of the graduation year. As I suggested in my school-leaving farewell speech (in March 1980), all I had learnt during my five years in the 'Best School of All' was to love people as they are.

**Prasant N. Choudhury**
Presco/Speedy Gonsaleze/Baldy | Nilagiri 1980 |1975–1980
Advocate, Guwahati High Court

# Interview – Mr S.R. Das

Handa, Bhullar and I chose to do a stint in journalism for our project. Bhullar and Handa confined themselves to topics like 'The Role of Journalism in the World of Today', 'Freedom of the Press', 'Origins of Journalism', etc. I also did something on similar lines and then decided to go on to do some reporting, which was why I had taken up this project in the first place. Interviewing is what I started off with. [The] headmaster was the first and most obvious choice—and so, I bearded him. This was the result:

Q.1. It is generally accepted that you are very temperamental—can you honestly say that this is never a handicap in your work?

HM: No! It's often a handicap.

Q.2. How long do you think it takes to become a Sanawarian?

HM: A Sanawarian? I don't think one can put a time limit on that but in my view, anyone who has finished his final exam from Sanawar should be an Old Sanwarian and being able to imbibe the spirit of Sanawar depends on the person. Even some of those who are Old Sanwarians may not have imbibed this spirit.

Q.3. Are you happy with the English system of running public schools in India—do you think they suit the native genius?

HM: I am happy with the way the public schools, copied from the English schools, have developed in India. Pity that [the] headmasters in public schools have stuck to the same old system that was established more than thirty years ago when society all around is changing rapidly. Although we provide an all-round education, I don't think we prepare children for the new society effectively.

Q.4. Has your experience shown that the effects are lasting or do you feel that a different system can or should be evolved? If so, how and what?

HM: You see, I think the role of the public schools should be to make young people into effective adults. That is, people concerned with their community and people who take initiative, express themselves against injustice, help the weaker sections and so on. This is because the children in public schools not only get a good all-round education but also come from an elite society. Our system should be such that they use their position of privilege to help society. Unfortunately, few children from public schools do this. Public schools should not be closed institutions and should play a leading part in the development of the community in which they exist and allow people of the surrounding areas to use their facilities by providing extension of services with the help of students.

Q.5. Don't you think that you should have greater and closer contact with the students and staff?

HM: Well! It would be nice if I could meet every student and every member of staff every day, but this is not physically possible. A lot of my time is taken up in meeting students and teachers but with 600 students and about 60 teachers and 150 other staff, it is physically impossible to do so. A balance has to be drawn in meeting people, spending time thinking about policies, and doing one's administrative work. As Chief Executive, I spend more time meeting them than most other people in my position.

Q.6. What is your reaction to criticism?

HM: I like criticism. I might get irritated but nonetheless, I appreciate it.

Q.7. We believe that you wanted to bring about some changes in the attitudes and working of the schools. How far have you succeeded and has there been an adequate response? Are the staff the obstacles or the children disappointing?

HM: The changes in attitude—to try to bring about greater rapport between children and staff and teachers and give greater responsibilities and greater opportunities for taking initiative to the students. To have less of a hierarchy and more of a community. But such changes cannot happen overnight and can take many years. I am generally happy with the response. As for the students and staff being obstacles and disappointments, neither are. As I told you, I am generally satisfied. There are some obstacles and disappointments, but these are a part of life.

Q.8. Are there any other changes that you would like to bring about?

HM: No, I've already given you my broad view on the role the public schools should play. Within that framework, whatever changes that can be made, after consultations with students and staff, will be done. But we must not be afraid of experimentation, nor should we change simply for the sake of changing. All changes must be done with the spirit of constructive criticism. And if generally found to be unconstructive or unsuccessful, should be modified or even abandoned.

Q.9. Do you think that there are any major shortcomings in the school? How do you propose to tackle them?

HM: No, there are no major shortcomings but I do wish to give children greater responsibility. This we hope we can do by providing a school counsel. It would also be less of a military atmosphere.

Q.10. What is your opinion on the students and their attitude towards the school, one another, staff and towards the opposite sex?

HM: I think that the girls tend to subdue the boys. I think they are afraid to express themselves and tend to take little initiative on their own. Though there should be more cooperation and activities between boys and girls, and less of the rigid demarcation between both the sexes in the activities organized by the school. For instance, Indian dancing is confined entirely to the girls while very few girls would dream of taking up electronics and motor mechanics. With women playing a greater part in the taking of life decisions today, the role of both the sexes overlap considerably. In Sanawar, we should keep this in mind when making changes so that girls and boys are prepared to take on each other's roles. For instance, if I introduce Home Science, I would like all boys to have a course in this. And equally, if motor mechanics is introduced, girls should learn something about motor cars.

Q.11. Do you always tell the truth?

HM: No! I am not a saint!

**Anu Bedi U-IV A**
Old Sanawarian (Vindhya 1979)

**Source and Acknowledgement:** *The Sanwarian* **(December 1977)**

# Ode to My Teachers

Long long ago, our quest for knowledge
Started in the cozy comfort of a school
Where the seeds of wisdom were sown
By the greatest teachers the world has known.
The wonderful magic you bestowed on us
The intricate maze of schooling years
Was a formidable task you chose as yours
Just gratitude and thank you!

A million times over
Would not be sufficient to cover
The skills that you taught us over and over
Trudging up and down the hill
To enter the sacred Birdwood school
Where the impressions of a lifetime
Were stamped in our schedule
The tryst with destiny had started with a song
Our odyssey of life had just begun
We knew not what lay before us inside those stonewalls
As curiosity and destiny walked us down the hall
Be it music or dance, carpentry or painting
The joy of learning was profound and captivating!

You held our hand and taught us some letters new
Barne Hall no longer seemed a lofty place hidden from our view
The prayer for New India was imprinted in our hearts
Pandit Ravi Shankar's sitar was the initial start
You painted the seven colours on the canvas of life
As we discovered VIBGYOR sitting upright
Your encouraging hand on our back

When we did the Hodson run
Gave us energy to conquer Tilley's Hill
With so much fun!

Cricket, football, netball and more
Was instilled in us for the years to come
Your presence, teachers, made all the difference
To our lives beyond the boundaries of the institution
You stood like the Rock of Gibraltar
Protecting us from the severe harsh winter
Guiding us with your beacon light
Supporting us with all your might.

In reverence, Teacher, we bow to thee
Head, heart and soul in the years to be
'NEVER GIVE IN' has been our motto
'NEVER GIVE IN' it shall always be
As we hold our heads high and salute to thee!

**Champa Rani (Mukherjee) Banerjee**
Champs | Nilagiri 1964 | 1956–1964

# The Spartan Club

The Spartan Club was instituted by the Reverend G.D. Barne, fourth Principal of Sanawar on 13 October 1922. He is said to have named it after the ancient Greek city state of Sparta, which was renowned for its legendary and widely envied traditions of martial and sporting excellence. Here is a transcription of the order announcing the formation of the club, handwritten and signed by Principal George Barne himself:

It has been decided to form a Club in connection with the Past and Present Sanawarians called the Spartan Club.

Committee is composed of the President and Secretary of the Old Sanawarians Society and the following Old Sanawarians resident in Sanawar: -

- C.S.M. G. Foster
- J. Hale Esq.
- C. Teeling Esq.

1. Election to the Club is entirely in the hands of the Committee and will be by invitation.
2. Membership will ordinarily be confined to Sanawarians whose names appear on the Honours boards in the Lawrence Club but Old Sanawarians who have subsequently distinguished themselves on the field of sport, or Old Sanawarians who left before the Honours boards were put up will be eligible for election at the discretion of the Committee.
3. Present day Sanawarians are eligible for admission when still at School.
4. Membership may also be extended in certain cases to others who, themselves distinguished in games etc., have rendered service to Sanawar in this direction.

5.  The subscription to the Club will be Re. 1/- on election and no further subscription.

6.  Members of the Club will wear as the Club colours, a dark blue blazer with L.R.M.S. buttons and the School crest surmounted by the Royal Crown with the words SPARTAN CLUB underneath. The crest will be mounted on a red back ground to distinguish it from the blazer which every Old Sanawarian is eligible to wear whether members of the Spartan Club or not.

7.  The aim of the Committee both in the election of members and in the direction of the Club, will be to promote and preserve the best traditions of Sportsmanship.

[Transcribed verbatim from LRMS Sanawar Order Book Page 105 paragraph 630, handwritten and signed by The Reverend G.D. Barne OBE, MA, Principal, dated 13 October 1922].

The committee convened two or three times a year to consider candidates for membership. Election to the club required full consensus and the distinction of membership was keenly contested and highly prized. The club flourished for several years and in 1930, for the first time, ladies became eligible for election. In September 1934, however, the club was inexplicably closed down by Principal E.A. Evans. No reason was given for the closure. A convening notice for the Committee appeared in School Part II Orders on 25 September and was cancelled without explanation, less than three days later. The committee was dissolved and little or nothing was heard of the Spartan Club for the next twelve years. The club was eventually revived by Principal H.E. Hazell in August 1946 and lived on under Principal and Headmaster E.G. Carter until his retirement in 1955. Evidently, it continued well into the late 1990's and then appears to have ceased altogether.

**D.V. Boddington**
LRMS Sanawar 1942–1947
October 2005

**Sources and Referencess:**

- LRMS Sanawar Order Book, Page 105 paragraph 630, dated 13 October 1922
- LRMS Sanawar Part II Orders (NOTICES) dated 25 September 1934
- LRMS Sanawar Part II Orders (No. 207 CLUBS) dated 2 August 1946

# To Sir With Love

Yet another from the old guard has exited this world, having made the very best use of the role destiny offered him.

A passionate teacher, he left a strong imprint on his students. Humble, eloquent, articulate and impactful, he was a man of gravitas. His was a reasoning mind—enriching our lives with his knowledge while mentoring a whole generation of Sanawarians. How I admired the dexterity and methodical ease with which he solved difficult mathematical problems. And try as he might to shepherd his flock in the right direction, some black sheep always went astray and got lost and left behind in the mathematical labyrinths.

In spite of his best efforts, I remained inept at mathematics. However, what he was teaching his students outside the classroom was what I would call the feather in his cap: nurturing and developing young minds. Inspiring the future generations by setting an example to make a mark in life through noble means. In this sense, he was doing extraordinary work. Not one to believe in the rat race, he lived a chaste and morally upright life. His love for his students was selfless, encouraging and pure.

As Bursar, his warmth and spontaneity during my son's admission is clearly etched in memory, as are many other playful moments. He may not have become a man of success in the way we understand it, but a man of value, he certainly was. For me, his benevolence leaves behind an enduring legacy. As Ruskin Bond put it, 'Men like him leave a trail of legend behind them because they give their spirit to the place where they have lived and remain forever a part of the rocks and mountain streams.' Sanawar will never be the same without such icons.

With him gone, a part of our childhood is gone forever. We'll miss his benign smile and his very special way of calling out to us. We'll remember him with reverence and as a teacher and fine human being. He will always be Numero Uno.

Copyright © Kripang Kashyap | Himalaya | 2021

May he always remain in 'Chardi Kala' (high spirits). Shakespeare's words do justice to his simple and honest way of life:

'My crown is on my heart, not on my head;
Not decked with diamonds and Indian stones, nor to be seen;
My crown is called content, a crown it is that seldom kings enjoy.'

Rest in Peace, Gore Sir!

**Dilbagh Singh Sidhu**
Dilby | Himalaya 1969 | 1960–1969
Retired D.I.G. – Border Security Forces | A decorated officer | Keen Sportsman, passionate horse-rider | Won Gold at the All-India Police Duty Meet 1991, New Delhi

OS Children – Son – Manpreet Singh Sidhu | Himalaya 1998 | 1989–1998

# Remembering a Guru

'I liked the article you wrote a few days back'—coming from a person considered to be an institution in the academic fraternity, this was an accomplishment of sorts. Unfortunately, this was the last time I met him as he passed away, a few months later. Tall, slim, with a limp in his gait, Dr Harish Dhillon was an educationalist par excellence, who shaped thousands of young minds spanning over two generations, with his warmth, wit and sense of discipline. He was affectionately called 'Yoodee', as his initials 'H.D.' looked more like 'UD' when he signed.

An Army aspirant, his dream was cut short due to an accidental discharge of a rifle during his training, which forced him to spend the rest of his life with an artificial leg. This, however, did not deter his indomitable spirit—he once accompanied us on an arduous trek in the interiors of Himachal Pradesh. While we, then budding teens, hitchhiked after walking some distance, this man, in his forties, walked the entire stretch with a wooden leg, putting us to shame. He did not admonish us but his silence conveyed a strong message of 'taking the harder right than the easier wrong'.

'Use simple language to communicate, but while putting your thoughts on paper, use the best vocabulary you have', he would propagate. A good accent would not impress him if the spoken English was not up to his literary standard. 'Pack as much punch as you can in as little words possible' was the only mantra for scoring marks with him.

In those dark days of militancy in Punjab, when the militants' writ ran large, he was at the helm of affairs as Principal of YPS Patiala. One heard of the resistance he offered, well aware of the consequences, to an edict passed by militants for observing a specific dress code in schools and colleges. He was a man of great conviction; his actions spoke louder than words. A few years later, he was recalled to Sanawar as its first 'Old Sanawarian' Headmaster.

He authored over a dozen widely acclaimed books, but was loved most for the 'middles' he penned down for newspapers. He was brutally honest in his writings, not even sparing himself on several occasions. 'Correct combination of style and substance is perfect. But with choice only between 'substance without style' and 'style without substance', go in for the former'—this was his advice to writers attempting to emulate him. No wonder his articles were spontaneous, coming straight from the heart, making an immediate impact on the reader.

It has been five years since he transcended to the other world. His students and fans remember him for his literary acumen, which presents fascinating slices of his own life. I fall short of words in my attempt to preserve some footprints he left behind and create a measure of immortality around him, no matter how small. He must be smiling up there, content and happy that one of his disciples is trying hard to give permanence to something that is essentially transitory. We miss you, UD Sir.

**Col. Harvinder Pal Singh**
Harry Paul | Nilagri 1989 | 1983–1989
Vishisht Seva Medal (2012) – Commanding Officer in Siachen Glacier

OS Children – Daughter – Mannat Bir Kaur | Nilagiri 2019 | 2011 – 2019
Son – Agam Bir Singh | Nilagiri (Present Sanawarian) | To be Batch of 2025

# Ah! Those Were the Days!

I am a Sanawarian virtually from birth, having been born in Kasauli in July of 1939. I could boast of only two parents, the technology of the day not enabling the possibility of five, as is the case now. Both were part of the teaching staff, my mother joining in 1933, and my father, a few years earlier. They had never known each other before. My father taught chemistry, and my mother taught maths and geography. My father later had the title of 'Headmaster', but that did not make him 'The Boss'. In those days, the top man was the principal, who had to be an ordained minister in the Church of England.

In Sanawar's dark ages, boys and girls were taught separately. My father was responsible for the abolition of this practice, as he had to give the boys one lesson and then repeat it for the girls. The Army (the ones who ran the school) agreed that this was wasted effort and the old order was swept away for good. Soon after my mother's arrival, the principal, Rev. Edgar Hunt, died of a heart attack during a late evening swim in the pool where the CDH now stands. Malicious tongues spread the rumour that my father and Sammy Cowell had thrown him into the ice-cold water as a prank. This was soon quashed as both had sound alibis. My father resigned from his position at the end of 1944, on my mother's insistence, as he was losing his battle with alcoholism, a very common failing in those times. I rarely saw him after that.

The following year, 1945, was the most miserable of my life as I was entered as a boarder. The food was vile and meagre in quantity. In later years, I understood the reason for this: the purpose of Sanawar was to produce well-disciplined young thugs for the army. In this capacity, Sanawar was a fabulous success. Toughened by meagre rations and severe retribution for minor misdemeanours, Sanawar's graduates were everything an occupying army could wish for. (A story was put up about how when an Old Sanawarian was stung by a king cobra, it took the reptile fifteen minutes to die. That can't be true, five minutes tops). In the succeeding years, I found my situation to become more tolerable, as I developed sound survival strategies. Foremost among these was a genius for telling a shameless lie with a straight face. I can't count the number of scrapes this got me through. One of life's valuable lessons was accidentally learned here: that when faced with a long list of accusations, it was a good idea to confess to a few of them. That way the accuser-in-chief would accept the compromise and just a couple of strokes of the cane served to satisfy the honour of all concerned.

As I progressed through school, my scholastic achievements failed to keep pace. I found studying tiresome and uncreative. I would do the barest minimum to avoid repeating a year. This was in stark contrast to my older sister, Lesley Coombes, who was a good scholar and in 1950, was awarded the Nelly Lovell Prize. She spent the next two years at St. Bede's in Simla, getting a teaching diploma, and then returned to Sanawar as a teacher for the lower forms of the Upper School. To keep tabs on our academic progress, or lack thereof, an event was held about four times a year, which even the most seasoned work; shy slackers and bad marshes anticipated with chronic apprehension. This was called 'Mark Reading'. Those (often myself included), who were deemed to be under-performing, would be commanded to stand up when our turn came. Our fifteen seconds of unwanted fame, surrounded by a sea of smirking faces, would be accompanied by verbal blasts of 'shocking', 'words fail me', 'Never in all my career', 'bone-idle waster' and more besides. When an explanation for my dismal performances was demanded, I wish I had possessed the head and the heart to say that not even a wise man could answer a question posed by a fool. To reinforce our humiliation, the mark lists, together with the scathing comments schoolteachers excel at, would be pinned to a board in the main corridor so others could relish our discomfiture at leisure. I sat my Senior Cambridge examinations at the end of 1954, my sole distinction being in mathematics, thanks to my instructor Mr M.V. Gore (later School Bursar), who despite being the butt of the ribald humour of some of my classmates, successfully led me through my first steps in the differential calculus. This fired up my interest in a subject that had hitherto baffled me. Calculus made previously hard problems vanish like magic.

Pre-1948 Sanawar had its own dairy farm, which was actually army property. But it was staffed entirely by Indians, manager included. In my pre-school days, it was a favourite visiting spot for me. The cowsheds were located just below the tennis courts, and I believe have now been converted into staff quarters. The chief fascination for me was Shamsher, the enormous bull. He had to be handled with great care, as any stranger was seen to be competition for his harem! He performed his arduous duties with great dedication, and has to be lauded as a true Sanawarian. At milking time, each cow's yield was measured and recorded by the manager, and signs of a falling-off meant that Shamsher was required to swing into action. The regular appearance of new calves furnished ample evidence of his professionalism.

In the early 1950s, China started flexing its muscles near the Ladakh border of India. Some 2,50,000 well-armed Chinese had to be stopped by 12,000 Indian troops with near-obsolete weapons. The time was ripe for a futile gesture: I was dragooned into the NCC. The chief military attribute required was a talent for polishing one's boots to a high gloss. As even a Sanawar-trained liar like myself would flinch at the idea of including this claim on his CV, I could not see of what further service I could be to halt the march of communism. Nevertheless, my superiors placed great faith in my potential and I was not allowed to resign. There was a compensation: the NCC camp at Poonah at the end of '53. Despite the long train journey in Dickensian conditions and the hectoring by army instructors who had seen combat in North Africa, Italy and Burma, I got to mingle with chaps from several schools across India. Sanawar was well-known and highly regarded by almost all. There was also a day trip up into the wilds of the Western Ghats and from the rugged terrain, you could understand why even the formidable Mughal Empire had found handling the local tribes to be a tricky job. The experience broadened my outlook.

Others may have commented on the school diet. I hereby add my one rupee's worth. 'Dire' is one adjective, others are not printable. We did not go so far as eating each other, like shipwrecked sailors have sometimes done, but that was probably because there was too little flesh on our bones to make the exercise worthwhile. Presumably to sharpen up our survival techniques, a plate of sliced bread would be placed on the dining tables at mealtimes. The number of boys exceeded the available number of slices. As soon as grace was said, a swarm of boys would pounce on the bread. The slower went unrewarded. A visiting member of the Board of Governors was entertained to this sport, and failed to respond in the way his hosts had hoped. In the future, everyone had to be guaranteed his slice. Sanawar reeled under the shock of this decree. One slice for EVERY boy!? Holy Saint Ignacious, whatever next?

For the dinosaurs on the school hierarchy, worse was yet to come: a new school bursar was appointed. By some administrative oversight, they actually appointed a man who had heard of double-entry book-keeping. The man, J.K. Kate by name, rapidly and ruthlessly identified the leaks in the pipeline. Contractors who had been engaged in creative sleight of hand were either told to cease their sharp practices or simply given the boot. As a result, there was a marked improvement in both the quality and quantity of the diet. Rice could be confidently consumed without the risk of shattering one's teeth. Chicken curry was served every Sunday, instead of twice a year. Some of us actually started to put on weight. The downside of this was that we had to handle getting punched harder in the boxing ring. This was some consolation for the diehards who thought we might be getting soft.

Founders' was a time some pupils looked towards with a mixture of dread and hope, caused by their parents' proposed arrival. Other boys, safe in the knowledge that their own parents would not be showing, would lounge against the gymnasium wall, wearing that expression of jeering contempt which sits so easily on the faces of adolescent boys, and passing their (often accurate) opinions on some of these elders: 'Just look at yonder fat old jerk; smells like a whisky factory; should have a fire warning notice hung round his neck; that's X's dad', or 'That heavily made-up dame being fork-lifted out of her Rolls Royce; that's Y's mum'. This psychological torture was partially offset by the Rs. 25 illicitly slipped into the victim's hand, thereby bracing him/her against the likelihood of death by malnutrition, and briefly widening his/her circle of friends!

Sporting activities were deemed to be the way to prepare youngsters for citizenship. The covert reason for tiring us out, boys especially, was of course never mentioned, and has never worked anyway. The ideal of sportsmanship only seemed to apply to those on the winning side. I have to say on behalf of Sanawar, that in this regard, we behaved the most honourably of all and lost with good grace. Tournaments against other schools, our oldest foes – BCS, in particular – were fought with almost insane passion. When Sanawar played host post 1948, there would always be a 'Special Tea' to follow, so this added to the sense of occasion. My own sporting endeavours met with only sporadic success, mostly in athletics. However, the jeers and hoots of derision accompanying my bowling of wides on the cricket field, and to catches fumbled and dropped, still ring in my ears.

Returning briefly to my long-suffering mother, she eventually became headmistress. She taught us geography in the Sixth Form despite being under the incurable delusion that the Earth was round. God knows where she picked that up from. She clung to this crazy idea till she passed away in July 2005, aged ninety-five. Our biology master, Mr N.K.S. Rao, was possessed by another delusion: to wit that mankind had evolved from the apes. Such was our education and ah! those were the days!

Did later life teach us more than Sanawar ever did? Yes, but the fees was infinitely higher. The maxim 'Never Give In' has kept me on the rails.

**James L.C. Coombes**
Jumbo (Hathi) | Nicholson and Himalaya 1954 | 1944–1954

Parents – Mother – Joy Coombes | Staff 1933 – 1954 |Mathematics and
    Geography teacher | Headmistress 1953 – 1954
    Father – James R. St. M. Coombes | Chemistry teacher 1928–
    1944 | Headmaster | Officiating Principal in 1942

OS Sibling – Sister – Lesley F. Coombes | Nicholson and Yellows 1950 |
1940–1950 | Teacher 1953–1954

# Frames Etched in My Mind's Eye

Goodbye home. Tears, backward glances, guilty parents, iron trunks with white names and House labels laboriously stitched by tearful mothers. Winding roads, clashing gears, get out and push through the last climb, to the new home, through its gates.

Cloudy skies, yellow flowers, grey rocky buildings, a sea of faces, the chitter-chatter of girls, eyes following you, a new girl. The New Girl. Sadness and trepidation, loneliness, parents depart, you're lost to be found anew; short hair, shining black eyes, a happy face, a friend at the start, a new homecoming.

Sounds of whispers under the sheets, muffled sobs and sporadic giggles, raindrops crashing on the roof like a grand orchestral crescendo, mist rolling in through the window like an eerie ghostly apparition that engulfs everyone and everything it touches, the sound of the rouser bell, PT, brekka, classes, the loud voice of a prefect to be obeyed, or else, be chastised; cold arms and knees, crunchy snails under black brogues, trudging our way through serpentine, covered passages.

Say grace for what we are about to receive, may the Lord make us truly grateful (for the lumpy porridge?!), the clatter of plates, and 'elbows off the table', if with Miss Chatterjee, 'mind your p's and q's!'

March and march some more, Assembly, the Chapel resounds with young voices, 'Abide with me', fast falls the eventide, prayers etched in ancient stone, winged gables and jewel-toned windows, red-carpeted stairs, newly painted masterpieces on the wall, cloisters of stone, silent sentinels to stories untold, 'All things Bright and Beautiful', stern-faced portraits casting their gaze at young, unfettered minds, the crash of folding chairs before settling down, giggles in the next row, lovelorn looks tossed across the aisle, life is beautiful!

March out, to class we go, scarred desks, carve out your moniker, the graffiti of endless names that have come and gone, the clatter of desk tops, raised and dropped with a bang, Camel geometry boxes, Chelpark-inked fountain pens, 'Good Morning Mr Benedict', blue-tinted glasses and quizzical looks, 'can this lass with long plaits amount to anything?', secret notes passed through gaps in the fireplace, a date after hobbies behind the art room, failing abysmally in Mr Gore's math class, a flying duster propelled at you.

Sixth Form, a new teacher, tall, long hair, a George Harrison moustache and a limp, Dr Dhillon, *To Kill a Mockingbird* and *Julius Caesar*, deep impressions on young minds, Mark Reading, shaking knees when called out by Mr Kemp in front of the whole school, milk break, hang out on the wires of the fence, skirts hitched up, faded blue shirts tucked in, the cannons and brass bell—witnesses to hundreds in grey and blue uniform, yesterday, today, tomorrow!

The airy, light art room, a haven for dreamy young artists, the smell of the smoky cigar wafting through the corridor from Mr Bhalerao's den, cross stitch and crochet with Mrs Mundkur, the Naga dance with Mr Brajamani, endless lessons on the sitar, music wafting from the piano cells, Mrs Sawhney inducting young souls . . .

Letters written home, blue inland letter forms, 'Dear Mummy & Daddy, How are you? I am well. How is the weather there? It rained here.

OK, have to go'; sitting on the sundial trying to tell the time, hungry, always hungry, dog biscuits at dawn, ice-cream on Sunday, wash hair once a week, spend the day in the sun, carefree in the company of friends. Fire in the middle of the night, scurry out, Peacestead, daylit at night, BD to the rescue, buckets of water and panty raids!

Long, skinny legs, easy to jump hurdles with, pass batons, plaits flying in the wind, flappy blue shorts, Come on Vindhya!

Camp at Gaura, tents on the river bank, idyllic days sitting by the stream, bus rides with voices raised in song, classes and teachers a far cry away . . .

End of the year, bittersweet, goodbyes and tears, midnight parties in the bogs, watery coffee in enamel tin cups, whispered conversations, dressing up for the last Social, lighting up the dormitory fireplace, faces aglow in the ebbing light, burning books, turning words to ashes, unwilling to end it all, stretching each moment as far as the last bugle call . . .

Experiences of a lifetime, frames etched in my mind's eye . . .

**Amrita (Singh) Nakai**
Vindhya 1972 | 1969–1972
Teacher | Trekker | Wanderer | Photographer

# It's the Way We Have In Sanawar . . .

I was admitted into Sanawar a week before Founders', 1951. There was a mad rush to get me kitted out in all the different uniforms, before the festivities began. One of my earliest memories is of the school tailor measuring me from waist to just above the knee, and me thinking, 'gosh, they wear short dresses here'. The tailor then explained that he was measuring me for shorts. I tried to move the measurement up at least six inches, when I was caught by Mrs Coombes, who said, 'in Sanawar, we do not expose our thighs'. And so I had arrived . . . after spending five years in Woodstock, the all-American Mission school in Mussoorie; very few could understand my broad American accent and I was lost in all the classes, as the courses were so different.

I survived. I couldn't believe how bad the food was and how little we got. At night, it was a scoop of dal and stringy, lime-green *arbi ki sabzi* with three chapatis. One night, Mr Carter did a round and asked me what I thought of the food, and I said 'it's punk'. He kept a straight face and asked if we could eat more and when we said we could, he asked the kitchen to carry on making chapatis till we could eat no more. I remember eating thirteen!

I survived the 'bogs' (our dreadful outside toilets), the uniforms (never having worn one before), being given clean uniforms only once a week (yuck), the pine-needle mattresses, the horse-hair blankets, and the fact that, in spite of being a co-ed school and knowing quite a few of the boys who had just joined, the girls and boys were not encouraged to speak to one another. I not only survived, but loved every moment in Sanawar. I loved the bugle, the marching, saluting the War Memorial—all the military traditions; I loved hearing about Honoria Lawrence's ghost wandering about Peacestead with a lantern; the multi-denominational prayers and songs at Assembly . . . I loved Sanawar . . .

We had the most incredible staff, who not only taught academic subjects, but also taught sports and were on duty for meals and hobbies.

They were there for us for all twenty-four hours. Their teaching was excellent and they were disciplinarians, but with a sense of humour and fairness. This was important, as I was always doing something I shouldn't have been, and getting caught . . . whistling in the corridors of Birdwood ('young ladies don't whistle'); jumping out of the class window, giving chase to one of the boys with a pair of dividers ('young ladies don't jump out of windows'); breaking bounds; talking to the boys; ducking the Head Girl in the swimming pool; bringing down the curtains around the basins where we had our five-mug basin baths in the summer when there was a water shortage. You got ticked off and punished, but no one tried to break your spirit.

Mrs Carter taught us to love maths; Mrs Coombes' geography is still with us; Mr Cowell taught English language with such precision; Miss Chatterjee arrived from Oxbridge to teach us English literature; Mr Vyas taught us enough Hindi to pass the S.C. exam, though all I remember is being read stories to in class; Mr. Saleem Khan . . . I didn't hear a word he said . . . we girls just gazed at him in adoration; Mr Kemp delighted in making us smell all the horrid gases; Mr N.K.S. Rao taught Biology; Mr Chicky Evans taught physics (most girls took hygiene and physiology with Mrs Kemp); Mr Mitra taught art and laughed at one of my drawings . . . I promptly gave up art and took additional maths instead.

Then there were the Housemasters and Housemistresses, the bursar, the matrons, the doctor, nurses and Mastoo, the PT master, the games coaches, the bearers who gave us extras, 'Charlie', the Quartermaster and all the other wonderful people, who were there for us all the time. And above all, Mr Carter, who devoted his whole life to Sanawar and was one of the finest human beings I have ever known (in spite of summoning me to his office and showing me, what he said was, the special cane for erring girls).

There were all the special occasions . . . the Dagroo Picnic, the ten-day breaks when you weren't allowed to leave the Simla Hills, the Hodson Run, the Socials, the House plays, and, of course, Founders', with all the excitement of the play, the tattoo, the dance, the ADS, the parade, the pagal gymkhana and the fete.

And then there were the mountains to climb, the whispering of the pine trees to listen to, the scent of pine needles or wood-smoke to smell, the twinkling lights of Simla on a clear night and the clear, clean air to breathe and grow in.

What Sanawar gave to us were friendships that have taken us through life, a value system that has stood us in good stead, the happiest of memories and the art of survival. 'Never Give In'.

**Gita (Bery) Bhatia**
Siwalik 1954 | 1951–1954
Senior Management – International Airline | Export Consultant – Handicraft/Handloom promoting India to Galleries Lafayette, Bloomingdales, Harrods, La Rinascente, Magasin du Nord, JC Penny

OS Spouse – Ashok Bhatia | Shoki | Vindhya House 1953 | 1951–1953

OS Children – Daughter – Premika Bhatia | Siwalik 1991 | 1987–1991
Son – Adil Bhatia | Siwalik 1993 | 1988–1993

# To Be a Sanawarian

In essence, the quality of schooling provided to the youth of a nation determines the nature and efficacy of institutions, thereby ensuring the future of the nation. Sanawar has been constantly churning out top-grade leaders, covering practically every sphere of human endeavour, over the past 175 years. I live by our motto 'Never Give In', every moment of my life, and take immeasurable pride in the education and the values I imbibed in school – from teachers and administrative staff to friends that shaped the six-year-old toddler in PD, into what I am today.

We all are familiar with the name of Gorkha Fort, a feature pointed out by knowledgeable seniors to famished juniors eagerly awaiting the bugle call to line up for dinner. Many will also recall the punishment run, for not being in line in ten seconds down to Barne Field, touch the far end of the wall and run back up the stairs because of an irate Head Boy or a senior prefect. To put my random thoughts into context, I am the first Nepali from the land of the Gorkhas to have entered the portals of this glorious institution. The care and instructions I received in school moulded me into what I am and ensured my journey to the apex of my profession, as the Chief of the Army Staff, Nepal Army (2012–2015). I never could figure out why the geographical feature, within hike-able distance from school, was named so.

February 1962 is a time firmly etched in my memory. Two Nepali boys, one nine and the other six – my elder brother, Gorakh, and I – visited an uncle, a political refugee at that time in Simla and somehow ended up at our enrollment to Sanawar. The question: how and why Sanawar? Well, our maternal grand-uncle, the venerable one and only, Mr B. Singh, was teaching there and our maternal uncle and cousins – Mankotias, Pathanias and Jamwals – were all studying there.

This roster is a pretty depictive show of familial strength, particularly in Himalaya House. However, I had one major problem: I could speak in Nepali only. My second and only other spoken language was English, in

134

which my vocabulary was limited to a maximum of half a dozen words. My older brother in BD, on the other hand, had far more developed communication skills and was better-equipped than me to tackle the strange environment we were suddenly placed in. My cousins took care of me—dressing me up, tying my shoelaces and making my bed. However, there was a caveat, this would be done for a timeline of one week only, by which time I had to become self-reliant. Fortunately, I had a fallback position in the form of Mariam ayahji. She is the one who taught me how to make my bed.

Upon reflection of the adage coined by Rudyard Kipling in *Kim*, 'Send him to Sanawar and make a man out of him', I was pleasantly surprised to discern that the basic foundation of my manhood rested upon the teachings and lessons imparted by ladies of tremendous stature, Ms Rudra, Ms Suri, Ms Harbaksh Singh, Ms Cherian, Ms Kaveri and many more. The only male input in this crucial formative stage was – a sporadic and very muscular one – from Mr Jagdish Ram Acharya, our PT teacher.

In my journey through life, thanks to Sanawar and my teachers, I have a firm understanding of the wholesome and true nature of masculinity and being a man. An understanding that sees a woman as an equal. An understanding which is adorned with a deep awareness of the importance of empathy, compassion and care—an invaluable leadership trait. An understanding laid brick-by-brick by ladies responsible for enabling individuals to develop fully by creating a secure surrounding—one of home and hearth—everywhere they went. Under their supervision and attention, I discovered and developed the qualities of diligence and commitment; essential while striving to make the world a better place to live in.

Mr Jagdish Ram (Jagga), on the other hand, was instrumental in creating an interest and love for soldiering in me. Having firmly implanted the importance of physical fitness in my impressionable young mind, he turned me into the best gymnast in school and subsequently, equipped me with the necessary tools to lead from the front in a robust and professional physical environment.

Those of us who joined the profession of arms were trained and groomed in the scientific military system that develops individuals who are fully committed and dedicated, to provide selfless service to the nation. What better example can I give than that of our greatest hero, Lt. Arun Khetarpal?

The underlying traits inculcated in such individuals are duty, honour, courage, loyalty, adaptiveness, reliability, humility and so on. However, the most important trait that constitutes the core element of leadership is character, which was hammered into my psyche by the old war-horse of Sanawar, Mr B. Singh (Chacha, Mama, Mucchoo or whatever names we called him, depending upon the intensity of our emotions) himself. On being caught in an act of improper behaviour, the invaluable sermon would begin with the delivery of a light tap on our head directed at enabling greater receptivity, followed by his indelible dialogue, 'No buts, my lad, there is something known as DECENCY, DIGNITY, DISCIPLINE, and DECORUM . . . and you have none. Now what do you have to say?' These basic '4Ds' have been the four pillars on which I built my character and subsequent leadership traits.

Words cannot describe my gratitude to Sanawar, the ever-progressive institution, the school fraternity, my friends and my teachers. As a tribute, I lay my successes at your feet.

Never Give In.

**General Gaurav Shumsher Jung Bahadur Rana**
Himalaya 1972 | 1962–1972
Royal Military Academy Sandhurst (UK) | Command & General Staff College, Fort Leavenworth (USA) | National Defence University, Islamabad (Pakistan) | Chief of Army Staff – Nepali Army 2012–2015

OS Sibling – Brother – Gorakh SJB Rana | Himalaya 1969 | 1962–1969
              Brother – Gautam SJB Rana | Himalaya 1976 | 1969–1976

# Carpentry and the Mad Dog

S A N A W A R—that's the way we spell it, that's the way we YELL IT! And that's the way it still reverberates within me every day of my life.

I joined Sanawar not by design, but pure accident. Fifty-nine years ago, I went up to the hilltop to see off my cousin, Rohit. His grandma, with five other grandchildren – Arun, Ameeta, Anita, Anil and Atul, all Sobti(s) – studying there, had a great influence on the Heady, Major Som Dutt.

She explained how Rohit and I were inseparable. Heady agreed to take an impromptu test. I don't really know how I fared, but Ms Kavery and Ms Suri were bowled over with my having a pencil and eraser ready in hand. So I was given a week to join . . . a whirlwind affair for a seven-year-old: buying a GI trunk, hold-all, blankets, dressing gown, undergarments etc. marked with dhobi ink and name labels . . . the painful and depressing inoculations . . . and teary-eyed parents, grandparents and sisters, surprised by my sudden going away for four months.

We were homesick, but new friends helped. And Ms Kavery, with her smiling, warm visits, to check whether our cheeks were well-plastered with Charmis cream and whether we had taken our daily dose of Celin tablet.

As a child, I was always inquisitive and opened up every toy given to me. On being reprimanded, I would promise to fix it when I got older. It was perhaps because of this inclination to build that I chose carpentry as a hobby. With modest beginnings from wooden carvings and sculptures, I progressed to a chair fashioned on a wooden lathe, with a jute-cord-knitted seat, which adorned my grandpa's room till his last day. The high point was to come in my final year—a guitar that I had built with all the right curves, brass frets and strings . . . quite the eye-catcher at the Founders' exhibition, though alas, I didn't get to learn how to play it. My obsession, however, paid me rich dividends through life, giving me an architectural and aesthetic bent of mind.

Cash Work was on Wednesdays—three consecutive classes post milk break. In order to maximize my time in the Carpentry Room, I would forgo tea. The pre-break class was English with Ms Harinder Kaur, the young daughter of the quarter-master, Mr Mohinder Singh. She read from the *Readers' Digest Red Book*, a story of a baby in a pram and a rabid dog: the nanny runs away, the pet duck flaps her wings to shoo away the mad dog, the baby survives. Ma'am explained how dangerous rabies was . . . a rabid dog froths at the mouth; puts its tail between its legs; gets hysterical near water and the only treatment for it is getting fourteen painful injections in the stomach, or else one could go mad.

Just then, the bell rang and I headed for Cash Work. I had recently changed my route to avoid (senior) girls who hung around the school bell, and perpetually giggled at us juniors. So I went down to the Chapel and as I was passing by the Nilagiri House quad, I saw a black dog . . . frothing at the mouth and his tail between his legs. Babban, the Nilagiri House attendant, was there with a big broom in hand. I called out to him, 'this dog is MAD!' He just smiled and shooed the dog away, into the khud. I continued up the stairs, next to the swimming pool, a spring in my stride, that was suddenly cut short by a sharp pain in my calf. I turned around to find that the black dog had dug his fangs in! I screamed and Babban came running, struck the dog on its head with the broom handle, causing the dog to let go of my calf and attacking my ankle, before fleeing.

The commotion brought Mrs Mukherjee to the scene, '*array, isko toh paagal kutay ne kaata hai . . . pate mein injection lagega*'. At Hospital,

Dr Sakuja and Mastu bandaged me up and contacted Dr Thomas, head of the Central Research Institute (CRI) in Kasauli. Dr Thomas lived on campus and Mrs Thomas was my teacher. Mastu carried me on his back all the way to Bakery, into Mr Manley's (School Bursar) shining green Chevrolet. I vividly remember Mr Manley driving with me sitting beside him and Mastu in the rear . . . a blood-stained khaki seat cover and a loaded pistol between us. Villagers stopped us at Garkhal to inform us that the black dog had been found. Apparently he had bitten some cattle, too. A little ahead, we reached the gasping dog and Mr Manley shot him in the head.

Mastu once again carried me up the unmotorable steep CRI. Mr Manley recalled having been bitten by a mad dog when he was fourteen, and getting fourteen injections. He then tried to assuage me, 'Science has progressed a lot . . . maybe you'll get only five'. Dr Thomas confirmed that there would be fourteen, plus a booster. He was however, visibly disappointed, 'My research will suffer with a damaged (dog) brain.'

I endured the injections surprisingly well. However, the blood extraction twice a day, with boiled-sterilized blunt needles was excruciating . . . Dr Sakhuja wriggling around to find a vein . . . OUCH! The silver lining was countless helpings of ice cream, twice a day . . . but sadly, no mangoes. I'm happy to say that the episode did not traumatize me. I have never been afraid of dogs, whether pets or stray. In fact, I have had Cocker Spaniels, Labradors and now Mila, my third Boxer, my constant companion in Mukteshwar, after Laila and Zara . . . the loves of my life. But for those who think I am crazy – and there are a few – don't blame me . . . it all started in Sanawar.

To end, I would like to give a shoutout to my inseparable gang, Suren Hira (our Head Boy), Ritu Badhwar, Rupinder Sidhu and Anil Das . . . alas, we lost Suren in college to an automobile accident. I dedicate this piece to his memory.

**Vivek Mehra**
Himalaya 1971 | 1962–1971
B. Com (Hons) SRCC | Chartered Accountant | Partner – PR Mehra & Co. and PwC | PwC Governing Oversight Board | National leader – Tax, M&A and Regulatory Practice | Independent Director – prominent listed companies & SEWA NGO
Member – LSSS (1997–2000), (2007–2010) & (2017–2020) | Member – Board of Governors (2007–2010) & (2017–2020) | Chairman – FOSS

# Requiem
## Down From The Hill

There was peace on the hill;
The quiet broken by raucous crows,
Leathern thud of ball on bat,
The hum and cries of children
And rasp of heaving breath, at run's end.
Well, we were so young then.

When we came down from the hill
The air was thick with smoke;
Dust blotted out the sun,
Our ears a percussion madness—
Thundering bombs and screaming shells.
Well, we were so young then.

HE took us from the hill
Leaving faded pictures framed on walls,
Names cut into stone,
Sepia smiles frozen in albums
Stored in dark cabinets and forgotten.
Well, we were so young then.

Bells had tolled for us
And many others too;
Perhaps HE needed more young than old—
Tipping scales heavily towards youth
To balance less eventful years.
Well, we were so young then.

When old and grey you come down the hill
You will know us not unless,
Those dusty albums have told their tales
Of smiles, glances and hope long lost.
Well, we were so young then—
And we are so young, still.

Memorial, Sanawar, 2 October 2008 | A Fellow Warrior

**Lt. Gen. Tajinder S. Shergill PVSM**
Taji and Maun | Vindhya 1958 | 1951–1958

OS Sibling – Brother – Lt. Gen. M.S. Shergill PVSM, AVSM, VrC | Vindhya 1957 | 1951–1957

OS Children – Son – Jaimal Inder Singh Shergill | Jami | Vindhya 1985 | 1977–1985

# Random Reminiscences

Dharampur Station on a cold, wet February morning in 1933. A tonga with one other passenger dropped us at the bakery. I had travelled with Mr Burge, the school secretary.

This was my first introduction to a 'mixed' school, but in those days, there was precious little mixing of the pupils. Boys wore Khaki uniform, but I thought the girls' outfit was terrible, and those dreadful bonnets, which they tied round their waists when indoor. Goodness! I soon proceeded to do a lot I had never tackled before . . . hockey, lacrosse, playing in mixed teams. I still bear a scar for my pains. I found an old acquaintance on the staff, Eileen Brisley, who had been with me in school in Nainital. Her boys, Chris and Oliver, were at Sanawar. Chris set the high-jump record in 1929, which still stood when I left Sanawar in 1954.

My first home in Sanawar, after my marriage, was at Garden City with Captain and Mrs Burcher and the Ecclestons, as neighbours. Then I lived in the Gables. Mrs Tilley who taught Urdu and was later headmistress, was next-door and I can picture Violet and Nina (two of her six children) in their round solar *topees*, being escorted to Prep School by Mary Ayah. Mrs Tilley was the spouse of Sgt. James Tilley, one-time school secretary, after whom the notorious 'Tilley's Hill' is named. Mrs Tilley was herself an old Sanawar girl, and therefore probably well-attuned to the subterfuges of scrimshankers. My next move was to the Pines, then Fort Suji, and then the bungalow over which the school dining rooms now stand. Here, I had as neighbours, first Miss Smith, who became the second Mrs Basil Wiles, then Mrs Howie, until she retired in 1949, followed by Mrs Alice Sircar (mother of Raj and Asha), and last of all, by Miss Romila Chatterjee.

Life was very simple but pleasant. We played tennis and bridge and trekked off to the cinema in Kasauli and organized Socials and picnics. Occasionally, I filled in if a member of staff was absent. And then the war broke out. Gradually, the men on the staff began to leave and wives were drawn in. A half-time job soon became a full-time assignment. We also

142

started knitting furiously – socks, balaclavas – and making many-tailed bandages, as our war effort. We even took our knitting to the cinema. British-manufactured goods began to disappear, but we soon got used to the local products. Open cans of bacon, margarine, Christmas pudding, milk and fruit, could be had from the Central Research Institute in Kasauli, after a spoonful had been removed for testing. And I wore dresses made of Khaddar (coarse woven cotton) bought in Gurkhal—very cool and hard-wearing.

During the war years, we were very isolated. All the pupils went down for the Christmas holidays and there were no celebrations, as of old. Troops were billeted in the school for the winter weeks, as a precaution. Being on an isolated hilltop, we had to be vigilant. There were incidents of lights flashing across the valley from Kasauli, of people with foreign names, i.e., Continental European, being interrogated for suspicion of espionage. Staff armed with rifles paraded the estate at night. There were no lights after 11.00 p.m. The Americans established a rest centre at Subathu. Women were much in demand for their weekly dances and transport was always provided. I thanked our hosts for the lifts I had on my way to visit Lesley in the British Military Hospital and for the chocolates they gave me, when they came to know I had children. The Yanks constructed a small dam at Dagroo gorge, where we used to have an annual school picnic in our days. It had, of course, silted up by then.

Independence Day in 1947: we gathered near the old gym and the Union Jack was lowered and the Indian colours raised. We sang 'Jana Gana Mana', a tune I had to learn to play. Some members of staff donned Gandhi caps and went down to Gurkhal to join in the festivities.

School life didn't change much until Founders' Day in 1947, when nearly all the pupils left in lorries with armed escorts, on their way to join their parents in Bombay, awaiting repatriation to the UK. But we carried on and the staff play took place that evening to a depleted audience. A skeleton staff and forty-seven pupils, including staff children, began the term in 1948. The new intake of pupils was slow to arrive, as we were not an establishment which advertised, but we gradually grew in strength. Parents were diffident about sending their daughters to a mixed school, so the Girls' Department remained small for a long time. The new pupils adapted well, once they got over the language barrier, to Sanawar's customs, for we made little concession to their different lifestyles. Morning Assembly moved to Barne Hall, but the format didn't change. A special book of prayers without the word 'Jesus' was printed and hymns were sung. There were more lentils (dal), vegetables and goat meat in our diet. Indian festivals were observed—no Guy Fawkes, but a Deepavali bonfire.

Harking back, several principals came and went in my day, the Reverends Hunt, Evans, O'Hagan, Hazell and Mr Carter. I was too late arriving for Bishop Barne, but I met him on several occasions, for he made frequent trips back to Sanawar from Lahore. He christened my daughter, Lesley, in the cathedral in Lahore. His last visit to Sanawar had to be cancelled (in 1949), because of ill health, but we were able to meet him in Kalka, where he confirmed the candidates presented in the very small church. These candidates included my sister Lesley, E.A. Rhind, John 'Pelican' Wiles and Thomas 'Buckra' Sanford. We then took over the refreshment rooms at the railway station and had one of our famous pulao and chicken curry lunches, which had been cooked in the school kitchen.

I visited the school again in 1981, puffing and panting a bit in the rarefied atmosphere. Much had changed, but much was the same. The grounds were looking beautiful, but the buildings were very shabby. I am glad to hear that things have since improved in that respect. The pupils were very polite and helpful, and were amused when I told them I knew my way around. The daughters of the incumbent Charlie Bootlace invited me to tea and were intrigued that I knew so much about their father's House in Moti's Corner—a source of illicit cigarette-buying in the old days.

So what did I find in Sanawar? Many friends, many happy days and I am left with many happy memories.

**Joy Coombes**
Staff 1933–1954
Mathematics and Geography teacher | Headmistress 1953–1954

Spouse – James R. St. M. Coombes | Chemistry teacher 1928–1944 | Headmaster | Officiating Principal in 1942

OS Children – Daughter – Lesley F. Coombes | Nicholson and Yellows
          1950 | 1940–1950 | Teacher 1953–1954
          Son – James Coombes | Jumbo | Nicholson and Himalaya
          1954 | 1944–1954

# Art at Sanawar

In 1950, at twenty-four, I was a young art teacher at Daly College, Indore. I was selected by the All-India Public Schools Committee to organize an art exhibition for their Annual Conference at Osmania University, Hyderabad. Here, I met Mr E.A. Couzens, a teacher from Sanawar, who was attending as an observer. After 'observing' me from a distance, he approached me and asked, 'Hello young man, how is it that at a tender age you run Daly College? What is the secret?' I replied, 'Sir, the reporter (*Deccan Chronicle*, 30 December 1950) who reviewed the exhibition must have made a mistake, designating me as Principal.'

Before we parted, he extended me an invite to come visit Sanawar, casually mentioning that the school was looking for a full-time art teacher. At Daly College, I was a substitute for their art master, who was on leave for a year. I decided to apply to Sanawar upon the completion of my term here. Surprisingly, before I could send a formal application, I received a brief note from Mr Couzens, inviting me to 'visit Sanawar and meet the Principal'.

One fine morning, I reached Sanawar. The school was closed for winter holidays. Mr Couzens greeted me. He introduced me to me Mr S.C. Cowell, the senior-most teacher, who after a brief chat, took me to Mr E.G. Carter, the Principal. I learnt that this was previously called the Lawrence Royal Military School and that before Independence, only British children studied here. It later took after the name of the village, Sanawara. After Independence, children of Indian Armed Forces personnel started coming into the school. When I reached, the change in management from the Ministry of Defence to the Ministry of Education was still on.

Mr Carter showed me the main blocks and other parts of the school campus. I was impressed and loved the environment. We sat for a while in his garden, where finally, he handed over my appointment letter to me. My interview was over.

Copyright © Rathin Mitra | ART MASTER | 1950–1953

I landed up in Sanawar a day before the children were to arrive after vacation. I was allotted a suite in Esquire Hall, designated for four bachelor masters. The other three were Virender Vyas, Bhupinder Singh and N.K.S. Rao.

The next day, the school transformed into a battlefield. The sound of the bugle could be heard now and again. The quadrangle was full of young boys in military uniform marching in heavy boots to Birdwood for classes. Prefects were the commanding officers, escorting their troops. While passing by the Chapel, they saluted the War Memorial with an 'eyes left'. I was thoroughly confused. We four (masters) followed the troops in black gowns, the uniform of the teaching faculty. Thank God we were not forced to wear the General's uniform. After hearing 'All things bright and beautiful, all creatures great and small, all things wise and wonderful, The Lord God made them all' at Assembly, I began to settle down.

Half of the library, next to Mrs Carter's office, was allotted to the art class. Sixteen desks crammed next to each other, with no space to move around. I complained to Mr Cowell about the dingy atmosphere. Luckily, the Art Room was shifted to a new building on the first floor next to the Principal's House. Children could see the sky through the window, sit on the long veranda and draw nature. Community work was introduced and a mural was put up on the wall. Gradually, aero-modelling and pottery design were introduced. My less imaginative pupils took interest in such crafts.

I would take my senior students out of the classroom to give them a wider perspective. The authorities disapproved of the idea. Rigid regimentation came in the way. I persisted, making a strong plea that to live in pristine surroundings, appreciate exquisite sights and Nature's bounties – the blue sky, the green foliage and trees, the golden sunset – was the right of every child. By putting together an exhibition 'Sanawar on Canvas', I made my point and made the authorities see reason, and also became aware of budding talent. I vividly remember the works of Aruna Vasudev, Doreen Field, Yograj Palta, Sita Bhai, Harpreet Gill, Aditya Nehru, Suresh Malik, Harjit Kochhar, Bul Bul Singh, to name a few.

Next year, the Art Room was again shifted. This time, I got an entire double-storey building, with finished works displayed in the ground floor hall, an art gallery for visitors. It was very satisfying to see Mr E.G. Carter escorting VIPs and introducing budding artists. Dr Tarachand, Prof. Humayon Kabir, the Maharaja of Patiala were amongst the first visitors. I never looked back from then onwards. Three successful art exhibitions were organized in Amritsar, New Delhi and Calcutta. A large number of parents attended to appreciate and acknowledge the talent. The media took notice and commented favourably. Sanawar came into the limelight, especially for Calcuttans.

I would like to conclude with an extract from Mr E.G. Carter's note on art activities in the school: 'We find that although the school was founded in 1847, it was not till 1949, when the Ministry of Education took over, that any serious attention was given to the subject Art. It figured in the school curriculum but we were compelled to work within narrow confines. After Mr Rathin Mitra's arrival as an art master in the early 50s, all that changed. I am not an expert on art but merely an interested amateur, who learns much from Mr Mitra and his pupils. His enthusiasm has inspired many of our children and their work today has reached a very creditable standard. Rathin's keenness is infectious and our little colony gets increasingly art-conscious. Our art now provides one with an outlet for expression. Art today is accepted as a pleasant and satisfying feature of life in school, and our debt to Mr Rathin Mitra for making the school art-conscious is great.'

**Rathin Mitra**
Art Master | 1950–1953
Head of Art Department – Daly College Indore (1949–50), The Lawrence School Sanawar (1950–53), St. Paul Darjeeling (1954–55), Doon School (1955–1981). Also taught at Bryanstan Public School, Dorset, England on a teacher exchange program, in 1959.

Among India's eminent artists – visual essayist, writer and teacher | The Youngest elected member of The Calcutta Group at twenty-one years in 1948 | A prolific Traveler and Explorer, dedicating the last forty years of his life documenting in pen and ink line drawings (his signature style) the heritage buildings of India (mostly Kolkata) | Created the longest mural (312 feet) at Air India building, Nariman Point, Bombay | The first living Artist to have exhibited in Victoria Memorial Hall (1983–1984) | Oil Paintings displayed in the National Gallery of Modern Art, New Delhi.

# Magic

For me, life in Sanawar was dynamic and magical. Like dynamite, even a small amount had a huge impact. My brief – sixteen-month – stint there cast a spell on me that continues to hold me captive. It also imbued in me an ethos that has often guided my decisions since I left school.

In August 1974, halfway through the school year, when Mr Das ([the] headmaster at the time), agreed to consider our application, my mother did not hesitate. She packed all four of us into the car, and we headed up the long and very windy road to Sanawar. I have no doubt I failed the entrance exam, because I was a lousy student; but I suspect Heady was so charmed by my beautiful mother that he accepted all four of us.

I was a hypersensitive and immature fourteen-year-old, who had never lived away from home. Thus, putting me into an institution not necessarily known for providing a nurturing, homely environment was a recipe for disaster. Yet, the magic of the hilltop, the juxtaposed experiences, and the 'Never Give In' motto shaped who I became. For example, I hated waking up for Chota Hazri, especially on chilly winter mornings, when the only thing we could expect was tepid tea and K-ration-type tasteless 'doggies' or 'sweeties' masquerading as biscuits . . . but that's when I discovered how beautiful and peaceful early mornings are.

I am a dawdler and very easily distracted (ADHD was not a recognized condition in the mid-70s). With thirty-five of us sharing six or seven toilets and a limited number of sinks, I quickly realized that to be on time, I had to wake up at 5.30 every morning, fifteen minutes before our matron rang the rouser bell. Like the rivers of humans that flow through India, we flowed and rushed around each other as we attempted to get ready. Surprisingly, most of us even managed to be on time most days!

My memories of mealtimes in Parker Hall were of organized chaos. Dishes filled with our favorite foods did not float down to the tables. The food was apportioned onto plates in the kitchen, and juggling three plates at a time when it was our turn to serve, we brought the plates from the kitchen to our House tables. And delectable aromas from exotic foods rarely wafted up from the table. But because I was generally famished, I ate everything that was served and frequently also what others at my table did not want to eat! So, despite our daily exercise and traversing the very hilly 140-acre campus all day, by the end of the semester, I wore uniforms that were two sizes larger than the ones I had got at the beginning of the term.

Dinners at our House mistress Mrs. Solomon's home and then invoking ghosts as we walked back to the dorm across milky-white moonlit Peacestead; the moment of pitch black, pin-drop silence before Peacestead was flooded with light announcing Tattoo; dates behind the Hospital, in Holiday House and Warrior's Grove, among other places; lunches and teas at the Gores', Dr. Dhillon's, Ma Chat's and other teachers' homes; puffing and panting up and down steep hillside trails to avoid having to walk down the longer roads through campus . . . the memories are endless. But other than dissecting frogs and being woken up during prep with a sharp tap on my head by Mr B. Singh, very few are academics-related. Having to sit still and learn at a desk had always been torturous for me. Fortunately, life in Sanawar offered many other modes and means of instruction, that lead to valuable lifelong lessons.

Sanawar, my first experience of living outside a major metropolitan area, was where my love affair with nature truly began. I can still see the mountains framing the horizon in the north, feel the tranquility and wonder while exploring local trails, and recall the exhilaration of my very first real hike with Mr and Mrs Solomon, who took us to Chor Peak for camp in 1975. That was also the first time I slept on cow dung. I marvel at the memory because it's not something I would do voluntarily (then or now). But it also proves that our anxieties frequently prevent us from experiencing life completely. I'm not any shorter because of the experience, but definitely wiser.

Most importantly, I don't recall any specific moment or occasion when we were told that we were to 'Never Give In'. It was simply a part of the ethos. The image of the words – painted in bold, white letters across a red banner in the quad – were soon firmly etched in my mind. The school song, which we sang daily, began with those three little words. And it wasn't long before 'Never Give In' became the mantra that flowed through my veins.

Long after I finished high school, on days that do not seem to end because the challenges seem insurmountable, remembering to 'Never Give

In' has helped me negotiate those challenges. While slogging through an MA thesis at the age of fifty-seven and an MFA thesis at fifty-eight, the 'Never Give In' chant played (in an eternal loop) in my brain, helping me cross the finish line every time. It also kept my feet moving, one painful step at a time, as I dragged myself through the final stretches of my first marathon at the age of fifty, and while wishing a bear would put me out of my misery towards the end of my first gruelling sixteen-hour hike up 14,505 ft. Mt. Whitney, the tallest peak in the continental United States.

The magic of Sanawar continues to bind me, like most other OSs, to the 'hilltop'. But Sanawar gave me much more than magical memories. Notably, the community service program provided me with my first opportunity to help others—a passion that continues to drive me many decades later. I'm grateful for the opportunity to have been a Sanawarian and am proud to be an OS.

**Mrinalini (Dhadha) Watson**
Dimple | Himalaya 1976 | 1974–1976

OS Siblings – Sister – Jyotsna Dhadha | Joy | Himalaya 1979 | 1974–1979
Sister – Ayesha Dhadha | Himalaya 1982 | 1974–1981
Sister – Indrani Dhadha | Himalaya 1985 | 1976–1979

# The King and I

Takes me back to 1981–82, when we were in Lower Five, first term, camps were approaching, and so Pande wrote home asking for a camera to be sent to him via post. God bless his sister, the parcel got delivered a week later during lunch at Common Dining Hall. It was one of those lovely click-3 cameras—hassle-free for the person using it, for the one and only button on the machine is that which says 'click'.

Anyhow, being an early riser, and in a dorm adjoining the Tiger's Den, I was kicked to find our man in just the position that he usually loved to put us in. Before I can actually engage my brain, I find myself standing in His backyard, armed with the click-3.

'What is it that you want?' the Tiger roared.

'One photograph, please,' I could hardly hear my own voice.

'NO!' He was not pleased one bit, to say the least.

'Please Sir, just one . . . photograph,' I couldn't believe myself.

'GET BACK TO YOUR DORM, NOW,' the majestic glare in his eyes was doing most of the talking.

Realizing that he was not going to get up and interrupt 'nappi' (who, by now, had stopped chopping and was awaiting the kill), I said, 'please Sir, I'll never enter your backyard again', beginning to tremble. Then, upon an enlightening afterthought popping up, I added, 'I'll never show it to anyone, Sir . . .'

That I think, to this day, is what did the trick, for I could clearly see a tiny bit of a smile appear at the corner of His lip. But being a master of camouflage amongst other things, doubt always played a significant role when one was standing face-to-face with the Tiger. Moreover, I was in His den.

Wondering whether He would permit me another breath, I completely surrendered to whatever was to follow . . .

I could swear I saw a twinkle in His eye, even though His tone was as stern as ever, 'Go on then. One and be gone.'

'Nappiji, *aap please deewar ki taraf ho jaaiye,*' I said. Suddenly, I knew I would survive it.

Now I do think that the photograph could have been much better in terms of the angle and so on . . . but, mate, I tell you this, it was an outstanding, amazing achievement to have got it just right in terms of focus.

Tigers like Mucchoo come by only once in a lifetime. I actually miss Him, sometimes.

I know a lot of people have this and that to say about Him, and have done so over the years, but I, for one, love Him to date for his unparalleled qualities of ensuring fairplay, humour and justice for all.

Every kid deserves to have a Mucchoo in his/her life . . .

**Dhiraj Sapru**
Himalaya 1985 | 1977–1985
STAFF 1989–1996

OS Sibling – Brother – Pankaj Sapru | Himalaya 1983 | 1976 – 1983

# Saved by the Whisker

In the summer of 1980, being a 'junior' in the Soccer First XI, I was bestowed the 'honour' of collecting the inflated soccer balls from Jagdish, who sat below the staircase leading to the Science Labs. I collected them after lunch and was on my way down to the dorms, and then onto Barnes.

Nirvik Singh, a year senior, and in First XI too, was known for his exceptionally accurate kick and was on a date at the Cannons. Seeing me and with the obvious intent of impressing his date, he yelled, 'Oye, kick!' I tried to caution him but, quite obviously, he was in no mood to listen to reason. He barked, 'Don't worry, fool, just kick.' So I kicked as hard as I could and sure enough, the ball sailed over his head, past the silver-painted fence, towards the War Memorial below.

I ran to see where it had landed. Peering through the hedge, I froze in my tracks as I met Mucchoo's bewildered gaze. He was seething with rage; his hair dishevelled; his right hand suspended in mid-air, the Charminar missing from between his index and middle finger webbing. It was still lit, lying mournfully by his feet; while the soccer ball was tranquilly resting against the parapet wall. I quickly put the pieces together—I had hit Mucchoo smack on his head, while he was on his way down after lunch. That explained the tousled look, the 'abandoned' cigarette and above all, that dazed yell, 'Hyeeeeee, how dare someone knock me out . . . cold . . . in SANAWAR?!'

He summoned me with his famed 'Hyeee LAD!' I doubled over on the Golden Staircase, dreading being greeted with a resonating slap, the kind that rings in one's ear for some time. I apologized and picked up the miscreant soccer ball. For once, he too was a tad embarrassed and at a loss for words. Sensing the opening, I took one step, following it with more quick ones. Barely thirty steps later, I bounced the soccer ball just once. He summoned me back and bestowed yet another beauty upon me, advising, 'Do not let go of the ball till you reach Barnes. Have I made myself clear?'

'Yes Sir.'

Two years later, in U-VI, we had 'double Eco' with Khalid—the last two 'schools' before lunch. For no particular reason – except enduring Khalid for 90 minutes, and that too just before lunch – felt insufferable so we decided to bunk. The list comprised the who's who – Vivek Kaul (Head Boy), self (M.I. Prefect), Dhyan Mayadas (DHM's Asst.), Bunny Jamwal (House Captain, Himalaya), Alam Khara (House Captain, Nilagiri), Amolak Gill (Prefect, Vindhya), Ranvir Dhillon and Sanjay Aggarwal.

In the classroom, Khalid realized something was amiss – it was unusually quiet today; surely, some people were missing. When he enquired, Sangha volunteered and wrote the list of absentees, which Khalid promptly dispatched to the DHM's office. So, just before going into lunch, we were told about what had happened. Sangha justified his tattling, saying, 'fools, you think he would not have found out?'

Thus our fates were sealed – creating khup, that too in U-VI, and, getting caught – it was only a matter of time before Mucchoo would order, 'hyeee lad, report to Dhani Ram at 0500 hours for morning drill. And, yes, till further advice . . .'

Understandably, we had lost our appetites and sat waiting for Mucchoo. However, for some strange reason, he came to our table (Heady's group) twice – once asking Dhyan to finish the dal only on his plate and another time, enquiring after something from Kaul. Bunny felt that Mucchoo had no right to 'torture' us like this and that he should have just stated upfront whether he wanted us to report for drill or not – 'This is pure harassment!' I too got excited, summoned the Server to our table, asked him to go to Mucchoo and say – 'Sir, Sapru's saying that if you want to say it, then say it, otherwise ***'.

As our luck would have it, the Server on that historic day was Keshav Chander, a raving lunatic. Mucchoo was somewhere between the Himalaya House and Vindhya House tables. Keshav went around him, pretending to be speaking to him and reported back saying that he had passed on the message. Impossible—no one could go up to Mucchoo and say all that. So I, continuing with the fun, told him that I knew he had not said it and that if he did not do so this time around, I would be left with no other option but to break his ***. So, Keshav marched back and actually had a tête-à-tête with Him. Apparently, Keshav said, 'Sir, Sapru is saying: "Sir, please say it, if you want to, and Sir, if you do not want to say it, then don't say it, Sir".'

Seconds later, Mucchoo was charging across CDH with bloodshot eyes and venom on his tongue. As my back was towards him, Bunny kept updating me from across the table: 'he's coming, he's closer, here he comes!' His right hand forefinger dug into my shoulder blade as he barked – 'Hyeeeee, what is it that you want me to say?' To that, I could only manage a 'Sir, I was only joking . . .', he cut me short, 'Hyeeeeeee, you and your utterly silly jokes, you misguided humourist . . . hyeee, I had to come all the way from the other end. Hyeeee, you see me after lunch, in my office.' Shomie Das finally realized that something was going on, and enquired, to which Mucchoo said, 'Hyeee, never mind . . .' and walked away. He was, quite obviously, beside himself.

Having to see Mucchoo after lunch, in his office, is not good news. All of us who have had the distinction of getting those beauties (canes, especially linseed-oiled ones by Jagdish) know better. But what had to be done, had to be done. There was no time to put on those extra undies, even. So, I was standing outside his office door, anxiously waiting for the beauties. Shortly, he came along, obviously still very upset, because he did not reply to my 'Good afternoon, Sir'. He unlocked his door, went behind his desk, sat down and shouted, 'Hyeeee, come in.'

I walked in with my head down, hands behind my back, looking really sad and 'innocent'. He said, 'Hyeeeee, close the door'. Now there were two doors – the one with a mesh on the outside and the solid wooden one on the inside. When he asked me to shut the wooden one too, I got really worried. He was probably so hassled that, maybe, he wanted to deliver his beauties to me with my pants down. He narrowed his eyes and peered at me through his thick-framed glasses (flashing me that trademark look of his) and said, 'Now, man to man, what is it that you want me to say?' Grabbing the opportunity, since he had not, right away, taken out the canes, I remarked that there was nothing that I could say to him, and more importantly, I never thought that anyone, Keshav included, could walk up to him and say any of it.

'Hyeeeee, but why is it always you, who is perpetually playing the clown?'

I promptly replied, 'I'm really sorry, Sir!'

He stared at me for a few seconds, and then said, 'Hyeeee, GET OUT!'

I couldn't believe my luck. I had been saved by the whisker.

**Pankaj Sapru**
Himalaya 1983 | 1976–1983
Senior Management – Petroleum Downstream sector | Travel & Street Photographer | Member – OSS Executive Committee 2019-21 | Vice President – OSS 2021-23

OS Sibling – Brother – Dhiraj Sapru | Himalaya 1985 | 1977 – 1985

# Gleanings From Major Som Dutt's
# Life and Work

*'Time goes, you say? Ah no! Alas, Time stays, we go.'*

Sanawar has been 117 years on the eternal field of Time. Contemplating our longevity as an institution, one is inclined to look for a justification for our being.

Whatever comes to stay, whatever is admitted by time to a degree of fellowship, attains immutability and a perennial state of being. Whatever is discarded, whatever goes having failed to stand the test of Time, deserves to go. Only true things last and become 'classics'; and especially is this true of educational institutions, for age may not be credit to individuals but to institutions it certainly is. It is the nature of Time to accept only verities and lend them long continuance. So in union with Time stay the significant works of men, things of lasting value, institutions, traditions, ideas and aesthetic creations.

And those that abuse their allowance of time, recede into the irrevocable past, pass out of existence: they do not cultivate the everlasting relationship with Time, they fail to be its instruments and are thrown out of being as refuse.

Whatever true has taken roots in Sanawar in 117 years of its history remains and will remain with Time; it has survived the eliminating factors of change and Time has still some use for it. If we appear to be continuing the traditions which were laid down over a century ago, we are doing so in conscious or unconscious obedience to the perennial reality in them, embracing all that is of genuine merit.

A happy blending of the old and the new is rendered possible only by the element of truth in both. Truth is neither old nor new, it is eternal, it is one with Time.

The false, the frivolous, the trivial, the trite and the insignificant have passed away and any effort to seek permanence for them could not but have failed. Our self-preservation, therefore, lies in recognizing the demands of Time, realizing the truth and achieving harmony with it; and, if we fail to do so, we cannot but be refused like all rejected things that fail the test of Time and are expelled beyond the limits of existence for good.

## Extract from Founders' Speeches

### 1956

May I conclude, Sir, by giving you briefly my own first impressions of the school. I have found it friendly and wonderfully well-disciplined— not the discipline of the drill-square nor yet the discipline of flags, slogans and exhortations but disciplined in the truest sense of the word. The children appear to do instinctively what is right and good and just. This, I feel, is because of a traditional way of life, a way of living and developing together, the very young learning from the very little older, who themselves have learnt from those who have gone before. And then there is the tremendously refining influence of education, which makes children feel almost at home with the balance and sense of security it gives. And I feel the school is achieving its purpose, which is not merely to fit a child for life, for that alone is insufficient because the life a child will lead is obviously conditioned by his education, but rather to send out into the world young men and women who have learned to exercise their powers and talents to the full in conditions of unity and amity with their fellows.

### 1957

Before I close, Sir, I should like to pay a tribute to the children, to their sense of discipline and their friendliness. Sanawar has always been famous for its sense of right conduct and has never required resource to the use of phrases and slogans to maintain it. There is an almost tangible body of protective tradition with roots that go back more than a century and this is what makes Sanawar what it is. Their sense of confidence comes from an inner assurance of their own developing talents and their friendliness from genuinely cooperative living, and this, I feel, Sir, is the basic aim of education.

## 1958

I should like to refer also to the cases of those children who are weak in studies. I am mentioning this because parents, I am sure, would like to know how we tackle this problem. We ourselves are very much alive to it. The children who are weak fall into two categories: those we know are weak and those whose parents feel they are weak. In the latter case, I would ask parents to bear with us. The essence of our system is that a child should develop as a whole. No amount of high marks will compensate a child, if in his attempts to secure these, he is found lacking in efforts or interest in his fellow students, his environment, his games and his hobbies. The experience he gains in the enjoyment of these activities will stand him in good stead all his life much more than knowing that Mt. Pappa, in Burma, is an extinct volcano or that H20 is another term for water. But we do have with us the problem of the genuinely weak children. These, in almost every case, are limited to late entrants.

Parents write to us asking that private tuition be arranged and express their willingness to pay for it. Private coaching as such is not a very good thing except in the case of new admissions who may be weak in one or two subjects. Otherwise, it makes a child dependent on a crutch, when our main object is to make children rely on, and trust, their own developing talents. In Sanawar, we do not permit private coaching on payment, as it leads to a number of abuses. But this does not mean that nothing whatsoever is done. Our results in the Overseas School Leaving Certificate Examination alone belie this. The problem is tackled in two ways. Firstly, new admissions are definitely helped to reach the standard of other students in the subjects in which they are weak. Secondly, the senior master Mr Kemp, is making a start with a system that will make our present tutorial classes a part of the school timetable, when weak children can and will be given extra instruction, without either cutting into the normal timetable of instruction or cutting into those precious hours which are available for games and out-of-class activities. This system has merit, achieves results and has none of the demerits of private coaching. It will, undoubtedly have to be limited to the lower forms and will also mean that fewer subjects will be learned, but these latter will be the really important ones.

## 1960

Over the last year, we have tried to make Sanawar a truly co-educational school. Many restrictions which were imposed formerly by the British, on the assumption that the lesser breeds had uncertain morals, have been done away with. In the PD, boys and girls now feed together with remarkably good effect on the table manners of the boys and on their choice of topics for conversation. And the girls, too, have discovered that little boys are not the horrid monsters of their imagination.

In the Senior School, all cultural activities, other than the essentially masculine ones such as carpentry and the band, are commonly shared. The result is a general raising of standards, e.g. where formerly Saturday Club Concerts were confined to four shows by the boys, one by the girls, and one by the PD, today these concerts are the joint productions of all children, regardless of age or sex. I am sure you will agree that girls make for more charming girls on the stage than do boys dressed for the part, no matter how hard you try to camouflage knobby elbows and incipient moustaches.

Boys are beginning to take an increasing interest in Indian dancing, much to the amusement of the conservative Sixth Form, though even here, the barrier is breaking down. It has been whispered that no less a personage than the Head Boy has been seen shaking a foot, more suitable for soccer, with the delicate nuances of an Indian Folk dance.

I am often asked by visitors, and you can almost sense that the question is farmed in block capitals, 'Are there no incidents?' as though the lack of them would amount to an unnatural phenomenon. It is rather hard convincing people that children are basically good, true idealists, and that it is a far more natural state of affairs to be free of incidents whether in block capitals or the lesser case.

## 1961

Firstly, I should like to talk on how we spend our spare time. In order that my words make sense, I must say, at once, that our guiding principle is that in learning to enjoy leisure, a child is going a long way in becoming a cultured and civilized being. I feel this has particular application today when there is a growing feeling in the country that parading up and down a square in an NCC uniform is a major means of inculcating a sense of discipline and responsibility in a child. In my view – and I have been a soldier for over twenty years – parade grounds offer little that is of spiritual value. They serve no more purpose than to teach you to conform to certain basic movements and patterns to the accompaniment of words and combinations of words you never knew existed. Professional pride comes much later, when you join your regiment which has a soul and is fiercely jealous of its honour.

In Sanawar, school gets over by 1.00 p.m. and therefore, we have the whole afternoon in which we can get down to doing something agreeable, whether on the games field or in a form that really interests us; and this, I am happy to say does not exclude reading for pleasure in the liberty.

So many people wistfully refuse to take up a hobby on the ground that they have no talent. We feel that this attitude is wrong. It is not really necessary to be gifted with a talent to enjoy a particular art or skill. For example, not every child is blessed with a voice or a musical ear, though many more possess these than think they do. But you can get much more from life, if by making an effort, you begin to understand the rudiments of music and signing; your appreciation of good music will be all the keener.

Neither need you be an artist to enjoy playing with paints and brush; and it is the same with anything else you care to work at, carpentry, modelling needlework and so on. I am sure that those who drive a motor car would enjoy driving far more if they knew a little more of what goes on under the bonnets of their cars other than that their engines need petrol, oil and water from time to time. There is an undoubted thrill in the feel of an engine, sweetly responsive to an educated foot on the accelerator pedal.

The important thing is not that you have talent. It is that you have tried and by trying, understood. You would be surprised at the number of boys who, under the inspired teaching of Mr Rajamani, have taken to Indian dancing; boys who were convinced that their feet were more suited to kicking a ball at soccer, or certain parts of the anatomy in the course of normal life. And with the effort, has come understanding.

## 1964

And now if I am not jumping too widely, I would like to talk on a subject very close to the hearts of our parents. We are asked by many for advice on the subjects their children should offer and what we consider a likely choice of career in the light of our knowledge of the child. I am afraid this is very difficult question to answer, for essentially, our purpose is not necessarily to prepare a child for a particular career—and we feel that to oblige a child to take certain subjects, or to make a child adopt a particular career which might be found unsuitable, would be to do him or her great harm.

Equally, many of our parents do not ask for our advice. They tell us quite frankly that young Gopal will take Maths, Physics and Chemistry, and that he is going to be an engineer, or doctor or be going into the army. Such decisions do not always help and cause acute misery to a child who has to, in deference to parental insistence, switch over from a subject which he likes to a subject he detests.

## 1965

Before I request Mrs Indira Gandhi to talk to you, I feel it is my duty to answer many unspoken queries which must be in the minds of the many parents who have defied the Emergency to be with us today, and those queries must relate to how safe their children are in Sanawar.

That is question I cannot answer – parents, Mrs Indira Gandhi could tell you more about this – but I can tell you what we have done and the possibilities for which we have prepared. Forgive me for using the royal and headmaster's 'we'; when I say 'we' I mean the staff as a team and nothing else.

Firstly, parents have an absolute assurance from us that we shall look after their children to the utmost limit of our capacity to do so.

Secondly, we have practised the children in drills to safeguard them against fire and against an attack by air, whether by day or night, and whether they are in their classrooms, sleeping in their dormitories, or otherwise engaged. Those drills have been practised to such an extent that the children can now be in their allotted positions of safety within a minute to a minute and a half to an alarm being given.

Thirdly, every member of the staff, including the senior members of our class-IV staff, have been instructed in the more practical forms of first-aid. First-aid boxes have been installed wherever they might be needed throughout the school and in all staff quarters. We have also, as you know, our own school hospital. Firefighting parties and firefighting equipment have also been arranged. We have also had to consider the remote possibility that it might be necessary, should the situation worsen, to evacuate the children and staff in case of a threat of real danger.

The plan for this evacuation includes the possibility of evacuation along the Kalka–Ambala–Delhi route if public transport is available and

if the route is open. It also includes the possibility that this route might
not be available. As an alternative, we have mapped a route through the
hills to Dehra Dun, viz., Dagshai–Kumarhatti–Nahan–Paonta Sahib–
Dehra Dun. We have contacted all the important civil officials in this area
and also those others in a position to help; very fortunately, the Deputy
Commissioner of Nahan was a Cadet in the IMA when I was an instructor
there, and we are satisfied that we could trek the distance involved, a little
short of a hundred miles, in twelve to fourteen days, walking at a rate to
suit the smallest of our children. Supplies and water are adequate, and the
Deputy Commissioner at Nahan has volunteered every assistance possible,
including the prospect of transport for the very young.

## 1966

It becomes increasingly difficult each year for a headmaster to find what
to say at Founders'. Ritual demands that [the] headmaster give a report
on the working of the school. I observed the ritual for about two years and
then gave it up for the reason that I found that a headmaster's report was
the best means of putting his audience to sleep. I feel there is a market for
tape-recordings of 'Headmaster's Report at Speech Day'—those could be
played back to you, in lieu of aspirin when you find you are unable to sleep
at night.

## 1967

The second subject I should like to speak on is with regard to the fears
expressed by some parents concerning the future of public schools in India.

May I begin by saying that few public schools go out of their way to
call themselves public schools. We really are private schools; and even if the
better of us are members of the Indian Public Schools' Conference, and the
country continues to call us public schools and the children of these schools
consider themselves to be public school boys and girls, we are nevertheless
private schools. I trust I am not being too shaggy dogged.

There are slightly over twenty-one private schools in the country which
are qualified to be members of the Indian Public Schools' Conference; and
I must say that few as we are, we attract more than our fair share of criticism
based largely on hearsay evidence. A certain Mr Malhotra, for example,
whose car bears the number plate: New Delhi One – this represents a

form of snobbery of which no public school boy could be guilty – would abolish us and, if this is outside the scope of his authority, he would like to see public school boys and girls debarred from public service. He is not alone in his way of thinking. I fail to see any justification for his animosity. As I've said there are only twenty-one of us. In what way have we thrust ourselves forward? No more than two of three prime ministers have been and are products of private schools. Pandit Nehru was the product of a private school in Harrow and Mrs Indira Gandhi was educated in, broadly speaking, a similar school in Switzerland; two out of three is far from being disproportionate.

There is reason why I am stressing the fact that public schools are private schools. As long as the Constitution of India does not debar a private citizen from buying a public school education in a private school, no one, not even Mr Malhotra, can prevent these schools from functioning.

**Major R. Som Dutt**
Headmaster 1956–1970

**Source and Acknowledgement:** *The Sanawarian*, 1975

# A Day with the Som Dutts

We had made it a point to visit them during our visit to Goa and so we did it. They had come to Goa just a few months earlier as the climate of Ooty didn't suit Major Som Dutt. About a month before we met them, he had survived a very severe attack of bronchial asthma, when doctors had almost given up hope. Our visit was a surprise and he was so visibly moved that he could hardly speak. His condition was pretty bad even then as he had an oxygen cylinder kept by his bedside and he had to use it often. He was moving about in the House, not giving any indication of the suffering he was undergoing.

All the time during our stay, he was talking about Sanawar. Never once during his conversation did he ever give an indication that he did not like so and so. He was feeling very bad that he was not able to attend the Founders', as they had planned to do.

Even at dinner on that day, when Col. and Mrs Simons were also invited, he was talking to us most of the time. There were occasions when he appeared to get exhausted and needed to go and rest.

It was a moving parting when that morning, he asked Merle (Mrs Som Dutt) to see us off at the Panaji harbour as he could not do it himself.

I can still visualize his spirit moving majestically in Sanawar as he did when he was with us.

**U.A. Mundkur**
Staff 1957–1981

**Source and Acknowledgement:** *The Sanawarian*, 1975

# Staff Kids

The Gidwani invasion of Sanawar started in 1950 with our mother, Siwalik House Mistress Mrs Dru Gidwani, teaching Prep School, Harish Gidwani (age nine years) and Shirin/Sheila Gidwani (age five years), followed the next year, in 1951, by Aroon/Anu Gidwani (age five) and Reeta Gidwani (age four)—all boarders in Nilagiri House!

Sanawar was our home away from home . . . a place where we studied, played, made lasting friendships, made mischief and revelled in carefree laughter. It was also the setting for our youth, our formative years and our core values.

We were Staff kids; boarders with families within the school bounds: the Gidwanis, Kemps, Carters and Coombes. We lived by the same rules as the rest of our peers, but had additional memories of escapades and events during short school holidays when the other kids left Sanawar to go home, while we remained on that glorious hill, but in our parents' homes rather than in our dorms . . . indulging in alternate fun capers. We chased each other on the covered rooftops, ate mangoes outside, defying greedy monkeys, exchanged hilarious stories of sliding horrid food into the huge brass pots in the dining room, breaking bounds and being punished with 'saline' on our return, Mrs Hickey's 'brush' for our misdeeds; midnight feasts, plucking raw mangoes from fruit trees while walking along with the little train down to Dharampur, picnics at Eagle's Nest. Our major exception to the reigning rules while school was in session, was that we had the run of the estate during those days of unfettered freedom.

On a Sunday in 1952, James (Jim) Coombes, Timothy (Tup) Carter and Harish Gidwani decided to go roller skating from Sanawar down to Garkhal. All set to go down the hill, Harish discovered his toddler sister Reeta, then five years old, had followed them all the way to the gate of the school! She was standing there looking up at them, holding up one skate in her little hands! The boys looked at each other and decided they couldn't forfeit their escapade. Quickly looking around the area, they found a piece

167

of wood and strapped Reeta, with one of their belts, onto the skate . . . and whoosh! Away they all went whizzing down the hill, the three boys on roller skates and Baby Reeta strapped onto her skateboard! Believe it or not, all of them – including Reeta – survived without a scratch!

A while later, the same three boys managed to climb into the Barne Hall attic and hoisted a sheet painted with the Jolly Roger from the flagpole. The flag was seen as far as Kasauli, and someone called Principal Carter and asked him if Sanawar had been 'taken over by pirates'. Needless to say, the elders were 'not amused' and, notwithstanding Tup being Principal Carter's son, each of the boys got 'six of the best'.

Harish was supposed to babysit his three sisters one afternoon in Holiday House (Mom's residence for a while). He, Tup and Jim asked us if we wanted to play cowboys and Indians. Of course, we were excited! Little did we know what these three had planned. They made a tent out of old blankets, told us we were Indian squaws and to get into the tent. Once we were in there, they collapsed the tent over us and told us we were their captives! Then they sat down to a game of cards!

There was a tradition in the girls' dormitories, to frighten the new girls when they first came to Sanawar. During the day, we would prepare them by telling them that Lady Honoria's ghost walked the dormitories on certain nights. All of us had white nighties anyway, so half the battle was won. Then, after lights-out, when it was pitch dark, one of the 'old' girls would leave her dark hair loose and walk around, close to the new girls' beds, while several of us made soft, occasional humming sounds. Then, the girl pretending to be Lady Honoria would let out a shriek and quickly dive into her own bed. The new girls were petrified!! One of them wet her bed, another cried, others trembled and pulled blankets over their heads.

My sister Reeta was always getting into trouble and being punished. We always marched to our meals, marched to school, marched everywhere. Reeta decided she didn't want to keep in step and repeatedly put her left foot forward for the right, completely screwing up the rhythm of that particular group. The prefect-in-charge shall remain unnamed, but that evening, after prep, she punished Reeta by making her stand in the dorm with her arms outstretched, holding gumboots filled with water in each hand while simultaneously reciting Lady Macbeth's speech! One of our visitors from Lovedale was in the dorm and after twenty minutes, begged the prefect to stop the punishment. She did so. However, Reeta refused to say sorry despite having trembling arms after that ordeal.

Every morning, the entire girls' school lined up on Peacestead for PT. Practically every morning, Mr Jagdish Ram shouted 'GIDWANI!' I froze, looking guilty. Mr. Jagdish Ram called me to the front, yelled at me and I returned red-faced to my spot. Meanwhile, my sister, Reeta, who was the real culprit, grinned. This happened fairly often. I was yelled at, while Reeta grinned. Jagga never figured out the difference between the two sisters, and I never had the courage to tell him that he was yelling at the wrong person. Reeta thought it was very funny, as did most of the others.

One day, we were march-practising for Founders', when Mr Jagdish Ram said 'Salami Do!' Everyone saluted with their right hand. Reeta saluted with her left hand and Mr Jagdish Ram shouted 'GIDWANI!' Everyone looked at ME instead of looking at Reeta, who just switched to her right hand! Since I looked guilty, I got punished!

All four Gidwani siblings spent their entire schooling lives in Sanawar: Harish (Nilagiri '55), Shirin/Sheila (Nilagiri '60), Aroon/Anu (Nilagiri '61) and Reeta (Nilagiri '63). We love Sanawar and often reminisce; 'remember when . . .', giggles, amused chuckles, excitement of memories long forgotten . . . lots of tales to share. Perhaps, one day, we will get a chance to sit around a warm fire and relate all the wonderful stories of our long gone youth in the best school of all!

**Aroon (Gidwani) Shivdasani**
Anu | Nilagiri 1961 |1951–1961
Executive and Artistic Director, Indo-American Arts Council, New York, USA

OS Parent – Mother – Dru Gidwani, Teacher | Siwalik House Mistress | 1950–1961
            Professor of English, Head of Drama at Bombay University, India
            English Teacher, High School, Toronto, Canada

OS Siblings – Brother – Harish Gidwani | Nilagiri 1955 | 1950–1955
            Sister – Shirin (Gidwani) Hira | Nilagiri 1960 | 1950–1960
            Sister – Reeta (Gidwani) Karmarkar | Nilagiri 1963 | 1953–1963

# Weekend Excursions

For most of us in the Boys' School, a holiday was best spent lolling around in the dorm or at most, going to Kas for a movie and lunch at Daily Needs or Kailash Hotel, all in the two-rupee pocket money, which later went up to a princely five rupees.

It is to the credit of Sanawar that weekend treks were encouraged. Two popular excursions were Gurkha Fort and Simla, although the prospect of adventure had little to do with it. The driving impulse was a change of scene, a chance to get some 'outside' grub and of course, the opportunity to brag later.

The Gurkha Fort trek was a challenging proposition. It entailed a steep descent and a stiff climb both to and fro, that needed to be completed in a single day. Armed with a meal packet at 'Cocoa' the previous night, we made an early start at 5 a.m. The beaten track took us to the village below Barnes, and along the ridge, to a point directly above Jabli Railway Station. This could well have been a ghost station—not a soul in sight, barring of course, the sleepy railway employee. We walked along the track till the Koti Tunnel, descending to the Koti Rest House below, and further down to 'Meet', the stream flowing in the valley. The clear water was most tempting but a dip was best avoided, given the daunting climb that lay ahead—uncharted territory at that, as none of us actually knew the way. Initially, it wasn't all that bad as the route was populated for a little more than half the way and we easily found someone to provide us with the directions to the next village. Things would have been a lot easier if the fort had been visible as we climbed. Having known this before we started, some juniors had been engaged to stand on the BD pavement and shine small mirrors in our direction, but unfortunately, we were none the wiser. The choice before us was to either abandon the trek and return (unsuccessful) or continue climbing. A council of war on this delicate issue, after considerable debate, chose the latter. It was a steep climb with no footpaths, and so we clambered on. Jagga's PT kept everyone going.

Finally, nearly at the top, the fort was sighted and everyone heaved a sigh of relief. It speaks volumes for our navigation by instinct as we had missed the fort by just about half a kilometre. Having set off from the river below close to three hours ago, we entered through the portals of Gurkha Fort. That the fort was a complete disappointment would be an understatement—a tumbledown structure with a solitary pine tree. Taking turns, we scratched our name on the pine-tree trunk with a pen knife. Nobody told us that our bid for immortality would be shortlived as a new bark would erase all traces of our names in a year or two.

The return was a shade better. The descent was easier than the ascent had been, and added to that was the luxury of a dip in the stream. For all the endeavour, the reward was that we failed to make it for dinner, got yelled at by Mr B. Singh for being late, and went to bed hungry. But that was par for the course at Sanawar!

In contrast, the hike to Simla was fun. The trick was to obtain permission to leave school after Friday lunch so that we got two nights out. Surprisingly, this didn't prove too difficult. However, there was a trust deficit and so it was a conditional approval. A staff member, a young school leaver, was to accompany us.

We collected our all-crucial meal packet and departed. From Long Back, we plunged straight down onto the Garkhal–Subathu road, onward to Broken Bridge, downstream from the Dagroo picnic spot. A brief but steep climb followed but in a little over an hour, we had left Sabathu behind. The good progress made was rewarded with tea and a samosa each at the next dhaba. It was agreed that as the better part of the route up to Simla was at a low altitude, we would walk late into the night to avoid the day's heat. Shortly after sunset, we crossed the Gambhar river at Iron Bridge. It was a moonlit night and the walk along the shimmering river was actually quite romantic, but I doubt any of us thought along those lines then. As it usually happens, the group soon broke up into twos and threes, with each walking at their own pace. An hour and a half later, the ones in the lead wisely decided to take a break and allow everyone to catch up. We discovered that the staff member was nowhere to be seen. To those of us who had read Jim Corbett, the thought of marauding tigers and panthers sent a chill up the spine. Fortunately, Sir finally caught up but didn't look too pleased. He suspected that the conversation in Punjabi and the subsequent guffaws were at his expense. He was absolutely right.

After another hour of walking, night halt was called. We were in the middle of nowhere with no habitation or shelter. A stony ploughed-up field on a terrace just above the road was selected, and the single sheet we carried was spread out. Continuous practice on pine needles-stuffed mattresses had prepared us well for such eventualities. Even the mosquitos weren't a bother. Everyone slept soundly.

We were up at 5.30 a.m. The brightening sky and the flies taking over from the mosquitos had sounded the Rouser bugle. After parantha and tea at a wayside eatery, we soon reached the bottom of the forbidding Jutogh mountain. Ahead lay a 3,000-feet climb on a bare mountain offering no shade from the baking sun. There was dire talk of everybody being on their own and those not being able to make it being left behind. Nobody seemed to notice that the staff member was growing redder and redder in the face. At last, his reserve broke down and in a low voice, cold with rage, he laid down the law. 'Enough is enough', he said, 'from now on, everybody will walk at the pace of the slowest.' He readily admitted that to be him. There was stunned silence but it quickly dawned on most that we had been needlessly inconsiderate towards this gentle person. This broke the spell and apologies were readily offered and graciously accepted. There was much backslapping and for the first time, our newfound English friend actually smiled. Much later, it dawned on me that the niceties of life which are now taken for granted are often imbibed the hard way.

The rest of the trip was a breeze. India Coffee House, the cheapest eatery on the Mall was duly visited and masala dosas partaken of. After an English movie sitting on 8-anna seats, we hunkered down in the YMCA, on beds costing 16 annas a night.

Next morning, things got even better. While looking for an affordable place for lunch, I bumped into a close relative, who quickly figured out our problem, and promptly fished out a ten-rupee note. I had never seen so much money before. The generous addition to our pooled resources meant a lunch at Baljees' became possible. What could be more satisfying for the perpetually hungry?

**Jai Singh Gill**
Himalaya 1961 | 1954–1961
St. Stephens' College, M.A. History | Indian Administrative Service – 1968 Batch – Punjab Cadre | Served in different capacities – State and

Central Govts. | Chief Secretary, Punjab | Chairman, Pay Commission, Punjab

OSS President 1993–1995 | Member, LSS Board of Governors 2004–2007 and 2011–2014 (Second Term)

OS Sibling – Brother – Inderjit Singh Gill | Himalaya 1960 | 1955–1960

OS Children – Daughter – Ismat Gill | Vindhya 1993 | 1986–1993
              Son – Chiranjiv Singh Gill | Himalaya 1996 | 1988–1996

# Speaking to Sir Henry

I joined Sanawar in the middle of 1981 since a vacancy opened up during the summer hols. I was handed over to Ms Kapila and Mrs Ram Singh. Within days of joining, all preppies were lined up outside the Assembly hall. Auditions for the Prep School Founders' play were held. That year, it was going to be *Aladdin and the Magic Lamp*, that too a musical. We trooped in one by one and stood next to the piano. A key was struck and we had to hold the note. I must confess that I had a bit of an unfair advantage here. I had come from Burn Hall, a missionary school in Srinagar, where the Christmas nativity play was a big deal. I had cornered the role of the Angel Gabriel and belted out carols with much gusto, year after year. Following a scale on the piano, therefore, was really no big deal for me. I was immediately cast as the Genie.

That marked the beginning of my love affair with the Barne Hall stage. Over the next seven years, there wasn't a House show or school play that I didn't perform in, playing Tin Woodman in *The Wizard of Oz*, Maitland in *The Chalk Garden* among others. But the one part that sort of found me repeatedly was that of a butler. I really don't know why. I was the butler with such regularity that a parent, watching me perform one Founders', remarked to my mother, tongue firmly in cheek, that she hoped this wasn't indicative of a career choice on my part.

But, coming back to the Genie. I loved everything about my debut performance in Barne Hall. I remember being fascinated by the lights with their dimmer wheels, the screens on the side of the stage, the rickety steps that led to the platform below the stage and the grand piano to the side of the covered orchestra pit. I'd never been to Broadway or the West End but surely this is what it must have been like. One of the first instructions I was given was to deliver all my lines as if I were speaking to Sir Henry Lawrence (immortalized in a white marble bust at the far end of Barne Hall). This was a lesson I remembered and followed through every single of my performances over the years. I remember one year, just about a fortnight before the final show, I had a bit of an accident with a cricket ball, breaking my carpal bone of the right wrist. I wore a bandage that looked like a boxing glove, and could be seen from under the long-flowing sleeves of my robes. Captured for posterity by Sharmaji, the school photographer from Kasauli. Thankfully, however, the performance went off without a hitch and the play was very well-received. This was also the year of the epic *Kim* and I've never said this to anyone, but I'd secretly desired I'd been cast in that. I was one of the few lucky Prep School students, though, who were taken to see it twice. Even after four decades, I still sometimes catch myself humming the lines from those songs. That said, I'm really glad I started with the Genie and though a star wasn't born that day, performing in front of an audience certainly laid the foundation for a choice I would make later in life. But that's a story for another day.

Although most of my time on stage was spent performing in English, it wasn't always so. In a surprising turn of events, Dr D.C. Gupta chose to cast me in a Hindi play, a musical no less, that he was directing for Founders' one year. I can't for the life of me remember the name but I do remember, true to form, I was cast as a singing waiter. I had a very tenuous relationship with Hindi, having barely scraped through in my U-V board exams in spite of Dr Gupta's best efforts. So, the first challenge was to read the script. It took me a while to work my way through the first few readings but after that, things fell in place. Of course, once the rehearsals started in the right earnest, Dr Gupta hit me with his next challenge. It had been a few years since I'd last sung on stage and in the interim, my voice had cracked and I wasn't able to hold notes that had once seemed so easy. I remember Dr Gupta struggling at the harmonium as he worked to change the notes and almost had me rapping some of my musical lines because my singing was so bad. This play was memorable for another reason. It turned out to be the only one which I performed outside school. We took it to Kasauli and performed in the army auditorium. I don't know what they made of our efforts but all of us on stage had a great time.

By far the most memorable stage experiences was to be a part of a production directed by either Mr B. Singh or Mrs Pheroza Das. Regrettably, I never got to be part of a Mr B. Singh production, but I was fortunate to be picked by Mrs Das for a Founders' play. I was cast as Maitland in *The Chalk Garden* and I simply loved the entire experience. It wasn't just that Mrs Das was a fabulous director who got the absolute best out of her actors, but the chance of walking into Heady's House without having to be scared out of my wits was a revelation. The initial script-reading sessions and rehearsals would take place in the glass-panelled veranda facing the garden and on Sundays, it would include lunch. I had my first Khao Suey while rehearsing with Mrs Das and I bragged about it in the dorm for days after that. All I can say is, thank goodness for the opportunity.

**Omar Abdullah**
Vindhya 1989 | 1981–1989
Corporate career – ITC Limited and The Oberoi Group | Youngest Member of Parliament (Twelfth Lok Sabha) | Union Minister of State, Commerce and Industry | Youngest Union Minister (of State for External Affairs) | President – National Conference Party | Eleventh Chief Minister of J&K

OS Sibling – Sister – Safia (Abdullah) Khan | Vindhya 1990 | 1988–1990

# UP SGT. Tilley's Hill

My first day in Sanawar, after having spent three years at the Doon School, was a big culture shock. I did ask my father why before trudging up the hill and he said that Gen. Cariappa and he had decided that both Nanda and I should move to Sanawar, as Doon was getting populated by a lot of 'funny people' not from Services backgrounds, and not likely to have a good influence on us. I was not sure what that meant, but back then, one did not argue with their parents, and so all I said was 'Yes Sir'. However, it wasn't just Nanda and I who moved, but my sister, Indu (President's Medal 1952), cousins Ranjit and Ravi Bhatia, the three Nehru brothers, Ashok, Adit and Anil, Gita Bery (who would later become my wife) and her brother, Arvind.

Despite the influx of the 'clan', the Sixth Form of 1953 had only ten students, and not a single girl. We practically walked into every First XIs, and as a class of Prefects, were up to all sorts of pranks. I was demoted from a House prefect to 'other ranks' because Bhardwaj and I decided to go for a 'short back' in the middle of the night, and came face-to-face with the staff taking Mr B. Singh from the school hospital to Kasauli. He had hurt himself playing football earlier in the evening and Mastu's mixture had not helped his knee.

Sanawar was still growing and Mr Carter, [the] headmaster, was the guiding force to transform it from a military asylum to an Indian public school. Getting ready for Sanawar was very easy. On asking about the school uniform, I was told to bring a dressing gown and a cake of soap (optional, as baths were once in two to three days). The school would provide the rest. On arrival, I was dispatched to the Quarter Masters' store to be 'kitted out' – and horrified to find that my uniform was to be Battle Dress, Ammo Boots, a very funny-looking side cap straight from the First World War, a great coat – all khaki, of course, and a striped pyjama suit, and so on; reminding me of Oliver Twist rather than a public school.

The real shock came when I was sent to the Hospital to be put 'in quarantine' for a week. Fortunately, the Inter-House Swimming

Competition was on and my Housemaster, Mr Vyas, learning that I was a good swimmer, got special dispensation for me to participate. So if you walk away with a couple of medals within a week of arriving at a new school, it makes for a very good first impression.

Having spent the first few days in the Hospital, I was to find myself in the dorm, on beds with strips of metal, mattresses which had pine needles sticking out of them, and 'horse blankets', that had definitely been rejected by the Veterinary Corps. I turned to my neighbour to say goodnight and was at once confronted by, 'Who is talking after lights-out?' asked in this rather booming voice. 'Yes,' I said. 'And who were you talking to'? asked Dileshwar, the House prefect. At this point, I figured this conversation was not going well. So, I pleaded the Fifth and decided not to answer the question. But Dileshwar was not happy and figured that I must have been talking to my neighbour, a small little boy called David Frank, who was pulled out of bed and given a 'knock' on the head, which resounded in the whole dorm. 'You are new, but Frank should know better . . . No talking after lights-out. Understand?' said Dileshwar. *Welcome to Sanawar*, I said to myself.

The food was Spartan, to say the least. I think the Quarter Master counted and issued four beans per student. We had to say grace before attacking our plates and after we had finished our meal . . . which in our

hearts, went, 'We thank you for what we have had, give us more and we'll be glad.' The menu was easy to remember: fish on Friday, followed by fish cakes on Saturday, as not many could eat the fish. Charlie was the source of our food supply and of course, the few tuck parcels sent from home. It was not till my last year in school that an angel called Mrs Nanda came to Sanawar. She took over as matron and started feeding us real food. The change was so dramatic that we actually started putting on weight. Not only did we get grub that was cooked properly, but we could eat as much as we wanted . . . we even started getting chicken curry and dal that could be identified and traced to a suitable origin and not something the cat had just brought in.

Very soon, one fell into the routine and it was then that I started really enjoying Sanawar. It was a tough school, for sure. We were woken up with the bugle and given a dog biscuit and a mug of tea and sent off for PT. Quick change, breakfast and then marching up to Birdwood for classes. Dining was separate for boys and girls, so lunch was back in BD, followed by hobbies, games and prep, before dinner and lights-out. I'm sure the routine has not changed.

What made Sanawar different and memorable was the interest created by the teachers in the subjects that they taught. Mrs Carter made math fascinating by starting a 'Magic Square' competition, in which the numbers down, across and diagonal had to add up to the same total. She showed us how to master geometry and quadratic equations and if you couldn't, she called you a 'Solan Goose' (whatever that was). The result was that we all did very well and got distinctions in math. Mr Vyas introduced us to the works of Premchand, if not for him, I would not have read any Hindi literature. Mr Kemp took us through the difference between $H_2O$ and $H_2SO_4$, which gave rise to the rhyme: 'Ramma was a scientist, Ramma is no more, for what she thought was $H_2O$, was $H_2SO_4$'. Mr Evans chased the magnetic poles forever and used his divider to make his point. In Sanawar of the 50s, whilst Sports was compulsory and given great importance, doing well in studies was equally important. In our Senior Cambridge Examination, failure was out of question, in fact, three out of seven people got First Division.

In all, I was given a classic good education by my father: Doon, Sanawar, St. Stephens' and then a short spell selling jute goods in Calcutta, before chucking it to do chartered accountancy in London. I returned to India and joined ITC Ltd., retiring as the Director, Hotels, Power Generation and

Environment. I owe my achievements to the grounding I got at Sanawar, and gratitude to all those wonderful teachers, who moulded our characters to prepare us for the world outside the sheltered umbrella. Play hard, work hard, be honest . . . perhaps it did 'make a man out of me'.

Our children, Premika and Adil, went to Sanawar, too, and greatly benefitted from the experience.

**Ashok Bhatia MA FCA**
Shoki | Vindhya House 1953 | 1951–1953
Director ITC | Chairman Welcomgroup of Hotels | Author *A Little Bit of Heaven: The Gulmarg Hut* (self-published)

OSS PRESIDENT 1984–1985

OS Spouse – Gita (Bery) Bhatia | Siwalik 1954 | 1951–1954

OS Children – Daughter – Premika Bhatia | Siwalik 1991 | 1987–1991
                            Son – Adil Bhatia | Siwalik 1993 | 1988–1993

# Boys School (1902 – 1927)

On resigning from a mastership in Bishop Cotton School, Simla, I was appointed Headmaster of Sanawar on 1 December 1902, when the Rev. A.H. Hildesley was principal. In my previous school, there was a qualified master for each class. In Sanawar, I found that I had to try to educate 250 boys with the assistance of only three masters-a formidable job! All schools inspected or given grants-in-aid by the government were divided into three departments: High (ex. VII, roughly corresponding to matric); Middle (Stds., VII, VI, V); Primary (Stds. IV, III, II, I). Promotion from the primary to the middle department and from the middle to high depended on passing written examinations conducted by the Education Department. Scholarships were granted on the basis of the results of these examination and the names of successful Sanawar candidates were placed on the Honour Boards.

I found that there was no High Department in Sanawar in 1902, so I was determined to make one, as higher education was necessary for our boys if they were to compete successfully in civil or military life. I staffed Stds. VII, VI, V, IV with masters and Stds. III, II, I, were taught successfully by pupil teachers. I selected six promising boys from Std. VII for this purpose. They received lessons in teaching and tuition for the high school examination from me out of school hours, and some studied and passed the qualifying examination into the Survey of India Department. These pupil teachers, who took their responsibilities very seriously, were rewarded for their extra work by concessions of various kinds. Technical instruction took place during school hours, thus liberating the services of masters for work in the high department after it was formed. Military instructors took band practice, gymnastics and carpentry. A telegraph class was instructed by a post office official and printing and bookbinding by an Indian master of the staff in the old printing shop near the stores. This class was a farce and gave a lot of trouble. I was being continually sent for to read the Riot Act. The instructor did not mind boys going to sleep or getting into a corner to read a novel, but he objected to type being thrown about and other forms of rowdyism. The band, under Mr Ricketts, was excellent, and on several occasions, the Viceroy's bandmaster came down to Sanawar to choose boys for his band. In my early days, our band attracted the most promising boys, and many of these were lusty fellows. I remember one, who played the bombardon, telling me that when the band marched up to Church on Sunday morning, he blew his instrument so forcibly that the weather-cock on the Church tower turned round and round.

Between the years 1903–1906, the high department grew into a fairly large class. In 1906, a radical improvement was made by the Education Department. Pupil teachers and unqualified assistants were no longer to be employed in schools, and all teachers were to be trained. To implement this order, a training college for teachers was opened in Sanawar in the old Boys' School building, on the site of the present Birdwood School. Many of our boys after passing the high school examination, proceeded to the Training College, became qualified teachers and joined the school as masters.

In addition to my school and pupil teacher work, Mr Hildesley asked me to organize games. I asked him to show me the sports gear. He took me to a small room behind the Barracks, where I saw a few broken hockey sticks. When I murmured at the inadequacy of material, I was told that the sum of Rs. 200 a year could be spent on sports gear. This was not liberal for 250 boys, so games were restricted. The first thing necessary was a suitable ground, and coolies were put on duty to enlarge the present parade ground and make it a suitable shape. A corrugated iron pavilion to House the sports gear was provided. I formed sets for the senior boys to play hockey, football and cricket in their seasons. As our ability to play these games improved, we were able to challenge teams from the neighbouring cantonments, and had many enjoyable matches. After the Rev. G.D. Barne became principal, organized games for the whole school became possible.

As organist, it was my duty to select boys for the choir. There were few volunteers, mostly conscripts. Their work in Chapel was not arduous as the principal (Mr Hildesley) and the organ provided the music, with the choir rendering a modern obligato. If singing in the choir was not popular, the annual choir picnic was. The day was usually spent at Barog, travelling there by train in the morning and returning in the evening. A good midday dinner in the Refreshment Room was much appreciated—a change from the usual school diet.

'Home Day' for the Christmas holidays was the most popular day in the school year. Before the opening of the Kalka–Simla Railway, the wards had to make their way to Kalka to entrain, either by pony, tonga, rickshaw, or on foot. In the early mornings, a concourse of horses and rickshaws were packed at the Kasauli entrance and senior boys in funds made for the ponies (tats) and in the morning before dinner, exhibitions in horsemanship, both elegant and otherwise, were given to the not-so-fortunate on the road below my House. After dinner, the exodus to Kalka took place. What a happy crowd! Riders and pedestrians proceeded via Kasauli, and the tongas along the tonga road.

I often enjoyed the walk to Kalka, but always rode back. In those days, the holidays only lasted three weeks.

In 1912, Mr Hildesley resigned from his post as Principal. There were not many amenities in the barracks. Life was hard and discipline strict, but this training made the boys manly, fit to tackle any emergency and as the Americans would put it, 'tough guys'.

The Reverend G.D. Barne was appointed Principal to succeed Mr Hildesley. Improvements were speedily made in every department of the school, a full teaching staff, better qualified and better paid; better conditions in the barracks; improved clothing; properly organized games and money for adequate equipment. As now I had a fully qualified staff, I was able to give more attention to supervision than I had in my early years, but I always reserved to myself the teaching of Scripture in the upper classes.

I have dwelt mainly in these notes on my early days in Sanawar, not on the later, as these will be better known. The greatest educational development before I left Sanawar was the affiliation of the school to London University, up to the Inter BSc Examination. Two graduates in science were brought from England and laboratories were equipped in the old band Room. I only saw the beginning of this experiment, but I am sure wonderful progress will be made in the new school building where I am told all equipment is first class and up to date. I hope all boys at present in the school will take full advantage of these educational opportunities.

I shall never forget my loving and happy service in Sanawar and the hearty cooperation I received from staff and boys alike.

**W. Gaskell**
Staff | Headmaster, Boys' School

**Source and Acknowledgement:** *The Sanawarian* **(December 1960)**

# The Diary of a School Boy

| | |
|---|---|
| 1 May | Tumbled down the 'Khuds'. Had to attend MI. |
| 6 May | Discharged at last! Celebrated the occasion by not doing prep. |
| 7 May | Got the 'sticks' for a bad report from a master. |
| 10 May | Attended a party on the 9th. Got stomach ache from eating too much cake. |
| 16 May | Out of Hospital. Rejoiced by buying two chocolates. |
| 29 May | Mark Reading! Result: a huge 'F' marked in red ink. |
| 7 Jun | Drank a bottle of ink. Not so tasty. Had chalk in it! |
| 18 Jun | Sunday! Given a black eye by a prefect. |
| 20 Jun | Got my own back on the prefect by putting a pin on his chair and had the satisfaction of seeing him jump. |
| 27 Jun | Wrote 'Fool' on a prefect's back. Had a good laugh over it. |
| 2 Jul | Wrote an article on 'How to drink ink'. Rejected by the editor of the newsletter. |
| 11 Jul | Learnt about Akbar, why was he ever born? Making us write notes miles-long. He ought to be put in prison. |
| 21 Jul | Had a fight. Got another black eye! |
| 30 Jul | Had a Maths test. Marks as usual - a big zero on a smaller ten. |
| 12 Aug | Made paper-chains for the 15th. Useless work! A plate of chicken curry looks better than a thousand chains. |
| 15 Aug | Marvellous supper and delightful pudding. Every one enjoyed it (except the prefect who could not get any pudding because we had emptied the bowl.) |
| 16 Aug | Prefect took his revenge by eating three shares of pudding. |
| 21 Aug | My birthday. Received a great many knocks. Head swollen by noon! |

| | |
|---|---|
| 22 Aug | Come to class with a huge bandage as big as the parcel I received on my birthday. |
| 23 Aug | Parcel raided by prefect. Nothing remained in it! |
| 24 Aug | Prefect went to Hospital with a stomach ache. Hurrah! |
| 30 Aug | Prefect came out—misery of miseries. Got a hiding because he said my 'grub' had poison in it. |
| 6 Sep | Tampered with the electric meter, so that the light would fail for prep. But to no avail. One minute before prep, the electrician appeared and ten seconds before prep the lights came on. |
| 23 Sep | Wrote another article for the News-Letter. Heading: How to play Cricket. It was rejected. It seems a busybody called Don Bradman had written a book on this subject before. |
| Note: | Because someone took the unused pages from my diary I have to stop here. |

**Karam Sheel Oberoi, L-IV**
Old Sanawarian (Nilagiri 1960)
**Source and Acknowledgement:** *The Sanawarian* **(December 1956)**

# The Shortcut

The long Hodson run – as the cross-country run was called – was gruelling, and taking the one shortcut available had become such a common practice that, as children, we took it without a qualm of conscience.

As a teacher, it was another matter. I was a Housemaster and when the qualifying took place for that event, while other houses each had only four or five boys qualifying, my House had eighteen beating the qualifying whistle. The truth was there for any fool to see—while the boys from the other three houses had not been able to take the shortcut, perhaps due to the presence of a zealous and vigilant member of staff, my boys had had no such disadvantage.

A protest was lodged, a meeting of Housemasters called and I was forced to agree to a re-run for my boys.

That evening, I had a meeting with the boys and in an emotionally charged speech, brought home to them how the honour of the House was at stake. If eighteen boys failed to qualify, I would have no option but to acknowledge my failure at not being able to inculcate the right values in my boys and with that acknowledgement, I would have no option but to resign from my Housemastership.

The next day, the race was run again. I stood nervously at the finishing line, wanting desperately to bite my fingernails. After what seemed an eternity, the first boy turned the last bend and came into sight. I went wild with excitement.

One, two—fifteen, sixteen, seventeen, eighteen. My heart lifted with relief. But it didn't stop there—twenty-two, twenty-three, twenty-four, and yes, twenty-five came in before the whistle blew.

To this day, I do not know how they did it. To this day, when I meet these boys, they keep poker faces and say: 'The honour of the House was at stake, Sir. This was the least we could do.'

I would like to believe that my emotionally charged speech had endowed the boys with superhuman physical strength and speed—it does happen in myths and legends, and myths and legends are always drawn from real life. But the cynic in me will not believe this and I hope, someday, in an unguarded moment, one of the boys will tell me how exactly they achieved this 'miracle'.

I came back to the school, one last time, as [the] headmaster. On the day of the qualifying for the Hodson run, I found, to my surprise, that no official had been posted at the point where the shortcut rejoined the main course. I took up position there and soon enough, I heard voices and three heads appeared at the top of the shortcut. They were horrified to see me and turned back.

There was only one reaction to this incident, a consensus amongst the senior boys, that no old student should ever be appointed as [the] headmaster!

**Dr Harishpal S. Dhillon**
UD | Nilagiri 1957 | 1949–1957
STAFF 1971–1986 | HOD English | Housemaster | Headmaster 1995–1999 | Headmaster YPS Patiala 1986–1995 | YPS Mohali 1999–2010

OS Sibling – Sister – Yogindra (Dhillon) | Nilagiri 1956 | 1951–1956

OS Children – Daughter – Priya Dhillon | Himalaya 1988 | 1979–1988
Daughter – Naina Dhillon | Himalaya 1988 | 1979–1988
Son – Jai Singh Dhillon | Nilagiri 1991 | 1982–1989

OS Grandchildren – Granddaughter – Mannat Tipnis | Himalaya 2013 | 2006–2013
Grandson – Abhay Tipnis | Himalaya 2017 | 2009–2011
Granddaughter – Inaaya Kumar | Himalaya | 2018–To Date
Grandson – Rehaan Kumar | Himalaya | 2020–To Date

**Source and Acknowledgements:**
Published as a Middle in *The Tribune* on 11 December 2006 and reproduced in *Of Cabbages and Kings – A Book of Middles*, (New Delhi: Picus Books, Hay House Publishers India, 2014).

# Humility by Rotation

Moving to Senior School inspired a combination of hope and fear. Hope that you'd get a nice prefect in your dorms; fear that you might get bullied a lot. Stories of bullying had found their way to us from the boys who had gone to Senior School the previous year.

It was good preparation for the circle of life. Humility by rotation. Humility aside, there are many things that boarding schools teach you. They have their own unwritten laws which you learn very, very quickly. The first and most important law is that you never tattle on a fellow student. It is the easiest way to ensure that you instantly become a social outcast. The second is that you can do anything you want, but if you get caught, you have to face the consequences. So you either tow the line, or learn how to not get caught, or learn how to bear the consequences. And the consequences in those days were far more severe than you can imagine nowadays.

On a Sunday, the last place you wanted to be spotted as a junior was on the quad outside the L-VI and U-VI dorms. A senior would call you to do a 'favour' and once you'd serviced his needs, another would spot you, and your entire Sunday was to go in being 'useful'. They were called 'favours', but in no way did any of those activities ever leave the senior feeling obligated to you. Also, in no way was the favour optional, whether it was polishing shoes, getting water or fetching something from Tuck Shop. If the senior was someone you particularly hated, before you served him the water, you'd carefully stir it with your penis. Some seniors began asking the juniors to sip the water first, like ancient kings who had tasters to ensure that they weren't being poisoned. Eventually we downgraded our invisible protest by spitting in the water instead.

The 'official' punishment was Drill, and took many forms. You ran down and back up to Barnes in five minutes. If not, you would have to do it again. Others were 'murga', 'legs-up-hands-down' or handstand. If you somehow managed a medical certificate saying you were excused physical activity, you would get it far worse. You'd have to write one sentence a thousand times over by the next morning: 'I (name) promise that I will never ever go for Assembly without my Assembly Book'.

These were the official punishments. However, our seniors and prefects did not want to waste time administering such long drawn-out drills, and suffer the grovelling of struggling juniors. So they came up with swifter forms of punishment. The more psychotic ones were innovative with the torture they doled out, that included a specified number of slaps across your face, whacking with a squash racket, or worse, cricket bat or a hockey stick on your arse. Some of us got whacked so hard with hockey sticks, we were left with Nike swoosh marks and could barely sit for an entire week. One senior would pair us up and make us give each other five slaps each. If he thought the slap wasn't hard enough, it wouldn't count, and he would slap you instead. Given that he was a national-level boxer, we whacked the shit out of our partner. Also, choosing your partner could be tricky. The skinny were often the worst because they would give what we called 'skeleton slaps'.

Strangely, though, in those days, we didn't see this as abuse. It was understood that that's how things were. We never felt victimized or singled out because that's how it was for everyone.

Nilagiri House was a different story though. Away from the other three Houses, and often in their own world, they were called 'Commies' due to their over-enthusiastic approach to the mundane (like winning the PT Cup). One day at Assembly, Gulbagh Singh, my House Captain, a national-level boxer and the strongest guy in School, got pissed off with the Nilgarians in my batch and pronounced, 'You Commies, come see me tonight.' When you had to see Gulbagh Singh tonight, you knew you were dead. He was our version of a WWE wrestler. The Nilgarians were shitting themselves. Unable to eat or even entertain any thought besides the fact that they were about to get the thrashings of a lifetime, they came up with a plan. They caught hold of                          a batchmate who'd joined school recently, and scared the living daylights out of him.
bro, Gulbagh has asked us to see him tonight. You know what that means, right? We are going to get a bad hammering. We guys will still be able to take it. But what will happen to you? You will die.' Convinced that his death was imminent,                sought advice on what to do. The batch convinced him that he should run away from school. When Gulbagh would learn of this, he would get scared that the teachers would find out

why, and refrain from beating up anyone.              thought this was a great plan. But where could he go? His grandmother lived in Chandigarh, ninety minutes away by bus from Dharampur. That's where he would go.

The bus ticket cost thirty-two rupees. The batch chipped in with one rupee here, two there, till they got to the magic figure. It then dawned on someone that since              was going to Chandigarh, he might as well get them some Hot Millions burgers and pizzas. Suddenly fifty- and hundred-rupee notes started flying out. Soon,              had enough money to feed a small army. They escorted him to 'Stinkies' and waved him goodbye.

News of              flight was strategically delivered to Gulbagh Singh via the grapevine. Meanwhile,              found his way to Hot Millions, bought all the burgers and pizzas he could, and then arrived at his grandmother's House. She found it unacceptable and promptly sent him back to school. He was back late afternoon, with all that food, which was downed with great gusto.

That night, when the Nilagirians went to see Gulbagh Singh,              was the only guy who got a hammering!

**Papa CJ**
Chirag Jain | Siwalik 1995 | 1986–1995
Stand-up Comedian | Author | Executive Coach

*Excerpt from Papa CJ's autobiography titled* Naked.

# Names, Nicknames and Place Names

A Glossary of Familiar (and Not-So-Familiar) Names for Sanawar's Faces and Places (1900–1947)

**Ajax:** the impressively endowed Ongole bull that lived a 'life of Riley' in the old school Dairy, across the gulley from Small Plain (Lower Barne's). The bull was acquired by the school in the late 1930's and it was rumoured that his prowess and reputation for never 'firing a blank' soon spread far and wide. By all accounts, he was still going strong in 1948 when the school dairy was finally closed down.

**Back Road, the:** the long, twisting bridleway to Taksal and Kalka down the west face of Kasauli hill. Before the days of the train (Kalka–Simla Railway, 1905), it was the main route to and from school for those who lived in the plains and went home for the long winter breaks. Cut into the hillside around about 1843, it soon became the favourite route into the hills for Simla and other hill stations, replacing the old, and much longer route via Nalagarh, Baddi, Haripur and Khadli.

**Bakery, the:** the group of buildings at the west (Kasauli) entrance to the school. Known simply as the Bazaar in the very early days of the Asylum, it became the main service provisioning and business centre for the school, comprising the bakery, 'dharzi' (tailor) shops, 'mochi' (shoemakers, repairers), general stores and visitors' quarters. It was also, (and still remains), the site of the 'Village school', [q.v.].

**Barbary Bull:** no, nothing to do with Ajax and the school dairy but the group of farm buildings just below the Pavilion on the *pagdandi* going down to Sanawar Village. The name goes back a long time, and if anyone knows its origin, please get in touch.

**Barney:** the nickname given to the Reverend George Dunsford Barne when he was Principal from 1912 to 1932. The name continued to be used after he became Bishop but was always spoken sotto voce, never to his face, of course, and never within earshot of the staff.

**Big Plain:** the familiar name for the Boys' playing field, constructed in about 1904 during the reign of Principal Hildesley. It was formally named 'Barne's' in April 1941 by Principal Charles George O'Hagan, who named it after his mentor and exemplar, the Right Reverend George Dunsford Barne, Bishop of Lahore and fourth principal of Sanawar, in order to '. . . perpetuate, in a small way, the name of one who had laid the foundation of Sanawar games and raised them to heights unequalled by any other school in India'.

**Birdwood, or Birdwood school:** the academic centre of learning for girls and boys built on the site of the original 'School Hall' and former Teacher Training College. The foundation stone was laid on 25 August 1927 by the Rt. Rev. Henry Bickersteth Durrant, Bishop of Lahore, and the buildings were formerly opened on 22 September 1929 by the Commander-in-Chief, Field Marshall Sir William Riddell Birdwood (Baron Birdwood of Anzac), after whom the new school was named.

**Bleak House:** the staff quarters built on the northeast side of the east (PD) ridge and said to be the highest point on the school hilltop. It has the best view of the Shivalik ranges to the east and snow clad Himalayas beyond. It was the family residence of the Coombes' family for many years (see 'Bobuck').

**Bobuck:** the nickname for Mr J.R. Coombes BA, BSc, much loved and respected Physics teacher who came to Sanawar from Bishop Cotton School for Boys in Bangalore and the University of Madras in 1933 and left us in 1944 for a teaching post at Armidale Teacher's College, University of New England, NSW Australia.

**Bolthia's or Boota's Plain:** an area of fairly level terrain about the size of a hockey pitch on the 'Chota Dharampur' spur of Eagle's Nest, just below the huts of the old Consumption Sanitorium. At the north end of the plain near to the huts, there was a spring-fed pond that was named 'Doomer's'.

Origin unknown but perhaps a 'spooky' reference to the nearby sanatorium. The name goes back to the early 1900's.

**Boss:** Principal

**Bootroom:** the place where one exchanged worn-out boots, shoes, socks and other bits of 'kit'. Originally in a storeroom off the veranda of what is now the gymnasium (Gaskell Hall), at the top of the broad steps leading down to the lower dormitories (Block 12). It was moved down to the south end of the juniors' dorms, (near the bathhouse and washrooms) around about 1943.

**Bouncer's Rock:** a large rock overlooking 'Hart's Pool' [q.v.] in the stream below Choir Bridge at Dagroo valley. Said to have been named after 'Bouncer' Morton (Nicholson 1913–1920) who, one year during an early Summer Camp, evidently attempted a 'swallow-dive' from the rock, and flopped somewhat inelegantly (not to say painfully) on his belly in the pool below!

**Bounds (Short, Long and Roving):** Self-explanatory. Places where one could or could not go. Bounds were specifically defined for each department and regularly published in school Part I Orders. Short Bounds referred to particular parts of the hilltop where one could safely go, and others that were strictly 'off limits' during 'normal', day-to-day school times. Long Bounds permitted short forays onto the hillsides a little beyond the estate boundary markers, and were applicable to weekend free time, half-holidays, etc. Roving Bounds, applicable only during official school holidays, defined the boundary limits for 'roamers' permitted to ramble even further afield. There were certain conditions, however. One had to be at least fourteen years of age and in a party of three or more. Moreover, you had to say where you were going and roughly what time you expected to get back.

**Broken Bridge:** the bridge across the lower reaches of Dagroo valley on the old bridleway between Subathu and Kasauli. It was said to have been constructed by the Gurkhas in about 1812. The Lawrences would have crossed this bridge on the overland journey from Rupar (Rupnagar) to their summer cottage in Kasauli before the 'new' route from Kalka was developed (See Back Road). The bridge fell into disrepair sometime after 1900.

**Brown Sahib:** origin unknown but it was the name given to one of Mr Ulavi's delivery 'boys' from the Bakery who displayed and sold his wares on Wednesday and Saturday afternoons, on the BD Pavement by the Bath House water tanks. He carried his wares in a large tin trunk, balanced on his head. In one hand, he carried a bell that he would ring to let us know he had set up his 'stall', in the other, a stick to ward off the flies—and thieving hands!

**Butchery, The:** the school abattoir, run by the IASC. The butcher's name was Ishmael so our meat was at all times, strictly 'halal'!

**Butts, the:** the 'target' end of the old 200 yard, full-bore firing range between Garden City and the main road. Following disuse in 1938, the trench and embankment became overgrown with 'Spanish Flag' (Lantana camara) and was latterly a favourite spot for butterfly collectors.

**Camp:** Annual Summer Camp held during the first week after Easter, and usually at Dagroo on a fallow piece of farming land, just a little upstream from the bridge on the road from Dharampur to Subathu. See also Choir Bridge.

**Camp Pie:** a culinary concoction of the camp cooks, consisting of yesterday's leftovers with added chopped vegetables and a few tins of corned beef (if you were lucky)! The ingredients were arranged in large, shallow metal pans or trays, topped with a thin crust of mashed potato, and warmed up in large, cast iron 'Dutch ovens' set over the camp kitchen *chulas*.

**Cannons, the:** aka 'the guns'. The two captured Turkish 13-pounder field guns on Birdwood quadrangle, sited in front of Gaskell (Barne) Hall, on either side of Birdwood staircase, and overlooking the Cenotaph below. They were presented to the school by the Indian Government as trophies in 1928 in recognition of Sanawar's contribution to the Great War, and to commemorate the Sanawarians who fell during the conflict. For some time, they were the favourite meeting places for senior boys and their girlfriends during morning milk breaks.

**Centre Court, The:** following Wimbledon tradition, the Girl's new Tennis Court built in the dip between PD and the main ridge was formally named 'The Centre Court' when it was opened in June 1922 by Principal George Barne, who was himself a keen and accomplished Tennis player in his time. Strictly out of bounds to the boys, of course, except when officially appointed as 'fags' (ball boys). (Order No. 383 dated 27 June 1922 refers.)

**Charlie Bootlace** – Real name Ram Lal, maker and vendor of various sweetmeats (badam barfi, doodh peda, laddoo, mithai etc.) He also sold channa, chevda, poori and roti of various sorts. Charlie Bootlace came to us from Ghora Gali in early 1943 and was formally granted permission to sell sweets on Sundays '. . . to the girls between 11.30 a.m. and 12.30 p.m. on Peacestead, and to the boys in the afternoon on No. 11 Pavement' (School Part I Orders dated 9 March 1943). He later opened his first 'shop' at the top end of the Bakery, a second in the upper level of the rebuilt Tuck Shop on the Chapel slope, and a third in the little hut just below the road leading up to Peacestead from the 'tank'. After independence, he became known simply as Charlie and continued selling his wares to Sanawarians until about 1956.

**Chelmsford Training College:** the name given to the former Government Training Class and Teacher Training College built by the government on the site of what is now Birdwood school. The college moved to Ghora Gali in 1923 and the vacant building was taken over by the asylum as its first 'school Hall' (See also Birdwood school).

**Chikku/Chikki:** origin uncertain but it was the nickname given to Mr M.C. Evans, BA, well-liked and respected science and maths teacher, who came to us from the Chelmsford Teacher Training College, Ghora Gali in 1941, stayed on after independence and finally left in 1954.

**CI:** Chief Instructor. The most senior member of the military staff, and the only one of them who was authorized to award and administer corporal punishment. Appointed by Army GHQ in New Delhi and selected from the ranks of serving staff sergeants and warrant officers, he was seconded to the post of Chief Instructor and granted the local rank of WO I (RSM). The CI would directly report to the Principal for all matters pertaining to good order, conduct and military discipline in BD.

**Choir Bridge:** the bridge on the old cart road between Dharampur and Subathu at the head of the Dagroo valley. Evensong was held here on the final Sunday of most summer camps. The school choir generally assembled on both side of the stream, under this bridge, with the congregation seated in groups on the banks upstream. Hence the name 'Choir Bridge' which goes back to the early 1900's. This old bridge has since been by-passed by a more substantial structure of steel and concrete to cope with today's modern traffic loads. However, when the author last checked in September 2012, the familiar old cart road bridge was still left standing alongside the new edifice. Long may it remain there.

**Church Barrack:** Block 10, the original Girls' Dormitory; the school building next to the Chapel. It was the very first of the three-storey dormitory blocks to be built. The building underwent many changes and modifications and got the name 'Church Barrack' after it was completely rebuilt in the early 1920's.

**Creepie:** the familiar name for the tiny white-eye (Zosterops palpebrosa), a common bird of the gardens on the hilltop and the broad-leaved woodland below Big Plain. Origin uncertain but thought to be nicknamed after its creeping manner when foraging. Its nest is a beautiful little purse-like structure of silken web, suspended in the fork of a slender branch.

**Dagshai Gate or Entrance, the:** the formal name for the entrance to the school on the east side of the hill at Jamuntu Village [q.v.]. The name appears to have been dropped in favour of Moti's Corner [q.v.] since about 1930. Visiting sports teams from BCS Simla and elsewhere were generally welcomed and 'sent off' at this gate. The school band played them in and out.

**Dairy, the:** the school Dairy Farm established in the late 1870's across the gully from 'Small Plain' as a private venture by the asylum, and later taken over and managed by the Indian Army Service Corps. It provided fresh milk and dairy products for the school until about 1948, when it finally closed down.

**Dhobi Ghat:** on the same small ridge as the Dairy but just a little higher up the hill.

**Dhom's Plain:** a small plain or piece of level terrain just above the cart-road at 'Chota Dharampur' (present-day Chhahar). It marked the eastern limits of the Boys' 'normal' bounds.

**Dock:** the Hospital.

**Donkey Slant:** the gentle, sloping path between the Short Back and the Long Back on the north side of the hilltop starting just below the old power House. Origin unknown. The junction of the path with the Long Back also marked the Girls' eastern Short Bounds.

**Doomer's Pond:** a spring-fed pond just below the Consumption Huts on Bolthia's or Boota's Plain [q.v.].

**Drinkies:** a spring conveniently located near boundary stone #38 on the pagdandi between Sanawar Village and Big Plain (Barne's). The water ran sweet and clear for most of the year, and it was a welcome stop off for 'roamers' on the long, uphill trek from Jabli valley and beyond.

**Durrant Society:** the school Debating Society founded in March 1929 and named after Rt. Rev. Henry Bickersteth Durrant, Bishop of Lahore, staunch friend, patron and benefactor of Sanawar throughout his incumbency.

**Eagle's Nest:** the familiar pine-clad peak immediately to the east of the school estate, on the southern lower slopes of which the 'new' school cemetery was built in 1886–7. Eagle's Nest was inside Long Bounds for all departments and a favourite destination for PD nature walks.

**Flat, the:** the first of the playgrounds to be constructed on the hilltop. Said to have been started in Principal Cole's time from a level and even bit of terrain on the east side of the estate, beyond the infants' accommodation. Subsequently levelled and graded even further to form a small playing field. Also known as 'PD Flats'.

**Followers' Lines:** the name given to the four blocks of living quarters provided for the families of Indian employees. Two were on the southeast side of the hill, below Moti's Corner (buildings 58 and 59) and the other two (buildings 33 and 34) were located just below the Long Back (now MDR-10) on the north face of the hill.

**Foxie's Cave:** a small cave in the rocky khud-side of Horseshoe valley, about 60 metres above the old stone quarries.

**Fundoo:** the nickname given to Mr H. Fernandez, BA, first Asst. Master and Art Teacher.

**Garden City:** the name given to the Teacher's accommodation and Mess on the west face of the hill between the Mall and the former 300 yd. full-bore Firing Range.

**Ginger Jacks:** the name given to one of the school chowkidars. He was a Muslim, whose real name was Irfan, who at some time in his life had performed Hajj and dyed his whiskers with henna. He had very obviously spent a lot of time in British Army barracks, because he had a phenomenal vocabulary of good old-fashioned Anglo-Saxon expletives and used them like a trooper.

**Golden Staircase:** aka the 'Birdwood Steps'. The stone stairway leading up to Birdwood from the Chapel road below. It was formally opened on 22 September 1929 at the same time as the unveiling of the War Memorial and opening of Birdwood school.

**Graveyard Corner:** the sharp bend in the Short back at the northwest corner of the former (original) cemetery.

**Gurkha Fort:** a familiar sight on the southwest horizon and a much-prized destination for many a budding 'roamer'. (More to follow.)

**Hart's Pool:** a large and deep pool situated about 400m below Choir Bridge, in a steep section of the valley and course of the stream. Formed naturally from a series of small waterfalls, it was deepened considerably more over the years by many generations of Sanawarians on Summer Camp, using rocks, small boulders, stones etc., to dam the flow. Said to have been started off by a ward of the Asylum named Hart, after whom it was named. See also 'Bouncer's Rock'.

**Herbert-Edwardes Library:** uncertain, but said to have been the original site for the school library which was formerly housed in Block 10/1 (the small building between the Chapel and original Girls' Dormitory). The library was moved up to Birdwood sometime after 1928.

**Hodson Runs:** a series of three long distance runs, instituted by Principal George Dunsford Barne in 1916 and named after Brevet-Major William Stephen R. Hodson who was a well-known runner when he was at Rugby school. Competed for annually, they comprised the Little Hodson for boys below the age of twelve, the Short Hodson for boys under fifteen and the Long Hodson for boys aged fifteen and over. The runs were held during the athletics season, in the latter part of the school year, and prizes were distributed during Founders' Week. The annual Long Hodson, which started from the top of Monkey Point (Tapp's Nose), was open to all and attracted many 'guest' runners from army units stationed in the garrisons nearby. The runs were dropped after independence but were reinstituted by Mr E.G. Carter in 1949.

**Hodson's Slant:** the bridleway slope from Graveyard Corner on the Short Back, down past Step House to the east end of the Bakery or Bazaar, where it joins the Mall. It was renamed 'Secretary's Slope' by Principal Agard Evans in the mid-1930's.

**Holiday House:** origin unknown. The familiar bungalow (Building No. 22) with the makeshift viewing gallery on the northwest corner of Peacestead, built during the late 1870's or early 1880's, it has served as staff quarters, a temporary dining hall and girls' accommodation in its time. Evidently now known as 'Holiday Home'.

**Honoria Court:** the new dormitories for the senior girls. It was built between the years 1943 and 1944 (same time as Wavell in BD), on the site of Jubilee Gardens and the old school cemetery. It too was built of modern concrete blocks and not the quarried and dressed stone of the earlier school buildings.

**Horseshoe:** the sharp bend in the bridle way (now road) between the Boys' Department and the Hospital.

**Iron Bridge:** the old, disused and broken-down iron bridge across the stream in lower Koti valley, said to have been built by the Gurkhas when they ruled in these parts.

**Jamuntu Village:** a small settlement of rural dwellings and one or two local shops on the east side of the hill that had been there since before the days of the asylum. See also Moti's Corner.

**Jubilee Gardens:** the name given to the gardens constructed on the grounds of the old cemetery by Principal A.E. Evans in 1935. The bandstand built there by his predecessor was retained and the gardens remained in use until they were built over to make way for Honoria Court in 1943–44.

**Lady Grace:** the wife of an eminent Administrator on the staff of the Commissioner for the hill states. She lived for part of the year at the family summer residence in Kasauli. She was a highly accomplished horsewoman and was frequently seen riding along the bridle ways of the hilltop. Rumour had it that one evening, having ridden her mount to the top of Monkey Point via the gentle climb from the south, she foolhardily attempted to descend by the precipitous path of the north face. Tragically, both she and her mount plunged to their deaths, 150 feet below. A small pavillion with a spring-fed fountain was erected in her memory among fruit and ornamental trees at the foot of the peak. The grove became known as 'The Lady Grace', and for many years was a popular spot for picknickers. (Addendum: There were a few who uncharitably remarked that Lady Grace was also partial to a 'chota peg' or two in the club before setting out for her evening rides!).

**Lawrence Arch House:** No. 30. The small bungalow on the Mall, immediately to the west side of the Arch, generally assigned to one of the married sergeant instructors of the Boys' Department.

**Little Building or Barrack:** the smaller dormitory block for girls just behind and up the khud from the girls' main building (Block 10).

**Monkey's Playground:** the name given to the piece of level and open terrain just below Stone View Staff Quarters. Very few trees but lots of Berberis, Medlar and other fruits of the forest in their seasons. Large troops of macaques often seen foraging here. Presumably, hence the name which goes back a long time. The area has since been cleared, graded and extended and has served, among other uses, as a helipad.

**Moti's Corner:** the junction of the 'Long Back' and the Kasauli-Dagshai bridle way, (now part of MDR10) on the east side of the hill at a small village previously known as Jamuntu. It was also the east gate or entrance to the school estate. It got the name 'Moti's Corner' sometime in the early 1920's. Origin unknown but theories abound! Some said that it was named after Moti, the long-serving and popular jemadar chaprasi who worked in the principal's office and lived in quarters near the village. Others said Moti was the cemetery chowkidar who lived in a hut on the same corner. After many years of loyal service, he was found dead at the cemetery gates early one morning. His ghost now reportedly haunts the corner, which was named after him. Yet others say it was not Moti's Corner at all but Mochi's Corner, after the contracted shoemaker and boot repairer, who also lived and worked in the village on the corner. There were other theories swapped by the winter evening fires, some more fanciful but all just as implausible!

**Muddlers, the:** the name given to the annual school concert. It was customarily performed during Founders' Week and all three departments took part. The Muddlers Concert of 1947 was attended by Lord and Lady Mountbatten and their daughter Pamela.

**Musthoo:** one of two Dispensers who ruled the roost in the MI Room and always took morning Sick Parades.

**Nazareth:** origin unknown but it was the familiar name for the village of mostly white-washed dwellings that appear to tumble down the Kasauli hillside, just below, and to the south of 'Palpitation Hill' (present-day Kimughat). In the summer of 1944, a huge landslide took away part of the village. The scar remained visible for many years after.

**Nicholson's Corner:** the sharp hairpin bend in the Chapel road, just beyond the War Memorials. It led up to Birdwood Steps and beyond to the school Admin Office and Headmaster's House. It also marked the southern limit of the Girl's Short Bounds [q.v.].

**Nurse Softly:** Mrs Elizabeth Softly, Hospital Nurse, Sister and Matron, whose eleven years' untiring and selfless work endeared her to all. Her understanding and kindliness made her a true mother for all sick people. She died of pneumonia on 24 June 1929 at the age of fifty and lies buried in the school cemetery. There is a plaque to her memory in the North Aisle of the school Chapel.

**Office Quarters:** until 1926, one half of the school Office building was originally staff quarters. It became the principal's (personal) office in 1926 and latterly served as the Teacher's Common Room and school Admin Office.

**Palpitation (Hill):** the steep climb from the main cart road at present-day Kimughat up the east face of Kasauli hill to the junction with the Lower Mall.

**Parker Memorial Arch, the:** aka The Lawrence Arch, or simply and more familiarly, 'The Arch'. This is the stone archway erected to the memory of the Reverend William J. Parker, first principal and superintendent of Sanawar in about 1864. The arch is located on the 'Mall' [q.v.] below the Girls' Building and the Chapel, and for many years, served as the official entrance to the Boys' Department. It has also been the finishing post for all three Hodson Runs [q.v.] since they were instituted in 1916. The original arch had a false tiled roof (see pictures), thought to have been removed in the late 1920's. Some said that the present-day Birdwood Bell originally hung in the aperture above the arch but there is no evidence to support this. The adjoining building, known as the Lawrence Arch House (No. 30), continues to serve as staff quarters to this day.

**Parker Hall:** the Girl's main school building or Hall, it was built on the site of the original infant girl's dormitory (Block 4) circa 1923 and named in honour of Miss Ada Parker, long-serving and much loved headmistress from 1890 to 1923. Her farewell telegram to Sanawar reads as follows: 'Goodbye Sanawar, many thanks, much love and every good wish'. Her last few words have since become a favourite closing salutation for many a Sanawar Girl and Boy.

**Peacestead:** Originally, the small area of even terrain, or 'maidan' just below the main ridge, where the very first tents and temporary buildings of the asylum were said to have been erected in 1847. In much later years, it was extended, levelled and graded to make the Girl's playing field, and eventually, the principal venue for all ceremonial parades and displays. It was given the name 'Peacestead' in about 1928, and was named after the sacred field and playground of the Norse Gods of Aesir, from the book *Heroes of Asgard*, (*Tales of Scandinavian Mythology*) by A. and E. Jeary, 1857.

**Peter Buck's:** a spring-fed pond on the Sonwara spur, just above the old cart road, and directly opposite the quarries. Origin uncertain but once again, theories abound! A favourite yarn claims it was named after Peter H. Buck (Nicholson), a former ward of the asylum who was found drowned there after the long winter break of 1903. (Records show that there was indeed a P.H. Buck who was admitted in 1938. However, he was apparently hale and hearty when his parents withdrew him from school two years later. Ed.)

**Pooh Corner:** Origin unknown. The name given to the staff quarters at the junction of the Mall and the Chapel slope. It was usually assigned to one or other of the military instructors.

**Power House:** the building constructed at the top of the main ridge in March 1923, which housed the two Crossley 96 bhp diesel engines and belt-driven generators that provided electricity for the hilltop.

**Quarries, the:** the original granite and sandstone quarries that provided the stone paving and masonry for the early school buildings, pavements, quadrangles and retaining walls.

**Ridge, the:** the familiar name for the Preparatory Department (PD).

**RMO:** the Resident Medical Officer or school doctor.

**Rose Cottage:** the delicate and refined sobriquet for the girls' outside lavatories, in particular those built in 1926, next to Block 10, the original Girls' Building or 'Church Barrack', and latterly the junior girls' dorm.

**Sammy:** Mr Samuel Charles Cowell, BA, BSC, former pupil and Bandsman, (Lawrence House, 1920–1925), graduate of the Teacher Training College, Ghora Gali and Sanawar teacher (1928–1956).

**Small or Little Plain:** the smaller, levelled playing field located on the north side of, and a little below Big Plain (Barne's). Unsurprisingly, also known by some as 'Lower Barne's', it was not quite large enough for any of the major field sports but was widely used for non-track athletic events. In the season, it was also a favourite venue for 'goolie dunda'.

**Spadge, Spadgy:** the 'Sanawarese' for Sparrow. Yes, the common House Sparrow (Passer domesticus), that ubiquitous, chirpy commensal of man, and its slightly wilder relative the Tree Sparrow (P. montanus) were popular pets for many chaps. Stolen from their nests as fledglings, they were nurtured and mollycoddled into maturity by the most unlikely of foster parents. Who knows how long they lasted after being released back into the wild? It is not surprising that the term was also used as a sort of familiar diminutive for anybody with the surname Sparrow.

**Spartan Club:** instituted by Major the Rev. Canon G.D. Barne, fourth Principal of Sanawar on 13 October 1922 to encourage, preserve and promote the best traditions of martial and sporting excellence. Membership of the club was ordinarily to be confined to Sanawarians past and present, but also extended to others who, themselves distinguished in any of these fields, have rendered service to Sanawar.

**Square, the:** aka 'BD Pavement', 'Quad 11'. The granite, paved quadrangle in front of Barrack Block 11. The square is where one 'fell-in', or assembled for parades, PT, meals, musters, roll-calls, fire practices: in fact, any and everything! Whenever 'Assembly' was sounded by the duty bugler, the square is where one would immediately head for: always at the double.

**Squire's Hall:** the male equivalent of Trafferd House (see below).

**Step House:** the bungalow at the lower end of Hodson's Slant. It was built in the 1920's and became the permanent staff quarters for the school Secretary.

**Stonehenge:** (No. 20)

**Stone View:** The staff quarters just above Monkey's Playground with the grand view of the old quarries, Foxie's, Peter Buck's, Clay Valley [q.v.] and beyond.

**Tin Huts, the:** the Hospital's 'isolation wards' and/or quarantine quarters. A line of tin-roofed huts down a bit from 'dock', where anyone with anything remotely contagious was confined. Visitors were not allowed, and meals were brought in by the Hospital kitchen staff.

**Trafferd House:** aka 'Virgin Villas'. The block of Staff Quarters especially built for unmarried female teachers. (See also Squire's Hall for the male equivalent)

**Warrior's Grove:** a small copse of broad-leaved hardwoods and ornamental shrubs planted in the the early 1930's. Location uncertain.

**Wavell Court:** the Boys' new Dormitory building built on the site of the old Gymnasium (Block 13) during the long winter break of 1943–44. Somewhat disappointingly (for some), it was built of modern, pre-fabricated concrete blocks and not the quarried, dressed stone of its neighbours. That said, the new dorms provided all the modern amenities that the older buildings lacked. The rubble from the demolished gymnasium was tipped into the old, disused swimming pool, where it remained, home to snakes, lizards, bandicoots and other denizens of the jungle, until some time after Independence. See also Honoria Court.

**Wickie:** one of the two school barbers. Specifically, the one with the very sharp tongue, blunt clippers and impossibly tight-fitting *patlun* (However did he get them on?). Any *'gup'* from you resulted in a violent and painful yank of the clippers which left you half-scalped, or at best, with a 'gunja' you hadn't bargained for!

**D.V. Boddington**
LRMS Sanawar 1942–1947
3 March 2005

# School Girlfriends

Going back five decades, I remember being terrified of the Sanawar girls. It needed all our courage to speak to them. Socials would largely be embarrassing memories of squarely stepping on the girls' toes in a mechanical square dance. I am reminded of a short story I once wrote, called 'A Matter of Prestige!' about my last year in school. 1963, Vindhya House.

It so happened that I was promoted to School Prefect in my final year and got the private cabin in the senior dorm of Vindhya House, which I had coveted for years.

The problem, though, was that I did not have a girlfriend. The problem was of my own making because it was not necessary to have a girlfriend. But in the cockeyed traditions of school hierarchy, fifty years ago, of which I was a part, a true Sanawar hero needed a girlfriend.

Mind you, girlfriends in that distant past, subject to the strict watchful discipline of school, did not resemble the girlfriends of today. Far from dating or kissing (for which a daring junior was expelled from school! He did extremely well for himself later, perhaps because of that), the girlfriends and boyfriends of that distant era did not touch or even speak to each other.

So how did the connection even take place? Quite simple. The boy, most of the time, confided the fact of his infatuation in his friends, who in turn would take it upon themselves to tease the object of his attention during class hours. Normally, they would be swiftly and sharply rebuffed, but if the girl had even a passing interest in the lad, she might blush or simper shyly, which would confirm her reciprocation. *Bas!* The deed was done. Boyfriend and girlfriend were confirmed and the teasing would continue for the rest of the term, to be taken up even by the girls, if the young lady in question took notice and became seriously interested.

There was one major pitfall for a skinny bespectacled school prefect like myself, aspiring for hero worship, which was that I aimed too high. There existed an informal rating system for the girls in school, known to a privileged few, and two of the girls I knew from my class, both friends, both beautiful and talented, one an accomplished dancer, scored well over 8/10. To aim for them was to commit harakiri, as they were already courted by handsome college studs in comparison with whom, a gawky fifteen-year-old schoolboy was a snivelling joker not to be taken seriously.

No, a girlfriend selection had to be perfect for it to hit the target, neither too high to be unattainable, nor too low, as to invite ridicule. And in the private rating system, in my head, I chose a smart young lady whom I figured was rated 7/10, and threw out the first tentative suggestion into the melting pot by trying to borrow her school notebook to complete my homework. My friends enthusiastically took the hint and began teasing her. Apparently, she was not entirely averse to the idea, because she lent me the notebook. And thus the deal was clinched. Our boyfriend–girlfriend status was confirmed without us ever exchanging a glance and in my private universe, I believed I had achieved my imaginary hero status before graduating from school.

But there is an interesting footnote to this story. At best, I may have pulled her pigtails or caught her arm, chasing her around Kalka Station on Home Day and chattering with her in the compartment. She may have smiled sweetly at my non-jokes. Perhaps, we may have exchanged a few

letters in the year or two after we graduated from school. We never met. This was the extent of our relationship, yet its penumbra lingers about us even today.

We got busy with our own lives, our careers and our relationships. She became a successful food author and I found my niche in television.

Many years later, travelling around the world, we had an opportunity to meet again. We were both happily married and yet more than forty years later, why was there an awkwardness between us?

I attribute it to a certain fundamental innocence of the age we lived in. Perhaps I should have labelled my short story 'A Matter of Innocence' and not of prestige. How could a boy or a girl take the lending of a notebook so seriously that its repercussions should echo for more than half a century! I believe our lives and upbringing in Sanawar, in a remote time hundreds of years ago, kept us naïve and allowed for the tenderness of innocence to flourish.

I remember that even after I left school, it took me many years to engage unselfconsciously with the opposite sex. I can now understand the inexperienced nervousness of a young boy when confronted with a confident woman. I recall walking around the House of a female Sanawarian colleague in Delhi, trying to pluck up courage to meet her. I was able to even consider the audaciousness of the attempt simply because she was a tomboy! Still, I needed to walk three times around her House before I could gather up the nerve to enter her garden and ring the bell. She will never know this because tragically, she is no more, but I am grateful that she accepted me as a friend and helped me understand friendship in a big city.

Except her, of course, I believe that the ladies in question may perhaps recognize themselves if they read this story. To them, I would like to say: thank you for having indulged me, six decades ago. You gave me something to live for. Each one of you lives on in my memories and affections today.

**Siddharth Kak**
Sid/Jimmy | Vindhya 1963 | 1957–63

Delhi State Athletic Team 1964–69 | National Award, Best Exploration Film, 1984 | National Award, Raj Kapoor Biography, 1987 | Award-Winning Series, *Surabhi*, 1990–2001 | Author, *Surabhi ke Sau Sawaal* (Rupa Publications, 2005) | Award-winning thriller series 'Mano ya na Mano', Star TV, 2005–2007 | Author, *Looking in Looking Out*, collected poems, 2014 | Chairman, National Documentary Awards

# Will You Square Me?

In 1937, the impossible happened. The most unthinkable change took place in the school's history. I returned from the winter holidays, which I had spent in Lahore with my mother and stepfather, to find coeducation had impacted the school with the force of a Category 4 hurricane. Girls and boys were to be taught in the same classroom by the same teacher! A concept that sent me screaming into Foxy's cave, if you know where that is.

Then a truth hit me, that has remained indelible for the rest of my life: girls were cleverer than I was. My masculine pride has never recovered from that shock, however much I recognize the fact as being indisputable, like discovering that the earth is not flat. When I later went to London University, I conceded: Girls are cleverer and the earth is round.

1937 was also a time when something else happened to me. I noticed that girls had chests that stuck out and they walked in a funny way, especially if you saw them from the back. I was a senior. They called us 'big chaps' in our day. Most big chaps belonged to an elite club from which I appeared to be excluded. I eventually discovered why.

On Sundays, boys were allowed to meet their sisters on Peacestead (did you know this name was given after World War I?). Certain boys were given permission to meet their girl friends – who were not their sisters – provided they did so in the open and with proper decorum. This relationship in our day was called 'squaring'. Boys often asked a girl to square them and sent their letters of request via a boy who had a sister. Chaps who were squaring belonged to the elite club. They spoke a silent language that only they understood. I was envious. I resolved to belong to the club.

But gaining membership proved monumental. I had to find a girl to square me. My brother had squared a girl. He was four years older than I and had left school. I could not draw upon his experience, but he had told me that he had once actually kissed a girl. I remembered her name. She had a sister called Joan, who was still at school. Joan was in a form below me. She had the chest and walking attributes I had noticed and also a pretty face.

That was enough. I decide to write her a letter. I was reading a spy novel at the time. I wrote her a long letter of adoration, asking her to square me. When prep was over that evening, I intended to find her and slip the letter into her hand. My plans suffered the blow that fate often delivers to mice and men. I could not get close to her before she left. Clutching the incriminating letter, I was afraid it may fall into the wrong hands. Like the spy in the novel, I ate it.

'Never Give In' is a great motto. I wrote Joan another letter. This time, I kept it short. The last one had given me indigestion. After hours of chewing the top off my pencil, I wrote four words, 'Will you square me?' Remembering the spy, I left it unsigned. This time, I was successful and slipped the letter into her hand. The contact was sufficient. I did not wash my hand that night. The next evening, after prep, she slipped a note about 4 centimeters square into my hand. On it was a single word, 'Yes'. I could not sleep that night.

Romeo was a nutcase and so was I. 'Will you meet me on Lovers' Hill?' I stated the date and time. The answer on the usual stationery came back 'YES!'. After lights-out, the capital letters and exclamation mark created fantasies better left undescribed.

I ran around the Long Back to Lovers' Hill. Joan was standing on the path. Suddenly, my knees went weak. Her cool, clean beauty made me realize what I looked like. The sides of my eyes were blue and bruised, my lip was swollen and cut from boxing training. I was sweating and probably didn't smell too good. We walked up the khud side and sat cocooned in long grass. I did not know what to talk about or what to do. Nor did she. We sat there in strained, fidgety, uncomfortable silence, looking across the valley below. Then I remembered my brother. He had kissed her sister. I grabbed Joan and kissed her. I thought she would push me away. She didn't. She kissed hard against my lips. The cut opened up and I could taste the blood in my mouth. My lip was hurting. The more she pressed, the worse it got. 'How long do we keep this up?' I asked, out of the corner of my mouth.

She shoved me away and stood up. 'Not a moment longer,' She brushed the grass from her skirt, my blood from her lips and left. That was the worst memory I have of school. I never tried to square anyone again. Hockey, football, cricket and even boxing were better than girls, even though their chests stuck out and they walked in a funny way.

Also, think about it, if I had been caught, I would have been flogged and expelled. I would have been a disgraced cad and bounder, and obliged to kill myself and I would never have written this. Did I hear you say, 'Pity you didn't get caught'?

Someone speculated that Joan of Lovers' Hill may have been the Joan Collins of Dynasty. I stood next to Joan Collins in a lift at Heathrow Airport. Time distorts memories, but the Dynasty chest appeared more substantial and obtrusive and her funny walk as she exited from the lift (as a gentleman, I let her out first) also appeared more oscillating. But comparisons are odious and often unfair.

About twenty years ago, I once again met Joan of Lovers Hill. I didn't recognize her. I understand our bodies change completely every seven years. She did not have grey hair in school. It was a really sad meeting. She was dying of cancer. But she told a friend of mine from school that she wished she had married me. Now, isn't that more romantic and sweeter than Noel Coward's *Brief Encounter*?

**George Browne**
Havelock 1937 | 1930–1937

# Ten Chocolates

No matter in which direction you looked, Moti's Corner or Garkhal, for the 'outside' biosphere, the 'Sanawar School boys' were the world's most fortunate teenagers . . . residing in the oldest, the most well-recognized, co-educational 'paradise' on this planet.

The moment we stepped out of the campus, we would notice that begrudging smile—be it the firecrackers shopkeeper in Garkhal; Kallu, the paanwallah at his kiosk adjacent to the black dog sitting outside Kalyan Café; the 'authentic' Bun-Sum guy (sixth shop down the cobblestoned-pathway); the Military cinema ticket-window clerk; the timeworn, billiards room manager at the Grand Maurice Hotel; or the penny-pinching Daily Needs bespectacled, *mooch-wallah*, notorious for declining even one extra gram of salami or smoked ham. And it was the same look we got when 'outsiders' visited our school: teams from Bishop Cotton School, Simla; Yadavindra Public School, Patiala; Punjab Public School, Nabha; and Doon School, Dehradun found it exceedingly challenging to keep their eyes on the ball. With our lips sealed, faces smug, noses in the air, and swaggers a little more pronounced, we all chose to play along—silently regaling in the make-believe perception.

Contrary to what others believed, in reality, the boys on this side of Sgt. Tilley's hill were a different kettle of fish. Barring a trifling minority, referred to as the 'Pump-pies' (by the rest), BD, by and large, was mortally scared of the presence of 'Dames'. We had our self-determined *Lakshman Rekha(s)* – not a stride beyond the swimming pool, Parent's room, printing press, QM stores, or the Cannons (during evening prep). Self-imposed 'out-of-bounds' restraints for stipulated time intervals were strictly observed, which affected our behaviour even within our own 'territory' – for instance, all paths leading to Tuck Shop were to be avoided between Mondays to Saturdays, between 1400 to 1530 hours. At the morning Assembly, during classes, or Sunday movie in Barne Hall – essentially, all formal congregations – if they sat in the northern hemisphere, we occupied the southern.

There was nothing innocuous about the girls. Two or more of them breaking into a giggle (never when alone), while passing somebody by felt far crueller than being subject to the death chair. God forbid if one ever got 'caught' talking to a girl, they would face harsh sanctions, at times, leading to social ostracization. Your closest pal would interrogate you, 'Oye, why were you talking to that chick?', to which you would unvaryingly answer, 'She was asking for my Maths prep work' or some such thing.

'Forget her, what did you say?'

'I said . . . (thinking hard) Go to hell!'

No matter what the answer, dark clouds of suspicion would engulf you. The trust, earned over years of abstinence (read self-denial) vapourized in that one moment of failing to do so. For boys with sisters in GD, life was far easier, and thus, the concept of 'rakhi' sisters emerged.

The opening of CDH was catastrophic. It plainly moved the goalpost, forever redefining the boy–girl terms of engagement. And if that wasn't enough, someone decided to seat one girl for every three boys – the most insensitive, gruesome idea. Many of us lost between five to eight kilograms in the first month. It was an insufferable paradox—hungry as a wolf but shy as a fawn. As the self-consciousness quotient rose exponentially with every served meal, the giggles got louder, reaching ear-splitting decibels. Caution was thrown to the wind; chapati-trafficking reaching unparalleled magnitudes. Charlie found himself toiling twice the manhours, but he wasn't complaining, registering unprecedented windfall gains. Mr Behl and Billu, manning the Tuck Shop counter, felt the heat too.

Despite all the fuss and the feigned melancholy and trauma, practically everyone fell in love. Covertly but unabashedly! And, as luck would have it, Cupid came knocking on my door, too.

Now, school Socials or the House party (in case the 'infatuated' and his love interest were 'colour-coordinated') were the safe havens—the best arena for testing waters. There was, however, one other impediment – the weighty prospect of being blackballed by diffident, never-talk-to-a-chick batchmates; one's best buddies. So to wade past the blockade unnoticed, a plan had to be devised. Once the dance floor was 'warmed up', Chaudhari (my co-conspirator) would throw open a challenge. And that would be my passage to the dreamland . . .

The Himalaya House party was soon jiving. We, Lower Fivers, sat huddled in a dark, sheltered corner under the Barne Hall balcony, away from the prefects' peering eyes.

'Oye, go and dance.' It was time! Chaudhari excused himself from the dance floor, walked over to us, and announced, 'I challenge anyone to ask Noor Jehan (name changed to protect identity) for a dance'.

Sangha laughed out loud. Pandey said that Chaudhari was in the wrong place, and should get back to his business (waiting on the dance floor). I (unexcitedly) probed, 'What's the bet?'

'Ten chocolates!', came the rehearsed response.

'Big ones?', I clarified.

'YES.'

Sangha was scandalized, 'Bastard, for ten chocolates, you will sell your . . .? You, PHUK-KHE. I'll give you twenty if you don't go.'

I had to think quickly. 'Sanghey, listen. Chocolates from Chaudhari's money! Think, man!' Surdie nodded hesitantly, with the anticipation for the Fruit and Nut chocolate shining in his greedy eyes. I had my gate pass. Before Sangha could dissuade me any further, with his virtues of rising above pettiness and greed, I stood up and strode towards the smiling Mahatma (Noor Jehan was sitting below his portrait).

'Could I have a dance?'

'What?'

I yelled back, certain that the whole of Barne Hall had heard me. A few giggles (for others) later, the sweetest smile appeared and she said, 'Sure!'

I had barely begun my *kadam-taal* (1,2, slight left. 1,2, back home. 1,2), when the music suddenly stopped. Strategic timeout? A dreadful 'slow' number came on.

She asked, 'Do you know Ballroom?'

'Noooooo,' I told her.

She wasn't surprised.

'I can teach you.'

'OK.'

'Here, give me your left hand.' She gently placed her left hand on my shoulder. 'Now put your right hand around my waist.'

'Right!'

She tried her best to explain the four steps, but I was soon back to my *kadam-taal*. But I was in seven (hundredth) heaven.

Back under the balcony, Sangha was overcome by self-reproach. His most trusted comrade had sacrificed personal well-being for the larger interest of the 'gang'. He should have protected Sapru. 'How do we save him, guys?'

'I can go and tap him', Bhaiyu offered.

'What's that?'

'OK, go man. Save the poor guy.'

By now, I was on cloud nine. All of a sudden, I felt (another) hand on my shoulder. I turned around and saw Bhaiyu. 'What?'

'I'm tapping you.'

'Meaning?'

'You have to go.'

'Why?'

'Arre, tapping means . . .'

'Funny rule. not fair, Bhaiyu!'

I certainly believe that Noor Jehan was sad too. Sangha was relieved when he saw me and gave me a tight hug. Paying for the ten Fruit and Nuts the next day hurt, but not as much as . . .

**Pankaj Sapru**
Himalaya 1983 | 1976–1983
Senior Management – Petroleum Downstream sector | Travel & Street Photographer | Member – OSS Executive Committee 2019–21 | Vice President – OSS 2021–23

OS Sibling – Brother – Dhiraj Sapru | Himalaya 1985 | 1977–1985

# The First Indian Head Boy

Gurbans Jasinder Singh Pahuwindia (GJS) was the first Indian Head Boy (1949) of The Lawrence Royal Military School, Sanawar.

For GJS, it all began with his ancestor Baba Deep Singh, whose valiant sacrifices are well-documented. His great-great-grandfather, Sardar Karam Singh, along with his three brothers, took possession of the country between the rivers Satluj and Beas in the latter half of the eighteenth century. His great-grandfather, Sardar Gulab Singh Pahuwindia, joined Maharaja Ranjit Singh's Sikh army in 1806 as an adjutant, to soon become a commandant. After the capture of Multan in 1818, he was promoted to the rank of Colonel and took part in various actions against the Afghans in the Peshawar Valley. In 1826, he was given command of three infantry and two cavalry regiments with a troop of artillery. In 1839, he was promoted to the rank of General and in 1847, appointed Governor of Peshawar.

With the passage of time and following the India–Pakistan partition, a number of families in and around Punjab found themselves uprooted. GJS and his younger siblings had to abandon their education at Aitchison College, Lahore (Chief's College). His maternal uncle, Sardar Harbans Singh Guron of Ladhran, ADC Simla, took it upon himself to gather all the displaced relatives at Subathu. He was instrumental in enrolling the young boys at The Lawrence Royal Military School, Sanawar. Unbeknownst to Gurbans then, he and his extended family were placed in the care of the institution founded by the same General who once was diplomatically engaged with his great-grandfather. Years later, finding a photograph taken in the early 1850's, of his great-grandfather, General Gulab Singh, with General Henry Lawrence at Jamrood Fort in the North West Frontier Province (now Pakistan), he would remark, 'This was way before my tryst with Lawrence School began . . . my connection with the name Lawrence seems to have percolated through my genes'. He would chuckle to add, 'The Lawrence relation didn't stop here . . . the granddaughter of Henry

Lawrence was also studying with me and was one of my best friends. I remained in touch with her even after she migrated back to England.'

However, the newfound life at Sanawar was a rude awakening for the lads of Chief's College as they had left their personal assistants behind and were introduced to the phrase coined by Rudyard Kipling, 'Send him to Sanawar and make a man out of him'. The young lads found themselves doing their own chores and being toughened into manhood. Gurbans did not skip a beat while effortlessly mingling with the British and Indian boys. He was a hard-to-ignore boy, as he would strut around the campus the whole day, jumping, playing games and winning matches for the school. It appeared his bloodline was serving him well as he was appointed captain of the hockey and football teams, vice captain of the cricket team, excelled in Athletics and Hodsons, breaking the half-mile and mile records that had stood for several years. The school newsletter mentioned, 'In the One Mile Race, Gurbans lowered the school record by no less than 11 seconds. It was an amazing feat. Gurbans deserves our very hearty congratulations. He is an athlete of considerable promise and we hope very much that he will persevere with athletics on leaving school. If he does, he should have no difficulty in representing India in international fixtures. In case Old Sanawarians are tempted to think that he was timed with the help of the old clock that used to hang in Parker Hall, perhaps we ought to mention that we had, as usual, three timekeepers whose stopwatches were carefully tested for a fortnight and synchronized. Gurbans is built on the right lines

for a runner. He has speed and staying power and was the outstanding athlete at the Sports.'

During the summer vacation in 1949, the Head Prefect T. Chillmaid, left to join his father in Australia. In a frantic search for a replacement, Headmaster E.G. Carter wrote to Gurbans' father, Sardar Gurvaryam Singh, asking for Gurbans' early return to take charge as the Boys' Head Prefect. It appears his leadership qualities hadn't gone unnoticed as Mr Carter wrote of the time he had witnessed him successfully mediate and end a 'violent' pillow fight in the dorm. Carter mentioned how he had been impressed with his 'moderating' skills, and that he thought he could do well as a manager of the schoolboys. The school newsletter (June 1949) records, 'Trevor Chillmaid left on Sunday, the 26th. A farewell lunch was given in his honour by a number of the boys; a gesture which was like a tribute to "Chilly", a deservedly popular Head of the school, and to the fine feelings which actuated the hosts. We all went out as far as Moti's Corner to give him three cheers and say goodbye, after which a few of the bigger boys walked down with him to Dharampore to see him safely on the train. Gurbans Jasinder Singh is now Head of the school, and we are certain that he enters upon the duties of his new office fully assured of the loyalty and support of all in the Boys' School.'

James L.C. Coombes, Himalaya 1954 recalls, 'I remember him, but as he was very senior to me, there was no common ground for us being pals. His surname in school was Sandhu, which he later changed. His nickname was Jassy Jee, I guess derived from Jasinder, his mid-name. I have a photo of him in a combined Sanawar/BCS football clash of 1949. The photo includes Ruskin Bond of BCS, now a well known author in India. He was sound as a Head Boy, but there were ways of getting 'round him. His chief brilliance was as a hockey forward, and he had the potential to play professionally, if hockey had been as well organized as cricket in India.'

Upon graduating from Sanawar, Gurbans joined his family in their effort to tame their newly allotted fallow land for agriculture. The tenacity and leadership skills inherited from his valiant forefathers and further honed by the strict discipline at Sanawar, successfully guided him. It certainly was no easy task with little to no mechanization at the time. 'I always knew I wanted to do this . . . I am originally from Pahuwind, a village now on the Pakistan border . . . I came from a family where land was worshipped. It was my duty to enrich it with my skills. Never Give In – our school motto – guided me through my days of struggle as a farmer.'

Staying true to his winning spirit, he ran his final marathon on 13 September 2015, at the age of eighty-six, to leave us all breathless in our tracks. One would think this pronounces the end of his journey, but his legacy will live on forever . . .

Farewell, Head Boy, till we meet again. Never Give In!

**Himmat Singh Guron**
Siwalik 1984 | 1974–1983

OS Parent – Father – Harkrishan Singh Guron | Siwalik 1954 | 1949–1952
OS Sibling – Sister – Amrita Guron | Siwalik 1980 | 1969–1978

*Source and Acknowledgements*

- Sohan Lal Suri, `Umddt-ut-Twdnkh, Lahore, 1885–89.
- B.R. Chupia, Kingdom of the Punjab, Hoshiarpur, 1969.
- Derek Boddington | Roberts 1947 | 1942–47.
- Dr Timothy Carter | Yellows/Himalaya 1953 | 1944–1951
- James L.C. Coombes | Nicholson and Himalaya 1954 | 1944–1954
- Pankaj Sapru | Himalaya 1983 | 1976–1983

# The Admiral's Usher

I remember our former Headmaster Dr Harish Dhillon's farewell speech to the sesquicentennial batch, where he said, 'As we grow, our emotions dry up and tears freeze.' The credence would have several connotations to cherish with dried emotions but penning memoirs from various phases at Sanawar wouldn't hold that to be true. The hilltop is perhaps the only place on Earth that generations of Sanawarians have experienced, where no bruise from 'life's stern game' could supersede the ethos evolved within one as a schoolchild.

In 1997, Sanawar celebrated its sesquicentennial year of magnificence. That year, when India was celebrating her fiftieth year of independence, Sanawar had innumerable pertinent events scheduled in the calendar to mark the occasion with a greater degree of enthusiasm—from paying homage to Sir Henry Lawrence at the Residency in Lucknow, to releasing a book and postage stamp by the then Hon'ble Prime Minister and the Governor, respectively. Each event was meticulously planned and conducted after several rehearsals.

In fact, there were exceptions to the rule only for Sanawar. Prince Charles sent his good wishes from St. James's Palace, reminding us about his father doing the same during the centennial year in 1947 (co-incidentally, the letter arrived around the same time as Lady Diana's demise); Prime Minister Mr I.K. Gujral delayed his departure for Calcutta to attend Mother Teresa's funeral because the schedule of the book release at Vigyan Bhawan was overshot by an hour, and to place on record, Dr K.R. Narayanan, the then President of India, had once considered releasing the stamp himself in spite of his seniority in the order of precedence to the Chief of Navy Staff, who was invited to be our chief guest.

I was in L-V. On joining Sanawar in 1995, I was enamoured by the roles and examples [the] headmaster, staff, students and especially the prefects displayed on various occasions. I admired the Head Boy, Amitya Sharma, for he had the opportunity not only to command the parade, but also to lead and act as an ambassador of the school amongst students, staff and distinguished guests visiting Sanawar the entire year. Subtext, the Head Boy and Head Girl, Nanki Mann's appointments in the landmark year were special, and we envied them, understandably.

Admiral Vishnu Bhagwat, the then Chief of Naval Staff and an OS (Siwalik 1954), was invited to be the chief guest for Founders' Day. Dr Dhillon and Mr Sukhvinder Singh, our NCC instructor, appointed me as the student usher to the Admiral. This meant that the parade commander would command the troops to march to the ground and be prepared for the general salute only on my instructions, and so, I was tasked to inform the commander once the Admiral was prepared to leave [the] headmaster's residence.

This was an important responsibility and I felt more privileged than fortunate that it was assigned to me. I waited outside [the] headmaster's residence, nervous but filled with immense pride. Soon after the Parade, I was to receive the governor for releasing our postage stamp and first-day cover. So it was important that the parade commenced on time, otherwise the governor would have to keep waiting. When it was evident that we were running late, I gate-crashed at [the] headmaster's residence to ask if the Admiral was ready to leave. Mrs Bhagwat and Dr Dhillon were frantically annoyed, at which I explained the protocol mentioned on the sheet handed over to me, read otherwise.

I ran to have the parade march to the ground. Soon after the Trooping of Colours and the Admiral's speech, the governor's chopper begun landing at Barnes. The governor's reception at Sanawar is also an episode, but I shall leave that for another story. Dr Dhillon took a deep breath for all of it happened just on time.

I accompanied the Admiral to the exhibitions and the formal lunch hosted by Dr Dhillon, as a silent usher. I was unsure if the Admiral would welcome any more courtesy, for a senior-most serving defence officer running late for a parade was not acceptable. Dr Dhillon remarked briefly, 'Maneet, how could you mess up?' and to Mr Sukhvinder Singh, while showing the protocol sheet, '*Kar diti na jattan wali gal!*'

He noticed what I was going through and called me in for a quick cup of coffee. On such a busy day, it meant the world when he ensured that I felt good about the wishes and messages of congratulations coming from visitors, parents and guests, and not let the incident cloud my vision. That evening, the Naval band was to perform at Birdwood, and I was asked to take charge of the unit settling in.

The unit had a few requirements and the arrangements had to be made in very little time. I worked closely with the quartermaster and ensured the performance was successful. All their needs were met to the extent that the class-four staff had to rush to Kasauli over three times, for which the unit was grateful.

After the show, the Admiral, Mrs Bhagwat and Dr Dhillon, with all their heart, stepped up to say, 'Well done, Maneet, that was a very nice show!' I was moved by the gesture followed by a warm hug and hand shake. I broke my silence to thank the Admiral for his patience and enjoyed conversing with him while escorting him to [the] headmaster's residence. His ADC gifted me a badge of the United Services, which I proudly wear even today.

**Maneet Singh Sarla**
Nilagiri 2001 | 1995–2001
Education and Publishing Consultant

OS Sibling – Brother – Prabhjit Singh Sarla | Nilagiri 2008 | 2000–2005

# My Love for Music

My love for music began in 1974 when, in Upper IV, I started my Siwalik House senior dorm journey. Being the junior-most, my bed was next to the LP player table, and seniors would shout out to me to play a record. LPs available were a mix of Hindi and English albums. Frequent requests included the Beatles' 'Abbey Road' or Paul McCartney & Wings' 'band on the Run'. For no reason in particular, I started memorizing names, songs and albums. Artworks on these covers fascinated me. I became a huge fan of actor James Coburn, who was on the cover on 'band on the Run'. I remember the famous Polydor graphic on many LPs that we had.

In 1975, I became a close friend of Tutu Gill's (V-1979). His family lived in Kenya and he brought his favourite album 'Dark side of the Moon' by Pink Floyd, the following term. As the Vindhyans did not have any record player, Tutu would ask me to play it on the Siwalik House LP player. Initially, the music sounded weird. Tutu would insist that I replay the album, or he would ask me to move the needle to the third song, 'Time'.

A few of us got together and built a homemade speaker for the Vindhya House senior dorms, wired to the LP player on the floor below.

Often Gurinder (Daka) Ahluwalia would show off his fast-paced dance moves to the Black Sabbath song 'Paranoid'. Sanjay Dutt's favourite album back then was 'Smoke on the Water' by Deep Purple. Rajiv Bali's contribution to the collection was 'KC & the Sunshine band', bought by his dad on his USA trip. We all loved to shake our bodies to the KC music.

In 1975–76, we started listening to music on shortwave radio. Every Friday afternoon, we would listen to Radio Australia 'Count Down' by Glenys Dickson. Jasmit had an infatuation for Glenys. She had a very sensuous voice. We would write letters to her.

We often listened to 'Voice of America' that played American Country and Blues. A song appealed to me instantly as it played, getting stuck in my head. But I did not get the name of the singer or the name of the song. All I remembered were the words 'New Orleans', sung repeatedly. Decades later, I searched for those words on Google and after a few hundred attempts, finally found the song I was looking for: 'Magnolia' released in 1972–73 by J.J. Cale, a legendary Blues singer, songwriter and guitarist. It remains my all-time favorite—very easy-breezy song and, in my view, the most romantic song ever. Check it out.

My love for music is intense—deeply ingrained in my heart, mind and soul. I romance to music, often dreaming about it, and love to move my body to it. My Spotify dashboard informed me that I had listened to 40,000+ minutes in the last twelve months. My favorite genres are Blues, Jazz and Country Rock. Now I am expanding my horizons. Music is therapy and meditation for me. Not a day goes by without it.

Sanawar, this is a wonderful gift you gave me.

**Harjaspreet Singh Gill**
Clay | Siwalik 1979 | 1969–1977
Lives in Seattle, USA; passionate about golf, music, dance, real estate development and software engineering

# The Old And The New

'If only!'—the words of a dreamer. Young men have their ambitions, old men have their dreams. If only—if only I could capture and present to you the spirit that prevails at the OS reunion in London.

There is a room over a select hostelry in the centre of the metropolis and once a year, in early May, it resounds to the noises that are peculiar to Sanawarians. Most have studied their Omar Khayyam, it seems, the glasses filled to the brim indicate 'better be merry with the fruit-full grape than sudden after one—or bitter fruit!' The coherence of sentences uttered make sense only to those in the immediate vicinity. The babel sees that.

The years have disappeared. A bristly moustached retired General becomes 'Ting-Ting' once again—he used to play the triangle in the school band. A successful businessman, his success denoted by the increase in his girth, becomes 'Tanky' again. Balding heads are greeted as 'Curly', but should a master have the temerity to attend, there is nothing lost in respect when 'Sir' greets his presence. They don't live in the past entirely. Mrs Tilley is bombarded with questions about the present and her fund of knowledge is inexhaustible. She can tell you just what Pichkowrie's youngest is doing. She can tell you the date the Head last went to Delhi – and why – and she can tell you who entered the matrimonial stakes and the odds offered that it would ever come through. What a huge debt of gratitude we owe to her.

Every year, Mrs Tilley says, 'This is the last!' The response is characteristic – 'Never Give in!' – and the following year, we all turn up again. She can still lead us in the school song. Never do sopranos become so ultra-soprano; never do baritones descend lower than those profound basses. The emotion is choking. How we manage to read the small print of the pamphlets through misty eyes beats me. But I know you're just the same. As Major Som Dutt used to say, 'OS are such an emotional bunch when it comes to school matters'.

What a Founders' we have had. Three years ago, at the OS Meeting here, I frothed about the 'tamashas' that did nothing for the memory of the founder. It is so gratifying to see a return to the true meaning of this hallowed week with Sir Henry ever in the forefront of events throughout the programme.

How many years ago was it that, unbeknown to me, a very diminutive Sanawar boy joined me in the Chapel when I was taking photos in the Font area. I only knew of his presence when he asked, 'Is that the founder, Sir?' He indicated Sir Henry's marble bust and I said, 'Yes'. 'When did he die?' 'In 1857,' I said and added, 'It's written there.' He repeated the date, '1857!—did you know him?' I must have looked old even then, but the years have made me realize the wonderful tribute he paid me—and to all OLD Sanawarians. Of course we know the founder, that's why we are here, and I'm certain he knows every one of us.

The present occupants of his shrine have not lagged in their endeavours to fulfil Sir Henry's earnest wish. Your achievements in his name are astounding. No wonder the Head spoke with such conviction during his address today. We are indeed proud to belong.

There is a marked significance in the figures that make up this 130th anniversary, particularly figure 3. We have had first the 'Barne' era;

secondly, the 'Som Dutt' era; and thirdly the 'Das' era, which will be as successful and fruitful as its predecessors'.

Let me quote Middleton in conclusion:

'And I, who with expectant eyes,
Have fared across the starlit foam,
See through my dreams a new sun rise,
To conquer unachieved skies,
And bring the dreamer home!'

And there let me rest—this is home.

**William H. 'Bill' Colledge (Bilkul)**
Old Sanawarian (Roberts 1917–1927)

**Source & Acknowledgement:** *The Sanawarian* (December 1977)

# Mastoo and Kundan

Not everyone can claim to have worked under seven heads of an institution and when the institution is one like Sanawar, such a claim makes you sit up and take notice. Mastoo (Mast Ram), who retired on 1 December 1971, made this claim just before he got onto the school bus for the last time as a school employee. He had served Sanawar for forty years and was off to a well-earned rest.

People who have been at Sanawar for a long time tend to become a part of the Sanawar landscape and Mastoo, in his Khaki uniform, his khaki turban and his ever-smiling face, had very much become a part of the landscape. He was always very affectionate, very gentle and over a span of forty years, he endeared himself to generations of Sanawarians. Sanawarians everywhere carry in their hearts a picture of the cheerful little man, with his medicine bag slung over his shoulder going from one department to another.

It was 1949. There was a flu epidemic and the Hospital was full. Mrs Page, almost out of her mind trying to keep everyone in bed, chanced upon the simple expedient of confiscating everyone's pyjamas. Shamefaced and bored, the patients tried to pass the time playing 'geography' and 'word-building'. But it was no use. Mastoo finally came to the rescue. The next morning, Mrs Page was horrified to see 'lungi'-clad figures darting all over the place and untidy beds stripped of their sheets.

Over the years, Mastoo had accumulated a vast fund of medical knowledge till he had become very accurate in his diagnosis. It was not unusual to find people who had trudged up from places as far away as Sabathu, to seek the benefit of Mastoo's opinion.

When I returned to Sanawar, last May, one of the first things I did was to go and visit Mastoo. I was a little disappointed that he was not able to recognize my face. But I told myself that I really hadn't been outstanding in any way and had not even been a very regular visitor to the Hospital. It was natural that Mastoo should have forgotten me but as I came away, he called after me. 'You were in Nilagiri House, weren't you? And you used to tie a turban.'

In spite of his advancing years, Mastoo didn't look old and had always been in the best of health. But during these last two years, he had had two heart attacks and he knew that the time had come for him to retire from active life.

Compared to Mastoo's forty years, Kundan Lal's twenty-nine seem very few. But in themselves, they are long enough, especially when they span the period from his boyhood to adulthood. Kundan came to Sanawar at the age of thirteen. After Independence, he was attached to the Prep School, of which he soon become a permanent and indispensable part. In the true Sanawar spirit, his duties embraced anything and everything and he performed them all cheerfully without any grumbling and complaining. He was always very helpful to the Preppers—little children living away from home for the first time, who needed the friendship which Kundan gave them. All those who have been in Prep School in the last twenty-four years remember Kaunda with affection and with gratitude.

The Prep School used to go on an annual picnic to Eagles' Nest. In 1950, on this picnic, Mr Sircar devised a very interesting and complicated game of attack, ambush and planting of flags, which involved a lot of running up and down the khud-side, of sneaking from cover to cover. During the course of this game, I sprained my ankle and Kundan carried me on his shoulders to the Hospital and all the way, he talked and joked to take my mind off my swollen and painful ankle.

Mastoo left because it was his age to retire. Kundan, at forty-two, still had long years ahead of him and one wonders why he left. Whatever the reasons, the fact remains that the he was one of that band of totally selfless and dedicated workers which is rapidly becoming extinct.

When teachers leave, there are farewell parties – touching and sentimental – and there are farewell presents. Mastoo and Kundan left without presents and parties. But in the final analysis, I suppose this is more true to the Sanawar tradition: to give of yourself completely and sincerely, without any thought of reward, and when you have nothing more to give, to slip quietly and unobtrusively away, leaving in the hearts of those who have known you, the only true and worthwhile tribute that any man can have.

Thank you, Mastoo and Kundan, for all that you did for Sanawar, goodbye and good luck.

**Dr Harishpal S. Dhillon**
Staff | Headmaster 1995–1999
Old Sanawarian (Nilagiri 1957)

**Source and Acknowledgement:** *The Sanawarian* **(December 1971)**

# The Somnambulist General

Some of the older OS had told us that buildering or sky-walking in secret had been a hobby for some schoolboys for decades and their patron saint was George Herbert Leigh Mallory, who had reputedly climbed into Magdalen College, Oxford, over a wall after the gates had been shut. In June 1924, along with Andrew Irvine, he was lost at over 26,000 feet on Mt. Everest. His body was eventually found by an expedition in 1999 at 26,760 feet. Through the late 1970s and early 1980s, the romantic mystery of Mallory's disappearance almost at the summit of the mountain had spurred many sky-walkers to do the impossible; some even believed he had reached the summit.

The fact that [the] headmaster during this period, Mr Shomie Ranjan Das, who had been a tutor to Prince Charles at Gordonstoun School, was also a Magdalen man, brought the mythic Mallory closer to sky-walker boys. There were many ways up to the tin roofs at school. If the roof was close to a retaining wall, a short jump would do the trick. An obliging branch of a tree that led to the roof was the easiest. Climbing drain pipes was another option but required a reconnaissance to see if they were well pegged-down; this was however a difficult climb towards the end, entailing having to leave the support of the pipe and tackle the overhang of the tin eaves, and without climbing equipment, almost impossible. Using the lightning conductor strip was perhaps easier, but again it had to be ascertained that the iron pegs clamping it to the wall were securely in place. The many troops of monkeys showed the boys how it could be done! Making the climb with eyes open and senses fine-tuned was difficult enough but climbing at night, eyes shut and senses on neutral, was something else!

My father told me that in April 1955, Mr E.G. Carter, the principal, had gone to England a very sick man. The following year, he had written to say he was not returning to India. In his absence, Mr Kate, the Bursar, had officiated ably as the Head, till autumn of 1956, when Major Ravi Som Dutt loaned from the Army, became the first Indian headmaster of the school. The 'Major', as he was fondly called, had served for long in the Army, seeing action during World War II. A thrill passed though the school when he arrived in a red MG convertible motor car with Mrs Som Dutt, who had also served in the Army during WWII in the Indian Medical Nursing Service, along with their Daschund Mitzi. His stature jumped several notches when the boys discovered that the Major had been a boxing 'blue' at Cambridge University. This was also the year when Mr Sam Cowell, who had been a schoolboy, then having served for thirty-three years as a teacher and senior master, left the school, with his set of 'sticks' or canes, that had names: Biter, Slasher, Nipper, Cutter and Smasher. Major Som Dutt's departure from school after many successful years was a sad occasion for all, however, he donated photos, memorabilia and his uniform to the school museum, complete with hat, jacket, trousers, Sam Browne belt, brown shoes and shiny medals attached to colourful ribbons. Schoolboys down the years used to view this uniform with wonder and a whisper would go around: 'he was a boxing blue at Cambridge, too.'

At school, hunger was as ever-present as breathing. Like a pride of lions, pack of wild dogs or troop of monkeys, the boys had formed their own groups to forage and 'raid' to satisfy their hunger and if truth be told, more for thrill and excitement. Like the heavily muscled king monkey that always has its thick tail up in the air, each group of boys also had a group leader. Normally, these informal groups comprised boys from the same House, class, or Team XI. One group had boys from more than one House or class. The group leader, Keshav Chander, after intense internal discussions, allotted tasks and the loot. He had been given the sobriquet 'General'. He had many leadership attributes but was not a sky-walker.

The boys had, at times, been woken up at night by what they thought were monkeys running and jumping on the tin roof. This was unusual since the Macaca radiata, or the red bum monkey, is a diurnal creature and sleeps at night. Occasionally, the entire dorm would be awakened by heavy drumming of feet running across the roof; it was concluded that perhaps a troop of gray langurs or Hanuman langurs were loping their way across. This was plausible because gray langurs weigh, at an average, about fifteen to twenty kilos and can leap twelve to fifteen feet horizontally and forty feet descending! The missing piece of the puzzle was that langurs are diurnal animals, too. It was impossible that some sky-walkers were up to nocturnal tricks; nobody would try that at night even on a 'grub' dare.

There was a furore one morning when the museum was opened; somebody had broken in and removed all the Major's accoutrements.

There was huge commotion and Mr B. Singh, Mucchoo's moustache bristled furiously with a life of its own, wanting to catch the culprit. Who in abomination would commit such a treacherous act? We had barely fallen asleep that night when we were woken by loud rhythmic thuds on the tin roof of the dorms and thought it were the langurs again, having a late-night celebration. Hoping to catch sight of them, we rushed outside and to our utter astonishment, we saw General in the full-dress uniform of Major Ravi Som Dutt, complete with parade hat, nonchalantly twirling a swagger stick marching to perhaps 'Sons of the Brave' atop the roof of the U-VI dorms! After a few smart turns at the very edge of the roof that brought our hearts to our mouths, he suddenly marched again towards the end of the roof, leapt onto a retaining wall, bounded up the khud, and disappeared. A frantic search for him in the khud with makeshift flame torches, yielded nothing other than causing an inadvertent khud fire. Wearied, some of us came back inside, only to find the General sleeping soundly in his bed in full-dress uniform.

Our somnambulist General awoke to find all questioning eyes on him, wondering how the General, who was not a gifted long or high jumper and yet, had emulated the grace of a champion langur at his peak best and that too at night? He, of course, had no idea how he had come to acquire the uniform or wear it. Many other strange happenings that had taken place earlier were answered and laid at the feet of the General, including a decapitated chicken found in his locker. There must have been intense discussion in the Staff Common Room and the conclusion reached was that somnambulism was a medical condition and that the General was quite innocent. Mr Sam Cowell's collection of canes had long since left the senior master's office and Mr B. Singh had no need to recall for them, thus there was no retribution.

We did get to hear that at a secret conclave, the OS Skywalkers got together and the General was made an honorary Skywalker; the Skywalker who waltzes with langurs.

**Jaimal Inder Singh Shergill**
Jami | Vindhya 1985 | 1977–1985

OS Parent – Father – Tajindar Singh Shergill | Taji | Vindhya 1958 | 1951–1958

# The Sunshine of Sanawar

1955. That was the year my brother and I (six-and-a-half years old) joined Sanawar. We were dropped off by our father, and the only thing I clearly remember is that after a day of fun and games, when evening came, he did not return to collect us. The next time we saw our parents would be nine months later.

The best part of Prep School was that one didn't have to think for oneself (not that we could). The school routine took care of everything. All one had to do was follow the crowd, and you ended up getting your baths, meals, education, sports, and when they shut off the lights, your sleep. But outside the regimented routine, there was lots of unsupervised time, and that was when the fun started. It was during these hours that we made friends, experienced 'epic' adventures, explored places, listened to tall stories (and believed most of them), and honed 'essential' skills like throwing stones, scaling walls, racing down khud-sides at breakneck speeds, walking on our hands—one of my proudest achievements was being able to walk the entire length of the PD Pavement on my hands.

The memories of our escapades still make me laugh. I recall one Saturday evening, the movie being screened was *Robin Hood*. The very next day, every Prepper had made a bow from bamboo procured from the khud-side, and had strung the bow with his school shoe laces. That Sunday, the arrows flew thick and fast in every corner of PD. At some point during the day, there was this guy from Form-II, who claimed to have curved an arrow round the corner of the Dorms to hit his fleeing target. We were too young to doubt this 'incredible feat', and spent the next hour trying (albeit unsuccessfully) to bend an arrow to go round the corner.

I guess it was only in Senior School that I realized how lucky I was to be in an institution like Sanawar. Our campus in its sylvan surroundings undoubtedly made it one of the most beautiful schools in India. We were so proud of the school's traditions and they were zealously upheld. The most significant being the military traditions left over from the times the school was The Lawrence Royal Military School, Sanawar. But it was also the little things that made a difference—like when it was time for us to don our winter uniform, the teachers wore gowns to classes; during Assembly, on alternate days, we sang in English and Hindi, and on Fridays, we belted out the national anthem. One of the songs '*Chisti ne jis zamin pe*', written by Iqbal, has stayed with me, and which I now realize had a lasting impact on my image of India.

No Sanawarian can ever forget the excitement in the dorms before a 'Social'. There were three Socials scheduled in the year—one before the summer break, one at Founders' and one before school closing. However, [the] headmaster, at his discretion, could award the school a Social, if the school team performed some exceptional feat in the sports arena.

For most of us (and here I speak on behalf of all my male batchmates), Sanawar is the 'Best School of All' because it is a co-educational boarding school. Now, in the Humanities section the girls to boys ratio was 4:1, so there was enough opportunity for exchange of conversation. So also for the boys, who took part in the plays could interact with girls during practice. But for us in the Science stream, where the boys to girls ratio was 10:1, the Socials were the only time we could not only talk to a girl, but even got to hold a girl's hand during a dance.

In soccer, I remember that BCS had beaten us for four consecutive years, and in 1963, we drew the match. The soccer team went to Heady's House to ask for a holiday and a Social, but was turned down with a 'but you didn't win'.

Then in 1964, after a long time, the school had a strong and talented bunch of sportsmen. Recognizing this windfall, Mr Kemp thought it worth his while to take on the coaching of the school cricket team. That year, we convincingly beat BCS, YPS, Khunjpura Public School, but lost the Social when Doon School beat us by two runs. In soccer, after five years, we beat BCS 2–0 ( I missed a penalty shot when the score was 0–0). The School team trooped up to Heady's for a holiday and Social—they were granted. We came sprinting down to the Quad yelling 'he said Yeeeeeeeees'. And at the Social, the emcee announced that the first dance would be a 'Snowball' to be led by the soccer team.

From its inception of the Inter-Public Schools Athletics, YPS (with the National Institute of Sports coaching available to them) had always come first, while Sanawar and BCS competed for the second position. Their dominance was such that in 1963, the principal of YPS had even suggested that perhaps they should withdraw from the event. But in 1964, Sanawar performed a miracle by coming first. Heady declared a holiday and Social before our athletics team had even boarded the bus at Patiala. 1964 was a very good year—it will be recorded in the school's history books as the 'Year of Five Socials'.

Sports has always been a big part of my life, and it was on the playing fields of Sanawar that I was given the opportunity to develop and nurture this passion. I clearly remember the scramble to see the 'Friday Order' to check if you had made the team. And, before the match in front of the whole school, the feeling of nervousness magnified to the point that it got difficult to breathe. Ironically, the recognition of my sporting pursuits at Sanawar came after I had left the school. I was in college when I received an envelope from Sanawar. Inside was a Spartan Club badge and a two-lined letter, which said, 'Congratulations, it gives me great pleasure to inform you that you have been inducted into the Spartan Club'.

Apart from the memories of fun and laughter that filled our school days, I also have fond memories of some of the people who were instrumental in our upbringing and proved worthy role models. I remember Mr M.V. Gore (on and off the Housemaster for Vindhya House) for his unique methods of trying to discipline us into improving our performances—he always had our best interests in mind (though we didn't recognize it then). Mr Jagdish Ram, who held the portfolios of PT, gymnastics, boxing, shooting and NCC, was a perfectionist and shaped the discipline of the school. Mr and Mrs Kemp, who strove to polish us country urchins into future leaders. And, above all, at that impressionable stage of my life, I was hugely influenced by the principles of governance practised under the leadership of Major R. Som Dutt (Headmaster since 1956), which involved rules being framed and followed, merit recognized and rewarded, and most importantly, fairplay, which was the overriding principle governing every action. They all took pride in their work, and led by example.

If someone was to ask me what I took away from my ten years in Sanawar, the answer would be, lifelong friends, good health and my life's guiding principles, namely 'Fair Play' and 'Never Give In'.

**Lalit Varma**
Lallu | Vindhya 1964 | 1955–1964
Squash – Asian Championship 1981 – Silver Medal | National Champion (Veterans) for three years | World Masters (45–50) 1996 – Ranking 5 | Captain – West Bengal | Inter-State Squash Champions 1985 (Delhi Squash Team) | Assam State Tennis Champion 1971 | Northern India Wills Golf Championship 1980 – Winner

OSS PRESIDENT 1987–1989

OS Siblings – Sister – Malti Varma | Vindhya 1960 | 1953–1960
　　　　　　　Brother – Anant Varma | Vindhya 1964 | 1955–1960

OS Children – Son – Umang Varma | Nilagiri 1992 | 1983–1992
　　　　　　　Daughter – Ambika Varma | Nilagiri 1988 | 1986–1988

# Mrs Sehgal

'I refuse to do it, Mr Joshi. Just what do you think I am? Go and get someone else to do—what did you say? No—I care two hoots. What's this? I don't want any menu-shenu,' and with magnificent anger and scorn, Mrs Sehgal tore up Mr Joshi's menu and threw it into his face. Mr Joshi only smiled. Without a word, he pulled out another copy of the menu from his pocket. 'And if you tear this, I've got another copy at home.' Mrs Sehgal burst into hysterical laughter and the next day turned out to be what was, even by her standards, an extraordinary dinner for the Siwalik House party. That was her way, always: loud, pushing, but at heart, so very kind. She was willing to do anything and always gave her best.

She wasn't always BD Kitchen Matron. During my schooldays, she was the Nilagiri House Matron and what a matron she was! Such tongue-lashing she gave us and when it was something beyond her, Mr Saleem Khan was summoned and he was always quick with the cane. But it was a small price to pay. Nilagiri House boys were the best turned-out boys in the school. She took a personal interest in our clothes and one Sunday afternoon, I remember fifty-three school pullovers hung out on the railing to dry—each one of them washed by Mrs Sehgal herself. A boy had an attack of allergic asthma and all through the dark and quiet night, she sat beside the suffering boy—her very presence a source of warmth and security.

Her room was a haven for the homesick, the losers and the insecure, and comfort from her usually took more substantial from than words—it could be an apple, a '*pinni*', a slice of cake, or even just Charlie's barfi.

Sundays and holidays found her sitting on the pavement wall, knitting, and more often than not, there would be a crowd of boys around her, eagerly telling her about their homes, their families, showing her letters and photographs and cars. In this way, she substituted in for all the absent mothers. Even amongst the staff, she was always willing and eager to lend a helping hand, especially in a crisis.

Is it any wonder then, that all those who came into contact with her will remember her with the fondest affection?

**Dr Harishpal S. Dhillon**
Old Sanawarian (Nilagiri 1957)
Staff | Headmaster 1995–1999

**Source and Acknowledgement:** *The Sanawarian* (December 1972)

# Sanawar, Cricket and I

Ever since the age of about six, my most prized possession was a cricket bat. I have fond memories of those days when we played cricket after school or hung around watching seniors play the game. At the age of nine, in 1958, I joined Sanawar. Cricket was not very much in focus, except for a few net practice sessions. However, watching Sangram Singh Gaikwad play exquisite cricket in 1958–59 was a delight and a great source of encouragement and inspiration for me. Not to forget Ajit Bhargav's leg-spin bowling, which I tried to emulate. In '61 and '62, I got the opportunity to play for Colts and Lalit Varma was the captain, while Arjun Batra was the wicketkeeper-batsman. Those were good times. My only regret was that the cricket season was much too short for my liking.

The following year of 1963, when I was in Lower Five, cricket playing actually blossomed because much more emphasis was laid on it and opportunities were provided to the First XI. Access to Barnes field came more often. From this period, a couple of changes and incidents come to mind that have had a bearing on how cricket is played today. House matches were a tedious and time-consuming affair as each match was played for two days, consecutively, after lunch and the result would be invariably decided based on the first innings' total. Since Barnes was the only field available, the Round Robin stretched on for a couple of weeks. Now Trevor Kemp, our senior master, came up with a brilliant idea. Each innings of a team was limited to twenty-five overs and the result was decided on that very day. Mind you, this was way before Kerry Packer came up with his pyjama cricket in 1970–71 and the current very popular T20 format came into existence.

Another interesting development that I can recall is that of the reverse sweep or flick, that is an integral part of today's cricket. We were playing a practice match on Barnes and Lokinder Verma, fondly known as Loki, was batting right-handed and the late, lamented Ajit Jayaram was the lone slip fielder as a spinner, and was bowling. As the ball was delivered, Loki switched his grip and smashed the ball towards slips. Ajit was taken by surprise and came in the way and was, unfortunately, hit where it hurts most.

The cricket XI held their own against most opponents. When Doon School visited us in 1960, the wiles of Ajit Bhargav flummoxed them and we won our first encounter with them. Unfortunately, that was our first and last victory against Doon till my time in 1965. In 1963, we were to visit Doon and were to go down to Dehra Dun in our brand-new bus. The route to be taken was via Jagadhari, now known as Yamuna Nagar, where Inderpal Singh Bhusri, our Head Boy and our head prefect, owned a saw mill.

He promised our captain that if we took him along, he would host a royal lunch for the team at Jagadhari. Since Bhusri was not a cricketer, a compromise was reached and he was taken along as the official scorer. And boy, when we reached Jagadhari did he live up to his promise! His father had organized for a cook from the famous Moti Mahal of Delhi and unlimited quantities of tandoori chicken and oranges and Coke on ice were offered to us to gorge on. And we did justice to the fare laid before us. Jugnu, if I remember correctly, went through twelve bottles of Coke.

Despite our rapacious appetites, we couldn't quite clean out the table and the leftovers were promptly packed and put on the bus for us to partake later on. We had barely travelled another hour or so when we attacked the leftovers and annihilated them with a flourish. Satiated, at last, we eventually reached Doon School and I was exposed to a full-sized cricket ground for the first time. Needless to say, we were soundly thrashed and in fact, their captain, Mike Dalvi, sent us on a leather hunt and scored a remarkable double century.

Without sounding like a lame apologist, I would like to state some facts that gave Doon a distinct advantage over Sanawar. They had several full-sized grounds, where games of all types could be played throughout the year. Compare that to our Barnes, where we played cricket, football, hockey and athletics—which necessitated short seasons for each sport. Doon's cricket season lasted for over four months as compared to our barely two months.

Moreover, while we bid adieu to Sanawar after Senior Cambridge, Doon had a system wherein after SC, the boys could come back to school for Inter before joining college, which obviously added a lot of strength to their teams.

In 1964, our cricket coach was away on study leave and the reigns were taken by Mr Kemp (called Kempy behind his back). Despite holding the responsibility of a senior master and actually running the day-to-day affairs of the school, it was indeed creditable that he found time to coach us. In fact, he fractured his foot and even then, would hobble up and down to Barnes on crutches. Mr Kemp used to play cricket in his younger days and imparted a few tips to us on the game that were good advice. Under his tutelage and the able captaincy of N.S. Pannu, we probably formed the strongest team ever. We won every match that we played that year. The last match was against Doon, our nemesis. After the first innings, Doon had a meagre lead of a couple of runs. So far so good. But then disaster struck in the second innings and for reasons I still can't fathom, Doon ended the match with a facile victory, much to our disappointment and that of Mr Kemp.

Come May of '65, we were back in Doon. Due to intense summer in the plains, the match was played at six in the morning, till eleven, and then there was a break; the match was resumed at four in the evening.

At the end of first day's play, the first innings had not been completed and it looked like a certainty that the match would end in a draw. After the first day's play, some juniors suggested that we go to town and watch a Shammi Kapoor starrer called *Janwar*. After a bit of cajoling, I agreed, keeping in mind that the match was sure to end in a draw and that we would be in bed by 9.30 p.m. in any case. However, there was a power failure during the film and we were assured that it would be restored shortly. No one was ready to leave the movie incomplete. Eventually, the power was restored rather late and the movie finished around 11 p.m. We found no transport to take us back to Doon and trudged in after 12 p.m.

The next day 6 a.m. start proved disastrous for us and we ended up losing the match. Mr Mundkur, our coach, was furious and I never heard the end of it. It was a shameful display of a lack of discipline and I take full responsibility for that fatal mistake.

Our last match was against BCS, which unfortunately was rained off. Despite frequent interruptions and trying conditions, our Ashok Masand scored a century.

Another significant event of 1965 occurred when two gentlemen from the Punjab Cricket Association landed in Sanawar in September to hunt for talent bolster the strength of the state team. The matting was laid out on an unprepared pitch and after nets, three of us – Marwah, Masand and

I – were selected to attend a coaching camp in Jullundhar. The problem was that the camp and matches were to be played in October and early November. Unfortunately, those dates clashed with our forthcoming final SC exams that were to be held on 20 November. However, our Headmaster was very keen, as he said, to put Sanawar on the cricketing map of India. A letter was shot off to my grandfather, who agreed, knowing how keen I was on cricket.

Masand, the other sixth former, was from Jullundhur, so his parents were only too happy and even volunteered to look after the boarding and lodging of both Marwah and I. After athletics on 4 October, we made our way to Jullundhur. After enjoying a few days of Masand's hospitality, Marwah and I were told to fend for ourselves and we ended up staying for a month at the pavillion of the Burlton park stadium. I think the reason we were ousted was because Masand's parents felt we would prove a hindrance to their son's preparation for SC. Anyway, being Sanawarians, we took it in our stride and subsisted on buns, omelettes and tea, that were available at the local dhaba—the only food joint in the vicinity of the cricket stadium. We practised hard for a month on a matting wicket only to be told two days before the match that the game would be played on a turf wicket! So much for the sports administration. Anyway, Marwah and I were selected in the team against stiff competition, that included the soon-to-be famous Amarnath brothers, Mohinder and Surinder. We beat Delhi in the finals to win the North Zone trophy.

We finally landed in Sanawar fifteen days before our exams. I was a nervous wreck and somehow went through the exams as best as I could. The holidays were harrowing, awaiting the results which finally came three months later. And would you believe it, I topped my class in biology/ humanities section and the icing on the cake was that I scored distinctions in History and English literature! I became a firm believer in 'All's well that ends well'.

However, this was not the end of my cricketing saga. In the early 70's, I went to Kasauli with some friends for a holiday. I visited S'na to find Mr Mundkur at Barnes with the boys playing cricket. I joined them and had a whale of a time. Mr Mundkur suggested that I bring up a team and provide much-needed practice to the boys (the Doon School disaster of '65 was long forgotten by then). Thus was born the Sood's XI. From mid-70's to the late 90's, I brought up a team every year. The team comprised of not only old Sanawarians, but other enthusiasts, too. The format was informal and often we had an incomplete XI, wherein reserves of the boys team and some staff members were inducted in our team. As we grew older, the rules were tweaked. For one, no matter who won the toss, we always batted first. This was done to ensure that our fielding was minimal, at best. There was so much enthusiasm amongst the OS to play, that once a player flew in from Bombay to Delhi, and then drove up to Sanawar just to play. He was a left-hander and the first ball he faced he was declared LBW. Much to his chagrin, he trudged back to the pavillion. Keeping in mind the trouble he took to come all the way from Bombay, we felt it was rather unfair, so another rule was tweaked. No LBW decisions would be made against us. All in all, it was just fun and games. Unfortunately, sometime in the late 90s, I rose on my toes to square cut a ball and ended up snapping a ligament in my foot.

And that, my friends, was the end of my sojourn in the realm of Sanawar cricket. I must say, till the very end, it was wonderful playing with youngsters and later celebrating with them after the match at the Tuck Shop.

Never Give In.

**Rakesh Sood**
Vindhya 1965 | 1958–1965

OS Sibling – Sister – Manju Sood | Vindhya 1961 | 1958–1961

OS Children – Daughter – Mansi Sood | Vindhya 1997 | 1988–1997
                 Daughter – Meghla Sood | Vindhya 1999 | 1992–1999

# From Sky to the Ocean on Hero Bicycles

At last, the day had come. The day we had been waiting for so anxiously. 30 November 1977—the day we were to leave from Sanawar on our adventurous expedition.

All the preparations had been made the night before. We had tied our rucksacks securely to the bicycles, and with frantic efforts and suggestions from all sides about how to tie them, we had finally succeeded and hit upon a clever method of tying them. We had been practising with our bikes before in the mornings (and of course 'ducking' morning prep). It had been fun and once we had even gone quite close to Dharampur (this made people more confident that we'd never reach Dharampur—the pessimists, of course, and 'The Beard'). There had been some terrible moments too, like the day when we had our inoculations.

And finally, D-day came. It was supposed to be 1 December but had changed by Mr K.J. Parel (the big boss) to the thirtieth. We were all lined up in a semicircle on the Quad.

## Part I

Extract from JP's log book:

12.00 noon: Everything was ready. The bikes all lined up. One of the most exciting moments of the trip. I could see the happy and worried faces of my brother and parents, who were full of advice and last-minute warnings.

12.15–1.30 p.m.: A hearty send-off. The chief guest said a few cheerful words and flagged us off at 12.40 p.m., followed by 'Rasgullas' five minutes afterwards from Mr Hegde at the Bakery. We were stopped by the manager of the Oriental Bank at Garkhal, (he had partly financed us for the trip), to give us signboards advertising the bank which we unwillingly hung on our bikes, followed by a photograph which the manager took.

Extract from Gautam's log book:

While we were going from Garkhal to Dharampur, we could see and hear the Sanawarians screaming cheerio (red jackets were more in number). We had a distant look at them and prayed to God, though somebody had warned us not to look off the road (a cause of accidents).

While going down to Kalka, many thoughts were racing through our minds and the major one was whether we'd be able to do it. These thoughts we never revealed to each other and with doubts still creeping through our minds, we reached the destination of our first day: Mohangram. We had done it in spite of the fact that we had thought that it would be Sanawar to Kalka.

The second and the third day we had indigestible food (because it was so good) at Kulu's and KD's place.

Extracts from JP's dairy:

2 December 1977: The first puncture. We had been quite afraid of punctures but never showed our feelings to each other about it. After crossing Panipat, we decided to go fast as it was getting dark and we were going at quite a speed when Gautam suddenly shouted to me from behind, 'Something's happened to your tyre, JP. It's punctured, the air is coming out.' I got down and was distressed to see that the first puncture of the trip had been suffered by my bike.

The third day was a tiring one, as that day, we did 140 kilometres. The first three days were tiring too, as our knee joints got used to pain.

3 December 1977: We reached Delhi around three o' clock. We went to Monty's place first and then moved on to Gautam's, where we were received by his cheerful parents and afterwards, we had lots of cake and cold coffee, and then we went to see a movie called *Samson and Delilah* after a heavy supper and went to sleep around 1.00 a.m.

We left Delhi on the fifth and in the evening, reached a place called Kosi, where, unfortunately, we stayed in a place which had toilets fitted with Kipp's apparatus and so the result was that we had a troublesome night.

6 December 1977. We had hardly gone about 10 kms. from Kosi when we experienced bad roads which had been devastated by the floods last year.

Suddenly, Pixy had a puncture. We all came to a halt as we were in the middle of nowhere. We all started getting brilliant ideas about how to fix the puncture. As we didn't have sufficient material to repair it, we finally decided to change the whole tube and took the wheel off the bike. But to our distress, air couldn't be filled in the new tube by the small pumps which we had. So, Mr Parel and Mr Hassan had to take it to the nearest village and to their horror, it was discovered that the new tube had seven punctures. Anyway, it was fixed, and we all moved on to Agra, where we reached in the evening. The sixth day of our journey was over.

Our gratitude goes to The Hero Bicycles Ltd., Ludhiana; Lt. Gen. I.S. Gill P.S.V.M., M.C. GOC–IN–C, Western Command; Mr S.C. Soneja, Manager, Oriental Commercial Bank; Mr B.D. Bali, Manager, Mohan Meakins Breweries Ltd; Mr Ashok Mehta (Tubes India Ltd.) and many Sanawarian parents and OS for the immense help they extended to us.

**J.P. Singh and Gautam Shaunik**
Old Sanawarians (Himalaya 1979)

## Part II

Our stay at Agra was a lot of fun. We stayed with Col. Pental. The highlight was our visit to Fatehpur Sikri and the Taj Mahal. The other attraction was the movie which we finally succeeded in persuading Mr Parel to let us see (it was *Juggernaut*). We were, however, in for a few disappointments as well. One of these was the para-jumps which we were meant to be seeing. The day for the jumps commenced with our waking up early (i.e. six o' clock). After a quick breakfast over Mr Hasan's protests, (who didn't want to go), we were dumped into an army one-ton and rushed off to the landing zone. There, we discovered, much to our distress, that the para- jumps had been postponed. We returned cursing our luck (Mr Hasan was the loudest). The rest of the day, we spent making the best use of our last day of rest at Agra. The day ended with a shopping spree, during which Mr Hasan, Mr Parel and Gauty showed their romantic natures by buying loose floppy (ladies') hats in colours ranging from purple to bright pink. The ostensible purpose of these purchases was to protect them from the sun, though the rest of us were suspicious.

The next day, a police van arrived at our doorstep. Their purpose was to escort us through the dacoit-infested area of the Chambal ravines.

The appearance of the police escort confirmed Pathak's worst fears and he made no attempt to hide them. The run continued with quite a few halts since tins of juice (courtesy Mohan Meakins) insisted on finding their way out of our haversacks and taking their own path. The day's run was very interesting since we crossed many state boundaries (UP, Rajasthan and MP) and much to everyone's irritation the police escort changed every time we crossed from one boundary to another. The transport for the police ranged from vans to bicycles. The excitement of the day's journey reached its zenith when we reached the Chambal river. The ravines were a fascinating sight. As we reached Gwalior, we saw to our horror that Scindia School, where we were supposed to spend the night, was on top of a high plateau. The walk up (with our bikes) was excruciating and was performed in total silence. However, the situation took a reverse trend when suddenly, out of the blue (rather black, as it was 8.00 p.m.), the sound of a bike falling was heard, followed by loud groans. When we turned around, all we could see was JP's face twisted with pain and the green body of his bike lying over him. The rescue operations were performed quickly, amidst much laughter.

Still followed by the police escort, the next day's journey ended at Datia, where we were warmly received by Taru's grandparents.

The rest of the journey to Nagpur was exciting. The people of the region are very hospitable. In fact, at places, we were offered sweets and other comestibles (free of charge, of course) which we accepted without hesitation. On the way, we were also showered with a number of questions from all sides regarding our arrest as we were being accompanied by an armed police escort (arms ranging from lathis to 303s). People often viewed us and our haversacks with suspicious eyes. Some of them even asked us what we were trying to sell.

The day before we reached Nagpur, we stayed at a fascinating place called 'Khwasa'. The place, Pixy claimed, reminded him of Africa since there were many date trees (which our friend mistook for palm trees) and the name also resembled 'Mombasa'. Since we reached Khwasa early, Mr Parel proclaimed that it was high time we did some constructive work. He handed us a paper and pencil and threw us out of the rest House. We were forbidden to enter until we returned with at least three sets of questionnaires duly filled in with the answers of the local inhabitants.

The next day was quite a bright one, since all of us were looking forward to a break at Nagpur. 20 kilometres from Nagpur, we stopped at a place called Kamptee (where there is the Guards' Training Centre). We were supposed to have lunch with the Commandant (Col. Sodhi), i.e. Arunjeet's father. Since he was away on urgent work, we were invited to lunch by the second-in-command, Lt. Col. Sharma. After a delicious lunch, we proceeded to Nagpur. Our entry into Nagpur was not what one can call enjoyable, since the first thing we did was go get lost. After spending an hour or so finding our way through the network of roads, we finally reached the maintenance command of the IAF.

**Monty Khanna and J.P. Singh**
Old Sanawarians (Himalaya 1979)

## Part III

As most of us in the expedition had an affinity for the Air Force, we were glad to reach Nagpur, where we stayed with the Air Force Maintenance Command. We still cherish the memories of our stay in Nagpur and the delicious lunch we had at Col. Sodhi's place. We attacked the food voraciously that day, and got nightmares at night (due to overeating).

On the twenty-first, we left Nagpur and Mr Goswami tied the transistor, which he had bought in Nagpur, securely to his bike and thus we were pedalling on to the rhythm of the Indian music playing over it, when we suddenly heard a thud followed by a crunching sound. When we looked back, we saw Mr Goswami picking up his transistor off the road – his rear wheel had gone over it – and, as you might have guessed by now, it had stopped working.

Hardly had we gone a few kms. further when we heard the familiar voice of Sanjay Batra greeting us from his car. After chit-chatting with us for a short time, he left us to go on with our long hard journey.

On the way to Hyderabad, which we reached on the twenty-fifth, quite a few interesting incidents occurred. One day, we had our breakfast at a place called Gudi Guntoor, where we ate no less than 200 pooris. The shopkeeper was so astonished that he didn't have any words to express his astonishment. The same day, we met many carts on the way, carrying cotton to the local factories, and Mr Goswami being a mathematician, counted them all and afterwards solemnly declared that the total number was 658.

Mr Parel got very excited as we reached a place called Nirmal, as the place had many South Indian restaurants, with the result that he forced us to have dosas for all the meals we had there. The following day was a bad one for Pathak. Early in the morning, before anybody woke up, his bike somehow fell down, creating a lot of 'thunder' and 'crash' sound and also waking us all up. The second time, it fell down while he was cleaning it. Poor Pathak's reflector broke and he was almost shedding. In the afternoon, as Pathak was trying to do some acrobatics on the bike, he again fell down but this time, he blamed Gautam for it as he claimed that Gautam was trying to frighten him.

On X-mas day, we reached Hyderabad and in order to cheer up Mr Parel, we started singing Christmas carols. The result was that Mr Parel bought us a huge cake at Hyderabad, which we enjoyed. We stayed at Hyderabad for four days but we didn't show any signs of indolence by relaxing etc. Instead, we explored different parts of Hyderabad, went for a savoury dinner at Col. Bhalla's place (Amita's father) and also visited the Military College of Electrical and Mechanical Engineering (MECE). Here, again, those of us interested in Electronics were on pins and needles, looking at and examining every minor detail of the tanks and complicated electronic equipment which we saw.

On 30 December, when we left Hyderabad, we came across many newspapers carrying news about us.

We reached a place called Kurnool on New Year's Eve and in order to celebrate, we stayed in a 'posh' hotel, ate 'lavishly' and the next day, witnessed Mr Parel paying the bill 'sneakily'. On our way to Bangalore, we stayed at Anantpur with Father Ferrer and the people at his place really looked after us very well. The next day, we passed through a place called Gooty, where we stayed for some time and saw the fort there, followed by Mr Hasan's lecture on the Persian influence on fort architecture. But unfortunately, it was a bad day for him. Just before lunch, he had a puncture which was nicely repaired by Gautam. Hardly had we gone a few kms. when we heard an explosion equalling that of a truck tyre bursting—alas! It was Mr Hasan's tyre bursting due to excessive air in it. After long and tiring efforts, we repaired it and Mr Hasan told me to check it. I climbed on to the saddle but could hardly go a few yards forward when the tyre burst open again due to excessive air. It was Mr Hasan's fault. We fretted and fumed but couldn't express our anger, Mr Hasan being an adult.

We reached Bangalore on 4 January, and stayed at the MEG Centre but had troublesome nights there due to the bugs. From Bangalore, Mr Hasan, Mr Goswami and I went to visit some historical temples at Belur and Halebed, and as they were quite far from the city, the whole way I had to sit quietly listening to Mr Hasan's speech on 'Indo-Persian trade relations' and the fall of the Mughal empire.

Mysore was our next stop. Mr Parel was again quite delirious on the way from Bangalore as the landscape around was full of coconut plantations. We passed Srirangapatnam on the way (just before Mysore). This time, it was Mr Hasan's turn to go into fits of excitement. Srirangapatnam had a fort belonging to Tipu Sultan and Mr Hasan knows the history of the period like the back of his hand, so you can imagine what must have happened. I suppose there is no need to tell you.

At last, we reached the historic city of Mysore with Mr Hasan nearly dancing on top of his bike and Monty and Pixy trying their best to calm him down.

**Jatinder Pal Singh U VI A**
Old Sanawarian (Himalaya 1979)

**Source and Acknowledgement:** *The Sanawarian* **(December 1978)**
Note: Despite our best efforts, were unable to retrieve the concluding part (Mysore to Kanya Kumari) of this expedition.

# Tank

Lyrics by Mr S.C. 'Sammy' Cowell, Headmaster written for the Muddlers
Concert of October 1947 and sung to the tune of a popular rhumba of the
time.

You know that we have a swimming pool
And it's filled with water blue and cool
All the boys just love to go in 'tank'
But the girls stand on the bank.

(Chorus)

So their bathing suits never get wet
They pose on the sides looking pretty
And say it would be a great pity
If our bathing suits ever got wet!

When the time for swimming heats comes round
For each race some entries must be found
But the question is can this be done?
If the colours are going to run

(Chorus)

For their bathing suits musn't get wet . . . etc.
　　There are three more verses all in a similar 'ragging' vein, but I have
forgotten them.

**D.V. Boddington**
LRMS Sanawar 1942–1947
October 2001

# The School Barber

He had a small wiry frame and his face was wrinkled and creased like the skin of an apple that has remained on the shelf too long. He exuded the musty odour of age and this led you to believe all the fifty-year stories that he told you. He was a living history book as far as the school was concerned, going right back to the 1920s, when Bishop Barnes was the principal. He told of how Rev. Hunt, the fifth headmaster, had not suffered a heart attack and drowned while swimming as he was supposed to have, but had been murdered by his daughter and her two lovers because he had objected to her going out with two men at the same time.

The school authorities insisted on severe, army haircuts and Sukh Ram, or Nappi, as he was generally known, found sadistic delight in chopping away at the boys' hair till he was in danger of scalping them. One year, shoulder-length hair for boys was all the rage and the boys returned from the winter vacations sporting long, scruffy hair. Nappi proudly proclaimed: 'See, how the boys love my haircuts. Not one of them went to another barber during all these months.'

Sometimes Nappi would soften and let some boys off with slightly longer hair than prescribed. On one occasion, for some mysterious reason, he succumbed to cajoling and blandishments and did the unthinkable. He cut a Sikh boy's hair. All hell broke loose. The boy was hauled up by the deputy headmaster, Nappi was served a show-cause notice and the boy's father arrived, armed with a double-barrel BSA twelve bore, determined to shoot Nappi.

Nappi went into hiding and we thought that his services had been terminated and we would never see him again. But he returned one morning and all seemed to have been forgiven and forgotten and I, for one, was relieved and glad to see him again. Somehow, he more than anyone or anything else, served as a bridge between the Sanawar which the British had owned and run as a military school, and the Sanawar which was now a totally Indian public school.

One cold, Sunday morning, while he cut my hair, my mother sat in the sun nearby, reading the newspaper. Nappi kept up a running chatter for her benefit.

'Your son is now a mature, responsible man,' he said. 'But when he was a student here, he was a rascal. He would never sit still in my chair while I cut his hair.' I suddenly realized that Sukh Ram could not be assumed to be a walking encyclopedia of Sanawar history or a bridge between the past and the present. All his stories needed to be taken with more than a pinch of salt. You see, while I was in school, I had never been to him because I had long hair and a turban.

**Dr Harishpal S. Dhillon**
UD | Nilagiri 1957 | 1949–1957
STAFF 1971–1986 | HOD English | Housemaster | Headmaster 1995–1999 | Headmaster YPS Patiala 1986–1995 | YPS Mohali 1999–2010

OS Sibling – Sister – Yogindra (Dhillon) | Nilagiri 1956 | 1951–1956

OS Children – Daughter – Priya Dhillon | Himalaya 1988 | 1979–1988
             Daughter – Naina Dhillon | Himalaya 1988 | 1979–1988
             Son – Jai Singh Dhillon | Nilagiri 1991 | 1982–1989

OS Grandchildren – Granddaughter – Mannat Tipnis | Himalaya 2013 | 2006–2013
             Grandson – Abhay Tipnis | Himalaya 2017 | 2009–2011
             Granddaughter – Inaaya Kumar | Himalaya | 2018–To Date
             Grandson – Rehaan Kumar | Himalaya | 2020–To Date

**Source and Acknowledgements:**
Published as a Middle in *The Tribune* on 11 December 2006 and reproduced in *Of Cabbages and Kings – A Book of Middles*, (New Delhi: Picus Books, Hay House Publishers India, 2014).

1964 Final year Students group

Dear my Children,

This is the year 1964. I have entered my 36th year in life. This means I am close to your double of your age. Finishing the schooling, you are now due to leave Sanawar.

You have added to that 50 years — the most productive years of your life. All of you as of now, must have crossed 65 years of age. Those of you who joined service must have retired, now leading a peaceful retired life. In business and manufacturing industry, one never retires.

You have given me the privilege of to address you all as my children. This way I come closer to you, with greater affection. I am trying to recollect myself, as I was in 1964, especially in the nature of my thought processes, in particular as a teacher.

Some of you carried conspicuous talents, and forbearance. You then showed great patience, and sound integrity, and a very high sense of honesty. I have learned a great deal, from you all.

In 1973, I took over, in the office; though it was necessary for me to do so, I greatly missed

257

teaching. My association with the children was was broken, & and I missed my games and sports.

I joined Sanawar in March 1953. I took over Housemastership in Sept 1957. I retired as Bursar in Aug. 1992.

I have learned that there is no profession in the world, more rewarding than teaching, especially in a residential school of Sanawar type, where children respond to discipline like the magnetic needle.

My fortune that brought me to Sanawar, a hill-top, where I spent some 40 years, the most pleasant time of my life. I am living in Baroda, with my son; he is in Merchant Navy; he has set up an establishment in this city; his family (with 2 daughters) live in this city. I am running 87th year of my life, engaged with finding an answer to the unswered question: "Where do I go and with WHOM!"

———— x ———— M.V. Gore

18 - 21 - 2015

**Madhav Vishwanath Gore**
Staff 1953–1992
Mathematics teacher | Housemaster 1957–1973 | School Bursar 1973–1992

Spouse – Sunanda Gore | House Matron 1963–1992

OS Children – Daughter – Indurekha (Gore) Prakash | Vindhya 1972 | 1962–1972

Son – Anirudh Gore | Siwalik 1972 | 1962–1972

Daughter – Varsha (Gore) Dharwadkar | Vindhya 1976 | 1966–1976

Daughter – Meera (Gore) Oke | Vindhya 1977 | 1967–1977

Daughter – Saisha (Gore) Khanna | Himalaya 1986 | 1976–1986

Son-in-law – Mohit Khanna | Himalaya 1985 | 1976–1985

OS Granddaughters – Gunjali (Trikha) Rana | Vindhya 1998 | 1989–1993

Shalghniya Khanna | Himalaya 2003 | 2002–2003

# Sanawar – A Dream

My father, Mr U.A. Mundkur came to Sanawar in March 1957. It seems like a dream when I think of the chain of events.

One afternoon, a stocky guy came looking for my dad. Instead of calling him into the House, Dad walked down to his office. He painted a vivid picture of this place he wanted to take us to. This was Dad's interview. That man was Mr J.K. Kate.

Dad was happy, but a bit vary about the prospects. Dad had only one thing in his mind and that was to give the best education to his kids. So he decided to give it a try. He came to Sanawar. He was enamoured by the grandeur of Sanawar and stayed on. Two months later, my mother Mrs K.U. Mundkur, brother Vivek and I followed him there.

Dad was a man of simple habits and high thinking. Teaching was his passion and he loved to play outdoor sports. He was basically a cricket player (best all-rounder) from Bombay University's Wilson College.

We arrived in this heaven. Dad was allotted a British-style villa at the Garden City. We were thrilled with the surroundings. Vivek and I enjoyed running around the villa, though it wasn't so great walking up a steep slope four times a day, sometimes accompanied by monkeys. First year of school was tough for me as I was from a vernacular school.

Winter vacations of 1958 were a great experience—the first time I saw snow. One cold snowy evening, Major Som Dutt and Mr Kate trudged down to Garden City to offer the matron's post to Mom. Nervously, she accepted. She was nervous because she was not fluent in English. In the remaining two months, Dad had made my mother a master in English. Thereafter, she could write a loving letter to the Quarter Master or bullshit her way through anything. At this stage, I was shunted off to GD dorm.

In the years that rolled by, I had very good friends and a very strict but loving and compassionate House mistress.

One Sunday morning late-rouser, two of my friends and I had a brilliant idea. We gathered our blankets and pillows, jumped out of the bathroom ventilators to go and sit in the warm sun on the Chuna-room roof. We had just about perched cosily in the sun, when Mrs Able, our matron, and Croaky, the sweeper woman, arrived. Before we could scramble, they caught us by the scuff of our necks and we found ourselves in front of Mrs Kemp. We three were petrified. Ma'am took charge of us and asked us why we had been so foolish as to get 'caught'. She made some hot Bournvita for us and sent us back. Thereafter, extra bars were fixed on ventilators.

Several years later, my daughter, Arati worked as a matron in GD. My granddaughter had told her friends of the 'masti' I had done, and the resultant bars on the bathroom ventilators.

Anyhow, the Mundkur family holds a record of sorts—four generations associated with Sanawar.

Life goes on, leaving you with beautiful memories.

**Aruna (Mundkur) Kodical**
Siwalik 1964 | 1957–1964

Parents – Father – Umesh Anand Mundkur | Staff 1956–1981 | Biology
          Teacher | Cricket & Athletics Coach | Housemaster
          Mother – Kumud Mundkur | Staff 1957–1981 | Matron

OS Sibling – Brother – Vivek Umesh Mundkur | Siwalik 1961 | 1957–1961

# The House System

The Rev. G.D. Barne (Principal) made a firm decision, one of many, and in this case, he even decided to take the first step, introducing the public school system of Houses in place of the prevailing military division of the Boys' School into Companies. Nothing else was to be changed, just names for letters. And the names . . . military, of course . . . and what a wonderful selection.

The erstwhile 'band' Company became Lawrence House after the Founder. 'A' Company enjoyed reflected glory in the accomplishments of Lord Roberts of Kandahar. Then came two names that were inseparable in the formation of Indian history—Sir Herbert Edwardes and Sir John Nicholson guided 'B' and 'C' Company, respectively. Lastly, who better than Hodson of Hodson's Horse to take over 'D' Company. He built Sanawar and these buildings that stand today.

Sir Henry Lawrence—no pen can do him more service than what is already carved in cold marble beside his bust in the School Chapel. Sanawarians, if you haven't already done so, go there and read. If you have done so, go again and be refreshed.

Lord Roberts of Kandahar (1832–1914) was Commander-in-Chief in India, a position that crowned forty years of devoted service to the country. Kipling, in the same book in which he wrote, 'We will make a man of him in Sanawar', wrote of him as 'Bobs Bahadur'.

Frederick Sleigh Roberts, Earl of Kandahar, Pretoria and Waterford, was born in Cawnpore. He went to the same school as the Rev. G.D. Barne, viz., Clifton, and then went on to Eton and Sandhurst. He entered the Bengal Artillery in 1851 and took an active part in raising the siege of Delhi and was also at the relief of Lucknow. He won the Victoria Cross for Gallantry in 1858. As a Major-General in the Afghan War in 1878, he forced the seemingly impregnable fortress at Perivai Kotul. He finally defeated the Afghans at Charasa, took possession of Kabul and assumed the government.

Two years later, on 9 August 1880 he set out on the memorable march that led to numerous legends being wound round his head. Short, wiry, dapper, his spirit was indomitable and it was infectious. His force of 10,000 marched through Afghanistan to the relief of Kandahar. The march was completed in three weeks and the enemy was routed. After a short spell as C–in–C Madras Army, he was appointed C–in–C India.

The troubles facing the British in the early stages of the Boer War faded when 'Bobs Bahadur' assumed chief command. He returned to England after the relief of Kimberley in 1901 to become C–in–C. He retired in 1904. Mahatma Gandhi visited him in 1914 and taking the advice of his friend regarding his health, the Mahatma returned to India to recuperate. 'Bobs Bahadur' died in Flanders Field while visiting troops, in the early stages of World War I.

Sir Herbert Edwardes and Sir John Nicholson, together with the Founder, were known as the 'Titans of Punjab'. The three worked closely together. Sir Henry was their mentor in the years of successful administration of Punjab. Both Sir Herbert and Sir John shared Sir Henry's mantle of conduct—'. . . to do as much justice as possible in judicial matters, under the trees, before the people. In material improvements, to go ahead at a tremendous pace and cover the country with roads, bridges, etc. In policy, to be very conciliatory, very friendly. Promptness, accessibility, brevity and kindliness to be the best engines of government. To have as few forms as possible. To be considerate and kind, not expecting too much from poorly educated people. To make no changes unless certain of decided improvement . . .'

There was warm love between these men of more than mortal stature; they were knit together into one family by their work, by their fierce restraint and by their puritanical religion. 'Next to his mother, John's (Nicholson) thoughts turned towards you,' wrote a mutual friend to Sir Herbert. Wrote Sir Henry to Sir John, 'Let me advise you as a friend to bear, and to forbear. I think you have done much towards conquering yourself and I hope to see the conquest completed'. Wrote Sir Herbert to Sir John, 'What a loss we have sustained in our very dear friend (Sir Henry). How his great purposes and fiery will and general impulses and strong passions raged in him . . .' And, said Honoria Lawrence to her husband of Sir John as she lay dying, 'Tell him I love him as dearly as if he were my son, tell him I love him very much'. Finally, Sir Henry writing to them both, 'Daily and nightly she talks of you and of the others of the Punjab as her sons and brothers'.

## Sir Herbert Edwards (1819–1868)

Soon after the new protectorate system began in the Punjab, the Council of Elders suggested to Sir Henry that it was time to send an army to Bannu. Sir Henry would agree only on condition that a British political officer went with them, to settle a reasonable revenue and to get the Bannuchis to pay it without coercion. The Sikh elders smiled in their long grey beards. They said that a political officer was welcome to try.

Herbert Edwardes, the political officer chosen, was still a lieutenant, not yet thirty years old. He was used to working for Sir Henry, even so, it seemed to him that what he was now asked to do was difficult. He was expected to reach a settlement with a people utterly untamed, a thing neither Greek, Afghan nor Sikh had done, and in barely six weeks. He was in the valley from 15 March to 1 May, when the sun burnt them out, but on this first brief visit, he achieved a good deal. He wrote, 'I look back to these months in Bannu as the hardest grind I ever endured. But the peace that ensued came home to so many and the cultivation it permitted sprang up and flourished so rapidly under the genial sun, that one's good wishes seemed overheard by angels and carried out upon the spot before charity grew cold.'

## Sir John Nicholson (1822–1857)

Sir Henry Lawrence, as Resident, kept a guiding hand on Sikh affairs, while his young men, including Herbert Edwardes and John Nicholson, scoured the country, advising, exhorting and from time to time firmly and without any authority taking things into their own hands, and administering. 'The protection of people against oppression will be your first duty,' wrote Sir Henry to Nicholson. Sir John's administration of Bannu was a golden age when there was less need to punish for theft or murder than for paying divine honours to a ruler who did not care for them. He could not prevent his apotheosis and a religious community known as the Nikal-Seyni Faquirs, lasted at least ten years after his death.

Sir John was reported by the Board in the following terms, 'He saw that substantial justice should be plainly dealt out to a simple people, unused to the intricacies of legal proceedings. His aim was to avoid all technicality, circumlocution and obscurity; to simplify and abridge every rule, procedure and process. To form tribunals which were not hedged in with forms unintelligible to the vulgar and only to be interpreted by professional lawyers, but which shall be open and accessible to a Court of Justice where every man may plead his own case, be confronted face to face with his opponents, may prosecute his own claim or conduct his own defence.' That Sir John adhered to the admonition given him by Sir Henry is clearly found in what he wrote after the Battle of Gujarat, 'I have allowed all the prisoners made after the action to go quietly to their homes'—a merciful and chivalrous man.

Yet, a decisive mind forced him to take a risk when troops mutinied in Nowshera and he ordered their disarming. 'As we rode down to the disarming, a very few chiefs or yeomen of the country attended us and I remember judging from their faces that they came to see which way the tide would turn. As we rode back, friends were as thick as summer flied and levies became from time to come in.' It was a triumph for the policy of the risk taken by the throat.

The crisis at Delhi in 1987 forced Sir John southwards and he led the storming party to raise the siege, but he himself was mortally wounded.

## Major William S.R. Hodson (1821–1858)

William Hodson joined the Indian Army in 1845. He possessed many talents and soon came under the notice of Sir Henry Lawrence. One of the talents was engineering and in 1847, Sir Henry trusted him with the erection of the first buildings in Sanawar. These still stand, eloquent of the high standard employed by Hodson. His military duties saw him serving in the first Sikh War with great distinction and some years later, he took command of the North West Frontier Guides.

He was the fourth of that famous quartet to be recalled to the crisis in Delhi and he became head of the intelligence service. He raised the irregular cavalry known as 'Hodson's Horse' and formed part of the relieving force at Lucknow. He was mortally wounded on 11 March 1858 and died the day after. Sir Henry's own death shroud seemed to cover him as well as Sir John Nicholson.

The principal had chosen wisely—the five were leaders, selfless, devoted, loyal; and all-embracing as the School Anthem is the memory of the five, ever part of the line that forms the title of the anthem: 'Let us now praise famous men'. The words were sung fortissimo by a full choir and later in the anthem, the soprano solo echoed the words, 'There be of them

that have left a name behind them, that their praises might be reported.'
So be it, their names live as durable and as firm as the majestic ranges that
have taken their place—Himalaya, Nilagiri, Vindhya, Siwalik. These are
forever India – so in the memory of five famous men – forever India.

House Colours

| | |
|---|---|
| Lawrence | Yellow |
| Roberts | Dark Blue |
| Herbert Edwardes | Red |
| Nicholson | Light Blue |
| Hodson | Green |

**William H. 'Bill' Colledge (Bilkul)**
Old Sanawarian (Roberts 1917–1927)

**Source and Acknowledgement:** *The Sanawarian* (December 1972)

# The Robbed That Smile

It was not for nothing that Shakespeare wrote in *Othello*, 'The robbed that smiles steals something from the thief.'

During my final year at Sanawar, we were trying to revive relations with the Round Square International Service (RSIS), a popular initiative amidst public schools in India and abroad, to promote International Understanding. The RSIS hosts exchange programs, conferences and projects across the world to support communities in need. Although Sanawar is one of its founding members, it was beginning to lose its decision-making capacity in the year 2000.

We had a British Headmaster Mr Andrew Gray, who like all headmasters, was fondly addressed as Heady. He is a distinguished Fellow of the Royal Society of Arts (FRSA) and interestingly, by academic specialization, an accomplished pianist. His wide exposure allowed him to communicate in a manner and language that was beyond the execution capability of most of his contemporaries.

I was MI Prefect, number three in the prefectorial hierarchy, and Heady and I often discussed issues such as these. In a few months, we uncovered that two exchange students, girls from a reputed South African school transferred to a developed nation, were being discriminated against on the basis of their colour. Their performance and health were deteriorating because of the emotional turmoil, and with that, their merit of representing their school and country in another nation was being dishonoured.

Heady saw this as a well-meaning opportunity and wrote to his counterpart in South Africa. He did not mince a single word while stating, 'Let the exchange opportunity of these children not go waste. Send them to India and Sanawar will look after them. Please remember, we have lost relations with the RSIS. Should the children wish to be with us, the RSIS and your school would owe us a favour.'

The leadership and students in the South African school appreciated a proposal as truthful and candid as that. Their happiness knew no bounds

amidst all the admonition they continued to face. The fear of discrimination ebbed away as the students prepared to live their dream and flew to India.

With time and experiences, the girl students groomed themselves into women of substance. Currently, they are teaching communication and imagination in a special school in the same country where they were discriminated against. Their single greatest achievement so far is that they have brought two differently abled children back into the mainstream. Where the rest would be lead is unimaginable. One of those children is the daughter of a former discriminator of theirs.

The robbed smile through their lives with hearts of gold, fulfillment and honour, being referred to as the godmothers of the special child.

**Maneet Singh Sarla**
Nilagiri 2001 | 1995–2001
Education and Publishing Consultant

OS Sibling – Brother – Prabhjit Singh Sarla | Nilagiri 2008 | 2000–2005

# A Passing Thought

My first impression of Sanawar is still fresh in my mind. The same cool breeze among deodar, fir and chir trees greets me affectionately whenever I step out for a stroll in this fascinating place. My memory goes back to the good old days, when we lived like a joint family with boys and girls, teachers and administrative staff.

The murmuring of pine trees fills my thoughts as I look through the cirrus at Monkey Point. Reaching the Quadrangle, I hear the boys' ammunition boots marching to Birdwood, passing by the Chapel and War Memorial. The rich voice, like a general's, of the Head Boy, Macintosh, commanding 'Eyes Left', still echoes and vibrates through the Golden Staircase. E.A. Rhind, the Head Girl, follows with the girls' squad, also saluting the Memorial smartly.

I see Sam Cowell, Cuzens, Paige, Trevor Kemp, Virendra Vyas, Bhuppi, Saleem Khan emerging from their houses and heading to Birdwood. As also, Romola Chatterjee, Piloo Rudra, Alice Sircar and Pam Ahuja from the other side of the hill. The school bell rings. Assembly starts. The notes of the piano are drowned by Sam Cowell's voice . . .

'All things bright and beautiful,
All creatures great and small,
All things wise and wonderful,
The Lord God made them all.'

Did C.F. Alexander have Sanawar on his mind while penning this?

The loveliness of our surroundings cannot but have an effect on the impressionable minds of children in our care. Here, the picturesque merges with the splendid, the radiant with the sublime. Beauty, elegance and grace bloom around us. We live in an aesthete's paradise. Beauty is a child's heritage; to see, to feel, to express beauty, to own lovely things and to live in beautiful surroundings, to appreciate the exquisite and the dainty.

These rights of children will be enjoyed more fully if we can give them our wholehearted sympathy, understanding and guidance.

I still remember the creative work of some of the budding artists – Harprit Gill was one of our more mature artists. His pastel and oil paintings showed great promise; Sita Bhai was a dancer of repute and an actress of ability, and her paintings often drew inspiration from the stage or ballet; Aditya Nehru was a budding portrait painter and did some good likenesses of his teachers and fellow students. His pen-and-ink work is characterized by its detail; Nanda Cariappa preferred naval battle scenes (in spite of his army upbringing). His portraits showed promise; others whose works were displayed at successful art exhibitions in Amritsar, New Delhi and Calcutta include Ashok Desraj, Brijinder Singh Bala, Gay Butler, Gita Bery, Gurdip Singh Bedi, Gurdip Singh Kalyana, Kulbir Singh Soin, Aruna Vasudev, Doreen Field, Yograj Palta, Suresh Mallick, Harjeet Kochhar and Bul Bul Singh.

I conclude by narrating an amusing incident. The annual auditors arrived to inspect the accounts. They objected to 'missing' cricket balls being written-off in the books and expected them to be collected somewhere for inspection, before being replaced. Cuzens, in-charge of cricket, was asked to answer to the auditors' objection. He first served them a large meal and then took them down to Barnes, asking some of us to join him. Quickly setting the field, he proceeded to demonstrate how cricket was played at Sanawar. I bowled to him and he hit the ball so hard, that it went over the iron net and down the khud . . . down, down, down, perhaps all the way to Kalka. Cuzens pulled more than a dozen balls over the net and then informed the auditors that when a ball gets lost, it takes its skin with it. Therefore, missing balls are written-off in the books. The poor auditors, after that hearty meal, had to trudge up the steep hill from Barnes.

We took the shortcut and had a good laugh, applauding Cuzens' presence of mind and wit.

**Rathin Mitra**
ART MASTER | 1950–1953
Head of Art Department – Daly College Indore (1949-50), The Lawrence School Sanawar (1950-53), St. Paul Darjeeling (1954-55), Doon School (1955-1981). Also taught at Bryanstan Public School, Dorset, England on a teacher exchange program, in 1959.

Among India's eminent Artists – Visual Essayist, Writer and Teacher; The Youngest elected member of The Calcutta Group at twenty-one years in 1948; A prolific traveler and explorer, dedicating the last forty years of his life documenting in pen and ink line drawings (his signature style), the heritage buildings of India (mostly Kolkata); Created the longest mural (312 feet) at Air India building, Nariman Point, Bombay; The first living Artist to have exhibited in the Victoria Memorial Hall (1983–1984); Oil paintings displayed in the National Gallery of Modern Art, New Delhi.

# The Last Bastion

'Send him to Sanawar and make a man of him', wrote Joseph Rudyard Kipling, in 1901, in his book *Kim*. Seventy-five years later – on Tuesday, 17 February 1976 – I read it for the first time, written in red bold letters on a white wooden plank, perched high on the Gaskell Hall wall. I couldn't help but wonder why Kipling had said so. What was it about Sanawar that had prompted this distinction? How could he be so certain? By merely admitting me here, how did my parents know that I would learn and imbibe all that there was to, in order to metamorphose into a man? How did one become a man? Didn't everyone, in time, anyway grow up to be a man (or woman), or was there more to it? Imagine my dilemma, away from the safety and solace of home for the first time in eleven years, intrigued by countless uncertainties thus triggered by one seemingly straightforward, innocuous sentence: 'Send him to Sanawar, and make a man of him.'

I did not get to meet Rudyard, and so could never figure out why *he* had said it. However, it was still in the early days when I comprehended the how one was made a man of him. For those who studied in Sanawar between the '50s and the '80s, the one name that not just epitomized the maxim (coined by the illustrious novelist), but that single-handedly sculpted the moral fibre and instilled the value of true character within the students – honesty and integrity; discipline and courage; valour and camaraderie; justice, equality and fairplay – was Bhupinder Singh Rathore, aka Mr B. Singh to one and all, and Mucchoo (in whispered references). It is to Rudyard Kipling's credit that he wrote those words without having had the *kismet* to have met Mucchoo, who made Sanawar the very core of his existence for forty-two years with dedication and selflessness. Joining in 1951 as a young sprightly Assistant Master, he was elevated to Housemaster, Himalaya House in 1953 and took over the reins in 1973, from Mr Trevor Kemp (another stalwart and DHM since 1962), adeptly serving in that role till his retirement in 1993.

It was easy to mistake Mucchoo for God as he was omnipresent across the 139-acre picturesque campus. Come rain, hail or snow, the Rouser bugle went off at 5.45 a.m. As you ran out for PT squad formation, he would be standing, leaning against the Gaskell Hall pillar. That was his first sighting of the day. Two drags later, he would stub his filter-less Charminar and commence his inspection of each PT shoe to check whether it was 'properly' polished or not. When in the slightest of doubt, he would ask the boy to stamp his foot hard on the pavement, and if powder emitted from the shoe, he would receive a well-deserved whack. While House squads began the PT table, he would inspect the dormitories, checking on the 'sweepers', and return to each House to check on the PT.

On one such morning, in August 1982, when I was House Captain, he took me aside and quipped, 'The person you told to make your bed, *forgot!*' I tried to assure him that there was no such person and that I'd woken up five minutes late and that was the reason—but he cut me short, 'Never mind, make sure he doesn't forget again', and walked away.

Half an hour later, he was at the vantage point outside his residence (aptly called the Tiger's Den), as one marched past him. After the first school, at the fall-in for breakfast, you could see him from the corner of your eye. As you walked into the Dining Hall, in single file, he would be standing near the food counter, ensuring pin-drop silence before grace was said. He then did the rounds to ensure that no one missed out on one's rightful share of the cold, lumpy, tasteless porridge. It was only post Assembly, from the second school till lunch, that one got some respite – i.e., if one managed to keep out of trouble during classes. Given his already chock-a-block schedule, he rarely took classes, but there would be one or two 'lucky' sections (usually L-V onwards) that he'd teach. Dictating notes, he would go, 'The Romans, yes, were great warriors, yes . . .'

Post lunchtime was hectic. Boxing or gymnastics at Gaskell Hall; cricket nets at staff courts or Bottleneck; 'full' games at Barnes, New Field or Lower Barnes; hobbies – art, bamboo work, clay sculpturing, papier maché, batik, ceramics, carpentry, Indian classical music and dance, piano, weaving and needlework, photography, bugle and brass band, poultry farming – a wide array of skills that one could chose to acquire; and, finally NCC with rifles. No matter where you were, he would find you. It was said that Mucchoo never turned around and that one could follow him all the way, without being caught. However, it remained folklore and nobody dared to push their luck.

Evening Prep meant, once again, forming squads and marching up. To come to think of it, we rarely 'walked', either we marched or we ran. Going up the Tuck Shop slope, we crossed the Chapel, did a '*baye dekh*' at the War Memorial, were dismissed at the Golden Staircase and ran up to the Cannons, as the prefect shouted, 'Last guy up, see me tonight'. On days when there was no prep work to do, one could read a novel (neatly tucked into a textbook) or simply idle away time playing Book Cricket. All this went on till 6.43 p.m. when the guy on watch either coughed or cleared his throat to signal Mucchoo's arrival. Each classroom had a fixed time. For once, he was predictable and never late or early. In that minute or so, while he went around the class, all storybooks were put away and everyone would be seen 'seriously' studying. End of prep [time] meant falling into queue in front of the school bell and walking into the CDH in single file.

So, the day began with Mucchoo, standing against the Gaskell Hall pillar at PT and ended with his round, to the dorms past 'lights-out'. There was no escape whatsoever. He even visited the Hospital wards to check if your fever had come down.

He bid you farewell each Home Day, disappointed at having to let you go. Come School Day, he would be all excited and raring to go, waiting for the school parties at the B.D. Quad, rejuvenated after the holiday break, ready to counter any 'pandemonium' and end up 'knocking the living daylights out of the bloody nincompoops'. Through all this, probably the only stillness that he permitted himself was to settle down on the cushioned bench in the quaint, old-world Pavilion at Barnes, on a brilliantly sunlit Sunday morning, immersing himself in a game of cricket.

As all good things must come to an end, so did the best days of our (Class of 1983) lives. Farewells galore – House party, school Socials, Heady's dinner and breakfast at Tiger's Den. And then, the last hour before the bus would take us away. With sorrow-filled hearts and lumps in our throats, some of us clicked open the brass doorknob and walked down the curved stairway of Tiger's Den, one last time. Mucchoo, a little teary-eyed himself, but not one to display emotion, managed a smile and hugged us. We pulled out our autograph books and he painstakingly wrote personal notes for each of us. Walking out, I opened my book to read what he had said. All the lessons learnt over the last seven years seemed somewhat trivial in comparison to his parting diktat, imprinted in his inimitable handwriting—'As you have played on the playfields of Sanawar, play, and play it fair in the game of life.'

Thank you, Sir. You continue to live on, in our hearts and souls, and will always guide us truly till the game is through, and for time, the whistle blows . . . till the last bugle call!

In closing, I would like to say that Kipling was a tad off the mark. So let me rephrase the adage for him – 'Send him to Mucchoo, and he'll make a man of him'.

**Pankaj Sapru**
Himalaya 1983 | 1976–1983
Senior Management – Petroleum Downstream sector | Travel & Street Photographer | Member – OSS Executive Committee 2019–21 | Vice President – OSS 2021–23

OS Sibling – Brother – Dhiraj Sapru | Himalaya 1985 | 1977–1985

# Endless Adventures

**A Trip to Kasauli:** We would start after Sunday breakfast with a 'to-go' lunch, courtesy Mrs Sehgal. Pocket money was a handsome sum of Rs 1, and that would be all the money we had to spend. The walk to Garkhal was easy, followed by the more challenging climb up the hill to Kasauli. The first stop was usually Daily Needs, with their renowned ham and cheese sandwiches. A luxury which only a few could afford. The precious Rs 1 pocket money was spent on a movie ticket, a samosa with chutney, *aampapdi* and bubblegum—a sumptuous meal. We could only afford the cheapest movie tickets and had to fight our way into the theatre to bag the best seats. Needless to say, we were always in the front three rows and too close to the screen. After the movie, we would started the trek back to Sanawar. Along the way, we enacted the movie scenes and quoted the movie's dialogues. The road back to Sanawar from Garkhal was steep and usually covered in silence.

**Bhutta and Nashpaati:** During the Bhutta (corn) and Nashpaati (pear) season, we would head off to trade with the farmers of village Sanawara. The favoured item of barter, for the villagers, were tennis shoes. While most kids transacted honestly, there were a few who would raid. Mr Kemp always got to hear the 'breaking news', and justice for the guilty was swift and painful.

**Collecting Pinecones:** When the weather started to change and evenings became cold, it was time to collect pinecones from the khudside below Barnes. Pillowcases came in handy and served as convenient containers for hauling the pinecones back to the dorms. Of course, the pillowcases were very itchy until the next issue of linens. On Saturday nights, typically, friends and foes came together to enjoy a cracking, warm fire. 'Doggie biscuits' swiped from the Dining Hall, 'orange drink' and 'baked beans' from the Tuck Shop, purchased with pooled resources, made for a lovely

feast. These were some of our best times there which are forever etched in my memory.

**Home Day – Walking To The Kalka Railway Station:** Another favourite activity was to walk down to the Kalka railway station. There were at least three routes to consider. The most popular being the dirt road from Kasauli. A second, not-so-popular option was to go to Monkey's Point and rough it down the hill from there in the general direction of Kalka. The third option was the least popular and most interesting option. It involved a walk through the Koti Tunnel – the second longest straight railway tunnel on the Kalka–Simla track, being over a kilometre in length. The one and only time that we took that route, we were well into the tunnel when we heard the rumbling of a train entering the tunnel. The tunnel opening closed off and only the train's headlights were visible. We panicked and ran for the tunnel exit. Fortunately, we had already traversed three quarters of the tunnel. All but two of our group made it out of the tunnel. These two had found a wide spot in the tunnel to wait out the passing of the train. We had been terrified our companions had been run over and spent anxious minutes waiting for the train to manoeuvre its way out of the tunnel.

**Annual School Camp:** The school camp, held at the banks of the Giri River, was indeed a memorable event. The entire School – boys, girls and staff – attended. The weather was warm, the water was cool, and hours spent hiking up and down the river were great fun. The best part of it all was the singing by the campfires. It was wonderful—cool evenings, a crackling campfire and the lovely voices of kids singing. I distinctly remember Virender Singh V-66 and Ranjit Nagrath S-64 singing romantic songs and touching the heart of many a fair maiden.

**Movie Nights:** Movies were screened in Barnes Hall on a single 16mm projector. When a reel finished, there was a break while Mr Mukherji switched reels. Sometimes, the film wouldn't wrap around the spool and fell to the floor. Occasionally, the film would break and Mr Mukherji would scramble to address the problem. During these breaks, the din would reach a high pitch and continue even after the screening resumed. The Head Boy would then yell, 'QUIET' at the top of his lungs, and there would be pin-drop silence. After the movie, we would exit Barnes in an orderly fashion. As we walked back to the dorms, the conversation centred around the movie—the dialogue, the mystery, the plot and enactment of the same. On occasion, a student would pick up a nickname from the movie because of a random event or likeness to a character. A batchmate is called 'Abdullah', even sixty years later.

**House, School and Staff Plays:** We were fortunate to be exposed to and act in plays at Sanawar. Participating in plays, be they Prep School, House or school show plays was part of the Sanawarian experience. Learning to play musical instruments, singing, dancing and acting were skills all students were expected to possess. Our teachers excelled at drama, music and dance, and helped prepare for the Saturday night event. By far the most enjoyable was the staff play. Bhupinder Singh, Mr and Mrs Kemp, and many of other staff members whose acting was memorable, were well-loved and appreciated by the students.

**Zafarullah Khan**
Zafar | Siwalik 1965 | 1957–1965
Landed in the US (BS Chemical Engineering, University of Nevada; MBA, Washington University) with $200 and a semester's fees | Brought parents to the US for mom's successful open-heart surgery | Worked for forty years in positions of increasing responsibility in Africa, Asia, Australia, Europe, North and South America for Monsanto and Coca-Cola | Served as President IFN | Chairman of the Board ECIC | Board of Directors, Amana Academy | Semi-retired | Consultant.

# The Red Armchair

It was a wingback armchair made in the seventies – yellow and brown, striped vinyl, stretched over a wood frame on yellow-painted wooden legs. It probably sat in a room with a shag carpet for years before it was covered with a bright red corduroy fabric. The fabric was dusty, the edges frayed. I wondered how many garage sales it had been in before I saw it sitting in the corner of a House on a wet Saturday afternoon in the mid-1990s. I was immediately drawn to it. I paid the full asking price and took it home.

The red armchair went by the fireplace in the kitchen. Almost immediately, it became a jungle gym for the not-quite-five-year-old Bani. She would bring her toys and books and scatter them around, and then climb up onto the seat clutching her pink *niny kamball* (blanket). While our youngest daughter, Preeti, only months old at the time, would be napping. I would tuck Bani and Simi, our middle daughter, in on either side of me and, with dogs curled up at my feet and my arms around each of the girls, I would open a book on my lap and read to them. Bani would point to pictures and chatter about her version of what was happening, while two-year-old Simi would lean into the curve of my body, her little fingers stroking my earlobes, content to just lie there. It became a ritual; all three of us cradled in the arms of that red chair. It would take another three decades to understand why I was drawn to that chair.

For most of my childhood and all of my teen years, I lived in a dormitory in a boarding school with sixty other girls. It was a long, two-storey building made of wood. Wildfires came close to destroying it, one year. The smell of smoke and the tense excitement of that night is still with me; but I digress. The Nilagirians and Himalayans slept on the top floor and Siwalikans and Vindhyans on the bottom floor. I was in Nilagiri House. There were four rows of beds. Each bed had a little cupboard next to it, where we kept everything we were allowed to have, and even some things we were not allowed to have. Now and then, our House mistress, Miss Ling, would conduct surprise checks to see how clean they were.

Once, a nest of tiny baby mice was discovered in one of those cupboards. Some of us thought it was the cutest thing, while others complained about how dirty the person was. I don't think she ever lived that down.

Beds lined up from north to south, two rows for each House—bathrooms and stockroom on the North end and Miss Ling's suite of rooms overlooking Peacestead on the South end. The Eastern and Western walls had many windows. I don't remember the curtains. I do remember how the sun setting behind the Himalayan peaks transformed the dorm into a bright orange universe at dusk—every single object ablaze. Some afternoons, I lay on my stomach watching the edge of shadows move along the wooden floor boards. I notice such things; I always have.

Adults referred to me as a 'sensitive' child. It scared me, because it sounded like a reprimand and I didn't understand what they were disapproving of. I was maybe five, when I first talked to my father about this. I came home from pre-school in a bad mood that day. Ayah was fussing over me trying to get me to eat Marie biscuits and drink a glass of milk on the porch, when my father asked what was wrong. My teacher had been mean to me, she had used this word and I didn't like the way it had made me feel. 'Don't listen to her,' he said, 'she doesn't know what she is talking about.' He brought his bearded face close to mine and tweaked my nose. And then he swung me out of my chair and threw me up in the air. I flew upward, too surprised to be scared before tumbling down into the safety of his arms. An unforgettable, exhilarating experience. Teacher forgotten, everything made sense in my world again.

The idea that 'sensitivity' was not desirable was reinforced in school. I was ten, maybe eleven, years old, when our House mistress pulled me out of class one day and admonished me to 'not be so sensitive'. There was that word again. I had no idea what she was referring to and was too afraid to ask. My life had changed dramatically by then. Papa ji had died a few years earlier. The world no longer made sense in the way it once had. Adults were inconsistent, unpredictable and dangerous. They confused and scared me. Contrary to what my father had said, their opinion mattered and they hurt you if you challenged them. I had retreated into the shadows and learned to be quiet, compliant, and vigilant.

A few days after this event, I was alone in my dorm. It was the rare afternoon where I had nowhere to be. I had just returned from the library with an arm-full of books. Mostly Nancy Drews and The Famous Four, but Mr G.C. Arora, our librarian and my personal hero, snuck in some

P.G. Wodehouse. I made myself comfortable on my bed and opened a P.G. Wodehouse.

One moment I was reading words on the page and the next, I was flying in the air—blue skies, sunshine on my face, and wind in my hair. My stomach dropped into my toes and I squealed with delight as I circled above the clouds. Below me were green fields dotted with white mounds, which could only be sheep grazing, I thought. I flew over a stone House with a quintessential British thatched roof. A man wearing a hat came out the front door and waved at me, as if it was the most normal thing to do. And yet, how could this be? I looked down at my hands and they rested on the armrest of a large red wingback chair. And just like that, I was back in my bed in the dorm again. The only evidence of my adventure was a heart beating so hard, it threatened to jump out of my chest and a huge smile on my face. Over the next few years, I had many adventures in that red chair. Each one joyous and every single one connected in some way to a book I was reading.

The daydreams stopped just as suddenly as they had started. Perhaps puberty and boys had something to do with that. But for many years, I forgot the days I flew in the arms of a red armchair.

**Dr Mininder Kaur**
Mini | Nilagiri 1975 | 1966–1975
King George's Medical College, Lucknow | PG Internal Medicine | Practicing Zen Buddhist | Trained Soto Zen Chaplain | WHO Community Health & Development volunteer – Haiti, S. Africa, Zimbabwe

OS Siblings – Sister – Rupinder Kaur | Pedro | Nilagiri 1968 | 1966–1968
Sister – Navneet Kaur | Neeti | Nilagiri 1977 | 1968–1977

# Friday, The 13th

On one of the rare occasions that my name was entered into the dreaded 'red book' that contained the names of every day's petty criminals for their slight misdemeanours, I reported to BD quad in front of Gaskell Hall at 9:40 a.m., as soon as study hour ended, for drill. The purpose of drill was to atone for our crimes by facing the punishment (Dostoevsky would be proud). We were ordered to run a circuitous route that took us up the steep flagstone stairway from the BD quad. It was a covered staircase that began right next to the scaled-down battleship replica and the full-sized body of a fighter jet. At the middle of this stairway, there was a path that led to the War Memorial and the Chapel. Our route involved taking a left at the Chapel, running down the slope in front of Tuck Shop and back to BD quad, and then the final sprint to Gaskell Hall could begin. The masters of the drill would decide who was to be let off and who had to repeat the circuit, depending on two factors: the perceived heinousness of our 'crime', and our relative finishing position vis-á-vis our compatriots.

When I reported for drill on that silent night, there were more than a dozen of us apparent khup-creators. Since the drill circuit was predefined, we took off sprinting below the battleship and fighter jet as soon as one of the House Captains (that night's master of the drill) signalled us to begin.

The first lap went by quite fast for most of us—at least for those of us who were accustomed to Hodson's Runs and cross-country races. As a couple of people took 'too long' to stumble back to Gaskell Hall, all of us were asked to do one more lap. Grumbling at the injustice of life, we took off once again, albeit slower than the first time around. One of my friends who was also part of the Criminal of the Day list in the red book casually mentioned that it was Friday and the date was the thirteenth. We joked about how scared we used to get on Fridays the thirteenth as kids—referring to our Form II days, when we both had joined in 1994.

Seniors would regale us with fantastical and completely nonsensical ghoul tales, and would even go to quite some lengths to put on a show for us, so to speak. The long corridor that ran along the rear of the Prep Department dorms served as a nice staging area, lined as it was with dressing gowns hanging on those huge pegs. Were they brass? I would be grateful if any of the Sanawarians, both old and present, who are reading this, could confirm whether I'm remembering correctly or my memory is just playing tricks on me.

While we reminisced, we jogged down the path to the War Memorial. Just seconds later, as we started the sprint down the Tuck Shop slope towards BD quad (so that we would be at the head of the pack after this second round, thus increasing our chances of being considered punished enough), a few screams rose from among the stragglers, and we heard their pounding feet as they redoubled their efforts while sprinting past the Chapel. So spurred on they got that they nearly outran us—it was all I could do to maintain a slender margin at the end, nearly stomping on the flabbergasted Captain's feet.

It was, of course, short-lived hysteria. One panicky junior thought he saw the Headless Chowkidar lurking on the Chapel's porch. We all know there isn't such a thing as a ghost. Or is there?

Ghost stories were fun, though, especially on Friday the thirteenth. One story, narrated to us by none other than my favourite Headmaster Dr Dhillon, persists in my memory. Would you like to read it for yourself?

They say (not of the acropolis where the Parthenon is) that during the British Raj, the foothills of the Himalayas were teeming with feral fauna. It was not unusual for livestock to go missing, and even humans would fall victim to dangerous animals if they were unlucky. Keeping this in mind, travellers to our school were strongly advised to plan to reach their destinations before nightfall.

Despite taking this advice, unavoidable halts and unpredictable events (as they generally do) on the journey upwards from Delhi brought our Headmaster to the gates of Sanawar way past dusk. As he began the final climb towards Charlie's, he heaved a sigh of relief at having made it into the better-secured school premises. It was tough going up the steep slope with his luggage, heavy with woollens for the winter. It did not help that he had a war injury in his leg which worsened in the cold and damp weather, and so it was relief he felt when his eyes were stabbed by the flash of a kerosene lamp splitting past the light mist of the gathering night.

The guard carrying the flickering lamp hurried to our Headmaster's aid the moment he recognized him, and accompanied him to his bungalow door, with deference. Since it was the end of the holidays, the children were expected in a day or two for the new winter term and there was only the caretaker inside the premises, who rose from his slumber and warmed the evening meal for the famished Headmaster, in his half-stupor.

Late, the next day, with the sun peeking fleetingly through the overcast sky, our Headmaster sent for the guard-on-duty, the night before. The now-awake caretaker, who listened with increasing alarm to his master's tale of being aided by the night guard, informed him that the post had been vacant since the day before yesterday, due to the incumbent having been found mauled and partially eaten by a leopard.

Dismissing the caretaker's aghast cries about all sorts of supernatural curses descending upon Sanawar, our Headmaster tried to find the man himself. To his consternation, the caretaker's horrified reaction was condoned by everyone. As the next logical step, our Headmaster assumed he had a case of mistaken identity on his hands in recognizing who had helped him get to the school, blaming his travel-induced tiredness for his mental slip-up. No matter how much he sought the actual man who had helped him out, there was no one who came forward to receive his thanks, even when he had spent a week futilely trying to track down the (apparent) man who had greeted him jovially and helped him up Sergeant Tilley's Hill with his luggage.

There were other popular tales that did the rounds, about the aforementioned Headless Chowkidar. Endless variations of his nocturnal habits, his favourite haunts (pardon the pun) and his origin stories existed— still do, I'm certain. One involved an over-confident girl who took up the dare of playing basketball at midnight on the Honoria Courts near Girls' Department, only for the ball to mutate – or as Calvin (from *Calvin and Hobbes*) would say, 'transmogrify' – into the missing head of the Headless apparition. Another put the paranormal patrolman in the Chapel, the one 'sighted' at the beginning of this tale from Sanawar.

**Aradhye Ackshatt**
Himalaya 2003 | 1994–2001

DCE and FMS, Delhi University | Author, *A Life Afloat* (2020)

# The Hodson Runs

The Hodson Runs were instituted by Major The Reverend G.D. Barne, fourth principal of Sanawar in 1916. Over the years, these long-distance runs became important annual events in the school sporting calendar and a feature of school life that continues to this day. In addition to the regular, inter-House runs which became part of the Annual Inter-House Athletics Competition, an 'open' version of the Long Hodson Run took place several times a year. It became a very popular event and many teams, each of eight runners from the surrounding districts competed. The Garrison at Kasauli regularly produced six teams every year, Dagshai five and Subathu also five, two of which were from the Gurkha battalion stationed there. Sanawar itself boasted as many as four teams: LRMS (Boys), LRMS Staff, Squire's Hall Harriers (bachelor teachers) and the Mandi Harriers (school coolies). Here is a transcription of the handwritten order that started it all off:

A new feature of Founder's Week this year (1916) will be 3 long distance runs. These will be called after Hodson, who was a famous long-distance runner when he was at Rugby. They will be known as

'the little Hodson'
'the short Hodson' and
'the long Hodson'.

'The Little Hodson' for boys under 12 only. The winner will receive a bronze medal and 10 marks for his House. The second will receive a prize and 5 marks for his House. The third will receive a prize and 2 marks for his House. Any boy coming in within 2 minutes of the winner will receive 2 marks for his House.

'The Short Hodson' for boys under 15 only. The winner will receive a bronze medal and 15 marks for his House. The second will receive a prize and 10 marks for his House. The third will receive a prize and 5 marks for his House. Any boy coming in within 2 minutes of the winner will receive 3 marks for his House.

'The Long Hodson'. Open. The winner will receive a bronze* medal and 25 marks for his House. The second will receive a prize and 15 marks for his House. The third will receive a prize and 10 marks for his House. Any boy coming in within 5 minutes of the winner will receive 5 marks for his House. (From the point of view of counting towards the championship silver medal for Athletics, this event will count only as one of the other open events in the sports).

All 3 'Hodsons' will finish through the Archway near the entrance to the Boys' School ('The Lawrence Arch'). The courses will be as follows:

'Little Hodson' start at Boys' School: go up to the Chapel; round to right in direction of the Principal's office; sharp to left ['Nicholson's Corner'] in direction of Girls' School; 'short-back-way' round Head Master's House and so home [1 mi 459 yd].

'Short Hodson' start at Boy's school: halfway up to Chapel; sharp to right [Lower Chapel road]; under Principal's House; horseshoe and Hospital; 'long-back-way' through Kasauli gate [main gate] and so home [1 mi 1070 yd].

'Long Hodson' start on top of 'Tapp's Nose', otherwise known in Sanawar by some as 'Monkey Point'; on to upper mall; past Club; through bazaar; round lower bazaar (Kasauli), above Pasteur Institution to Kasauli–Dharampur cart road; through Gharkal and so home [3 mi 550 yd].

The 'Long Hodson' will be considered one of the coveted athletics honours of the year. It will take a boy of grit, endurance and stamina to win the race.

The Order continues for several more paragraphs, prescribing in detail the training methods and programmes to be adopted and strictly adhered to for all three Runs. The three Hodson Runs as described above, continued to be run regularly until 1939 when they were radically modified by Principal the Rev. Agard E. Evans. He decreed that 'in view of the falling ages of the boys and of strictures passed by the Medical Officer and others

---

* Prizes for the Long Hodson (Open) event were revised shortly after the end of WWI. Thereafter and until September 1939, the winner received a silver medal and a bronze medal was awarded to the runner-up. There were no changes to the junior events, and for all three runs, the number of points gained for the annual inter-House Athletics competitions remained the same.

henceforth there was to be one race only, the HODSON RUN, and that once only around the Long Back starting and finishing at the Bakery.' The course was to be along the Mall, through the Arch to Boys' barracks, on to Horseshoe bend, past the Hospital to Moti's Corner, turn left onto the bridle road (now part of MDR10), continue on to junction with cart road at foot of Crater's, sharp turn left up Sgt. Tilley's Hill and so home. Teams would be limited to eight runners from each House and there were to be no runners under twelve years of age. All runners home were to count and the House with the lowest score to be declared the winner. There would be no individual awards.

The highly successful and widely contested Long Hodson from Tapp's Nose (Monkey Point) was run only once again after this, and that was in a 'run-off' for third place between two runners from the coolie team, the 'Mandi Harriers' in September 1939. The official open record time of 19 minutes 7¾ seconds for this long-distance run, set by Fusilier P.J. Risso, 2nd Bn. Lancashire Fusiliers (Subathu) in 1934, was never bettered.

Upon his arrival in 1941, Principal the Rev. C.G. O'Hagan partly reversed the changes made by his predecessor. He retained the run that had been recast as 'The Hodson Run' but adjusted the course to make it almost

2 miles in length. He also re-instituted the junior run for nine- to twelve-year-olds. The two runs were renamed the Long and Short Hodson Runs respectively, and both started at the south end of the Boys' quadrangle (No. 11) and finished at the Lawrence Arch. He also reintroduced individual awards and prizes. The two events continued as part of the annual Inter-House Athletics Competitions until 1947.

The Hodson Runs were revived and reinstituted in a slightly different format by Principal Mr E.G. Carter, MA (Oxon) in 1949 and still take place annually today.

**D.V. Boddington**
LRMS Sanawar, 1942–1947
13 May 2001 (Revised 18 Feb 2020)

**Compiled from:**

- L.M.A. Order Book Page 84, Order No. 269, handwritten and signed by Maj. the Rev. G.D. Barne OBE, MA, Principal, dated 7 July 1916.
- L.R.M.S. ORDERS by The Rev. E.A. Evans, MA, Principal, Order No. 167 dated 6 April 1939.
- L.R.M.S. ORDERS by Maj. the Rev. C.G. O'Hagan, BA (Oxon) IEE, Principal, Order No. 156 dated 29 April 1941.
- Lawrence School Orders by Mr E.G. Carter, MA (Oxon), Principal, Order No. 191 dated 17 September 1949.

# The Tilleys

Whoever 'The Butcher of Kanpur' may have been (presumably c. 1857) he certainly was not Sgt Tilley. I should like to correct that notion right away. Staff Sgt Tilley of the MES was seconded by British Army HQ to Sanawar during the reign of George Barne (1912–1932). Sgt Tilley, a pillar of strength in the administration of the school at that time, helped George Barne to make permanent in Sanawar the imprint of an English public school.

Sgt Tilley was the school's chief clerk. His responsibilities were to see that all the daily needs of Sanawar were taken care of: food, shelter, clothing, all were under his care, down to the laces in our boots. Barne regarded him as his right-hand man, keeping the school running, while he tackled the monumental task of transforming the school to become the best school of all.

Sgt Tilley was a handsome man, upright, honest, smart and dedicated to his duties. He lived on the hill that bears his name. He was a man who did his duty and was cut short in his prime. He died in the winter of 1928, leaving a wife and seven or eight children, three boys and four or five girls. Mrs Tilley was a school teacher. Jim, the eldest boy, became the school's Head Boy in 1934. His sister Betty followed him a year later to become Head Girl. His second son, Bill, was a friend of mine in Havelock. All the Tilley children distinguished themselves at school. As infants the last of his daughters, who were twins, were admired and fussed over when their Ayah wheeled them daily across Peacestead in a pram. Unfortunately, one of the twins did not survive for long.

Mrs Tilley retired and came to live in London. In 1948, she organized and started the OS reunions and hundreds of OS from the UK and the four corners of the world flocked to them. She kept a register of all who attended. Each year, she would send personal invitations to everyone. I never missed a single reunion. I recall that George Barne came to one of them. At the sesquicentennial, there were over 300. I will post a copy of the late Sir John's speech soon.

When Mrs Tilley died, her daughter Betty continued the tradition. When Betty died, her sister Phyllis continued and when Phyllis died, Violet, the last survivor of the Tilley family, continued and became secretary of the OS Association, which was a formalized version of the reunions. I was elected the first president of the OSA. Violet lives in Wiltshire in England. She has promised me she will be at the Reunion in London on 17 October.

The reunions continued in London, unbroken for sixty years, when time took its toll and the ageing members of the OSA started finding it hard to travel. Aruna Mongia has picked up the baton and everyone who can make it, should attend and keep this tradition alive. I have missed two reunions since 1948, one of which was last year.

The name of Tilley is rightly immortalized in our school song. Tilley is part of Sanawar's history. George Barne asked Bishop Durrant of Lahore to write the school song and the music master at the time (I have forgotten his name and so has Jock) wrote the music. The song of the best school of all has been sung all over the world. Doesn't it make you want to stick your chest out?

**George Browne**
Havelock 1937 | 1930–1937

# A Macrocosm of Experiences

A rowdy set of OS, having fun, a class lunch in progress . . . every sentence starting with 'do you remember . . .', followed by peals of laughter! Here are some cherished memories; wish I had a cup of tea and doggies to munch on . . .

I joined Sanawar in 1952, at age six. We were barely twenty girls in PD, with many from some or the other royal family of India. Much showing-off happened. One of them, Shayla, would always boast about her elephants, while others about their mountain kingdom. It all sounded very intriguing, and made the rest of us six- or seven-year-olds feel like we were not quite right. During one such chatting session, I piped up, 'I am also a Princess,' at which, many an eye turned towards me. One of the older, maybe eight-year-olds, of real blue blood questioned, 'but you are from Sonipat?' 'Yes! My mother is the Queen of Sonipat'. Aghast, a sneaky one reported me to the matron, who put me across her knees and spanked my bottom. Come to think of it, this spanking happened to one of us in that dorm on a regular basis. Next day, invariably, the spanked would find a paper cone filled with sweets on the bed. Not enough compensation, I think. But believe me, we were not left psychologically damaged by it later in life. It felt as though we were living in an Enid Blyton fable.

The PD sardar boys wore two plaits. The ends were tied with shoe laces, and then folded up like a swing just below the skull. One of the plaits of the guy who sat in front of me in Form I (let him remain nameless), would always come down. I would quietly tie it to his chair. The fun of seeing him trying to get up would cause a flood of giggles among us girls. Now when I think of it, I realize what a meanie I was.

The House shows, in the 1950s, were girls-only and boys-only. The Boys' House shows had the young sardar boys, with their long open tresses, cast in girls' roles. They would wear saris or dresses, as the role demanded. The worst, as they tell us now, was wearing lipstick. And how we called them by the names from the play.

'Hungry as hell' was our perpetual underlying state. We walked up and down the dales the whole day, with our tummies rumbling. We looked for wild berries and medlars and hold your breath, junglee palak, that grew all around. We would pluck the leaves and without bothering to wash them, take a bottle of coconut hair oil, go down to the boiler-room, and fry them on the rusty little platform and *gobble* them up. Another delight was jelly packets from Tuck Shop. We would empty them into our mugs, fill hot water from the bathroom basin tap, and leave them by an open window. Next morning, one had a mug full of wobbly pink jelly to eat. Ambrosia! Nothing has ever tasted as delightful. We all remember our midnight feasts, sitting in one of the large claw-footed tubs in the bathroom. Most happy stories in Sanawar have food woven in somewhere or the other.

The Socials were the highlights of our lives. We were given party school clothes—a red silk long shirt, a white dupatta and a white salwar. We spent the entire day getting ready, and ended up looking just the same. Only for that evening, we were allowed to make a single plait, as it was high fashion. It was all a mixed batch, sometimes daring, other times wallflowers . . . but in its own way, an evening of music and dance and imaginary boyfriends. We did the four-step foxtrot and later, in our senior years, the rock & roll. The Kemps would perform the most delightful waltz.

Diwali was another fun time. One time, boys from my class bought rockets and other such projectiles, stuffed them into the cannons, and lit the fuse. Fortunately, they were neither caught nor punished.

A memory that jumps to mind is from geography class in Sixth Form. Mr B. Singh would stride in, look at Shashi and me, and say, 'Go to your places, Shashi and Vinay'. And both of us, heads hanging in shame, would go stand inside the wooden wastepaper baskets, on either side of his table.

It was a pitch-black September night. I was the MI Prefect. In the middle of the night, the Matron shook me awake, 'Leena's eye is bleeding really badly—her stye has burst. Take her to the Hospi'. Without a second thought, conditioned not to question orders, I changed and Leena and I set out for the Hospital, which was really at the other end of the campus. As I said, it was a pitch-black night. Crossing Peacestead was scary as hell, but we were walking at a quick, steady pace. In any case, no one strolled in Sanawar—always at clippity-clop, always in a hurry. We reached the Hospital. I deposited Leena with the Sister and started running back, expecting a ghost to come out of the floaty misty air. It was like walking through cottonwool. I knew the way like the back of my hand, mist or no mist, but what about the ghost?

And just as I was thinking that, I saw a wavering light coming towards me. I had goosebumps, a scream was choking my throat. I walked close to the wall on the hillside, almost hugging it. I thought I heard a high-pitched wail. The voice was calling out my name. After almost puking with fright, I saw it was our matron, who having realized she shouldn't have sent me alone, had come looking for me, huddled in her dressing gown. A head bobbing in the white cottonwoolly mist. She finally appeared in human form. I remember hugging her and gasping. Hairy-scary night of my life. Tumbling into bed was a relief like no other. For the very first time in ten years, I appreciated the hard comfort of a pine needle-stuffed mattress.

Mark Reading in Barne Hall was particularly traumatic. Those who didn't do well were coldly told by Heady Major Som Dutt, that they would perforce have to graduate from a Sonipat College. And every time he doomfully declared that, he would look directly at me . . . the Sonipat girl. I would want to rush out and jump off the Chapel tower.

Another doomsday scenario had to do with my huge feet. Brogues would be issued by the School, but GD never had my size. I would be marched off to BD to be fitted out. I would die a thousand deaths as the boys would stare or laugh, and tease me the next day. However, today, when I look back, it was character-building, really. Nothing in my life thereafter has scared or embarrassed me.

Sanawar is like no other. To have grown up in Sanawar was a learning way beyond books. We have a bonding blind to age or gender. And that was the best part—no difference between boys and girls. We were brought up as equals. The last stanza of the school song says it all: 'come what may . . . we will live with dignity and honour till the Last Bugle Call . . . never say die . . . we are too tough for all that'.

Love you, Sanawar! The best school of all . . . Never Give In!

**Vinay (Chopra) Tuli**
Chops | Siwalik 1961 | 1952–1961

OS Sibling – Sister – Vijay (Chopra) Narang | Siwalik 1964 | 1955–1964

OS Children – Son – Atul Tuli | Siwalik 1983 | 1974–1976

# A Tiger at Barnes

Barnes was and still is the centre-stage for all sports in Sanawar; a revered ground that one aspires to perform on and outshine the lot; from School Atoms to Colts to ultimately, the First XI. The mood at Barnes changes with each season; from Cricket to Soccer to Hockey and of course, the focal point of the Athletics finals at Founders' every year. Not surprising then that Barnes holds a treasure trove of memories for all Sanawarians, though essentially a mixed bag—the recollections of triumphant victories and conquests; to the bittersweet reminiscences for those who didn't make the cut. Nonetheless, it was a happy place for both the participants as well as the spectators alike.

In 1979, while Mallik's XI were 'having it out' at Barnes, I took the opportunity to (successfully) sneak off to my grandparents' home in Delhi via Moti Corner. Upon my return a few days later, I chanced upon Mr B. Singh outside his residence. Glint-eyed, with a Charminar cigarette dangling between his nicotine-stained fingers, he asked, 'Back in one piece, Lad?'

Other memories at Barnes include watching Mr B.P. Joshi, opening the batting for the Staff XI, dressed up as a bridegroom in an 'achkan & pugree'. Quite the sight he was. Also etched in the mind is my batchmate Harbinder Purewal breaking my cousin, Mukul Chopra's 880m record (1973). Forty-two years on, Purie's record still stands. 880m is unique to Barnes since it is an unconventional alternative for the 800m. The track is actually 200 metres, as opposed to the standard 400 metres, given that Barnes is fairly narrow in width. In fact, a boundary to the on or off side in cricket is scored as a 2 as against a boundary of 4. 800m translates to 880 yards (give or take a few).

In the new millennium, the hard-gravel, stone surface gave way to grass top under floodlights, giving a new life and feel to the hallowed ground. Something we could never have dreamt of in our time on the hilltop. In fact, it was the harsh playing conditions here that gave us a very clear edge when we visited other schools to compete. I recall visiting YPS Patiala in 1980 with the Cricket First XI and witnessing our fielding rise to another level altogether. It was not possible to take a dive in the outfield at Barnes during our time, unless of course, one was aiming for an injury that would allow them to visit Hospi and duck Prep.

Perhaps, it is now time to seal the field and track records set by those from the pre-grass era for posterity and start a fresh set for the new millennium, yes?

1980 Inter-House Cricket. Kim Sinha (N-83) works his way through a formidable Vindhyan batting line-up—Arun Chandra, Subroto Mallik, Nirvik Singh, Rohit Tangri (to name a few). I walk in as the potential #4 wicket to be 'had' at the end of a hattrick. However, I proceed to smash Kim over the net to Dhobi Ghat. Non-striker Piyush Malaviya watches in disbelief, as I rub the Nilgarians all over Barnes, to wrap things up in a couple of overs. Sweet! So sweet!

Later that year, the Nawab of Pataudi leads his Tiger's XI (me included), taking on the School First XI. Twenty-one of the best cricketers on campus and one Tiger from Pataudi facing-off, with all of Sanawar in attendance at Barnes.

Tiger huddles his team by the sight-screen adjacent to the Pavilion, for a spot of catching practice—his 'method' of quickly assessing our agility to place his fielders accordingly. He placed me at the run-saving mid-wicket. I managed a run out as well! Anand Pathak opened the batting for Sanawar. Notably, at one point, he unleashed a cracking cover drive which Tiger pounced upon and before you could say 'S-A-N-A', the ball smacked into wicket-keeper, Iftekar Hasan's gloves, like a tracer bullet. Anand recalls being 'paralyzed in his crease'.

With most staff drafted into playing the match, there were slim pickings for umpires. Was one of them Mr Bhalerao, who famously called an over up, after declaring the previous delivery a no-ball? Perhaps, it was Mr K.L.K. Solomon, with a reputation for dozing off while umpiring. My batchmate Arjun 'Bunty' Bedi was the other umpire, despite being clueless about the game of cricket.

Tiger took the crease early and proceeded to tear into the Sanawarian bowling attack in a swashbuckling display of his legendary batting prowess. I can't forget an effortless leg glance that he executed with such ferocity, that it almost decapitated Ranjan Roy in the scorer's box. How did he manage to generate such velocity off a leg glance? Baffling!

Subroto Mallik brought himself on, hoping to halt Tiger's assault. Pataudi went into defensive mode, trying to read Subroto's wily quickish spin. One of the deliveries spun out, down the leg, which Tiger padded away. No harm. No foul. Subroto appealed weakly. Umpire Bunty Bedi, who was clueless about deliberate padding or the finer nuances of LBW decisions, hesitated. Subroto appealed again. Bunty's finger came out of his jacket pocket. 'HOWZZAT!', Subroto appealed strongly this time, sensing he could bag the prize wicket of Tiger Pataudi, with the right or wrong of it being lost in the heat of the moment.

Tiger of Pataudi is pronounced 'out' by Bunty Bedi.

A deathly silence descended upon Barnes. There was a very brief but palpable pause in time . . . after which all hell broke loose. Tiger stormed off the field in sheer disbelief, flinging his bat at some hapless soul in the pavilion, ripping off his pads, as Heady (Shomie Das), tried to calm him down. Perhaps a tall cold beer was suggested and the Tiger of Pataudi was whisked off to Heady's den. Game over.

With Tiger gone, so did the interest in the match. Soon, the stands at Barnes were empty while the rest of us went through the motions of completing the game. A damp squib ending, but certainly not anticlimactic.

A day not for the record books, but certainly one for memory lane.

**Arvind Hoon**
Vindhya 1981 | 1979–1981
Advertising Professional (1984–2008) | Photographer

OSS Vice President 2005–2007

# Send Him to Sanawar and
# Make a Human Being of Him

I vividly remember the day I joined school. My parents came to drop me. The minute I got there, I knew I belonged – the exquisite campus, the old stone buildings, the red roofs, the wooden floors, the fresh crisp air and, above all, the smiling faces around me. I felt completely invigorated and eager to immerse myself in the life my new home away from home had to offer.

I couldn't wait to get my uniform. And the best part? I got a top bunk in the dorm! I'd always had a desire to occupy a top bunk. Next, I had to learn to fit in, along with other newcomers, into a community, and still stand out. I soon realized how important those weekly inland letter-writing sessions were. The bonds I formed with my family back home grew stronger each week. As I look back now, it was a good idea to join in Prep School. It gave me time to get a foothold before being thrown into the big, bad world of Senior School.

Senior School was different. There was an exacting hierarchy to be respected. Seniors were seniors, having worked their way up to earn their place in the sun. Respect for one's elders is another lesson I learnt, one that has stood me in good stead, and sadly, a virtue that has been forgotten in today's oh-so-casual world.

Memories abound—running at night, all alone, across Peacestead, once a graveyard, to SSC for badminton practice with a head full of ghost stories; waking up at 5.30 a.m. for study, sports and extracurricular activities, travelling for inter-school, state, and national competitions, trekking and white-water rafting during hikes and camps, the exciting build up to Founders' every year. School really packed in a lot. I also remember pining for holidays while in school and then itching to go back to school before the end of the holidays.

There's one heartbreaking memory that remains. During my first year in school, I was doing exceptionally well in my age group in athletics. I had one last race before I won the championship. I was running a mild fever after athletics practice, and my English teacher insisted I was admitted to the Hospital. That was the end of my championship! A huge regret . . . but such is life!

We lived like a family, forming enduring relationships. Till date, my most intimate and reliable relationships are those that were formed in School. Outside school, their homes are my home and vice versa. I am yet to meet an Old Sanawarian who doesn't have that signature good heart.

True, it can all be quite rough, but that's part of life, and I believe that being in Sanawar not only gave me an well-rounded education, but it set me up to deal with anything that life threw at me—and for that, I am eternally grateful. Sanawar whips, beats, kicks, smack us all into shape, in the best, most fun way possible. There's a reason it's known as 'the best school of all'. This is where we truly learnt the necessary attributes of a good, well-balanced personality—patience, resilience, courage, willpower, commitment, optimism, self-confidence, teamwork and leadership. Precisely what it takes to be a better human being.

I took my children recently to visit my beautiful school and it still filled me with so much pride as I showed them around. As we drove out after our visit, my daughter announced excitedly, 'See you when I join Sanawar!' I understood exactly where that came from. It's still the most magical place ever . . .

**Mahima (Anand) Mehta**
Himalaya 1998 |1991–1996

OS Siblings – Brother – Arjun Mehta | Himalaya 2002 | 1994–2002

# Thirty-Seven Years in Sanawar

Oh My God! Thirty-seven years, so long that I myself just can't believe it. My intention was to spend just a summer in Sanawar, and return to Lucknow University to continue my teaching. I had also submitted my thesis for a final perusal.

Initially, I was not happy at Sanawar. I wanted to quit. Mr M.S. Sinha advised me against it. I decided to consult Mr J.K. Kate, the officiating Headmaster at the time. Mr Kate was very warm and before I could say anything, he mentioned that he was giving me a very important task to escort twenty girls and fifteen boys to Nainital on an excursion along with Ms Chatterjee and Ms Joshi. This was to be the turning point of my career at Sanawar.

I joined Sanawar along with Mr Sinha, Mr Atma Ram and Mr M.P. Gopinath, and was a tutor in Vindhya House. Mr Virendra Vyas was the Housemaster and also Head of Hindi Department, as well as the Hockey Coach. He inspired me to direct a Hindi play for the Vindhya House show. This was a new beginning and I went on to direct many plays for House shows and school plays. I remember Mr Vyas directed *Kabuliwala* and Mr Balraj Sahni, who was in the audience, was so impressed that he took the script and later made the movie with the same title. If I have to name the best teacher Sanawar has produced, I will name Mr Vyas. He was selected into the Civil Service and left us. I was made Head of Hindi Department and the Hockey Coach in the wake of his departure.

The Amateur Dramatics Society (ADS) produced plays of very high production quality. Mr Kemp, who was in-charge of ADS, was the best producer, director and actor. I was the stage manager. There was good chemistry between Mr Kemp and Mr Sikund and after Mr Kemp retired, Mr B. Singh took charge of ADS. He was an equally good producer, director and actor. Mr Shomie Das asked me to do something new for Founders' and I decided to stage a nautanki for the first time in a public school. It was a great success. Mr Shammi Kapoor and Mrs Nargis Dutt also had great things to say about the plays we staged in Sanawar.

Major Som Dutt took over as Headmaster in August 1956. He was very fond of Bridge and he, Mr and Mrs Kemp, Mr Bhalerao, Mr Sikund and I often played Bridge in the Staff Club or at [the] headmaster's or Mr Kemp's House. Major Som Dutt's personality was such that even after many years of knowing him, I could never dare talk to him about anything apart from Bridge. When I joined Sanawar, I was told about Mr Carter and Mr Cowell, '*Jidhar se* Carter *nikalte the, udhar patta bhi nahi hilta tha*' (Wherever Carter passes, not even a leaf dares move). But what I saw for myself, 'Birdwood *mein jidhar se* Major Som Dutt *nikalte the, udhar bacche aur staff chhup jaate the*; *pata nahi kab aur kya pooch baithein aur aapki samajh mein na aaye*' (Wherever in Birdwood Major Som Dutt passed by, there, staff and students would both hide in fear of what he might ask you and you may not understand or know the answer to). In one incident, after a staff meeting, even Ms Chatterjee, who was Senior Mistress and Head of the English Department asked me, 'Dr Gupta, Major Som Dutt *kya keh rahe the*? *Meri kuch samajh mein nahi aaya.*' (what was Major Som Dutt saying? I couldn't understand a thing.) I replied 'Madam *jab aap ki samajh mein nahi aaya, toh aap* Hindi teacher *se kya ummid rakhti hain* . . .' (Madam, when you couldn't understand a thing, what do you expect of a Hindi teacher?) Major Som Dutt was a special kind of headmaster. He was soft-spoken and yet people were afraid of him.

I had many interests, but preferred to maintain a low profile ever since I joined Sanawar. I was a known poet in U.P., a sitar player of merit. I would quietly go to Simla for radio programmes on poetry. I was interviewed by BBC, London. I, a Hindi teacher, was selected by the British Council to teach English as a Foreign Language, and for the TEFL course at the University of Wales, for a year.

My Hindi class batches did exceedingly well. In my last year's batch of 1992, there were seventeen students with Hindi, out of which fifteen passed with distinction.

**Dr Dinesh Chandra Gupta**
STAFF 1956–1993
Head of Department, Hindi | Hockey Coach | Housemaster | Director – Dramatics

OS Children – Daughter – Meera Gupta | Nilagiri 1969 | 1958–1969
              Daughter – Nirja (Gupta) Jain | Nilagiri 1972 | 1963–1972
              Son – Ashok Gupta | Lovey | Nilagiri 1977 | 1966–1977

*As narrated to Pradeep Sharma, Vindhya 1967*

# Random Thoughts

I am privileged beyond my deserts to be asked to write a short monograph on Sanawar. The man who should do this, and who would do it much more ably, is Mr S.C. Cowell. My association with the school dates back only thirty years to 1941. Mr Cowell's span – as boy, assistant master, Housemaster, and finally headmaster – covers a much longer period.

In 1941, a young master entering the august portals of Sanawar was assailed – and I use the word deliberately – by the surprising number of ladies on the staff. The war was on and many of the men-staff had been called up or had volunteered—hence the preponderance of the women. My first impressions of the school were overwhelming. Everything seemed to be on a grand scale. One could get lost quite easily on the estate. And I did. The boys wore military uniforms, boots, putties, side caps and local badges of rank. I was never able to get used to the sight of little Johnny, nine years old, resplendent in full military regalia, coming up smartly to the salute three paces before he passed me. My mild 'good morning' was always an anticlimax.

Pride in their school was an outstanding characteristic of all age groups, boys and girls. They were all-India boxing champions, all-Empire shooting champions . . . they were Sanawarians. Three generations of Sanawarians were often present at Founders', son (in school), father and grandfather, each as proud as the other and of one other. 'Ba Gum! What wouldn't I give to have my Regiment see that!' was one comment I heard from an old sweat watching the school Trooping of the Colours. Nothing was impossible for that old breed, or for that matter, to the new breed. We were without an orchestra for the Old Sanawarian Dance, one year. Within forty-eight hours, a plane circled Barnes and dropped a message that the dance band wired for by one of the OS Girls had arrived from Karachi by military plane, and would motor up from Ambala. As I sit and think of the old school and all that it stood for – stands for – the floodgates of memory open and I can scarcely marshal my thoughts fast enough to maintain coherence. I wonder how many know that Sanawar was, in a small way, a marriage mart for the eligible bachelors of the surrounding cantonments of Kasauli, Dagshai, Sabathu and Solan. The girls (those who were fed up of school life) paraded, the young man appeared, cupid cast his dart, and the man and the girl were allowed to sit and chat and walk for a bit, while they each decided whether or not the other would be a suitable mate for life.

1914–1918 and the First Great War! Boys from Sanawar, at eighteen, were drafted straight into the fighting line without any preliminary training. They were trained already, and then the memorable occasion, in Rev. Hildesley's time, I think, when the whole Boys' school protested – was it against the food? – and marched down to Kalka in orderly array, with rifles and bayonets. Those were the days when Sanawar could only be approached on foot, or on horseback, or in a dandy. The days when few children went home for the winter holidays; the days when a boy was paid four annas a month for singing in the choir; the days when the brass arrow embedded in the wood of the Barne Hall floor was embedded in the Gaskell Hall floor, and marked the spot where you stood to face North and collect your 'six of the best' on the spot where it hurt most. Those were the days a lovely little wood stood with its paddling poll, where

Honoria Court now stands, a tin shed gymnasium occupied the area now forming Wavell Court, and each of the double-deckers (Dining Room, Him., BD Nil., Lib.) was a triple-decker, and the present gym was the main classroom building for the boys. Those were the days when the non-academically inclined girls were given a preliminary nurse's training in the school hospital and the romantically inclined boys soon developed sudden undetectable aliments. Cold compresses over the eyes and massive doses of castor oil cured that epidemic.

In April 1847, seven boys and seven girls with a master- and one mistress-in-charge, pitched their tents on a piece of flat ground near Peacestead, and Sanawar was born. In 1947, thirty-three boys, seven girls and seven Preppers contributed in their own way to a second birth. A small band of devoted kids and staff strove mightily to rebuild a recognizable image of the heart of Sanawar from the shattered debris in the aftermath of Independence, and the departure of 500 children, almost overnight. We who were associated with that effort, are proud of the products we have produced, fiercely proud of the pride and the love and the emotions which the name Sanawar engenders in all those who have been privileged to be called Sanawarians.

Bishop Barne was the architect of the modern Sanawar and all it stands for. He laid the foundations solidly and well, and when he moved to Lahore on becoming Bishop of the Punjab, he handpicked his successor. Unfortunately, death intervened within a year and Rev. Hunt died of a heart attack while swimming in the pool (now a water reservoir) below and behind the needlework room. He was followed by Aegard Evans, and he, in 1941, by Charles O' Hagan. Harold Hazel, Billy Carter and Pat Som Dutt replaced each other after short spells, and it is Pat Som Dutt's Sanawar that most of the present generation are familiar with. He was the first Indian headmaster and it was in his time that growth was great and grand and phenomenal. The fact that Sanawar is so solidly representative of the traditions of the past and the hopes of the future, is a lasting memorial of Som Dutt's genius. He was the right man in the right place at the right time. He was, to quote Bill Colledge, 'the Indian Barnes'.

**T.C. Kemp**
Staff | Deputy Headmaster

**Source and Acknowledgement:** *Souvenir Brochure 1847–1972*

# Amritsar to Sanawar – And Beyond

In 1955, I was admitted to Form I in Prep School. I was born in a village in Amritsar and Sanawar seemed so distant and isolated in the hills. It was as if the British were sending rebellious natives to the Andaman Islands, from where there was no escape.

We were fortunate that Ms Kaveri and Mrs Tikaram looked after us all with great care and compassion. The school environment was a strong contrast to the circumstances in which I was born and raised. My yearning for home was paramount and I could never understand why one must be sent to an alien environment to help grow into a wholesome being. I recollect that Headmaster Mr Cowell would occasionally come to Prep School and give us an oration on discipline and growing up. He reminded me, later, of a character from one of Charles Dickens' novels, for he would scowl at all the kids and brandish his cane as an absolute egalitarian discipline tool. It was quite terrifying.

In Prep School, the buildings seemed large, but in BD, the senior students seemed equally large and Barne Hall seemed colossal. When, as an Old Sanawarian, I went back to walk down memory lane, the same Barne Hall building seemed just normal in size. My perceptions constantly changed in the ten years I was at Sanawar, from 1955 to 1964.

We wore battle-dress school uniforms and marched to classes. Discipline was extreme and corporal punishment quite harsh and frequent. However, it was rarely taken to heart, as it was just a part of the system at the time.

My Housemaster was Mr M.V. Gore, a very articulate and fair man. He wrote in my House report when I was in the Boys Dorm Vindhya House, simply, 'Disobedient. Defiant to corrective measures'. Thank God my mother could not read English and I was spared a sound thrashing when I returned home for the holidays.

I remember a funny incident. Each morning, we had to get up and go for the Hodson Run. I wasn't athletic, unlike my elder brother, O.J.S., five years my senior. I was constantly compared to him for his athletic performance by my Housemaster Mr Jagdish Ram, who was very disappointed that I was not a chip off the old block. While doing Hodsons, I would take a short cut up Sgt. Tilley's hill, which would spare me the agony of wanting to kill myself. On this occasion, however, everything went wrong. I did not know that the semi-finals were on and the whole school was cheering all the front runners. Having taken a shortcut as normal, I suddenly ended up in front on the 'last bend'. There was no way I could pretend to slow down. As I crossed the finish line, many students rushed up, hugged and slapped me on the back and even lifted me over their shoulders with a little 'hip-hip-hooray'. How sheepish I felt is hard to explain. What made it a disaster was that I did not have a wrist watch and the calculation of the time I had taken was absurd. My Housemaster eventually caught wind of what had happened and I assure you, I was subjected to corporal punishment with interest by him.

Sanawar's best gift to me was the English language. I rebelled within myself on how I grew up and wanted more than just the confines of the military discipline. In 1982, I discarded all things Western. Today, I travel all over the world in my kurta pyjama and an open flowing, beard. True aristocracy is not by birth, it's in your thinking.

**Maninderjit Sandhu**
Manny | Vindhya 1964 | 1955–1964

OS Sibling – Opinderjit Singh Sandhu | Vindhya 1957 | 1952–1957

# Thappo

Sanawar conjures up a million memories—and as we grow older, the memories take on shades of happiness and nostalgia. Of course, there are some incidents which stay with one forever, like nicknames.

I joined Sanawar in 1977 after being home-schooled for a year in Bhutan—there were no schools to speak of in Bhutan back then and I was mischievous enough for my father to pull me out of the one school there. And so, after a year of boredom at home, my parents looked for a boarding school and I landed up in Sanawar. On 12 February 1977, my mother left me with Mrs Soloman outside Parker Hall (just before lunch), who promptly handed me over to the nearest group of girls: Sheshe, Mandy and Hoofy—my best friends for the next seven years.

Less than a month after joining, we were all assigned prefects who would check our prep work and ensure that we were adjusting well. I was assigned to Payal Singh, who at that time seemed quite strict and scary. One afternoon, she called me to the Upper Sixers' area and while browsing through my notebooks, glanced up at me and said, 'Anjali, your face is quite dry. Go and *thappo* some cream on it'.

I raced out of the cubicle and stood outside in panic, as I had no idea what exactly she had asked for and none of my friends were around to help. After an appropriate amount of time, I returned and rather sheepishly said, 'I don't have any Thappo cream . . . I only have Ponds Cream'. The entire dorm erupted with laughter and I got my 'lovely' nickname for life: THAPPO.

Today, I am 'Thappo *maasi*' to all my friends' children and it is a rare Sanawarian who knows who Anjali Khosla is.

**Anjali Khosla**
Thappo | Nilagiri 1984 | 1977–1984
Documentary Filmmaker and Editor | Work on Conservation, Environment and Livelihoods

# The Ghost of Red Field

At any given time, it just takes me a millisecond to transport myself back to school to those good old days. The typical Saturday night Senior dorm setting. As lights-out approaches, the senior prefect shouts, 'Guys, settle down!' The ongoing banter about who all are off to Kas for the Sunday movie, tapers down to pin-drop silence. There's a stillness which is broken by gestures and whispers . . . 'come to the Senior Bunk' is the message that reaches me.

I venture out of my corner. In the bunk, Rana (Jasmit), the senior prefect and Dutt (Sanjay) are hatching a plot. Tonight, the Ghost of Red Field—the Chowkidar carrying a lantern and a large stick, will make an appearance. Dutt, given his acting skills, is to be the Chowkidar. Rana is to take on the task of ensuring that everyone hops into bed and the lights are switched off. The question is: how do we get Dutt to sneak out of the dorms as the only exit is in full view of more than half the dorm? Solution: I am to open the door while staying concealed behind the curtain, in my corner—the Senior sidey bunk, so that Dutt sneaks out unnoticed.

The plan is that Dutt will appear menacingly at the window next to Baggage's (Sanjiv Bajaj) bed and scare the living daylights out of him, as well as the others, whose beds are in that row—by the windows facing Red Field. Dutt and I regroup at the night pans for the emergency lantern, and tidily separate the broomstick from the broom. The two of us coolly walk across the dorm to my bunk, I call out, 'guys, light out now . . . hop into bed'. As some of the ones who are still loitering scamper to their beds, we move to removing a blanket, one of those army-issue rough and stiff woven ones, from the bed. Dutt then slips out of the door; Rana once more announces, 'Oye, lights-out!'

The stillness of the night is broken a few minutes later. An indeterminable shadow of what appears to be a faceless, headless beast, striking a stick on the ground—thump, thump, thump . . . falls on Baggage's window. The lantern sways eerily left to right in the night breeze. Some of the guys let out a barely audible shriek: 'Ghost . . . guys, Ghost!' The somewhat braver of the lot scramble towards the windows to catch a glimpse, while the rest slip deeper under their quilts. Dutt, apparently thrilled with his performance, decides to improvise and strays from the script. He tosses a mug full of water through the window that lands on Baggage's bed.

Now, Baggage, the true boxer that he is, is not to be intimidated and that too by something which appears to be not of human form. He grabs a hockey stick lying nearby and scoots off towards the exit, determined to give the roguish 'ghost' a sound thrashing. Panic strikes! How do we save Dutt? The same 'supernatural' mode of communication comes to our rescue—hands gesticulating wildly now and signalling to Dutt from inside the Senior bunk, we manage to get him to instantly recognize the looming danger. We instruct him to make a dash to the door near my corner. So while Baggage goes yelling and screaming out of the exit at the far end, Dutt runs for his life and enters the dorm through the sidey bunk. He then nonchalantly walks across to his bed with a theatrical swagger, as if nothing happened. Meanwhile, we watch Baggage run across the length of Red Field, menacingly waving his hockey stick, puzzled and disappointed at the mysterious disappearance of the apparition.

Baggage returns empty-handed. Dutt, Rana and by now, the others, cannot stifle their laughter. The cat is out of the bag. After a hearty round

of laughter, applause for the Dutt's acting skills and Baggage's courage, the dorm slips into deep slumber. Just another Saturday night. And another exciting tomorrow to look forward to.

A few weekends later, we were back to hatching yet another devilish adventure . . . 'who will go to the graveyard?' Challenge accepted. But there's a twist. A sub-plot to the main plot: some of us left surreptitiously as advance party, carrying our white bedsheets, and hid near the graves. One or two of us managed to fit right behind the headstones and stayed completely out of sight.

A short while later, we heard the chatter of the 'brave' who had accepted the challenge coming towards the graveyard. Torchlight beams lit the road as well as the hill-side, the trees casting ominous shadows. Each shadow causing the challengers to become louder, more boisterous, as if sheer noise would keep the 'spirits' at bay and personal safety secure. One particular challenger could be distinctly heard singing some garbled song. Closer and closer they came, completely unaware of the fact that some others were already in waiting.

Loud shouts about what an easy challenge this was ensue, and the skittish ones shine their torchlights at the graves. Then, as a sign of absolute bravery, they egged each other on into the graveyard. Their decision to carry their bravado to another level and boast of their feat, drove them unsuspectingly closer to the centre. That is when, as if on cue, we rose up as one from behind the headstones and the graves. Something like the ghosts in ghostbusters: white sheets flapping and shrieking as we ran towards the brave ones!

I can still recall some of my dear friends running for their lives and one in particular, who had come in singing songs, but was now running chanting prayers at the top of his voice, torchlight lighting every tree along the way, making for an even more eerie setting!

There is a never-ending string of memories that come back to me . . . reveries that remind me, as all of us, of the special place: school. The memories remain firmly nestled within our hearts.

**Maj. Sanjeev Sharma (Retd.) Sr. Advocate**
Sherms | Siwalik 1977 | 1974–1977
Trial Judge and Advisor – Military Law with the Judge Advocate General's Deptt. (Indian Army) | Independent practice – Himachal Pradesh Bar Council and Punjab and Haryana Bar | Senior Advocate – Litigation,

arbitration, advisory roles for corporates | Additional Advocate General Punjab | Senior Standing Counsel for Chandigarh UT | Principal Law Officer – Chandigarh Housing Board | Editor, *Indian Law Reporter* – Punjab Haryana High Court

OSS President 2021–2023 | Member – Board of Governors (LSS)

OS Siblings – Sister – Neelu (Sharma) Jyoti | Vindhya 1964 | 1961–1964
Brother – Pradeep Sharma | Chesty | Vindhya 1967 | 1961–1967
Brother-in-law – Kunal Batra | Vindhya 1985 |1976–1985

# The Windfall

One of the many interesting things that mark the age we live in is that almost everyone you meet is an expert on all subjects. And education, it appears, is what all of them seem most eminently qualified to comment and advise all and sundry on. Learning seems to be one of those things that everyone seems to know much, much better about than those who are in education. And of course, it goes without saying that each of these sentient beings is most vociferous about the right they have to display their opinion on the mechanics of learning. The best learning and that too learning for life, takes place not through books but through life itself!

Of the many things that were way ahead of their time at Sanawar, was the immense learning that took place on our 139-acre sylvan campus in our natural surroundings. Nature was our unstated curriculum and the great outdoors the entirety of our syllabus. Truly, it taught us lessons for life! Some of the greatest lessons cannot be learnt only from books and what you learn from Mother Nature is learning for life; often comprising lessons which cannot ever be forgotten. And of course, we had an array of stalwarts whose very presence was a life lesson. Mr Shomie Das was one such legend.

One of the iconic events in the calendar was of hikes or camps. Students would travel with their tutors to the pristine, unspoiled interiors and remote, high-altitude wilds of Himachal Pradesh, where this wonderful learning would be extended. This took place in early April, each year, when the severity of the winter was replaced by the cool breezes that preceded the summer. Arguably, the very best time of the year to be outdoors enjoying the joys of Nature. Indeed, this was one of those pillars of the Sanawar experience that everyone seemed to take for granted, until one left the school. It definitely pre-dated fashionable initiatives like the Outward Bound movement.

One iconic memory that stands out is of our tutorial group taking the toy train up to Simla in a delightful interlude that was spent gazing out of the window and admiring the carmine rhododendron blossoms! Literally, we were relishing what was, to our young minds, the lap of luxury. The train journey was a most unexpected windfall as we were rather used to roughing it out. However, we were hardly aware that we had arrived at Simla station, before we began our long march, first to the outskirts of Wildflower Hall—at which point one of our more worldly-wise batchmates extolled the delights that were to be found inside. No sooner had he started than our tutor indicated a narrow rocky path and we started our trek to Chakrata!

Not an easy prospect, but what an adventure. At a certain point amidst oak and rhododendron thickets, we came across a shy animal with a long bushy tail that scuttled away even before we really had a good glimpse of the creature. The face was like a mixture between a cat and a bear, and it had big eyes and long whiskers. It was the shy and elusive red panda.

However, it was the rare villagers that we encountered who were even more surprised to see a group of tired and hungry school boys on the remote trail through the forests to Chakrata than we had been at the sight of the red panda!

So here we were, clambering onto a bus at the BD Quad at first light. As the cold light of dawn broke, we found ourselves amidst a host of seniors and not just any seniors; these were the prefects, led by none other than the formidable Mr Das, our headmaster. Truth be told, the Heady's group was most kind and did not even acknowledge the presence of us, lowly U-IVers. Apparently, our tutor had requested our magnanimous Heady to let us ride along and the large-hearted gentleman had acquiesced.

We reached the Sangla Forest Rest House very late in the evening and our tutorial group was billeted in an outhouse. We were very happy to be sheltered from the cold wind that had suddenly begun blowing.

The next morning, we discovered that Heady's group had left for their next destination at the crack of dawn. That meant that we lesser mortals could move in and occupy the Forest Rest House. And it was a grand old building embodying the best facets of colonial architecture. Most of us had possibly never seen such a large expanse of space at our tender age, let alone had the luxury to occupy such expansive lodging. Like excited little ferrets, we forayed into every room and, in one enclosed veranda, we happened to chance upon some cartons, and, being curious, we proceeded to rummage through them. Lo and behold, not all were empty! In one carton, we came across a treasure—cans of tinned fish in tomato sauce and, thereafter, every meal became a feast fit for a king.

It was a blissful time spent exploring streams, quaint villages, hiking up hills and trekking to forts and temples, taking in the rich culture and heritage of Kinnaur. Alas, even before we had comprehended the treasures that were laid out before us, it was time to head back to civilization and to school.

On our return to school, we were filled with a sense of trepidation centering on the tins we had stumbled upon. However, the denouement could not have been better—Heady maintained a stoic silence on the subject and there was no inquisition. His generosity of spirit was truly a great part of his being a legendary headmaster. In fact, there was no mention of the windfall at all by any of the parties concerned. Nobody referred to the canned fish and there were no awkward questions asked regarding whether we had come across any, either.

I guess what happens in Sangla, stays in Sangla.

**Himmat S. Dhillon**
Vindhya 1989 | 1984–1989
Principal, The Gandhi School, Jakarta, Indonesia | Principal/CEO, GEMS Our Own English High School, Fujairah, U.A.E | Executive Principal, GEMS Modern Academy, Gurgaon | Headmaster, The Lawrence School, Sanawar

OS Siblings – Sister – Diviya Dhillon | Vindhya 1997 | 1987 –1997

OS Children – Daughter – Aafreen Tara Dhillon | Himalaya (Present Sanawarian)

# The First Couple

The Lawrence School, Sanawar would no longer be on the world map had it not been for the Carters' fight for its survival.

Mr Carter was born in India and did his initial schooling here, before being sent back to England to complete his education. He then went on to Cambridge to study for his degree and play Cricket for the university, when he fell ill and had to spend six months in a sanatorium. He was diagnosed with ankylosing spondylitis, back then considered a terminal disease. Given only months to live, he was in a quandary as to what to do with the short time at hand. His friend, Bishop Barne, advised him to go as the cricket coach to Sanawar, 'A wonderful school in the foothills of the Himalayas', he said. Mr Carter applied for the job and was accepted, and so left for India.

This was in 1926. It was love at first sight . . . with the mountains, with India, with the school and eventually, with Violet Haddock, who was teaching maths at Sanawar. They courted. However, Mr Carter had to tell her that he was not going to live long, and so could not marry her. However, better sense prevailed (did Mrs Carter call him a Solan Goose?), and they did get married. Anne was born, and despite the doctor's verdict, he was still alive. So the Carters returned to England. He went back to Cambridge to complete his degree. He was offered a rather good job in the UK, but had lost his heart to Sanawar. So back they came and, soon after, their son, Tup (Timothy), was born. Although his illness took its toll (we remember him being stooped), he continued to teach and coach cricket, and eventually, became [the] headmaster of the school.

This, at a crucial time—1947! Sanawar was being threatened with closure, as most of the students had returned to England with their parents after Independence. There were only forty-eight children left, but with the benedictions of Lord Mountbatten, who was a frequent visitor to the school and chief guest at the Centennial Founders' in 1947, the school was kept going by the Ministry of Defence. Eventually, Sanawar was transferred to the Ministry of Education, in 1952, changing from a British military school to an Indian public school.

It was the Carters who kept the school going against all odds and who were responsible for the Indianization of Sanawar. Indian food, music, dance and history were introduced. In 1952, the new formal uniform for girls, red and white salwar-kameez, was designed by Mrs Carter and she insisted that the school play at Founders' be Tagore's *Shakuntala*. More and more Indian staff were taken on and as the school became famous, more Indian students enrolled. When our class finished in 1954, the strength was 400, the school was financially viable, and for the Carters, it was a job well done. Mrs Carter left for the UK at the end of 1953 and Mr Carter retired in 1955, after twenty-six years in Sanawar, handing over the reins to the first Indian headmaster.

### Gita (Bery) Bhatia
Siwalik 1954 | 1951–1954
Senior Management – International Airline | Export Consultant – Handicraft/Handloom promoting India to Galleries Lafayette, Bloomingdales, Harrods, La Rinascente, Magasin du Nord, JC Penny

OS Spouse – Ashok Bhatia | Shoki | Vindhya House 1953 | 1951–1953

OS Children – Daughter – Premika Bhatia | Siwalik 1991 | 1987–1991
Son – Adil Bhatia | Siwalik 1993 | 1988–1993

# Birdwood: School

The foundation stone for Birdwood School was laid by the Rt. Rev. Henry Bickersteth Durrant, Bishop of Lahore on 25 August 1927. The ceremony was also attended by the Officiating Chief of the General Staff (CGS) Major-General W. M. St. George Kirke, CB, CMG, DSO and Colonel Commandant P.R. Gervers, the Chief Engineer, Northern Command who was also the chief architect and in overall command of the construction project. The service was conducted by the Principal, the Reverend Canon G.D. Barne, MA.

Before the stone was laid, the principal handed the Bishop a copy of *The Pioneer* of the day, a copy of the School Order of the day, a copy of the service, and a complete set of silver and copper coins bearing the King's head and the date 1927. These were placed in a lead casket, which was then soldered down and sealed. The casket was then set in a cavity in the stone footings of the main building, so that when the foundation stone was laid, the casket would be left built into the wall.

Colonel Gervers then handed the Bishop a silver trowel bearing the Arms of the School, with which the foundation stone was ceremonially laid. A mallet made from cedarwood timber from the old school building was also used to symbolically set the stone in place.

Construction of the new buildings, the quadrangle and the granite staircase from the Chapel road below, was completed in late 1928 and the new classrooms were brought into use in early 1929. At about the same time, the two Turkish field guns presented to the school as World War I trophies by the Government of India were delivered and installed in their present sites. On Sunday, 22 September 1929, following the ceremony for the unveiling of the War Memorial, the new school buildings were formally opened by the Commander-in-Chief, Field Marshall Sir William Riddell Birdwood, (Baron Birdwood of Anzac), after whom the new school was named.

**D.V. Boddington**
LRMS Sanawar 1942–1947
March 2011

**Compiled from:**

1. 'Annual Report on the Lawrence Royal Military School' for the year ending 31 March 1928.
2. LRMS Orders Part I, Order No. 770 dated 17 September 1929.
3. Lawrence School Orders No. 261 dated 26 October 1951.
4. *Civil & Military Gazette*, Lahore, August 1928 (Citation) and September 1929, (article).

# Old Sanawar

I have no notes or records to guide me and must trust entirely my memory for such facts as might be of interest to a younger generation of Sanawarians. At this distance of time, some events are apt to be forgotten or but dimly remembered, and one cannot always make a statement with any marked degree of finality. However, such impressions of mine as are at all hazy, I have tried to avoid. Looking back on my schooldays in Sanawar, there are certain features which stand out more vividly than others, and it is these, in the main, that I record.

In 1869, when my sister and I joined the school, we came up by bullock cart. The journey was comfortable, if a trifle long drawn-out, but if we lacked the speed and efficiency of modern travel, the leisurely rate at which we moved had some advantages, and I'm sure we had as much excitement as the present-day girl has in her journey to and from school. When we left Sanawar, in 1876, we went down in 'dandies' to Kalka whence we transferred to the inevitable bullock cart at Ambala, however, by way of variation and because my father was short of time, we obtained 'tikka gharries'. These were faster, though not as comfortable as the bullock cart, but comparing it now with the railway and the motorcar, it does seem a painfully slow mode of travel. Still, not knowing any better, we enjoyed our journeys and look forward to them with no little pleasure.

Perhaps the most bewildering change in Sanawar is in the number of buildings that have sprung up in the course of the years. Of the buildings we had, and they were comparatively few, most have disappeared or have been entirely changed to suit some present needs. The principal's bungalow remains very much the same. The medical officer occupied the same House then as now. The House at present occupied by the quartermaster was [the] headmaster's, but Ms Tait's bungalow is that of her predecessors—now the office. Bleak House has changed but little. The present stores were the Hospital, the Music School and the Dispensary. The 'barracks' in both departments were built after my time. We certainly did not occupy them, though we had buildings on the same sites.

Though I do not think there have been any great structural alterations in the Chapel, yet there are one or two changes which have made a difference. The reredos and the 'Hunt Memorial' are both new. We had two pulpits and one lectern, near the priest. The organ and choir were in the gallery, and, as far as I can remember, Church music was well-rendered. The verger was a Mr Wittaker. He sat in the front pew and answered the versicles when the children were sleepy or lazy or both.

Our staff was small in numbers. We had two matrons in the GD, Mrs Stevens and Mrs Anderson. They were assisted by sub-matrons, usually senior girls who were paid Rs. 1–4 a week. Below the sub-matrons were orderlies, who received Rs. 4 a week for their services. The teaching staff consisted of Mr and Mrs Mellor and Ms Escott, Mrs Mellor's sister. Later, Mr Mellor was transferred to the Boys' School, his place being taken by Mr Burgess. This Mr Burges was an excellent teacher and was thoroughly interested in the school. He evinced his love of the GD by marrying the Head Girl, Elizabeth Gibson.

The Principal, the Rev. J. Cole, would read the Bible in class to the children on given mornings, but did know other teaching. The Hospital was in the charge of Major Smythe, who had Miss Scanlon as his Nursing Sister. We seemed to keep fit in those days, in spite of the fact that medical science had not advanced as far as it now has.

We took the Punjab examinations, going as far as the Middle School, but I am not quite certain about this. The schedule of a day's work might be of interest. We rose at 6 a.m. From 7 to 8, the senior classes attended morning study. Breakfast was at 8.15 and school work began at 9 a.m. We worked, with a short break, till 12.30 p.m. and went into dinner at 1. A further spell of classrooms followed from 2 to 4. At 6 p.m., we had supper and that ended our working day. We went early to bed.

Organized games did not exist and except for occasional walks under the charge of a matron, we had to provide our own amusements. A 'giant's stride', standing where the Centre Court now is, was extremely popular with the younger girls. Skipping and 'hopscotch' were pastimes which had many adherents, while a number of girls found amusement and recreation in hoeing and manuring little plots of ground, which they proudly called their gardens and which dotted the khud-sides.

Child's nursing provided a career for many, and the Mission at Delhi, a training centre, was always ready to receive our girls. They had an enviable reputation for good work and did well as a rule, though occasionally, a girl was returned as being unsatisfactory.

Matrimony, however, then as now, was the most popular of careers and considerable matchmaking was carried out in Sanawar, often to our great amusement. A man would write to the principal enquiring if he could obtain a wife in Sanawar. His letter would be handed, or read out, to would-be-wives. In due time, the prospective husband would arrive in Sanawar, to interview and be interviewed. Questions asked by the girls were a strange mixture of clear-eyed acumen, blind dreams and sly humour.

These interviews were good fun and provided us, often enough, with much laughter. When a couple came to an agreement, the wedding arrangements were left to the principal. The wedding would eventually take place in Sanawar, and would provide the necessary excuse for little hilarity and jubilation. Weddings were always welcomed by us. Sanawar, in those distant days, now seems to me to have been a very happy and leisurely place.

In 1876, I left Sanawar. I had been extraordinarily happy and left not without much regret. In the last fifty years, I have seen many changes in Sanawar, changes which have spelt development and progress. I hope, for she has a warm place in my heart, that Sanawar will go from strength to strength, and that the pages of her history will be records of her continued happiness and prosperity.

**Mrs A. Crunden**
Old Sanawarian (Batch of 1876)

**Source and Acknowledgement:** *The Sanawarian* (December 1972). Reprinted therein from *The Sanawarian*, December 1934.

# The Blooming of the Wisteria Bush

*'Spirituality need not be grandiose in its ceremonials. Indeed, the soul might benefit most when its spiritual life is performed in the context it favours— ordinary vernacular life. But spirituality does demand attention, mindfulness, regularity and devotion. It asks for a small measure of withdrawal from a world set up to ignore the soul.'*

—*Thomas Moore,* Care of the Soul

On rare occasions, Joy, the kind that defies logic and reason, would interrupt our tightly structured lives in Sanawar. These instances were as precious as they were transformative. On a dreary spring morning, fifty years ago, I experienced just such a moment. I was about ten years old. It was my first year in girls' school.

I woke up grumpy that day. I resented being forced out of my warm bed more than usual. My mood matched the weather. It was grey, overcast and cold. The downstairs bell rang early. I dragged myself through the morning exercise period. Breakfast tasted like cardboard. My friends were getting on my nerves. I wanted to be left alone, but there was no chance of that happening. I had been in school long enough to know there was no point in complaining. No one was interested in my funk. So, I withdrew and resigned myself to another interminably long, boring day.

Yet another bell rang and I fell in line with the rest of my Housemates. The senior prefect would march us to morning Assembly in our usual four-row military formation. On this particular day, we were going to the beautiful old stone Chapel with stained glass windows, instead of the large wood-panelled hall in Birdwood. The last part of our journey was downhill on a paved road with a stone wall built partway up the hill on the left. Vegetation grew from that part not covered by concrete and spilled over the embankment. To our right, was a low retaining wall, also made of stone, over which you could see the cobblestone pathway which led into the church below. I had gone down this path many times before.

I had only recently learned how to march. So all my focus was on getting it right; arms swing up to the shoulders each time, match my steps and keep a constant distance from the person ahead of me. As we turned the corner, a splash of colour suddenly appeared in the periphery of my vision. My head jerked up. 300 feet away, plumes of bluish-purple flowers growing out of brown gnarly branches were cascading over the moss-covered stone wall. I was transfixed. Spellbound, I stopped short in my tracks. A bush, I later identified as Wisteria, had started to bloom.

My body lurched forward as the person behind me collided with me. Nevertheless, quiet waves of joy welled up in my body, and I was filled with an almost unbearable sweetness of belonging. The closer I got, the more blissful I felt. My legs and arms went through the motions and marched under and past the bush, turned the corner and stopped in front of the Chapel. But every other part of me was looking up at the flowers, wonderstruck. I thought of nothing but those flowers the whole day.

Over the next week, I returned to the wisteria bush often, and each day, more purple and blue blossoms greeted me. Very soon, I began to smell their fragrance before I even turned the corner. Eventually, the petals dropped on the paved path below, transforming it into a purple carpet. We crushed the petals into a brown slippery mush with our feet. Eventually, one day, just as dramatically as it had started, the show came to an end. Nothing was left of the flowers; only the stems and delicate green-coloured leaves remained. But for that week, I was in bliss. I did not know it then, but I had stumbled into the reality of just this.

Half a century later, I am reading the Japanese Soto Zen sacred text *Shobogenzo*. In 1240 AD, Zen master Zhiquin saw peach blossoms in full bloom in a distant village and wrote this:

'For thirty years I have looked for a sword master.
Many times leaves fell, new ones sprouted.
One glimpse of peach blossoms—
Now no more doubts,
just this.'

Every year, I would wait for my wisteria to bloom again. Looking back, I see how I clung to the possibility that I might be able to relive that week again, desperately seeking my sword master. Zhiquin's peach blossoms and my wisteria blossoms are one! Just this, they said to us both: No more doubts. Just this moment.

I visited my wisteria one last time before I graduated. I have not seen it since. I do not know if it has survived the years. It doesn't really matter. When my stomach is in knots and my mind is a tangle of contradictions, when my heart is heavy with doubt and despair, even a hint of that distinctive floral scent of wisteria brings me home to my body. I have to stop, breathe as I recall: 'Just this. This moment is as it should be and all is well'. For this reason, I use wisteria-scented candles for my altar and have planted a wisteria in every single home I have lived in, with, I must admit, marginal success. But the memory endures.

Sanawar did not ignore the divine mystery. She just did not make a fuss about it. The structure and discipline of our lives was an invitation to attend to every moment with regularity and devotion. A training to consciously find the stillness in the middle of movement. Not by turning away from movement but by turning into it so deeply that conditions appeared where our soul could satisfy its own longing.

**Dr Mininder Kaur**
Mini | Nilagiri 1975 | 1966–1975
King George's Medical College, Lucknow | PG Internal Medicine | Practicing Zen Buddhist | Trained Soto Zen Chaplain | WHO Community Health & Development volunteer – Haiti, S. Africa, Zimbabwe

OS Siblings – Sister – Rupinder Kaur | Pedro | Nilagiri 1968 | 1966–1968
Sister – Navneet Kaur | Neeti | Nilagiri 1977 | 1968–1977

# The Ghost of Birdwood,
# Home Day and Other Tales

From the day I reached school, I kept a log of the number of days left for Home Day on a chart scratched with a pebble on a large stone slab, under a pine tree below the boys' bogs. There would be a breeze blowing and I would dream of being back home. Luckily, that same breeze would blow away the scents from the bog and it was a pleasant enough place to spend an hour daydreaming!

Sometimes, this dreaming would turn into nightmares! I remember the night I was woken by a friend in the dorm stuttering with fright.

'There is a ghost in Birdwood!' he stammered.

It was past eleven at night! Reluctantly, I got out of bed and with a few friendly reinforcements, hurried past the ghostly War Memorial and stopped fearfully just by the steps leading up to the cannons at Birdwood. And then we heard it. Our blood froze. It was a frightful wailing sound, a moan that emanated from the bowels of the dark and deserted Barne Hall! We were chilled to the bone! We lingered for a few seconds to make sure the sound was real. It was. Overcome with fear and excitement, we rushed back down towards the safety of our dorms.

Next morning, the school was agog with the story of the Ghost of Barne Hall, as we stepped in gingerly for morning Assembly. I mentioned it excitedly to the British Exchange student, who was volunteering at Sanawar that year.

'Oh! That was me!' he said apologetically, 'I was practising my saxophone for the school concert when the lights went out. I needed the practice so I continued in the dark until the lights came on. I didn't realise anybody had heard!'

We were disappointed. For some time, we had really believed that the Ghost of Birdwood had arisen again—its stories had spread like wildfire. It might even have been the ghost of Sir Henry Lawrence keeping a benevolent eye on his school!

But it was satisfying to know that what we had heard was real, that there was a British connection, and that we had mustered up enough courage to stand and listen to the eerie sound in the middle of the night in a deserted, desolate Birdwood, without immediately scooting to safety!

The school concert signified that Home Day was drawing near. The days were shortening and growing colder. This was the time for school plays in which our teachers would act, becoming subjects of hot gossip and merriment among the girls and boys of Upper Five and Sixth Form, who would read meanings into their lines and imagine liaisons between our beloved staff members. It also meant that apart from foraging the woods for pinecone bonfires, the winter term was soon ending and the stone slab behind the school bogs had only a few squares left for the pebble to scratch out.

Home Day meant piling all our packed steel trunks in advance near the boys' gym veranda, to be picked up by the school buses which would arrive to ferry the students down to Kalka station in the afternoon. The trunks would be marked in chalk and stored together on the veranda by destination: Delhi, Bombay, Calcutta. Just reading these names in the haphazard jumble ignited a spark of happiness within me.

Home Day, for me, also meant not waiting for the buses that would arrive to ferry us to Kalka Station but instead walking down to Kalka via Monkey Point, starting at about 6 a.m. on a cool morning. It was an exhilarating walk. The sense of freedom from school carried one down and across Garkhal in half an hour and then up the Kasauli hill to the Lower Mall, where a brief detour was felt required and we'd head towards Daily Needs, that supplied, among other things, bread to Kasauli residents and also stored cold cuts. It opened early because it was, after all, for daily needs, and the swarthy owner who sported a gold earring that made him resemble a benevolent pirate, was not averse – though perhaps he was a vegetarian himself – to frying the bacon in a small attached pantry and stuffing the greasy rashers into roughly cut chunks of bread, a substantial sandwich for hungry schoolboys from Sanawar! The bacon sandwich was useful as there would still be quite a trek ahead.

Back along the Lower Mall, one hurried along towards the deserted Monkey Point, just before which one had to locate a rough trail that wound down through maize fields and farmers' cottages, until it deposited you on the last stretch of the main road going down to Kalka. This took another two hours or so.

This was the time now to savour the sandwich and a sense of freedom, seated on a jutting boulder on top, and looking down over the pine trees to catch a glimpse of the vast plains that stretched beyond the Siwalik Hills to Chandigarh, and the world that beckoned beyond!

Sometimes, one got lost and wandered around on the khud side until a glimpse of habitation helped align oneself again. But one knew that all one needed was to keep going down. We would reach Kalka eventually!

I liked to make this journey alone, full of my thoughts, overcome with the happiness of going home.

Upon reaching Kalka, the first refreshment we were offered was Shikanji in huge glasses with salt and sugar and crushed ice from a number of dhabas situated outside the station. All forbidden pleasures!

Kalka Station would be fairly deserted when I would reach. My first destination would be the Railway canteen on platform 1, to order tomato sauce along with omelette and bread in that order, since we never got tomato sauce in school. The idea was to finish one bottle of tomato sauce in that one food order. In later years, the Railway canteen got wise and gave us the tomato sauce separately in a small bowl. We now had to pay if we wanted more. I wonder if anyone had a similar experience?

I now had time to myself to walk up and down the platforms, and wait for the rest of the school to reach.

By late afternoon, the school buses would arrive and the two platforms would soon be full of boys and girls walking up and down and over the connecting bridge in wild excitement.

On the siding at the end of the first platform, was a metre-gauge line for a quaint toy train that would travel up to Simla. It had only three or four carriages and would depart with a few passengers in the early afternoon. It was the first train to leave from Kalka that day. Thus the exodus began.

When would my train arrive to take me to Lucknow, I would wonder? I was always envious of the Bombay and Calcutta travellers, who seemed to come from a more glamorous planet.

By evening, the arriving trains would set off and a new excitement would break out, as we searched for our compartments.

Our exodus would begin at night.

The whole Home Day hike to Kalka took about three or four hours. But it was a heady trek. It was travelling home. It was a voyage to freedom!

**Siddharth Kak**
Sid/Jimmy | Vindhya 1963 | 1957–63

Delhi State Athletic Team 1964–69 | National Award, Best Exploration Film, 1984 | National Award, Raj Kapoor Biography, 1987 | Award-Winning Series, *Surabhi*, 1990–2001 | Author, *Surabhi ke Sau Sawaal* (Rupa Publications, 2005) | Award-winning thriller series 'Mano ya na Mano', Star TV, 2005–2007 | Author, *Looking in Looking Out*, collected poems, 2014 | Chairman, National Documentary Awards

# Back to School

Gone the British Raj, gone the sour memsahib. His chota peg is a dream of the past, and if she takes Chota Hazri, still she has to boil the kettle herself in her neat semi at Eastbourne. All is changed, changed utterly, except for Sanawar. We always knew that Sanawar was part of the eternal scheme of things, and to prove it, there it is twenty-one years after Independence, still rousing the boys with reveille blown on a bugle, still holding the annual race around the bridle tracks, and calling it still the Hodson Run.

The Lawrence Royal Military School, Sanawar, started as an asylum for the British Soldiers' children. Kipling wrote that if you want to make a man of your son, 'send him to Sanawar'. When I reached Sanawar at the age of seven because in the plains, I was a sickly child, it was a school for sons of regular soldiers, and it was dedicated to the cause of the greater glory of the British Empire.

It was 1,000 miles from home, three days and two nights by train. First, the Lahore Mail from Karachi Cantonment over the Thar Desert. Change at Lahore, under the huge girders swarming with monkeys. Across the rice and mustard crops of the Punjab plains to Kalka. Finally the narrow-gauge railway climbing into the Himalayan foothills, and the last couple of miles on foot over the bridle parts.

Each long, three-storeyed dormitory block sheltered one of the school houses, their names a roll call of the glorious victors of the Indian Mutiny: Lawrence himself, Hodson, Herbert-Edwards, Nicholson, Havelock, Roberts. In class, too, we dwelt on the achievements of Lucknow, and when we had exhausted that, they told us about Sparta (but not Athens) and when he had heard about the boy who let the fox bite him to death rather than admit that he had it under his shirt, we learnt about the Carthaginian wars.

It may be only my memory that persuades me now that we spent an entire school year on the exploits of Achilles, Ajax, Hector and the Patrocles. Certainly those lessons so fired our imagination that we youngsters, the under-elevens, spent all year fighting up and down the khud-sides, reenacting Agamemnon's just cause, with only one detail forgotten. Helen.

## 6 a.m. Reveille

For the over-elevens, war games were more authentic. Until the age of eleven, we all rose at 6 a.m. and went for a route march or PT. We all drilled under an army sergeant or warrant officer (cushy posting Sanawar must have been for him); we all suffered the equivalent of a works parade. But after eleven, they dressed the part as well; left off the grey flannel shorts and grey shirts with floppy grey funnel hats that the rest of us wore, and donned gurkha hats, khakhi shorts and shirts, puttees and boots, broad leather belts and for (I think) House captains, Sam Brownes. They drilled with rifles and learnt to fire them on the range, they marched to martial music by the school military band, and every year, on Founders' day, they submitted to inspection by the Viceroy, Wavell, or C-in-C India, Auchinleck.

It seems now that if we were not honouring the founder, we were honouring the Empire (Empire Day Parade), or God (church parade every day, twice on Sundays). We never maligned the memory of Guy Fawkes, but one memorable evening in the same season, descended instead to a village of mud godowns in the valley to join the Hindu celebrations of Diwali, the festival of lights, to splash our pocket money of four annas a week on yellow, sweet, sticky jalebis and soft white bricks of barfi.

Normally, our money went into the pocket of Charlie Bootlace, the Tuck Shop wallah. My older brother Peter taught me to supplement pocket money by stealing a loaf from the bakery while he distracted the baker (later, Peter hollowed out the loaf and poured in the contents of a tin of guava jelly); Charlie Bootlace was protected from similar depredations by his prestige. His brother had been a circus-strong man, lying on a bed of nails while men carrying great weights stood on his chest.

Peter was fourteen and everything to me than what an older brother should be; in return, I gladly stole for him or ran errands. One day, a convalescing airman came with the cricket team from the town on the next hill, Kasauli. He scored 37, caught and bowled de la Rue Brown, and Peter, too shy himself, sent me to the pavilion to collect his autograph. 'All the best, Denis Compton.' So what? The man I was too shy to speak to was the Sixth Former, de la Rue Brown.

## Seasonal Competition

Our life was bounded by the seasons, conker season, alley (marbles) season, beetle season (we caught rhinos and by stroking them firmly between the wings, enraged them so that they would fight and kill each other), lathi season (you hit a short sharpened stick at one end with a larger stick, and as it flew into the air, whacked it as great a distance as you could), butterfly season. Even butterflies encouraged competitiveness, over who could make the best collection of these exotic insects: swallowtails, oakleaves, sunsets. We collected jam and fruit in tins and allowed it to rot. Then we smeared it on the bark of the pines and watched the butterflies settle and gorge themselves into stupefaction so that you could simply pick them off the bark.

For official entertainment, we marched annually to the little Kasauli Cinema, once to be bored by a musical, either called *This is the Army, Mr Jones*, or with a song of that title as refrain; once to be stupefied by *Tripoli Victory*, all animated maps; once to fall asleep over a documentary on the Tennessee Valley Authority; once to sweat with terror over a thriller about wife murder, *Suspect*.

We organized our unofficial entertainment better. The school authorities never did discover that the reason the soap periodically vanished from the wash houses was that the visiting snake charmer took payment in soap; used or unused, it was all currency. How we thought we could do without soap, I cannot imagine. There were no sewers in the latrines, and until the sweepers made their daily visit, the stink made a late visit a real challenge.

Mental challenges can be no severer than elementary arithmetic in class, and American comics in the dormitory. When we ran out of Captain Marvel and Superman, my friend Robert and I made our own comics. I would not admit that he could draw better than me (he could), but I could not deny that he was illiterate, so did the artwork and I did the conversation balloons. It was not a difficult form to master.

Soon after taking up comic paper production, our humane English teacher praised me for using the word 'lumbering' in an essay about a bear. Then a sergeant showed us the *Times of India* front page, all about a new bomb that destroyed a city in Japan. This concatenation of experiences made me determined to be writer; I saw that the occupation of fighter pilot would not long remain fashionable (Peter, however, maintained his original purpose and earned a fleeting peacetime fame with a pilotless aircraft that somehow became airborne and he shot it down into Sydney Harbour). Peter is still in the Air Force but RAAF.

Copyright © Rathin Mitra ART MASTER | 1950–1953

One day, at Napier Barracks, Karachi, I mentioned my plan to become an author to a group of paratroopers, who had asked, 'What are you going to be when you grow up?' Because of their reaction to my answer, I have never since disclosed my vocation to another soul. But I left Sanawar a solemn, dull boy, swinging my arms to regulation height, a butt to my new schoolmates in the North-east of England, until I had adjusted. Peter left school and England as soon as he could. Things might have been different had we been born and brought up in Darlington, but Kipling had a word for that kind of profitless speculation. If.

**Michael McNay**
Old Sanawarian (Havelock 1943–1945)

**Source and Acknowledgement:** *The Sanawarian* (December 1972). Reprinted from *The Guardian*, 6 September 1968.

# Close Encounters

We had some really interesting teachers in Senior School.

Mr Sibbal taught English. He was quite a spaced-out sort of chap; we called him 'Zap'. One day, Zap took his wife to Chandigarh for a dental appointment. While he was away, four boys from Nilagiri House broke into his House. They stole a CD, raided his fridge, and took all the food they could find. Zap came back to find his House burgled and, as you might expect, was deeply upset.

However, it turned out that Zap wasn't as spaced-out as we had thought him to be. The following day, he announced an essay-writing competition for the School, titled 'The mystery of Mr Sibbal's House robbery'. The four who had broken in wrote exactly the same story. They changed the names but described, in great detail, how the perpetrators entered through the ventilator, raided the fridge, then the cabinet and left with two packets of Maggi noodles, four packets of chips and a Bryan Adams CD. Needless to say, they were caught and got the thrashing of their lives.

Twenty years later, I was narrating this anecdote on stage at the Chandigarh Golf Club. One of the four happened to be there. I asked him why he had written the truth in his essay. His response stumped me: 'Brother, I thought I'd get full marks.'

Ms Shonu Mukherjee taught geography and was a Housemistress. One night, three of us broke into the swimming pool complex. Since we didn't have costumes handy, we went skinny dipping. A while later, Ms Shonu was passing by. She peeped in through the window and reprimanded us severely for breaking rules and being there at 10 p.m. We apologized profusely. She asked us to get out immediately. We responded saying, 'Sorry ma'am, we *cannot*'. It took her about thirty seconds to figure it out and walk away, leaving us with our tiny dignities.

Mr Sukhwinder Singh was our hockey First XIs' coach. The team travelled to Bilaspur in a local bus for a district-level tournament. Exhausted, we crashed on reaching our destination. The following day, we played well, winning most of our matches. As a reward, Coach gave us the evening off. Instead of roaming about town, the bunch of us went in search of a video parlour that screened porn. We found it in a dark, dingy basement and settled down with our heads covered by shawls. When it was time for the parlour to close, the lights were turned on. We found Sukhi sitting in the rear corner of the room, with a shawl wrapped around his head. We didn't get a firing that night. However, we did get a dressing-down after we lost our matches, the next day. The Coach believed we hadn't spent our time, at the tournament, most appropriately.

Mr Abraham called me to his House, one night. He told me that some boys had gone to the girls' dormitory and while he knew who they were, as Head Boy, he needed me to confirm their names. I told him that I had been in the school for nine years and while I did not know their names, I was surprised he expected me to actually tell him who they were. He warned me that there were significant awards coming my way and that if I didn't tell him the names, I'd lose those. I didn't budge, and neither did he. I did, of course, know the name of every single boy who had gone to the girls' dormitory. But when you grow up with a code, you honour that code. I lost the Chief of Army Staff's Medal (erstwhile President's Medal) by one point on account oh the weighted teacher's vote that Mr Abraham had as Officiating Headmaster. Maybe that's why *Scent of a Woman* remains my favourite film. Maybe secretly, I wish that I had an Al Pacino or Colonel Frank Slade speaking in my defence: 'I can tell you this: he won't sell anybody out to buy his future. And that, my friends, is called integrity. That's called courage. Now, that's the stuff leaders should be made of.'

I really did want to end with this, to make me look good. However, I did once tattle on somebody. In fact, one of my closest friends. During the U-VI board exams, my friend KD wasn't really putting in the kind of effort he should have been. So, on the sly, I called up his father in Calcutta and told him to fire KD, without of course, revealing the source of his information. I happened to be with KD when he was called to his Housemaster's residence to take the call. He came out crying and deeply upset about the dressing-down his father had given him. Being the good friend I was, instead of telling him his father was right, I said, 'Don't worry, bro. You'll be fine.' Face palm.

But KD did start to focus a little bit more on his studies after that. So much so that he decided to break up with his girlfriend. Since he was so focussed on his lessons, I was assigned the responsibility of writing the break-up letter. It was pretty standard format. 'You're a lovely girl . . . this isn't going to work out . . . I hope we can still be friends . . .'

**Papa CJ**
Chirag Jain | Siwalik 1995 | 1986–1995
Stand-up Comedian | Author | Executive Coach

*Excerpt from Papa CJ's autobiography titled* Naked

# In Hindsight

What mattered the most
The structure, the order, the rules
The bounds, protection, a warm embrace
Limits to test, each for oneself

Within these hills, we found our wings
Nurtured in the pines, to become who we became
Buoyed by friends, their support, a lift
The foundation for life, they continue to be

Actions had consequences, justice was swift
Self-reliance a necessity, no choice to make
In search of depth, hollow words were shunned
Valued what mattered, ignored the rest

We walked away with character and grit
A yearning for friendship, true and deep
Shared history, bonds and memories abound
To our future selves, may this be an encore.

**Mytri Pritam Singh**
Himalaya 1985 | 1976–1985
Public Health Professional in New York City | HIV/AIDS Prevention
and Research | Population Health Measurement and Improvement

OS Parent – Father – Pritam Singh | Himalaya 1952 | 1950–1952

OS Sibling – Sister – Mimi Pritam Singh | Himalaya 1984 | 1976–1984

# Obituary

## The Rt. Rev. George Dunsford Barne, 1879–1954
## CIE, OBE, VD, MA (Oxon)

It is with the very deepest regret that we have learned of the death of The Right Revd. Dr G. D. Barne, in London on 17 June 1954. As is well-known, Bishop Barne was Principal here for twenty years from 1912–1932. What Arnold was to Rugby, he was to Sanawar. He took over an institution and left it a flourishing school based on public school principles and moulded in the public school tradition. No tribute could possibly do him adequate justice but there is no doubt that he was a legend in these parts and that his name will live on for many years in Sanawar. Though changes have been considerable since his departure, the basic principles on which we work today are largely his. We remember with pride and gratitude his devotion to, and affection for, Sanawar. In his last letter to me, written in March of this year, he sent greetings and good wishes for a successful year and wrote nostalgically of 'The Hilltop'. Sanawar was very dear to him and Sanawarians throughout the world will be joining us in mourning his loss. He was a great man in every way and we who are built in a humbler mould, can but strive to maintain the standards set by him and thus ensure that we continue to be what he made us, one of the premier schools in the country. Thus, we shall be serving not only Sanawar but, in a wider field, India. He passed on to us a very worthy heritage. Our consciousness of that fact must make us, one and all, all the more determined to preserve it.

**E.G. Carter, OBE, MA, (Cantab.)**
Staff 1922–1955 | Principal, 1947–1955

# The Hills Come Alive

Today, as I go down memory lane, nostalgia overwhelms me, the hills and valleys beckon. The fresh fragrance of the pines and the mist engulf me and send a chill down my spine. My memories are vivid – crystal clear – my parents and Sansar Chand, our trusted driver, driving up Sergeant Tilley's Hill. The black Ambassador holding my grey trunk with my name boldly printed across it in black.

My young, six-year-old mind was confused about where I was going and what the future held for me. Miss Kaveri and Miss Rudra were both welcoming and friendly, yet stern. They shaped our future and inculcated in us qualities which have held us in good stead even today.

I was tall and lanky. Almost built wiry—a target for humour by my co-fellows.

My parents cut short their vacation and came up to school to celebrate my seventh birthday. Arms filled with goodies for me and my friends—what joy it brought me. Birthdays were simple affairs . . . we tried to be friends with the birthday boy to get a coveted invitation. Good old Charlie used to give us the goodies to enjoy.

Being a part of the choir and concert was an honourable part of school life. The Naga dance and Himachali play, I remember, I loved participating in.

Baths in 6 minutes! Or a dry bath if you were in the second lot – and that scramble for the best working shower.

That rouser bell! It still rings in my ear, no matter where I am in the world; early to rise, even today.

The Hodsons' run! What one didn't do to qualify for this prestigious run around short and long back. The cheers of the girls made our day.

The warmth of the tea in the aluminium mugs at Chota Hazri—a kickstart to every chilly morning. And the hot cocoa at night.

*The Man in the Bowler Hat*, a play I was so proud to be the lead of.

Going down to Dhobi Ghat to get our blazers ironed. And shining our shoes to look dapper at the Socials was all that mattered, even if it ended up with us dancing at an arm's length with our favourite girls.

The Bhutta raids in the cornfields down the khud invited the wrath of Mr B. Singh and we got six of the best.

Mr Kemp's duster being thrown at us was something we dreaded in the chemistry class.

Ms Douhati's and Mr Fustey's English lessons and the passion for reading they inculcated in us. Then the nuances of learning Hindi and Sanskrit.

The effort to master the handstand. The bullying and the friendship. The bonding. All part of being at the best school of all—the Lawrence School Sanawar!

**Dr (Prof.) Rakesh Chopra MD**
Chopsy | Himalaya 1969 | 1961–1964 and 1966–1967
Senior Director and HOD, Medical Oncology/Haematology, Fortis | Chairman and HOD, Artemis Hospitals, Department of Medical Oncology/Haematology/BMT-(V) | Senior Consultant and Professor, Apollo, Indraprastha and Sir Ganga Ram Hospitals | Adjunct Professor, University of Nebraska, Omaha, USA | Ex-Board of Directors, American Society of Clinical Oncology

# Rajan Grows Up

My parents and I journeyed from Meerut to Kalka by train. A taxi drove us the twenty-two miles from Kalka, labouring up the steep, winding road that forked at the village of Garkhal. The one and a half mile from Garkhal to Sanawar took us from rural India into a world that was an offshoot of British India. Perhaps no other stretch of road is etched so vividly in my mind. The taxi eventually drew up to a board that read 'The Lawrence School, Sanawar'. It then struggled up a steep slope, as if it was going to die—a sensation I was to experience scores of times thereafter, up Sergeant Tilley's Hill, finishing last in Hodson's in my final year, and being cheered all the way to the finish line.

We were met by senior master Mr Kemp, an Anglo-Indian gentleman in his late forties. Besides handling administrative matters, Mr Kemp also taught chemistry. He was an accomplished batsman, too. He was tall, broad-shouldered, bald, pink-complexioned and bespectacled. His academic, black gown was venerable with age and chalk. Once, sprinting down a corridor in Birdwood, I turned a corner and headed full tilt into Mr Kemp's midriff. He side-stepped neatly, swatted me on the head with the register he was carrying and said, 'Watch where you are going, dopey'. I guess he must have had a lot of practice.

Mr Kemp gave us breakfast and took us on a tour. I was assigned to Vindhya House, which occupied the two top floor dormitories of a building, named after Field Marshal Wavell. The dormitories were connected to the quadrangle by a stepped walkway. In Sanawar, everything is up or down.

During breakfast, my father informed Mr Kemp that I was exceedingly sensitive. To this, Mr Kemp replied, 'Parents rarely understand their children. I have three and I am not sure I understand them'. We were served in a guest dining room adjacent to the main hall. While we were eating, boys filed into the main hall and stood at their places in order of height. A prefect intoned, 'For what we are about to receive, may the Lord make us truly thankful'. The whole company sat down and ate in controlled pandemonium.

Mr Kemp led us through the gymnasium, that contained a vaulting horse, parallel bars, a high bar, a beam like a high bar and floor mats. There were about thirty boys practising boxing under the supervision of a coach, who was six-foot-plus, massively built man of almost sixty, named Jagdish Ram Acharya. In private, the boys called him Jagga. It was known that he had retired from the Indian Army as a Subedar Major. Rumour had it that he had been the heavyweight boxing champion five times running, in the Army. Here, he was in-charge of physical education, boxing, gymnastics and marksmanship. From my second year at Sanawar, till I graduated, he was Housemaster for Vindhya (Senior).

That gym and the 'ropes' outside were the stage for many trials and tribulations of my boyhood. On that spring day, however, I accompanied Mr Kemp and my parents on the tour feeling a mixture of pride, joy and trepidation. The tour included the War Memorial to old school fellows that had fallen in the Great War, 1914–18, the school Chapel, Birdwood School with the Barne Hall, classrooms, and the art and crafts and woodworking shops.

My parents left that evening.

My first year was pure hell. I got branded a sissy and a tattler. Nobody would talk to me. Prefects slapped, buffeted and sometimes even caned us. Other punishments inflicted included push-ups or jumping jacks. One night in my first year, someone left faeces near the washroom sink. The prefect reasoned that since this had not happened before, the culprit must be a new boy. Six of us new boys were rounded up and questioned. No one confessed. All of us got six of the best: six slaps and six strokes with a cane on our butts apiece.

Homesick and friendless as I already was, this punishment and humiliation was more than I could bear silently. So when the Housemaster Mr Gore asked me how I was getting along, I told him about this incident. In doing so, I committed the cardinal sin—I 'tattled', which was taken as threatening the power of the prefect. The Housemaster told the prefect that I had complained. Since he was otherwise an intelligent and well-meaning man, I can only assume that he was subject to a random fit of stupidity. The prefect assembled the House and singled me out. As a result, the boys in my House either cut me dead or amused themselves by bullying me. I didn't mind the ostracism; I spent most of my leisure studying or reading.

This habit further fuelled the derision of my Housemates. My books were snatched and thrown away.

Life, however, got a little better after the results of the first Mark Reading. Progress in class was measured by tests administered periodically. There were no scheduled final examinations, so that we studied for the whole year instead of just before exams. Three times a year, test scores were aggregated and announced at Mark Reading. Each House competed on the basis of the total scores in scholastics, games, gymnastics and boxing. In that first Mark Reading, I achieved the highest score in Sanawar's history.

The other fallout of this ostracism was that I took no part in social activities. It was a co-educational school. Every month, there were Socials, where the staff and students would dance. The school had its own band and orchestra. The school band led the Founders' parade. The Drum Major marched, tossing up and whirling a baton. It was quite a tradition. That's where I first heard 'Colonel Bogey', a march with the line 'Hitler has got only one big ball'. It is the theme song of the movie *The Bridge on the River Kwai*. At the Socials, they mainly danced the foxtrot and the waltz, and sometimes, the twist. Teachers from England or Peace Corp volunteers were encouraged to show us their dance moves. The final item in our PT display used to be dancing the Scottish Highland Fling. I only attended Socials in my final year at school. My parents, like true Tamil puritans, considered ballroom dancing immoral. However, once I started going, it was a lot of fun. How it worked was that you went up to a girl and asked her to teach you to dance. Sonali, who sat just behind me in class and teased me all the time, taught me. She was the kind of outgoing, vivacious personality that is the life of any party. When she took my arm and put it around hers, I realized that there was more to life than spherical trigonometry. Her sines and cosines were magnificent.

There was little opportunity for hanky-panky. The girls' dormitories were at the other end of the school campus. There were thirty girls sharing one large room, rather like a military barrack. Then there was Cerberus, a fierce spinster named Miss Chatterji, who watched over the girls like a mother hen. However, there was one attempt at getting to the girls during the years I was at Sanawar. Five boys from Vindhya, led by Rana, visited the girls' dormitory at night, climbing in from the roof. They were caught in flagrante delicto by Cerberus, who had been tipped off by one of the other girls.

The entire Boys' School was assembled on the quadrangle. The offenders were marched in and publicly caned by Jagga. It was a steep price to pay for a stolen kiss. They were lucky not to be expelled. The fact that Rana's girlfriend, Roop, was [the] headmaster's niece may have had something to do with it. I silently cheered Jagga on with all my soul. Rana had been my chief tormentor. He said of me, 'This guy will just become a frustrated scientist and kill himself'. On another night, his gang waylaid me as I was going to the washroom. I was made to strip and could not help weeping. Rana commented to a sidekick, 'It is not the pain that makes them cry, it is the humiliation'. The same treatment was meted out to my best friend, probably because he was my friend.

As I moved up, life became progressively better. Classes were easy. There was an excellent library that I used extensively. I read Stevenson, Scott, Kipling and acquired the habit of studying mathematics on my own. My favourite teacher was Miss Pamela Dougherty (later Mountford), an Anglo-Indian about twenty-two or -three, our form teacher in L-V. She taught English and we read *As You Like It*. Due to her encouragement, I acted as Raja Jaichand in *Samyukta Swayamvar*, a Punjabi play staged at Founders'.

My boxing improved. The very first time, I got hit on my nose and started crying. My father was a pacifist who didn't believe in boxing. The fact that he sometimes beat up people didn't seem to be inconsistent with his beliefs. He suggested that I should somehow wriggle out of it. This wasn't possible since you could only be excused boxing on medical grounds. The categories were based on weight, height and age, rather than just weight. This was to prevent older boys from dominating the groups. A bout was of three one-minute rounds in the lower weights and one-and-a-half-minute rounds in the higher. Bouts were decided on points or by Technical Knock Out (TKO). No boxer was ever knocked out during my years in school. In between rounds, the spectators cheered on the boxer representing their House. During bouts, pin-drop silence prevailed.

I got to the quarterfinal round, one year. My opponent was T. Vungalalian, from Nilagiri. He was short, strong, agile and cheerful. Jagga encouraged me greatly before the fight. He said that I could go on to win the weight. I pointed out to him that I would have to beat Naresh, his own son, who had won the weight in the previous year and was favoured to win again. Jagga assured me that I could win. The fight started and Vunga came at me. Being shorter, he would keep trying to close in while I moved away and tried to hit him at long range. He kept smiling throughout. It was not a supercilious smile at all. It was just the happy smile of someone playing a game that he loves. Some natures enjoy contention. The three rounds went by very quickly. [The] headmaster declared, 'Well-fought Green, Red is the Winner'. I went back to the middle of the ring and congratulated Vunga. He went on to win the weight.

At our Sixth Form (farewell) party, I was mostly looking forward to going out into the world. Addressing the audience, Jagga said, 'This boy has improved greatly since first coming to Sanawar. I am sure he will do well in the world.'

I have treasured his words all these years, for no one else ever said any such thing.

**Narayanaswami Rajan**
Vindhya 1965 | 1961–1965
BTech (E.E.E.), IIT Kharagpur, 1971 | MTech Electrical (Control Systems), IIT Kharagpur, 1973 | PhD, School of Automation, IISc, 1979

ISRO Satellite Centre Employee 1978–81 | National Research Council Associate, NASA Ames Research Center 1981–83 | Postdoctoral Fellow, Deptt. of Aeronautics & Astronautics, Stanford University 1983–86 | Software Development 1990–2014 | Apple Software Developer 2014–2017 | Coding Coach, The Coder School, Palo Alto – 2018 onwards

# Idyllic Musings

It was a cold morning in early March 1951, when my father and mother drove me up to be admitted to this new school. We negotiated the 'narrow' turning at Garkhal (a shabby hamlet, alleged to have the highest number of TB cases in the world), and then the onward climb to Sanawar—with the powerful engine struggling to climb the final bend to the school gate. My father, an experienced and good driver, had to resort to the power gear. As I look back now, I cannot stop thinking that we had driven up in our light-blue Chrysler fluid-drive car, and thus I was in some strange way, ordained to join the Blue House.

We parked at the school Bakery and trudged up to the school office. Formalities completed, Bursar Sardar Mohinder Singh met, we were sent off to Honoria Court, the PD dormitory, to meet with the matron, Miss Woodward, and the senior mistress Mrs Sircar. I was allotted a bed in the lower dorm and issued my kit that included the battle dress, games kit, underwear, stockings, PT shoes and Ammunition Boots. Finally, a tearful farewell! I remember weeping in bed after lights-out, for many days after. Where had my parents dumped me? Moving from Welham Prep School in Dehradun to this dump in the wilderness. I wasn't alone though—Vijay and Vinod Nair, Jitinder and Surender Daulat Singh, Tej Pratap S. Mamik all had come from Welhams'. And the next year, Mr Vyas also joined as a Hindi teacher.

Soon, one settled down and fell into routine. Classes for Preppers were in Upper Birdwood. I was assigned to U-KG. In the first Saturday letter-writing class, Miss Rudra noticed that I was writing in joining hand, and so I was sent to Form I. A few days later, Mrs Curzon decided to push me another rung up and sent me to Mrs Sircar, the Form II teacher in-charge. I remember Mrs Sircar handing me a coloured chalk and asking me to draw on the wall above the chimney, a cuckoo in its nest (it was the beginning of spring, and the cuckoo could be heard loud and clear, all over the campus). In the first Mark Reading, I secured 98 per cent. My cousin, Tej Pratap, was aghast. Wow!

Our annual picnic was at Eagles' Nest. Obviously, there were two teams—Yellow and Blue. We collected pinecones and then battled over them. If hit, you went to the 'Camp Hospital', manned by the girls. I vividly remember 'soldiers' intentionally getting 'wounded' to be attended to. The injured were made to lie down, while Nalini Cariappa, Jasbir Kaur, Praveen Kumar (a renowned doctor today) and others (names I cannot recall now) put damp swabs on our forehead.

The little spare time went in playing marbles, tennis-ball cricket, and rounders. One Sunday, H.S. Sodhi, on his weekly visit to his younger brother, R.S., hit the ball from Peacestead, all the way over the powerhouse.

We preppers would watch in awe as the Senior School marched smartly in battle dress, shining ammo boots and berets tucked under the epaulettes, led by the Head Boy, D. Mackintosh. In 1952, I moved to Senior School, into Sparrow Hawks dormitory, what eventually became Himalaya House. Mr Cowell was our Housemaster there. Amarinder (of Patiala) was on the bed next to mine. Courtesy him, I was often invited to [the] headmaster Mr Carter's House for Sunday lunch. I captained the Sparrow Hawks cricket team against the Maharaja's XI in Chail. It was a cemented pitch and the ball often bounced over our heads. Max Guyga's band played in the pavilion with Coke for us and beer for the adults.

The two houses, Blue and Yellow, were housed in the Wavell Court, upper and lower dorm respectively. The dining hall was on the BD pavement (Nilagiri House today). The food was spartan and quite horrid—somedays, pooris leftover from the previous night's dinner were served with porridge. A pumpkin pudding, on another day, gave loosies to the whole senior boys' school. We were running to the loo all night. We had dry loos. What a nightmare! Mrs Nanda, mother of Bubbly and Asha, was a godsend. The food improved by leaps and bounds when she took over the catering.

One year, at the school picnic (held annually at Dagroo, midway from Dharampur to Subathoo), while others frolicked around and a few chatted up the girls, we heard a loud bang, followed by a shriek and then, a thud. We ran to the spot to find that Nankoo, the cook, while riding his bicycle, had lost control, hit the railing of the bridge and gone over it to land some thirty feet below. He was hurt badly and quickly taken to the Hospital in the school truck. He survived, but had an unmistakable limp thereafter. Today, I shudder to think that we skated down from Dharampur to Dagroo. Luckily, there was hardly any traffic back then.

In 1955, the House system was reorganized. Four Houses came into being. Mr Kemp became the senior master. Both Mr Carter and Mr Cowell left. Nilagiri moved up to number 10, the building next to the Chapel, to the envy of all. Mr Saleem Khan was our Housemaster.

In 1956, Major R. Som Dutt joined as the new headmaster, and was welcomed by the school lining up on both sides from the Green Gate to the Arch, as he drove through in his MG convertible, accompanied by Mrs Som Dutt and their dog, Mitzi.

Life was fun, easy and we were always up to a lot of mischief. Veer, Amol and I were caught by a peon doing experiments in the chemistry lab on Sundays, and got an earful from Mr Khan. Saravjit Lorai and I sabotaged a PT drill (for the entire House) called for by our prefect, Hardip Brar. The two of us printed formal invites (at the printing press) to a PT display by Nilagiri. So as the House fell-in on the pavement, Brar, to his horror, saw the girls watching from below the Art Room and the boys from around the Chapel. He had no other option but to dismiss us.

In 1958, my final year, I was appointed the school prefect (House captain) for Nilagiri. We had a glorious year with successes in almost every field, to deservedly lift the Cock House Cup.

I am happy that both my sons, Arjun and Gauravjit, were also at Sanawar, and last year, Gauravjit's son, Manavjit picked up his 'Old Sanawarian' stripes.

Never Give In . . .

**Harjit Singh Kochhar**
Nilagiri 1958 | 1951–1958
M.A. History, St. Stephens College | Pioneer in corporate gifting in India | Set up the Giggles chain of Stores

OSS PRESIDENT 1989–1991

OS Children – Son – Tej Arjun Singh Kochhar | Nilagiri 1989 | 1982–1989
Son – Gauravjit Singh Kochhar | Nilagiri 1992 | 1985–1992

OS Grandchildren – Grandson – Manavjit Singh Kochhar | Nilagiri 2021 | 2015–2021

# Fishing at Renuka

As part of the school annual camping tradition the Siwalik House, boys and girls from Sixth Form (1977 Batch) and Upper V (1979 Batch), went to Renuka Lake near Nahan, HP in 1976. The girls and the lady staff stayed at the guest House and the boys pitched tents in the front yard.

One afternoon, Sanjay Dutt, Rajiv Bali and I borrowed our Housemaster Mr BP Joshi's (Joey) fishing rod, informing him that we were going fishing in the Giri river nearby. Instead, we went fishing at the lake. Renuka was a religious lake, hence fishing was banned there.

The fish were huge and plentiful. Dutt took the rod and flicked it into the water. With abundant fish around, he immediately hooked one. Dutt started to struggle trying to reel the fish in and he was getting tired. Bali and I sat laughing our heads off, seeing Dutt struggle with the fish. After many attempts, Dutt asked me to take Mr Joshi's knife from his fishing kit, and swim towards the fish and kill it. The dumb guy that I was, I did exactly that, holding the handle of the knife tightly between my teeth.

Getting close to the fish, I got the knife in my hand. At that very moment, Dutt starting to pull the rod and the fish started to thrash about in the water and landed on my face. I panicked and started to stab the fish in a frenzy, as if my life was in danger. As I was stabbing the fish, the guest House guard saw me and started running towards us. Dutt cut the line and along with Bali, ran towards the guest House. The guard got close, yelling profanities and threatening to have me arrested and put in jail.

I got scared, got the fish to the shore and ran towards the guest House, with the security guard running behind me. He went straight to Mr Joshi and pointing at me, he explained what had happened. Mr Joshi, seething with rage, picked up a long broken tree branch, asked me to bend over, and started swinging the branch at my butt, back and legs. By now, a crowd of boys, girls and staff had gathered around. Given the macho boys environment, I did not plead or squeal in pain as Mr Joshi was beating me. This got Mr Joshi even more mad. The beating went on for quite a while and the stinging pain was becoming unbearable. Finally, the security guard and Mr Abraham (Abu) came to my rescue and stopped him. I could barely walk and Dutt stepped forward to help me. At that time, the security guard pointed to Dutt and Bali and stated that they were there too. He explained to Mr Joshi that it was, in fact, Dutt who had been holding the rod, while I was in the water stabbing the fish. Mr Joshi then worked on Dutt and by the time it was Bali's turn, he was exhausted. The security guard saw our plight, felt sorry for us and said he would not pursue the matter any further.

We got back from camps and Heady (Mr S.R. Das) was equally enraged upon learning of the incident. He called us to his office. As I entered, he threw a punch at me, which I ducked. He lost it completely and beat us with a piece of wood he kept in his office.

Just for the record, I am, by choice, a vegetarian and have never tasted fish in my life. In my early childhood, I was raised by my grandmother on her farm that was full of animals that she loved.

**Harjaspreet Singh Gill**
Clay | Siwalik 1979 | 1969–1977
Lives in Seattle, USA; passionate about golf, music, dance, real estate development and software engineering

# The Foreign-Returned

With much dread, we greeted our foreign-returned. Our visions of them coming back in tight Levis' transparent halters and blonde curls were sadly dashed when we saw them approach in slushy PT shoes and familiar old salwar-kameez. They were perfectly recognizable and hadn't changed even a wee bit. They were all given welcoming thumps on the back and Kabir must have got an extra-enthusiastic welcome as he had an enormous blotch of mud splashed right across his trousers.

They all arrived in lots, the first among them was JP, who being disgusted at his extra early arrival, went straight back home.

The rumour that Nixie, Payal and Praneet had acquired an accent was proved wrong, much to our disappointment. An assortment of tales poured out. Oh! the midnight parties, the discos, the fantastic departmental stores, the scrumptious eating joints—they were all too good. Trunks spilled goodies from swimming costumes to heavy coats. We looked on in amazement, and I daresay in jealousy, too.

The foreigners seem to have been thoroughly impressed by our Indian beauties—their charm, height, tan, long black hair and sophisticated dresses. Someone was most enchanted by JP's 'top hat' (as they called it) and even requested him to wear it down to breakfast.

The many broken hearts left behind, of course, have been accounted for, Nixie having already received what might fall in the category of a love letter. Mr B. Singh, I learnt, had quite a time fending off the extra-affectionate admirers. 'At an arm's length' was his advice to them. Gauti, as usual, was up to his craziness and was caught in the girl's quarters! Not very surprising, is it? Keeping him away from girls is like keeping Jughead away from Pop Tates' hotdogs.

**Mohyna Khurana U-V A**
Old Sanawarian (Nilagiri 1981)

**Source and Acknowledgement:** *The Sanawarian* (December 1978)

# Little Girl Lost . . . And Found

A little girl, barely eight years old, is sitting on a bench feeling sad and emotional. She can see her father sitting on a staircase close by, holding his face in his hands. She tip-toes up to him and timidly asks what the matter is. When he looks up, his eyes are filled with despair and sadness . . . from the fact that his wife, her mother, has been diagnosed with cancer and requires surgery at Chandigarh. She sits beside him, holds his hand and tries to reassure him, searching in vain for some words.

This bleak picture was the precursor to her journey as a student at Sanawar, her home since birth. As her parents left for the surgery, she was left in the able care of the school's resident engineer, Mr Surendra Kochhar, and his endearing wife Mrs Dhanbir. A fair share of teething troubles ensued, as is common when one is initiated into Prep School life. This rather lost little girl was me.

I went through varied emotions at that point in time, feeling lost without my parents around, so anxious about my mother's health and of course, the newly minted peer pressure! Gradually, I started getting involved in the academics and extracurricular activities. To my utter surprise, I won many prizes in athletics, especially in long jump and high jump, which I had never done before. I started looking forward to classes owing to my able teachers—Mr Ramchandani, Mrs Rampal, Mrs Joseph, Mrs Zutshi and Mrs Batish, who were not only good at their subject but also very loving and caring people, which resulted in a lifelong bond of respect and admiration.

Graduating to Senior School was pleasantly surprising because it was here that I befriended many boarders. Owing to this, the feeling of inclusion engulfed me, whereby from a smaller tribe of day scholars, I became a part of the larger tribe of boarders. Gradually, a lot of my friends like Ismat, Iram, Shagun, Gaurika, Tahira, Hemantika, Natasha and Yogini started visiting home, where they got a glimpse of my family life. Even my sister's friends like Tavleen, Ayesha, Ruplekha and Japna started visiting us. Boarding life was all about being independent and self-reliant and having to hack it without one's parents. The kids would constantly find emotional wellness in the faculty and my parents, because of which there was a semblance of love.

My mother's kitchen became a focal point from where she would churn out all kinds of goodies and extra breakfast every Sunday, for a dozen hungry girls.

Festivals, especially Diwali, came alive with my friends and their siblings helping with all the decorations and rangoli. We improvised the rangoli colours with spices such as turmeric, deghi mirch, rice flour, etc. For the Diwali Socials, there was a regular bevy of girls from afternoon onwards, inviting themselves over for baths and getting dressed. My mother's silk sarees were a big hit!

This influenced me in a very positive way whereby both my worlds coexisted. My home was my oasis, which was at the periphery of the main campus. It became my launching pad. From here, I would step out into an entirely different world with an eclectic mix of kids from all walks of life. I started excelling in my studies and sports.

Hailing from the naughtiest section, I started getting involved in all the pranks that we played on our teachers. We made Mr Mehta, our maths teacher, sit on a broken chair; scattered fart spray in the Hindi class which disgusted Dr D.C. Gupta no end. He would often send me to get the Drill Book, at which I would regularly come up with some excuse or the other. Despite being naughty, we were also the most intelligent section, with tremendous unity amongst ourselves. No one dare tattle against each other, the result of which was that almost every day, our entire class was put on drill. Time just flew by and before we knew it, it was time for us to enter college.

Sanawar imbibed in me innumerable values. I saw myself budding from a shy, lost girl to a confident, competitive go-getter—one who lives and abides by the school motto, 'Never Give In'.

As always, life does come full circle. I came back to Sanawar to admit my daughter, who transitioned from a small-town girl to a world citizen with bright stars in her eyes. The culmination of this beautiful journey was when I admitted my son in the school. I had always dreamt of sending my children to Sanawar. As we were heading towards the school, my son was full of enthusiasm. Upon entering the school gate, the welcoming staff, with their ever-smiling faces, the bright sunshine on the beautiful hilltop which I called home for so many years, brought on a feeling of intense gratitude and nostalgia. I dropped my son at school knowing that he will surely carry forward the great legacy.

Thank you, Sanawar, for being 'The best school of all' and for making us the best versions of ourselves.

**Namrata (Gupta) Sood**
Namru | Vindhya 1993 | 1985–1993

OS Parents – Father – Subash Gupta | STAFF 1967–2005 | Physics Lab Assistant | School Quarter Master

OS Siblings – Sister – Nitika (Gupta) Sandhu | Vindhya 1995 | 1986–1995
                Brother – Abhishek Gupta | Guppi | Vindhya 2001 | 1992–2001

OS Children – Daughter – Tanvi Sood | Tavvy | Vindhya | Present Sanawarian
                Son – Aarav Sood | BTS | Vindhya | Present Sanawarian

# 'Sanawarese'

## A Lexicon – A Glossary of old Sanawar Slang and Common Expressions

**artsie:** [n.] an eight anna coupon in School 'cash' [q.v.]. Adapted from the Hindi *'aath'* meaning 'eight'.

**ballyole:** [n.] the small, round and shallow depression in the ground used in a particular game of marbles. The game was known by the same name. (See 'taws').

**bed-roll, -pack, -block:** [n.] a neat and precisely folded parcel of one's bedding 'made up' daily for inspection (Sundays and holidays excluded). The standard issue of bedding comprised four blankets, two sheets, one pillowcase, one mattress (filled with dried pine needles) and one pillow (same). Three of the blankets were dark grey, very hairy and rough, and the fourth was a softer bluish-grey with a darker stripe (one's so-called 'best' blanket). Beds were 'made up' thus: the bed was stripped and the mattress folded back in half. The three rough blankets are folded to the same dimensions (approx. 28" wide and 14" deep) with the two sheets, similarly folded, sandwiched neatly between them. The whole parcel is then neatly enveloped in the outer (best) blanket folded longitudinally and displayed on the folded mattress at the foot of the bed. Finally, the pillow (cleanest side up) is placed on top. Beds were permitted to be 'made down' for sleeping, after evening prep.

**bed-space:** [n.] the whole area immediately under one's bed and 'kit box' [q.v.] extending halfway to one's neighbour's space on both sides (if applicable) and midway into the centre aisle.

**bobuck:** [n.] a sort of 'knock' [q.v.], but not quite the same. It was the speciality of Mr J.R. Coombes, BSc, the science master who was fondly

357

known by the same name, 'Bobuck'. (No one seems to know which came first) but a 'bobuck knock' is delivered thus: using one's favoured hand, the thumb and middle finger are held together, directly opposed as though to 'click' one's fingers. The heel of the palm is then placed on the crown of the miscreant's head. Pressure is applied, and the thumb is suddenly removed: resulting in the middle finger coming down like a miniature hammer onto the skull of the recipient. The 'bobuck' was latterly adopted as another form of prefectoral punishment for minor misdemeanours, giving 'gup', 'skunking off', etc.

**bobs**: [n.] pinecones, usually mature, opened cones fallen from the tree and collected for burning during the cold months of the year. The larger the cones, the better. A common punishment dispensed by prefects towards the end of the school year, was to collect X many 'bobs' for burning in the evening fires in dormitories. (See also 'chiligoja').

**bone/boning/boned**: [v.] the procedure employed for the removal of surface dimples when 'bulling' [q.v.] a brand new pair of boots. The leather of the toe-cap and heel is first softened by setting fire to a generous application of boot polish and methylated spirit. The molten polish is then allowed to spread around the surface of the toe-cap or heel, and while still hot, is rubbed hard with a bony substance (usually the bone handle of a toothbrush, sometimes a shoehorn). The procedure is carried out two or three times until all the dimples are flattened and smoothed out, ready to receive the final gloss.

**bosom**: [n.] not quite as in 'Abraham's bosom' but the space between cloth and flesh, inside the front of one's shirt. School regulation shorts and trousers were by design without pockets, so whatever one could get away with, whether animal, mineral or vegetable would be carried or stored in one's 'bosom'.

**bootroom**: [n.] the place where one exchanged worn-out boots, shoes, socks and other bits of 'kit' [q.v.] It was also the place where the Chief Instructor dished out 'lobs' [q.v.]. The original bootroom used to be in what is now the gymnasium (Gaskell Hall), on the veranda at the top of the broad steps to the lower dormitories (Block 12). It was moved down to the south end of the juniors' dorms (near the bathhouse and washrooms) around about 1943.

**bra':** [n.] no, nothing at all to do with ladies' nether garments but one's brother. Origin uncertain but presumed to be derived from bro' or brer as in 'Bro or Brer Fox' (Uncle Remus Folktales). When referred to by others, brothers were distinguished by the prefixes 'big', 'small' or 'little', e.g., 'Big Cook', 'Small Cook' etc. See also 'sas' (one's sister).

**brain:** [n.] as the word implies, a 'brain' was someone who was studious, industrious and who consistently came top, or near the top of the class. With a very few notable exceptions, 'brains' were not very good at sports, PT, marching about, shooting, drill, and all that sort of stuff.

**bull/bulling/bulled:** [v] the application of 'spit and polish': just the same as in Army slang. The toecaps and heels of one's 'best' boots were 'boned' [q.v.] and 'bulled' to a mirror-like gloss. So was one's leather belt. All brass buttons, badges, collar-dogs and buckles were burnished until they glistened and gleamed like miniature suns. Inspecting SNCO's expected to see their faces looking back at them. And heaven help you if they didn't!

**butch:** [n.] a particular form of game with marbles, 'taws' [q.v.] but played against the wall.

**buthi:** [n.] borrowed directly from the Hindi 'batti' meaning light, lamp or candle, but referring specifically to the lighted kerosene lamps placed at both ends of the dormitory aisles each night after 'lights-out', when the generators were switched off. They were used to light one's way to the outside 'tatties' [q.v.].

**butt/buttnet/butt-collector:** [n.] butterfly/butterfly net/butterfly collector. Butterfly collecting was a popular summertime hobby and sport for many a Sanawar boy, and there were quite a few who became 'chokes' [q.v.] at it. This 'free-time' pursuit was generally encouraged by the staff, who considered it a commendable and healthy interest in natural history.

**butts, the:** [n.] no, nothing at all to do with the above. It was the target end of the 200 yard, full-bore 'Long Range' near Garden City. Use of the Long Range was discontinued in about 1938 but the trench, mound and partly demolished safety wall of the butts remained well into the 1940's.

The entire range, up to and including the 100-yard firing point has since been levelled, graded and made into another playing field.

**camp**: [n.] the Annual Summer Camp. Usually held for seven days around Easter and nearly always at Dagroo valley, by the 'Choir Bridge' on the Dharampur–Subathu road.

**cash**: [n.] money, dough, dosh, paisa etc. (as in general parlance); but in those times, the word cash had two meanings. 'Hard cash' (i.e. real, or proper money) and 'Soft Cash', or 'school' money. Hard cash was officially not permitted during the school year in a vain attempt to prevent children from buying food, sweets and drinks from the local village bazaars and unauthorized vendors. Anyone arriving for the school year with hard cash was required to hand all of it in to the Housemaster/mistress. A receipt was always given, and the money went into one's pocket money account. Soft cash consisted of coupons or vouchers, negotiable only among authorized contractors on the hilltop. It came in rolls in the form of old-fashioned, perforated bus tickets and was issued to those with pocket money allowances in lieu of hard cash. There were half-anna, 'halfsie', one anna, 'onesie', two anna, dowsie, four anna, charsie, eight anna, artsie and twelve anna denominations, and a Re.1/- coupon, all in different colours. (By the way, Rs.13/8 = £1 in those days)!

**catty**: [n.] a catapult, painstakingly fashioned from a carefully selected forked branch growing on the 'khud-side', rubbers cut from the inner tube of an abandoned truck tyre, and a suitable piece of leather (generally the tongue removed from one's shoe). Again, some chaps were natural 'chokes' at making 'catties' and, for a small consideration, would produce them for others.

**chap(s)**: [n.] boys of all ages in general but more specifically one's fellow Sanawarians. There were 'Big Chaps' (seniors), 'Small Chaps' (juniors) and 'Little' or 'Titchy Chaps' (PD/infants).

**charsie**: [n.] a four anna coupon in school 'cash' [q.v.]. Adapted from the Hindi 'char' meaning 'four'.

**chew**: [n.] big eats; a great feast. Not surprisingly, uncommon in Sanawar! Occasionally, some chaps got together and saved up their pocket money for communal midnight 'chews', usually close to 'Home Day' [q.v.]. Chaps with parents living close by sometimes provided weekend 'chews' for their special chums, or perhaps even, 'grub-chums' [q.v.].

**chiligoja**: [n.] the common, edible pine nut, the winged seed of the edible pine tree, Pinus gerardiana. If you knew how, these could be harvested during 'bob-gathering' forays. They could be found between the scales of the fallen female cones or scattered about, under the trees on the khud-side: but you had to know what you were looking for. Some chaps became 'chokes' [q.v.] at it.

**chip**: [n.] a Rupee (16 annas) in hard or soft 'cash' [q.v.].

**chirricks**: [n.] diarrhoea, the 'runs' or 'squits'. Generally caused by a surfeit of 'inky-berries', 'jammy-jallopers' [q.v.], and/or other dubious fruits of the forest but occasionally too by one or other of the kitchen matron's culinary concoctions.

**choke**: [n.] someone who is exceptionally good at something/anything; an 'expert of experts'.

**chuck/chucks**: [n.] sweet/sweets but not the local 'mithai'. They were the boiled sweets and candies of the West such as 'Acid Drops', 'Humbugs', 'Bull's Eyes' etc. They generally came in food parcels from home (if you were lucky) or could be bought at the Tuck Shop. See also 'Salt-Sayo' and 'Sweet-Sayo'.

**chuff/chuffed**: [n.] [adv.] delight/delighted; pleasure/pleased, much the same as in general parlance.

**chuff-chart**: a sort of makeshift calendar produced by some chaps towards the end of the school year. They were used to mark off the number of days left until 'Home Day' [q.v.].

**chum**: [n.] same as in general parlance but with special reference to fellow Sanawarians, with whom one had strike up a special, friendly accord.

**coggage**: [n.] from the Hindi *'kagaj'* meaning paper but specifically school-issue toilet paper. (See 'tatti-coggage').

**conk/conks/conkers**: [n.] much the same as the English schoolboy's 'conker' and used in the same manner but in Sanawar, it was specifically the ripened fruit (nut) of of the Himalayan Horse Chestnut (Aesculus indica), found growing at various locations on and about the hilltop. Collected in October, they were seasoned, hardened and stored over winter for use in the following 'conker' season. Again, chaps had their own, closely guarded methods for seasoning and toughening the conk, including rubbing it daily with butter, ghee and other strange substances.

**crut/crutty**: [n/adj.] dirt or dirty, as in unwashed (usually behind the ears).

**crust**: [n.] the crown of one's head where one might receive a 'knock' [q.v.]. ('Pass your crust, you crutty little scob')! See also 'dome' and 'nut')

**culcher**: [n.] probably borrowed from the Hindi kulcha, a form of leavened flatbread baked in the Punjab. In Sanawar, it was a sort of bun or biscuit; product of the school kitchens and often served in lieu of hardtack. It was fashioned from iron-hard, brownish coloured pastry, sometimes sparsely embedded with raisins. Evidently, the raisins were edible, if you knew how to remove them. Again, some chaps became 'chokes' at this. Culchers were remarkably long-lived and evidently non-biodegradable. Tales abound of ancient specimens being found down the 'khud-side' below Big Plain while 'fagging' [q.v.] for cricket balls; and in other places as far afield as Dagroo.

**cushy**: (adj.) same meaning as in old army slang, and since accepted in many other walks of life. Adapted from the Hindi *'khushi'* meaning joy, delight, pleasure, happiness etc., it was used to express any chore or task that was easy to perform, comfortable (pleasurable even), and not too onerous. There was not much of that sort of thing in Sanawar, so the word was not very often heard. (Also spelled 'khushy').

**dame(s)**: [n.] girl/girls of all ages in general but more specifically the ones who lived well out of bounds (and out of reach!) beyond the Chapel on the far (north) side of the hill. Origin uncertain but no doubt borrowed from American slang.

**decent**: [adj.] the word had two meanings: [1] A 'decent' chap: someone who is fair-minded, considerate, friendly, helpful etc. (i.e. a nice guy, quite the same as in conventional usage). [2] When used in the context of numbers, quantities, amounts of anything at all: it became a synonym for 'considerable', 'substantial', 'reasonable', 'sizable', etc. e.g., 'a decent gang of chaps/dames at the Tuck Shop' = a fair-sized crowd of boys/girls at the Tuck Shop, 'a decent chew' = a pretty good feast, 'a decent dole' = a fair or goodly amount (of something), and so on.

**dent**: [n.] a hit, 'knock' [q.v.] or strike, ranging from a hard punch with closed fist (very serious), to a light cuff or blow about the 'lug', head or 'dome'. (Also used as a verb: to dent/denting/dented).

**dew-drops**: [n.] the small, telltale and embarrassing patches of damp occasionally appearing on the front of one's shorts, indicating a recent, hasty and rather careless visit to the 'tatties' [q.v.].

**dhup**: [n.] as in 'dent' above but borrowed from the Hindi and preferred by many. Also used as a verb, to strike (dhup/dhupping/dhupped).

**doggie**: a hardtack biscuit, usually served with a mug of tea at 'Chota Hazri'. (See also 'culcher').

**dole**: [n.] an amount, quantity; a portion, helping, or a dealing out of something. E.g., 'a decent dole' = a fair amount; 'a heck of a dole' = an awful lot).

**dome**: [n.] one's head. (See also 'crust' and 'nut').

**dowsie**: [n.] a two anna coupon in school cash [q.v.]. Adapted from the Hindi '*do*', meaning 'two'.

**egg-collector**: [n.] also 'bird-nester'. Not strictly slang expressions but included for their historical and social interest. Of course, the practice is widely deprecated today, and in some countries it is illegal. However, in those far off days it was many a Sanawar boy's spring-time hobby, with its roots deeply buried among the collecting traditions of the Victorian naturalists. The Staff considered it a commendable and virtuous interest in Natural History (or Nature Study, as we knew it then), and openly encouraged the activity. Again, many chaps became 'chokes' at it. See also 'butt-collector' [q.v.].

**fag/fagging** – [n.] the traditional practice in English private, and public boarding schools of the time was never prevalent in Sanawar. In Sanawar, 'fagging' was a wearisome, boring but necessary chore. It was generally carried out by minor offenders and miscreants as a form of punishment. However, if there were not enough wrongdoers, one could find one's self detailed off to perform the task as a necessary, community service, duty or fatigue. During the cricket season, for example, one might be detailed off to 'fag' for cricket balls. 'Fags' were stationed around the outside perimeter of Big Plain (Barne's Field) during the major matches, and would retrieve any balls struck over the boundary fences. Sixes onto Small Plain or over the Pavilion end were quite easy to 'fag'. However, the 'khud' [q.v.] on the west side of the field was quite steep and balls struck squarely over the wire here might easily end up on the main road far below. Thankfully, it seldom happened! 'Fags' were also employed for Tennis matches and major tournaments. Needless to say, there was never a shortage of 'fags' when the girls were playing. Details for 'fagging' duties regularly appeared in School Part I Orders until about 1937, when the term seems to have been deprecated. The practice continued quite overtly, however. Compulsory 'bob' collecting [q.v.] as a punishment dispensed by prefects, was also a form of 'fagging'.

**feet 'n' knees**: [n.] a brief and perfunctory form of bathing for small chaps, usually carried out under strict supervision during dry spells when water was scarce. One sat 'nanga panga' around the rim of a communal bathtub with half a dozen others, feet dangling in a few inches of lukewarm water until deemed clean.

**flick**: [v] to steal, purloin, 'swipe' or misappropriate. Serious offences, e.g., stealing of cash or valuables were punishable by expulsion.

**fizzog**: [n.] same as in general (English slang) parlance, meaning one's face. Said to be an eighteenth-century derivation of the term 'physiognomy'— also spelled 'physog'.

**flicks**: [n.] aka the Pictures or the movies (same as in conventional usage). As a rare treat, the whole school would take over the bioscope in Kasauli for a matinee performance of some carefully chosen and approved epic or other. It happened maybe three times a year.

**gaff**: [n.] fun, enjoyment, merrymaking, lots of laughs (lol), e.g., a 'dole of gaff' = a lot of fun.

**gang**: [n.] any two or more 'chaps' together, or 'dames' together. (Usage: 'Hey, you gang!')

**gid(s)**: [n.] borrowed from the Hindi *'giddh'*, meaning vulture(s). Large numbers of 'gids' assembled in the trees about the school butchery whenever there was a slaughter. They were fed the offal. The gids were mostly Himalayan Griffons with a few Black (King) Vultures here and there. Once in a while, a Bearded Vulture would turn up, causing much excitement.

**gogs**: [n.] spectacles, glasses; as in 'goggles'.

**goolie-dunda**: [n.] borrowed directly from the Hindi *'goli'* meaning ball and *'danda'* meaning stick. A game played on a reasonably flat open space or 'maidan'. (Also known elsewhere as 'Tip-cat', 'cat and dog', 'one-a-cat' or 'piggy'). The 'goolie' is a small stick, about 4 inches long, sharpened to a point at both ends. The 'danda' is a stout stick or rod about 2½' long. While resting flat on the ground, one of the sharpened ends of the goolie is struck with the danda, causing it to rise, twisting into the air, at which point it is again struck forcibly with the danda. The object being to hit it as far as possible. Sounds easy but it is harder than it would seem. The rules were variable according to the standard being played. There were quite a few 'chokes' at it, in the season.

**grub**: [n.] food, same as in common parlance but specifically the simple fare and rather frugal diet that played such an important part in the life of the school. Some meals were good, some bad; but whatever, there was never enough of it!

**grub-chum**: [adj./n.] one who made friends with another for whatever he could get from him. 'Grub-chums' would appear out of nowhere, like 'gids' [q.v.] at the butchery whenever a food parcel was received from home.

**gunja**: [n.] borrowed from the Hindi *'ganja'* meaning bald and used to describe a shaven head or a very short haircut. 'Gunjas' were the speciality of 'Wickie', the school barber. [q.v.]. A 'gunja' is also what one was immediately given on the faintest suspicion of head lice!

**gup**: [n.] backchat, to answer back impudently (not to say imprudently)! Giving 'gup' to a senior chap generally invited an immediate and painful response in the form of a 'knock', 'dent' or 'dhup' [q.v.]!

**gut/guts**: [n.] one's stomach, as in the common parlance.

**halfsie**: [n.] a half anna (2 paise) coupon in School 'soft cash' [q.v.].

**hard cash**: [n.] proper, or real money. (See 'cash')

**Home Day**: [n.] it speaks for itself. The magical, exciting, rowdy and joyful final day of the school year. It usually came around about the second week in December. See also 'school day'.

**home kit**: [n.] normal (civilian) clothes; 'civvies' or 'mufti'. The clothes one arrived in on 'School Day' and which were then taken off and stored away in boxes or suitcases until permitted to withdraw them a day or so before Home Day. It goes without saying that they no longer fitted and 'hummed' [q.v.] of camphor mothballs, or at best, mildew. 'Bum-freezer' jackets and trouser cuffs flapping around the ankles were common sights on the bridleway down to Dharampur on Home Days.

**hook (hoof) it**: [v] to 'move it'; take off quickly or urgently without delay; to 'shift one's backside'.

**hum/humming**: [v. or n. and adj.] to smell, smelling. It has to be said, some chaps 'hummed' almost to high heaven, usually at the height of summer when water was scarce. (See 'feet 'n' knees').

**inky-berry**: [n.] the ripe fruit of the Indian or Asian Barberry (Berberis asiatica), too many of which can result in stained fingers, mouth and tongue, and very, very loose indigo blue or purple coloured stools for several days to come (See 'chirricks').

**jacks**: pubic hair. Origin unknown but evidently goes back to the early 1900's.

**jammy-jalopper**: [n.] the common Medlar (Mespilus germanica), edible raw only after much bletting. Used extensively by 'butt collectors' to make 'sap' [q.v.] and by others to supplement the school diet (See again 'chirricks').

**jeebie-jeebs**: [n.] meaning to tuck in, muck in, help oneself or 'free for all'. Said to be derived from GBG, short for 'Grab Boys Grab' and dating back to the early 1900's.

**jongs**: [n.] swimming trunks. Not included in one's issue of 'kit' [q.v.]. One had to supply one's own, borrow from another, or simply do without! On summer camps, many a chap went into the pools 'nanga-panga'.

**KV (kayvee)**: [v] an exclamatory verb meaning 'watch out', derived from the Latin 'cave', to beware! 'Kayvee chaps, here comes Boss'!

**khud/khud-side**: [n.] borrowed from the Hindi '*khadd*', meaning gully or ravine. In school parlance, it applied generally to the banks, slopes, heights and inclines of the hilly terrain all around.

**kit**: [n.] any item of Government (WD) property issued to one, including all items of apparel, accoutrement, footwear, mess tins/mugs, eating irons etc. One was expected only to provide one's own toothpaste, soap, boot polish, Brasso and 'jongs' [q.v.]. Kit was inspected randomly and without any notice at all by the CI to ensure that nothing had been sold or bartered for food, mithai, *sigret*, *birisor*, whatever. See also 'home kit'.

**kit box**: [n.] the 3 x 2 x 1½ ft wooden box at the bottom of one's bed where all of the above was supposed to be stored.

**knock**: (n) a form of prefectoral punishment meted out between boys, usually for trivial offences or misdemeanours. The clenched fist, with the knuckle of the middle finger extended is brought down with varying force (according to the severity of the misdeed) on the crown of one's head, 'dome', 'nut' or 'crust' [q.v.]. Notice was generally given, 'Pass your crust,

I'm going to give you a knock'. One could respectfully decline and appeal to go before the CI, or even higher authority for justice but it was never really worth it!

**kunni**: [n.] mistake, error. Origin unknown.

**lob/lobs**: [n.] Corporal punishment, as administered to boys in those days. One to six full-blooded strokes to the backside with a well-oiled and highly polished Malacca cane. Dispensable only by fully qualified members of the teaching Staff and the Chief Instructor. Very occasionally administered in public (extremely serious); at other times privately, under the stairs in Birdwood Science Block, where Sammy Cowell kept his collection of fine Malacca canes, or else in the 'bootroom' down below in BD. Sammy Cowell was a real 'choke' [q.v.] at dishing out lobs. Nowadays, people would be sent to prison for doing this!

**lug/lugs**: [n.] one's ear, or ears.

**manhole(s)**: [n.] the safety niches or recesses built into all the tunnels on the Kalka-Simla Railway. They occurred every 50 yards or so on both sides, staggered, so one only had about 25 yards to run in order to find one. Tunnels made excellent shortcuts and were extensively used by 'roamers' [q.v.]. Given that no one had a clue about train timings, it's a wonder there were never any fatalities! Needless to say, hair-raising 'manhole' stories abounded around the winter evening 'pine bob'[q.v.] fires.

**modest**: [adj.] exactly the opposite of the accepted meaning! Modest chaps were brazen swanks, braggers, boasters and know-alls. Usually extrovert, they knew always how to guide any conversation back to themselves. They generally came in all guises.

**nippie or nappie**: [n.] the generic term for school barber. There were two, sometimes three, of whom 'Wickie' [q.v.] was the most well-known.

**nut:** [n.] one's head. (See also 'dome', 'crust').

**onesie:** [n.] a one anna coupon in school cash.

**orders**: [n.] following standard military practices and protocols, Orders were published and promulgated periodically as required (usually every four or five days). They were the written instructions, issued and signed by 'Boss' himself, which governed almost every day, hour and minute of one's school life. They came in two Parts: Part I Orders were 'disciplinary' and prescribed such things as daily routines, duties, timings, punishments, movements, itineraries for visiting officers, etc. Part II Orders were 'administrative' and dealt with matters pertaining to increases and decreases in departmental strengths, staff appointments, promotions, demotions, fag duties (prior to 1938), leave, fines, notice of shop opening times, commodity price lists, entertainments, etc. Orders were posted on Notice Boards in the Birdwood corridors, the verandas of all dormitory blocks and at both ends of the dining rooms. Everyone was expected to read Orders. There were no excuses. School Orders continue to be issued in a similar form to this day.

**puck/puckdundi**: [n.] borrowed from the Hindi *pagdandi* meaning literally, different or difficult path; and referring specifically to the winding, mountain footpaths and trails found everywhere on the slopes of the Siwalik. Often abbreviated simply to 'puck'.

**paisy**: [adj.] used to describe someone who is frugal, canny, parsimonious and reluctant to spend money. Borrowed and adapted from the Hindi 'paisa' of which there were four to the 'anna' in those far off days.

**pipe/piping**: [v./n. and adj.] to whinge, whine, bleat or cry; to complain self-pityingly.

**polly's dirt**: [n.] the delicious chevda or chuda, resembling parrot's droppings that was made and sold by Sri. Known today in the west as Bombay or Punjabi Mix, it now comes with peanuts, chickpeas, raisins and such-like added.

**press/pressing/pressed**: [v.] the standard procedure for obtaining a fine crease in one's shorts and/or trousers without the aid of a hot steam iron. The item in question is liberally sprinkled with water, carefully folded along the desired creases and placed overnight between one's bottom blanket and mattress. If one could then manage to spend a sleepless night without moving around too much, the result might be a finely pressed pair of shorts or trousers for the next day's wear. The smarter chaps among us were chokes at this and frequently appeared 'all pressed up'. Needless to say, however, most preferred to wait until Saturday mornings, when they could be exchanged for a clean, highly starched and ready-pressed pair from the school dhobi.

**pump/pumper:** no, nothing to do with the school water supply which was entirely gravity fed from reservoirs at the top of the hill but relating to the hand pumped organ in the Chapel loft. From time to time, one was detailed to perform 'pump duty'. The detail usually lasted a week, and simply involved pumping furiously at the hand bellows whenever Miss Jones, the organist nodded vigorously in one's general direction. Happily, one was not required to pay any attention at all to whatever else might be taking place on the floor of the Chapel down below. A khushi number, you might say. Not surprisingly, a lot of chaps were known to volunteer for this particular fag or duty.

**poori-tac:** [n.] a favourite staple food from 'Charlie Bootlace'. It consisted of a spicy but relatively mild potato curry stuffed in a delicious poori. Served hot and eaten at once, it helped fill many an empty stomach. With a little lena-dena, one could get three for a 'charsie' [q.v.].

**rag/ragging:** [v] to tease or 'take the Mickey'.

**raid/raiding:** [v./n. and adj.] same as the English 'scrump/scrumping'. The stealing of bhuttas, pears, figs etc., from nearby pahari farmer's terraced khet and fields. There were always lookouts, however, and if you were spotted, the cry 'Aieee, *bhutta lena!*' would go ringing around the hilltops. One had to 'hook it' back up the hill to avoid getting caught. The experienced paharis would go for your hat because they knew your name was written inside the headband. It was very shameful, not to say subsequently painful, to lose one's hat.

**ringtack:** an ancient form of marbles, 'taws' using a small depression in the ground with a circle drawn around it. The complicated rules are buried somewhere in the annals of Sanawarian folklore. If there is anyone still alive who remembers them, please get in touch.

**roam/roaming**: [v./n. and adj.] to ramble, rove, wander, trail and explore the surrounding hills and valleys. One generally stuck to the well-trodden 'pagdandi', bridle paths, cart roads, railway lines and highways but some would venture off the beaten track. The practice was encouraged during the main term breaks because it helped to keep one fit. There were rules, however. Small chaps were restricted to places nearby like 'Eagle's Nest', 'Foxy's' and 'Monkey Point'. Bigger chaps could wander further afield but only in parties of three or more and one had to say where one was going. At certain times, well-known GD destinations, e.g., Lahli's', 'Lover's' and 'Crater's' might be pronounced out of bounds to all boys. Haversack rations (usually sardine sandwiches and a 'culcher' [q.v.] ) were generally issued after breakfast or Chota Hazri, if one gave sufficient notice. A good day's roam could take one to Subathu, Solan, Kalka or Gurkha Fort, but one had to really hoof it to get back in time for supper!

**RMO**: [n.] the Resident Medical Officer. A staff appointment by GHQ New Delhi, he was usually a medical officer in the Indian Army Medical Corps (IAMC).

**Rose Cottage**: [n.] the delicate and refined sobriquet for the girls' outside lavatories, in particular those built in 1936 next to Block 10, the original Girls' Building or 'Church Barrack', and latterly the junior girls' dorm. (See 'tatties' for the somewhat coarser BD equivalent).

**salt/sweet sayo**: [n.] a variety of 'chuck' (western sweet or candy) available in the Tuck Shop, and popular with some.

**sap**: the word has two meanings: [1]: [n.] a concoction of fruits and sugars, well-fermented and matured to provide an alcohol content of about 5 per cent by volume. This mixture was smeared onto the bark of certain trees to attract sap-eating butterflies such as the Oakleaf (Kallima inachus) and other nymphalids. The 'butts' were said to become drunk and were easier to catch. Butt collectors had their own closely guarded, secret recipes, often with rare, outlandish ingredients. Some also observed curious and somewhat cabbalistic rituals in the making of their 'saps', which was said to improve the efficacy of their brews. [2]: [n., adj.] a 'softie' or 'sissie'; a denigrating label no boy wanted. A sap 'piped' when given 'knocks', 'lobs' or 'ragged'.

**sas:** [n.] one's sister. It goes without saying that chaps with pretty sisters in GD were widely courted as 'chums'.

**school colours:** [n.] not to be confused with the school Colour, the official school (Regimental) standard that is paraded every Founders' Day and sometimes on Sunday church parades. The school colours are red and white, taken from the cross of St. George emblazoned on the Lawrence shield, and the flag that flew permanently from the Chapel flagstaff. The 'school colours' referred to here are humble sweetmeats or 'chucks', sold by 'Charlie Bootlace' and also available in the Tuck Shop. Made from sugared coconut candy, they came in bold red and white coloured blocks or slices. Sickly sweet but favoured by some.

**scrap:** [n.] same as in everyday parlance, a bare-fisted fight between boys.

**School Day:** [n.] the first day of the school year and start of a new term; the very opposite of 'Home Day' [q.v.]. School Day generally fell on the first Monday of February.

**scoff:** [n.] to eat eagerly, quickly and with relish. Same as in common parlance.

**scob/scoblobber:** [n.] a term of derision, sometimes applied to 'small chaps' (e.g., 'You little scob'!) but more often to scroungers, sneaks, tittle-tattlers etc. See also 'snitch'.

**shugs:** [v] a demand for retribution and/or reimbursement between chaps for the loss of, or damage to an item of one's personal possessions. The word had to be stated loudly immediately after the incident and preferably in the presence of witnesses. Most chaps paid up without quibble, usually in kind.

**sister-boys:** [n.] officially these were supervised meetings between boys and their sisters after Sunday matins. One and a half hours, usually on Peacestead. Latterly, the rules were relaxed and bent a little to allow boys to meet with other boys' sisters! (See 'squaring/squarers').

**snick:** [n.] specifically a school cricketing term and not used in general parlance. It referred to a distinct edge of the bat that is caught behind the wicket but not given. Snicks are distinctly heard by everybody, including folks living across the valley in Kasauli but not, evidently, by the umpire.

**snitch**: the word has two meanings: [1] [n.]: one's nose. (From an Old English expression). [2] [n., v.]: same as in common parlance. An informer; one who informs on another. A 'tittle-tattler'. To tell tales in order to cause trouble. Also used as a verb, snitch/snitching/snitched.

**skotch**: [adj.] a few; a little of something; a small amount or a tiny bit. Strictly non-racial and absolutely nothing to do with the Scots, their reputation for prudence and frugality, or their fine whisky! (See also 'dole')

**skunk/skunk off**: [v., n.] to sneak away from some collective chore, job, fag or duty; to steal off surreptitiously. Most Sanawarians were very good at this. Also used as a noun for chaps who consistently 'skunked-off' and so were labelled 'skunks'.

**snotty-bobs**: [n.] this rather disgusting term referred to the sticky, purple-black, ripened berries of the Black Nightshade (Solanum nigrum). Said to be mildly toxic by some, it was considered edible in our part of the Siwalik and widely used as a diuretic by the local hill people. It commonly occurred in open waste ground and the fruit was consumed by many a chap with predictable consequences! (See again 'chirricks')

**splung**: [n.] a term for a greedy person; one who stuffed himself with food, or anyone having an immoderate appetite. Given the frugal school diet of those times, this term was not often heard.

**square/squaring/squarers**: [v./n.] publicly acknowledged boy/girl, or sweetheart relationships. Generally of short duration, although quite a few 'squarers' are known to have carried the association into adult marriage. Squarers met publicly at morning 'milk breaks', discreetly at 'Sister-Boys' [q.v.], and clandestinely at other times and places.

**stewks**: [v.] an expression of derision, spoken loudly and usually accompanied by a forefinger behind the ear and a flick in the direction of the chap to whom it was directed. It could mean anything between 'told you so!', 'so there!', 'bollox!' and 'up yours, chum!' A sort of precursor to the present day (Anglo-Saxon), two-finger gesture.

**sunshine hol, a**: [n.] an adhoc holiday or half-holiday occasionally given at the first clear break in the annual monsoons. The sole gift of the principal, they were generally announced after Chapel, at morning class Assembly. The resulting cheer from Birdwood might be heard as far afield as Subathu.

**swack**: [v] to eat satisfyingly and with relish. Sadly, an activity rarely witnessed or experienced in Sanawar!

**tank**: [n.] the swimming pool.

**tatties, the**: [n.] derived from the Hindi '*tatti*' meaning call of nature. Borrowed and adapted to describe the outside toilets, latrines, privies, 'bogs' or in Oz parlance, the 'dunnies'. In particular, the long row of tin-roofed closets with urinals at each end, located just below the quadrangle of the lower, junior's dorms (Block 12; present-day Himalaya). In compliance with the primitive hygiene standards of those days, every surface (except maybe the wooden bit you sat upon), was liberally coated with creosote.

The smell was overpowering. At dead of night, it was a long walk to the tatties with a dimly glowing 'buthi' in one hand, and three sheets of 'tatti-coggage' [q.v.] in the other. If the jackals suddenly sounded off nearby, you could easily fill your pants before you got there. Today, there are convenience 'loos' in all the dormitory blocks. They are all flushable and there is no longer a strong smell of creosote (or anything else)! wafting up the 'khud-side'; or at least, so one is told. The GD equivalent of the boy's 'tatties' was the rather more elegantly named 'Rose Cottage' [q.v.].

**tatti-coggage**: [n.] from the Hindi 'kagaj', meaning paper, but in combination with 'tatti' (see above), it refers to toilet paper; specifically the 'bog' standard, school-issue Bronco brand. Hard, shiny, unforgiving stuff that came in ridiculously small sheets. The story goes that in the early days, one was issued with just three sheets per diem: one for wipe, one for polish and one for shine. Ah Andrex! Whither wert thou?

**taws**: [n.] the game of marbles; in the 'taws' season, any reasonably smooth and flat bit of 'maidan' on the 'BD' side of the hilltop would have its small groups of 'taws' players. Several forms of the game were played at school. (See 'ballyole', 'butch' and 'ringtack'.) Again, some chaps were 'chokes' at it.

**thug**: [v] to cheat, deceive or defraud. Probably from the Hindi *thagi* (trickery, skull-duggery). What can one say? This sort of thing only happened in library books or at the 'flicks'! [q.v.]

**titch/titchy**: [n., adj.] a small person; a youngster; small of stature; same as in general slang.

**vatican**: [v] a mysterious and rarely used suite of rooms with its own washing and toilet facilities situated on the northeast corner of the gymnasium block. Boys who had been publicly expelled from school were accommodated here in total seclusion until they were removed from the premises by their parents or guardians.

**wink, the**: [n.] the momentary dimming of the lights that occurred every evening at 2110 hours, warning that you had just five minutes to make your bed 'down' (if not already done), get undressed, brush your teeth, say your prayers, and get into bed before the lights went out.

Compiled and edited by:

**D.V. Boddington**
LRMS Sanawar 1942–1947
August 2013

**With grateful acknowledgements to:**

- Noel Hadley. 'Hey you Gang', a short discourse on the use of 'Sanawarese', in *The Sanawarian*, Summer 1944.
- L. Vaughan, V. Hipkin and H. Hewetson. '"A Decent Dole": A Concise Dictionary of Sanawar Slang', *The Sanawarian*, circa 1946.
- John Dixon. 'A Personal Memoir in the Form of a Lexicon', *The Old Sanawarian* magazine, June 2001.

**Contributions gratefully received from:**

- Stella Beatty née Owen (Hodson 1947) (whose idea it was)
- Jim Walker (Hodson 1947)
- Bill Hyde (Lawrence 1945)
- George Browne (Havelock 1937)
- Dave Williams (Hodson 1947)
- Tony Cook (Hodson 1946)
- Jack Harper (Nicholson 1945)
- Gladys Spencer née Lowe (Nicholson 1945)

# Miss Chatterji

The '78 Sanawarian would not be complete without a mention of Miss Chatterji, who left Sanawar this year, after a long and successful innings.

I did not know Miss Chatterji for very long but the impact of her personality did not require the length of time to make itself felt or be remembered and even now, though she's been gone a few months, many's the time that one remembers what she'd have done, said or worn on many different occasions.

My first memory of her was of a very helpful and considerate person who took me and my rather scatty ways in hand and proceeded in the most tactful manner to show me the ropes – how to organize myself on both the domestic and school fronts – inviting me to a never-to-be-forgotten cup of excellent coffee (freshly ground beans and all) and a piece of the most delectable apple pie, one sunny Sunday morning, out in her little garden with the first sweetpeas and petunias just appearing, and then a large hunk of cinnamon bread carefully wrapped that I must take home for my children. Such kind gestures are not easily forgotten.

I remember her punctuality, her ease of manner, sense of occasion and her style. She combined in her persona the best of a lady and a teacher and by her strong sense of duty and dedication to her work, she set an example for both the students and the staff.

'Miss Chatterji is coming' was often heard down the corridors of Birdwood, on Peacestead, even in the MCR and her light, quick step and smiling 'Well, dear . . .' was a familiar and reassuring sight. Often a reminder of duties forgotten or delayed! And one misses the neat, little hurrying figure with the parasol sometimes, with a bunch of violets in her hand.

We would all like to wish her joy and pleasure in her new life.

**Manjari Khan**
Staff

**Source and Acknowledgement:** *The Sanawarian* (December 1978)

# The Story of Sapru

I first met Mr Sapru when I was eight years of age, having just joined the boarding school, The Lawrence School, Sanawar. He emerged as a kindred spirit in an otherwise authoritarian school system and was truly inspirational during my formative years.

He left school within just a few years of my enrolment and though I never met him again, his memory stayed close to my heart. Eventually, when I started writing *Meghdoot* in 2010, he inspired a central character with the same name. I imagined him garnering much wisdom during his travels and now returning to the boarding school where he once studied and later taught, to conduct a photography workshop—and facilitating a sensory and emotional awakening of the students.

Out of curiosity, I reached out to the real Mr Sapru in 2016 and unbeknownst to me, the fictional backstory for the character which I had constructed turned out to be almost in line with reality. Overwhelmed at the coincidence, he himself agreed to play the character. For nearly two years, he grew his beard in preparation, and due to our very frequent communication, the fictional character in the script transitioned into the real one.

In 2018, doctors discovered that Mr Sapru had cancer. He instantly reached out to me, fearful that his beard may fall off due to chemotherapy and he was very worried about the character. Deeply moved with his concern for the film at such a grave time, I felt a great urgency to return to India from LA to commence pre-production work on it.

As I put all the wheels for the film into motion with rigorous travels across the country, I fell really ill one night, and the morning after, received news that Mr Sapru had passed away. This fated day also happened to be my birthday (8 June 2018), so all of it felt quite uncanny and overwhelming. In spite of a sense of uncertainty and grief, I felt a greater urgency than ever before to complete the film. *Meghdoot* now, in many ways, is also a tribute to Mr Sapru—his spirit is an intrinsic part of it.

**Rahat Mahajan**
Siwalik 2004 | 1995–2004
Filmmaker

OS Parent – Father – Ajay Mahajan | Maggie | Siwalik 1975 | 1965–1975

OS Sibling – Brother – Ambar Mahajan |Siwalik 2002 | 1993–2002

# The Underdog

Every House was forming their teams in preparation for the 1960 Annual School Boxing Championship. I was a complete novice and had absolutely no clue about this bloody sport, except for a few compulsory, introductory lessons under the watchful eye of Mr Jagdish Ram, the legendary, ex-Army PT Instructor. I tried to remember his advice to keep my eyes open when the opponent was trying to hit, a very difficult thing, since we instinctively wince and close our eyes.

My friends were jokingly tempting me, trying to talk me into being part of the team. They said that in my weight category, I had no chance of winning because last year's best boxer from another House was in it. Other teams were also not fielding their good boxers in my category. The best boxer was well-known for knocking out his opponents. In fact, his reputation was such that other House team boxers in that weight category were reducing weight to fit into a lighter category. My friends told me that I would earn a lot of respect if I lasted one round before a knockout. It would be quite painless, they assured me. I would not feel a thing as I went down with stars circling around my head. That sounded like a challenge.

And so, like a foolhardy fellow that I have become famous for being, I agreed. I reached the finals easily because other Houses had also fielded dummies. Last year's best boxer was a handsome lad who looked and even sang like Elvis Presley. The girls swooned and cheered when he entered the ring. I looked around and found my House cheering for me, too. They were quite sure it would be a short and painless exit for me.

Major Som Dutt, [the] headmaster, was the referee. He was a great boxer himself and had earned a Boxing Blue while studying in the UK at Cambridge. 'Seconds out of the ring', he said. The bell rang for the first of three rounds and there was total silence. I could hear a few giggles as I cowered in my corner while my opponent stood in the middle of the ring, waiting for me to come there, too.

I decided to try to hit my opponent first before going down. He was standing with his gloves down, hands at his side, tempting me to make the first move. I knew that he would pulverize me soon anyway. So I walked towards him timidly and then made a wild swing with my right arm. It connected and there was stunned silence. There was blood spattered on his white vest. The referee stopped the fight to examine what had happened. My punch had hit the opponent's nose and he was bleeding profusely. Doctor Sakhuja was called in and said it was bad. It was a broken nose, better to stop the fight he said. Major Som Dutt could not believe it. It seemed unfair, declaring a TKO (technical knock-out) of last year's best boxer to an absolute novice, who had just landed a lucky punch. But that would have been a correct decision. But he let the fight continue after asking my opponent whether he wanted to fight on.

My opponent was quite dazed and rushed at me angrily. I tried to keep him away by stretching my arms and clumsily throwing straight left and right jabs. But he was very quick and managed to hit my face many times with no result. His punches were not having any effect. Keeping my eyes open, I was instinctively taking those punches on my head, instead of my face, by ducking a few inches. People wondered how I was able to take so much punishment. Major Som Dutt noticed my trick and warned me several times not to duck low as it was against the rules. But my survival instinct was so strong that I ignored the warnings and continued to keep my eyes open to duck and avoid punches on my face. It was a mystery for the spectators. There was no blood on my face while my opponent was bleeding profusely.

As he recovered from the shock and initial setback, his punches got harder and I backed off. I barely lasted till the end of three rounds. I made a stand to fight and land a few wild punches, which connected again during his reckless assault. When the bout ended, I was still standing on my feet and somehow made it back to my corner in the ring.

There was no doubt about the decision and the referee, Major Som Dutt, known for his short sentences, said, 'A hard-hitting fight and a plucky loser' and declared the winner, who won by narrowly outscoring me on points. The boys cheered me on lustily even though I lost, but the girls were in tears, although their hero had won. He suffered two black eyes and a broken nose, and was rushed to Kasauli Military Hospital. There was spontaneous cheering later, in front of the boys' dining hall.

Mr Jagdish Ram asked me to report for training with the School Boxing Team. I declined. I had realized that this crazy sport was not my cup of tea. I did not want any more blows to my head which could cause internal damage. I did not want to risk brain injury, which happens to many boxers. I was right. We all know the tragic end of famous boxers. It is exactly what happened to Muhammad Ali.

We had no protective head gear and tooth guard in those days, but nowadays, boxers wear it and the chances of injury are much less. That boxing bout was a big turning point for me and gave me a lot of confidence to face adversaries later in life and follow the school motto to the tee.

## NEVER GIVE IN!

**Lt. Col. Vivek Umesh Mundkur**
Siwalik 1961 | 1957–1961
Army Engineers, Innovator – built and flew India's first hang-glider in 1976 (Limca Book of Records) | Built a Hovercraft; designed a portable Solar Pump for small farmers to win Greenpeace Innovation Challenge 2013 | Installed windmill at Komic Monastery at 4582 m, the highest in the world.

Adventure fanatic in Aero sports and Water sports.

Parents – Father – Umesh Anand Mundkur | STAFF 1956–1981 | Biology Teacher | Cricket and Athletics Coach | Housemaster
Mother – Kumud Mundkur | STAFF 1957–1981 | Matron

OS Sibling – Sister – Aruna (Mundkur) Kodical | Siwalik 1964 | 1957–1964

# Sanawar – My First Home

Sanawar was my first home to later become my school. I was born at the British Military Hospital, Kasauli, and my parents were school staff. We lived in the House named Pooh's Corner in Garden City, followed by the secretary's House (above the school gate), and eventually, the principal's House in 1947. The present one was built after the original burnt down. We occasionally went away during holiday breaks, ordinarily preferring to stay back in school, especially for the winter break. But we would go to Delhi to stay with Mr Raja Ram, then the Principal of St. Stephen's College and an old friend of my father's from their days together at Cambridge University. Also to Bombay, to stay with a very keen Old Sanawarian called Horace McCarthy. He used to visit Sanawar frequently and organize parties and bring treats and the latest records to play. His brother was Ken McCarthy, a most famous band leader in India. I learnt to swim in Bombay at Breach Candy and also had my tonsils taken out there. We went to Karachi as well, to a beach House on Sandspit, only reached by boat; Simla, of course, and Chail—the highest cricket ground in the world.

In 1952, I was sent to school in England and made one last trip to Sanawar in 1953. To say that I love Sanawar would be an understatement. I have nothing but the happiest memories of a glorious childhood there. For others, Sanawar was a boarding school, and so I would like to reminisce the 'less-encountered' Sanawar.

I started out in Prep School, walking with my ayah from the secretary's House, past the classrooms for servants' children, the bakery, the cobbler, Ulavi's sweet shop, and along the Short Back, where my sister and her friends had found a secret cave. I was sometimes allowed to go into it. At some stage, I fell backwards, off the road looking up at the girls' dormitories then being built at Peacestead, and was saved only by the seat of my shorts catching on a shrub. My ayah was very frightened and thought she would be in trouble, so she told me not to mention it to anyone. I didn't. In the garden of the same House, my father built a tree House for us children in a large eucalyptus tree. From it, I remember vividly watching a mongoose and cobra fighting, but not what happened at the end.

I learnt to roller-skate in the corridors of Birdwood School, and during the holidays, would ride down to Garkhal village, sitting on a book strapped to a single skate; there was no traffic and the ride was terrific and well worth the climb back. In the winter holidays, there were very few children about, but there was small gang of us who got up to mischief. Probably the sort of mischief that would now be considered hooliganism, so I won't go into detail! It did snow quite often, always providing a lot of fun.

I had an airgun and also a .22 rifle and was allowed to shoot pigeons. Our cook was called Gulah and he would cook just the breasts, which were delicious.

School was simply a lot of fun. We were always being given a 'school holiday' by appreciative visitors, mostly for no good reason as far as I can tell, but especially on Speech Day. I even have a vague recollection of someone awarding us three days, but we didn't have them all at once. Even my father gave us one, once, on the first sunny day after a heavy monsoon had ended.

I do not think there was a school truck (an army vehicle) till 1948, so we mostly walked everywhere, including Kasauli, to go to the cinema.

Perhaps, coming back by tonga. Otherwise, I was free to roam all over the hilltop, often collecting butterflies. I used to make 'sap' – a mixture of fermented fruit – to paste onto tree trunks, which attracted butterflies and made them drunk and easy to catch. I would then stand by the pavilion on Barnes, waiting for the butterflies to fly down the valley. I learnt to play tennis and billiards at the Tennis Club and to shoot at the range. I loved all sport, perhaps cricket above all—my father had built a practice net in the garden. We had a spaniel called Rajah, a gift from good friends in Kasauli, the Honourable T. and Mrs Sinha. Rajah walked either the Short or Long Back every day with my mother, though I would often go with them.

Picnics at Dagroo and Eagles' Nest were a real treat and I loved collecting the biggest pinecones I could find, taking sacks full back home for crackling winter fires. Diwali at Moti's Corner was something special, too.

In the principal's House, we had many famous visitors as well as people who have become well-known since. I particularly remember Bishop George Barne (Sanawar's most famous principal), the Mountbattens, General Sir Arthur Smith, who was Commanding Officer British Forces in India and Pakistan, Compton Mackenzie, the writer, Archie John Wavell, son of Earl Wavell, the penultimate Viceroy of India. And of course, General Cariappa, the first Indian C-in-C and father of Nanda, an OS who is famous in his own right. Baldev Singh, the Defence Minister of India, Maulana Azad, the education minister, Ashfaque Hussein, who also served as a school governor, the Maharani of Kashmir and the Maharaja and Maharani of Patiala, whose two princes were at school for a while, and Amarinder, who is now Chief Minister of Punjab, I think.

Our head servant, Gurditoo and our cook, Gulah, both liked to put on a good 'show' for them.

**Dr Timothy Carter**
Tup | Yellows/Himalaya 1953 | 1944–1951

Parents – Father – E.G. Carter O.B.E. | 1922–1955 | History teacher |
      Secretary | Vice Principal | Principal 1947–1955
      Mother – V.W. Carter | 1928–1955 | Mathematics teacher |
      Headmistress

OS Sibling – Sister – Anne Carter | Himalaya 1951 | 1938–1951

# Keep Fighting the Good Fight

My story begins on a cold March morning in 1960. By a quirk of destiny, I segued from my mother's warm embrace into the equally warm and deep embrace of Miss S.T. Kaveri. She was, henceforth, to be my foster mother for the entire duration of my stay in school, and along with other staff members, would play a key role in defining who I am today. As teachers of the finest vintage, they recognized the fundamental truth, that to make a better world, our children should be cherished and nurtured. We had unflinching faith in our teachers.

An institution with an ambit that stretches across the canvas of pre- and post-Independence India, Sanawar was a heavenly abode set amidst sylvan surroundings. It was to be my home for the next nine years. Little did we realize then that as we took our fledgling steps, we would not only strike up bonds of friendship and camaraderie transcending time and space, but the past would also bequeath unto us a bagful of memories.

In the Sanawar of yesteryears, life was a different paradigm from what it is today. Life was spartan, devoid of unreasonable demand. School life revolved around friends, classes, games, hobbies and weekly films, generally cartoons, to the great delight of the preppers. Mickey Mouse, Bugs Bunny, Woody Woodpecker, are all etched in my memory. American Wild West movies with fight sequences (*The Fastest Gun Alive*) were our favourites. All films were shown on a 16mm projector manned and operated by Mr Mukherjee. The only thing missing was the aroma of *moongfalis* and fried *chanas*. I remember once how worried Mr Mukherjee got when he had to screen *A Night to Remember* as he himself had not ascertained its actual contents. What a sigh of relief for the staff when the film turned out to be about the sinking of the Titanic.

Other childhood memories still vibrant are of nature-walks along forest trails to exotic-sounding places like 'Eagle's Nest' and 'Lover's Pond', to name a few, to be followed by a picnic lunch; the painful introduction to the wild, thorny 'bichu buti'; inculcating the love for reading that only increased as the years rolled by, passed down by my seniors, due to an accidental borrowing of an Enid Blyton's *The Boy Next Door* from the library; the entire school gravitating towards the limited faucets/taps available at key locations, especially after sports in hot weather, leading to a lot of pushing and jostling, and at times, squabbles for the seniors to step in; playing the clappers/triangles/bells in the Prep School orchestra, which for us was no less than playing for the Royal Philharmonic Orchestra; and the pièce de résistance—sashaying across the stage in plays like *The King Who Could Not Smile* and the hilarious *Uncle Podger Hangs a Picture*.

After the most fulfilling two years at Prep School, it was time to move on to the real world: Boys' Department. My favourite memory, though, is the smell and sound of raindrops on the dormitory tin roof, which during a heavy downpour, could be deafening. Life was tough to begin with, but what I remember is that I willingly and wholeheartedly attempted all competitive sports that formed the foundation of group activities in school. Though I did not excel in the classroom, to some extent, I compensated on the playfields. Sports introduced me to many virtues—discipline, tolerance, harmony and most importantly, fair play, preparing many of us in the best possible way for a life of service in uniform, and to overcome life's challenges with fortitude and determination. On the bucket-list of every Sanawarian was to win the Cock House. Himalaya had come close in previous years, but it was only after an all-round display by the House that this landmark was finally accomplished in 1969.

To me, Sanawar is akin to an ancient palimpsest on which successive batches have added fascinating chapters of the history of their times. Chris Le Doux wisely said about life: 'It is not the years that count, it's the miles'. We have travelled on a long and tumultuous journey of adventure. I believe the best is yet to come and henceforth, my motto is to 'Live, Love and Travel'. To keep fighting the good fight till the final echoes of the last post have faded.

**Dilbagh Singh Sidhu**
Dilby | Himalaya 1969 | 1960–1969
Retired D.I.G. – Border Security Forces
A decorated officer | Keen sportsman, passionate horserider | Won Gold at the All-India Police Duty Meet 1991, New Delhi

OS Children – Son – Manpreet Singh Sidhu | Himalaya 1998 | 1989–1998

# Hike to Dehradun

After the strenuous two months at school, everyone was looking forward to the camp break. Thirteen Himalayans including myself had decided to undertake a hike to Dehra Dun with Mr B. Singh and Mr Solomon.

We started off on Monday morning and managed to catch a bus from Garkhal to Simla. From Simla, we changed buses and loaded our luggage on a Jubbal-bound one. The journey was long and sickening. The road was uncomfortably narrow and it gave me the creeps when I glanced out of the window. Before my eyes stretched steep cliffs with valleys, thousands of feet below. We reached Jubbal completely exhausted. It had been a trying experience.

At Jubbal, we went to see the Maharaja's palace. Though the better part of it had been incinerated by a fire, the remaining portion looked very majestic. The interior was very ornate and spectacular. After a hearty dinner at one of the Tibetan 'dhabas', we dozed off in the PWD rest House.

Next day, we started walking. The weather was just perfect and we walked at a brisk pace. Quite suddenly, the harmless-looking clouds in the sky burst into rain and we were forced to take shelter for two hours in a small village. Though this was a major setback in our plans, we were determined to reach Tuni, our next stop, about fifteen miles away, by nightfall. We had to prolong our stay at a village named 'Auntee', after having our lunch, again as a result of the rain. After the rain had ceased, we carried on, stopping at Arakote for a cup of tea. All this while, we had been following a big stream. The countryside looked clean and beautiful. Since we had lost more time at 'Auntee', we quickened our pace. Night fell and we were still walking. Finally, at eight o'clock, we reached Tuni, weary and hungry. We found accommodation at a rest House after arguing with the chowkidar.

Next day, we trekked through some very difficult terrain. The road was steep and we walked slowly. On the way, we met a number of nomadic

Muslims who had come to spend the summer in the mountains from Dehra Dun. We ran into a slice of hard luck yet again and had to wait for the rain to stop. After having our lunch, we set off for Kathian. It was very cold. We reached the place in the evening and stacked our luggage in a long shack, divided into small cabins meant for the foresters. After a sumptuous dinner besides a campfire, we went to sleep. The cold did not affect me since I was very tired and I slept soundly right until the morning.

The sun was warm and pleasant as we made for our next stop, 'Kharamba'. The way was tough. On the way, we passed 'Bamnai', which is at a height of 11,000 feet. We had a spectacular view of the snowclad Himalayas and the low, green valleys in the foothills. Unable to find accommodation for the night, we were advised to carry on to Buckkoti, which we readily did and we found accommodation in the Forest rest House there.

Early next morning, we set off for Chakrata. We walked against a very strong, warm wind. Chakrata was sighted in the distance and we walked on with renewed vigour. We reached in the late afternoon and had a delicious lunch.

Since Chakrata is a military base, we couldn't find a place to spend the night. On consulting the divisional forest officer, we were advised to carry on to Kalsi, where we could sleep at the Forest rest House. A bus was leaving soon and in order to catch it, we would have to hurry since most of our party was three miles away. So we had to make a dash up the slope to inform the others and then run back to the bus stop with our haversacks. We ran for 6 miles and only just managed to catch the bus for Kalsi. The journey was sickening and lousy, and we thankfully got down from the rattletrap at Kalsi. After our first bath on the hike and a good dinner, we slept peacefully under fans.

Next day, we made it to Dehra Dun and deposited our luggage at The Doon School. After a wonderful swim, we lunched with the Doscos, and then set off for the town.

We had a delicious meal and saw two movies. We returned to Doon School at midnight, completely exhausted. The change in weather was taking effect and we passed an uncomfortable night.

Next morning, we boarded a bus to Ambala, which unfortunately broke down on the way and we were stranded for two hours. Finally, we changed over to another bus and after a very hot and monotonous journey, reached Ambala. We had missed the train to Kalka and were therefore obligated to take the bus. After a long wait at Kalka, we boarded a bus to Garkhal. We reached Garkhal at night and walked up to Sanawar.

We had covered a good 105 miles on foot. The hike was very instructive. It helped us to learn to face difficulties with determination. It was an eventful, adventurous and thoroughly enjoyable hike.

**Gaurav Rana VI-B**
Old Sanawarian (Himalaya 1972)

**Source and Acknowledgement:** *The Sanawarian* **(December 1972)**

# As the Sun Set on the British Empire

Sanawar in 1953, the year I was admitted to Prep School at the age of eight, was an age and world apart from today's India. The country had just gained independence, only six years earlier, and the school was metamorphosing from being a school for other ranks during the Raj, to a public school in a new country trying to find its bearings. The trauma of the Partition, particularly of the Punjab, was reflected in the behaviour of some of my classmates. We were all, in some measure, children of the Partition, admitted into a boarding school as our parents struggled to bring stability and equanimity into their lives outside. Admission was gained through a competitive entrance examination. As my parents could not, at the time, afford my fees, I managed to win a Jawaharlal Nehru scholarship that supported my first four years. The great man called for me, and blessed me himself.

Our school, too, was struggling to find its bearings. My Prep School years (1953–55), were reminiscent leftovers of the now-outmoded British army and colonial traditions. It was not for some years, until I entered Senior School, that our headmaster and teachers gained what I may define as a more Indian confidence, which manifested itself in different ways; they began to transmit this new confidence to us in our middle years. Therefore, the nine formative years that I was at Sanawar, were broadly a period of transition for the school as it was for us in a new, free country. Sanskrit as a language was introduced. Learning the piano for a musical instrument soon gave way to the Tabla and Sitar. The morning Assembly had no conventional prayers, but Rabindra Nath Tagore's verses, and verses from the Gita, were gradually introduced.

Our daily lives were regimented by the bugle call and a thoroughly archaic military tradition. A modern school would never be run on those lines. But it left us with a strong sense of discipline. We had a varied day that incorporated classes, sports, hobbies and amateur theatricals into our schedules. The school permitted no singular focus. We learned to multitask.

We had no leisure time and as a result, the work ethos became deeply ingrained in us. Our small joys were hard-earned. The weekly Sunday visit to Kasauli, the annual ten-day camp to Dagroo. Our two-rupee pocket money was a great equalizer. We never knew who was rich or poor. We were all equally poor and as is the case of most children who attend boarding school, equally hungry! A major but invisible strength was that the school was careful that there was no mention, let alone discrimination, on the basis of caste, religion, region or creed. We grew up to respect each other for our skills and achievements alone. Nor did our teachers unduly glorify success or failure. In the process, we also learned to cooperate with one another.

Excellence in sports was a major achievement and the focus of popular admiration. The four-kilometre Hudson run was seen as a test of stamina. I was always last in the annual Hodson run. A polio handicap and incipient asthma were the main culprits. Yet, it did not matter. My far-seeing and wise Housemaster, Mr B. Singh, would invariably lead the rest of the class to the finishing line to cheer on for the last entrant. The school had taught us that someone was always first. Someone else last. But the strength of the school's unspoken mantra was to encourage and never discourage.

By the time I had reached the Sixth Form, the school had ingrained in me such a strong sense of confidence that by the time the year ended and we were to step out into the unknown, I believed I could conquer the world. Of course, at sixteen, one invariably has the exuberance of youth, but the self-confidence that the school gave me, has never left me.

Our motto, 'Never Give In', was so deeply ingrained in us that it has seen me and many of my classmates and school friends through 'downs' of life that have invariably accompanied the 'ups'. I share this indomitable spirit with all my classmates and schoolmates, whenever and wherever in the world I meet them.

Each of us Sanawarians carry our hosts of memories, some of which were more memorable than others – of breaking rules, of running wild in the hills on Sundays, of the pride of winning an inter-school match, or the disappointments of the reverse – leading to a strong camaraderie that carries to this day.

I remember an occasion when a friend's father had come to Kasauli, and this friend invited a bunch of us to join her father for lunch at the Circuit House. This was a great treat because a delicious lunch had been laid out in the beautiful lawns of the Circuit House. After we had eaten our fill, I was elected to say 'Thank You' to the friend's father for hosting us at the generous lunch. Not knowing what to say after thanking him, I asked him, 'Sir, what you do?' He smiled at us all and said he was the Chief Election Commissioner of India. None of us knew what that meant, and nobody was particularly interested in the explanation that he gave of what his obligations were to the country. Nor could we understand what a high Constitutional office he occupied. He was just a friend's father, and that was it. Ironic then that almost five decades later, I would find myself serving as India's Chief Election Commissioner, often enough on the same lawns, recalling my very first visit. Life offers many coincidences and this was one of them.

**Navin B. Chawla**
Himalaya 1961 | 1953–1961
Indian Administrative Service 1969 Batch | 16th Chief Election Commissioner of India | Writer | Official biographer of Mother Teresa

# Charlie's Law

Miss Jerath taught Physics for a very short time in Sanawar in the early 1980s—she was a relatively young, kindly teacher, but taught perfectly well. It was her gentle and mellow nature that we, as a 'rough-around-the-edges' batch took advantage of, relentlessly. We looked for any reason to not do our coursework, preferring to fool around and create 'gadar', making as much noise as humanly possible. Each day brought more disruption than the previous and each class had its own, unique master troublemakers, whose sole aim was to ensure lessons never got started at all.

Bearing in mind that this was our board exam year, it caused problems for Miss Jerath with the head of department as our coursework was seriously lagging behind. Not that this troubled us at the time, as we were oblivious to the competition (for marks) outside our little bubble universe, that was Sanawar. So mayhem always ensued. Many a times, Mukho or Heady would be forced to come in to exert some sort of control on us, embarrassing poor Miss Jerath in the process. Now thinking about it years on, maybe we should have paid more attention to school work, but then hindsight is always 20/20! Coming back to my story, it was generally acknowledged that the best trouble masters were, hands down, in our UV-D. We were terrors.

Every so often, Bonga would elegantly collapse in a faint, on demand by the trouble masters and this was as good an excuse as any, to stop 'work'. Those sitting around Bonga had an undeniable reason to hurl water with great gusto across the room. Water ostensibly meant to revive Bonga was used to drench everyone else, especially Miss Jerath. I don't know what it was that the boys found irresistible about a wet Miss Jerath, whether it was her wet saree or a very wet cotton blouse, one will never know. Invariably, Bonga escaped bone-dry. To make Miss Jerath's life absolutely miserable, at times, it was deemed necessary by the trouble masters that a stretcher be used to cart Bonga to the Hospital as he wouldn't come around. Just short of the Hospital entrance, he would miraculously revive or else, be thrown off the stretcher. You see, Bonga had this innate ability to faint at will, and being thin and spindly, he was just the perfect weight for boys to carry on a stretcher, giving them a perfect reason to skive from class. It's sad that Bonga passed away soon after school. Rest in peace, our resident thespian, you are sorely missed.

Basically, Miss Jerath's class was a merrymaking time. Another time, when the class wouldn't settle down, Miss Jerath shouted (inadvertently), 'Last bench, GET OUT!' So the boys seated on the last bench stood up, lifted the bench, carried it outside and marched right back in saying, 'Last bench is now outside, Ma'am.' I still cringe thinking how Miss Jerath must have felt at the time, but such things happened frequently, much to the annoyance of other teachers in the classrooms around. However, the worst was yet to come.

One fateful day, Miss Jerath, who normally spoke properly, happened to mispronounce a word, as one does sometimes. The class jokers pounced on it as only fifteen-year-olds can, making her even more miserable than she normally was when dealing with us. She was teaching us Charles' Law (on the behaviour of gases). Now the law states that the volume of a gas is directly proportional to the heat applied to it, keeping pressure constant, or at least that's what I think the theory is, going by memory alone. Do forgive

me if I've got it wrong. After teaching us the theory, she questioned, 'Class, what is Charlie's Law?' A small innocuous mistake one would think, but no, the D section thought it had to be capitalized upon. Charlie, as we know, is the name shared by many generations of the school *halwai*. That's all the class needed to burst out laughing raucously. The quick-thinking joker, Vivek Narang (who, sadly, is no more either), was bright as a button in all non-studious subjects; he stood up and in a loud voice said, 'Ma'am, Charlie's Law states that samosas are directly proportionate to gulab jamuns, keeping ghee constant.' The laughter that erupted was loud, very loud and it went on and on. What followed was the final straw for Heady, who was teaching in the room next-door. The loud guffawing could be heard across the Science floor above Mucchoo's office, and I don't think the noise and ruckus subsided when Heady walked into the room. From our vantage point next-door, we could hear Heady bellowing at them to shut up, but I doubt they heard him. We could hear Thappo laughing the loudest and the longest, adding further to the mayhem by falling off her stool and joining those already rolling on the floor.

I have never in my eight years in Sanawar, seen Heady as angry as he was that day. D-Section was in serious trouble and Heady couldn't let this pass without some form of punishment. So, UV-D were summoned to assemble outside Birdwood after lunch that day and were caned on their behinds. Thappo got two whacks because she laughed so much; this was the only time I've seen the girls being caned.

By the powers vested in the rest of our batch, UV-D (1981–82) were officially declared the rowdiest and the funniest class in school history, something to be proud of at fifteen, I suppose.

This is one story I'm sure a lot of us have told and retold over the years and now it's in the book, for posterity. Writing about it some forty years later still makes me nostalgic and very thankful for those carefree days and for my batch, who made school life so much fun, so worth it. That was Sanawar for me.

**Anuradha (Varma) Bhatt**
Verms | Nilagiri 1984 | 1977–1984

OS Sibling – Brother – Alok Varma | Loki | Nilagiri 1986 | 1977–1983

# Come On, Purewal . . .

The 1980 Hodsons Opens Finals were on the next day. Harbinder Purewal was not merely the bookie's favourite (by at least a mile); he was riding the wave of general perception that Ranjit Bhatia's record of 11 minutes 25 seconds, long-standing since 1952 (wow! Twenty-eight years!), was under serious threat. Many were aware that in preparation, Purewal would run down to Garkhal and jog up the shortcut to Kas and back. On other days, he would run all the way home (near the Kas turn on the Kalka–Simla Road), relish a glass of fresh juice and run back via Sukhi Jodi to Moti Corner and to the Vindhya House dorms.

Understandably so, the Opens course was a breeze for him. The starting point was from the Resident Engineer's office-cum-residence (Kochi's dad) instead of the 'ropes' outside Gaskell Hall, and hence, one had to cross the Lawrence Arch, not once, but twice. And, that's where our brilliant idea took seed.

Five Himalayans – Bassi, Pari(tosh), Cheel (Sandhu), Pandey and I – met in the 'night-pans', minutes before lights-out, to iron out the last detail (we didn't know the word 'strategy' back then). The concept design was very simple. As none of us were among the likely contenders for a position among the top ten, there was nothing to lose. The plan: the Five would go firing on all cylinders in the first lap (to the Arch), ensuring we stayed ahead of Purewal by approximately twenty paces. While the entire school, including Danny and the entire Vindhya House, would still be quaking in disbelief, we would pause under the Arch, turn around and roar, 'Come on, Purewal'. After that stellar performance, we would continue up to Gaskell Hall, take the stairs on our right, and crash land on our beds, while Purewal and the rest would be taking the trouble of completing the entire Long Back. What an idea, Sirjee!

The Five reached Kochi's House ten minutes before time to 'bagz' a front-row slot at the starting line. Purewal was getting into the zone, quietly warming up in a corner, concentration writ large on his forehead.

He was a bit surprised when we walked up to him and wished him luck. He smiled. Our prefects, too, were observing this newfound keenness of ours with some interest. Danny blew the damn whistle . . . we five and Purewal were the first ones off the block. We were neck-to-neck till Green Gate. However, with every passing stride, it was becoming more and more evident that our gameplan was a disaster. Why? Because at Warrior's Grove, Purewal overtook us. On the Last Bend, not only was he clearly ahead, but increasingly distancing himself from us. What the hell! Despite the fact that our final destination was the Himalaya House Senior Dorms, we were unable to keep pace.

However, this is how *we* saw our plan crumbling. Not the others. That's why they say that things are not always as they seem. What the entire school saw was that the five Himalayans were barely twenty strides behind the Numero Uno, and slightly ahead of the other 'assured' position-holders—Tula, Albert, Lama, Gautu, Rawlley. To be honest, while hatching the plot, this prospect had not, even for a moment, crossed our minds. Otherwise, most certainly, we would have reevaluated the pros and cons to decide whether to proceed or not. Because, at this moment, Himalaya House was 'on course', and poised to bag six of the ten positions (including Gautu, of course). UD was skipping with ecstasy . . . floating like a butterfly. He quickly calculated the Himalaya House tally and belted out his customary Victory Cry, 'Come onnnnnnn, Hiiii-maaa-liiii-yaaaaa!' as we went past him. In that very moment, all the glee and cheer disappeared from our lives. We together seemed to see the rush of what was to come . . . half an hour later, this butterfly would be stinging like a bee! And the five nincompoops would be forward-rolling into the wee hours until the next dawn! Thinking on our feet, we realized that it would be too dangerous to stay with the quit-at-Gaskell Plan. Now, we would most definitely be missed. We had no choice but to show up at the finish line. Mustering all our resolve, we somehow managed to crawl till the Horseshoe Bend, breaking into a canter from thereon, and finally picking up steam just short of Moti Corner. Needless to say, no one was in sight . . .

When we ultimately turned the Last Bend, the prize distribution was about to commence. UD was hugely disappointed, to say the least, but couldn't possibly unravel the plot, and so, not only did we emerge unscathed, but were also patted on the back for having tried 'so hard'.

But back to where the spotlight most deservingly belonged—on Harbinder Singh Purewal, the true legend. We learnt that he had finished in great style in 10 minutes 44 seconds, smashing the twenty-eight-year-old record by a full 41 seconds.

I narrated this anecdote years later, in fact at Purewal's Silver Jubilee Founders' party. He smiled and reasoned, 'But Sapru, you must take into account that we had a year's advantage over those 1950s guys'. Humility Personified. But on a lighter note, thankfully, Ranjit Bhatia did not get a whiff of the 'conspiracy' or he might have set right the 'Five Himalayans' for unintentionally pacing a Vindhyan, and stealing the limelight off a Siwalikan.

**Pankaj Sapru**
Himalaya 1983 | 1976–1983
Senior Management – Petroleum Downstream sector | Travel & Street Photographer | Member – OSS Executive Committee 2019–21 | Vice President – OSS 2021–23

OS Sibling – Brother – Dhiraj Sapru | Himalaya 1985 | 1977–1985

# The Annual Summer Camp

Traditionally held every year for about seven days around Easter and, with a few exceptions, always at Dagroo (with the kind permission of His Highness the Maharaja of Patiala, who owned the land). Boys of the senior Houses, 'Rangers' and Girl Guides went to 'camp'—but not, of course, at the same time! Annual Camp, as a regular event in the school calendar was instituted in 1916 by Principal George D. Barne, who was said to have been influenced and inspired by Lady Honoria's account of the Lawrences' 'gypseying' (sic) with forty children of the asylum, on a picnic to the same valley in April 1849. Thereafter, it became a regular and enjoyable feature of school life.

The chosen campsite was in a fairly even, fallow field near the Dharampur/Subathu road bridge over the Dagroo valley, about 2 kilometres from Dharampur. The tented accommodation, kitchens and latrines were set up in advance under the direction of the Chief Instructor and his staff. Everyone 'marched' down the old Dharampur/Dagshai bridle way to camp in noisy, excited groups. The requisite 'kit', baggage and rations went down by 'chakra' (bullock cart) in the early days, and latterly by lorry via the main road. 'Grub' was cooked on open fires, and the fare was no better, or worse than one got from the cookhouse, back on the hilltop. Over the years, several deep pools were formed above and below the bridge for swimming by damming the stream with large stones, boulders, etc. They were given names like 'H-E Skunks', 'HRS' and 'Harts', which stuck for many years. Rambling, 'roaming', swimming and other outdoor activities were encouraged. However, there were strict rules published in School Orders regarding behaviour and respect for the local farmers' property, livestock and standing crops.

On the last Sunday of camp, evensong or matins was sometimes held by the bridge. The officiating minister was usually the Chaplain but occasionally, 'Boss' (the principal) was known to take the service. The bridge was given the name 'Choir Bridge' in about 1918 or 1919.

LRMS Summer Camps continued to be held until 1944, when, for reasons of economy and the rising cost of the war effort, the arrangements for 1944 were cancelled. The practice was later revived, and the venue extended to other sites as far afield as Gaura and Sadhupul.

**D.V. Boddington**
LRMS Sanawar 1942–1947
March 2003

**Compiled from:**

1. The Journals of Honoria Lawrence, 'India Observed 1837–1854'
2. L.R.M.S. Orders No. 151 dated 22 February 1923.
3. L.R.M.S. Orders No. 84, dated 14 April 1944.

# Pakistani Paratroopers

On 5 August 1965, Pakistani soldiers dressed as Kashmiri locals, crossed the Line of Control. Simla was then the Western Command HQ. With military cantonments of Kasauli, Dagshai and Subathu within close proximity to us at Sanawar, it was a real challenge to distinguish through aerial survey, one from the other. Hence, we were very much in the danger zone. All blackout drills, including hitting the khud-side at the sound of the air-raid siren, were observed, day and night.

A few weeks later, in September, we Vindhyans decided to scale Ozark. It's been fifty-seven years since and I'm not getting any younger. My apologies if I miss out some names. Those I remember are Amar Talwar (Amro), Vinay Mehra, H.S. Pannu (Lumber), Ashok Saxena (Saxy) and me (of course). Ordinarily, the Ozark trek took two and a half days. However, the previous year, some fellow Vindhyans had made a maiden attempt of leaving after tea on a Saturday, to return by Sunday evening. However, they had fallen short, and had been picked up from Dagshai late on Sunday night by [the] headmaster, Major Som Dutt. We were determined to succeed.

The next Saturday, we left after tea to conquer Ozark. We were dressed in shorts, with haversacks and rolled blankets on our backs, donning Gorkha hats. We planned to descend to Dharampur, climb up to Dagshai and then descend again to the valley beyond. We had been promised a night halt in a villager's hut. However, on getting there, we found him to be rather cagey. In fact, he suggested that we continue our climb to the next hill, where we would find a place to stay. Darkness had already descended, but we had no choice.

On reaching the top, we were greeted by a gun-toting chowkidar. We introduced ourselves: 'from Sanawar . . . on a hike to Ozark . . . looking for a night's shelter'. He had never heard of 'Ozark' (can't blame him. After all, it was a Sanawarian name for the otherwise simply known as Bhursingh Mahadev Mandir . . . and sure enough, we hadn't heard of Bhursingh).

Still worse, he wasn't aware of Sanawar School. With some persuasion, though, he agreed to find us a place to sleep, but a couple of miles up ahead. Despite the fact that we were pretty tired, we, yet again, had no choice.

As we trudged along, we inquired whether he was aware of the ongoing Indo-Pak war. He replied that he lived in the back of the beyond and knew little of the 'outside' world. We had no reason not to believe him. He strung us along the proverbial country mile that didn't seem to end. We had been on our feet for over eight hours and were on the verge of collapsing when, all of a sudden, he yelled out in his native language and blew his whistle. And lo and behold, in a flash, we were hemmed in by more chowkidars, wielding guns belonging probably to the great Indian Mutiny.

Our repeated answer 'Sanawar' didn't hold much water. We were asked to furnish proof of identity. Vinay Mehra fished out his Delhi Gymkhana Club dependent member card. Even we were amused. We wondered why the hell was he carrying it, anyway. Seeing us agitated and perplexed, they clarified that they were patrolling the area as there had been a spate of dacoities recently. Eventually, after a full hour of marching in captivity, we were ushered into a building. Before we could bat an eyelid, we were locked up.

After an hour or so, a uniformed policeman arrived and once again subjected us to questioning. As the leader of the group, I reiterated, in all honesty, that we were students of Sanawar, and were out on a hike. He then asked if I knew Mr Manley, a retired DIG of Punjab Police, and at present the Bursar at Sanawar. Before I could answer, Lumber piped up that he knew his daughter as well. Coming from Lumber that was quite a statement and had us in splits. In any case, it was enough to lighten the atmosphere and the policeman became decidedly friendly.

Sensing a favourable disposition, we enquired what this was all about and why we were being treated like prisoners. He explained that these gun-wielding guards were on the lookout for Pakistani infiltrators. Suspecting that we were Pakistani paratroopers, they had contacted him at Nahan to come and interrogate us, while they held us in custody. Shocked and dumbfounded, we ended up complimenting the chowkidars' diligence.

By now, the sun had risen and we, being wide-eyed and awake, decided to continue on to Ozark. As a result of the forced march through the night, we reached our destination within an hour. We scaled up the mountain and came to rest at Bhursingh Mahadev Mandir. Leading to the temple was a large sloping rock, at a 60-degree angle, with a thousand-feet drop. Legend has it that on certain moonlit nights, ghee is poured on the rock and a *tantrik* dances on it in a trance, protected by the temple deity. We paid our obeisance to the deity from a safe distance, and made our way down.

With the entire day ahead of us, we made a rather uneventful trek back to school, reaching well before dinner.

**Rakesh Sood**
Vindhya 1965 | 1958–1965

OS Sibling – Sister – Manju Sood | Vindhya 1961 | 1958–1961

OS Children – Daughter – Mansi Sood | Vindhya 1997 | 1988–1997
                    Daughter – Meghla Sood | Vindhya 1999 | 1992–1999

# A Paean

It was three months before I turned thirteen. I had barely begun to question my place in this universe. 'What is your name?' I was asked.

'Latika,' I replied.

A thunderbolt struck. The look of complete amazement on my father's face, while my mother's huge eyes were ready to pop out in anger left my brother, nine-year-old Shirish, waiting to answer the same question, looking at me, puzzled.

I had adopted a new moniker, a far cry from the simple 'Lata', my name until a few minutes ago. In a single strike, I had taken revenge on the Irish Catholic nuns at Loreto who butchered my four-letter name 'Lata'—something Shirish delighted in distorting to 'Laathaa', or kicking in Marathi. Life had become pure hell for me as a preteen. In a flash, I had thus become 'Latika', a name stolen from Lotika Ratnam, an All India Radio newsreader—a household name at the time.

Though not yet in its classrooms, Sanawar had already given birth to this free spirit.

A couple of hours later, I walked up to the girls' dorm with my unusually quiet parents as we took care of what all new students needed to. That moment of bravado in the bursar's office ended quickly. For the next many months, I cried myself to sleep every night, holding tightly the secret that I still sucked my thumb. Each time I looked at the lights of Kasauli, across the hills, tears soaked my pillow because home seemed so far. Every morning, I counted the days till the weekend when I could escape from school, but before that could happen, the fierce dragon who later became a beloved teacher, 'Ma Chat', had to be confronted. If she gave permission, only then could I be afforded a few hours of reprieve.

Weeks passed and years too, carving indelible memories along the way. A science teacher once told me and my friends, 'Go find yourself an eligible bachelor and get married,' because we could make no sense of the formulas he rushed through. History class used to put me to sleep because of the incessant repetition of dates of wars, while the math courses were beyond the likes of me who preferred to create fantasies out of word problems. Numbers continue to be enigmas to me even today.

But there was plenty to read. The librarian allowed me to borrow as many books as I could carry. My infinite curiosity was constantly encouraged at every step, whether it was about asking questions at the Friday Forum, where no query was out of bounds, or in the countless discussions with equally nosy peers and a few teachers.

The morning Assembly sowed seeds of true secularism within us and was followed by a balance of academic, athletics and extracurricular activities. We marched from one place to another, fostering discipline and punctuality, though there was always room for playfulness and guilt-free wandering around the serene terrains of the hills. The student body was formed by varied geographical, linguistic as well as cultural differences. It was a genuine postcard-perfect picture of what the Indian subcontinent is all about.

I can write pages upon pages on the wide spectrum of programmes we were exposed to, which were seamlessly woven into our schedule. It was a lifelong journey of exploration, not only of the riches of our vast country, but transnational boundaries as well. The classical and popular

music concerts, the debates and speakers on different subjects, theatre, local and global, dance programs drew from our ancient heritage but also from the contemporary world, whether it be Bollywood or Hollywood. It was a smorgasbord—how is it possible to not learn anything?

Even in the equalizing grey-blue uniform, this middle-class Maharashtrian could never belong to the cliques or 'gangs', as we called them. Nor did she have a best friend. Yet, the planting of lifelong friendships had been initiated.

A daughter of a General, younger than me, introduced me to ways of the world. Another product of Indo-American, Hindu-Muslim unification, even more junior in years became my intellectual peer. A Kashmiri exile's progeny turned into a lifelong hero I'd admire, while another senior, an offspring of a major Bollywood legend, became like a loving elder sister and protected me from many a bully.

It was a difficult time for so many of us, as I discovered much to my surprise when a few of us met decades later. Over lunch, we commiserated as we recognized our basic humanity. We acknowledged how privileged we were, yet almost all of us still shoulder many social responsibilities. It is this awareness that Sanawar created in me and my cronies. Once I lifted the dark curtain that had kept me away from so many of my childhood peers, vitality was rejuvenated.

Today, when we are in our seventies, that synergy colours our exchanges; more honest than ever; the Never Give In spirit permeates us. Our numbers are decreasing but there is still a strong desire to stay involved. Occasionally, irritability also erupts but almost always, our dry sense of humour, recalling some incident or the other from our school days, lightens the mood.

Yes, I still grumble a lot, and complain about how painful the time on the hilltop had been, but as I continue to live in many different and changing environments and pass through life's different stages, it is the spirit of Sanawar I call on more than anything else. Sometimes to the aggravation of whoever I am with, but usually to be asked by the ever-curious something about that place we call 'Sna'.

**Latika (Tatwawadi) Mangrulkar**
Vindhya 1961 | 1958–1961
Social Worker/Therapist | Educator | Writer in the ancient tradition of the 'Kathakar' | Stories adapted into Dance and Radio plays | Published

anthologies include *Family Matters and Other Complications*; *Life Happens, and Death Too*; *Uneven Shadows*; *Tales around the Kitchen Table: the South Asian Immigration Saga through Recipes and Stories.*

OS Sibling – Brother – Gp. Capt. Shirish Madhao Tatwawadi | Tats | Vindhya 1964 | 1958–1964

# The Sanawar Shuffle

Sanawar is steeped in history: the oldest co-educational boarding school in the world, it boasts proud traditions not least as an institution with military connections. As early as 1853, it enjoyed the rare honour of being awarded the King's Colours. The strength of its sporting and academic traditions has also earned it wide renown. Yet, however, proud Old Sanawarians are well-aware of their school's reputations and we love the school even more than we esteem it: how could one have any but happy memories in such an idyllic setting, atop a beautiful hill surrounded by trees, with a climate as temperate as any in the world?

My experiences at Sanawar formed and shaped me, and left a more visible stamp on my character than any other period in my life. I am particularly grateful for the secular, democratic philosophy it introduced me to; if I am not myself enlightened or wise, then at least this philosophy was, and it has served me faithfully and well. Another great gift of this education was the English language. I not only read it, speak it, write it and think in it; I enjoy it as others enjoy music. This pleasure would have been unavailable to me had I not been gifted with the benefit of such a rigorous, thorough training in it. English is not just a language or a means of communication: it is a tradition and an art. I am glad to have been taught to appreciate it as such, and even gladder not to speak Babu English.

The school motto 'Never Give In' has served us particularly well. It inspired in us qualities of courage, calm, temperance, self-reliance – all the ancient virtues that steady us in the face of the vicissitudes – the changes and turns that ever unsettle human existence.

Sport was at the heart of our training. It taught us, among other things, teamwork, gentlemanly sportsmanship and the importance of physical fitness; but let us not neglect the beauty in sport. I relish my particularly fond memories of the weather at Sanawar during cricketing season. In my mind's eye, the picture remains undimmed by time: it was invariably sunny; on many days, not a cloud could be seen, whether in the middle of the sky or looming on the horizon. For some reason, I remember, especially vividly, the cricket trip to Bishop Cotton's School Simla, in May 1964. We started the day with a solid English breakfast: fried eggs, bacon, sausages and beans. The weather was perfect that day; we beat our hosts handily. Mr Brown from BCS told me afterwards that my fast-bowling action was the best he had ever seen. Naturally, I was flattered. Of course, we were not always victorious. In 1964, I think we should have beaten the Doon School. Unfortunately, the first day of the match was a washout because of unseasonal rain. Play started on the second day; because of the downpour, the pitch was exceedingly slow and we always did better when the pitch was fast and bouncy. Thankfully, we were taught how to lose magnanimously, like gentlemen.

At Sanawar, our classes were small and the teachers unusually committed. Rather than generalizing, I should like to pay homage to a few special favourites—more than a few. Let me single out Mr Hardip Sikund, a gem of a man—not only a great teacher, but my best friend. I could share my joys and sorrows with him. Not only was he utterly non-judgmental; he had the unique ability of making students feel comfortable—surely one of the most crucial qualities in a teacher. He encouraged us to learn in a relaxed frame of mind: stress could not develop our intellect or make our mind grow. This was a welcome contrast to the methods and manners of many of his colleagues (to say the least). I do wish we had more teachers like him. One of my happiest memories of Sanawar is of that magical hiking trip to Chamba with Mr Sikund. May God bless him and his family.

Our headmaster, Major Som Dutt, was a great man. A Cambridge graduate, he excelled as a sportsman and scholar (he read History at Fitzwilliam); though at heart, he was an army man, and served in the Armed Forces before transferring to the Army Educational Corps. School history remembers him as a sage and effective reformer, though we who were pupils at Sanawar between 1956 and 1970 were more conscious of his presence and authority, and the high standards he drilled into us.

But for all my admiration of Major Som Dutt, I cannot forget my first Housemaster, for whom my affection stands very high. Mr Saleem Khan was the one who got me into Sanawar. I had been studying at Sacred Heart, Dalhousie. My father was taking my elder brother, Balraj, to school after the winter break and decided to take me along. Mr Saleem Khan told the Major that he would make a place for me in Nilagiri House. He was a tall, handsome, aristocratic man and looked every bit as belonging to a grand, princely House. I have met House masters from Winchester and Eton; in my eyes, Mr Saleem Khan was every inch their equal, and stood head and shoulders above most. He was the best cricket coach we had, and at that time, we even had a great team, led by two princes, Sangram Singh and his cousin—the great leg spinner and googly bowler, Ajit Gaekwad.

A few other favourites may be mentioned with deep fondness here: Mrs Lyal, who taught us how to speak proper English—the most loving and compassionate teacher I came across at school; Mr Atma Ram: a sincere, genuine man who shared wonderful stories from the *Ramayana* and *Mahabharata* with us, once a week. He always had my best interest at heart. Mr Kemp, the best senior master of any public school, in his blue blazer, grey trousers and Peshawari chappals, whose honourable sense of justice even as a referee at football and hockey, demonstrated the soundness of his Christian upbringing; Mr Gore, the best mathematics teacher and Mr Sinha, the best geography teacher. Of course, not all the teachers left this strong an impression, and the staff were not without their occasional weaknesses.

My sacred place at Sanawar was near the gate leading from the Nilagiri House pavement to the Chapel, which was rightly at the centre of the school campus. It is a small, beautiful old church, filled with memories. Mr Parker, our first headmaster, never took a day's vacation in twenty years; one day, whilst preaching during a service, he passed away.

Mr Saleem Khan used to stand at the gate as we walked down for breakfast and check our uniform and shoes.

It makes me happy to revisit Sanawar; even in memory.

**Paramjit Takhar**
Nilagiri 1964 | 1958–1964
Doctor-cum-Farmer in the US

OS Sibling – Brother – Lt. Gen. Balraj Takhar | Nilagiri 1960 | 1956–1960

# Class Topper to Boundary Hopper

Nothing is more exciting than breaking rules at boarding school. Having grown up on a diet of books like *Mallory Towers* and *Naughtiest Girl in School*, which made boarding schools seem like a haven for pranks, strong friendships and ghost stories, I spent my years at The Lawrence School, Sanawar bringing those books to life.

I was inevitably always in the red drill book for one reason or the other, having attempted to sneak out of the class windows; caught loitering where I should not have been; flying paper planes behind the teachers' back; wearing nail polish; rolling my socks down to my ankles and hiking up my skirt to show off my legs; reading a storybook instead of a textbook during prep [time] . . . the list goes on! Many a times, teachers would admonish me with 'focus on your studies', and I'd jovially retort, 'but I'm already the class topper'. Signing the *Book of Honour* won me favour in my teachers' eyes, but to my seniors, classmates and juniors, I shone bright for my happy, naughty, bold and fun demeanour and sporting spirit. Must recount here how Mucchoo (a term of endearment for our very strict but much revered and loved, big-whiskered Deputy Headmaster), twisted my ear in the Dining Hall to get me to divulge the name of the person who had put a rat in the bowl sent to me as a prank. I had screamed loudly attracting pin-drop silence and his ire, but I didn't 'tattle'. Camaraderie and loyalty above all! However, nights spent with torches regaling and terrifying juniors with ghost stories, sneaking into the kitchen through the backdoor and taking off with whatever food we could grab, having boys pass us beer bottles and butter chicken through the window gaps (from their escapades to Dharampur), and other antics and rule-defying tomfoolery clearly wasn't enough 'khup', our word for playful, naughty fun in Sanawarian lingo.

It was time to up the game and do something far more daring and hopefully, even legendary, for our mischief archives. So one night, pre-Founders', Harsha, Ritu and I conspired to do the unthinkable. We hatched a plan to sneak out of the locked girls' dormitory and into the

Upper Six boys' dorms! Our boyfriends were in there and we wanted to surprise and impress them. Of course, they had no clue of our plan or how funnily and bizarrely it would pan out! The girls' dorms were locked at night, but the boys' dorms weren't. The plan involved smashing a large piece of glass in the lower part of the door in the Upper Six section of the lower girls' dormitory during the day.

Our windows had mesh and grill, the main door would have been impossible to exit from, so this permanently locked and unused side door in the quarters was our only option. We snuck back into the dormitory while everyone was at class, disposed of the broken glass in a non-discoverable manner, and covered it with a suitcase not only so it was not visible but also so that the cold air from outside wouldn't blow in. This was a brave start as that section belonged to our seniors and prefects-to-be. Getting caught would mean much more than a week in the dreaded red drill book. The next step was to break the lock on the mesh door and close it in a manner that it couldn't be detected by the guard on his daily rounds. This part was executed swiftly and surprisingly well. Of course, the last and greatest challenge of the exit plan was summoning the courage to actually sneak into the Upper Six girls' section, moving that heavy suitcase in silence and hope that all our wiggling and giggling our way through the broken glass opening wouldn't wake them.

We succeeded! The walk across the 'haunted' and foggy Peacestead was far more daunting. Our deeply ingrained school motto 'Never Give In' gave us impetus, but the tales of the dead colonel who smoked his pipe and watched over Peacestead, and the headless chowkidar who cavorted with *chudails* frightened us into holding hands tightly while tiptoeing across. We crossed the swimming pool complex in utter silence. It was 4 a.m. Our ready excuse to any living mortal we might encounter was that we had been permitted to practise for the Hodson finals. I still remember the adrenaline-thumping moments of that chilly journey, replete with goosebumps, giggles and shivers in the early morning cold, as we finally made it to the Upper Six boys' dorms.

We had never been in by day, and rather than an open dorm like ours, they had confusing cubicles, so we split up. I groped about in the dark, went inside one and shook someone and asked, 'Where is Andy's cubicle?' It was Vishal Dhar! At the same time, I heard a loud commotion as the other girls had probably done the same thing. What ensued was loud screaming, 'OYE! THERE ARE CHICKS IN THE DORM!', and then a volley of abuses by those that had been woken up by the ruckus. Suddenly, shoes were being thrown and went whizzing past our heads. Vishal, who was mortified, disappeared under his blanket and hurriedly explained how many cubicles I should be going down, when suddenly the dorm lights turned on.

Mr Puri, (Billa to one and all), roared, 'Ohhhhhooo, what are these noises, you know?' Oh heavens! No way was I going to be caught and punished, and to Vishal's utter horror, I jumped into his bed and disappeared under the blanket. That moment is indelible in my memory! Billa carried on talking loudly from afar, 'Ohhhhooo, talk slowly, you know' and 'Ohhhhooo, go to sleep, you know!' I'm not sure whether Vishal was shivering because of the cold or from having 'a chick under his blanket'. I did not hear him breathe.

Billa turned off the lights and left and we fled soon after, with laughter and tears of mirth all the way back. While we were unsuccessful in our objective, it was hugely successful for our archives. It became a legendary tale and a miracle that no one squealed, or that our names never entered the red drill book for what was clearly my most audacious rule-breaking moment on my beloved hilltop.

**Pooja Bedi**
Siwalik 1989 | 1982–1987
Actor | Television talk-show Host | Columnist

OS Sibling – Brother – Siddharth Bedi | Siwalik 1989 | 1982–1987

# Sanawar – Old and New

In the newsletter dated 1 June 1972, Old Sanawarians and teachers were asked to write about their work and achievements, and their memories of the school. I write as a former headmistress of the Girls' School after Independence—many years before both my husband and I were appointed to the staff by the late Bishop Barne, whose leadership has been so greatly admired. I was appointed to teach mathematics.

This 125th Founders' has very special significance for me. In 1947, the year of Independence, the principal was the late Rev. H.E. Hazell, and my husband was the vice principal. On 15 August, there was a ceremony in Gurkhal which Mr Hazell and my husband attended and enjoyed. My husband became the Principal on 1 October 1947, just before the centenary celebrations which were attended by such distinguished people as the Earl and Countess Mountbatten, General Sir Arthur Smith, Bishop and Mrs Barne, and Mr Compton Mackenzie, the writer and historian.

On my arrival in 1928, I was impressed by the beauty of Sanawar. I loved the mountains and the pines. My husband loved trees too, and to celebrate Independence, he held many tree-planting ceremonies and those trees, including those in Independence Gardens, must now be well-established. We also planted the gardens known as 'Leisure' and planned the rustic bridge. Mr Carter worked with determination and enthusiasm, blending new ideas with old traditions, and it is sad, perhaps, that he is not still alive to be aware of the fruition of many of his hopes. It is unfortunate, too, that during his last months in Sanawar in 1955, he was too ill to enjoy the hilltop he loved so much. Doctors confirm that his condition, even then, indicated the symptoms which led to eventual brain surgery and many years of illness.

Among letters Mr Carter kept and treasured, and which I still have, is a letter in 1955 from one of the first Indian girls to become a boarder, written after she had left Sanawar. If I may, I will quote extracts:

'I think I owe a very great deal to you—much more than in the ordinary way. Before going to Sanawar, I had a deep-seated resentment against the British and when I came to Sanawar, I resented the British as fiercely as ever. I was absolutely overwhelmed by the sense of fairness and justice and the spirit of tolerance and charm that you possessed. There is one thing that I shall always remember. You told us in a history class that no nation can ever be conquered—it may be for 50, 100 or 200 years, but a century is but a moment in the life of a nation. That made a tremendous impact on me; it restored my pride and I did not feel resentful any more.'

In the first century, or 'moment', of Sanawar's history, it shaped with pride the lives of many who have been, and still are, all over the world. In 1947, there was no gulf and the family of Old Sanawarians has grown with continued pride, with another quarter-century added to the history of the school.

Long years ago, there was a Girls' School magazine known as the *Honorian*, which I revived while I was the Headmistress, but I think this may have been discontinued.

It was during my husband's principalship that your hall was renamed Barne Hall in 1949. Because of this, I have asked for my contribution to be given to the expansion of the hall. I see that a workshop room is needed for the new maths. I have, from time to time, tried to interest Sanawar in S.M.P., which is so very challenging. I offered a small prize for a completion problem.

I associate Barne Hall vividly in connection with my husband's keen interest in the A.D.S. He produced several plays, among them *The Barretts of Wimpole Street*, *The Lilies of the Field*, *Little Ladyship*, *Laburnum Grove*, *Ambrose Applejohn's Adventure* and *The Ghost Train*.

I could write about so many things but I must not take up too much space. Many Old Sanawarians have been to see us here in Suffolk; my husband so enjoyed renewing memories, be they of his cricketing days, or of his period as Housemaster of the old Lawrence House, or of his final years in Sanawar as Principal.

I wish you a very happy Founders'. May the school prosper and go from strength to strength. My daughter, Anne, my son, Tim, my daughter-in-law and my grandchildren all join me in sending you our very best wishes for the years to come.

**V. W. Carter**
Staff 1928–1955 | Mathematics teacher | Headmistress

**Source and Acknowledgement:** *Souvenir Brochure 1847–1972*

# The Birdwood Guns

These two artillery pieces were presented as trophies to the school by the Government of India in 1928 in recognition of the school's contribution to the Great War of 1914–1918, and to honour the twenty-seven Sanawarians who fell in action during the conflict. They are early Turkish, 3.5", (13-pounder) breech-loading field guns reported to have been captured in 1916 in the Dardanelle, during the Gallipoli Campaign. The guns, with their carriages, were despatched from Ferozepore Arsenal on 20 March 1928, and after de-commissioning, were installed in their present sites on the quadrangle in time for the opening ceremony of Birdwood School and unveiling of the Cenotaph in September 1929.

The guns remain standing there to this day, still overlooking the Cenotaph and Memorials below—silent sentinels to the memory of Sanawar's fallen.

**D.V. Boddington**
LRMS Sanawar 1942–1947
August 2001

**Acknowledgements:**

1. *Civil & Military Gazette*, Lahore, August 1928 (Citation) and September 1929, (article).
2. Lawrence School Orders No. 261, '(NOTICES) TROPHIES', dated 26 October 1951.

# When the Earth Shook

It was a bright, sunny day in autumn. We were glued to the transistor, listening to the cricket commentary of the India–Pakistan Sialkot Test. It had been a feat to sneak in a pocket-sized transistor into school, to hear the match between the then world champions and their arch rivals. We were exasperated when the broadcast of the enthralling match stopped abruptly, only to be followed by dreary news on All India Radio.

In disgust, we switched it off to conserve battery. It didn't strike us then that it was not the normal hour for a news bulletin. Soon, the school bell rang (at that odd hour), and the entire school was asked to assemble at Chapel. Only then did we sense that something was amiss. Our headmaster addressed the gathering, informing us that our prime minister had been assassinated.

All this while, we had been impervious to the ugly occurrences in the neighbouring Punjab, which had been in a state of unrest for a couple of years now. No longer oblivious of the prevailing situation, we heard horrendous tales of arson, looting and gruesome killings following the assassination. Our mathematics teacher lost a close relative to the mindless violence and one can't forget the shock and grief on her face. With no cell phones or STD/PCO in those days, anxiety about the well-being of our parents and relatives was but natural. The telegrams received at the school office were the only way for us to learn about the safety of our near and dear ones.

We had always been taught that we were Indians first, and anyone else later. Overnight, the fault lines of faith appeared on the horizon and there was a general atmosphere of anger everywhere. What had happened and what was happening was absolutely unjustifiable, yet there were views and counterviews, leading to unpalatable heated discussions. It was very baffling at that impressionable age, to have to differentiate as to which side was right and which was wrong.

Those were the days when the teachers often went beyond their call of duty. They handled the situation with tact and dexterity, without offending anyone. They would interact with us frequently and keep a strict vigil on anyone who showed the slightest of tendencies of adolescent misadventure. Thanks to their personal indulgence and maturity, they were able to impress upon our young minds that 'an eye for an eye or a tooth for a tooth' would only make the world a gloomier place to live in. The scourge of communalism was thus nipped in the bud.

When the 'Big tree fell', the earth under it did shake, but the tremors caused could not shake the solid foundations laid by these selfless souls. While the whole region was covered with dust, it was our beautiful hilltop that stood magnificently above the commotion; I salute these unsung heroes who were institutions in themselves, for saving an entire generation from going astray.

**Col. Harvinder Pal Singh**
Harry Paul | Nilagri 1989 | 1983–1989
Vishisht Seva Medal (2012) – Commanding Officer in Siachen Glacier

OS Children – Daughter – Mannat Bir Kaur | Nilagiri 2019 | 2011–2019
Son – Agam Bir Singh | Nilagiri (Present Sanawarian) | To be batch of 2025

# Summer of '49

In the Summer of 1949 (June–July), I visited Dagshai with my grandfather, and there stretched out on a hilltop was Sanawar. With each passing day, my curiosity for this school, once out-of-bounds for Indians, increased. One fine morning, accompanied by my grandfather's chaprasi, I set foot on a trek to Sanawar—the journey took perhaps three hours. We reached [the] headmaster's office late in the morning. There, I was confronted by Mr Mohinder Singh. Shortly after, I was taken to Captain Wyles, the vice principal. A frighteningly thin, fidgety man of medium height, he asked, 'Yes, what can I do for you?' I answered, 'Nothing! I have come to meet the principal'. '[The] headmaster is busy . . . but I am the VP.' I insisted on seeing the boss, which further annoyed the Captain. With despair on my face and a sinking heart, I turned around to leave.

Suddenly, a hand gripped my shoulder. Scared and almost in tears, I turned around and there was the boss, E.G. Carter, who had walked in quietly. He said, 'Yes, young man?' He led me into his office, piled with furniture. A rather stern but kind look. I explained that I had walked all the way from Dagshai to have a look at the school and if I liked it, I would like to join. This was something new to a military-disciplined school. Sam Cowell was sent for and told to show me around—Birdwood, the Dining Hall and some more. He also clarified, in no uncertain terms, that it is not 'if you like it' but a case of 'if we are willing to have you'. Shortly after, we returned to [the] headmaster's office and he asked, 'How was the tour?' I replied, 'Looks nice.' 'Well, then you are admitted.'

July 1949 was the start of my date with Sanawar . . . No regrets . . .

**Rajinder Kumar Sondhi**
Rajondhi (to friends); Yank (to [the] headmaster) | Siwalik 1953 | 1949–1953

# One Misadventure

I came as a child who had never stayed away from family before, to Sanawar in 1962, and completed schooling in 1967, as self-disciplined, determined and confident – a complete man. After Sanawar, I studied Electrical Engineering at IIT Kanpur, leading to a forty-seven years' illustrious corporate life. I now live in France, having retired only recently, in November 2020.

Among the many memorable moments during my days at Sanawar, one incident clearly stands out.

In Sixth form, we, Jagdish (Gill), Sunil (Kalia) and me decided to go to Kasauli, one night. The three of us put on pagris thinking that it would be the perfect disguise. Our books and some other belongings were 'strategically' placed under the blanket to give the impression that all was well, and that we were in bed, fast asleep. Bhupi (Aggarwal) accompanied us up to the Bakery, where one of the *dhobis* saw us and informed the school authorities, which we learnt only later. I don't remember whom he tattled to. Anyway, oblivious to the 'treason', we carried on with our plan. While we were crossing Pir Kot House, the Nilagiri House dorms were checked, and the cat was out of the bag.

Returning triumphantly, still unaware, we were received by a reception committee, led by Mr Uma Prasad Mukherjee, our Housemaster. Needless to say, the three of us got a hammering of our lives, although Jagdish and Sunil took the major brunt. I was the last felon (in line) to be reprimanded. Mr Mukherjee, who liked me a lot (even inviting me home for the occasional 'macher jhol'), was visibly distraught, 'Oh Oh, Prosanto, you hab eestabbbed me in the back'. Next morning, we were rusticated. I was really scared to face my father, but it turned out alright and he said, 'if you don't do such things at your age, when will you do them?' After the reassurance, I was made to lead a jawan's life (as punishment), including eating at the langar in Pattan, where my father was posted. Fortunately,

Major Som Dutt was kind enough to take us back just after a week. But sadly, I was never invited for macher jhol again.

**Prosanto Das Gupta**
Fontu | Nilagiri 1967 | 1962–1967

# Paddy, the One From GD

I first arrived at the hilltop on a cold and rainy February evening, in 1978. I was scared and unsure of what to expect as I huddled closer inside my ill-fitting brown speckled coat. My parents were equally uncertain on what to do next, as we stood below GD, next to the Stores Department. We had a choice between being cheery and all-smiles or teary and emotional, and I don't think any of us were doing a good job of either. So I finally hugged them as tightly as I could and before the tears could fully escape the dams that held them back, ran up the steps to GD.

Now I was left to navigate this new territory on my own. After being assigned to Nilagiri, I went up to the first floor, sat on the blue counterpane-covered bed and looked around. Immediately, someone noticed a 'new girl' and came up to say hello. We exchanged names and a few tentative smiles. Others came around and asked questions, too. The tears sank back into my eyelids as it would be too embarrassing to burst into tears in a dorm full of strangers, even if they all seemed kind and friendly.

As we got ready for Prep, yes, it was evening, it was time to march to Birdwood to do our 'homework' and preparation for the next day. I got in line with my books and stuff. Everything still felt awkward and alien, though I constantly got friendly smiles and stares. The prefect came to inspect the lines and stared at each one of us. When she came to me, she stood and looked for a long time. I finally picked my eyes off my shoes and stared back at her. I wondered if she was looking at me because I was new or if there was something I was supposed to do that I hadn't. Before I could fathom, she let out a shout, 'Paddy,' she screamed, 'Paddy,' and pointed towards me quite hysterically.

Taken aback as I was, I looked around me to understand what she could possibly mean. There were three or four Upper Sixers around her, who too were now staring at me. Slowly, they began to see what she saw and they, too, began smiling and nodding in agreement. 'Paddy,' they said, pointing and smiling widely.

This was how I first marched in my NGD squad to Birdwood, my confusion completely heightened at the strange reaction I seemed to have evoked in the senior girls. By dinner, which was straight after Prep, I had dozens of seniors from various houses come up and stare at me and confirm, 'Paddy'. They all agreed and nodded and smiled. Soon, the girls in U-V, my class, and the juniors, too, took to parading before me chanting, 'Paddy, definitely Paddy.'

I could not take it any further and shy as I was, I finally asked, 'What is Paddy? What does it mean?' I think this made people around me realize I may be feeling a bit upset. They hastily retreated and I was left alone for a while.

When we got back to the dorm and were readying ourselves for bed, someone came up to me and asked, 'Do you have a brother in BD?' I was taken aback by what seemed like a pretty strange question. 'No,' I blinked. 'But why?' This kindly soul (and I wish I could remember who it was), sat down next to me and explained. 'Well, you see, you look exactly like someone in BD and his name is—'

'Paddy,' I finished, finally understanding what or who Paddy was.

The poor kind soul blinked, 'How do you know his name?' she asked.

'Never mind,' I replied, too weary to explain that the number of times I had been referred to as Paddy made it quite clear what my BD 'twin' was called.

Paddy, as it happens, was short for Padmanabhan Rangappa – quite a mouthful – so just as well that it had been sweetened to Paddy. He was the Head Boy, an important person by all accounts. Actually, he was quite cute and when I finally saw him, a few days later, he smiled at me and stared a bit harder than usual as if trying to understand from which angle I looked like him. It was the same for me – except for his mop of curly hair and that the lengths of our hair were pretty similar – and a ready smile, I could not find too much resemblance between Paddy and me.

Then Paddy, the other one, went and did something that sealed my fate to be called Paddy for the rest of my life. He posted a note on the School notice board (about something I cannot remember), and signed it, 'Paddy, the BD one'. From that day on, there was officially another Paddy in Sanawar, 'Paddy, the GD one', or simply Paddy, or the erstwhile Mohyna Khurana, never to be referred to by her name ever again, as long as she lived on the hilltop.

This is how I got my nickname. I now understand nicknames are a way at Sanawar to show people they belong, of accepting new folks and giving them a sense of familiarity to make them comfortable. I certainly felt that way when I was christened Paddy. Suddenly, I became part of the establishment.

Years later, Paddy (the BD one) came to IIM, Ahmedabad where, I too, was studying. I could scarcely believe we were once again sharing an academic institution. I hadn't been called Paddy for a while now, except by my School friends, and thankfully no one saw the resemblance between us anymore. Paddy and I would laugh about this and talk about the days gone by. No one else at IIM could really understand what happened at the hilltop anyway.

**Mohyna (Khurana) Srinivasan**
Paddy | Nilagiri 1981 | 1978–81

# 'Let There Be Light'

## The Switching On Ceremony for the
## School Electricity – 1923

Approval of funds for the provision of electric lighting for the school was granted by the Government in March 1922. Building of the school power station, engine rooms and workshop on the main ridge began later that same year. By the following March, two large capacity alternators, belt-driven by Crossley 126bhp, horizontal diesel engines were installed in the engine rooms and the necessary electrical wiring of all buildings on the hilltop was completed. The school 'lights' were officially switched on for the first time by General Sir Claude Jacob, KCB, KCMG, Chief of the General Staff, at a special ceremony held on the evening of 3 April 1923.

At about 7.30 p.m., the General and Lady Jacob were escorted to the newly built power station and after a short welcoming speech by the principal, the buildings were officially declared open by Lady Jacob. The General then turned on the main switch connecting the system to the generators. The party proceeded in turn to the Girls' and Boys' Schools, where all the children were seated at their desks in the dark with their form masters and mistresses present. All individual light switches had previously been turned to the 'on' position. The General then turned on the main switch and all the class rooms were flooded with light. There followed much cheering, loud cries and shouts of excitement from the boys.

The Chapel was visited next, the party entering from the main west door. The church was gradually flooded with light beginning with the chancel, followed in turn by the apse, the two side aisles and finally the nave.

Finally, the General and his party proceeded to No. 11 quadrangle in the Boy's Department, by the top of the steps leading down to the lower dormitories and, on the sound of a single 'G' from the duty bugler, all the boys' barracks were simultaneously flooded with light. By this time, the boys had all assembled on the BD pavement to witness the event. The

'Best School of All' was then sung, and the Heads of school called for three cheers for Sir Claude and Lady Jacob to conclude the ceremony.

Sanawar hilltop remained lit up and a blaze of light that evening until 9.15 p.m., when 'lights-out' was sounded and the generators switched off. Thereafter, although there were occasional failures, the electricity came on for everybody on the hilltop at 6.00 a.m. in the morning and was switched off at 9.15 p.m. every day until the early 1970's, when provision of the electrical supply for the school was taken over by the Himachal Pradesh State Electricity Board and the school was connected to the national grid.

**D.V. Boddington**
LRMS Sanawar 1942–1947
March 2002

**Compiled from:**

1. L.R.M.S. Sanawar Order No. 70 dated 30 March 1923.
2. Annual Report for year ending March 1924.
3. *The Sanawarian* magazine, February 1924.

**With grateful acknowledgements to:**
Alan Lane, former Crossley Service Engineer (Kilburn & Co., Calcutta) who kindly identified the engine for us.

# The Bloom of 1975

We, the batch of 1975 (meant to be 1974), began our journey in 1965 under the watchful scholastic guidance of 'heartbreakers' Ms Dudt and Ms Kemp in Prep School. Ms Suri, Ms Cherian, Mrs Harbaksh Kaur, and Ms Rudra kept us on our toes in our early years, which included memories of air-raid drills prior to the Indo-Pak war; midnight viewing of the Halley's comet tail; measles and chicken pox outbreaks; nature walks to distinguish keekar, elm and deodar; vivid imaginary weekend bang-bang attacks on enemy campsites nestled on hillsides, culminating in the hoisting of a handkerchief flag in victory; and our first crushes! The blue-jacketed boys and red-coated girls co-existed in harmony, barring some '*guth*-pulling'. However, I never understood why girls were brought to the boys' dorms to be 'punished', with the ayahs and matrons sternly supervising the bucket-bathing of playful boys. Of course, the tuck cupboards and 'doley' were veritable treasure chests. It was interesting how one had so many 'best pals' when a birthday party was coming up, because one could only invite fifteen 'friends' for Charlie's sweets and the birthday cake, with some spots already 'bagzzed' by the bullies. Early training in Machiavellian strategy! My grandfather always sent a *peti* of mangoes from Lucknow in late June, in time for my birthday. The Dussehris and Langdas were consumed quickly at the party, as Home Day would not be far off.

In 1968, we graduated to Boys'/Girls' Departments. There was some shuffling of houses and new classmates joined. We nervously adjusted to life at the bottom of the totem pole. Then followed seven years replete with too many memories, including that of DJS as Toby the Toy Soldier; Behti, the Kalinga winner; a good squad of boxers; the tragic khud-side jeep rollover; Naga dancing; Pahenga (Virk), the bugler; Mutty (Ramchandani) the maths whizz-kid; and our strong-willed and bright girls who kept the boys waiting for the proverbial 'knock three times on the ceiling', if not the head . . .

After graduating from school, our batch really bonded through the herculean efforts of the late Jerry (Bains) and Dhody, who generously and persistently organized regular, and frequent reunions. RIP.

Our talented batch has remained close and boasts of accomplished painters, doctors, writers, philanthropists and businesswomen. Our somewhat late-blooming boys (ahem!) have scaled impressive heights (and depths) in the armed forces, merchant marine (thanks to the carrot juice), finance and industry, hospitals and hospitality, technology, media, agri-business, politics, graduate teaching and entrepreneurship. We are particularly proud of two formidable women pursuing careers in peacekeeping and gender equality at the United Nations (UN); four, who have nurtured schoolkids at home and abroad.

And, we've had our fair share of surprises, too. A non-swimmer joined the navy, but chose submarines, as swimming was not a required skill; a witty debater trained to become a tank commander, and later, a defence journalist; a shy dancer is today an intrepid Himalayan rallies guide; a quiet, intelligent woman has opted to live in a commune; an active lad followed his passion for off-track motorbiking; and a third-divisioner has blossomed into a successful entrepreneur and venture capitalist. Our batch, unwittingly, has followed a neo-Stalinist model where a select few have become non-persons with nary a tear shed, or recollection. C'est la vie!

**Sanjiv Kapur**
Kapu | Siwalik 1975 | 1965–1975
St. Stephen's College, Economics (Hons.) | Thunderbird School in International Management | Harvard Business School: Corporate Director Certificate | Worked at AIG, HSBC, IFC/World Bank, AMP, Janus Henderson, and Wolfensohn Capital Partners | Non-Executive Board member and Consultant for GMAT, IDFC Capital, Fabindia, Ujjivan Microfinance, Hindustan Times | Travelled to over hundred countries across seven continents to pursue photography, culture, history, food, sports, languages and philately.

OS Sibling – Brother – Rohit Kapur | Kapu | Siwalik 1983 | 1972 – 1983

# Ozark in a Single Day – A New Record

One of the most popular hikes was to Ozark, a small hilltop *tibba* (a local deity temple), 7 kms ahead of a sleepy village, Naina Tikkar, on the Kumarhatti–Nahan road. The excursion was traditionally made over a long weekend, starting after Friday lunch and returning in time for Sunday supper.

I had been there once with other seniors from our House. We stocked our haversacks with tinned food, viz. baked beans, sardines, mackerel etc. bought from Tuck Shop, and bread loaves provided by Mrs Sehgal, the BD kitchen matron. We borrowed sleeping bags, packed towels, a night-suit, an extra change of clothes and water bottles. Reaching Dagshai at dusk, we were put up by the Principal of the Army Public School in their infirmary, and fed dinner and breakfast the next morning. Next day, we reached Ozark by late afternoon. All of us were simply stunned by the breathtaking view of the valley below the steep cliffs. We spent the cold night beside the tibba, safely tucked in inside our sleeping bags. We started back early on Sunday morning, halting at a tea shop in Naina Tikkar, and buying hot samosas and pakoras to make delicious sandwiches. We reached Sanawar just a little after tea.

Looking back at this Ozark trip, I analyzed that if we had nothing to carry and we started before the sounding of the rouser bell, it might be possible to convert the three-day hike into a single-day one. In 1968, we U-V Siwalikans took the bold decision to at least give it a try. A sporty junior, Jaspal Sandhu alias Sucha Singh, volunteered to join us. So on a Sunday, we woke up early, quietly readied ourselves, and left the dorm at 5 a.m. Walking down to Dharampur was no problem, and shortly, we were at Cherry Crossing, Dagshai. Taking shortcuts throughout the hilly terrain, we reached Naina Tikkar for a late chai and samosa-pakora breakfast.

Ajit Grewal was, by then, feeling tired and feverish. So, we gave him an Aspro and left him in the care of a responsible village elder. Reaching

Ozark, we spent an hour admiring the scenic beauty, had a light lunch of bread and baked beans, and started back. A three-hour rest had done Ajit a lot of good and he was now found fit to walk. We thanked the villagers. It was getting dark by the time we reached Dharampur. It was at the start of the bridle path via the school graveyard that Butch suddenly shivering and sweating, had clung on to me. The hallucinations of trickling white moonlight, coming through the swaying tree branches with a whistling sound, had reminded him of some haunting stories told to him by his father's orderly back home. We were yet to cross the graveyard and so to calm him down, all of us started singing loudly and cracking jokes, till we thankfully reached Moti's Corner.

Walking on the short back below Birdwood, we could hear blaring music from Barne Hall, where celebrations were on to mark the huge success of *Heer Ranjha*, the musical staged at Founders' that year. Rakesh Khosla, who had played the lead role of Ranjha, and Anil Auluck that of the villain Qaido, could probably enlighten us on the date of that Sunday in 1968.

We had reached our dorms before supper, thus successfully accomplishing a three-day hike in a single day, without lifts or hitchhiking. Our batchmates, the Himalayan Sixth Formers (of 1969), did attempt to match our record, but without success.

**Ravinder Raizada**
Chini | Siwalik 1969 | 1959–1969

OS Sibling – Ramakant Raizada | Kant | Siwalik 1968 | 1958–1968

# Arun Khetarpal

'Never Give In', the motto and the school song had a great impact on young Arun. Following the proud tradition of his family, he trained at the National Defence Academy and Indian Military Academy, and then joined a famous Tank Regiment, The Poona Horse.

16 December 1971, the War for the Liberation of Bangladesh.

*Never Give In is our Motto,*
*Strive till the set of sun,*
*. . . learn . . . truth . . . days of youth . . .*
*On the long Hodson run . . . heart seems bursting . . . may not win . . . yet*
*come in.*

First light. Exhausted from the harrowing task of clearing a mine field, the previous night. Almost deafened by the roar of exploding shells. Out of the blue, the words of his school song popped into his head. His heart was bursting, yet his mind was clear. He slowed his breathing . . . calming himself. Stillness. He zeroed in on who he was.

'I have been born into a family steeped in the traditions of the Indian Army. I studied in a school that taught me determination. I wear the colours of a regiment that has produced outstanding officers. Besides, in comparison to the NDA, clearing the mine field at Basantar was a cakewalk.' With his sense of humour intact, Arun Khetarpal answered the crackle of his tank radio.

'Enemy tanks approaching. B Squadron in urgent need of help . . . please send reinforcement!' Arun's trained ear recognized every voice of the men of his regiment. His unit needed him. Of his troop of three tanks, one was damaged. Reloading his personal weapon, he ordered the two remaining tanks to move to the village of Jarpal. Surrounded by enemy fire, his own tank roared into the heart of the battle.

*Never Give In Sanawar,*
*It's the cricket motto too,*
*Somebody's got to stop the rot,*
*And why not you . . .*

The enemy had been routed. At pistol point, Arun had captured some enemy soldiers. However, the commander of the second tank had been killed. Alone, in-charge and undeterred, Arun chased the enemy tanks . . . he thought, 'Somebody's got to stop the rot . . . so it may as well be me!'

The enemy was regrouping. He was now joined by two more of his regimental tanks. The ground shook as the mighty metal monsters roared onto the smoking fields of Basantar. He was on autopilot, his perfect training taking over, men and machine meshed in terrifying harmony. Load. Aim. Fire. Move. All synchronized in teamwork that needed no words. In the graveyard of tanks, four hits were by the crew of Arun's tank! The battle grew grimmer; one of the three Indian tank commanders was wounded. Then the gun of the second tank jammed. Arun was on his own for the second time.

*Never Give In, Sanawar . . .*
*. . . you're all alone and on your own . . .*
*With life's stern game to play.*

With steely resolve, he continued. The earth shook. They were enveloped in smoke. Arun's tank had been hit. It was immobile. The radio set crackled. His Commanding Officer ordered, 'Arun, your tank is on fire, abandon tank.'

Arun realized he was at the focal point of the enemy advance. It was only he who could stop the onslaught. 'No Sir, I will not abandon my tank. My gun is still working'.

Like a wall, he held back the enemy. He destroyed a tank just 100 meters from his own. He swung his turret towards the looming shadow of the enemy tank, there was a bright flash, a roar, his tank was hit for the second time. Light. Heat. And as darkness fell, he felt words more than heard them.

*For still the old school motto,*
*Till life's long journey close . . .*
*Will guide us true,*

*Till the game is through . . .*
*And for 'time' the whistle blows.*

Arun Khetarpal's courage has continued to inspire the Defence Services
and the Nation for fifty-plus years. His name adorns almost every
military station and cantonment. Back in Sanawar, where it all started,
the field of Peacestead has been serendipitously named after him because,
ironically, this brave young Sanawarian died in war, so that we could have
lasting Peace.

Copyright © Vashima Mansukhani | Siwalik | 2020

The citation of the Param Vir Chakra awarded to him reads:

"Second Lieutenant Arun Khetarpal, POONA HORSE (IC-25067)
[posthumous]
    Second Lieutenant Arun Khetarpal was dead but he had, by his
intrepid valour saved the day; the enemy was denied the breakthrough he
was so desperately seeking. Not one enemy tank got through.

Second Lieutenant Arun Khetarpal had shown the best qualities of leadership, tenacity of purpose and the will to close in with the enemy. This was an act of courage and self-sacrifice far beyond the call of duty."

This is an imagined account of how Arun Khetarpal must have fought. This fictional account now ends with three real facts:

1. A lot of army training is designed to empower people to work on autopilot. Arun was called to join his regiment on the battlefield actually with his training incomplete, as his batch of young officers had their YOs [Young Officers] course cut short. This speaks volumes for this young man who took on the might of the Pakistani Patton Tanks and won India the day.

2. In December 2021, as India commemorated fifty years of the 1971 War, Arun himself would have been seventy-one. Martyred at twenty-one in '71, and seventy-one in '21. How the word one (read won) rings through his numbers.

3. A more poignant firsthand account is when I sat by his gracious and dignified mother in Mathura, watching a shadow play being enacted to commemorate the Battle of Basantar. Arun's tank engaged with the enemy. The stage lit up as his tank was hit. The voice of the Commandant of Pune Horse call to him to abandon tank. A young voice calls out that the gun was still working. I heard Arun's mother, the same mother who had filled her son's heart with courage and pride, sigh faintly to herself, '*Haye Arun, tum ne kya kiya!*'

While generations of Sanawarians, and our nation will continue to draw inspiration from Arun, my heart belongs to a family that produced such a son.

**Preminda (Batra) Langer**
Vindhya 1970 | 1965–1970
Educationist

OS Sibling – Sister – Preeti (Batra) Singh | Vindhya 1975 | 1969–1975

# Mr W.G. Gaskell

'You think yours is the best school of all? Well, it isn't—mine is!' So said Mr Gaskell, when acknowledging a birthday gift presented to him on the veranda of Gaskell Hall, facing the boys' dining room. The 'pavement' was filled with all the boys of the Lawrence Royal Military School, the present water tank had not been built. Mr Gaskell made his acknowledgement with a wry smile, a rare thing for him, but I daresay Blundell's could be considered to be at par with Sanawar!

Mr Gaskell served the school loyally for many years, including the time that he took over the reins from Rev. G.D. Barne, the principal, and acted in that capacity. He never let himself go at any time. He preserved the quiet dignity of the traditional headmaster, caustic in his adverse comments, sparing in his praise, but inwardly as proud of the school as any rabid Old Sanawarian, who had the privilege of being taught by him.

His prowess on the sports field when playing for the staff, at cricket, hockey and tennis showed that he must have been a force to contend with during his school days but no one could say that he was absolutely at home as Second-in-Command of the Sanawar Detachment, Simla Rifles. It was evident that the Captain's uniform was immaculate, even if worn with a slight discomfort; it was evident that the mild voice of an educationalist did not do anything for his words of command, but the intricate detail of 'Officers, fall out!' was observed with the spirit and determination of a seasoned warrior, albeit with a sense of relief.

His was a familiar figure just before 9.00 a.m. daily, as it left the English bungalow now occupied by the bursar. The dress was correct for the occasion—grey flannel bags, tweed jacket and a walking stick. The latter never touched the ground. It was held mid-way along the shaft and the curved handle beat a measured tempo on the shoulder blade; the walker was always deep in thought and any salute proffered by a boy in passing was returned with a raising of the stick. Mr Gaskell would be on his way to the Chapel. He played the organ at all services; he conducted the singing and trained the choir. Somehow, he managed to keep the young interested in what he played. The 'voluntaries' were light and tuneful, Gregorian chants were noticeable by their absences but never was 'Onward Christian Soldiers' allowed to become banal with a military tread. Church festivals, such as Easter, Whitsun and Founders', were made memorable by anthems that were rendered with devotion and great care was given by the choir and soloists to the Founders' Day Anthem, 'Let us now praise famous men!' It was a feature of the entire school year. His very life and well-being were left in the tender hands of two boys from the Lower School, detailed as 'organ pumpers'. Frequent lapses of attention resulted in severe gusts of wind emanating from the organ and disarranging the set of the tweed jacket. 'Trying to blow me away, boy?'

It was in the classroom that Mr Gaskell truly came into his own. His was not an easy task. The school was 'Military', and 'Royal' at that, consequently much of the twenty-four hours was given over to bodily pursuits. Gaskell treasured the few hours, 9.15 to 1.00 and 2.00 to 4.00, in which to administer the three 'R's' and he was never more at home than when teaching. His fine, classical blackboard writing was copied by many an admirer and even his signature was reproduced by boys, but not for any criminal purpose, in spite of being so accurate.

His methods were straightforward, and I, for one, not blessed from birth with a gift for maths, found the 'unitary method' to be child's play when explained by WG. He commenced the school day with religious instruction for the Upper School, a combination of the senior standards. 'Line upon Line', 'Precept upon Precept', the Works of Josephus, The 'Homilies', The Articles of Religion were as much integral parts of the Bible readings and the history of the prayer book, as the learning of any Collect or Psalm; and those Old Sanawarians who entered the Church must have found this grounding to be without price.

W.G. gave the impression that he lived aloof of the lives of the boys. Nothing could have been further from the truth. He was aware of the pulse rate of any section of the BD. He shared our moments of anxiety. He revelled in our moments of elation—quietlike! He heard a boy singing in a barrack-room concert as he walked the path below the principal's House. He used the correct procedure to find out who the boy was and much to that boy's surprise, he was invited 'quietlike' to the principal's House to play with young Peter (WG was acting principal at the time). The 'play' turned out to be the boy's first singing lesson with Mrs Gaskell at the piano. Apart from this instruction, it was the boy's first taste of home life in the school's Spartan year. There were other lessons culminating in solos in the Easter, Whitsun and Founders' Anthems. WG showed no emotion outwardly. He flogged me, six of the best, for writing a complaint home instead of adopting the usual channels. I am of the firm opinion now, fifty years on, that the punishment hurt him more than it did me. Standing on the compass in front of his desk facing north, seemed to knock the bottom off my world.

A year later, he congratulated me, quietlike, for the first place in the government exams. 'Didn't do you any harm, I see!' I knew what he meant. Those marks on my posterior seemed to be indelible at the time. The hue changed from black to blue, to purple, through the spectrum to the yellows and then barely visible, but what has been indelible is the memory of a man who had the greatest influence on my life for the good. I'm an old age pensioner now, a senior citizen, but I go back often to the days when I sat spellbound under the direct gaze of WG when he expounded maths, science, English, geography or religious instruction. Somehow, I hear and feel the 'tap, tap' of a curved handled walking stick beating rhythmically on my shoulder blade as I wander through memory lane past Warrior's Grove, Leisure, The Lawrence Arch, The Church Slant and come to rest rather gingerly on the organ stool, listening for the sounds that help to bring back the vision of a great man.

**William H. 'Bill' Colledge (Bilkul)**
Old Sanawarian (Roberts 1917–1927)

**Source and Acknowledgement:** *The Sanawarian* **(December 1972)**

# The Stars Above the Chapel

One of the joys of being in Nilagiri House was its location. And one of our discoveries, in this location, was an amazing little perch on the Chapel roof next to the House of our Senior dorm Housemaster, Mr Mukherji. Everyone called him Mukho, including Mukho himself. And in true Sanawarian tradition, his wife was called Mukhi. For example, Mr Solomon was called Solo and his wife was Soli. Jalo, Jali. Katta, Katti.

There were some curious exceptions to this rule. For example, the Nilagiri House Junior dorm Housemaster, Mr Atma Ram, was called Lickto, but his wife wasn't called Lickti, but Licktini. Which sounds diminutive, but go figure. My dad, who could never resist playing on words, had his own nickname for Mr Atma Ram: Mr Atom Bomb. I'll never forget writing my first letter to my parents during the weekly letter-writing session on Fridays on an aerogramme. I wrote, 'Hello Mama and Papa, I'm very happy in Sanawar. I've made lots of friends already. Mr AB is my Housemaster.' As soon as I'd written it, Lickto, who was supervising the session announced, 'all the new boys, please don't seal your letter!'

When my turn came, I walked to the front of the classroom with dread. My mind was racing. Lickto read my letter. 'Who is Mr AB?' he asked. I'm still proud of my presence of mind. 'What?' I feigned complete surprise. 'Sorry sir, that B should be an R!' Close call. But I digress from the Chapel story . . .

On most nights, there would be a light breeze, and a spectacular night sky to boot. It was a great place to picnic. But it was 'out of bounds', which made it all the more fun, like our occasional midnight forays after dark into the graveyard, where we would try and scare each other without making too much noise.

Some of my 'hunting' friends would usually come back after the vacations with large vats of meat pickles, mostly venison and wild boar, preserved in heavy spices. The thought of these still makes my mouth water. My friend 'Fanto' was known for his especially delicious lineup, thanks to all his hunts with his 'tayas' and 'mamas' and 'chachas', who favoured wild boar and 'neel guy' (Nilgai).

While Fanto's supplies lasted, which wasn't for long, we would feast. In fact, food of any kind didn't last long in Sanawar. We felt perpetually starved. If anyone received a 'parcel' of goodies from home, like chocolates or biscuits or fruits – delivered at lunchtime so everyone could see it – it was consumed within a few paces of the dining hall. We were *always* hungry.

Our modus operandi for savouring the pickles was to sneak out some extra rotis under our shirts after dinner in anticipation of our late-night snack after lights-out. As we became more senior and friendly with the 'sixth formers', who had a special room of their own with ghee and heating equipment, we'd repurpose the rotis into parathas and make delicious picked rolls. But as 'junior seniors', meaning seventh graders, we didn't have this luxury, so we'd head out to our Chapel perch to make 'roti rolls'.

On this particular night after lights-out, three of us snuck out of the rear of the dorm with our supply of rotis and meat pickle. We tiptoed past Jerry Bains, better known as 'Mudge', who was being punished by his uncle who was the senior prefect. Jerry was in his usual 'murga' position outside the prefect's bunk, with his head facing backwards between his legs. Years later, I learned that 'murga' is an excellent yoga asana, and a great stretch for the hamstring!

A common reason for punishment was unpolished shoes. 'See me tonight', was the most dreaded sentence to come from a prefect. In today's world, the punishments would be considered excessively cruel, but we just toughed them out. Telling on a prefect or any senior who bullied you was anathema, no matter how cruel the punishment. As I learned quickly, 'honour' mattered more than anything else in Sanawar, which meant, among other things, never telling on anyone and being a team player.

Mudge was a regular murga. I don't think I could have handled what was meted out to him for unpolished shoes, bad grades, or a host of other reasons. But Mudge was more resilient than anyone I know, which earned him double respect from everyone forever. Years later, I recall his regular visits to New York fondly, which would invariably end with an all-night party at the apartment he always rented in the city.

Mudge waved at us from his upside-down murga position and grinned. He was in the early stages of his murga. The grunting would start later. The prefect was drinking coffee in his 'bunk,' getting advice from a classmate on how to approach a girl he had a crush on. The clueless advising the clueless. We slipped noiselessly out of a door across his bunk.

The rear of the dorm led into a narrow passageway, with a steep hillside on the other side. I have fond memories of playing 'pithoo' in that passageway, but that's for a different story.

We dragged our butts and supplies to our perch. As we sat down and laid out the rotis, I tipped the pickles onto my pyjamas! 'Oh fuck!' I cried. 'Shhhhh, you'll wake up Mukho!' Sure enough, a few seconds later, Mukho turned on an outside light and peered around. We barely breathed. He eventually went back inside. Phew!

But Mukhi was on to me. Twice a week, she would oversee our laundry exchange. The next time I went to collect my fresh 'kit', she asked slyly, 'Dhar, where did those pickle stains on your pyjamas come from? Surely, you don't wear your pyjamas to the dining hall?'

She smiled as I fumbled for an answer. 'Badmaash!'

(Dedicated to Jerry Bains, a larger-than-life friend. RIP Jerry.)

**Vasant Dhar**
Nilagiri 1972 | 1967–1972
Professor, Stern School of Business and Center for Data Science | Co-Director – Graduate Studies, PhD Program, Center for Data Science

OS Sibling – Brother – Krishen Dhar | Nilagiri 1963 | 1961–1963
               Brother – Upender Dhar | Nilagiri 1968 | 1963–1968

# The Silent Drum Major

It was the dress rehearsal for the big day, Trooping of the Colours Parade at Founders'. We were all decked up in our finest, especially the Brass band, in red-and-white uniforms—but the one who stood out the most was the Drum Major Kulpreet Singh (Kullu), with the big mace and all the stripes and accoutrements, along with a blazing red turban. The front row included Tarun Sawney (Taru) on the trombone, and Suryaveer Singh (Shorty, H '80) on the trumpet. They were at the front because they played the loudest and could just about hold any tune so that the others (in the band) could follow. Taranjit Singh Sandhu (Tarry) was the Parade Commander. Egged on by Taru, Kullu took on the challenge of being louder than the commands given out by Tarry.

All went well, for the first few commands of the day—Kullu was in full throat, his bellowing voice reverberating across Peacestead, making Tarry appear like he was giving a silent sermon. Kullu was glowing with pride. Then came the sequence wherein the entire parade stands still and all eyes are on the Brass band, as it does a slow march while playing. This is a pivotal moment in the Parade and Kullu was well aware of it.

A fair crowd had turned up for the Dress Rehearsal so there was some pressure on the band to be at its best. Kullu bellowed out 'BAND . . .' loud and clear. However, due to his earlier exhortations, the remaining part of the command, 'Dahine se, Dheere Chal' (slow march from the right), came out as an inaudible rasp, as he had LOST HIS VOICE! Only Taru and Shorty caught the command to march, and promptly set off with Kullu, blasting on their instruments. The rest of the band did not budge. Nearly five paces later, it dawned on us that things were not quite right. Now, the decision on hand was to either carry on as if nothing untoward had happened and let the rest of the band run and catch up, or to abort and restart. Mr B. Singh (Mucchoo) settled the dilemma (as always), ordering us to return to the starting blocks.

444

In hindsight, it was side-splittingly hilarious, but at that point in time, acutely embarrassing. As Kullu put it later, it is '*Hosh*' that sees one through adversity, not just '*Josh*'!

**Tarun Sawney**
Taru | Vindhya 1979 | 1971–1978

Mother – Josephine Winifred Sawney | Jo | 1970–1978 | Teacher – English and Piano

OS Siblings – Brother – Ravi Sawney | Mad | Vindhya 1976 | 1971–1976
              Brother – Sunil Sawney | Tommy | Vindhya 1981 | 1970–1978

# Dagroo – Ode To A Mountain Stream

All round the Camp wild roses blow,
A fragrant, wind-tossed, bank of snow
Alive with birds: and round about
The little silent tents peep out
Their curious peaks, as if to show
The reason for the noise below
In 'Massey's Valley', clear and cool,
Where waters move from pool to pool
In tinkling melody: or sleep
In drowsy shadows, deep
Beneath the pines the long day through.
And down in 'Hart's' the fish dive deep
In panic fear: or silent, creep
Beneath the rocks,
To watch, with round enquiring eye,
Lithe limbs, that there from 'Bouncer's Rock'
Invite the cooling water's shock
And all the air from Choir Bridge,
Right up to where the utmost ridge
Stands clear and black against the sky,
Is filled with youthful laugh and cry,
While fellows fish, and bathe and lie
And laze around. In happy, rare,
Fitful fragrant breeze, there
Comes the grave, imperial and fine,
Dim, memorial scent of Pine.
And oh! The long unmixed delight,
In the hushed and scented night,
Slowly to swim about the pool,

And feel the healing touch and cool
Caress of water. While the hill
Looms more vaguely huge, until,
The veils of evening dropping slow,
Fades all trace of sunset glow.
Dear Heaven! To see again the streamlets twist
Down purple khud-side crowned with mist,
All through the shimmering veil again
Of soft, baptismal, silv'ry rain.
To feel once more upon one's lips
The sweet spring water as it drips
Through moss and fern.
Say now?—standeth still,
Below the bridge, the ruined mill?
And are there still the groves of pine,
All broken through with eglantine?
And where the morning freshness calls,
Do fellows still climb up the Falls?
Still in eastern skies are born
Those lilac tints that come with dawn?
And doth the love of simple things
Sway greatly hearts? And sings
The vocal air when moving through
The wood? And is the sky still just as blue?
Great scheme! I'll go and see
And find the peace that pleaseth me.

**John 'Jack' Harper**
Nicholson House (1940–1944)

**Editor's note:** Jack started this poem during his last year at Sanawar. I still have a transcription of his first two handwritten verses. I don't know when he finished the poem but judging by the reminiscent and nostalgic vein of his last few stanzas, I guess it was some many years after he left in 1944. The poem appeared in full for the first time in the 2007 edition of *The Old Sanawarian* magazine and is presented here on these pages as a

lasting memorial and personal tribute to a good friend, true nature lover and kindred spirit.

**D.V. Boddington**
LRMS Sanawar 1942–1947
3 August 2009

# Kasauli in Sixteen Annas

I was one of the fortunate kids to have never been a day scholar. My father, being an army man, decided that army children shouldn't suffer from the continuous cycle of their parents' periodic posting, which resulted in perpetual school-hopping. So in 1949, at the tender age of five, I was bundled off to Bethany House in Lower KG at the Welhams' School Dehradun. I finished Upper KG in 1950 and happily moved to Sanawar in 1951, where many kids from our extended family, were studying.

After two enjoyable years as a prepper, in Form I and Form II, I moved to L-III in the Boys' Department in 1953. I was sent to Sparrow Hawks B, which was a Holding House, before I could move to the Siwalik House Junior dormitory.

The days of Prep School mollycoddling were far behind us and we were always expected to be a step ahead in our ability to survive the Sanawar discipline. We had Gurdip Singh Kalyana and Surinder Kalaan as prefects to ensure that we were always 'on the ball'. Mrs Thun, our matron, was the kindest person on earth. Prefects were like the proverbial Dracula sent to scare young children into disciplined robots or, at times, they were like consultants helping us realign our sense of prioritization. Yet, their flipside turned them into friends helping us unravel the mysteries of compiling a decent, well-constructed, loving and informative letter to our parents. Our matron was the epitome of kindness; but she also made sure that we learnt how to stitch our own buttons. Our school discipline was well in keeping with its military lineage.

Cutting a long story short, the much-awaited liberty to visit Kasauli was the only silver lining in our Spartan existence in Sanawar. There were four good reasons for anyone to walk down to Garkhal and up to Kasauli, past the mad woman's House, at the start of the climb, past Richard Mountford's grandmother's House and to our first stop—Alasia Hotel. This was our first reason, one of the four 'To-Dos'.

At Alasia, we would be greeted by Nikoo, the waiter in whites and a matching turban with the ubiquitous fan-like end jutting out and a black band tied obliquely around it, with the hotel's crest pinned stylishly in the centre. He would lovingly serve us an ice cream cone each, for a mere four annas, notwithstanding the fact that it was often the leftover custard dessert from the night before. We would lick and crunch the cones into oblivion. A quick rush to the cage of about thirty Budgerigars, near the lawn, was always refreshing. Their different colours, continuous chirping and screeching, kept us glued to the cage. A pity we weren't allowed to feed them. Leaving Alasia, we would trudge on.

The next To-Do was Daily Needs, which served the best ham sandwiches in the world—or so we thought at that very impressionable age of nine. It was a short distance up the road from Alasia and near Dr Arjan Singh's clinic-cum-residence. The tall, high-cheekboned owner, with a centre parting of well-oiled hair and small gold earrings, kept his best ham for Sundays; as he knew that no Sanawarian could go past his shop without decimating one or more of his amazing sandwiches at the measly rate of four annas each (there were sixteen annas to a rupee).

Our pleasant walk would then take us past the mini shopping centre with Indra Studios, Sharma Studios and a toy shop. We usually turned left and below us, on our right, were the bus stand and the road barrier. On our left and slightly above the level of the road, was our next To-Do destination: the Kalyan Hotel, whose proprietor was a kind old gentleman who always wore tight pyjamas, an Indian collarless kurta and a Nehru Jacket. He had an abscess-like bump on his forehead and a cheek full of betelnut. He adored Sanawar kids and waited the whole week for them. This is where we went to town on the Indian cuisine aloo poori. In school, we survived on bland English cuisine, except for the chicken curry and rice on Saturdays. Little good came of it as the weekend shot of saline was compulsory for everyone to clear their innards of dastardly amoebic parasites. Thus, the aloo poori was a celebration of sorts, much to the proprietor's delight. For four annas, we got a deep plateful of aloo curry, six pooris, with homemade mango pickle, and for another two pooris, there was never an extra charge.

Feeling satiated after a humongous early lunch and with our bellies bursting at the seams, we would descend, literally, to our last To-Do – the Defence Cinema, run by the Kasauli Army Garrison. For Sundays, they made it a ritual to show Westerns for the Sanawar kids. A ticket cost us four annas for the front stalls – rows were kept for Sanawarians and teachers. Watching Roy Rogers or the Lone Ranger was pure ecstasy. It wasn't unusual to hear a kid warning the Lone Ranger to be careful as the crooks were 'behind the boulder'.

As all good things, the Sunday fun too would suddenly end and we'd be trudging back to School before we knew it. By convention, we would cast a stone or two onto the roof of the mad woman's House on the right of the bridle path at Garkhal. When she came out screaming and showering us with the choicest epithets for our lineages, we ran with our tails between our legs, imagining the worst if she ever caught us. Hundreds of dents on her tin roof bore testimony to our weekly ritual.

The walk up Tilley's Hill and from the bakery to the Quadrangle was always solemn, signifying the return to the grind. The amazing realization would sink in that one rupee was well spent in Kasauli; from a monthly pocket money allowance of four rupees.

Kipling's 'Send him to Sanawar and make a man of him' rings so true. We Sanawarians are different from the alumni of other schools because what Sanawar made of us is still on the drawing boards of other institutions. The foundation of Sanawar rests on the bedrock of an education system both within and outside the classroom; based on self-confidence, discipline and a code of honour.

NEVER GIVE IN.

**Col. Rupinder Singh Brar**
Rupi | Siwalik 1959 | 1951–1959
1982 Asian Games Individual Gold Medallist (Equestrian); 1984 Arjuna Awardee (Equestrian); Captained the Indian Polo team in the 1990 World Cup Polo; 2000 National Seniors Golf Champion

OS Siblings – Sister – Gurshinder Brar | Guchhi | Siwalik 1964 | 1954–1964

OS Spouse – Roop Malhans | Mousy | Vindhya 1964 | 1956–1964

OS Children – Harpratap | Chutti | Vindhya 1989 | 1979–1989
Sherpratap | Sheri | Vindhya 1989 | 1980–1989
Virpratap | Viri | Vindhya 1993 | 1984–1993

OS Grandchildren – Govind | Gobi | Vindhya 2015 | 2009–2015
Mansher | Siwalik 2021 | 2014–2021

# My Tryst with Mucchoo

Mr B. Singh, fondly called 'Mucchoo' by all, was the backbone of Sanawar—a man of several qualities. He was a brilliant actor and director (ADS and Himalaya House Shows), a fantastic dancer, perfect instructor for the Founders' parade and, last but not the least, an extremely strict disciplinarian.

He made sure that everyone was punctual, not loitering around; dressed simply—in nothing extravagant; had their hair cut like IMA cadets (like a freshly mowed lawn); did not create 'khup' and of course, obeyed the 'lights-out' timing as if it were London under curfew during WWII. Anyone crossing the line was not spared, irrespective of gender, caste, creed, height or the amount of facial hair. I remember regulating my breathing on sighting him and my heart actually skipping a beat when it was evident that I was the one being approached! My mind used to race through the previous few hours to detect hints of 'crimes committed'. Acts of omission rarely went unnoticed. In a nutshell, he was seldom the bearer of good news.

While preparing for our Board exams, in the Sixth Form dorms, we would break from the gruelling study routine (which was seldom serious, barring a few 'Einsteins' in our batch) for a midnight meal. Mind you that this was after having full dinner at the CDH or the Central Dining Hall.

Never in my life have I seen such a well-oiled and efficient machinery to take care of our continuous hunger pangs! Each of us had taken up tasks to match our strengths! I was in-charge of beverages, which normally meant a horrible coffee, while others made omelettes fit to be served on the Queen's table and 'transported' bread or chapatis from the CDH.

We would choose the corner bunk and convert it into a makeshift kitchen. All food had to be made in adequate quantities to match the appetite of our batchmates. Thus, coffee was always made in large plastic buckets with a makeshift immersion rod (pencil and erasers strung together along with shaving blades on both ends). We also modernized our equipment, with me getting a hot plate for making delicacies like omelettes or simply heating the chapatis from CDH to be eaten as rolls with a dash of sugar thrown in.

While the chefs were hard at work, we used to have a number of hungry souls sitting on nearby beds waiting expectantly for the feast! Each of them carried their only utensil – a plastic mug – to drink my heavenly brew!

One day, I was making coffee in a bucket as usual while others were making omelettes with eggs from Mr Attri's farm and onions from Nankoo's CDH. These were to be devoured with bread brought inside our jackets from CDH. Everyone was hard at work with a sense of determination and excitement. Little did we know that this was to be our 'Last Supper'.

The onions needed frying, as per the omelette recipe. Someone chucked them to the Chef when Mucchoo entered unannounced—the onions barely missing him! We got a solid lecture—on the need to focus on our studies and acting as examples for others to follow. Why he spared us the dreaded 'drill' this one time, remains a mystery to this day. Probably, he had a change of heart and wanted us to study hard, or that he was simply overjoyed by the thought that he was finally getting rid of these nincompoops for good in a few weeks . . . Nevertheless, all our utensils were confiscated on the spot after we had cleaned them. Uncooked food had to be thrown away, much to our collective agony!

In the days and weeks that followed, all of us tried to focus on our studies, but our minds demanded nourishment, which was unfortunately not available anymore! Using our collective willpower, we managed to give our Board exams and then it was time to leave school for good and head home.

On the day we were leaving school, I went over to collect my utensils from his House. Naturally, I was apprehensive, picturing one last 'parting shot' across my face. I knocked on the door and was told to enter. He met me near his stairs. He just hugged me and tears streamed down his eyes! I WAS SHOCKED! The great man, who terrified all humanity, was crying as if he was losing his favourite son! It was a side of him that I had never witnessed in all my years at Sanawar.

It took me time to register all this and then I hugged him back. All time stopped. Till date, I remember him telling me how much he will miss me and to stick to the values that I was taught in Sanawar. Words that he had never spoken before. I was really surprised that I meant so much to him—an extremely ordinary and average student!

All fear or anger that I felt for this man vanished in those moments. I finally saw him for who he really was. My biggest mentor, guide and friend. He always meant well, taught us values to stick by and hardened us to meet the everyday challenges of life. The persona he had created was to instill discipline within us for our own benefit. Regrettably, it took me more than six years to really get to know him and that too on my last day in school! I really wished this wisdom had dawned upon me earlier.

Sir, wherever you are, just know this that whoever I am today, to a large extent, is thanks to you. You helped create a strong conscience that guides me to this day—your gift to me. Thank you, Sir . . . eternally . . . for everything.

**Sanjay Aggarwal**
Ghancha | Himalaya 1983 | 1977–1983
Founder and CEO – Clover Organic Pvt. Ltd. | Sustainable Aquaculture, Wastewater Treatment and Solid Waste Management

OS Sibling – Sister – Sangeeta (Aggarwal) Chopra | Agri | Himalaya 1984 | 1977–1984

# Make a Man – If Not a Boxer – Of Him

I was an oddity when joining Sanawar. Firstly, I entered in L-V, joining schoolmates who'd been there since the beginning of time (L-III). Secondly, being South Indian – a rare breed being spotted in the flesh by many students for the first time – I stood out like an idli in *rajma* (or the other way around, colour-wise).

Therefore, my feeling on day one was not excitement at joining India's premier boarding school, but raw, physical fear. Would I fit in, even survive, among these tall, muscular Sardars? Rudyard Kipling had perhaps written 'Send him to Sanawar and make a man of him' to reassure new students about the fine education they would receive. But it had the opposite effect on me. Reading the words as I passed the gym, my fear doubled.

As I met my Housemates, my apprehension abated—they were all decent, friendly fellows. And I loved their nicknames, creative concoctions of juvenile originality! Take Pankaj Sethi for instance. His Sanawar moniker was the imaginative result of replacing the 'S' in his surname with first letter of his first name. The resulting 'Pethi' would have been innovative enough. But, perhaps to make it sound more masculine (which, by the way, his calf muscles alone justified), it was changed to 'Petha'. Sheer genius, I thought. And when his younger brother Neeraj joined Sanawar a couple of years after him, the nickname name Netha was a fait accompli.

But as I met more boys with unique nicknames, I began to fear my fate. I learned that all Agarwals, irrespective of weight, complexion and athletic ability, were called 'Kiyo', the Punjabi word for ghee, apparently because, in a bygone era, the Agarwals were associated with its production. I began to sweat gently despite the cold mountain air. If they could transform an innocuous 'Agarwal' into 'Kiyo', what monstrosity would these creative rascals unleash on perhaps the school's first South Indian? But, though many of my friends experimented with 'Upma', 'Dosa' and 'Saambar', I managed to hang on to 'Paddy'. I attribute this accomplishment to pure, unadulterated luck. Of course, I had introduced myself as Paddy, not even attempting to subject the delicate North Indian tongue to the jawbreaker Padmanabhan, but this was hardly a guarantee of success: after all, Sanjay Batra had been decisively christened 'Bats' despite his many attempts to steer us towards 'Brat', including emblazoning the word across his notebooks.

Though a newbie joining in the middle of a relatively senior class, I found it surprisingly easy to fit into Sanawar life. Within two days, I was visiting the 'pan', ordering 'bun-samosas' and using 'are you mad?!' as a catch-all phrase to express shock, mild surprise, disgust, curiosity, confusion or amusement.

Having established my linguistic credentials and avoided the horrible-nickname-for-life, I began participating in extracurricular activities, the hallmark of Sanawar, with flourish. I joined during football season and, while playing in my set was fun, watching and cheering the school teams made me want more. During the winter break, having cajoled my father into getting an army soldier to coach me, I improved and made it into the Colts the next term. Similarly, I represented the school in cricket and hockey, wrote for the school newsletter and acted in plays.

In fact, the only activity conspicuously absent from my repertoire was boxing, exempt for boys wearing dental braces, like me, or spectacles. Frankly, I was grateful to my Chandigarh dentist: a fist fight with *hatta-katta* Sardar boys wasn't high on my wish list. But after two years, when my braces were removed, so was my apprehension. *I can do this*, I thought. I'm from Vindhya, House of the school's best boxer (Tarun Sawney) and heavyweight king (Poe Bhullar). So I replicated my proven football coaching model. And the boxer soldier assigned by my father responded with fervour. He trained me on posture, footwork, defence and offence; and made me pummel a punching bag with jabs, hooks and upper cuts.

Back in Sanawar, I entered the boxing ring for the first time in my life. And won my first fight on a technicality, when my opponent was disqualified for not being able to remove his *kada*. Two days later, I faced my classmate, Housemate and friend, A.P. Singh. The dong sounded. Immediately, I began prancing in front of him, darting left, back, front and right, on my toes, my eyes fixed on his. He watched me quietly for a while, then hit me in the face . . . and everything changed. My head flew back, followed by my arms and then AP's. Showing no recollection of our friendship, he pummelled me on my left and right flanks with his right and left hands, all very symmetrical. I staggered back. He stepped in. The gym seemed to be spinning around me; then things became black. Out of

the darkness, from time to time, I would see A.P. Singh and his gleefully active gloves. If I hit him, it was advertent and not more than three times.

After an eternity – that I later learned lasted a mere fifty-five seconds – the referee shouted 'stop fighting'. A.P. Singh, the only one doing it, stopped. The referee declared him the winner. I staggered out of the ring, never to enter it again. I graduated from school before the next boxing season.

Later, I introspected deeply. How had football coaching facilitated my entry into Colts while boxing coaching had left me with an ignominious defeat? I had been equally assiduous in following the coach's instructions in both cases, and had practised with the same intensity. Suddenly, like the law of floatation and Archimedes, the solution hit me. The army coach, in all his hours of coaching, had never, not once, actually hit me. He had, perhaps, believed that striking the commander's son showed a lack of decorum. Had he smote me a few on the face, I might have enjoyed the training less but learned boxing more. But now A.P. Singh had made up amply for his lapse. I'd had all the hitting I needed for a lifetime and was happy to put boxing behind me permanently.

**Padmanabhan Rangappa**
Paddy | Vindhya 1979 | 1975–1979

# Thank God I Am a Sanawarian!

In 1959 Major Som Dutt, Headmaster, Sanawar, interviewed my younger sisters, Sangi and Chingpi, and me, at Guwahati in the fourth and final round of the National Merit Scholarship for Scheduled Tribes and Castes. He was bewildered to find three children from one tribal family, in a hilly corner of Manipur, desiring to join the faraway Sanawar. Curiosity is probably what brought him to that hilltop. My dad knew nothing about Sanawar, except that it was in the hills, and a co-ed, so the three of us could be together.

Sanawar – teachers, students or the support staff – didn't worry themselves with tribes, castes, colour, creed, or chinky-looks . . . something that, sadly, our country today seems to be embroiled in.

My first brush with authority was in March 1960. I quarrelled with a boy (whom, try as I may, I just cannot recall). In the verbal dual that ensued, I soon ran out of words, and so blurted, 'ban chut' before running away. Calling someone 'BC' was the ultimate parting shot in Babu Para, the Bengali-dominated government colony in Imphal, where we quartered. My adversary bawled. I was summoned to the Dining Hall. Ma'am-on-duty asked me why I had hit him, to which I replied, 'I did not hit'. Then what did I say? I replied, 'BC'.

A click of the tongue! When she learnt that I did not know its meaning, I was gently informed, 'It is a very, very bad word . . . You mustn't ever use it again'. I apologized. We shook hands and ma'am – alas, I cannot recall her name either – gave us an extra helping of caramel pudding. Incidentally, by and by, in college at Delhi, her advice faded out—'BC' in its most bawdy, unsophisticated form became an expression one dished out – or received – without anyone batting an eyelid.

I salute all my teachers, starting with the Oxford Blue Major Som Dutt and Ma'am Merle, whose elevenses I can never forget; the Kemps, Mukherjees, Manleys, Mr Atma Ram, Mr and Mrs B. Singh, Ms Rudra, Mr Sikand, Mr Mundkur, Mr Jagdish Ram, Mrs Sehgal, Ms Doherty . . .

well, *all of them* . . . along with the host of unseen, unheard support staff who made life so comfortable at the hilltop.

I salute the wiry Babban, always in his dark blue outfit, waking us Nilagirians with the long, loud rouser bell every morning. He would have already swept and fired up the boiler by then so that we had running hot water. Yes, Sanawar had an army of unsung heroes, who were seen collectively only on Independence Day, when they came with their families to Barne field to race, jump, throw and play football, win prizes and enjoy the special treat. A great tradition, which I sincerely hope Sanawar continues.

Ah! It was 1963 or 1964. After a week of margarine-on-bread-and-milk diet, supposedly to starve my fever, I was discharged from Hospi to find myself on the brightly-lit Barne Hall stage for the Nilagiri House show rehearsals. There I was. A stern voice from the dark instructed me, 'Listen carefully and then follow'. The piano sounded and a few lines of a song were sung two to three times. I listened but I did not follow: 'Ma'am, I can't sing'. Ms Doherty would have none of that, 'I have been in Shillong before Sanawar, and one thing I learnt there was that all, repeat, all Mizos can sing—and play the guitar!' Factually correct. Warning me of dire consequences, she pounded the piano again. And I had really tried. But I proved to be an exception. An exasperated and shocked Ms Doherty cried, 'You are the first Mizo who cannot sing!' To my great relief, I was dropped from the opera.

Two years later, one Sunday afternoon, Karamvir, Bimbet and I were on the steep slope above the swimming pool, just below the library. Chlorine fumes from the swimming pool had scorched and seared the grass on the slope. So, the three buddies were just rummaging among the grass, God knows for what. Till one of us found a well-used toothbrush. I remember we passed it around and aired our views. One of us (only Karam can confirm who), with wisdom written all over his face, pronounced, 'This is Ma'am Doherty's toothbrush.' The other two, equally wise, agreed.

A stern voice from high above us asked, 'Now . . . what are you three doing down there?' We froze, drained of our wisdom and blood. We looked up to find Ms Doherty looking down at us. She continued, 'Go and play near the dorm. And don't roam about on the slope.' As we breathed a sigh of relief and turned to scoot, she added, 'And, by the way, that is not my toothbrush'. We vamoosed and have lived to tell this tale.

Life has been from one hilltop to another . . . to yet another . . . with testing halts in valleys. Our motto 'Never Give In' and everything else we learnt at Sanawar has made this life worthwhile.

I hug, of course, my batch, Class of '67, who I cherish, miss and salute. Those were the days, my friend . . . we thought they'll never end. And they certainly haven't ended, though some of us have moved on to a higher hilltop . . . where we shall meet again.

Thank God, I am a Sanawarian!

**Tonsing Vunglallian**
Vunga | Nilagiri 1967 | 1960–1967

OS Siblings – Tonsing Lalsanglian | Sangi | Nilagiri| 1968 | 1960–1968
Tonsing Ngaizaching | Chimps | Nilagiri | 1969 | 1960–1969
Tonsing Lianrammawi | Moite | Nilagiri | 1972 | 1969–1972
Tonsing Thanghminglian | Mingi | Nilagiri | 1979 | 1973–1979
Tonsing Khaisianmung | Mungpi | Nilagiri | 1980 | 1973–1980

# Form-I, an Initiation

As life goes by, the mind is overloaded with information, more so with the advent of social media. As is with all hard disks, the 'older' data starts getting 'corrupted', and so I have undertaken penning down as much as I can remember, before these precious memories fade away.

As I look back to my time in Form-I, I 'see' Mrs Harbaksh Kaur, Mrs Bhalla, Mrs Leela Thomas, Mrs Sidhu and Mrs Sakuja.

Mrs Thomas was the first member of staff I met when I joined Sanawar. It was 3 March 1971; it had snowed all night-long and well into the morning. I managed to jump the admission test line, as I was the only kid not hanging onto his mother. Mrs Thomas seemed quite pleased with my English. I had been made to practise hard before reaching school. She looked like a kind grandmother like those one sees in kindergarten storybooks. She had a very loving and happy persona, with tiny crinkles in the corners of her eyes, that immediately put me at ease. I was handed over a pink card with sums written on it – my maths test. I went about sorting them out in a jiffy as my mother, being a maths teacher herself, had kept me in line. I am not sure how many I got right, but I'm sure that the confidence with which I went about it made her happy enough to accept me. My English was well in control as I was determined to join.

Fortunately, she turned out to be my class teacher in Form-I A. I now remember her fondly as a very patient, firm, strict and nice lady, whom we were lucky to start our boarding school experience with. She had her very set systems in class that were clearly communicated to seven-year-old brats, a mix of homesick sobbers and sprightly bouncers ready for a fight anytime. We were to reach class before her, not to be naughty, complete and submit our prep work on time, and participate in all activities. If we were late or got into some other trouble, we were made to stand in a big dustbin in a corner of the class, with our noses against the wall. Standing in the dustbin hurt, for we were already developing egos (which we then understood as 'bad feelings'). The timetable for classes and prep work was

461

prepared well in advance. The good part about prep work was that only two subjects were given on a day. Even then, I could barely manage to keep my head above the water!

Our class was divided into four Houses—Tiger, Lion, Rhino and Elephant. I was assigned to the Lion House, with another 'as bright as' me. To our utter dismay, we found we were teamed up with four 'super-smart' Lionesses, who were meant to 'encourage' the two of us for the rest of the year. They were true achievers, and I particularly remember Ulka Puri and Shalini Bakshi, the 'distinction' types. With laggards like us in the House, Tiger, Rhino, and Elephant had some hope of catching up, but never really did so.

In class, the Houses were assigned different tasks—cleaning the blackboard; filling the chalk box; ensuring the cleaning of the dustbins by the sweepers; keeping the library in order; managing bio projects; updating the scoreboard and charts; and, in general, housekeeping of the classroom. As the House was collectively responsible, Sunny and I had no reason to complain and were, in fact, extremely proud of our super-efficient Lionesses.

This, then, was the sowing of the seed in Sanawar and the beginning of the process of 'make a man of him'.

**Grp. Capt. Sajan Sethi**
Srgt. Shetty; later, Sarge | Himalaya 1981 | 1971–1981
M.D. Aerospace Medicine | Officiating School RMO 2019

OS Sibling – Sister – Rajan (Sethi) Wahi | Petha | Himalaya 1972 | 1967–1972

# House Breakup Party

At the end of every year, and on the night just before Home Day, every House organized a Breakup Party, where House girls were invited to be the guests.

In 1963, my first year in BD, our Sixth Formers made the illogical decision to skip inviting the Siwalik House girls, and make it an all-boys Stag Party. Through the year, they had discouraged us juniors from talking to girls, and made fun of any boy doing so. We had been friendly with the girls in PD, especially with those from our class and House, but had now started to shy away from talking to them. The 'Bal Brahmachari' seniors requested Mr Waud, our Senior Housemaster to inform Mrs Kemp, the SGD Housemistress, of their decision. I still find it amusing and break into a smile when I remember the picture of Mrs Kemp trailing Mr Waud, repeatedly questioning, 'But how is this possible, Mr. Waud? This has never happened before . . .', and Mr Waud adamantly sticking to his lines, 'But Mrs. Kemp, the boys do not want the girls', a line he kept repeating again and again.

This was happening for the first time—the House girls were being denied the customary invitation to the boys' House Breakup Party. The Nilgarians were smart enough to take advantage, and invited our Siwalikan girls to their House Breakup. When word spread around school, everyone started to make fun of the Siwalik House and its Sixth Formers for their unchivalrous act, thus prompting a rethink on the matter. In a comic turnaround, our Sixth Formers requested Mr Waud to once again approach Mrs Kemp, and extend an invitation. It was now time for Mr Waud to run behind Mrs Kemp, repeatedly saying, 'Mrs Kemp, the boys want the girls to come', and Mrs Kemp snubbing him by saying, 'But Mr Waud, it is all over now. The girls are going to the Nilagiri House Party'.

I am pretty certain that 1962 was the only year when a House had a Stag Breakup Party . . . Never before, and probably never after.

In 1968, I was assigned the task of organizing the House Breakup Party. Rocky (Mohan) helped me greatly. We walked down to his brewery below Garkhal on a few occasions, picked up his Jeep and went shopping, to Kasauli and Solan, to place orders for ham, sausages, tinned food, etc., as well as to choose the farewell gifts to be given to our departing Sixth Formers, and our House Tutor Mr David Richard Anderson Mountford (an Old Siwalikan of the 1958 batch), who was leaving to join St. Paul's School, Darjeeling, as the vice principal. The gift we gave Monty deserves a special mention. As he was very fond of smoking, we bought him a king-size golden-coloured cigarette case, a silvery lighter, a cut-glass ashtray and a black smoking pipe, from Jakki Mull & Sons (above Indira's Studio and Kalyan Hotel, Kasauli). The Sixth Formers received a school necktie and scarf, bought from the Tuck Shop, a small wooden Siwalik House shield from the carpentry room, and one 78 rpm disc of the latest Hindi film songs, purchased from a gramophone shop in Solan.

**Ravinder Raizada**
Chini | Siwalik 1969 | 1959–1969

OS Sibling – Ramakant Raizada | Kant | Siwalik 1968 | 1958–1968

# Ghosts of Sanawar

It's been thirty-three years and I am still haunted by the memory of my first encounter with a 'Sanawarian ghost'.

I joined Sanawar in 1989, and, along with three other bachelor masters, lived at Stone View, above Monkey Field—truly a bachelors' paradise. Every now and then, we would walk to Kasauli on a Saturday night to have dinner and return before midnight.

On one such cold Saturday night, as we crossed the BD pavement and headed towards Horse-shoe Bend, we realized that someone was following us. It was rather misty, with no street lights and visibility of barely 10 metres. As we turned to look back, we saw a lone silhouette, draped in white from head to toe, following us purposefully. A shiver ran down our spines and by sheer telepathy, the thought of the fabled 'Headless Chowkidar' filled our collective imagination. We had all heard about him and his supposed encounters near the Horse-shoe Bend.

We were speechless but somehow mustered the courage to hurriedly continue towards Stone View. At a much-quickened pace, our heartbeats galloping, we could still clearly hear footsteps behind us. By the time we got to the Hospi slope, we were literally running. And then we heard the 'ghost' shout, '*Oye, ruk jao*'. We froze at that very spot. The ghost came closer and asked, '*Oye, kahan ja rahe ho?*' He sounded very familiar. We turned around to face him and realized that it was none other than Mr Sukhvinder Singh, Assistant Housemaster, Sixth Form House, draped in his white '*loi*' (woollen shawl). He had mistaken us for senior boys breaking bounds and heading to Moti Corner.

A few months later, I travelled to Delhi for my B. Ed. examination. On my return, I took a night bus for Simla but grossly miscalculated its arrival time at Dharampur. It was 2.30 a.m. when the bus dropped me off at 'Sukhi Johri'. I had no other option but to walk up all the way to Sanawar. There was no luxury of getting a cab in those days and that too at such an unearthly hour. So there I was, trudging up on that cold, windy night.

I knew about a shortcut that passed through the graveyard. Lots of 'ghost stories' flashed through my mind as I took the bold decision of taking that route. The rustling sound of pine trees and the crackling sound of the dry pine needles getting crushed under my feet set the tone for a 'ghostly encounter' to perfection. Suddenly, I thought someone was following me as I could hear a weird sound, *khizz . . . khizz*. I stopped and looked back but there was no one behind me. The weird sound, too, had stopped. I gathered my courage and resumed walking. Sure enough, the sound was back. I was certain that I was being followed by a ghost. I gathered pace only to find that the 'ghost' too was walking faster. I was close to the end of the shortcut by then and I literally ran all the way to my residence. As I sat on my bed, I realized I was sweating profusely on that cold November night. After catching my breath, I got up to drink a glass of water. I heard the '*khizz . . . khizz*' sound again. Good Lord, the sound was of my arms brushing the outer synthetic layering of my jacket. I had a hearty laugh then, though that 10–15 minutes' walk through the graveyard had been a harrowing experience.

Many would also have heard of the legendary ghost of a British lady who had drowned in the 'Red Field' swimming pool, behind the Siwalik/ Vindhya BD dorms. Rumour had it that one could hear water splashing on 'special' nights. Well, I had recently taken over as Housemaster Vindhya. YPS, Patiala Cricket (Atoms) were visiting and were due to play on Sunday. Sixteen beds in two rows were arranged in our Common Room for their stay. Around 9.00 p.m., my prefect knocked on my door to inform me that the Patiala boys were being too noisy and were refusing to listen. I went to the Common Room, spoke to them and assured my prefects that calm would prevail.

However, by 9.30 p.m., I was told that those boys were at it again and this time with greater enthusiasm. I went straight to the Common Room and pretended that I had no idea of what was happening. I told the boys that I have come to warn them against some possible 'ghostly' encounter. I gathered them around and began narrating the story of the British lady who had drowned in the pool, right next to the dormitory. I deliberately got the lights dimmed to create an eerie 'environment'. Towards the end of my story, I told them that this lady's ghost still visits the pool area at night and one can often hear her splashing about.

I then said a cheery good night to the boys and told them not to worry since this 'ghost' usually didn't harm anyone. On my way back to my

residence, I took one of my prefects along. I handed over a bucket of water to him and briefed him to turn out the lights of the dormitory and after some time, make splashing sounds with the bucket of water. The prefect was at my door again after about half an hour and said, 'Sir, you have absolutely got to see this to believe it'. I followed him to the Common Room to find that the row of the beds next to the windows (overlooking Red Field) was completely empty. The other eight beds across the common room were joined to accommodate all sixteen of our visiting guests, huddled together in complete silence, buried under their blankets.

I could easily go on and on but . . . I hope the other 'ghosts of Sanawar' don't feel left out and start wandering around the hilltop. They too will get their moment of glory, in some other time, space and dimension.

**Vinay Pande**
STAFF 1989–1997 | Teacher – Chemistry | Housemaster – Vindhya | Headmaster 2016–2019
Founding Headmaster, Sarala Birla Academy, Bengaluru 2003–2006 | Senior Deputy Headmaster, The Doon School 2013–2016

Spouse – Usha Pande | STAFF 1992–1995 | Teacher – Mathematics

# Sunday Movie Night, with a Twist

One would think that for Heady's daughter, life in school would be challenging. On the contrary, I was treated very fairly and was never really at the receiving end of any criticism about him. None that was directed at me, anyway. It was never personal. I put it down to my wonderful seniors, batchmates and juniors, who were very sensitive and kind. It helped me integrate better and be entirely immersed in school life. I often pleaded with my father to let me be a boarder but he always pointed out I would be taking up an extra bed. Despite being a day scholar, it was very satisfying to have made some good friends in school. Friends that I'm still in touch with to this day.

We four were very close friends – Mandy, Hoofy, Thappo and I – known to be a bit of a gang. We were often up to no good, but being rather clever at our work, as well as in all the sports teams, we were somewhat overlooked as simply naughty kids. This probably helped us get away with a bit of mischief . . . We were very outdoorsy, quite fearless, highly opinionated, tomboyish kids, who never let any boy get the better of us. In fact, many of the boys in our House (Nilagiri) were good friends (out of fear, but also some affection!). While I'm giving the four of us credit for these characteristics, in actual fact, Thappo was the most fearless and outspoken—the boss! You see, one can feel much braver than one is if fronted by a confident boss lady. Thappo always saw to it that no one, especially the boys, ever got the better of us. If anyone crossed the line, they were dealt with severely.

On Sunday evenings, a film was shown in the spacious Barne Hall. Heavy, thick velvet curtains were drawn together to make the room eerily dark to view the film. The films shown were often black-and-white, punctuated with the reel-breaking gaps, interlaced with booing if the film crew took too long to reinstate the film . . . etc. However, all this was too much to bear for the four of us. What a waste of time! Sitting in a dark hall, trying to watch a tedious film. To our minds, this was the most boring way to spend a Sunday evening. Thankfully, we were given the option of not seeing the film, provided we hung around near the girls' dormitories. This seemed like a far better option, with us spending time outdoors in the fresh air. Although restricted in our movements and obligated to stay within a certain boundary, the ability to enjoy an evening doing what we wanted was very refreshing.

With this newfound freedom, we enjoyed whiling away our Sunday evenings. What a relief to be freed from the tyranny of watching a boring film. One Sunday (I can't quite remember the background to this event), we invited some of the Nilgarian boys for a grand tour of the Girls' dorm. For the Nilagarian boys, this was just a short hop away from the field that divided them and the girls' dormitories. As the number of students (who didn't watch the films) was so few, we were confident that our 'guests' would go unnoticed. Nonetheless, the boys were given a firm and exact time for the visit. They appeared on the dot, as if by magic! Now the matrons' rooms were attached to the dormitory, so this was, in fact, a high-risk strategy we were engaging in. However, we had decided to take the gamble, knowing fully well that on Sunday evenings, when the majority of the kids were at the film, she stayed indoors and relaxed. Anyway, it was to be a quick whirlwind tour. There had been other examples of boys coming to the girls' dorms and successfully going unnoticed (just for brief periods). With this in mind, we were confident we could pull off a visit by our fellow Nilagarian boys. Also reassured with the knowledge that Thappo had given the boys strict instructions vis-à-vis the visit, and that therefore they would behave prudently.

So, on the appointed Sunday, the boys arrived at the girls' dorms, grinning from ear to ear (probably quaking in their boots, too!) They had adopted a laidback approach, hands in pockets, strolling around . . . however, we emphasized the importance of looking sharp and then exiting! We gave them a swift tour of the dorm and then sent them packing. They were certainly not allowed to ask too many questions or pass any comments! We ourselves were a bit scared at taking this risk. Fortunately, the tour went off without any incident; the boys left and it was all pretty innocent. We were, therefore, stunned to be summoned by our House mistress, Mrs Solomon, minutes before the film ended. How she ever found out is anyone's guess. She was livid and really told us off, her conclusive parting shot being: 'This is not acceptable! I am going to report you to [the] headmaster!' Thappo (our courageous leader) trumped her parting shot, by interjecting somewhat timidly (but in our eyes extremely boldly), 'But ma'am, you can't report us to Heady, She'She' is his daughter!' I think despite the tense atmosphere, even Mrs Solomon managed a sort of smile and said, 'OK, letting you off . . . but next time . . .' I think we also struck a deal with her not to report the boys to their Housemaster, so all in all, a pretty productive deal!

Our punishment: to religiously watch the Sunday Barne Hall films for the next six weeks. Back to boring reality! Aahhh . . . but it was well worth it. Nothing like some innocuous khup!

**Shiraz (Das) Vira**
She'She' | Nilagiri 1984 | 1974–1984

Parents – Father – Shomie Ranjan Das | Headmaster 1974–1988
                  Mother – Pheroza Das 1974–1988 | Batik teacher | Dramatics
                  – ADS and direction

# It Can Now Be Told

There never was a policy directive on the permissible pieces of luggage we could bring to school. However, the predominant, hence established practice was to have one military trunk and one hold-all, with the name of the owner, his House, and 'The Lawrence School, Sanawar – Simla Hills. Pin – 173202' prominently displayed on them. As an aside, there was a case of the painter engaged by the Pandey household in Kanpur bungling up the spacing between the alphabets, as a result of which Abhijit's trunk was found proclaiming: A P ANDEY. Occasionally, a duffle bag (then called Air-Bag, before they started putting those into 'fancy' cars), supplemented the possessions, excluding of course, the frequent *peepa*(s) of *Kayo* and *Pinni* from the Great Land of Five Rivers or the Apple di peti(s) from our very own Dev Bhumi, Kotgarh.

Now, as the word suggests, a 'norm' is for normal people. However, there were always a few extraordinary organisms around. Gancha, the pampered child that he was, always had two king-sized trunks. One, as for everyone else, to store his twelve handkerchiefs, twelve vests and the rest of the items clearly mentioned in the school prospectus (at the time of joining), with the little printed name tag. The second trunk was exclusively for his tuck from home. Yes, he rarely ordered anything at the Tuck Shop, other than the elaichi-flavoured Verka milk. However, he was a regular at Charlie's hole-in-the-door diner, going every other evening.

The primary task at the start of each term, for us Himalayan classmates, therefore, was to identify the 'real' one; the trunk holding the booty. It would take not more than two days to figure that out by simply maintaining a close vigil on Gancha's visits to the Box Room. The tuck trunk, invariably, had a new lock each term, ascertaining that Gancha was smart! No wonder he took up Sciences in L-VI. On the first Sunday, post Breakfast, Jaggo would be sent to engage the services of

471

the in-House locksmith, Duki (Anupal Bawa) of Nilagiri (for years, I've wondered why he was called that. But, as I write this, it suddenly dawns on me that Du-Ki, could be an acronym for 'Duplicate Key'). Armed with his toolkit, Duki would take a couple of minutes to crack the code. A detailed inventory of the 'treasure' would be taken, and the trunk would be locked up, for the time being. Du-Ki, on his next visit to Kas, would return with a newly cast key to Gancha's tuck. The week or fortnight-long wait was quite unbearable, but the taste of the pot of gold at the end of the rainbow kept us going. Meticulous inventory management helped us track Gancha's (own) consumption, thereby helping us plan a sustainable supply-chain model, until Gancha's parents' next stock-replenishing visit. We were, in effect, instrumental in the occurrence of most of those mid-term visits.

From 1977 to 1983, Gancha 'generously' but unknowingly shared all his goodies with us. And we all agreed that he had good taste. Understandably, there were bound to be periodic bouts of depression that called for stern resolve and discipline on our part. It was critical to accept, adapt, 'moderate' consumption or explore other avenues so as to tide over this challenging phase.

April 1983. The very last 'treat' had been planned, a week before we left School. Gancha's farewell . . . for us. The last remaining luncheon meat tin had been 'liberated'. We were gathered in Sangha's bunk in the U-VI dorms. Mucchoo had finished his rounds for the night. The tin-cutter was nearing the last curve, when Gancha walked in.

'Bastards, hogging alone?'

'No, no, Ganche! Come, join us . . .'

'You guys are damn nice, yaar. Always ready to share your tuck . . . and some bastard keeps whacking mine.'

All of us, in chorus, exclaimed, 'Really?!'

'Ya, for years now . . .'

'Shit, man! Why didn't you ever tell us?'

The luncheon meat tin was nearly licked clean. Gancha made an offer, 'Oye, I think I have one tin left in my tuck trunk'. We all knew that he didn't, and needed to dissuade him from his act of generosity. Surdy, jumping to his feet, said, 'I'm not that hungry now . . . Ganche, why not save that for another night?'

Everyone joined in, 'Good idea, Surdy!'
Tears of gratitude rolled down Gancha's cheeks.

**Pankaj Sapru**
Himalaya 1983 | 1976–1983
Senior Management – Petroleum Downstream sector | Travel & Street
Photographer | Member – OSS Executive Committee 2019–21 | Vice
President – OSS 2021–23

OS Sibling – Brother – Dhiraj Sapru | Himalaya 1985 | 1977–1985

# This Was the Time

This was the time, when children were not weighed down by a backpack full of schoolbooks, when knowledge was not belched out of digital screens, when equal emphasis was placed on learning from the playing fields under the open sky as inside classrooms. It was more than half a century ago, when I walked out of the portals of Sanawar for the last time (as a student), to join the glorious brethren of Old Sanawarians. There are so many experiences. Where does one start and where does one end?

What excited me about Sanawar initially was that my father was an old-world army officer, commissioned from The Royal Military College, Sandhurst in the Cavalry as a Kings Commissioned Indian Officer (KCIO). My brother Jayant (who later joined the army after Sanawar in 1962 and retired as a Maj. Gen.) and I spent our childhood living and imbibing the Fauji ideology and lifestyle. Sanawar, for all practical purposes, was rooted in those traditions—something that was natural for us, and we took to it like ducks to water! It felt like home, except for mother's cooking!

Maybe I was one of the luckier ones as one of a group of five brothers and sisters who were together for a large part of our nine- to ten-year Sanawarian adventure. I was also lucky that my parents were close by, in Surajpur, between Kalka and Chandigarh. That made us 'popular', because we served as a 'watering hole' for any Sanawarian who chose to stop over for any reason, whatsoever.

I remember a group of us were hiking to Patiala in 1963 for the Triennial Games to cheer our team. My parents had left Surajpur by then, but we were put up in the GM's House and fed before we took off, the next day. After an eventful short journey using tongas, rickshaws and the State Roadways bus, supplemented with a final dash on foot to the YPS school gate, we charged into their Sports Pavilion. As there were, I think, ten of us, we made more noise at YPS than the entire stadium put together, with our heraldic war cry of 'C'mmonnnnn SANAWAR!' It definitely worked because that was the first year we won the Triennial Games!

Elder sisters have great value, particularly in a co-ed boarding school. Malti (Head Girl, 1960) was a godsend, for not only did she add to our pocket money, but also was a conduit for us and our friends to reach Girls' School on Sundays—'to meet our sister'. I do not know if the Staff ever questioned her about her rather large gaggle of acquired 'brothers'—she never mentioned it and we never asked. When she was the Head Girl, she had asked us to suggest some punishment for some girls who needed to be hauled up. The good brothers that we were, we stayed clear of knocks, dhups and such like manly measures, and recommended some benign disciplinarian stuff like Murga, Chair and Scarecrow. It seemed the girls started crying when asked to do these acts, so Malti stopped them immediately. A few days later, we were hauled up by her during milk break and given a lecture on courtesy and etiquette towards ladies—'Murga is soooo unladylike!'

I think Sanawar can also claim some credit in making India healthy! The Central Research Institute, Kasauli, needed human 'Guinea Pigs' for clinical trials of the serums being developed, after they had finished experimenting on rats, monkeys and horses. Here we were, a few hundred nubile boys (I don't think the girls were a part of this) who would be periodically lined up and vaccinated. As if that was not traumatic enough, they would then come back over the next few days and measure the length of the inflammation 'bump' on our forearms with little plastic rulers! Actually, we felt quite macho comparing our bumps. And today, we see international outcry and nationwide strikes about being vaccinated against Covid! It IS an odd world, indeed.

During those years, forest fires were frequent during the dry summers. The carpet of dry pine needles was highly inflammable, given the turpentine resin exuded by the trees. A piece of broken glass, lying around carelessly, could act as a magnifying glass and ignite those needles into a raging flash fire. At night, someone would invariably wake up, notice the raging fire, ring the 'rouser bell' madly and we would be formed into teams. With nothing but hockey sticks and any other handy implement, we would fan out at night down the khud side, scrape away pine needles to make fire breaks and prevent the spread towards the buildings. Later, ingenious pine needle scrapers were designed by a staff member and the activity of pine needle cleaning was integrated into our afternoon curriculum as a preventive measure. No one ever got hurt, even though it was dangerous work.

Maybe activities like this instilled discipline, dedication and a feeling of responsibility towards our alma mater within us? Maybe this is what drove young 2$^{nd}$ Lt. Arun Khetarpal into battle in 1971 to display courage and maturity that is the stuff of legends. The highest battle honour, Param Vir Chakra (Posth) awarded to one so young, must have had some great seeds planted in them at Sanawar.

Since there was nobody left in Vindhya House (now that is a great offline story, my friends), I became a House prefect under the command of (Col.) N.J.S. Pannu, late in '64. My most memorable moment was telling Arjun, Lalit and Partha to 'come and see me tonight' on my first day as prefect and making them ask *me* for permission to come into B Dorm . . . pure bliss! They have not forgotten it till today and I make it a point to ensure that they don't!

There is so much more to the Sanawar life; learnings deeply embedded within us that are impossible to compress into a few pages. How can I describe the back-breaking Labour Quota we had to do to carve out half of Chocolate Hill and carry that grit so that Mr Kemp could raise the level of Barne Field by two inches? Or the rollicking visits to Kasauli to spend a great day seeing a movie, having bun samosas (or investing another Rs 1/- to get scrumptious bacon and bun at Daily Needs) and a Coke, buying some knick-knacks and coming back 'home', totally satiated. Our pocket money was Rs. 1/- per week (later going up to Rs. 2/-). We 'young' OS still talk animatedly about those glorious days whenever we gather, much to the amusing and condescending looks of our ever-suffering OS wives.

I am a true Sanawarian because I have been caned by the Sr. Master Mr Kemp and have hiked to Gurkha Fort and carved my name in the moss on the crumbling wall. Somewhere in my youth or childhood, I must have done something good to have become a Sanawarian.

Extracts from my School leaving Certificate written by [the] headmaster include: 'Played games with zeal but with no particular skill . . . I would rate him a thoroughly pleasant boy possessed of real integrity of character'. Even today, fifty-eight years later, nobody has ever doubted my integrity! Our teachers really did know us.

I wear my School Crest with utmost pride and try to live up to its motto: Never Give In!

**Sanjaya Varma**
Vindhya 1964 | 1956–1964

Colours in Shooting, University of Allahabad 1966–67; All-India Inter University Shooting Championships – Runner-Up (Individual) 1966 and 1967; Fellow of The Indian Institute of Packaging

OS Sibling – Brother – Jayant Varma | Jaggy | Vindhya 1962 | 1955–1962

# Baths

I joined School on 3 March 1971, a day when there was plenty of snow all around, making me forget that my parents had left me behind to face my future on my own. And the very next day, my tryst with destiny brought up 'Baths' in chilling, sub-zero settings.

Baths were in the evenings, on alternate days, which was perfectly fine with me as I was no bathing enthusiast. And so I found myself following a senior's instructions to undress in the middle of our dorm, wrap my towel around my waist, wear my dressing gown, carry my soap dish in a plastic mug and line up in the covered veranda outside the Bath House.

Two Ayahs executed the operations with a 'no-nonsense' precision, one ushering (into the Bath House) ten boys at a time, the other donning a plastic apron and sitting by a big hot-water bathing tub, meticulously soaping and washing each ward. She was Mariam Ayahji—a portly, loud, dark and warm-hearted lady.

The group of ten was further divided into two. One half lined up between the rows of washbasins with mirrors and hooks above. I hung my gown and towel on an unoccupied hook. *Now?* Now, I'd join the starkers, busy in various stages of bathing. Sensing my hesitation, a senior, strategically positioned, egged me on, 'The hot water will soon run out, and you will have to wait out till the day after tomorrow.' So setting aside all inhibitions, I plunged in with 'gay' abandon – no holds barred – soon learning that the more daring you were, the longer you would hang around the hot water tub, and enjoy the hot bath. These community baths went on for the next two years.

On coming home for the hols, my *Nani* and mom would whine about how 'unclean' I was, and subjected me to rigorous scrubbings (with a pumice stone, called '*Jhawan*' in Punjabi). A few layers of skin were scraped off, making me more red and less brown. Back then, the marvel of suntans or sunburns was yet to be discovered. Today, every kid in school comes loaded with sunscreen lotions and gels, and returns home as fair, though not so lovely.

We moved to BD, without a clue as to how Baths were conducted there. Frankly, we never enquired. There were so many more important worries to attend to. Finally, the briefing in the Himalaya House Junior dorm. Only the alternate-day frequency and evening timing remained constant. The Junior dorms of the three Houses went to the BD Bath House on the same day, in a sequence, by rotation. Nilagiri House did their own thing. The school orders mentioned the time as 1700 hours. Our fates were in the hands of Rulda, the boiler man who heated water in the coal-fired boiler room, polluting the clean mountain air. The Bath House, on the first floor, housed forty-two showers. A gangway from the BD pavement to the bath House door was the waiting area before the assault of the showers. This was also gainfully utilized (mostly on Sundays) to play 'Blindman's Buff', 'Catching Cook' or just hiding under when we played 'Kick the Can'. A shower was a cubicle with walls on three sides, and one's hindquarters open to public view. That was a great upgrade from being in a crowd around a tub. A shower was a cubicle with walls on three sides, and one's hindquarters open to public view. Being at the pit-bottom of the seniority ladder, we ran in first to find a vacant cubicle, checked to see the shower was functional

(both hot and cold pipes, and the mixer, so as not to be boiled or frozen), get booted out by a senior, and begin the search again. The SOP included walking to the Bath House (from the dorm) with just the towel around the waist, under dressing gowns; soaps and shampoos in pockets.

As soon as the water was turned on, one jumped under the shower and made the most of the four-minute bath—three to soap and scrub, and the last minute to wash it off. Some seniors would bully juniors out of their expensive soaps or shampoos. And then, we learnt how to smuggle 'our own stuff' in. The unlucky junior still looking for a 'good' shower was treated to sights aplenty. Just my luck, I managed to find a clogged shower (in a well-placed corner) that no one was willing to 'bagz'. Left with no other option but to innovate, I unwound the sprinkler to enjoy a free-flowing hot water fountain. A senior saw it. I resumed my search for it the day after the next . . . Pranksters never let go of an opportunity—and baths were no different. Towels and dressing-gowns were swapped to the other corner of the Bath House; soaps swiped in the middle of the act—all within the four minutes. However, all this happened within a given wing, as one dared not cross over the connecting corridor facing the main entrance . . . Mucchoo stood there, waiting to bark, 'one minute left!'

There were days when I missed out on baths for such reasons, but didn't 'tattle', fearing the obvious consequences. Better to be untidy than sorry. When I became a 'senior', the door to joining the surdies on their Sunday morning head-bath that lasted a full ten minutes, swung open.

The benefits of the 'Battles of the Baths' were learning how to crack wet towels like whips, in defence or offence; smuggling a favourite shampoo or Camay soap and using it without a senior or friend sharing its lather and fragrance. But the key takeaway was learning the value of time, utilizing each second of the four minutes.

With these bathing experiences, I was better prepared to face the challenges of the future. Thus, the pleasure of bathing as well as the necessity to conserve water will remain with me till my last bath.

**Grp. Capt. Sajan Sethi**
Srgt. Shetty, (later) Sarge | Himalaya 1981 | 1971–1981
M.D. Aerospace Medicine | Officiating School RMO 2019

OS Sibling – Sister – Rajan (Sethi) Wahi | Petha | Himalaya 1972 | 1967–1972

# And My Name Is . . .

All of 58 kgs, a ten-year-old walked down the Vindhya House corridor with trepidation and in fear of the unknown, on a cold overcast day in February to the tune of Santana's 'Black magic woman' – the song still gives me the chills as it barrels me back to that day. So much so as to exorcise the memory that this was one of the first live shows I saw in 1983, when I reached Washington DC to pursue my MBA at George Washington University.

Hodsons were a tough ask for this kid, as was the repeated 'down to Barnes, last two to go down again', a favourite with the Vindhya House prefect to correct our marching skills. Then come the Hodson Heats, everybody waits with bated breath in anticipation for this kid to roll in. Not known to the spectators, especially the Vindhya House prefect, this kid pulls a fast one at the start point by shamming (now I forget what ailment). The Vindhya House Under 11's come in, but no Fatty.

Man, I have never done a longer Murga as on that night—as you can imagine, to tuck in an ample tummy in that pose is kind of difficult.

Oh well, this 58-kgs Fatty came back from his summer vacations weighing all of 42 kgs. But the name endured. And, if that wasn't enough, my younger brother, Arun, who was all skin and bones, was called by the incredible nickname, 'Thin Fatty'.

Proud that we survived and thrived. Never Give In.

**Sanjeev Chandra**
Fatty | Vindhya 1977 | 1970–1977

OS Siblings – Sister – Anita (Chandra) Brar |Vindhya 1979 | 1970–1979
           Brother – Arun Chandra | Thin Fatty | Vindhya 1981 |
           1973–1981

# A Wonderland Called Sanawar

It's a windy day and the little gusts and eddies of wind are making you hold your wrap tighter. The tree under which you are standing is flowering and you can see a squirrel climbing up as if its life depended on it. The macadam road has cracks in it and you wonder how old it is. The sky has small clouds that you can touch and there are people looking at the herbaceous border outside the office; there are people sitting under sunshades sipping tea; there are people going down the road. People everywhere and it's spring and you've come to a wonderland called Sanawar.

Your first day at school. You enter a mammoth classroom that's actually quite small and thirty eyes stare at you balefully, inquisitively, mournfully. And you grin shyly and say: 'My name . . .' But you've lost their attention. Again, you try: 'I come . . . I come from Scindia'. 'The boys' school!' they whisper, 'must be a terrible flirt!' and there, you've acquired a nickname. You take your place and there's a little boy behind you who says, 'Hey you've got to change places every maths school, 'cause I want the brain sitting in front of me.' Of course you agree. There is no moral support and the colour has climbed high to your cheeks and your hands are trembling, ever so slightly. And then you remember who you are and put on the ridiculous, self-protective, supercilious façade again and pray that no one can see through it.

After a few weeks, you make your first friend. It's so simple, really. You just go up and say, 'Um . . . um . . . I'd like to walk around with you, huh!' and there, you have a friend for life. And she's really very nice, she has a sense of humour like yours and is much more level-headed and quiet. And you're happy—till the first and subsequent quarrels.

Meanwhile, class is not proceeding as well as you would have it. There are two boys on either side of you who ignore you throughout and you fail in Maths while they get great marks in English. And every time you read in Hindi, they cough politely and you wish you could die. Your friend sits at the other end and winks at you for the occasional show of support, but it really doesn't help.

In a few weeks is your first Social. And you want so desperately to look nice and you know something? You really do. But you still don't know how to accept compliments and there's a nagging feeling that they're being slightly sarcastic. But the Social is lovely and you realize you're very popular with the opposite sex; this comes as a surprise, for you've never mixed with the boys before and you wallow in a contented pastime—and he and he and he. You write home coy and smart, and get a jolt in reply, which brings you back to earth.

Founders' comes and you are in the Hindi play. You spend long afternoons making rockets out of Assembly book sheets, when you are not required on stage. You've made your first boyfriend and he's given you a white mouse, Pepito. Pepito shows his dislike for you and you avenge yourself by flying him in your rockets. On days when you get off stage, your friend is upset and tells you Pepito is dead. And there's a funny feeling in your throat and you want to say, 'I'm sorry, Pepito', but it's too late so you laugh and say 'so what, only a stupid old mouse'.

The end of term has come and you sit all cozy before a log fire and wonder what the Sixth Formers are doing upstairs in the Art Room with all those lights and streamers, and laughter drifting lazily downstairs. And then you look at your flannel nightgown and wish to be Cinderella for a night.

The end of the term has come and your friend is leaving. You wish him a tearful goodbye and then promptly forget, with the elasticity of a child and the joy of going home.

The holidays have fled at your coming and you're back in familiar surroundings again. You wake up one morning to the excited scream of the girls and see the ground is snow-covered. It's the first time you've seen snow and you've never been so thrilled and wonderstruck. But before you have time to admire it, it's gone and slush has taken its place and Sanawar is Sanawar again.

School is fun and you've chosen your subjects and you're first. And you've got a wonderful new teacher who makes up for the others; you know you're smart and he knows you're smart and that's all that matters.

Gaura welcomes you with hot sun and sparkling streams, and you wallow in sun's sand for a week at camp. But when it's time to go, you don't feel sorry at all—Sanawar still has its hold on you.

It's nearing the end of the term and something happens to you at a Social. Partly because of your brazenness and the half-pleading look in your eyes, a little boy asks you to be his girl. You're madly elated and the world feels like your oyster.

You come back to school and meet at a Social. And you don't know what to say because you don't know him well enough. And you sit rigidly in your chair and he sits rigidly in his and both of you are at a loss for words. You say, 'Say something' and he replies, 'Something' and you both laugh and suddenly, you're friends.

The Sixth Form party is around the corner and your class is arranging for it. Only, you have nothing to do with it as you're not prepared to take responsibility. At least that's what you tell yourself; of course you feel they were dying to put you in-charge of something, poor egotist, you. The party is stupid, the real fun was in making the snacks earlier, where for each two snacks you made, you ate one.

End of term again and you don't want to go home. In between sniffs, you order him to write, threatening to bash him up. You go for a tour of Sanawar with the school-leaving girls and it seems to you too, that you are leaving something dear; the trees look taller without any leaves and the buildings look more solemn without any people. Long Back seems longer when you walk on it for the first time, Leisure is out of bounds and you get a kick out of breaking rules, the Art Room has a funny atmosphere, the scent of old romances lingering on, Barne Field is so far but you walk on, blithely stopping to shake a few stones from your shoes—it was worth it. Gaskell Hall is full of trunks, you take a surreptitious peek into the boys' dormitories. Tuck Shop is crowded with last-minute shoppers. Just to be defiant, you cut across Nilagiri House and walk balanced precariously on a ledge at the edge of the swimming pool, drawing lines at the bottom of the pool with a stick. You're glad this is not your last year—so much remains to be seen.

Sixth Form is great, you're the senior most in the school and juniors run madly to fulfil your every whim. Studies are not important, there is so much else to do. And everything is done with the thought for the last time and there a queer mixture of pleasure and dread when you regard this last year. Your last House show and you're in the Hindi play. Last camp and you go to Simla. Last Mark Reading and you've come fifth. Last year and you're determined to enjoy it. Each moment is tinged with excitement and you know you'll hate leaving Sanawar.

Remember the fire one night? The dormitory was in flames and you changed quickly into a discreet flannel nightgown and stumbled out onto

Peacestead till the rescue boys had put out the fire. The situation was really quite amusing. A bucket of water was passed from hand to hand and when it reached the fire, it was empty. You shivered, shook and laughed, and wished and prayed your locker was locked.

Founders' has come and your friend from the last year has come, too. And out of obligation and half hoping to recapture some of your L-V memories, you walk with him, talk, laugh and everything is as it was. Founders' is over and you find you've broken up with your boyfriend and the world has come crashing about your ears. You pretend not to care and even when you're left alone at Social, you smile at the whole world and wave at imaginary people and play games on your fingers and sing songs softly—anything to restore your equilibrium. And the clock stays fixed on one number and you stay fixed in your seat and think of all the time that's been wasted having good times. When at last, you are on your way back, you give way to angry tears. But, like everything else, you still retain the fickleness of childhood and are soon out looking for new faces, the old one locked up and relegated to a dim playground of the very young.

You wake up heavy-eyed one morning and SC greets you with a slap on your face. And before you have time to say, 'wow!', weeks of writing before kerosene heaters and teachers peering over your back are over . . . and so are your days in Sanawar.

You end up in a party to bid you farewell. And you spend the evening putting make-up on, vainly, knowing it will run as soon as you reach the Art Room. And you form circles singing 'auld lang syne' and cry, wishing you were sitting before the fireplace again hoping for Cinderella's godmother to let you join the party. The clock strikes midnight and in its last gongs lies your finale.

It's a windy day and the little gusts and eddies of wind are making you clutch your wrap tightly around you. And the tree under which you are standing has lost its leaves and stands cold and naked. And the macadam road has cracks in it and you know how old it is. The sky has small clouds far away and you stretch vainly to touch them. There are no people anywhere and it's winter; and you've got to leave a wonderland called Sanawar.

**Maneka Anand VI–A**
Old Sanawarian (Siwalik 1972)

**Source and Acknowledgement:** *The Sanawarian* (December 1972)

# Ode to a Legend

W. Clement Stone wisely said, 'You are a product of your environment . . . so, choose the environment that will best develop you.' Forty years after graduating from Sanawar, this statement is a great reminder of the formative environment Sna' was for me and many of my dear batchmates (Class of '81), full of lessons, experiences and insights on the picturesque hilltop that shaped us, and that I continue to draw on.

And then there was Mucchoo, our beloved Mr B. Singh, Deputy Headmaster extraordinaire—the backbone of the school, the glue that kept things together. For those Sanawarians who weren't fortunate to experience Mucchoo, let me bring him to life in three words: goliath, phantom, omnipresent.

Goliath Mr. B Singh was indeed the Big Man on campus in more ways than one. First, he was twice as tall as most people, especially since you likely encountered him as a young person (as I did in U-IV). With his stern demeanour and reputation, his long and pointy moustache (hence Mucchoo), he was always a giant in our eyes, even after we physically caught up to him in height. The man instilled fear in you from the first day you encountered him, which fear would then evolve into respect with perspective and insight, i.e. around your postgraduation!

Phantom Mucchoo was literally the 'ghost who walked' on campus; I doubt the man ever slept. The Mucchoo equivalent of a Close Extra-terrestrial Encounter (C.E.T) was the U.M.E. or the Unexpected Mucchoo Encounter, illustrated in a mathematical formula (Mr Jack Kohli, our math teacher, would be so proud!) we devised:

$$\text{Wrong Place OR Wrong Time} + \text{Wrong Thing} = \text{Unexpected Mucchoo Encounter}$$

Breaking it down, if you EVER found yourself in the wrong place and/ or doing something at the wrong time or doing something you weren't supposed to do, the Phantom would emerge . . . there would be a U.M.E and it never ended well. What followed a U.M.E was often a sarcastic remark from the Phantom himself, in his deep, husky voice. Then just as you were ready to smile at his sarcasm coupled with wit, the wrath of his hand would descend on you (known fondly as 'Dhaps'); the recipient would be left seeing stars, and instantaneously reminded of what they were supposed to be doing.

Omnipresent Mucchoo somehow seemed to be everywhere all the time! I don't think science can explain it, but I am sure he had invented WiFi and wireless way before they were allegedly invented! His office, strategically located at one end, gave him an unhindered view of the entire corridor – he always knew who was coming or going, but you could never see him, as he was a chainsmoker (Charminar, unfiltered) and his office was always fogged – yes, with cigarette smoke. The only time you physically saw him emerge was through the smoke, which added to the mystique and drama of the Omnipresent Phantom.

It is often said that you aren't truly a Sanawarian boy if you haven't had a U.M.E. By that measure, I am truly one—and have many fond memories (and scars) to prove it. Two instances in particular come to mind:

I was in L-VI, and having a bad gastric week – perhaps the Ronak Combined Dining Hall (CDH) had failed to add fibre to the massive chapatis that week or it was serving the daal with too much H2O – I was clearly struggling through the day, I picked the end of my math class to run down to the pans (toilets) to see if I could get more comfortable. I sat crouched in (near) murga position, struggling with no success. Fifteen minutes elapsed. What was the point of going late to my next class, I reasoned? I didn't think Mr Khalid (our economics teacher) would miss me anyway, so I decided to just hang out till the next period bell. Perfect plan, right? Wrong! I failed to anticipate the U.M.E. At the sixteenth minute, I heard footsteps approaching my stall and then stopping. 'Oh Sh*t!' . . . I must have said it aloud, for a husky voice responded, 'Heee me Lad, oh Sh*t is about right!', then a long pause ensued and what followed was: 'looks like you are struggling to . . .' (pause again) 'get to your next class! I have asked Mr. Khalid to wait for you – and stop by and see me after school today!' Needless to say, any bowel issues were instantly cured. I hauled ass, both literally and figuratively, back to class. Such was the impact the man had. Thankfully, when I saw him after school, he was sympathetic to my condition and on a rare U.M.E., I was able to get away unscathed.

The next episode, unfortunately, wasn't that mild. Let me set the scene (names have been changed to protect the innocent!). We were in U-VI preparing for final exams. The seniors were allowed to study past lights-out, but had to be in bed by 10 p.m. Most often – OK, every day – Mucchoo would circle the dorms by 8 p.m. to ensure everyone was in bed and then again, often at 10 p.m., to ensure seniors were sticking to their extended privilege commitment. My Vindhyan batchmates, for the most part, were a very studious lot and most often obeyed the strict regimen. That evening, the mischievous Toto (Subroto) hatched a plan that got us excited, 'what if we have a party at midnight?' Purie (Purewal, who often obliged and spoiled us with culinary treats from his home nearby) could bring some treats, others could bring some tuck (goodies from the Tuck Shop) and our resident barista, Netha (Neeraj), could make us a fine midnight brew (Netha had perfected the art of making coffee in a plastic mug, with a make-do heater, with two old-style shaving blades separated by a small wooden pencil, with blades attached to the outlet and two live wires. (Note: Please do not try this at home it's both a fire hazard and potentially injurious to life and limb).

The plan was to be in bed by 10 p.m. when Mucchoo made his rounds and then, the party could begin around 11 p.m. Like clockwork, Mucchoo made his 10 p.m. rounds with no incident. Around 11 p.m., the midnight party commenced. We gathered in one corner of the dorm in Chandu's (Arun) 'make-do' bunk room, comprised of many lockers in an L-shaped configuration. A few lamps lit the party venue, while the rest of the dorm was pitch dark. What a bonus, to be up enjoying laughs with friends, with a midnight feast and some strong, hot coffee. It was close to midnight, when Purie cracked open a special cake his mother had baked. As the cake was being distributed, it dawned on Pixie (Vikram) to ask the seminal question, 'guys, what if Mucchoo were to show up now?' There was a burst of laughter, the party continued. Pixie, not giving up, persisted, 'no, seriously, what if Mucchoo were to show up right now—what would we say?' Hoon (Arvind) shot back promptly, 'We'll give him a piece of this cake and ask him to f*** off!' More laughter until a moment of stunned silence at a voice which emerged from the darkness: 'heee me lads, may I have my cake now?' Needless to say, many of us saw stars that night!

I know there are many, many U.M.E stories that can be told by Old Sanawarians who were privileged to be schooled by Mr B. Singh. In hindsight, he was truly the backbone of our school and a stalwart who made our experience at Sanawar memorable. In this 175th year since Sanawar's founding, may we remember and raise a glass to our beloved Mr B. Singh, who served the school for over fifty years, and to all the teachers and staff who made our school so special and left an indelible mark on our lives, teaching us valuable lessons we carry with us to this day, on the hillside of Sanawar!

**Arjun Bedi**
Bunty | Vindhya 1981 | 1976–1981
Accenture – Partner (2000) | Senior Managing Director (2017) | Accenture – Global Management Team (2020)

OS Sibling – Sister – Anu (Bedi) Malhotra | Vindhya 1979 | 1976–1979

# Sanawar: The New Old School

Exactly a hundred years after the school was established, the British Indian Empire and The Lawrence Royal Military School (LRMS) become history. From the ashes of the Empire, emerged independent India and independent India resurrected LRMS as The Lawrence School (TLS). LRMS was part of the ruling structure of the British Indian Empire and provided education to orphans of other ranks. It was so important to the British that every viceroy since the establishment of the school made a visit to TLS, including Lord Mountbatten, after India became independent. TLS, on the other hand, became a preferred school for the emerging elites of Independent India. The role of the school has changed significantly from one training students to join British regiments based in India as non-commissioned officers, to training Indian pupils for joining the military as officers. Moreover, with time, the school evolved from a military school to more of a modern Indian public school, while retaining its essential military character. The Trooping of Colours, even today, brings a lump to everyone's throat.

I write this because I was part of the change. Five years after Independence, as a lad of nine, I joined Prep School (Form II) in 1952, and slept the first night in Honoria Court: yes, Honoria Court, for that is where the Prep School dormitories were. Very soon, I found myself in BD, as I was promoted to L-III. The holding House for boys was called Sparrow Hawks and for girls, Sparrows. The school strength was about 200 at that time, and we wore Second World War battle dress—ammo boots that we had to keep shining. As the Head Boy S.P.S. Gill dramatically put it, 'I should be able to count my teeth in your toe caps.'

The shift from battle dress to blazers and flannels was more than a change of dress. It was the beginning of making Sanawar less of a military school while retaining the essential values: Never Give In; you will yet come in if you stick it still; House and school spirit, and much more, which distinguish Sanawarians from others. Much of the credit for this goes to the last British headmaster E.G. Carter, who made the difficult transition from essentially a British school to an Indian school. The first Indian headmaster Major Som Dutt (Boxing Blue from Cambridge) made a spectacular entry driving a red MG Sports Coupe, which impressed us no end. He was more than a worthy replacement for Carter and a key figure in making Sanawar one of the best schools of the country.

It was the time some of the best-loved teachers of the school first joined. Mucchoo or Mr B. Singh, Mr Mukherjee, Dr D.C. Gupta, Mr Gore, Mr Vyas (who left to join the IAS), to mention a few. The older teachers that mentored them were Mr S.C. Cowell and Mr and Mrs Kemp. One of the most dynamic was the PT teacher Jagdish Ram or Jagga, as he was called. The PT routine displayed at Tattoo is still about the same that he had set up. Then there was Dr Soin, along with compounder Mastu, who were an interesting pair. It was the time the band had just been set up and by some quirk, everyone in the band, including myself, was a Vindhyan. I don't know how much of that is true today.

For the first twenty years or so after Independence, OS were not old enough to be seen in top positions of society. They started coming into their own after that. By the time of the sesquicentennial celebrations, Rajiv Gupta, OS President, and I, as president-elect, saw the change as we were able to call on many OS to help organize the celebration, e.g., Admirial Vishnu Bhagwat, who helped us invite the then PM Mr I.K. Gujral, to release a book of pen sketches of school buildings by our old Art teacher, Mr Rathin Mitra and the text written by Dr Harish Dhillion. The PM speaking on the occasion said, 'Sanawar is not only a school, but an institution.' The nation acknowledged the contribution of the OS, especially in defence of the country, by issuing a postage stamp and first-day cover in its honour. It signalled that the school had fulfilled the trust of those who resurrected LRMS as TLS hoping that those passing out of there would help build a new India.

If 1947 was the defining moment that brought the new school into being, then 1997 was the moment when OS announced they had come of age, by persuading GOI to recognize that they were the main stakeholders in preserving the traditions and standing of the school. This resulted in the GOI expanding Lawrence School Sanawar Society to twenty members, including nine past OS presidents, the current president, president-elect and three nominees of the OSS. Effectively, the school was passed into the hands of the OS, though nominally controlled by the government through Secretary (School Education) serving as Chairman of the Board of Governers and the LSSS. Matching changes were made to the OSS by registering the society; setting up chapters and batch representatives, and bringing in the idea of a nominating committee to make policy and give direction to the executive committee. The credit for bringing this about has to go to Rajiv Gupta, OS President, while I assisted as well as I could as president-elect.

The enthusiasm and scale of the preparation for the dodransbicentennial celebrations drives home the point that changes made in 1997 have taken root. More than that, the willingness of OS to support the school by funding projects to make it a truly world-class institution demonstrates that to be the best, you don't have to be owned by someone. No one owns Sanawar and yet every OS, in a way, owns it. It is truly a unique institution, where the government provides the scaffolding and leaves it to the OS to be the conscience keepers and fundraisers to make it one of the best schools of all. The dodransbicentennial challenge facing the OS fraternity is to identify OS who understand the novel problems India is facing in school education and how the school should adapt to meet them. Such individuals need to brought on to the LSSS and the BOG, so as to provide leadership to make Sanawar a truly twenty-first-century institution. This requires the OSS to become more organized, professional and focused towards brining into existence a powerful freemasonry.

**Sarabjit Arjan Singh**
SAS | Vindhya 1958 | 1952–1958
Indian Railways Service of Mechanical Engineers (IRSME) | Deputation – Mozambique Railways and Ports | Established Rail Coach Factory, Kapurthala | Retired (2003) as General Manager | Member, Central Administrative Tribunal, Principle Bench | Consultant, World Bank – Public Financial Policy and how to transform commitments to Persons with Disabilities into outcomes

OSS PRESIDENT 1997–1999 | Member, LSS Board of Governors 2014–2017

OS Siblings – Daughter – Chitwan Sarabjit Singh | Vindhya 1991 | 1984–1991
Daughter – Simran Sarabjit Singh | Vindhya 1996 | 1989–1996

# A Vignette

How can one write about Sanawar without a tug at the heartstrings, and the notes of 'Never Give In is our motto' playing on the Chapel piano reverberating through the soul? What is it about that verdant hilltop in the Shivalik range, cradled in the lap of the majestic snowcapped Himalayas? We all cry when we go there but once we leave, we spend the rest of our lives loving Sanawar not just as an alma mater but as a Shangri-La when our horizons in the journey of life are obscured . . .

Prep School was about puddle-hopping in gumboots and raincoats after the pitter-patter of showers on the tin roof subsided, leaving wisps of mist floating through the pine trees. Midnight snacks of milk powder and Bournvita with whispered secrets. We learnt to dream on Eagles' Nest and we ran from the ghosts in the graveyard while returning from Dharampur. Later, when dreams would lie shattered all around me, and my demons would come to haunt me in the dark of night, somewhere, deep within, I would still know that I would dream again and that I would conquer the fears, just as Sanawar had taught me . . .

Senior School epitomized frugality and discipline. The crisp morning air as we warmed our chilblained hands around steel glasses with steaming hot chai during 'Chota Hazri'. The clapping and jumping in unison till our cheeks got rosy and the 'highland fling' were mastered during PT. The echo of the bugle and the sound of the Birdwood bell clanging . . . the memory meanders down the grey-pillared corridor as if it were yesterday. You could call it the beginning or the end, where there was Mr B. Singh's office, till today inspiring one to respond to the call of duty . . .

Sitting on the 'Golden Staircase' by the cannons, basking in the winter sunshine as Dr Dhillon read out 'Charge of the Light Brigade' during an outdoor class, I fell deeply, irrevocably in love with poetry . . .

One would easily have believed that the 'argumentative Indian' was birthed in the Political Science class of Mr M.J. Parel (Popa). He ensured that we knew what was happening in the world by drilling BBC news and

494

the newspaper editorials into our collective psyche, to the point where our class debates were so passionate that we could have been changing the course of world history. Oh, the arrogance of youth . . .

As one grows older, one realizes that one of the greatest blessings in life is probably to never have to eat alone. The Central Dining Hall (CDH) was an enormous arena of eternally hungry children with bottomless pits for stomachs. The calm before the storm as the Sanskrit prayer was chanted and then the cacophony of community eating as boys, girls and staff all partook in meals together. Surrounded by beautiful art on the walls, including the magnificent Hussain that had been painted by the legendary artist in front of an overawed audience of school children, we ate food that we professed to hate. And yet, how blessed were we to be surrounded by friends and teachers who wove a sense of security into those meal times, even as we often laboured as servers and cleaners to earn our meals . . .

We prayed at the Chapel, singing in Hindi and English, chanting Sanskrit prayers and Kabir dohas, and went to the gurudwara in Garkhal to eat kada-prasad. Oblivious of the harsh reality of the 'narrow, domestic walls' that Tagore warned us about, we blithely strove towards perfection, our faith strong. When I found myself lonely and helpless in life, I closed my eyes and softly sang 'Abide with Me' and was engulfed in an all-pervading calm . . .

Under the bright October sun, as we marched House-wise and took the oath to participate in the Annual Athletic Meet on Barne Field, butterflies in our stomachs, our hearts would simply burst with pride for the 'honour of our school and the glory of sport'. I often wonder that what could possibly be a better educator for life than the sports field. Here we learn to push past the farthest limits of our endurance, often failing and falling, learning to pick ourselves up, holding on to team spirit, playing fair, humility and grace in victory, and inner strength and outward calm in defeat. And finally, having run the race to the best of your capacity, to pass on the baton smoothly . . .

Walking back after dinner, the stark beauty of Peacestead as we skipped to some song about a soldier who got drunk and packed up his trunk; the twinkling lights of Kasuali, the flashing red light of the TV tower on Monkey Point right across, and a galaxy of stars above that— something only the mountains can offer. During tattoo, our knees were grazed in 'kneeling group' and our feet bled painfully during our folk dances. However, the excitement and sheer relief as my brother cleared the ring of fire in gymnastics, the thrill of the baton being thrown up in the air by the leader of the Bugle band, the joy of hot cocoa from large aluminium kettles, taught us that life is simply a play of pleasure and pain . . .

Our Athletics coach, once, while training, made the girls' school team take on the boys' Hodson run route. When we started, it was dark, the stars were still out, the bitter cold stung, and life was simply miserable and unfair. When we reached the end of long-back, our coach asked us to do stretching. Our hearts were pounding and racing, our limbs were dead exhausted and our throats were parched and then . . . dawn broke. Far away, first Simla was set aglow, and then, slowly, Subathu was bathed in a golden light and finally, all the hills and valleys woke up, incandescent, as we witnessed the most glorious, breathtaking sunrise ever. Just like that, I learnt that the darkness eventually does end . . .

In our final year before the board exams, I would sit by the very Monet-esque lily pond with my books. The pink and lavender water lilies were heralding spring, fluffy white clouds were floating across clear blue skies, brightly patterned butterflies fluttered around, the air was redolent with the scent of pine and a magical chapter was ending. Thus then, was learnt the greatest lesson of all—that of holding on to all the beautiful memories of life, and of letting go . . .

**Samyukta (Kumari) Gohil**
Simki | Himalaya 1987 | 1979–1987

OS Sibling – Brother – Suryaveer Singh| Binny | Himalaya 1986 | 1979–1986

# A Student's Valentine to a Great Teacher

## Thank you, Mrs Khan, for opening doors and giving me the love of language

Hair now as grey as scattered ashes, sari draped casually, slighter in figure at 72 yet incisive of mind, she remains distinctive in voice. In sound, it is maybe hoarser, as if age has sandpapered her larynx; in strength, it is a teacher's voice, firm, strong, deliberate and once, like an orator, able to envelop a room.

Thirty-five years since she taught me, her voice has stayed with me, not merely for its occasional flintiness - words so sharp she could part my schoolboy hair - but for what it carried to me. An unforgettable education.

In an Indian boarding school perched on a hill, in a room washed by the sun, she was my interpreter. Untangling a Shakespeare sonnet for me and unscrambling O. Henry. She was my opener of doors to W.H. Auden, she was my fellow traveller to Thomas Hardy's world, instigating romance without even knowing it. If I write now for a living, irrespective of standard, it is because she endeavoured to first teach me to love language.

This is my teacher. Mrs Khan. Never Manju. Mostly just Ma'am. In December in Delhi, as she visited her daughters, I met her after nearly 15 years and it struck me on reflection: I owe her. What precisely I cannot say and how you can repay the great teacher I do not know.

A Valentine's Day card may not suffice for I don't particularly care for its affected affection, its artificially inflated red hearts and its trite words. Yet neither, as scattered fundamentalists in India decree, should it be banned, for how love is expressed is a choice that cannot be dictated. Curious about her opinion, I call my teacher and while she is no admirer of the commodification of love, firmly she states: "I believe in inclusion, in accepting the rituals and customs of other cultures."

It is a sweet lesson and so let me, on this day, at least send her the student's simple equivalent of a valentine: Thank you, Ma'am.

Shunted across Indian schools, I was a lousy student paraded before an erratic array of teachers. Classes in India could be charmless factories, where for the most part we were indolent, nose-picking kids, scratching our initials onto wooden desks with geometry-set dividers much like prisoners inscribing theirs on a wall. Hunched over desks like a platoon of stenographers, we felt part of the herd that Lucia Perillo eloquently described in her poem Transcendentalism:

Like musk oxen we hunkered while his lecture drifted against us like snow.

If we could, we would have turned our backs into the wind.

Teaching often warrants connection, a chord that is struck almost by fluke in a crowded classroom between child and adult. As if somehow the teacher is speaking only to you. There is an element of luck to it, to find amid this posse of teachers - the slappers and the sensitive, the dictatorial and the determined, those of undying spirit and those just defeated - the one who calls you.

And if Plato had Socrates, and Aristotle had Plato, and Alexander the Great had Aristotle, then I was privileged to have Mrs Khan.

She didn't teach by strict ordinance, she wasn't some ancient guru requiring obeisance and obedience. Maybe she understood the absurdity of expecting dull conformity from her students even as we examined the originality and inventiveness of poets.

To take flights of imagination, you need initial help from a navigator, yet even as we comprehended cadence and voyaged with words, we were not allowed to be mute.

The best teachers offer you a voice, to question, to challenge, and she gave us the gift of her listening. Not just in class, but sprawled on the carpet of her home, where life itself might have been the subject, time winding away as she made coffee and I surreptitiously stole her cigarettes. She made me feel not like a lost boy, but a young adult on the cusp of possibility.

She wasn't an "imparter of knowledge" for even down the phone line last week, as we debated teaching, she grimaced at the "pomposity" of that phrase.

She was learning from us, too, telling me now: "It was equally enjoyable for me. I saw another point of view, a new way of thinking. I was also being educated." When I said "thank you" when our phone call ended, she replied, "No, thank you."

She is retired now to a village called Vythiri in Kerala, tending a vegetable patch next to a pond of lilies and I wonder if she thinks of reward. Is there any? It isn't money, for at the end of a teaching lifetime, excluding accommodation and food, her monthly salary was roughly $200. When she tells me the figure, I recoil, for it only confirms that society's veneration of teachers is pompous fakery.

Achievement for her was, as a single mother then, to give her two girls - now friends of mine - an education, a life, a chance. She taught for the most elemental reason, to make a living, but perhaps her triumph was to affect some of our lives. But if we never tell our teachers of their influence, if we do not confirm their significance, if we do not reach out in gratefulness, then we have not completed our education.

In December when we met, I was carrying a copy of Richard Flanagan's Booker Prize-winning book, The Narrow Road To The Deep North. I asked if she had read it, she said no, and I was thrilled to give it to her. Later that night, at the airport on my way back here, I wondered at the flickering symbolism of it. So much literature taken from my teacher and now by chance a little returned.

**Rohit Brijnath**
Binks | Himalaya 1981 | 1979 – 1981
Journalist with The Straits Times, Singapore | Published in India Today, Sportsworld, The Hindu, The Mint, the BBC South-Asia website and The Age in Melbourne

OS Sibling – Brother – Rahul Brijnath | Himalaya 1980 | 1978 – 1980

**Source:** *The Sunday Times* © **SPH Media Limited. Reprinted with permission.**

**Acknowledgement:** *The Straits Times* **(International Edition). Published 16 February 2015, 11.32 a.m. SGT.**

# Our Param Vir

## Second Lt. Arun Khetarpal PVC, Nilagiri 1962-1966

The Param Vir Chakra (PVC) is India's highest military award for exceptional gallantry and valour in the face of the enemy. It replaced the former British colonial Victoria Cross (VC) after Independence in 1947, and like the Victoria Cross, it is (more often than not) awarded posthumously. So it was to Old Sanawarian, Second Lt. Arun Khetarpal, during the Indo–Pakistan conflict of 1971. The official citation reads as follows:

On 16 December 1971, the squadron Commander of 'B' Squadron, the Poona Horse asked for reinforcements as the Pakistani armour that was superior in strength, counter-attacked at Jarpal, in the Shakargarh Sector. On hearing this transmission, Second Lt. Khetarpal who was in 'A' Squadron, voluntarily moved along with his troop, to assist the other squadron. Enroute, while crossing the Basantar River, Second Lieutenant Arun Khetarpal and his troops came under fire from enemy strong points and RCL gun nests that were still holding out. Time was at a premium and as a critical situation was developing in the 'B' Squadron sector, Second Lieutenant Arun Khetarpal, threw caution to the winds and started attacking the impending enemy strong points by literally charging them, overrunning the defence works with his tanks and capturing the enemy infantry and weapon crews at pistol point. In the course of one such daring attack, one tank commander of his troop was killed. Second Lieutenant Arun Khetarpal continued to attack relentlessly until all enemy opposition was overcome and he broke through towards the 'B' Squadron position, just in time to see the enemy tanks pulling back after their initial probing attack on this squadron. He was so carried away by the wild enthusiasm of battle and the impetus of his own headlong dash that he started chasing the withdrawing tanks and even managed to shoot and destroy one. Soon thereafter, the enemy reformed with a squadron of armour for a second

attack and this time they selected the sector held by Second Lieutenant Arun Khetarpal and two other tanks as the point for their main effort. A fierce tank fight ensued: ten enemy tanks were hit and destroyed, of which Second Lieutenant Arun Khetarpal personally destroyed four; just then Second Lieutenant Arun Khetarpal was severely wounded. He was asked to abandon his tank but he realized that the enemy though badly decimated, was continuing to advance in his sector of responsibility and if he abandoned his tank the enemy would break through; he gallantly fought on and destroyed another enemy tank. At this stage his tank received a second hit which resulted in the death of this gallant officer. Second Lieutenant Arun Khetarpal was dead but he had, by his intrepid valour, saved the day; the enemy was denied the breakthrough he was so desperately seeking. Not one enemy tank got through. Second Lieutenant Arun Khetarpal had shown the best qualities of leadership, tenacity of purpose and the will to close in with the enemy. This was an act of courage and self-sacrifice far beyond the call of duty.

## Source and Reference:

- *The Sanawarian – Souvenir Brochure* (1947–1972)

# My Elder Brother

My elder brother, Gurdip, and I joined Sanawar at the beginning of 1948. They placed Gurdip in L-III and because I was just a tad over nine years, and 'too old' for Prep School, I was placed in the same class. So we locked steps and went through school together, finishing in 1954.

My brother became school prefect, played cricket for the school, was the school bugler, and the president of the Science as well as the Philately Society.

In complete contrast, I did nothing notable in school, or thereafter. I was a klutz, the clumsiest kid in the school. I couldn't walk and chew gum at the same time . . . still can't. I have two Sanawar group photographs—in one, I have my head down, and in the other, my eyes closed. I wore glasses and if I took them off, couldn't see beyond the end of my nose. I am not sure I ever scored more than two runs in a cricket game. I would be the last one to be chosen and the last one to bat. I never saw the ball coming . . . nor going. How was I expected to hit it with a bat just four inches wide? The same thing happened in hockey and soccer. I would run around but I never got the hang of it.

I was in the NCC. You guessed it, in the junior-most squad. I remember going to the firing range and taking five shots at the target. Four of us went to retrieve the targets. I looked at mine. It was still pristine. No holes to show. I was a bit unnerved. We got back to show the targets to Mr Bhupinder Singh. I held the target in my right hand and saluted with the left. That was the end of my career in the NCC. Mr Bhupinder Singh never forgave me for that faux pas and I don't blame him.

I managed to get into trouble without even trying. I remember laughing during morning Assembly in Barne Hall and being thrown out by Mr Carter. I can't remember what was so funny but it was a long walk from one end of Barne Hall to the exit. I felt a thousand eyes glaring at my back.

I remember being asked to speak to the Science Society. The subject was 'Interplanetary Space Travel', about which I knew nothing. I stood before the society and uttered three sentences. 'If you throw a ball in the air, it comes back to earth. If you throw it with enough force, it can escape from the earth's gravitational pull and travel in space. This principle applies to spaceships and rockets.' And I sat down. My brother, the president of the Science Society, rescued me. He asked the Science teacher to speak. I was never asked to speak again.

I loved Sanawar.

**Devinderpal Singh Kalyana**
Siwalik 1954 | 1948–1954

OS Sibling – Gurdip Singh Kalyana | Siwalik 1954 | 1948–1954

# Clockwork Precision

Rouser bell/bugle at 0545; Chota Hazri; tea in mugs with bun/dog biscuit/ slice with margarine; PT from 0640 to 0720; BBC news from 0730 to 0740; inspection (in-school kit) at 0740; breakfast from 0745 to 0810; march up to Chapel/Barne Hall for Assembly; classes from 0945 to 1300 (with a milk break at 1100); lunch; compulsory sleep during summer; hobbies/ games; tea at 1600. Then a brief respite. Inspection again at 1740; dinner at 1745; march to Birdwood (Prep) till 2010; hot cocoa; lights-out at 2100. The only departure from this otherwise unchanged routine for eight long years was in 1962, during the Chinese conflict, when we listened to the AIR's 'India and the Dragon'.

Sundays were different. Rouser at 0700; Breakfast at 0845; (if Walking Out Pass) – picture at Kas; fried bacon/ham from Daily Needs; samosa bun/gulab jamun/NP bubblegum/aam papad/*churan* from the market; loiter at Alasia: browse through *Daily Mirror*, ogle at the pastries; run back to school for roll call. Bhutta/*nashpaati* raids for the brave or bartering old PT shoes to do the same. Hikes to Gorkha Fort, Ozark peak behind Dagshai, stick jaws from Baljis on trips to Simla; Friday orders for movie of the week; building bamboo huts; kicking the can; hide-and-seek; gully cricket; rounders at Barnes; scaling walls/roof tops.

Looking forward to your name being called for a birthday party; waiting for Charlie and his full basket; Saturday's compulsory letter-writing; annual weighing and measuring; cheering for your House in inter-House competitions, grabbing at others receiving a parcel of tuck. Sunshine holidays. Ice cream at 40p/cone or 50p/cup—so the weekly 2 rupees got you 5 cones or 4 cups.

Sleeping out in the corridor during summer; midnight feasts of baked beans, pineapple slices, sardines, sprat, jelly, Milkmaid cans; DLTGH; Home Day galata or making apple-pie bed; school party rush with the 'correct' sticker on luggage placed in Gaskell Hall; Kalka walkdown – decide from three routes – the normal bridle path from Kasauli or straight down from Monkey Point or via the Koti railway tunnel; the prized samosas at Kalka; Comics at A.H. Wheeler book stall.

Seeing prefects at night for punishment; writing lines: 'I will not . . .'; running down to Barnes; frog leaping.

Besides the school song, 'Lord dismiss us . . .' was sung loudest and 'Lord behold us . . .' with some reluctance.

All in all, a wonderful life . . .

NEVER GIVE IN!

**Gp. Capt. Shirish Madhao Tatwawadi**
Tats | Vindhya 1964 | 1958–1964
Thirty-three years in the Indian Air Force

OS Sibling – Sister – Latika (Tatwawadi) Mangrulkar | Vindhya 1961 | 1958–1961

# Roots of Sanawar

Starting out at Sanawar as I did at eleven years of age, life was too rigid, to say the least. Getting up at the crack of dawn, a grimy cup of tea with 'dog-style' hard biscuits beckoned the start of yet another day in school . . .

I vividly remember getting up each morning around 5 a.m. to go to the 'bogs', as that was the only time they were clean. At 6.30 a.m. was PT, which was always treacherous, under the watchful command of Mr Jagdish Ram. And at 7.30 a.m., when a devilish prefect uttered the dreaded words, 'See me tonight', the entire day was ruined. The punishments were always physical in nature: fifteen–twenty minutes of pure hell.

In U-V, I opted for Humanities: English, History and Hindi. Other than English and History being cakewalk, I was also in a class with sixteen girls and just two boys, both of us called Sanjiv. The girls to boys ratio certainly worked to our advantage.

My memories of Sanawar are still vivid. I was an average student and I was not a sportsman. But what I could do was think on my feet and speak good English. My life at Sanawar instilled in me a strong sense of discipline, a sense of survival, the ability to face adversity and to get things done, which I firmly believe has always stood me in good stead in life. That in itself, I feel, is a fine takeaway from my six years at Sanawar.

It was the Sanawarian discipline and the 'Never Give In' attitude that sustained me through the abominable time I had in Tehran, Iran, in 1977, when I was not quite twenty-two years old. The ability to claw my way out of trouble in Iran, and later in Russia (USSR), and a few months later, when I jumped the French border at Calais, France, I do believe, had their roots firmly embedded in Sanawar.

The ability to call one of the richest men in Saudia Arabia in 1985 – someone I did not know – and tell him that I could make money for him, and somehow persuade him to invite me to his Champs Elysees office in

Paris for a job, which I got, is something I attribute to the self-confidence and persistence I developed while at Sanawar.

In 1994, I started an SAP consulting company in Auckland, New Zealand. Here I was a total novice in computers and software, taking on the Big 5 Consulting Companies in the world and IBM in Australasia, India and Qatar. I setup my company in Orange County, California, in November 1997 and within six months, in April 1998, bagged two huge multi-million dollar SAP consulting contracts with RIL and TELCO (now Tata Motors) literally within one day of each other.

In 2009, I purchased a Portuguese villa in Goa, and fortuitously started selling property, and saw an opportunity in renovating old Portuguese villas for sale and went on to renovate, own and live in a huge House with one of the best river and ocean views in Goa.

My passion for restoring old Jeeps, has stayed with me for the last forty years and today, I have perhaps the biggest and best selection of old WWII-vintage petrol jeeps in Jharkhand.

Around 2010, I had my ears pierced; a few years later, I started wearing rubies in them, and in 2018, published my memoir *Rubies in My Ears*, a book I dedicated to those 'who do not know what they want to do in life'.

Avis rental car company's advert punchline in the 1960s, 'We try harder', epitomizes the success of the second grader, yes, we sure do try harder and that truly makes the difference.

I got a call from Tirupati a few months ago, from Sreenivas, who had met with an automobile accident, was confined to the bed and depressed. He read, *Rubies in My Ears* and said, 'It's one of the best books I have read in my life. It transformed me to get on the right path'. Living in a temple town, amongst gods and goddesses, Sreenivas was resuscitated by *Rubies in My Ears*.

It is a paradox of life that some of biggest success stories in business are of introverts, such as Warren Buffet, Bill Gates, Jeff Bezos, Larry Page, Steve Wozniak, Mark Zuckerberg, and the late Steve Jobs. Who said introverts cannot make money?

The most gratifying, humbling and emotional moment I have had was while addressing the students and faculty of Sanawar in March 2019, during a motivational talk—a moment in time I will never forget.

God bless Sanawar. Never Give In.

**Sanjiv T. Lall**
Fatty | Siwalik 1972 | 1967–1972
Motivational and Leadership Speaker | International SAP Consultant | Author of *Rubies in My Ears – A Memoir* | Presently renovating Portuguese Heritage villas in Goa| Restoring vintage World War II 4WD Jeeps in Ranchi

OS Siblings – Sister – Mala Tandan | Siwalik 1972 | 1967–1972
Sister – Gita Tandan | Siwalik 1970 | 1967–1970

# Gassy Dames

Sometimes, one made really odd choices in an attempt to escape mundane hobbies and boring things like Socially Useful Productive Work (SUPW).

My gang of four (Sheshe, Hoofy, Mandy and I) chose poultry farming, primarily because the farm was way down, near Garden City, and the walk to and fro provided us with extra time to chat, generally loiter and left less time for 'productive' work. And so the four of us would traipse down once a week to clean chicken poop and collect eggs, but mostly to chat and giggle and get some 'us-time'.

To our utter amazement, two boys joined us for this insane activity. One of them happened to be our batchmate Bonga (Harminder Sohi). As was the habit with several boys, he would invariably pass us, muttering

'gassy dames', a highly irritating moniker for girls who talked a lot, i.e., 'gassed'.

One day, he decided to take on the four of us. While we were cleaning the chicken pen, he locked us inside. Of course, he thought this was hilarious and frankly, it must have been – four 'chicks' clucking around with six to seven hens and no teacher in sight – I have no idea where Mr Attri had scooted off to.

This was unacceptable and way off-limit for our egos. So, on the way back, we hid behind a tree, waiting. A little later, our unsuspecting Bonga came whistling up the hill. The four of us pounced on him and gave him a proper hiding, ensuring that he would not repeat his unpardonable offense ever again. And sure enough, it was never repeated but the 'gassy dames' became noticeably louder each time we were in earshot.

**Anjali Khosla**
Thappo | Nilagiri 1984 | 1977–1984
Documentary Filmmaker and Editor | Work on Conservation, Environment and Livelihoods

# Parsi Priest

I met Shomie Das as a twelve-year-old in Hyderabad at the residence of his boarding school classmate, Mr Hussain, in July 1980. He was the father of four Sanawarians, Rafaat, Sabba, Sujhaat, Shafaat. I had just completed my Navar ceremony to become a Parsi Priest in Mumbai. His Parsi wife, Pheroza, was naturally impressed, so fifteen days later (regardless of the joint exam results, which I probably didn't master) I landed in Sanawar. Sanawar had a bunch of Parsis from Jamshedpur (Ghandy's and Bhasin's 50 percenters), Mumbai (Maneck, me and later on, Ness) and Pune (the famous Wadia), but no Parsi priests. I stayed well off the radar so far as the Das were concerned – unlike some other Parsi students – throughout school.

Then, in 1984, I got called to [the] headmaster's House one day. It was way past lights-out. I hadn't done anything that I could recall that might merit a call to his House at this odd hour. I had two options—follow the route Nadim took to Kalka or go meekly to Heady's House. I nervously crept past the Chapel, saluted at the memorial, past the steps up the slope and to the House. Mr Das called me aside, at which point I almost passed out from fear, when he said Mrs Choksey (his mother-in-law) had passed away. *That's all?!* I thought. It wasn't about anything that I'd done. I was so relieved, as any student would be. He probably saw my relieved face. But he then broke the sad news to me that I would be performing the funeral prayers for the dearly departed. My relief soon turned to 'what am I going to do now?' panic. If I performed the prayers, they would have been all wrong and God alone knows where her soul might end up, so I muttered, 'Sir, I don't remember my prayers'. He flew into a rage and said, 'The only reason I took you into Sanawar was because I knew this might happen, and you would be on hand' . . .

I stayed up all night sputtering prayers just to impress the Dases. I was completely exhausted by the morning. Fortunately for the dearly departed, some Parsi priests were summoned from Delhi by the early Kalka train and I was able to join them in the formal funeral prayers, later that afternoon.

**Reyaz Mama**
Nilagiri 1985 | 1980–1985 | Went back to Teach in 1989

# Jagga Sir

Mr Jagdish Ram, fondly known as 'Jagga' was loved and respected by all Sanawarians. He was born in 1910 and was brought up in a small village called Rakkar, tucked away in the pristine Kangra valley in Himachal Pradesh. He lived his life as high and straight as the Dhauladhar Mountains which overlooked his home. After completing his matriculation from St. Paul's Mission School, Palampur, he was directly commissioned as a Junior Commissioned Officer in the Balauch Regiment, a unit that was subsequently transferred to Pakistan in 1947. He showed immense talent in gymnastics and so was picked by the unit to be trained, and was transferred to the Army Physical Training School in Rawalpindi as an instructor.

He was a determined man—he was not allowed to practise in the unit gym as it was for higher-ranking officers only, so after lights-out, he would go to the football field and practise on the goal post bar instead. He was the National Boxing champion for five years running and was also selected for the 1928 Olympics in Amsterdam, but despite his immense talent, he could not go as he could not afford to pay his fare for the three-week-long journey. India, for sure, missed a medal.

After Partition, in 1948, he was posted at Indian Military Academy Dehradun as the PT and Gymnastics Instructor. At the same time, Major Som Dutt was also an instructor with the Army Educational Corps, teaching the cadets how to dot their I's and cross their T's. From there he was moved to Kasauli, to the Army Physical Training School, and as destiny would have it, the then Headmaster Mr Carter, requested the then Commander-in-Chief of the Indian Army, General Cariappa, whose two children were studying in Sanawar, for a PT instructor. The search zeroed in on Mr Jagdish Ram in Kasauli. He was offered the job, which he willingly accepted to work at Sanawar.

A job he took so seriously that he would walk down from Kasauli to Sanawar every day, till he got his permanent staff quarters at Sanawar. It was no surprise that a man of such high values, discipline and diligence was awarded the Spartan within two years of joining Sanawar, for raising the standards of boxing and gymnastics to a level at par with the IMA.

Air Marshal Nanda Cariappa, OS 1954, as the Chief Guest during Founders' narrated that in those days, to beat Sanawar at boxing was the dream of every public school in India. In the mid-'50s, Sanawar was also visited by Mr K.P.S. Menon, who was the then Foreign Secretary, and having spent five years in the USSR as an ambassador, also said that the Tattoo was at par with the performance of the Soviet soldiers—compliments that illustrate the perfection and prowess of PT and Tattoo at Sanawar then.

In 1961, Vindhya House was facing disciplinary problems and when the school reopened in 1962, Mr Jagdish Ram was appointed the new Housemaster. As the story goes, Major Som Dutt was asked by the Board of Governors to appoint a Physical Training Instructor as a Housemaster. Major Som Dutt, without mincing his words, said, 'where there is indiscipline, I will send Jagdish and I give him one month to stem the rot'. For the next three years, Vindhya House won the Cock House. In 1968, he was shifted to Siwalik House to 'discipline them', where he remained till his retirement in 1970.

**Govind Singh Pathania**
Himalaya 1967 | 1957–1967

OS Siblings – Brother – Narayan Singh Pathania | Himalaya 1962 |
                1952–1957
                Sister – Indra Pathania | Himalaya 1963 | 1953–1955
                Brother – Vasudev Singh Pathania | Himalaya 1970 |
                1962–1970

OS Children – Daughter – Richalaxhmi Pathania | Himalaya 2000 |
1992–2000

# Bugle Calls

## LMA and LRMS, Sanawar from ca.1854–1947

For the better part of a century, every day, at various times from dawn to dusk, Sanawar hilltop resounded with the unmistakeable cadence of an army bugle call. Although a tiresome nuisance for many, it came to be an accepted feature of daily life for anyone that lived and worked on the hilltop. Regular army bugle calls were used to signal and announce various events and activities in the daily routine and timetable of the Boys' School.

There were two bugle calls to get you out of bed in the mornings, one of them for 'school' time and another (less strident) for 'free' time (i.e., weekends, summer camps and holidays). There were also originally two Mess or 'Cookhouse' calls, one for the junior houses and one for seniors. However, in about 1928, they were combined to make one single Mess call for all. There was a call to get you on parade, report sick, fall-in for school, assemble for Chapel or prep, turn out at the double for fire drills, report for band practice, summon the duty sergeants and, in the early days, three different calls to pack you off to bed for the night. Again however, the customary practice of playing the First and Last Posts every day before the lights went out, was ceased in Principal Agard E. Evans' time. Thereafter, most working days ended with a short and simple 'lights-out'. The longer and more complex Post calls were heard only at Chapel on Armistice Days and on the occasional Sunday night when the Duty Bugler felt up to it.

There were always nine buglers in the brass section of the school band from among whom the school duty bugler was routinely appointed. Notable among these in the 1940's was Ronald Brodie (Lawrence, 1943–1947), three-time winner of the Waugh Challenge Bugle and much admired by all for his exceptional skill with both bugle and trumpet. Everyone knew when it was his turn as duty bugler.

The bugle calls routinely heard on the hilltop in those times are listed below. No, regrettably they are not played by Ron Brodie nor by any other

515

Sanawar bugler. Modern recording technologies were still a long way off in those distant times, and whatever wire recordings might have been made, have long since rusted away. The calls presented here were performed by a bugler from the Regimental band and Corps of Drums, First Battalion, The Duke of Edinburgh's Royal Regiment (Berkshire and Wiltshire) in about 1991.

**D.V. Boddington**
LRMS Sanawar 1942–1947
23 April 2002

**Adapted from an article in the midsummer edition of *The Sanawarian* Magazine, November 1939.**

# The Chemistry Paper

The quartet, Dipi (Dipender Dhaliwal–H), Kand (Suminder Khandari–H), Maini (Parminder Sandhu–V) and yours truly, could pick teachers' home door locks or enter their homes through open windows. We specialized in stealing test question papers or replacing answer sheets. Sometimes both, as it was too much of an effort to memorize the answers. We also had a well-defined process of deploying lookouts along the route to the teacher's home. We used hand-signals from vantage points to indicate if anyone was headed our way. We would typically do this during classes—undeniably the best time for these operations, while the staff would be in class, teaching.

One time, we stole the Chemistry test paper from Mrs Longman's home—we went through her desk, found the paper, and wrote the questions on a piece of paper. Today's iPhones would have accomplished the task in sixty seconds.

We were braindead. So, it was always one of those 'brains' who was 'hired' to write out the answers for us. This Chemistry paper was a tough one, and we were too lazy to memorize the answers. So we decided that after the exam, we would just go and replace the answer sheets. I wrote enough to score 65–70 on 100. My dear friend Kand said he was going to ace the test, and wrote an almost perfect answer sheet.

Mrs Longman distributed the answer sheets. I scored 65 per cent. Kand, sitting in the corner row next to the windows, smiled as he got 90+ per cent. Mrs Longman finished distributing the answer sheets and came back to Kand's desk with a set of blank papers and requested, 'Please write the answers to the questions again'. That look of horror on Kand's face is still etched in my mind. Through those entire forty minutes, Kand tried to fill out the answer sheet. He fought gallantly, but failed the test miserably.

Maini, Dipi and I got away as we scored enough to get by. Mrs Longman did not report the incident to anyone.

Just for the record, Maini and Dipi run successful agriculture businesses in Punjab. Kand is a very successful real estate investor in Delhi, also dabbling in movies these days. After much trial and tribulation, I finally settled down and made a decent life for myself here in Seattle in the software industry. Many of you and members of my extended family still scratch their heads, puzzled as to how I made it as a software engineer with a critical thinking mind and entrepreneurial drive to create a small real estate investment company.

**Harjaspreet Singh Gill**
Clay | Siwalik 1979 | 1969–1977
Lives in Seattle, USA; passionate about golf, music, dance, real estate development and software engineering

# Band House

Did you know that, for a number of years, Lawrence House was known as the band House? Anybody who could play an instrument, or was eager to learn how to play, was automatically placed in the band House: Lawrence.

The school band was, therefore, composed entirely of Lawrence House boys. Full members of the band were presented with a badge in the shape of a lyre, which was worn on the sleeve. Lawrence House was considerably disadvantaged when it came to the inter-House drill competition (the Cooke Cup), because they were unable to practise the requisite drill movements; all the members of the band would be at band practice while other Houses exercised their routines.

This handicap was recognized by those in authority, and so it was agreed to give Lawrence a start of 10 points on the day of the competition. It is of interest that this bonus did not help Lawrence House to come higher than fifth place; there were only five Houses then! They always accepted their performance in a good, happy, spirit—which all the other houses shared.

**Jock Howie**
Roberts 1922–37

**From an article in the *Old Sanawarian* magazine, 2003**

# The Mid-70s / Early 80s

The mid-70s and early 80s were a great time to be in Sanawar. The school's traditions were strong, the discipline tight, the punishment harsh, and yet khup was at its peak!

## Poxies

In Spring '75, half the school fell prey to a chicken pox epidemic. Four of us from Vindhya House Junior dorm – known to be a big khup-creator dorm – were admitted to the Hospital main ward as the first wave of chicken poxies. Food delivered from PD was disgusting, with having to be on a 'milk diet' for the first three days. Then a senior, a fellow poxie, and one of the most colourful of characters during my time in school, called Gunda, gave us a lesson in *hakeemi* that if you eat chicken – a rarity in those days at school – it eats away chicken pox from the inside, insisting, 'loha hi lohey ko katta hai'. By the way, he was the same guy who gave us detailed lessons in L-III about the female anatomy and also claimed they were *bhoots* whose feet would flip backwards after midnight—which left an impression on our budding adolescent minds at the time.

So, the next morning, while playing carrom to kill our boredom, we decide to steal a few chickens from a bearer called Laini, whose shack was just below Hospi, and who had domesticated a few succulent ones. The planning was meticulous and the execution brilliant! Our reward: three plump chickens! We skinned the stolen chickens in the bathroom tub, quartered them with an old Wilkinson Sword razor blade swiped from the M.I. room, and then roasted them over a pine cone fire. Gruesome as it was, the chickens were enjoyed by all admitted poxies after taking a blood oath never to tattle.

We eventually got busted afterwards and received a major thrashing from the M.I. prefect; but thanks to the prevailing student code at that time, we were never turned in to the staff for disciplinary action! Phew!

## Caning the Rowdies

I reminisce it as a picture-perfect day in early November '76 . . . bright blue sky, crisp air, the leaves bristling in all their natural splendour, and best of all, Home Day just a few weeks away. And then, in a flash of impulsive khuppiness, we made it all go to hell!

A few of us in Arts class (L-IV, Section B) were asked by Mr Bhalerao to corral ourselves at the top of Peacestead and sketch the beautiful panorama with Monkey Point and Kas as the perfect backdrop (how we ended up in Arts class with zero talent is another story for another time). As we sat there struggling with our sketches, dreaming about supper and the common room banter to follow, suddenly before us, walking past Peacestead, went a man (Mr Onkar Singh) who had given us the biggest hiding of our piddly little lives just the week before. Instinctively, the temptation to return the favour kicked in and we pulled a real devilment that landed us in the biggest trouble ever (details best left for a reunion). This was now the second bust in two weeks for us . . . and get this, when even your prefects tell you, 'YOU KLUNS ARE GOING TO HANG FOR THIS!' you know you're in really deep shit.

After a sham of due processes and numerous dunds (punishments), we were asked to report to Mucchoo (Mr B. Singh) for caning—and that too right after Saturday's kadhi-chawal feast! How cruel is that?! But having gone through caning before, we had a plan this time—or at least so we thought we could pull off a fast one on Mucchoo!

A few of our class Housemates (i.e., *asli langotiya yaars*) were asked to give up their undies and each one of us wore between six to eight of them under our shorts and showed up for caning; however, the strange swagger and bulge from wearing layers of undies didn't go unnoticed by a sharp-eyed Mr B. Singh. Told to strip down fully, we got double the caning from a very special rattan cane that our prefects had sick-mindedly informed us that Mucchoo had cured with the finest linseed oil procured from a place high up in the Himalayas called Reckong Peo—just for a special breed of rowdies like us!

The purple scars on our buttocks crusting into brown were still visible after a month . . . they even placed a handmade 'spectro-colour-o-meter' in the common room to show the turning of the colours on our bums for all to take heed . . . believe me, we could only sleep on our tummies for weeks and that too well into the winter holiday break!

## Cowboy

Many of us batchmates had a special affection for Abu the cowboy (Mr Abraham). On a lazy afternoon in late April '76, three of us, all L-IV backbenchers then, decided to take another *panga* with Abu, having been gifted a perfect opportunity too good to pass up.

A bit of context first: it was customary then, and still is today, for students to greet teachers first when passing them, and them reciprocating.

On that fateful day, however, we had something else in mind and we quickly finagled a plan to have Abu (the teacher) greet us first, and then and only then would we three students greet him back. This wasn't some adolescent tomfoolery for kicks and giggles; we just wanted to show him who was boss after the umpteen lickings he had given us in and out of class; it was a pure unadulterated power play on our part!

So as we began walking up towards the Chapel from the quad on our way to carpentry room for Hobbies, we spot Abu walking down; and just as we are about to cross each other halfway up the hill, near the Tuck Shop, the three of us batchmates come to attention, giving Abu the impression that we had already greeted him, to which he responded with a smirk and 'afternoon' in his typically contemptuous voice, especially reserved for us good-for-nothings!

Then two steps later – as we come parallel to each other – for our return greeting, the three of us, in sync, announce in an equally pompous, snide and drawly tone - 'GooooOOOOD afternoon ABU!'

Just imagine our gall! Suddenly, all hell broke loose as Abu realized what had just happened. He spun around in his Texan cowboy swagger and managed to catch me by the collar while my other two batchmates bolted like bats out of hell and somersaulted into UD's (Dr Dhillon) garden below the Tuck Shop; and off and away! For me, though, being in Abu's grabs, it was game over! He dragged me by the ear all the way back to the Vindhya House dorm while he sent the prefects to look for the other two miscreants.

The rest was not pretty! I tell you, even today, more than four decades later, my earlobes have not fully healed!

**Sanjeet S. Bajwa**
Bajja | Vindhya 1982 | 1973–1977
Chief Procurement Officer | Head of Manufacturing Market Sector, British Petroleum | Corporate Vice President, Covanta | Vice President, Siemens | Group Commercial Management, Honeywell | MIM, The American Graduate School of International Management | MBA and BSc, San Diego State University

OS Sibling – Sister – Madhvi (Bajwa) Zingde | Mini | Vindhya 1979 | 1974–1977

# Life of a Preppy

In March 1959, I was admitted to L-KG, and allotted Siwalik House. Little did I know then that this was to be my new home for the next eleven years. The PD Boys' Dormitory, as most of the other buildings, were old, sturdy and magnificent pieces of stone architecture, made of well chiselled-out boulders, with wooden plank floorings and red-painted tapered corrugated tin roofs.

Siwalik shared the Upper Dormitory with Nilagiri House, while Himalaya and Vindhya were housed in the Lower Dormitory. PD girls, being much lesser in number, were all housed in a single dormitory above the dining hall, a building of recent construction, next to the Assembly hall. Each of us was given a strong iron bed, with a mattress and a pillow, stuffed with locally procured pine needles, and a wooden kit-box for keeping our belongings, neatly folded.

Our L-KG class teacher Miss Raj Rani Suri and my Housemistress, Mrs Rita Gidwani, were so affectionate, loving and caring that very soon, all of us newcomers started to feel comfortable, and began adjusting to the new, and hitherto unknown, disciplined lifestyle of a boarding school in the hills. We were lucky to have Mrs Sehgal, a very kind lady with great motherly instincts, as our Upper Dorm matron. A year later, she was moved to BD, as the Kitchen Matron, and was replaced by Miss Pamela Chopra, a very strict lady who would just not stand any nonsense from us Preppers, and punished us often, making us stand in silence, on our kit-box, with fingers on our lips for long durations. (I still wonder why we addressed her as 'Miss', considering her husband often visited Sanawar in the summer for cool respite from the Delhi heat).

There was not much to study, and most of the time was spent in playing games, singing songs, listening to fairytales and other stories. Miss Suri once organized a wedding (Gudday Guddi Ki Shaadi) with the cute Jugi as the bride getting married to an imaginary groom. We, the 'baraatis', merrily sang and danced to the accompaniment of folk music. Refreshments served by the PD kitchen were gurpatta and nimbu pani.

Other games in which the entire class participated, included 'Visit to the Market', 'Money and Banking', 'Dog and the Bone', '*Chor–Sipahi*', to name a few.

In 1960, our U-KG teacher Mrs Cherian went to England under an exchange programme, to teach at Brighton and Hove High School, Brighton, Sussex. She sent back a list of the girls in her class there. I made my first pen friend, a tall, beautiful girl named Joanna Rooper. For the next six to seven years, we regularly exchanged (friendship) letters, written on thin airmail paper. I wished to meet her in person if and when I visited England. I still remember her address by heart, but could not visit Brighton (though I did go to UK in 2013).

Dramatics was encouraged, and everyone took part in some play or dance or musical event during their respective House shows, staged in the first term itself. The PD school show marked the start of Founders'. I was part of many plays, most notably the opera 'The Pied Piper of Hamlin', staged in 1962, where we PD children scurried across the stage dressed up as mice, wearing black conical hats made of drawing sheets, while Senior School girls and boys played the other characters. Another play I remember is where I played a Tommy Policeman. The helmet slipped off my head when I bowed before the magistrate. I was quick to catch it and place it on the table before him.

In the PD school show, a Hindi play was staged at Founders' 1962, where I played the lead role of a washerman in *Dhobi Ka Gadha*.

In Form I, we were taught how and what to write home. Having noted the dictation then, I had put it in my overcoat pocket and forgotten about it. A fortnight later, during tutorial, we were asked to write a letter to our parents. Now, all of a sudden, I felt lost. It was a cold afternoon and I put my hands in my overcoat, and by sheer luck, 'found' the forgotten letter. Feeling happy, I pulled it out, and started to copy it off word by word. A classmate, two desks behind, reported me to Miss Piloo Rudra (PD headmistress), who was taking our tutorial. This was a lesson learnt forever that has stayed embedded ever since. Till today, the very idea of cheating has never crossed my mind.

We celebrated 15 August with an assortment of games and eats. In 'Jalebi Race', we ran with our hands tied behind, to a vertical bar on which hung round and tasty Jalebis. We had to devour them quickly, and then run back to the starting line. I won this race twice. In 'Sack Race', we had to put both our feet in a sack, and hop to the finish line. In another race, a boy's left leg was tied to another's right leg, and the two had to run together, without falling.

We celebrated Christmas just a day before Home Day (for the twelve-week winter hols). To keep us warm from the extreme cold, all PD children were given one big tablespoon of the sweet and bitter ginger beer. Miss Rudra, along with other teachers, would hush us all to hear the approaching reindeers towing the chariot in the skies. We would shake our heads in confirmation. Mr Jagdish Ram, the school PT instructor, would then come dressed as Santa Claus. We would stand in lines, House-wise, to shake hands with and receive gifts from Father Christmas.

In 1961, for the first time, Preppers went to the Senior School camp at Kandaghat's 'Indira Holiday Home'. We were ferried in the school truck (in groups, on different days), and really enjoyed the single-day outing. We left after breakfast and had lunch and tea with the Seniors, whom we had never interacted with before. The most exciting part was watching them swim in the very inviting indoor swimming pool. In Senior School, Camps were different and more challenging.

**Ravinder Raizada**
Chini | Siwalik 1969 | 1959–1969

OS Sibling – Ramakant Raizada | Kant | Siwalik 1968 | 1958–1968

# The Ghost of Honoria

An eerie silence. What's happened? No sound. Why were the pines so silent? No sound of crickets, no *jugnus* . . .

Some of us moved, scared as hell, towards the window. Peacestead stretched in front of us; the empty tennis courts and then—a shimmer; a small cloudy form started developing; the silence got heavy, palpable, throbbing; a collective gasp and a couple of panicky squeals. The cloudy form started getting bigger; and then a swaying twinkling, flickering light—a lantern—attached itself to that form which just grew and grew; a bonnet, a velvety gown; a face? I think. With wispy curls around the forehead; oh God in Heaven, were we seeing the infamous ghost of Honoria Lawrence? The excitement was running high; the fright had our hearts beating overtime; we clutched on to each other's hands; some went and hid under their counterpanes; trembling, eyes shut tight: 'is it HER?' 'Mommy, I want to go home', yelled someone. 'Oh my God, there are more cloudy forms gathering; it's like an invasion. What's going to happen?' 'They are coming; we will all die now!'

It's not Founders', damn it! She is only supposed to appear then. Is it the figment of imagination of a hundred girls? We saw, we swear! We saw the legendary Lady with the Lantern . . .

Suddenly, someone screamed, 'she is coming here; her grave is right below the central pillar in the dorm.' We scattered, pushed and yelled but slowly holding our breath, we crept back to the window and peeped out from behind our hands; she had reached the bell beneath the big pine tree right in front of our eyes; a long, really long, ever-growing arm reached out to ring the bell. She lifted the lantern with what seemed like a third arm, slowly turned her head; turned it towards us and smiled. This terrified us. Screams everywhere! This time, someone whispered, 'Don't look her in the eye; you will turn to stone.' God, was this a nightmare? A junior bleated, 'Mummy, I am scared!' The prefect shouted, 'Shut up; she can hear you!'

Our matron, of course, slept through it all. We were totally mesmerized; almost turned to stone . . .

A cricket, a jugnu; a whisper of the pine; a thin voice trembling, saying, 'She's gone'; a suppressed scream. With frightened eyes, we all looked at each other, unbelieving. Not many of us slept that night. We called our usual conference around a midnight feast; we gathered, pulling our dressing gowns tightly around us, as though the warm snug feeling would cocoon us from the horror of that cloudy vision. 'Are you sure we saw her?' We looked at Sunita. 'Have you gone mad?! We all saw her,' we said, giving poor Gita a disdainful look.

Our matron was snoring loudly enough to wake the dead—oh no! Was her noisy snoring the reason that the ghost had been awakened?

Morning, at last; we peeped out from under our quilts; the coast was clear; no ghost, no mysterious sightings. Rushing through Chota Hazri, we went to Mrs Kemp and narrated the whole story. She looked at us and burst out laughing. Offended, we insisted, 'but Ma'am, we all saw the ghost!'

'Our secret is out,' she said, 'we were rehearsing for the staff play that we are performing at Founders' this year . . .'

No! Oh, no! The fright, the thrill . . .

Actually, it was all so much fun.

**Vijay (Chopra) Narang** | Siwalik 1964 | 1955–1964
OS Sibling – Sister – Viney Chopra | Siwalik 1961 | 1952–1961

OS Children – Son – Tarun Narang | Siwalik 1989 | 1981–1989
                Daughter – Priyanka Narang | Siwalik 1997 | 1988–1997
                Grandson – Shaurys Vir Narang | Siwalik (Present Sanawarian)

# Lessons for Life

To a girl who had only studied on her mother's knee until she was twelve, the prospect of going to a boarding school was scary. However, Mr Kemp immediately put me at ease with his warm smile and friendly chatter. That bright introduction to Sanawar is the first of many wonderful memories.

That day, fearing an entry test, I had stood mutely before Mr Kemp in his six-by-six office. But he immediately made me feel as comfortable as if I had found a friend. 'You can practise some sums before the test,' he said, as he wrote down a few for me to do. Then he handed me a book and asked me to read it aloud, 'Just for fun'. And that was it! To this day, I marvel at the wonderful way in which I was assessed and compare it to the trauma little children are put through today.

Mr Kemp was the vice headmaster and an institution in himself; yet, we never saw him throw his weight around. A cheery 'Morning Sunny' from him would be like a springboard for my happy soul. He ran the school like clockwork—managing it and our lives through the little wooden squares which he moved around on the timetable on his wall.

As I drifted in and out of classes, House shows, hobbies, Founders', I learned many things. My mother always said, 'It's because of Sanawar that you can do so much.' Yes, indeed . . . the calibre of teachers was instrumental in cementing the values we acquired; including valuing our friendships, because neither status nor wealth mattered.

Miss Ling, Miss Chuck and then Miss Pamela Dougherty took us under their wing. I don't ever remember being scolded, despite all our Himalayan naughtiness. We managed to test so many boundaries that there were times when Kavita Padda, who was 'one of us', pretended she didn't know us after she became the Head Girl. Once, Mrs Mountford got seriously riled up at me for writing home to 'report' that I had beaten up Mickey Sehgal outside Parker Hall for punching me after my first (of twenty-one) anti-rabies shots. My mother wrote back saying 'Well done!'

because she didn't believe I could said 'boo' to a mouse. That was the turning point in my life—I learned to stand up and fight for myself. After all, I was GD '85.

Mr Bhalerao didn't just teach me how to paint, he taught me to be an artist. '*Thora Thora*', he'd say while touching up our paintings in his five-by-five studio, giving life and a new dimension to our paintings and me, inspiration. 'She has a flair for water colours and has her own style.' I would sit on the warm tin roofs near the Art Room or behind it and happily paint poppies and trees. Sorry Sir! I put down my brushes at age thirty . . . inexcusable after you gave me the Yog Raj Palta. Will make amends now and paint away until the end.

Additionally, in school, one rupee felt like a hundred because of Charlie's best-in-the-world aloo poori, palang-tod and gulab jamuns. We also looked forward to the weekends when we would walk to Kasauli for a bun samosa and a bulls-eye or a Doris Day movie in the tin movie hall.

Sanawar is in our blood and the memories remain sweet. The lessons I learned and the friends I made there are mine for life.

**Sunaiyna (Chauhan) Dass**
Chau | Himalaya 1969 | 1964–1969

Father – Mr I.E.N. Chauhan (I.A.S.) – Composed 'Waltz of the Flowers' and other marches for the school parade on request from Major Som Dutt, Headmaster | Performed two classical guitar recitals in Barne Hall | Had earlier composed 'The Cariappa March' played on Republic Day at the Red Fort.

# The (Art) Room with a View

My introduction to Sanawar, as an almost thirteen-year-old, was not Birdwood, Chapel or my dorm. It was the Art Room and Mr Bhalerao, the art teacher. My mother, herself an Old Sanawarian, was dropping me off at school and couldn't wait to show me the Art Room, where she had spent a large part of her time as a student.

As we entered, an elderly gentleman emerged from the office to greet us. To my mother's great surprise, it was Mr Bhalerao, the same person who had taught her twenty-five years ago. He almost squealed in delight when he learned who my mother was—she had been one of his star pupils. He quickly ushered us into the main hall, an open space with art desks arranged in a square and art works – large and small – mounted on the walls.

'Look,' he said, pointing to a painting larger than any I had ever seen. It showed a prophet reclining against some cushions. The swirls of translucent paint gave the painting an almost mystical, dream-like quality. I would later learn that the man in the painting was the famous Mughal poet, Mirza Ghalib.

'That is your mother's painting,' said Mr. Bhalerao, patting me on the shoulder. I knew that my mother had painted over the years. Every now and then, she would hand-paint a sari, rendering a refined and pretty pattern of flowers or birds. But this? This was a serious work of art. I felt at once proud that I could now show off to my classmates that my mother's painting still hung in the Art Room after twenty-five years, but also daunted because I knew that the painting would almost be looking over my shoulder as I attempted my own creations.

Growing up, I had always loved to draw, experimenting with crayons and poster paints. But art was serious business at Sanawar, Mr Bhalerao instructed us in his high-pitched, wobbly voice, peering critically over his glasses. But he soon retired and was replaced by Mr Madhusudan, a young and avant-garde artist trained at M.S. University, Baroda. He couldn't have been more different from Mr Bhalerao; his shock of unkempt curly hair and the loose, checked shirt and faded jeans a complete contrast to

531

Mr Bhalerao's neat appearance and old-school style. While Mr Bhalerao introduced us to more classical approaches to art, Mr. Madhusudan encouraged us to push the boundaries of our imagination and to seek meaning in abstract art. Under his guidance, I soon discovered the vibrancy of dry pastels and the joyful messiness of oil paints. The arrival of a newer and younger generation of teachers in Sanawar was perhaps itself a sign that the school was evolving and changing, moving in a new direction from the post-Independence yet very British institution that my mother had known.

My most vivid memory is of being seated outside the Art Room at the built-in concrete desks, looking out over the pine trees at the snowy Himalayas in the distance. It was a view that I suspect has inspired many an artist at Sanawar. Bordering the Art Room was a small, dark room dedicated to oil paintings. The tables and even the walls were covered with streaks of paint and even now, when I encounter the rancid smell of oil paints and turpentine, I am immediately transported back to that small room where I spent hours perfecting my skills, seeking refuge from overbearing seniors and teenage squabbles.

Next to the Art Room was the Batik Room, where Mrs Pheroza Das (Heady's wife) taught tie-and-dye and batik. As I sat outside and sketched and painted, other students – mostly girls – twisted fabric and applied hot wax under Mrs Das's guidance. Across from the Art Room was also the ceramics studio, where Miss Seema Arora taught students to coil clay and spin a potter's wheel. This was our small artistic haven in Sanawar, inspiring us to engage with the arts—painting, crafts, ceramics or sculpture.

Perhaps my artistic sensibilities were also being honed subliminally; it was a time when we were lucky to be exposed to artists at Sanawar whose significance we would recognize only years later. I still have a small bowl bought from a sale of Miss Arora's ceramics but discovered only recently that she was a famous artist, widely regarded as one of India's pioneering potters of the twentieth century, having taught also at Shantiniketan. Then there was M.F. Hussain's flamboyant painting with the iconic horse. The story goes that while visiting his son at Sanawar in 1982, he was inspired to make the painting on the spot and subsequently gifted it to the school— it still hangs in Parker Hall, the school library. And finally, there was Muzaffar Ali, the well-known filmmaker, whose also visited his son at school and used the occasion to share his works with students.

I eventually made a painting almost as large as my mother's, one that to my seventeen-year-old mind, was my magnum opus. The painting went up on display alongside other paintings that the art teachers had deemed

worth exhibiting. I haven't been back to Sanawar since 1989, so don't know whether mine or my mother's paintings remain, but what I do know is that my time at Sanawar inspired a lifelong love for art.

But like many of my generation, I was taught to always be pragmatic and follow a tried and trusted path. I never pursued a career in the arts because I was fearful of becoming the proverbial starving artist. I redirected my artistic endeavours into the work of a social scientist and researcher, and whatever creativity remained was reserved for writing. But more recently, to give my brain and mind a rest from intellectual pursuits, I have once again turned to the tactile and restorative power of painting. And whenever I hold a paintbrush in my hand and struggle to seek inspiration, I have only to close my eyes and imagine that serene view of the Himalayas from the Art Room and inhale the deep smell of oil paints.

**Dr Rajika Bhandari**
Himalaya 1988 | 1983–1988
International Education expert | Author, *America Calling: A Foreign Student in a Country of Possibility*

OS Parent – Mother – Dr Sudha Anand| Nilagiri 1964 | 1955–1964

# Mr Jagdish Ram

One evening, early in 1952, stands out so vivid and clear as if it was only yesterday, for that was my first encounter with Mr Jagdish Ram and the beginning of the happy association which continued for twenty years.

I saw him in a flurry of white, going merrily round and round the horizontal bar amidst a crowd of admiring and somewhat ogle-eyed youngsters and I was to see him thus, in his spare moments for over a span of twenty years. For Mr Jagdish Ram was one of those to whom there was no hard and fast line between hours of duty and work and leisure. His leisure hours were in a large measure devoted to the service of the youngsters and to his profession.

A devoted, dedicated and a sincere man, Mr Jagdish Ram started PT and gym work in Sanawar almost from scratch and steadily built up a standard which vied with the best that the NDA or the IMA had to offer. It is the contention of our boys joining the NDA or the IMA that the PT side never posed a problem and they just sailed most smoothly through every aspect of the physical training. According to them, to this day, there are instructors at both the NDA and the IMA who swear by the name of Jagdish Ram.

Having been the chief Physical Training Instructor at the IMA, and if I am not mistaken, the first Subedar Major of the APTS Poona, he endeavoured to infuse the best of the army standards into the pattern of Sanawar PT, which being his own baby, he cradled, nursed and nourished to perfection. Mr K.P.S. Menon watching the torchlight Tattoo best summed up the achievement of Mr Jagdish Ram by referring to the PT display as one of the best he had seen anywhere. Some of the remarks during the Founders' PT and gym display which have wafted over the breathless hush of performances over the years include: terrific, stupendous, breathtaking and the like, almost began to appear commonplace. It is difficult to express and visualize the hard work, integrity of purpose and sincerity which went into these efforts.

Punctuality, precision and sweating it out were his passwords and there was very little that escaped his keen eyes. It is indeed remarkable that there were hardly any 'dodgers' at PT time. For that man in his spotless snow white and the extra-large whistle, which went by the name of Thunderbolt, and whose sharp notes could be heard from one end of the estate to the other, had the knack of really putting the fear of God in the hearts of all shammers. Through his dedication to his profession and devotion to duty, he became an object of veneration and respect amongst the children and the secret of his success was not merely his professional ability but his magnetic personality.

A great exponent of the educative value of boxing, he always scoffed quite openly at those who even hinted that this sport veered on the 'barbaric'. He always maintained that it is only by learning to give and take in the ring that one can really go through life giving and taking with a smiling face. Through his efforts, boxing today, believe it or not, is one of the loved sports and the standards attained by him at every well-planned and well-organized Inter-House Boxing Meet, to measure by any yardstick, were indeed of a very high-standard.

There was almost something uncanny in the way success walked towards him. After a successful innings with Vindhya he had only to take over as Housemaster of Siwalik and within a couple of years, he made it the Cock House after a lapse of many years. Down-to-earth and humane, he not merely helped the boys of his own House tide over their personal problems and difficulties, but was approachable to the whole of BD. He spent his time midst the boys and for the boys. Today, I would class him as the typical old timer—a class sadly dwindling away.

He said, last year, that now he had really reached the 'retiring age' and it was about time that he sat back in his easy chair in the village. Just a couple of days before the school closed for the winter, I happened to peep into the gymnasium and saw somebody sailing smoothly over the horse in a flurry of white. It was Mr Jagdish Ram doing it with the same vim and gusto as on the day when he first came to Sanawar. I wondered about the 'retiring age' part.

Anyway, Mr Jagdish Ram, we wish you every happiness in your retired life and may the memory of Sanawar be ever fresh with you. We will always think of you with fond affection.

**Bhupinder Singh**
Staff | Deputy Headmaster 1970–1993

**Source and Acknowledgement:** *The Sanawarian* (December 1971)

# First Over, Fifth Ball

The year is 1980. Inter-House Cricket is in progress. During the milk break, I run into Dagger, 'Oye, match today?' He asked.

'Ya.'

'Against?'

'Vindhya.'

'Hmmm . . . what down are you batting?'

'Four.'

'Ohhh, then you will face the fifth ball.'

'Fifth ball?'

'Fool, fifth ball of the FIRST OVER!'

'Seriously? Buzz off, man . . .'

'Bet?'

The bell rings. Geography Class. Preggy is reading aloud, 'the westerlies or anti-trades are prevailing winds from the west toward the east in the middle latitudes . . .' I don't hear a word. Instead, all I 'see' is Subroto Malik (Toto), on top of his bowling mark at the Lower Barnes end, flashing the deadly, shining cherry. He dislodges a pebble from his spikes, starts to— Preggy disrupts the run-up, 'Sapru, where are you looking?'

'Sorry, ma'am . . .'

Dagger's ploy to psych me out seems to be working. Bloody sadist! Somehow, I lumber my way back to the westerlies.

In the classes that follow, neither Chappu's 'Ram Kevat Samvad' nor Eeeeeeee Khalid's 'Lorenz Curve' (Max Lorenz, 1905) fail to find my consideration. In the last class before lunch, Eggy is belting out his customary, daily rant about how unfair and cruel the world is: 'Haaa, I tell you . . . Haaa, what good?' For once, I agree.

Near the school bell, just before the lunch fall-in, Jasmeet Judge, a Junior dorm prefect, is handing out inland letters from home. Subroto walks out of Mucchoo's office and seeing us, says, 'Best of luck for today's game, guys'. My favourite chicken curry is served for lunch, but my stomach has butterflies instead of hunger today. Gancha is rather happy that I'm not eating, so that he can . . .

Susham goes in for the toss and Subroto elects to bat. Vindhya lose an early wicket, and in walks the skipper, wielding his menacing Gray-Nicolls. He's in an atypical frame of mind today—going about thoughtfully constructing his innings, strolling across for a 'harmless' single, settling in before launching his characteristic go-chase-the-leather onslaught. Himalayans, including our 'cheerleaders' sense this calmness before the storm. Only UD is optimistic that 'his boys' will win. Not sure, how . . . but they will. 'They better', he tells himself. The Cricket Cup . . . and then the Cock House!

Subroto is on 7. The next ball is pitched outside the off stump. He square-cuts hard, but uppishly. The ball floats in a parabolic trajectory towards backward point, misses my cupped hands, lands on my right wrist instead, before settling down three inches from my foot. Ten tongues (on the field, excluding the two umpires) and another 108 off-field hurl the choicest expletives in unison. The first hint of doubt crosses UD's mind. In no time, Subroto blasts a swashbuckling 72. Next over, he dances down the wicket, skies the good-length delivery, to be caught at long off. But with Vindhya at 136 for 4, the damage is more than done. They inch to 143 after his departure.

After downing jugs full of nimbu pani, Amarjung and Bhupi Saklani, our two openers walk in. Jung, who'd troubled the scorers in the previous two matches, takes guard. Subroto marks his run-up, choosing the Lower Barnes end (I 'saw' that in Preggy's Class).

First Ball: Subroto Malik, starting his run-up from the sight screen almost . . . nice and easy strides, right arm over the wicket, bowls on off-middle, and through the Jung gate—the bails go up in appeal. Jung turns back and starts walking. Punda, an established slogger (in today's parlance, respectfully referred to as a pinch hitter), is the next man in. The reason he had been promoted to number 3 was that last week, he was simply sensational against Nilagiri.

Second Ball: Lightening-quick, full length, pitched on the middle, maintaining its line—Plumb! 0 for 2. Sajan, the solid in defense, orthodox bat-pad-together, walks in.

Third Ball: near-perfect yorker length, doesn't wait for the bat to come down and disarrays the woodwork. 0 for 3. A stunned Barnes welcomes Paritosh (Pari) to the crease. In the meanwhile, Bhupi has been a silent spectator at the non-striker end, thinking to himself that only if he had faced the first delivery. For Bhupi has been the most successful run-aggregator in Sanawar this season, with a batting average of 60-odd. Pari too is no pushover; he is an accomplished stroke-player and proficient run-getter. If Himalaya is to make something of this chase – at 0 for 3 – these two need to dig in their heels and play the innings of their lives.

Fourth Ball: Again slightly short of a good length, on the middle, but moving away this time. Pari commits to the front foot, makes a feather-touch contact, straight into the anticipating gloves of the keeper. 0 for 4!

Dagger, quietly watching all this while from the stands above, in now on his feet: 'Come on, Sapru!' Bhupi walks down to meet me halfway. 'Relax . . . Concentrate. We can do it!' Now, over the years, starting from Atoms at Lower Barnes, to Colts on New Field, Bhupi and I have had many noteworthy partnerships. In fact, only last season, we came together at the fall of the third wicket to carry our bats and register an empathic win against Nilagiri (Colts). But that was then.

I'm shaking, just a little . . . Solo smiles and I ask him for a leg stump guard, bend on my knee to chalk-mark, realize I'm already wearing both gloves, take one off, mark the leg stump, stand up leaving the removed glove on the matting. Bhanu, in the slip cordon, can't hold himself: 'Want me to help you (with the) bat?' I ignore the derision, wear the other glove, and inspect the set field.

My 'inner voice' repeatedly warns: 'No matter what, remember *front foot*, lad. FRONT FOOT!'

Fifth Ball: Perfect good length, on off-middle . . . me, head down, front foot forward . . . the bat twirls slightly on impact, but safely steers the ball through Bhanu's sleeping legs for two runs. At Lord's, it would have been four. Himalaya is off the mark. Iffy Hasan, the First XI Coach, who is an enormously talented, artistic and stylish batsman himself, cheers, 'Well played, Sapru!' Believe me, I regard that as the highest appreciation I've received in my otherwise not-so-illustrious cricketing career. I survive the sixth ball as well.

The Gods (from the Himalayas) empathize and toss the ball to the benign, kindly and gentle-paced Purewal. Bhupi and I made merry, but are inconsolable that it lasts only for six deliveries. Toto is back. Third ball – short-pitched bouncer on the middle-n-leg; Bhupi goes for a hook, misses; the ball strikes him on his right earlobe (remember it was the pre-helmet age); blood all over; he faints and is carried away on a stretcher.

Toto, passing me on the way to his bowling mark, smiles and says, 'these things happen, yaar.'

After another benevolent six balls from Herbie (Purewal), I'm facing Toto again. This one is short of good length, and really quick. It aviates on impact on the brand new green matting (especially laid for the Himalayans to bat on). I take evasive action, removing my bottom hand from the grip. The ball hits the shoulder of my bat and flies up. Toto, on his follow-through, dives and scoops it millimeters off the ground.

I walk back unhurt.

Dagger loses. Vindhya wins. And Himalaya witnesses a great all-rounder in action, definitely among the best to have ever set foot on Barnes.

**Pankaj Sapru**
Himalaya 1983 | 1976–1983
Senior Management – Petroleum Downstream sector | Travel & Street Photographer | Member – OSS Executive Committee 2019–21 | Vice President – OSS 2021–23

OS Sibling – Brother – Dhiraj Sapru | Himalaya 1985 | 1977–1985

# My First Choice

My parents, younger brother, and I, came to Delhi by flight from Karachi after Partition in 1947. Having no House to stay in, we moved to my grandfather's rented House in Meerut, who had also migrated from Rawalpindi, one month earlier. My father, who was in Civil Aviation, got posted to Safdarjung Airport, Delhi, and got a House inside the Red Fort. We shifted there and in 1949, I got admission in a school in Daryaganj, close to our residence. In late 1951, I cleared the All-India Scholarship Examination. I opted for a boarding school, with The Lawrence School, Sanawar, Simla Hills as my first choice, as two of my cousins were already there. And believe it or not, I got my choice!

In March 1952, my parents and I travelled to Sanawar, and stayed at the Parent's Room. The next morning, we walked down the road going to the Girls' dormitory and arrived at the small ground before Peacestead. I saw some young boys playing cricket. My father called out to one of the boys and told him that I was joining Prep School, and also loved playing cricket. The boys playing were also from Prep School. Later, I learnt that the boy my father had spoken to was Gurpreet Singh from Form II. My father requested him to let me bowl one over. The batsman, who I later learnt was Jaspal Mann, started laughing.

My father's request took me completely by surprise, as I was least prepared to play cricket at the time. I braced myself, took a long run-up, and bowled. Jaspal did not expect a fast ball and missed it. I bowled the second ball. Jaspal missed playing the ball again, and was clean bowled. This completely shocked him. All the boys clapped loudly. Seeing this, Gurpreet, ran to replace Jaspal. My next ball was snicked by Gurpreet. And the fourth ball was crossed the boundary for a four, amidst a lot of cheering. Gurpreet was all smiles, and stared at me with a sarcastic laughter. He was all set to hit me again for a four, or a six—judging by his posture and his laughter. I regained my composure and came running for my fifth ball. And Gurpreet was clean bowled! He could not believe it, as he was the best batsman in the Prep School at that time. The boys nicknamed me 'Fast Bowler', which stuck for quite some time.

We reached the school office and completed all the formalities for admission into Prep School. And guess who I met in the office? None other than Arun Maira, my classmate to be, who was seeking admission in L- III. Our parents got along very well.

I adjusted quite well to Prep School. I remember Ms Rudra, our headmistress, Ms Chatterji, who used to come often, and also Mrs Kemp. I was alright at studies and managed to complete my homework regularly. In the classroom, I could answer almost all the questions asked by the teachers. My English was not too good, as compared to some of the others. So I would sometimes give the answer in Hindi or Punjabi.

After a month and a half in Form II, Ms Rudra decided to promote me to L-III—a double promotion! I packed my bags and moved to Cock Sparrows in BD, located opposite the gymnasium, on the first floor of the double-storey building. Mr Williams was our Housemaster and Mrs Thun (Ma Thun), the matron. Mr S.C. Cowell, the senior master, and Mr Bhupendra Singh lived in the yellow-coloured, double-storey staff building right next to us. Mr Cowell inspired much terror in the school. Mr Gurdip Singh Kalyana from Karnal was our Senior prefect, and was another terror. He freely believed in giving us front-rolls and various other forms of punishments.

I, being a young Sikh boy, did not wear a turban, but plaited my hair. In Prep School, I had no problems, but in BD, Ma Thun did not know how to plait hair. Mrs Sehgal from Prep School and sometimes Mrs Nanda from GD, would come down to teach Ma Thun. And I would also get several warnings from Ma Thun that from the next year onwards, I would have to wear a turban, and that I better learn how to, during my holidays (which I did, from my uncle). Mr Vyas, who was in-charge of the photography club, was so fascinated by my plaits that he took a photograph and displayed it at the 1952 Founder's Day Exhibition. I still have a copy of that photograph with me.

In Cock Sparrows, we had a young Sikh boy, Amarinder Singh, son of the Maharaja of Patiala. Almost every Sunday morning, a smart driver in a white dress would drive up in a white Mercedes Benz with Amarinder's relatives, accompanied by a waiter and a servant, also in white ceremonial dresses. They would bring goodies for Amarinder, including the famous Coca Cola (very popular but a rare commodity in those days), snacks, fruits, juices, etc. After the relatives left, Amarinder would invite us for a royal feast. We really looked forward to Sundays. Also, every morning, a servant would come and help Amarinder to tie his turban, make his bed and polish his shoes, etc. This did not go down well with Mr Cowell or Mr E.G. Carter, our principal, who wanted Amarinder to manage everything on his own.

Next year, from Cock Sparrows on the first floor, we moved to Sparrow Hawks on the ground floor of the same building. And then to Nilagiri House near the Church, the year after, where I stayed till the end of my schooldays.

Life in Sanawar was very busy and interesting. We hardly got any time to ourselves. PT, a quick change and off to breakfast, march to our class with a salute to the memorial, attend classes, a quick lunch, games, followed by a quick bath, prep to complete our homework, dinner, change and off to sleep. And we attended hobby classes twice a week, too.

I joined many hobbies during my years at school—photography, music, dramatics and art. In music, I started by learning the sitar, then moved onto jaltarang, tabla and in the final year, the tabla tarang. Learning the tabla was good as we performed at the House shows and Founders' Day concerts. My classmate, Maninder Bhagat and I, were the two popular tabla players. We really enjoyed playing, especially for the dances by the girls, on various occasions.

In games, I represented the school in boxing, cricket, hockey and football, against Doon School, YPS Patiala and BCS Simla. It was real fun playing against them.

Well, folks, that is a brief account of my days at Sanawar. No regrets; I had a fabulous time from 1952 to 1958, when I finished my Senior Cambridge. Till date, we are a close-knit class (class of 1958), stay connected on WhatsApp and through email, meet often, and remember each other very fondly.

**Brig. Tejpal Singh Chowdhury (Retd.)**
Teju | Nilagiri 1958 | 1952–1958

Conducted Asian Games 1982 Yachting Championships at Mumbai and National Yachting Championships at New Delhi in 1983 and 1984 | Led the first Indian sailing expedition by wind only from UK to Mumbai: 12,000 kms in a thirty-seven-feet yacht *Trishna* (12 October 1984 to 1 February 1985) | Led the first Indian sailing expedition around the world in yacht *Trishna* – 54,000 kms with wind only, without auto pilot, GPS, or SATNAV (28 September 1985 to 10 January 1987) | Led the first millennium sailing expedition from Mumbai to Singapore and back (28 September 1999 to 10 January 2000) | Awarded Ati Vishist Seva Medal on 26 January 1987 for organizing the Around-the-World sailing expedition in yacht *Trishna*.

# Whatever Happened to Mr Ulavi?

Late one Saturday afternoon in mid-September 1947, our precious 'free time' was shattered by the sound of sustained gunfire, which seemed alarmingly close by and coming from down below, on the southwest side of the hill. Within moments, the entire BD (what was left of us) were up on the square pushing, shoving and elbowing for the best vantage point on the parapet wall. However, nothing could be seen down the khud-side or on the road below. We learned shortly afterwards however, that Mr Ulavi's 'convoy' of Muslim employees and their families that had left the hilltop less than an hour before had been ambushed just beyond the sharp bend below Peter Buck's on the Sonwara spur.

Later that same evening, a group of about ten Sikhs shouldering an assortment of firearms appeared from around the corner at the kitchen end of Block 11, and strode brazenly and calmly across the quad, evidently on their way back home to Garkhal. The following day, Mr Ulavi's car (a drop-head limousine of the 1940's) was found abandoned on the roadside near Sonwara. Reportedly, the windscreen was completely shattered, and the hood was in shreds.

For the rest of that year, all sorts of dreadful 'yarns' concerning the fate of Ulavi and his Muslim brethren were swapped around the evening 'pine-bob' fires. Different versions abounded, each one more macabre and bloodcurdling than the one before. The fact is, however, we never really learned what actually happened down the khud-side that day. If any of the staff knew anything more, they never told us. Stories of killings, massacres and atrocities on both sides were rife in those dreadfully troubled times. So, many of us left school in December that year fearing the worst for Mr Ulavi, believing that something terrible had befallen him, his family and all the other school Muslims that left the hilltop on that fateful day.

Here now, some sixty-five years later, following a chance visit to this website, is the true story, verbatim:

My full name is Abdul Haq Alvi, and I am the eldest son of Amir Ahmed Alvi, known at that time as Ulavi. I am not a Sanawarian like you but having lived there for 18 years, I do have nostalgia about Sanawar. We were happy there and were forced to leave. I did not have any pics of Sanawar but you have filled the void. God bless you!

First, hats off to your immaculate memory! My father was known as Ulavi at that time, and it is amazing that you mentioned it on the bakery picture. You are again correct regarding the driver—yes, his name was Mohd. Zubair.

Gurkha troops came to evacuate us from Sanawar. [13 September 1947] Small children and womenfolk were loaded into army trucks and men were told to march to Kalka via Garkhal-Kasauli. Father couldn't walk that far, and he decided to take a car along with the army convoy. The car was fired upon after passing Garkhal [actually the sharp bend in the road below Peter Buck's] and was abandoned there on the road. My father, mother, two sisters, driver Zubair and a bakery employee Sardar [he was very popular with the students and they used to call him 'Brown Sahib'], were loaded into the trucks and reached Kalka safely. I along with three younger brothers and our bakery employees walked to Kalka and were taken to a makeshift refugee camp. Father, Zubair and Sardar were there but not mother and sisters. We were told that they were taken to the railway station and sent to Lahore. Those were indeed, troubled times and we were fortunate that no harm came to us in the camp and later, on the train to Lahore. Sardar Mohinder Singh, a Sikh employee of LRMS bade us farewell when we were leaving. His House was right opposite the Indian Boys' School. We got our primary education in this school.

I was a 3rd year student of Govt. College in Lahore and at age 18, returned home to Sanawar for the summer break. Julian Fernandes [son of master H. 'Fundoo' Fernandes] was also there and needed company for his trips to Garrison Cinema, Kasauli to watch movies. So he asked my father if he could take me and my younger brother, Waheed with him to the cinema. Permission was given and we used to walk on and off to Kasauli with him to watch English movies. Things, however, deteriorated rapidly after August 14 and it was no longer safe to venture outside Sanawar. In fact, as you would have recollected, we used to sleep in your barracks at night. [Ground floor Junior dorms, (Block 12), after it had been vacated by the remnants of Outram and Havelock in July August].

After about a month or so in the camp (at Kalka) we were herded into a train and sent to Lahore. We arrived safely, thanks to the military special train following us carrying Baluch regiment troops. My uncle was already settled in Lahore and my mother and sisters were there with him. So we were spared the agony of searching for them in refugee camps in and around Lahore. After remaining with his brother for some time in Lahore, my father moved to Okara, a small town about 80 miles from Lahore and settled there. He ran a small business there and died in 1969.

I will post more details of my family in my next email. Tell me when you left Sanawar and what have you been doing all these years? Have you visited India/Pakistan after passing out from LRMS? Be my guest and come to Lahore.

**D.V. Boddington**
LRMS Sanawar 1942–1947
April 2011

# Memories, from the Andamans

In writing this account of The Lawrence Military Asylum of the early twentieth century, it is hoped to impress upon the reader the strict methodical principles of both military training and education, and also how that knowledge could be utilized after leaving. Throughout life, practically everyone puts to test the substance of the knowledge acquired during their school days. All in their different spheres of life were trained both physically and mentally to do their best. This was the steam age and you will see from the occupations of the school-leaving boys that many were successfully absorbed in all its various fields.

Admitted in the year 1905, I was thrown in among boys with vintages ranging from 1897 to 1904. The pattern of military routine and education followed by their predecessors was passed on to their successors. Principal The Rev. A.H. Hildesley was in office till about 1912–13, when he retired, and was succeeded by the Rev. G.D. Barne, who in 1922–23, became Bishop of Lahore. Both principals were excellent administrators. The policy of Rev. Barnes was to establish an English public school system, with a military facing.

Yearly, the Rev. Hildesley reminded school-leaving boys of their standard of education and how it could and should be utilized to achieve success. In one instance, he addressed a draft of twenty or thirty boys who had been handpicked for the army, 'You are all sons of soldiers. You have been educated as officers to keep up the tradition of this school and your regiments'.

Here are some of the services for which boys were handpicked: The Regular Army, Army Medical Services, Military Telegraphists, Small Arm Factories, Arsenals, Police, Forest Department, Railways; operating workshops, Maintenance, tea gardens, administration, cotton and woollen mills, leather factories, etc. Those boys whose parents were affluent, sought prospects for their higher studies in law and business.

Admission was granted to the sons and daughters of soldiers serving in India or to those who had been discharged and had settled down in the country. The combined strength of the school was between 500–600 boys and girls. Half in each department., approximately.

The school and staff buildings were situated on a hilltop in a plateau formation. The Girls' Departments being on the higher ground, to the North, and the boys' lower, towards the South. The Church and the residential quarters of the principal and administrative officers – residential quarters of faculty – and the school theatre, which was later utilized as a government training school for teachers, were clustered on higher ground and was in the centre, between Girls' and Boys' Departments. Only one barrack in the Girls' Department was separated from the centre. Known as the Ridge or Norman Hill, it occupied a spur to the southeast of the Girls' Department, two furlongs' walking distance.

Four three-storeyed and one two-storeyed barracks—complete with wash House, cook, House-ration depot, gym, carpenter's shop, band room, armoury were attached to the Boys' Department, which consisted of two three-storeyed barracks on the southern end of the plateau. Disposal areas for both boys and girls were attached to each department. A school House near each department accommodated the entire school and the army instructors and matrons. The girls' section was two and half barracks on the northern, higher-level side.

Playground for the girls was in the barrack compound. The boys had two: upper and lower—some 200 feet lower on the western side.

Sergeant instructors occupied quarters attached to each dormitory.

The division of the school was in companies of between fifty to sixty boys in each: band; A, B, C, D companies. Each company occupied a dormitory in one of the barracks. The dorms were completely furnished army-style, with trestle beds, mattresses, sheets, blankets, pillows with cases, wash bowls, towels, boxes, soaps, toothbrushes, cloth and boots and bottom brushes with clips, hairbrushes and comb and bath brick, and bath tubs. In the bathroom attached to each dorm, there was running water for purposes of ablution, and a farm boiler (fired twice a week for hot water for bathing) and a night-soil room attached to each bathroom.

Two or three hurricane lanterns supplied illumination till 'lights-out'. Much later, gas was installed and each dorm was filled with a 50 candle power mantle. The faculty residential quarters were on the upper rim, within easy walking distance from the centre. A fine network of roads, covered walks and steps covered the entire hill. The layout of the barracks and school rooms today must be the same, though some of the buildings attached to them may not serve the same purpose. The school stewards' stores was alongside the girls' class rooms. It was from here that the daily time gun was fired.

The power magazine was on the west side of the road going up to the Church. The dairy farm, school gardens, water works and tank (swimming pool) were all on the western slope at varying levels. The fixed boundary between the Girls' and Boys' Departments, was a small length of an eight feet thick wall with a door and a bell to attract attention.

The post and telegraph office and the telegraph training school were attached to the Boys' Department. Incoming and outgoing mails were received and dispatched by runners.

The Sgt. instructors played the greatest part in the training of the boys. Except for the schooling period, we were entirely in their charge. Sgt. Major Ricks of the Wiltshire Regiment held the overall charge. Only through him could the principal be approached. He was virtually responsible for the discipline and good behaviour of the entire school, a duty he carried out with military thoroughness. In addition, he was in-charge of the dorm alongside the Boys' Department stores. He took all parades or deputed one of his Sgt. instructors. All ceremonial drills were taught and executed under his charge, care and efficiency of all weapons and equipment, target practice and field firing for practice or competition were all under his charge. His staff covered all the main points from Butts to the final range. There was never an accident.

His school duties were as that of a Quartermaster Sgt. and included the upkeep and maintenance of all clothing, beds, blankets etc., their washing and repairs. The department tailors, cobblers, dhobis and scavengers took their grievances to him.

Bandmaster Rickets had complete charge of the band Room and all wind and reed instruments, bungles and drums.

Sgt. Instructor Cook Napper (unit not known) had complete charge of the ration stand, the receipts and issuing of rations, and preparation of each meal. Scale of rations drawn was 1 lb. bread, 1 lb. meat with bone, 1 lb. veg., 1/5 oz. tea and 2 oz. sugar per head. Extras consisted of 2 oz. ghee, 4 oz. wheat, 1 oz. rice, 4 ozs. treacle milk.

Sgt. Instructor Carpentry – Keeling – Devonshire Regt. – had complete charge of carpenter shop, tools and benches.

Sgt. Instructor-Gym-Costello (Bedfordshire Regt.), was in-charge of all fixtures and movable stock of the gymnasium.

All instructors were thorough in their trades. Leniency was never shown—either in discipline or trade tuition.

Daily, it was the same routine. Reveille at 6 a.m., wash, dress, followed by barrack room fatigues. Making or folding of beds, scrubbing, sweeping, window cleaning, polishing, wash bowls and taps – dorm, wash House and Night-soil room – verandas, two sets of stairs. 7 a.m. Assembly. Roll call – split into (a) and (b) groups. (A) group ceremonial drills (B) group PT 8 a.m. First Breakfast call.

| | |
|---|---|
| Breakfast | 8.10 a.m. |
| Assembly, Church | 8.30 a.m. |
| Class Rooms | 9.00 a.m. |
| First Dinner Call | 1.00 p.m. |
| Dinner | 1.10 p.m. |
| Assembly | 1.50 p.m. |
| Class Rooms | 2.00 p.m. |
| First Supper call | 4.00 p.m. |
| Supper | 4.10 p.m. |

A Sgt. instructor attended each meal parade and collected the all-present report from each company before marching into a meal.

| | |
|---|---|
| Retreat. All outside activities cease | 6.00 p.m. |
| First Post | 8.30 p.m. |
| Tattoo | 9.00 p.m. |
| Lights-out | 9.10 p.m. |

Period from 4 to 6 p.m. Both upper and lower grounds used for six-a-side football or hockey. Two companies to each ground, 25 minutes each way.

Band daily had two hours' instructions and preparation for the following Sunday parade.

Gym in full-swing, displays on parallel and horizontal bars. Trapeze-Foils-Ropes, prepare, walls, vaulting the horse, club swinging and boxing; in the 6 to 8 period, the big boys showed their ability in an inter-company format. The umpiring was very strict and the boxing neat and clean but aggressive. All disputes were settled here by strict observers and 4 oz. gloves. In all these scraps, no quarter was given or taken. Three two-minute rounds, under Queensbury rules. The referee declared the winner – the whole gym was full of excitement and the smaller boys would bet, their 2 oz. bread biscuit being the stake – on the company champions.

In the 4 to 6 p.m. period, time was occupied by the youngsters by playing ball alley against the wall of the gym or carpentry shop, seven-tiles, rounders, baseball (ragball) football, hockey, Tip cat, allies, Tops.

No games were compulsory.

8 p.m., all would make for their dorms to polish up for the next day— that over a yarn, a song or good jokes till the first post. Tattoo, in bed by lights-out and asleep.

The special uniform for Sundays (Church) and all ceremonial occasions was dark blue trousers, and tunic with crimson collar and cuffs. Double-line crimson piping in the tail, with brass buttons. Head wear was a Khaki colonial hat (slouch). For evening, headgear was a dark blue cap with a crimson frontal flash.

For daily wear in summer, Khaki corduroy shorts and in winter, dark blue velveteen shorts, boots, puttees and a blue patrol tunic.

Underwear: grey flannel drawer, vest and grey back shirt.

Each piece of clothing had the owner's school number stamped on it.

Shorts, shirts, vests, drawers, towels, socks were laundered weekly. Sheets and pillowcases fortnightly.

Uniforms and Blue patrols were the responsibility of the owner.

Boots were checked weekly.

The standard meals served only varied with dinner. Breakfast throughout the week, was porridge, 4 oz. bread, 1 oz. ghee, 2 oz. treacle tea.

Supper was 8 oz. bread, 1 oz. ghee, 2 oz. treacle tea.

Dinner on Sundays and Wednesdays: 4 oz. bread, roast meat-veg. Duff (pudding).

Mondays and Thursdays, 4 oz. bread, curry and rice.

Tuesdays and Saturdays, 4 oz. bread, stew.

Fridays: Kedgeree

On Founders' day, we had the same fare as on Sundays with a little colour and taste thrown in, and for supper, an extra bread biscuit or sugarless 2 oz. bun. All practice ceremonial drills were held from 7 a.m. to 8 a.m. daily, except on Sundays.

Half-day Saturday was given to target practice and lectures from field officers on the manual laid down for Mountain Warfare, offensive, defensive and enfilading actions, guerrilla warfare, map reading, ranging finding and other subjects of military value.

Once a month, each company engaged in field firing from ranges of 100 yds. to 500 yds. At 100 yds., Team fired (rapid) five rounds at a target (grouping) 200, 300, 400 yds. At running silhouette and 500 yds. At falling plates. Teams generally consisted of four men.

Once a year, an examination was set by the army on the *Manual of Mountain Warfare* and other items of military knowledge lectured on. Certificates were given to all candidates in their grades of proficiency as passed but 'not so clear', 'tolerably clear' and 'clear'. These certificates held weight both in the army and Voluntary Corps.

In the annual rifle course covering ranges from 100 yds. to 300 yds. and 500 yds., each boy covered the course. From this, the school marksmen were selected also the school 'shot', the boy who scored the largest score. I do not think that this name was recorded on the Founders' Day Prize list, though it carried the most costly prize; in 1912–13 and –14, this honour fell to me. The prizes collected were a three-barrel silver pencil, half Hunter Watch (silver) and a full Hunter (silver). These were presented to me on parade by the Sgt. Major (School). Medals for the winning team of the Sulivan Shield were presented in like manner.

The boys were upgraded on merit to such ranks as Corporal Sergeants and Colour Sergeant. Colour sergeants were the heads of companies and Board sergeant, the head of the band.

Twice or thrice a year, the school took part in army manoeuvres. We would form a side light to the operations conducted by the two main bodies. Our part was to either attack or defend, or hold a given position. Commonly known to the boys as 'sham fights' these were both occasions of fun and reality. Fun was the part where we fired as many blanks as possible, both our own and also those of the troops opposing us. No soldier would fire a blank cartridge, because it affected the condition of his rifle barrel. Reality was, we fulfilled the objective orders.

Every Sunday was a spit and polish occasion without being armed. After breakfast, the band would parade on the flats by the school rooms, nearest to the Church and entertain the boys with music. The opening piece would always be 'Church Cal', followed by a short programme of classical music until the Assembly was sounded. Led by the band, to the strains of Colonel Bogey – or Old Comrades – the boys would march to Church. After Service, a route to march round the back way, and then dinner followed.

Founders' Day was a day apart. No latitude was given before or after it. All preparations from decorating the dining room to running of heats up to the finals was done in the 4 to 6 p.m. period. This is the only occasion the boys carried arms and ammunition to Church. Bandoliers and belts (leather) were polished to reflect like mirrors. After breakfast, there was a general inspection, with the band in attendance. After the inspection, we marched to Church. Church over, we marched back to barracks, when band instruments and arms and ammunition were restored to their proper places. Assembled and marched to the Girls' School room for the distribution of awards and prizes. Dinner at 1 p.m. Sports to which the Girls' Department was always invited. One of the regimental bands would often provide music for the occasion. Prizes were distributed by the General or officer who took the inspection in the morning.

Followed by the 'King'. School trumpeter would sound the Retreat at 6 p.m.. Supper and the day would end.

The efficiency of the band was such that many of the boys were snapped up by regimental bands throughout India. Many also were enrolled from school into the viceroy's and governors' bands. Band Master Rickets was a very hard man to please, but he was extremely proud of his boys, who always put up a perfect performance. After his departure came a succession of band Sergeants.

Though the school timetable allowed a period for carpentry, the greater part of the training took place during the 4 to 6 p.m. period. According to the boys' hobbies, so would be the products turned out. Butterfly and egg collection-boxes of all sizes and shapes—trinket boxes and pencil boxes, beautifully lined and polished. Sgt. Inst. Keeling was proud that such boxes made under his tuition were sent to practically every country in the world.

The School of Telegraphy, providing military telegraphists was abolished in 1912–13.

The general health of the school was reviewed by a medical officer from Kasauli every week. An army compounder attended every morning with medicines and first-aid dressings. A twenty-bed Hospital staffed by a trainer matron and five or six auxiliary nurses (girls undergoing training) took charge of the seriously ill. Generally, there were no patients.

Throughout the year, visitors were regaled with gymnastic displays consisting of figures marching, club swinging, parallel bars, horizontal bars, vaulting the horse, etc. In this, practically the entire school took some part. Special displays were trapeze works and foils, in which the instructor took the leading part.

Easter Holidays. Seven days of practically complete freedom, spent in camp at Daghru or Dogra gorge, halfway between Dharampore and Subathu. This gorge was spanned by Choir Bridge, the stream abounded with freshwater fish and on the hillside, was an abundance of edible berries. The stream was said to be one of the head waters of the River Sutlej. Several meadows on the hillside formed the camp. Several 160-lb. tipi tents and marquees were used as shelters for the night and for protection against inclement weather. Each company had its allotted area and tentage. An open-air cook House was approximately centrally placed. All disposal pits were more than 100 yds outside the camp.

One of the sergeant instructors had the complete charge. All reports of the day were submitted to him and all orders were received from him.

Camp routine was simple. Reveille at 6 a.m. followed by scrub-up and camp cleaning. 7 a.m. inspection followed by breakfast, consisting of 1 lb. bread, ghee, treacle and gunfire (tea without milk and hardly sweetened) 4 p.m. Assembly for bathing. Combined dinner and tea at 6 p.m.. Retreat at 6 p.m. Tattoo and lights-out between 8.30 p.m. and 9 p.m. All reports submitted and freedom till reveille next morning.

The occupations of the boys between 7 a.m. to 4 p.m. varied from cooking halwa, curries, stews, in mud chatties, to hiking, fishing, exploring, visiting, egg collection, raiding, swimming. Boys with catapults would generally bring back a partridge or chickoor; all the boys had a catapult. All the money collected and saved was put to good use at this period. Unlike today, you could purchase a food milking goat for a couple of rupees and a kid for a couple of annas. Fruit in season was forty to fifty huge pears for one anna, apricots, as much as you could carry. Green gages and liquots, free. Figs we had to pay for, as the farmers dried and kept them for home use. The area covered was from Subathu, Dagshai, Barog, Tara Devi. Dinner depended on our ability to make friends with the paharis. If so, corn cakes, figs, curds and honey were always welcome. Never spending more than one piece a day for a gang of three boys for our needs and generally, two pies to settle disputes, for we spoke as lambs but just helped ourselves when unobserved. We avoided violence but if necessary, we resorted to our catapults. We always returned to camp at 4 p.m. hungry.

Christmas holidays lasted twenty-one days. Though spent in school bounds, we had complete freedom. Orphans and those who did not want to go home, numbered fifty to sixty in each department. All messed together, generally in the Girls' Department. Strolled together under charge, danced together in the evenings, held impromptu concerts in which the principal and staff participated, shared our hampers and pocket moneys.

Once a week, we were entertained by the pipers of the Scottish regiment stationed at Kasauli, with their national music and dances.

Time flew till the reopening of the School. This was in the Rev. Hildesley era.

On the educational side, the standard was extremely high for those days. Though the subjects were common to the syllabus, the faculty always taught beyond the limit prescribed. In mathematics, arithmetic, algebra, Euclid mensuration, geometry and trigonometry. Later, Euclid and mensuration were discontinued, but we always had to refer to them.

In English, composition and grammar in all their fields, from essays to journalism.

English Literature, too, covered a very large number of prose and poetry items as *Ulysses* and Cyclops from *The Odyssey*, The Trojan war from *The Iliad* and selections from Samuel Johnson, Wordsworth, Longfellow, Lamb, Shelly, Keats, Byron etc., etc.

Urdu: *Tales from Arabian Nights* and Daniel Defoe's *Robinson Crusoe* (unabridged).

Scriptures: One book of the Old Testament and one of the New Testament, plus certain Church rituals.

General Knowledge covered a vast field of practical knowledge, such as botany and biology (elementary), physics and chemistry (elementary), surveying and triangulation, topography and map reading.

History: British and Indian in particular, and a look-see into Greek and Roman.

Geography: British Isles and Commonwealth, including India, in particular, and the World in general. This was followed up to about the first half of 1915, when the complete set of textbooks were changed. The new books dwelt more on the commercial side.

Now to bring back to memory some of the faculty for whom I still cherish regard.

Kindergarten Mistress Miss Teal. Her patience, kindness and humour; discipline, without being whacked, and encouragement.

Mr Gaskell, Headmaster, Boys' School. Tall, thin, slightly balding with a nasal accent. A fine administrator and good disciplinarian. One who looked for perfection in his staff. He was himself a fine vocalist, pianist and organist.

Mr Rogers, First Assistant Master. Middle-aged, tall, robust, curt of manner and crisp of speech. A gifted teacher bestowing individual attention to each and every pupil and being rewarded with their finest performance in all exams. Taught his pupils the value of self-assurance.

Munshi Ram, Urdu Teacher. A short, squat, bow-legged individual, unassuming but very firm—a thorough scholar of Persian and Sanskrit. Never left anything to chance, but taught his students to read, translate and write anything written in legible Urdu. Corrected everything with a smile and encouragement. Many passed with honours in Urdu.

Mr Smith, Professor, Maths. Primed us with practical knowledge which came handy in after years.

Mr Prince, in the fields of botany and biology, physics and chemistry, taught us much put to use in after life without having to undergo special training.

Messrs Brandon and Britain. Both were temporary teachers but touring encyclopaedias. Much-travelled, both were excellent teachers with a thorough knowledge of humanity. Britain summarized world conditions and happenings of the day – the why and wherefore – and the pros and cons of areas on a basis of religious culture. Christian Europe, Islam Middle East, Hindu India and Buddhist China and Japan, with their wars and treaties. Brandon outlined Greek, Roman and Ottoman histories.

It is to these members of the faculty I render thanks for teaching us how others lived—and how much we would have to go through in meeting peoples of other nations if we had no inkling of their customs and culture. Today, I admire at their understanding and far-sightedness. I am able to appreciate the wealth of knowledge imparted to me more now than when I was unfledged.

The school library was attached to the boys' dining hall. Free to all from 6 p.m. to 8 p.m. and only the boy NCO's from 8 to 9 p.m. Indoor games varied from Ludo, dominoes, draughts for the young ones to chess for the bigger boys. Chess and draughts tournaments were common and each company had its champion, inter-company championship games were keenly followed and criticized.

The selection of books, poetry, history, fiction ranged from Lytton and McCauley to Ganpat, Sir Walter Scott, Marie Corelli, Baroness Orczy, Alexander Dumas, Stevenson, Defoe, Ballantyre, A.G. Hintz, Jules Verne, Shakespeare, Dryden, Byron, Dickens, Chaucer, Longello; in fact, it contained all the books worth reading for growing boys. A twenty-six-volume *British Encyclopaedia* and *Pears Encyclopaedia* were always handy. Han Anderson's and *Grimm's Fairy Tales*, *Tales from Arabian Nights* for the youngsters. During the rains, the library was best occupied.

I will not attempt to describe the Rev. Barnes era. There are many who are thoroughly acquainted with it who could give a good description. Nor will I attempt to convey to you the difference in the outlook of school-leaving boys of those periods.

Perhaps many of you will ask, what experience and knowledge did I gain from my education and military training to face the world and hard facts? This I do say that Messrs Prince and Smith impressed upon us that further studies were necessary and Messrs Brandon and Britain, that the world was full of humans, differing in culture, language and religion, that to get along with them, you had to understand them.

Lastly, the day before leaving the school the School Sgt. Major Ricks, when bidding us goodbye, said, 'Never underestimate your tuition or your abilities'. Never did I think that someday I would have to put both to the test in a Japanese POW Camp.

How many school-leaving boys are so informed and so advised prior to their departure? From the cradle to the grave, we are every day learning something and also forgetting. There is no limit to learning. Can the method of tuition keep pace with that of increasing knowledge and science?

**Source and Acknowledgement:** *The Sanawarian* (December 1972)

# Heady's Jeep

It all started at our Annual Camps at Sarahan. Heady (Shomie Ranjan Das), sitting around the bonfire, boasted of his boarding school (in Doon) escapades, including 'borrowing' his Headmaster's jeep. Ahhh, the gauntlet had been thrown, the challenge accepted, and the seed of a glorious adventure planted – by none other than our very own headmaster. The bravest of the brave, the most competent drivers and navigators who could guide the way using but a few stars in the cloudy sky were shortlisted. Post a rigorous selection process, the Four Musketeers soon got to work— conceiving of all imaginable scenarios and devising the perfect plan. Even the righteousness of Heady's daughter, Shiraz, was compromised to obtain critical information – the most important question – 'Where does he keep the keys to the jeep?'

The Plan was simple. Roll jeep downhill well past Mucchoo's House (very, very important). Start jeep. Drive to nearest town. Grab a beer. Head back. DO NOT, repeat, DO NOT GET CAUGHT. Q.E.D.

The Reality, however was that Driver #1 (self-appointed), Sanjeeva, took to the wheel and the three minions pushed the jeep silently past Tiger's Den (Mucchoo's House). A rough start, followed by squealing tyres around each bend, which the co-passengers braved without panicking, though holding on tightly to whatever they could. Sanjeeva stormed into Dharampur at 2 a.m., to find every shop closed. Change in plan: we head to Parwanoo. Driver #2 Farokh takes over. The co-passengers are now gripping on for dear life as the menacing sound of gritty, grinding gears grows louder, while Farokh brags of his father's rallying skills. Shutters in Parwanoo are down, too. Alas, and definitely by divine intervention, no beer tonight. The drive back with Driver #3, Shome, is somewhat smoother, other than the knuckles (of six hands) shining bright-white under every passing vehicle's lights, because Driver #3 insists on turning his head around when he decides to speak—which is far too often for comfort. Driver shift-change, our last hope, Driver #4, Hanut. Now, he is adept at driving on the right-hand side of the road (bloody firangi). All faces (including Hanut's) turn pure white, drained of any and all colour. No chitter-chatter, except for the loud echo of 'polite' reminders to stay on the 'right' side of the road. The roar of the jeep is deafening in the still of the night as we rattle past familiar staff houses and park a millimetre short of Heady's front yard hedge. Mission accomplished, or so we think.

A week passed before the Four Musketeers were summoned to Heady's office. Knowing what was in store, we brainily wore a couple of extra pairs of underwear, which, in our view, was the second-best decision of that month. The 'earned' caning, suspensions and stripping of prefect-ship followed. However, how we were found out remains a mystery to this day. Suspicions remain, but memories have (thankfully) faded.

A memorable event we enjoyed talking about for years – actually, still do – it almost certainly triggered a sense of adventure in our consciousness . . . more than we realized then. Sanjeeva and Shome (who owns a Jeep Wrangler today) went on to do serious off-roading, flying, parachuting; Farokh followed in his father's footsteps and got into car rallying; Hanut is doing his own brand of the crazy in Colorado – skiing and off-roading in his Land Rover . . .

This prank, as with everything Sanawar, left an inedible mark on our lives.

Never Give In . . .

**Hanut Ewari**
Nilagiri 1984 | 1975–1984

OS Siblings – Sister – Feroz (Ewari) Gujral | Nilagiri 1982 | 1976–1982
          Sister – Anisha Ewari | Nilagiri 1987 | 1979–1987

**Suranjan Shome**
Bong | Himalaya 1984 | 1980–1984

# Confessions of a (Non-)Hobbyist

I joined Prep School in 1958. After two months, I was sent to L-III in Senior School, where I encountered art as a subject, soon earning the dubious distinction of securing an 'F' in the final exams. How I managed that is a story for another day, but when I took the results home, my mother and sister laughed their guts out. Be that as it may, Mr Bhalerao saw to it that I do not expend my energy on art anymore.

So now what? Next day, while walking up Jacob's ladder from Barnes, I passed the band House and saw a 'welcoming' Khurmani (apricot) tree within the precincts. It would be band! Many a Vindhyan had walked this path before. On my first visit, Mr Pillai, the band Master handed me a bugle to blow, like others were devotedly doing. After a few failed attempts ending in blowing hot air, interspersed with occasional weird sounds, I contemplated how tossing pebbles in the air and catching them in the funnel of the bugle would be far more interesting. That became my favourite distraction for the next few weeks. Occasionally, a real tiny pebble would make its way around the bend of the bugle and get lodged there. This experiment went on merrily undetected till a significant number of bugles had developed that uncharacteristic rattle. One day, I was at the swimming pool and saw Mr Pillai purposefully advancing towards me. He hauled me by the ear, delivered a few swift kicks, and admonished me to never again come down to the band House, not even for the Khurmanis. Till today, I do not know who had tattled.

Anyway, never one to lose heart, my next stopover was Carpentry. In the first hour itself, I fathomed that woodwork was not my kettle of fish, but I stuck around as I was able to stay out of trouble. Until a week later, when I was particularly bored, and ran a saw over my shoe, damaging it irreparably. Now in those days, shoes, like most other belongings, were issued by the school and these ill-fitting brogues had to be accounted for. Mr Ward, stroking his goatee, suggested I try my hand at some other hobby.

Major Som Dutt, [the] headmaster, one morning during Assembly, expounded his thoughts that we should develop social skills. He reasoned that later in life, if we were at a social gathering and were asked to participate, we very well couldn't roll up the carpet and rearrange the furniture and perform calisthenics or gymnastics. He suggested that the morning hours must be devoted to learning how to sing or play musical instruments (for the boys), and Indian classical dance for the girls. For us juniors, it was a welcome thought, (skipping the 6.30 a.m. PT under the ever-watchful eye of Mr Jagdish Ram, an undefeated Services heavyweight boxing champion. He was an absolute stickler for discipline and ensured PT took place every morning, come hail or sunshine. One morning, it was snowing lightly and we were sure that Mr Jagdish Ram would find it in his heart to cancel PT. No such thing happened. The only concession made was to allow us a cardigan over our vest. However, the idea was shot down by the seniors, who insisted that physical fitness was integral to overall development.

By now I was in U-IV, and taking Major Som Dutt's thought forward, decided it was time to try out an Indian classical instrument. I approached Mr Thakkar, the paan-chewing, moustachioed guru. 'Sir, I think I'd like to learn to play the *esraj*'. He stared at me in part bewilderment, part exasperation. I explained that my mother played both the *sitar* and the *esraj*. He was adequately impressed and took me under his wing. Time elapsed . . . I started showing signs of settling down . . . maybe I had found my true calling. I was selected to play in the Founders' orchestra. Chuffed! The following Monday, my prefect told me to get a haircut. In those days, you did what you were told. Else, you booked a seat for the prefect's 'tonight-show', which at times, continued well past lights-out. So I made my way to Naapi's, famous for his Topi-cut. There was an unusually long queue—maybe all the prefects were being 'watchful' that week. Anyway, the inordinate wait resulted in me missing Music practice. Next day, Mr Thakkar pulled me up and asked why I hadn't turned up for practice. I explained my predicament (and about my prefect). His next question was, 'What is more important, your haircut or music?' In all honesty and after considering all pros and cons, I replied, 'Sir, haircut'. That was the end of my tryst with Indian classical music.

After a brief stint with the piano, the sweet, motherly lady (I can't remember her name anymore) encouraged me to test my true talent elsewhere. I had just one hobby left to try my hand at. So, next afternoon, I turned up at the Crafts department. Displaying steel-like resolve, I refrained from exhibiting my expressive talent and found contentment in pounding waste to allow others to express themselves at papier-mâché. This was truly my calling—chatting with guys and chicks, and pounding away at paper to glory . . .

NEVER GIVE IN!

**Rakesh Sood**
Vindhya 1965 | 1958–1965

OS Sibling – Sister – Manju Sood | Vindhya 1961 | 1958–1961

OS Children – Daughter – Mansi Sood | Vindhya 1997 | 1988–1997
Daughter – Meghla Sood | Vindhya 1999 | 1992–1999

# Thank You Sanawar

I joined Sanawar in the mid-term of 1949 and was promptly quarantined for observation. On release, I was put in Blue House (later Nilagiri) with Mr Couzen as the Housemaster. The Principal was Mr Carter, the vice principal Mr Wiles and the headmistress Mrs Carter. Mr Cowell was the senior master and Mrs Sircar was in-charge of Prep School. The Head Boy was D.I.R. Mackintosh, the Head Girl Deserie Kauferauth and the school was all of forty-nine boys and ten girls.

There was no formal ragging but I was initiated into the House with an apple-pie bed (the under sheet doubled up and filled with stinging nettles). I did not know how to tie putties or march, so I spent hours on the Quad learning to do so, to the general merriment of everyone. It was a tough and very active life except the 'rest' period after lunch. The school authorities believed that the 'Devil found work for idle hands to do'. We did everything by the bugle and by marching.

We are lucky in that we had wonderfully dedicated staff who often took extra classes, sacrificing their Sundays. I still remember Kempi's 'pot so cal'; Couzen's 'Henry, Henry Willi, Ste'; Mrs Coombes and her long walks pointing out the hills, valleys, saddles etc.; Mr. Om Prakash and Ms Chatterjee. Sammy Cowell was a strict disciplinarian—he once had us close our boxes after inspection and run up to the Quad till we did it fast enough for his liking. He used to make surprise 'visits' at night to check whether the lights were actually switched off and we were in bed. Mr Kemp also made visits and regaled us with his dog, Paddy's tricks.

The years in school were truly formative, not just for me but for the school itself, which grew and prospered. We got our first lot of Indian staff and what a great lot they were: Vyas, Salim K., Kate, Rawat, Rathin Mitra. So many eventful moments, it is impossible to remember or relate them all—Dugroo Picnics, the hikes to Gurkha Fort, the raids for bhuttas, the walk-downs to 'Drinkies', the water spring below Barnes used for wash-ups and brushing our teeth during days of acute water shortage, the khud fires which we fought so bravely . . . I could go on and on.

The BCS Match in 1952, at BCS. They batted first and piled up a huge score. Our batting failed miserably, till Ratan Kaul and I, at number 11 came together at 50 for 9. We batted, or rather, he batted and I stonewalled for three hours till we got to 100, when Rotty got carried away, and got out. Following on, I was promoted to open along with Rotty. We did a repeat performance till lunch. The sledging we faced would have put the Aussies to shame. The BCS boys and their staff were not amused and threatened to call off the match and all future fixtures. Seeing how bad things were, our coach, Mr Kemp, asked us to go and hit out. We did and how, but lost our wickets in the process, and the match. Ironically, the skies opened up shortly thereafter. To cheer us up, Kempi took us all to ice-cream at Quality. He must have phoned the school, because the entire school had lined up from the bakery onwards, to cheer the 'conquering' heroes. We were a proud bunch!

At boxing, I was once fighting Aditya Nehru, when the elastic of his shorts came loose. He instinctively dropped his hands (to hold onto his shorts) and I impulsively got in a few punches. Aditya was not amused.

Our social service included clearing the khud so that the Jacob's Ladder to Barnes could be built. We boys also built Leisure, to be then informed that it was only for the girls. We decided to declare a boycott of the girls. No boy was to speak to any girl, be it his sister or classmate. This carried on for a long time, much to the amusement of the staff.

It was decided to divide the two Houses into four. The entire BD was lined up on the Quad and Housemasters went around turn-by-turn, choosing their wards. Mr Vyas picked me among others and so was born Vindhya, with Vyas Sahib as our Housemaster. I became the school prefect and Ashok Bhatia, the House prefect. We were the proud winners of the Cock House, in both the Boys and Girls School, and we also won the Gen. Cariappa Cup. As always, the girls were favoured. Indu carried the Cup as I stood alongside.

Hobbies were rather limited. There was a photography club, but they were not very active. We learnt printing, went for hikes and collected butterflies. Of course, there were the girl-boy crushes, sometimes involving the younger staff members, too (no names). The Sanawar 'Shuffle' was invented at Socials, as none of us were great dancers and deployed the 'box step' – 1,2,3,4, shuffle – for every tune that played. It earned me my nickname, 'Eddi Chuk', as I dragged my heels on the dance floor. Thank God it was short-lived.

And then, there was the non-teaching staff, without whom Sanawar would not have been. The Robins, Mastoos, Nankoos, Bansis, Nappis, Hansrajs, Girdharis and countless others who looked after us and the school.

To end, I will say that my years in school have left an indelible mark on me and I owe a hell of a lot to Sanawar. I was very lucky to have been a member of the best school of all. Thank you, my teachers, thank you, my schoolmates, thank you, Sanawar!

**Vikram Soni**
Vindhya 1952 | 1949–1952
Tea Planter | Factory Manager IWP Barielly | Chief Executive Officer, Waldies Ltd. | President (Pigments) Gillanders Arbuthnot | Retired since 1995

OS Children – Daughter – Geetanjali Soni | Nilagiri 1983 | 1976–1977

# The Roof Climbers

When and how this became a favourite pastime on Sunday evenings, memory fails to recall.

In the few hours before Sunday supper, Sanawar is at its quietest. Teachers in their respective homes having a drink, soaking in the peace before the chaotic upcoming week. Kids busy with the Sunday movie or for the few hours of free time away from the hawk eyes of teachers, doing whatever they want, mostly within the confines of the dorms. This was a tad tame for Sandy Chand, who suggested that we go roof climbing. A few of us 'bored' ones thought it was a brilliant idea and went looking for the closest roof to conquer. We started off by scaling the GD outside-bathroom roof. One tiny roof, a mere ten or twelve feet off the ground, but a thrilling achievement for us.

Of the initial larger group, the bug stayed on with the five – Sandy, Aarti, Surabs, Pulli and me. Discussing which roof to scale and how to pull it off without being caught, was an adrenaline rush we thrived on. Name of our club? I forget. However, this became a weekly pastime. Sunday movies could not compete with this forbidden activity layered with the excitement of evasive tactics to be taken to avoid being caught. Strategic planning usually commenced mid-week, debating which roof to climb, based on how popular the Sunday movie would be. We boiled it down to a science. First, we would push and pull each other up to the lowest accessible point of the roof to be conquered. After establishing that we were off the ground and on the prohibited territory, came the climb. We thought we were no less then Edmund Hillary, off to conquer Everest. Hook our fingers under the metal pattis covering the nails for grip, creeping up slowly to ensure the nails don't come off. Sandy would lead the way, shushing us, telling us when to duck and stay still to avoid being seen, figuring the best approach to the top, while Aarti or I would bring up the rear, to catch any one of us slip-sliding down (a common enough occurrence). Within a few weeks, we had covered pretty much all the nearby roofs.

Having scaled the Art Room and its environs, our eyes were now set on Parker Hall, the old GD Dining Hall, which is now the library. This was a challenge we relished; with an open sightline high above the ground, on offer was a droolworthy view. So, off we went on a Sunday evening shortly before the end of term. Slips, scrapes, halfway up, recalibrate—no way to reach the top this way, back down, start at another point, too high cannot do it, metal patti loose, coming off the roof, try another route, pulling, pushing each other; we were finally atop. Giddy with laughter and delight, we basked in the 360-degree view. Was that Simla we could see in the distance or just snowclad peaks far away?

'GET DOWN HERE IMMEDIATELY!'

A loud, angry bellow cut us to the core. Shoot, it was Heady (Shomie Das), quivering with anger. He was going to tell our parents and we are going to be expelled. These thoughts raced through our heads as we fearfully scrambled down from our latest conquest (it probably scared the living daylights out of Heady, to see us slipping in our haste to come down).

What bumbling luck, to get caught by none other than Heady. We thought we were done for. Quaking in our boots, we lined up before him in the covered passage, fearing what was to come next. Heady was yelling in a thunderous rage, but my terrified mind was racing with thoughts of 'which school will take me in just for U-VI?'; 'my parents are going to slaughter me, more so for being irresponsible enough to take my younger sister along' etc. First in line, I could not comprehend Heady's order over my frenzied thoughts until it was shouted one more time. 'Bend down!' Without registering what it meant, I did so. WHACK! a hard slap on the tush. Phew! Heady was not going to kill us. In shock, a giggle escaped me, the other four followed suit (typical of girls and giggles, always a chain reaction). Everyone took their slaps and off we ran to the dorms with palpable relief. Winter layers of thermals did defray the intensity of the hurt we should have experienced.

At the end-of-term House party, Heady approached us dancing culprits and told us how his soul almost left his body when the Beraji's from CDH notified him of five girls perched atop the Parker Hall roof. He had run all the way from his House, fearing the worst. This was definitely not on his or the school's agenda. Heady asked if he had hit us too hard. Maybe he meant to apologize, after all, a few years ago (again led by Sandy) we had successfully marched to Heady's House to get him to outlaw spanking girls, but me, the genius, responded with, 'No, Sir, barely felt it'. Heady was dumbfounded, 'Maybe I should punish you, after all'. Before my wise mouth could respond with another imprudent remark, multiple feet bored into mine simultaneously. Sandy, the smart one, responded, 'No Sir, we promise not to do it again'.

Heady's immense relief at not having five dead or seriously injured girls, meant we escaped with simply a warning, a somewhat tender tush, roofs scaled, incredible memories, the badge of honour of being spanked by none other than Heady himself, and the end to our roof-climbing expeditions. Those were the days, my friends . . .

**Suishta Saigal**
Siwalik 1983 | 1973–1983

OS Siblings – Sister – Surabhi Saigal | Saltie | Siwalik 1985 | 1974–1985
Brother – Sudanshu Saigal | Panther | Siwalik 1988 | 1980–1986

# A Leopard in Sanawar

I was just seven when I joined school in 1951. Back then, the school had only two Houses—Nilagiri and Himalaya. The following year, these were split up with some from Himalaya being moved to Vindhya, while half of us from Nilagiri went to Siwalik. Luckily, I remained in Nilagiri, as Blue was, and remains, my favourite colour. We Nilagirians were on the ground-floor dorm of PD.

In those days, it was the school policy that during the short summer break, students were not allowed to leave the Simla Hills. So during my first summer hols, my father took leave and we spent the time in Mashobra and Simla. Since my grandparents from both sides and my parents had lived in Simla for decades, they were essentially Simla walas. Thus, when my grandfather retired, he took a cottage at the Kasauli Club every summer. Hence, during summer hols in my second year at school (1952), I simply moved across Garkhal to Kasauli.

As I remember, it was a hot summer night in June that year, quite soon after we had returned to school from the summer hols. Our Housemistress came around the dorm at bedtime. She stood gazing out of the window North towards Simla (which was behind the high Ridgeline). Some of the more curious boys also gathered around her. She pointed to a hillside about three or four ridges away, where there was a small glow. 'Look! That's a forest fire,' she said, 'I hope it doesn't spread to Sanawar.' As last words go, these were destined to become one of the more memorable ones.

It must have been at about 4 a.m. when there was an ear-splitting pounding on our main door, which was towards the south of the building. Uppal (if I remember correctly) was the tallest among us eight-year-olds and his bed was near the door. While many of the boys were apprehensive, he unhesitatingly, in true Sanawarian spirit, got onto a stool and undid the latch. Since I had been holding the stool, I happened to be right behind him. We peeped out of the door and a few others, too, followed suit. In that brief moment, I glimpsed the unmistakable spotted tail and hindquarters of a leopard going down towards the bogs. Then we moved quickly back inside and Uppal hurried to latch the door.

At four in the morning, it should have been pitch dark. But instead, I vividly recall that there was a peculiar amber glow. As we turned back from the door, the reason for that unusual light became clear. The whole hillside opposite was ablaze!

The forest fire from three or four ridges away had crossed the intervening hills and was now burning fiercely on the ridge directly facing us. As we watched transfixed, we saw some dark lines eroding into the fire. The housemistress, who had come down to the dorm again, said, 'See those dark lines—that must be where the fire-fighters are fighting the blaze.' In fact, as I learnt afterwards, all the neighbouring fire brigades as well as the Army Garrisons of Subathu, Dagshai and Kasauli had been mobilized to fight the fire. Our BD boys and most of the school staff, including masters, were also activated to clear away any grass and foliage from the fire lanes that had been created around the school. Teams of younger students with water buckets stood by to douse any embers that may leap across the fire lane. We PD guys could only look on wistfully, longing to be part of the action in combating the blaze.

By mid-morning, victory had been declared over that massive fire! But after the flames had been put out, all that remained of what had once been a verdant pine forest were just blackened tree trunks and a soot-black forest floor. It was such a depressing scene! Nevertheless, the event had indeed been a fine practical lesson on fighting forest fires. Perhaps Australia and California could draw some lessons!

In hindsight, I realize that the leopard which we had spotted must have been terrified of the flames and had probably taken refuge within the safety of our school campus. Therefore, over the next few days, school work was briefly suspended as the staff grappled with the fact that a leopard was on the prowl in our vicinity; also due to the aftermath of the forest fire. Our freedom to move around was curtailed severely. We could only move in groups and mostly only when escorted by an adult. During all those days, Mr Carter, [the] headmaster, went around the school several times a day—I suppose, to reassure everyone. I don't know about the girls (I still don't!) but we boys did not need reassuring. In fact, most of us eagerly looked forward to the leopard appearing near us again. How thrilling would that be! But we learnt that some of the masters had been sitting up in a *machaan* for several nights, probably with a goat as bait. Disappointingly, in only a few days, Mr T.C. Kemp, the chemistry teacher, succeeded in shooting down the leopard.

But those days before the leopard had been shot were rather fun. Many of our parents, who were spending the summer in the hills, were allowed to come and see their wards. Charlie, the *mithai wala*, made roaring business as each parent visit was especially sweet for all friends and Housemates. I got doubly lucky because, apart from the 'sweet' visit of my parents, I got to spend a weekend in Kasauli. It was there that I learnt that the army garrisons had been called out for fire-fighting on that night. Then all too soon, the school overcame the disruption with characteristic Sanawarian efficiency and life returned to its humdrum normal.

Some ten days later, the rains came and life sprang forth again from the burnt trees and the forest became lush green once more.

## Maj. Gen. Pushpendra Singh
Pushi and Jotan | Nilagiri 1959 | 1951–1952
GOC MPB&O Area – Rescue and Relief operations in Orissa Super Cyclone 1999 |DG Disaster Management, Govt of MP | Authored forty-nine published monographs and middles | *Handbook for Earthquake-resistant Construction*, 2003 | *The Hawk Hunters – Banda Bahadur's liberation of East Punjab from the Mughals* (Leadstart Publishers, 2015) | *Securing India's Strategic Space*, (KW Publishers, 2019)

# One Hundred and Twenty-Five Years

It wasn't long after I had taken over as Headmaster of The Lawrence School, Sanawar, that I began to realize how all-embracing the vision of the Founder, Sir Henry Lawrence, had been when he created in Sanawar—an institution to provide a refuge and an asylum for the underprivileged children, whether of mixed parentage or not, of British other ranks serving in India. And that vision, implemented through the years, has continued to provide, though in different forms, that same fostering care to the children of today; for while Sanawarians – post 1947 – are not the deprived persons of yesterday, in so far as the status and means of their parents are concerned, they too – not all, but far too many of them to justify complacent thinking – find in Sanawar that refuge and sense of family, which the busy lives their parents lead, deny them in their own homes.

Again, the threads of tradition and history, the patronage – Royal and Viceregal, the deep imprint of past personalities; in particular, that of Bishop Barne; the calibre of boards of administration, composed as they were, later, of the principal staff officers at army headquarters, under the chairmanship of the Commander-in-Chief himself – left the legacy of dedicated interest in the welfare of the children, so ably continued today by the Govt. of India and the board of governors nominated by it.

These, in essence – the vision and the implementation thereof – constitute the mystic of Sanawar, which links the Sanawar of today with the strange shades of a contrasting past, the sense of belonging and being cared for, which enables very few people to walk the same paths on this lovely hilltop, as their predecessors, with gaiety and high spirits, gallant and unafraid.

And it is by virtue of that same mystic that old Sanawarians, whether pre- or post-1947, revisiting the school, find themselves to be instantly at home.

I could not conclude better than by quoting from a letter written by a post-'47 Sanawarian, which exemplifies what someone said, 'The children don't think of the history of the school, they feel it'.

The year draws to its close—and it is with mixed feeling of regret and pride that I write this. Regret at having at last to say goodbye to my school among the whispering pines and rainbow-hued hillsides, and pride at having had the honour to live and learn for many years in this wonderful place.

Some of us who are leaving Sanawar this year, feel as if we will be leaving a part of ourselves behind. We have yet to discover that mysterious, magnetic power Sanawar possesses, which binds both children and staff to it.

Perhaps that power has been handed down the years; perhaps it is present in the buildings, in the wind that blows across it, but wherever it is, it always affects all Sanawarians.

And we look out of the window; we notice the leaves are changing their tints, there is a cold spell in the air. Soon, winter with its gusts of wind, its snow and clouds will descend upon Sanawar, and some of us will have left for over, to depart to another sphere of life.

With reminiscence, I recall my early days here, five years ago, and I often wish I could relive those days all over again. No matter where we go, what we do, Sanawar will always remain a poignant memory with us, as fresh and as lovely as ever.

Rina Charan Singh

**Major R. Som Dutt**
Headmaster 1956–1970

*Source & Acknowledgement : Souvenir Brochure 1847-1972*

# Let's Conserve Energy

Bongo, Navdeep Kindra (V-82) from Bhopal and I were Siamese twins – born on the same day (22 February), we joined Sanawar on the same day in 1972, in the same House (Vindhya—we occupied adjacent beds for nearly a decade), in the same Section Form I B, all the way to Upper VI B, (even in L-IV/U-VI when they segregated us first by academic excellence and then into the science stream), we were always together, even choosing the same hobbies. After being kicked out from Cheru's Sculpture, Bhale's Art, Sattu's Carpentry, Sudha Arora's Ceramics, to finally roost in Attri's Poultry farm . . . needless to say, we always got into trouble together.

It was the first day of PT in the first term in 1979. PT followed by the mandatory Hodson's Long-back. Bongo has a thought, 'Oye, let's conserve energy'. I was perplexed, 'Conserve energy?' Sounds interesting, but a voice within is warning me that nothing that comes out of Bongo's brain is ever kosher. I allow my wild side to prevail, and ask, 'How?' Bongo explains, 'Why go the long way? Let's do it like this: we start last, run slowly and remain behind . . . then, we climb Charlie's slope to Birdwood, get to Chapel, and via the swimming pool, down to the Last Bend; we pretend that we are panting and hold on to our stomachs pretending we have a stitch. Voila, lots of energy saved!'

So, while the 'unfortunate' were running past Moti's, Bongo and I reached Birdwood, only to discover seven more energy conservationists there with the same intent.

Shortly after, we hear the most dreaded words, 'Oye, Mucchoo', just as in the Phantom comics, where the message is relayed with the help of jungle drums, from one ear to the next. Ahh, those pre-GPS times, when there was no way of knowing where Mr B. Singh was coming from or going to. We scooted in all directions. However, with limited latitude, most of us hid behind one of the many pillars in the corridor below Barne Hall, with our eyes darting in all directions to successfully intercept the incoming torpedo. Pin-drop silence! The crows and sparrows too fell silent . . . just the wind gushing, making our haunches stand up. Then we hear the words, 'Heeee YOU, hiding behind the pillar . . . Step forward!'

Unluckily, Ranjit Rawlley's (V-83) left white toe was popping out from behind one of the pillars. But, sure enough, eight of us stepped forward. Despite being safe (hidden behind huge pillars), each one of us thought that Mucchoo was calling out to him. Bongo, who is behind me, thinks only I have been caught and so he continues to hide. His logic is simple and straightforward: 'Why should two of us get punished when only one can take the blame?'

We were made to line up in front of the school bell, facing the school office (bearings important, for what is to follow). The slaps commenced. Two for each person, delivered with time-honoured one-liners, 'Heee, you good for nothing'; 'Heee you, utter disgrace to society'; 'Heee, you guttersnipe'; 'Heee, you misguided humourist'—not one insult was repeated; like a social security number to carry to one's grave: 'Here lies Bhanu Virmani, the root of all pandemonium' and more.

In the meanwhile, while the slaps were getting more intense (and the one-liners more colourful), Bongo realises that he cannot continue hiding for long and makes a dash from behind the pillar, through Hassan's history classroom (adjacent to Soli's geography classroom), jumps out of the rear window to head towards the post office. Mucchoo sees a white shirt flash past, 'WHO IS THAT? LAD, COME BACK!' Bongo is gliding past Birdwood Pans with reflections of freedom flooding his mind: 'I am the Monarch Butterfly, lazily fluttering in the summer breeze . . . daintily from flower to flower, sipping the nectar of life'. At that very moment, Mucchoo has finished with my quota and is about to take a step forward to 'greet' the next guy . . . when that fleeting white shirt recurs. Mucchoo turns to me (again), 'Heee, Bhanu, who was that?' Two more slaps! 'Heee, Bhanu, who was that?' and more slaps. Hearing my name from behind Mrs Channa's classroom, Bongo knew his Nelson Mandela moment was not to be. So, he abandons his escape, runs past the post office, the lily pond and comes and stands behind Mucchoo.

Mucchoo (still facing Heady's House), continues to slap me and asks, 'Heeee Lad, who was that?' No answer . . . Two more slaps with the same question repeated, 'Heeee Lad, who was that?' Bongo was standing quietly behind Mucchoo, smiling at me . . . a Kafkaesque moment. Unwilling to break the Omerta code of silence, I wait for Bongo to own up and break the cycle of two slaps, same question, two slaps . . . Instead, he continues to

Copyright © Kudrat Kashyap | Himalaya | 2014

smile and now, winks too. So I speak up, 'Sir, he is behind you!' Mucchoo spun around, saw Bongo, and stared at him for ten long seconds. No words. Grinding his teeth and getting redder in the face, he spins around again and presents me with not two, but three slaps, (Mucchoo - 13 : Me - 0). He finally turns to Bongo, who gets four! That's it?! Just four?!

The nine of us were put on drill, yes, till further orders . . . under the strict supervision of Ash Bhatia, Head Boy, whose pet hate was a (bloody) Vindhyan!

So much for conserving energy . . . clearly a myth on the hilltop. And lastly, a word of caution: please don't take any advice from Bongo, even if it is for free – even today – don't tell me I didn't warn you . . .

**Bhanu Virmani**
Vindhya 1982 | 1972–1982

OS Sibling – Brother – Manu Virmani | Shaggy | Vindhya 1975 | 1965– 1975
          Sister-in-law – Panita ( Malhans) Virmani | Pan | Vindhya 1986 | 1979–1986

# Mrs G.E. Cherian

Mrs G.E. Cherian joined Sanawar in March 1957. By coincidence, I had the pleasure of travelling up from Kalka with her in the mail car that used to ply in those days.

As Mrs Cherian had completed her junior school training at St. Mary's College, Poona, with a coveted first in Practice Teaching and Handwork and a high second in Theory, it was but natural that the winds of change blew over our Prep School. Within a few months, I noticed attractive charts adorning the walls of the various Form rooms, for not only did Mrs Cherian transform the teaching in her own class, but she was a source of inspiration for her colleagues as well. Trained in the activity method, Mrs Cherian found plenty of scope for her newlyacquired skills. Environmental studies, centres of interest, nature walks and corners in the classroom, interesting projects in which the children made their own models, all helped to make the Prep School a very happy place. Another welcome trend initiated by her was her special script writing.

Mrs Cherian also made a valuable contribution to the Prep School shows in the first term and at Founders', the English play being her special sphere. We not only learned to expect fascinating plays, but looked forward to seeing effective props which Mrs Cherian fashioned herself.

For many years Mrs Cherian looked after Nilagiri House with care and affection.

It was but natural that she was sent by the British Council to England for a brief spell in '60–61 as an observer/teacher. She made many friends there in the teaching world, as well as amongst the parents of her pupils.

This year has proved a challenging one for Mrs Cherian. Not only did she carry a full teaching load, but she was asked to look after the Prep School as well, as Miss Rudra, who was formerly in-charge, had left Sanawar at the end of 1970. To her administrative duties, Mrs Cherian brought her wealth of experience and her logical brain, with the result that she has succeeded in her task of seeing that the Preppers are looked after properly. In addition, she initiated the teaching of New Maths in the Prep School with her usual effective approach.

We are sorry to lose this dedicated worker, but our good wishes go with her as she plans to join Mr K.I. Thomas, as headmistress of the day school he proposes to start in January 1972 in Madras.

Thank you Mrs Cherian for all you have done for Sanawar.

**Romola Chatterji**
Staff

**Source and Acknowledgement:** *The Sanawarian* (December 1971)

# A Memory

## (with apologies to Harper Lee)

February . . . in my mind, the holidays had faded. It was February and we returned to school. Trains were packed, the station was buzzing and for a moment, parents were forgotten. The whistle blew, handkerchiefs waved, an unruly tear dripped down but it was soon forgotten in the smoky possibilities of a term to come.

Sanawar—we came back to tin-roofed dormitories and sagging beds; to another season of baggy skirts and harassed matrons. We walked up covered staircases, to the familiar fidgeting, through 'graces' and the scraping of chairs. We saw lacy cobwebs and admired distant mountains. We played in the evenings, talked in classes, dreamt during prep—and prayed at Assembly! We thought and never did; we did and never thought . . . We added to our well of memories! We visited camps; we ate and slept . . . it was a strange little drama with sun-filled moments and water-filled games. We returned home; the term's woes and triumphs on our minds.

It was August and we returned to a rainy and gloomy school. We adjusted ourselves again to fit old routines, old friends and old sagging beds with damp mattresses. We jogged through athletics, feigned nausea through tests and hobbies, and slept through PT. We groaned during movies and 'studied' through our last Mark Reading. We enveloped Founders' in nostalgia as we saw it all through proud eyes, we felt a part of it and tried to forget that we wouldn't be remembered. We drowned it all in the significance of exams—we still remembered.

November; there were ten days left to go home. We forgave people for counting the days, we strengthened friendships and exchanged snaps and autographs. We went for walks around Sanawar and we tried desperately to remember every stone in the graveyard. Every time we looked out at the lights of Simla, we tried to make ourselves believe we'd see them for more than just nine days. We looked at the Memorial, the Chapel,

Birdwood with a sinking feeling; far away, we heard the whistle and clank of a disappearing train.

Ten days later – and our hearts broken – February again, we needed to come back.

Schools give lessons to be learnt, disappointments to be borne and triumphs to be well-worn.

Sanawar was our school—it gave us a motto to live by, it gave us close friends and it gave us happy memories to look back upon. It gave us the time to guiltlessly stand and stare, to ruminate over the future; to laugh and play and listen to music. It showed us people, it showed us how different they all were; it showed us how to come unscathed through ridicule and criticism. It gave us the wonderful feeling that each of us was a special part of it—it helped us write the first chapter of our lives. And it helped us make that chapter memorable—one we could always refer to and smile at, even when we reach the end of our book. But we never put back what we had taken from it; we had given it nothing and that made me sad.

As we made our way home; it gave us its name—a name to be proud of. The last bugle sounded to end the brief day in school life. But we knew that it would be there all night and it would be there when we woke up in the morning.

**Rohini Arora VI-A**
Old Sanawarian (Vindhya 1972)

**Source and Acknowledgement:** *The Sanawarian* (December 1972)

# Fatso in Green Pants

I was feeling glum. My mom had hauled me all the way from Addis Ababa to Sanawar. After a teary goodbye, she was heading back to Ethiopia, where I had spent two amazing years with my parents. My dad was the Indian military attaché in East Africa, which had involved lots of travel across Ethiopia in a Land Rover: Axum, Gondar, Lalibela, Asmara, Massawa, Harar, Sodere, Assab, Adwa and Dire Dawa, the birthplace of coffee. All those wild lions and wildebeest that we drove by, in vast sanctuaries, seem like a dream now.

I had learnt some Amharic from the maid and the houseboy on evenings when my parents went to cocktail parties, several times a week. I remember Emperor Haile Selassie's parties for the diplomats' kids on his Palace grounds on every Ethiopian New Year. I shook the emperor's hands on two occasions. One time, I did a curtsy which I had practised diligently, to which he responded with a 'namaste' seeing my mother in a saree. Decades later, in Jamaica, where I made friends with some Rastafarians and told them about my meetings with the emperor in my youth, one of them said with much envy, 'you met God, maan.' Interestingly, none of the Rastas knew that Haile Selassie's real name was 'Ras Tafari' Makonnen. Bob Marley would have been most disappointed in them for not knowing their 'istory!'

The yummy Ethiopian food, like 'Injera' and 'doro wat', had turned me into a pudgy ninety-pounder at the age of nine. The boys I was joining in Sanawar looked lean and hungry, like Cassius from Julius Caesar. They did chin-ups and handstands with flourish in the gym while waiting for the dinner gong. Over the holidays, my older brother, Upi, who was already a senior, had warned me—'your fat will disappear in Sanawar double quick, you chubby dimwit.' No kidding. Thanks to his constant reminders that I was a fat shame to the family, I huffed and puffed my way to the finish line at the daily cross-country runs. I did lose twenty pounds by June, for which he received a sharp rebuke from my mother when she saw us.

The Junior dorm was on the second level with amazing views of Kasauli, a cute little village on the hill across the deep valley. I had just been assigned my bed and locker, and stood admiring the view. I saw this little blonde kid, Peter Price, go gliding down the twenty-foot rails along the stairs to the ground level and land elegantly on his feet. He had grown up in Kasauli, like other Brits across India, who had become too 'Indian' to go back to England post-Independence. I decided to give the rails a try in my favourite green pants. I almost fell off and barely managed to hang on, before landing hard on my butt on the stone pavement outside the Senior dorm. Close call. 'A man's gotta know his limitations', I learned much later from Clint Eastwood.

'Hey, what's going on, dimwit?' my brother Upi emerged from the Senior dorm on cue as I picked myself up and readjusted my pants. For some strange reason, I had liked the sound of 'dimwit' in Ethiopia, so I had not discouraged him from calling me that at home, but now, in front of other kids, I was not pleased with that greeting. Good thing there weren't too many kids within earshot.

'Nothing.' I was feeling alone. Lonely. Sorry for myself. I missed my mom.

He read my mind. 'Hey, come with me.'

I followed him, past the 'yellow labs' and the bamboo bushes to the swimming pool. It was empty of water—a dozen or so kids were playing 'Kings' inside the pool, making creative use of the walls with the tennis ball carroming off the sides.

'Hey Robbie', my brother singled out an impish little kid with a buzz cut who looked like he was designed for mischief, 'this is my brother, yaar.' As I would discover later, designed for mischief was an understatement. Five decades later, I still recall fondly one of the cleanest dirty jokes I learned from him.

'Hop in, we are just starting a new game', said Robbie.

We positioned ourselves in a two-foot diameter circle with one foot on the imaginary circle. Robbie dropped the tennis ball at the center. It bounced around and hit a foot belonging to a surd with a little bun that had gone slightly off-centre from the running. 'It's Sukha!' someone cried. Everyone darted away from Sukha, whose eyes doubled in size as he started whacking people gleefully as hard as he could with the ball, successively enlisting his captives to whack the others and get them 'out'. The last person standing was the 'King'.

Guess what? I dodged and snaked around the pool during the game, panting, exhausted. I lasted until the end! I was 'the King'! Wow, I must be good!

New game. Again, we stood in a circle. This time, the ball hit another surd with a large mass of loose hair that wasn't long enough to tie into a bun. 'It's Sam!' Again, everyone darted to the four corners of the pool as Sam started replicating what Sukha had done.

And then I hear Robbie yell out to Sam, 'Hey Sam, whack the fat bugger in the green pants!'

Thwack! That was it. In an instant, I was one of the guys. I'd learned their names already. Next game, when the ball hit yet another surd, I yelled, 'Hey, it's Moga!' Moga was more Zen-like and cerebral in his approach, and unlike Sam and Sukha, took his time.

'Oy, its dinner time,' said Kalia, when Moga was finally done. Kalia was one of the kindest souls I discovered in boarding school, and a great role model.

We clambered out of the pool and headed down the slope past the Tuck Shop towards the dining hall. I felt like one of the boys already!

I made a dozen solid friends that day. Friends for life. I just didn't know it then.

I dedicate this memory to Sukhminder Sekhon, 'Sukha', who lived hard, but not long enough. RIP.

**Vasant Dhar**
Nilagiri 1972 | 1967–1972
Professor, Stern School of Business and Center for Data Science | Co-Director – Graduate Studies, PhD Program, Center for Data Science

OS Sibling – Brother – Krishen Dhar | Nilagiri 1963 | 1961–1963
            Brother – Upender Dhar | Nilagiri 1968 | 1963–1968

# Seasons in the Sun

My Grandma decided to send me a cake. She must have made quite an effort, getting a box of the right size and shape; wrapping and stitching a white cloth around the box; register-posting it to school. The parcel took its own sweet time arriving. By the time I got it, it was an unbreakable rock. We tried smashing it against a wall, punching it till our fists bled . . . but it refused to yield. Any cake that came thereafter was called a rock . . . hard or edible made no difference.

Morning inspection meant a clean hanky and even cleaner nails. Innovation being the name of the game, I decided not to wash my hanky the night before and instead, tore a square piece of white cloth from the one used to cover the cake parcel. Next morning, quite pleased with my genius hack, I held out my hands with the cloth spread between them. Mrs Kemp, our Siwalik Housemistress, looking her strict self, stopped in her tracks and exclaimed in an icy voice, 'Vinay, open that hanky and show me'. Trembling with fright by now, I unravelled the edged piece of nothing. One look from her froze my blood, set my heart off into an uneven thumping. Barely concealed tears and a choked throat completed this utter debacle. Swift punishment followed, of course, no Saturday movie for two weeks . . . sit on your chair the whole evening . . . alone in the dorm. Gosh, I haven't had a dirty hanky ever since.

Manju Sood was my best friend. We would pool in our pocket money and buy biscuits or Charlie's together. Little did we know that we would be doing so later in life as well, going dutch at all our lunches and dinners. But I digress. For the Sunday Kas outings, we got extra money. On one such outing, we pooled in to buy a lipstick—shocking, horror, if anyone ever found out. It was to be our secret. With great enthusiasm, we chose a bright orange lipstick, costing all of five rupees. Manju, as the Vindhya House Prefect, had a cubicle; there would be no onlookers when we pouted in front of the tiny mirror. After lights-out, pretending to be studying, we would paint our lips and look like one would after eating an orange bar.

However, it was extremely exciting . . . almost as good as breaking bounds. And now in retrospect, extremely funny.

Four of us were walking down the covered passage from Parker Hall to the dorm after lunch. A group of teachers were ahead. One of them had a peculiar way of walking. The four of us started imitating her walk and giggling like the schoolgirls that we were. Behind us was this girl (let's call her Veena). Veena dear went and sneaked on us. Of course, this was a major breach. First, we got a yelling from Miss Chatterji, then by our Housemistress, and if this wasn't enough, were taken to BD, where for whatever reason, some hundred boys lined up to watch and laugh at us. Mrs Sehgal, a BD matron, was like a banshee out of hell when she wanted to be, but otherwise a very sweet person. She knew my mother well. She stopped in front of me, nose to nose, and screamed in her scary voice, '*Vinay, tera toh mein keema banakar sab boys ko khila dungi . . . aaj hi mein teri mummy ko letter likh rahi hunh, batameez ladki!*' The four of us pricked our fingers with a needle, mingled our blood and swore a blood oath, 'Even if it took us a lifetime, we would take revenge . . . Veena could not be forgiven.'

Saturday movie nights were so special, even if it was a documentary. Mr Kemp or Mr Mukherji, and at times Mr B. Singh, would man the 16mm projector. Whenever we got to a kissing scene, a hand would cover the lens. This one Saturday, Mr B. Singh was in-charge and the movie was *Mirza Ghalib* (I think the Staff must have wanted to see it). The movie started with what we thought was wailing, but it was actually a song. In chorus, we let out shrieks. In utter disgust, Mr B. Singh stopped the screening and in his Sergeant Major voice, asked us to 'GET OUT!' We ran. The following Saturday, to make up for the Misery Ghalib, Elvis Presley (*Jailhouse Rock*) came visiting. We nearly crushed the Barne Hall floor with our foot stamping (to the music). It was utterly delightful.

I could go on and on . . . Life in Sanawar was, for want of another word, exciting. Each day was a new experience. We learnt many a lesson: resilience, confidence and to stand up for ourselves. Sixty years on, I still feel a great sense of nostalgia. My absolutely wonderful school Sanawar!

**Vinay (Chopra) Tuli**
Chops | Siwalik 1961 | 1952–1961

OS Sibling – Sister – Vijay (Chopra) Narang | Siwalik 1964 | 1955–1964

OS Children – Son – Atul Tuli | Siwalik 1983 | 1974–1976

# A Very Unusual Sanawarian

I was a very unusual Sanawarian, joining U-V, from a Hindi-medium school, Birla Vidya Mandir in Nainital. Initially, I was lost in Sanawar . . . I had to struggle in a very different system to the one I had been accustomed to, and found it difficult to cope with the academic curriculum. Fortunately, for me, most of the teaching staff showed great sympathy and consideration for my predicament. They were not put off by my inability to read English—much entertainment it provided to my classmates. There were those like Mrs Violet Carter, the Mathematics Teacher, who encouraged me to be a high-flier in class. There was Mr Virendra Vyas, who would complement me in the Hindi sessions and ask me to translate essays into simpler Hindi for the benefit of others.

My initiation into long-distance running by my Housemaster Mr N.K.S. Rao and success in the Hodson run, was to be the forerunner of what became a lifetime obsession in the realm of big-time athletics. Greatly encouraged by the incentives I received in these areas, I thrived in those difficult two-and-a-half years at Sanawar. By the time I joined Delhi University as an undergraduate, I had got over my weaknesses and could face my B.A. studies with confidence. It was that version of Sanawar that stood me in good stead all through the way. Edward Carter and Sam Cowell were the two towering personalities at Sanawar who made my schooldays memorable in more ways than one. Mr Kemp and Mr Cuzen, with their inimitable sense of humour, invariably livened up the proceedings in the classroom and on the playing fields. And finally, the Housemaster N.K.S Rao, with whom I spent an all-important year as Head of Siwalik in 1952, prepared me to face the wide world with a great measure of confidence.

**Ranjit Bhatia**
Siwalik 1953 | 1951–1953
Rhodes scholar | Represented India in Rome Olympics 1960 | Awarded O.B.E.

# Camp: An Exaggerated Account

The bus staggered to a halt. The signpost said Simla; Halt . . . stand and deliver. An enthusiastic young man clambered aboard. 'Smallpox epidemic,' he squeaked frenziedly waving a syringe in the air. A general moan went through the bus and everybody lifted trembling arms to show recent inoculation marks. After a perfunctory examination, the disappointed inspector left. An auspicious beginning to camp.

The bus stopped in Tara Hall and thirty tired yet eager girls jumped out. We were staying at the Police rest House in Kaithu. Shouldering airbags, we made our way down tiny alleyways, leading, it seemed, to the bowels of the earth. When thirty girls had mentally consigned the rest House to Avalon, a bleak grey building surrounded by deodars emerged . . . Thirty females chortling with joy in a most unseemly manner, ran down to their temporary home and selected their rooms . . . small cozy ones smelling of pine wood but alas, no beds; unrolling their beddings, they dropped off to sleep. The week at Simla promised to be an effective summer with all that climbing to do.

The rain woke us up and thirty sleepy-eyed girls peered out of unfamiliar windows and wondered where they were. It stopped for breakfast obligingly and thirty hungry girls gorged on sausages. The sky sulked and the clouds looked fit to burst into tears any minute. With the weather being uncertain, the scheduled hike was postponed and we wended weary to the Mall . . . a short walk of three kilometres.

The Mall was a narrow street with shops fringed on one side. We divided up into little groups to add the money burning in our pockets and set out to explore its numerous shops. There were three of us and thirty rupees between us. We looked forlornly at the handicrafts in the shop windows, wishing for a fairy godmother to appear . . . or a convenient bank with its tellers fast asleep. After wandering around for an hour, we decided to 'blow the dough' on Chinese soup.

The sign outside the restaurant said: 'New Experiment: Chinese food from today' We sat in a dingy hall and ordered. The chicken soup tasted like horsemeat (a new thing to do, indeed!); the soyabean sauce like water and onions. We emerged sadder and wiser.

An antique shop beckoned. A musty, old world perfume hid in the corners. A wizened old man, as antique as his belongings, sat at the back. I fell in love with an exquisite bell with a carved Buddha on it. 'Very cheap, Miss.' He cackled, 'Only 150 rupees.' Old Buddhist rings lay spread out on the counter. We examined these but finding none particularly appealing, made our way out of the shop. As we reached the door, a worried voice summoned us back, 'Girls, please wait. There are three of my rings missing'. We froze and then turning back, insisted on his checking our pockets. The ghastly old man soon found his ghastly old rings under the showcase and three relieved girls marched out.

The next day, we were taken to Prospect Hill where, apparently, there was a very holy temple. We toiled our way up the hill and entered a small shrine. The priest sat on one side, clothed in saffron. 'Yes, girls, what can I do for you?' he said in impeccable English; a telephone sat mute at his side. We made our way down again.

The Viceregal Lodge was nearby and we visited that as well. A magnificent House with beautiful gardens all around it. The sight was breathtaking. I emerged after an extensive review of the place; I had never seen so much beauty in my life and I wanted more . . . and then I tripped over something—a dead dog lay at my feet, its eyes gouged out by the army of red ants that crawled over it greedily.

Jakhu, the highest peak in Simla and the site of yet another temple was our destination for Thursday. It was a journey into monkey land—apes gibbered and shrieked in every tree and at last, provoked into madness, I gibbered and shrieked right back. We arrived at the base after a three hours' sojourn, went for lunch and then saw a Hindi movie. The day was over.

Friday morning, we took a walk to Summer Hill. By now, we had lost all hope of reaching home alive and gave in meekly. However, after walking halfway, the teacher lost heart and we returned to the Mall to spend another day shopping. This one passed uneventfully, having very little money, we spent it all on cold coffees and pastries. On impulse, I entered a teeny-weeny alley shop and got a wooden key chain with 'creep' inscribed on it, for someone whom I know it would fit perfectly. In the evening, we saw yet another movie.

We had a dinner date that night. Mr Ahluwalia, the police chief, invited us. I choked on my first Limca and nearly died of ecstasy when I saw the pulao and chicken. I wasn't the only one either. We left at 11 p.m—our last day was over.

Saturday awoke and we faced it with mingled feelings. After packing hastily, we went to take a look at Tara Hall. It is an exquisite miniature of a real school—a fairy land for tiny tots.

The bus was waiting, the driver was a raving lunatic after having missed his lunch. After venting his anger on the already broken-down bus, he finally calmed down and the journey passed uneventfully. We were back in Sanawar.

In retrospect, camp was fun—but only in retrospect.

**Maneka Anand VI–A**
Old Sanawarian (Siwalik 1972)

**Source and Acknowledgement:** *The Sanawarian* (December, 1972)

# House Plays and School Dramatics

I'm sure each of us has a clear recollection of the first-term House shows, and of course, the raison d'être of this whole elaborate effort – the Founders' Day gala – spilling across several days. The shows had variety. Plays in Hindi and English, skits, musical recitals, dances, the works! And rehearsals were fun, a break from routine. The participants could skip hobbies and games, but classes and tests (who says life is fair?) continued as usual. All high spirits were methodically and relentlessly channelized. To me, the prompter's job was utterly thankless. They never got to strut their stuff despite being the most focused and alert of the lot.

House shows were fun, but Founders' was a ball. It was showtime. Akin to preparing for a big fat Indian wedding. The whole school participated in something or the other. And the ones who didn't, the 'shammers' and the malingerers, were okay too, because they were flying under the radar.

The Staff (ADS) Play was always a big ticket event. We only got to see the dress rehearsals, but the big day created a huge buzz. I can recall only one title, *Arsenic and Old Lace* starring Mrs Lyle and Mrs Kemp. They were a riot. Mrs Lyle was a natural. The other constants: Mr B. Singh was always Mr B. Singh, with great comic timing and a poker face. Mr Kemp had a stage presence and a naturalness that disarmed and won over the audience. Their wholehearted commitment and enthusiasm were the viewer's delight.

The annual school plays were elaborate productions and generated high levels of energy and excitement. Then we had the iconic plays of our times, *My Fair Lady* (1966), *Heer Ranjha* (1968), starring our very own Adonis, Rakesh Khosla, who played the lead role. And, who would believe it now, our man of few but telling words, Anil Auluck, as the villainous Mama Kaido. Then there were any number of us as the 'sidey' background dancers and singers. It was quite a production. There was our Sixth Form hit, *The Ghost Train* with Ashali Bhagat, Shekhar Kadam, Vijay Lalotra, Rajan Syal, Sunaiyana Chauhan, Kavita Padda, Rocky Mohan and Arjun

Rastogi. Our tastes in music were not so well-developed. Hence Mr Pratap's elaborate and faultless orchestras did not get the appreciation that they so deserved.

Classical dancing took a hit with the departure of Mr Rajyamani. The curtains came down on Bharatnatyam, Manipuri and the dance dramas staged by him. Enter Mr Brajamani and the era of the Naga dance. It was everywhere, and everyone danced it.

Our very talented and dedicated teachers deserve a vote of thanks and a standing ovation. They were producers, directors, music directors and even musicians when required, providing live scores for all the stage productions. We salute their individual and collective endeavour, their versatility, commitment, values and all that they gave and taught us.

**Jaspreet (Mann) Garewal**
Jas | Nilagiri 1969 | 1962–1969

# Memories Freeze

Memories freeze and are no less vivid.

Perpetual hunger. We would count the steps to the Dining Hall from the dorm, and there was a back-of-the-mind tally of the calories expended. The meal was, therefore, dismissed as being as good as no meal. No wonder Charlie was popular. On our side trip sneaked in between tea and games, more than once, we were caught desperately trying to hide the samosas behind our backs while wishing teachers passing us by near Peacestead. Confession was invariably followed by a sort of good-natured reprimand.

The water shortage in summer. It was the height of luxury to be allowed five mugs of water to have a wash, or should one say a bath, for that is what it was counted as. There were no deodorants in those days, yet I don't recall any of us complaining of B.O.

The memory of water that still terrifies me is associated with the swimming pool. I remember standing there and wishing I could disappear. Suddenly, I found myself in the deep end. The pressure of a pair of arms told me I had been pushed. I was damned if I was going to let go of those arms. If I drowned, I would take those arms with me. It seemed like forever that I had my breath held, with my eyes tightly shut. Then cautiously, I opened them to see what was going on. A pair of legs were kind of kicking away. I followed suit. We both surfaced. Me sputtering. Indignant. Outraged. Wiping my eyes, I saw Gita grinning, 'Hey! Let go.' I didn't and we went down again. Finally, Gita figured out that she had better get me something else to hold onto and so, the third time we bobbed up, she manoeuvred me towards the edge of the pool. I have to confess that till date; I cannot manage an over-arm, but I do quite well with the breast stroke, sticking my head out of the water at all times.

What else are memories made of when one is thirteen, going on fourteen? Boys. There were lots of them in class. Some remain memorable. But what was astonishing, even then, was that anyone should find me to be of any interest. Yet I remember little notes being left in one's desk.

Sidelong looks. Someone actually wanting to sit next to one at a play or whatever, or wanting to dance. I'm afraid that is about the extent to which friendship with the other sex extended in those days of innocence, or shall I say 'backwardness'. I guess puberty was still waiting in the wings, so to speak. My last two years of school in Delhi, at the Convent of Jesus and Mary, did nothing to help it along. It caught up to me only in my last year in school. I remember sitting in the veranda moping. Raj Sircar came by to see my brother – both two years senior to me. He waved cheerfully from the drive, and asked, 'Have you started?' I was absolutely mortified. How could people tell merely by looking at me? I sat there squirming, tongue-tied and no doubt, blushing. He continued, 'Which college?' The relief. My secret was safe.

Friendships lasted through the years at the university, then gradually, they began to loosen as our lives went on different tracks. I renewed my association with Sanawar more than twenty years later, when my daughter, about twelve, felt she was missing out on something and expressed an interest in studying at a boarding school. Where else but Sanawar?

One summer I took her and her brother, a year younger, though already at Doon School, to get a preview. It was then that the nostalgia really hit me. We walked up from Dharampur. The smell of the pines was intoxicating. Past the cemetery, which was to take on very personal overtones barely another twenty years later. The rear entrance through Moti's Corner. Past the Hospital, the playing fields. 'I was quite good at netball,' I told them. They looked skeptical. 'Mother,' they seemed to say, 'Good at Games?'

'Ouch!' Oona exclaimed suddenly. She had been stung by a bee. Just then, we came to a cottage with a red roof. A couple was standing in the garden. It was the Solomons, who kindly invited us in, offered us something to drink and attended to Oona's hand, which had begun to swell alarmingly. It was the summer vacation and they were the only people we met as we walked through the school. I showed my kids Birdwood, the old Dining Hall, which had by then been turned into the Art and Crafts place. For Oona, it was love at first sight. She took her entrance exam the following year, joined and proceeded to have, as we would say often, the best time of her life. A life that was cut short. She died when she was thirty-three. She always paid tribute to Sanawar for inculcating her love for the mountains – where she chose to make her home and do her life's work, though in a different region.

Mr Carter, Shomie Das and Harish Dhillon are three headmasters with whom I interacted in various stages of my life.

The wonderful thing about having been at Sanawar, let us say over two generations, is the links it forms and how it brings people together. I expect that it is true for any school, but somehow, it seems that Sanawarians all over the globe, are, indeed, a special lot.

Thank you, Sanawar.

## Jasjit (Kaur) Mansingh
Nilagiri 1954 | 1951 – 1952

Nanda Devi 1980 (Sapper Adventure Foundation 1981) | Co-Author, *Lt. Gen. P.S. Bhagat VC* with Lt. Gen. Mathew Thomas (Lancer, 1994) | Contributor, *Delhi City Guide*, 1998 | Author, *Oona: Mountain Wind* (Srishti, 2001) | Editor, *Time Out* | Author, *Stories from Punjab* (Srishti, 2002) | Author, *Oona* (National Book Trust, 2002) | Contributor, *Walking with the Gurus*, 2004 | Author, *Living Light Biography – Devinder Kaur Assa Singh 1906–2013* (Knowledge World, 2015) | Author, *Oona: Mountain Wind* (revised edition, Academy of Fine Arts and Literature, 2021).

OS Sibling – Brother – Sqn. Ldr. Pritam Singh | Himalaya 1952 | 1951–1952

OS children – Daughter – Oona Mansingh | Nilagiri 1981 | 1977–1981

# Send Her to Sanawar . . .

It was 1976 and I was in Form II. Supper was on in the Prep School dining hall—*dal*, *tinda* and those leathery, hard-to-break *chapatis* were being passed around amidst the deafening cacophony emanating from the 200+ kids' chatter and the spoon-on-plate and in-donga clangs. Every piece was made of stainless steel—I guess nothing less could have survived us.

Omi (Omindra Singh) sat next to me. He was, and still is, a good friend. His elder sister, Gitanjali Kumari (GK), my classmate, was the batch 'toughie'. Sanawar had a few girls who could give the boys a run for their money. In that melee and animated conversation, my elbow, of course unintentionally, managed to find Omi's nose. It started bleeding profusely. We did what we could to try to stop the bleeding, and Omi was whisked away to the M.I. Room. I, once again, turned my attention to the *dal* and *chapati*, staying clear of the *tinda*. Shortly, a message was passed down the line: 'Oye Dollar surd, GK's GOING TO GIVE YOU A CRACKING AFTER DINNER'. My heart skipped a beat and I got worried sick because, as I explained earlier, GK was a real tough one. I quickly consulted my buddies and asked for their help. I learnt that she had a big gang, and my only hope was to make a dash for the dorms, straight after grub.

Now, there were three doors in a row, leading out of the Dining Hall. After we entered and sat down, all but the first door, closest to the Girls' dorms, were bolted, leaving just one exit for everyone. Dinner got over and I felt like a scared hare being chased by hounds. My intelligence-gathering agents (Parry & Co. Ltd.) informed me that GK (and her gang) were waiting outside. The Boys' dorms were approximately 100 m from the Dining Hall. I would have to literally run like hell for leather to get past GK's gang, unscathed. By this time, I was the only one in the Dining Hall. Doing a quick situational analysis and thinking on my feet, I ran to the bolted door at the far end, placed a chair against it to reach the bolt, and high-tailed it. It had completely slipped my mind that GK was also

*Copyright © Rathin Mitra | ART MASTER | 1950–1953*

the 50 m champ. She and her gang tailing her, chased me like a swarm of hornets. Now I, too, was a good runner, but as luck would have it, I slipped and fell at the turn next to Mrs Ram Singh's House, all thanks to my untrustworthy, smooth-soled 'Naughty Boy' shoes. And the swarm was all over me . . . The rest is history. I am the only guy in my batch, or probably across batches, to get a cracking by the dames. Send her to Sanawar and . . .

**Col. Adeshpal Singh Randhawa**
Dollar/AP | Vindhya 1985 | 1974–1985

Commissioned to Fifth Battalion (Sikh Regt.) in 1989 | Part of all Army notified operations in J&K, Siachen, North East | Awarded COAS, VCOAS and Army Commander (EC) Commendation Cards for Gallantry and distinguished service | Accomplished shooter | Mountaineer | Cycling enthusiast.

OS Children – Son – Capt. Dilsher S. Randhawa | Vindhya 2014 | 2008–2014

# A New Life

I joined school on a raw and windy day in March 1960. But slowly, the sun shone as I learnt the ropes and how to survive in a boarding school.

Then came Senior School. L-III was a learning experience – learning to tie a turban overnight; keeping a locker tidy; knees oiled; nails cut; shoes polished; counterpane wrinkle-free – which were all essential to stay away from the dreaded 'see me tonight'. Slowly, I learnt how to take the good with the bad, and by L-IV, I had tried my hand at all the hobbies. Indian classical dance, piano and Indian classical music, which 'boys' generally stayed away from.

I discovered that I loved reading. I spent a lot of time in the library where *The Boy's Own* magazines were a must-read in the lower classes. After that, I read everything except what I needed to for my studies. I passed in all subjects except Hindi and Sanskrit.

I made a lot of friends, of whom I have very fond memories. They made my life complete. I loved the school and would often take long walks. Breaking bounds was a hobby; it was nature that drew me. The moods of the mountains—sunny, dark and forbidding; browns and fawns of winter; the burning summer with its water shortage; the gorgeous greens of monsoon. The wind sighing through the pines and the pitter-patter of rain on the tin roof, whilst I was snug and warm in bed. The best time was after the monsoon, as the grey clouds parted and gave way to fleecy clouds on a clear blue sky. Just as suddenly, monsoon was gone. Greens gave way to the winter and the nip in the air rejuvenated one. Pinecone collection was another looked-forward-to activity, as I got to go as far as the fourth hump legally.

I wish I had kept the Assembly song book. I still like the hymns, especially after Mr M.V. Gore explained the Sanskrit part to us. He even gave me a Gita with English translation. Gore was the epitome of a guru. He instilled in me the essence of the Vedanta and taught me a lot without any of the chest-thumping which is common these days. The other teachers too, had their effect on me in their own diverse ways. I am fleetingly reminded of these in my journey through life.

My sports prowess and career were limited to scoring a self-goal in a Colts match, against Himalaya and that too, from the half line.

Jagga made me a prefect. I sometimes wonder what he saw in me when he chose me for this exalted position over the others.

**Ajaypal Singh Gill**
Jae | Vindhya 1969 | 1960–1969

OS Children – Son – Abhaypal Singh Gill | Pali | Vindhya 2002 | 1993–2002
Daughter – Harpriya Kaur Gill | Hippo | Vindhya 2004 | 1996–2004
Daughter – Anup Kaur Gill | Vindhya 2009 | 2002–2005

# The Rev. A.H. Hildesley

## 1857–1939 | Third Principal of Sanawar

Reverend Alfred H. Hildesley came to Sanawar on 1 April 1884 from the Bishop Cotton School for Boys in Bangalore, where he had been Warden since 1882. He was accompanied by his young wife, Alice, and three daughters, Audrey, Avis and Dorothy. It was not till 1912, some twenty-eight years later, that he finally laid down his new and onerous charge as Principal and Chaplain of the asylum. When he came, educational standards were low, discipline was rough and the school grossly understaffed; there were indeed, only eight teaching staff to 500 children and some of these quite unqualified. The task before him might well have deterred a more timid man but Mr Hildesley threw himself wholeheartedly into his work and, ultimately, was able to overcome these difficulties which had first appeared insuperable. But it was no easy matter. Radical changes in outlook and education could not be effected without opposition. The boys did not take kindly to his ideas, and on one noteworthy occasion, went on strike and marched down to Kalka. Mr Hildesley met the situation with great tact and skill and never again was there a recrudescence of indiscipline. Academically, Mr Hildesley was a man of many interests, chief among them being music and English literature. His interests were reflected in the school, and the Glee Club, which he founded in 1885, flourished under his encouragement.

It was during his long tenure that many of the original school buildings were repaired, completely rebuilt or refurbished, and their ageing shingle roofs replaced with more durable corrugated iron. Several new buildings, including the Boys' School (now Gaskell Hall), the new band Room and two new water reservoirs were constructed. He oversaw the move of the old school cemetery to its present site beyond Moti's Corner on the old bridle path to Dharampur in 1886. It was he, too, who first conceived the boys' playing field, and in about 1904, 'Big Plain' (now Barnes), was born. He was also responsible for the planting of many 'hundreds of trees and thousands of cuttings' (sic) all over the hillside; and the myriads of naturalized dahlias and carpets of cosmos that one sees every spring and summer today, are believed to be part of his legacy.

He reigned in Sanawar for over a quarter of a century and served under three sovereigns. His children grew up on the hilltop. Sadly, one died there and was buried in the school cemetery. Another was born there and two were married in the Chapel. On his retirement, he was awarded the Kaiser-i-Hind Gold Medal for his labours for the welfare of Sanawar. He was, however, too indefatigable to remain idle and, on return to England, accepted the incumbency of Wyton in Huntingdonshire, where he spent most of his remaining days. He was of great service to John Drinkwater, when the latter was preparing a biography of parliamentarian Charles James Fox and the author acknowledged his debt.

He retired as Rector of All Saints Parish Church, Wyton in about 1925 and died at his home in Buckley, St. Neots, Huntingdonshire on 19 April 1939 at the age of eighty-one. Evidently, he had been ailing for some time and his end was not unexpected. His was a life given to service and we pay our humble tribute to him in these pages.

**D.V. Boddington**
LRMS Sanawar 1942–1947
23 April 2002

**Adapted from an article in the Midsummer edition of** *The Sanawarian Magazine*, **November 1939.**

# Plywood Canes

We were in U-IV then. Classes were on. We had to go for cash work in the hobbies section. There were four of us who had chosen Art, under the tutelage of Mr Ashok Bhalerao.

As we were walking towards the Art Room, we looked down and saw the Swimming Pool. It was shimmering and all quiet under the midday summer sun. In the spur of the moment, we decided to enjoy a swim instead of going for art. As the swimming season was on, we walked into Nilagiri House and picked up swimming trunks that had been hung to dry.

We were enjoying our swim, when all of a sudden, the booming voice of Mr Kemp thundered, 'What are you chaps doing?'

We ducked underwater. As we surfaced, he asked us to see him in his office. We were sure that we would be caned. He asked where we were

supposed to be. 'Art, Sir', all of us echoed. Mr Kemp then ordered us to go and see Mr Bhalerao. A sigh of relief.

Mr Bhalerao was waiting in his office, cane in hand. Instead of being frightened, we were amused because the cane in his hand was made of plywood. All four of us were accustomed to the hardest caning from Mr B. Singh, and to a lesser extent, from Mr Kemp.

One by one, Mr Bhalerao called us and gave us two or three whacks. After the canes, each of us would say, 'Thank you, Sir' because they were too mild. When the last one amongst us was being hit, all of us burst out laughing. This angered him so much that he brought his cane down very hard and it snapped into two. Our laughter became even louder. In great anger, he ordered us to get out and never come for Art again.

What wonderful memories of our years on the beautiful hilltop at Sanawar!

**Ajai Singh**
Himalaya 1964 | 1957–1964

OS Children – Daughter – Avantika Kumari | Himalaya 1996 | 1988–
        1996
                Son – Abhyudai Singh | Himalaya 2000 | 1992–2000

# Memories Are Made of This

The beauty of monsoon clouds mounting the Kalka gap; the scent of pines as we drove into the hills; being ragged, gently, on arrival in mid-term 1951 by boys who've remained close friends since then; excessive regimentation, which I didn't like, and marching about, which I did; Chapel services with psalms; being pummelled in the boxing ring; acting on stage; failing in English and geometry, initially, my English recovered but math never did; growing up with girls and my emotional ups and downs, though easier than friends who struggled in boys-only schools; surviving Garkhal's barking dogs to see the beauty of the sunrise from Monkey Point; fierce sports rivalry with BCS; camaraderie on school buses and trains from Delhi to Kalka; swotting at night by petromax in freezing cold rooms for the exams; friendships which have survived and strengthened over the course of fifty years.

We were privileged to be in a class of only eleven. The population explosion began with the next form, which had twenty-five people, reflecting the school's near-death in 1947 and revival as a public school, a year later. It must have been an extraordinary change for Principal E.G. Carter, who managed with grace, style and a gentle touch, the school's transformation from teaching children mainly of B.O.Rs to those of a new Indian elite, while maintaining high standards, discipline and morale, founded on his own strength as a history teacher and his wife's sharp skills in mathematics.

He was backed by a fine team of English and Anglo-Indian teachers, led by the legendary Sam Cowell, senior master of the Boys' School, who'd spent almost his whole life at Sanawar; Trevor Kemp, Nilagiri Housemaster and chemistry teacher with humour, quieting a rowdy group with 'only one fool at a time; now it's your turn'; E.A. Couzens (English history), whose 'Willy Willy Henry Stee' de-confused royal chronology; and Mrs Coombes (geography) insisting that our maps of Liverpool and Newfoundland were clearly drawn and accurately coloured.

And the first and close-knit batch of Indian teachers, extending our background of India: Viren Vyas (Hindi) who introduced us to the delights of photography and the Hindi stage; Salim Khan (history), Rathin Mitra (art), who went on to delight the world with his sketches of Calcutta and of Indian life for the next half-century; Romola Chatterjee (English) and 'Bhuppi', a rookie Housemaster when I was a prefect, and a caring and much-loved Mr B. Singh, who was the deputy headmaster by the time my daughter went to study in Sanawar, thirty-five years later.

To use the clichéd phrase, 'memories are made of this'.

**Ashok Nehru**
Pip Pip | Nilagiri 1953 | 1951–1953

OS Siblings – Brother – Aditya Nehru | Nilagiri 1954 | 1952–1954
                    Brother – Anil Nehru | Nilagiri 1957 | 1952–1957

OS Children – Daughter – Malavika (Nehru) Gupta | Siwalik 1992 | 1985–1992

# Broken Bridge

Yesterday's OS Reunion Lunch in London was well-attended by over fifty OS with Sir Henry Lawrence and his daughter Isabelle (Izzy) as our honoured guests. We are all so grateful to Anu (Aruna Mongia, OS 1967) for arranging such a happy occasion when we all shared our schooldays memories and once again glimpsed the joys of childhood. The delicious Indian cuisine and splendid ambience added to our appreciation of all that she had arranged for us.

We did mention Broken Bridge, on the right-hand side of the road from Dharampore to Subathu. It has been in the news on Sanawarnet, recently. To us, during my time at school, it was called Choir Bridge. We used to camp in Dugroo in the spring of every year for ten days' holiday. We marched down from school and broke ranks on Choir Bridge to proceed single file along the *pagdundee* to the camp site. The white tents were aligned on a flat plain in a valley near the stream. We slept fourteen to a tent, seven on each side. We had no beds or mattresses; we slept on bunched up piles of pine needles.

One Easter Sunday lives on in my memory. It was time for evening service and the choir assembled on Choir Bridge. In the soft light of the evening, I saw, from where we sat on the hillside, the Rev. George Barne, our Principal, in flowing ecclesiastic robes, emerge along the pagdundee, leading the choir boys in red and white cassocks, singing a hymn of praise to God. The church service took place under the open sky and I recall nothing of George Barne's sermon. I saw only the long shadows of the trees in the glow of the setting sun that touched the tips of trees with gold as we sang 'Abide with me'.

After breakfast, we were free. Free to roam the hills, explore the valleys, and swim in the cold fresh waters of the mountain stream. It was the time that birds were nesting, singing and darting across the valley and pretty butterflies, like flowers, floated against a blue sky blobbed with cottonwool clouds. The wilderness was painted in nature's fresh, bright spring colours and the air was crisp and clean. Our happiness was more than money could buy. We were full of joy and the innocence of youth.

Our favourite place to swim and have fun was Hartz Pool, that was fed by a silver waterfall in the stream that tumbled through the mountains from the melting snows. The water was clean and bracing. I remember a boy named Denziel Weeks dived into the pool and struck his head against a rock and came to the surface with his head full of blood and half his scalp hanging over his forehead. He brushed it back. 'It's only a leaf,' he said and passed out. He was carried to the school hospital where he recovered with no ill effects.

The cadence of jackals' calls at nights penetrated our deep dreamless sleep. The sleep of healthy, tired bodies that had roamed far and wide for miles and miles over and across the pebbled stream, stripped off for a dip in crystal clear ponds and explored up and down the mountain sides. There were many stories to tell as we sat around campfires in the evening.

For me, those ten days in camp were the happiest days of the school year. It is hard even now, nearly eighty years later (I am ninety-three and have lived a full life in seven countries on four continents and visited sixty countries) to recall any events that touched the depths of my being so deeply or have given me greater joy than the ten days' annual camping holiday in Dugroo.

The memory 'abides with me' . . .

**George Browne**
Havelock 1937 | 1930–1937

# Time Stood on Its Head

It was 1954. I was on the upper floor of Honoria Court and Mrs Hickey was our matron.

I will never forget a hilarious incident, or more accurately, a hilarious incident in *retrospect*! Lights-out was done with at 9 p.m. and the dorm was silent, except for the gentle snores of a few, or the intermittent fragments of conversations in someone's sleep. I was asleep, in happy oblivion of any sounds, until I heard the wake-up bell being rung frantically, all the lights being switched on, glaring into our tightly shut eyes, and Mrs Hickey screaming at the top of her lungs.

'Get up girls, we're late, it's nearly six o'clock. You should be up at Parker Hall for Chota Hazri! Hurry! Hurry!' This was punctuated by the awful clanking sound of the bell, literally in our ears, as she went as fast as she could down the length of the dorm until, it suddenly became pitch-dark all around us. The outside lights, whose comforting beams always fell on the dorm floor through various windows, went out abruptly. Just the dim light of the kerosene lanterns glowed gently at each end of the dorm, their flickering shadows lighting up the linoleum on the wooden floor. In the pitch darkness, a sea of stretching arms and tousled heads were at different stages of getting into shorts and blouses, preparing to go down for tea and a slice of bread, prior to our 6.15 a.m. PT. As we yawned and nodded sleepily, trying to get ready in the dark, Mrs Hickey's voice boomed *again*, loud and clear.

'Girls! Get back into bed! It's 12.30 a.m. I read the clock upside down and thought it was 6 a.m., fifteen minutes past our Rouser! The power House just switched off at its usual time of twelve-thirty. Sorry, girls. Go back to sleep. Hurry up, my mistake! Change and jump back into bed!'

I had a word with my best friend, Jasbir, and we conspired to go to sleep in our PT clothes and save time when the next bell would rudely interrupt our sleep of merely a few hours at 5.45 a.m.

One last memory connected with this fiasco was of a loud knock at the dormitory door, which had been relocked once Mrs Hickey had realized her mistake! There at the door, was Gay Butler, who had somehow got up and got dressed before the power House shut off. Of course, there was no Chota Hazri when she got there, and she managed to race back in the darkness in the light of the moon!

This is an indelible memory of Gay's swiftness and a reminder to always look carefully when looking at the time in the dead of night!

**Lila (Kak) Bhan**
Siwalik 1958 | 1953–1958

# Reminiscences of My School Days

I was born in a small town, Arifwala, now in Pakistan. At the time of the Partition, in 1947, I was studying in Class 6 in a Govt. High School where the medium of instruction was Urdu.

My younger brother, Devinder, and I, joined The Lawrence Royal Military School, Sanawar on 20 May 1948. Two dormitories were in use in BD at the time. He was put in the Junior dorm, while I was downstairs in the Senior Dorm. We both wore plaits. Harkrishan Singh 'Kitchu' put me in a turban right away, while I continued to go upstairs to do Devinder's plaits.

Mr Cowell put me in U-III, instead of L-IV, while Devinder joined L-III. Within a few days, I was hauled up by Mrs Robinson, taken to Mr Cowell and relegated to L-III, as I did not even know the English Alphabet.

A total of forty-five boys and sixteen girls comprised the school in 1948. Morning Assembly was held in Chapel with a march past salute at the War Memorial, on our way up to Parker Hall or Birdwood. All meals were served in Parker Hall. Four to a table—three boys and one girl, were served by bearers with gloves on. After dinner, every night, there was a Social in Barne Hall. It was the blonde bombshell, Joy Bellamy, who taught me to dance 1, 2, 3 to the waltz.

School provided everything – uniforms, night-suits, underwear, towels, shoes – even toothbrush and toothpaste. But no turbans. The annual fee per child for full board, lodging and tuition was Rs. 1,200/- with a 5 per cent concession for the second child.

Given our background, we yearned to converse in Punjabi—going down to Barnes to talk and abuse each other. One day, Joginder, Chaman Lal and I were caught by Mr Cowell, speaking in Punjabi. We were to report to him that night. Our friends told us that we would get 'laddoos'. So, we went up eagerly to Mr Cowell—only to be told to pull down our pyjamas. Six of the best were given to each of us and we were told to not only speak, read and write, but also think in English. Next morning, Joginder called me, 'Gurdip Singh, you is wanting wenting, tuck shopping?' Me – 'I is no go.' Joginder, 'Go go, go go, no go no go—I is wenting.' Me: 'You is went.'

Ten pianos were kept in the 'Music Cells', below the school office and above the Honoria Court. We had an excellent teacher. I too learnt and in the year-end Test, secured 98 per cent.

Our primary sports rival was BCS, with the venue for the matches alternating between Simla and Sanawar. We attended the All-India Public Schools' NCC Camp – Delhi 1952, Poona 1953 and Lucknow 1954 – and were adjudged the top all-round school, given the sporting prowess inculcated at Sanawar. At the Delhi Camp, in the Cross Country Marathon, Ranjit Bhatia and Tony (Doon School) were in the lead with Sardual Singh (Doon School) and I at their heels. They took a wrong turn, ending up doing five miles instead of three, and arriving at the finish line from the opposite direction. Sardual and I, having realized the mistake, had turned around.

A memorable incident occurred during the rehearsals for Founders'. Mr Cowell was very particular that the National Anthem be sung in precisely 52 seconds. Nanda Cariappa, Rattan Kaul and I were then the senior-most in school, and would sing from the rear end of Barne Hall, with great gusto. We were always the loudest, but unfortunately, out of tune and would invariably be told to 'shut up!'.

In another incident, when I was the School Prefect of Sparrow Hawks B. Dorm, I was caught dancing after lights-out, by the matron Miss Thun, in her room. I remember how I stood my ground and agreed to be transferred, but not expelled or demoted.

India's first Commander-in-Chief, General Cariappa's both children, Nanda and Nalini, studied at Sanawar. So we were fortunate to have him unofficially visit Sanawar a few times. He was punctual to the minute, and we would line-up on either side of the road from the Arch to the Quad to welcome him. Once, it started drizzling minutes before his scheduled arrival. So we ran and assembled in Gaskell Hall. He went around shaking hands with all the children and saying, 'I am disappointed to see the future of India in your limp handshake.' He went right back shaking hands with everyone again. 'That was good. I see India in safe hands'.

Amarinder Singh and his younger brother, Malvinder, were in Sanawar. Their father, Maharaja Yadavindra Singh, was the Chief Guest at Founders'. He also invited us to play cricket at Chail, the highest cricket ground in the world, and a 'royal' picnic at Pinjore, including conveyance from Sanawar to Pinjore, specially cooked delicious Mughlai food from Moti Bagh Palace in Patiala and Maharaja's personal band, under the excellent direction of Herr Max Geiger, to entertain us. The boys being boys, repaid his hospitality by stripping bare trees of their delectable fruit.

In the early '50s, every year, Jeffery Kendal's Shakespearana Company with Shashi Kapoor and Jenifer Kendall came from Bombay and captivatingly enacted plays from our Senior Cambridge syllabus. In 1954, it was *Macbeth*. They also performed in the green room and many schools in Simla.

The old guard comprised of E.G. Carter (Principal), S.C. Cowell (senior master), T.C. Kemp, Vic Evans, Paige, Curzon, Mrs Coombes, Mrs Robinson, Mrs Kemp, Mrs Carter and Miss Thompson. Then came Bhupinder Singh, Salim Khan, Virendra Vyas, M.V. Gore (the fabulous quartet) and Miss Romola Chatterji from Cambridge. There was Mr Ram Singh Varma, the art master, who would yell, 'sound the bugle and blow the light out'—he did not last long. Then there was N.K.S. Rao, who came to teach English, but his 'yum you yum yum yahe' made him our biology teacher.

Our Class of 1954 was the largest, comprising twenty-four children (six girls and eighteen boys) to have appeared for Senior Cambridge. Twenty-three passed—I was not the one who failed. Today, nine of us twenty-four have sadly passed away. May their souls rest in peace.

Our three children went to Sanawar—Tandip (OS 1983), twin boys Sandip and Shivneet (OS 1986). During Shomie Das's tenure, I• was asked to formulate the Constitution of the Old Sanawarian Society. In consultation with [the] headmaster, other reputed public schools and some Seniors, I prepared the same. I also put together the OS Directory, rummaging through records kept in gunny bags in the school office. The Old Sanawarian Society's elections were held for the first time at Founders' in 1979, where I was elected the President. Later, when Andy Gray was Headmaster, I served as a member of the Board of Governors. It was then that the quartermaster's store was dismantled. Among the numerous items found therein, was an heirloom violin made by Antonia Stradivari.

Our Class of 1954 set a new benchmark with an elaborate Golden Anniversary celebration in 2004, with classmates coming from Ireland, UK and all over India. On 29 September, we had a Golf Tournament at ITC Classic Golf Resort at Tarru, near Manesar, with the President of

India's band in attendance, thanks to Harinder Sodhi, followed by booze and a sumptuous lunch. Mrs Shobhi Wahi, wife of ex-Chairman, ONGC, accompanied by Mr Rathin Mitra, our art master from Calcutta, gave away the prizes. Dinner, that night, was hosted by Gita Bhatia. On 30 September, lunch was hosted by me at our home at Kulwehri, followed by dance and dinner hosted by OS Society at Chandigarh and a Golf Tournament at Chandigarh Golf Club, the next morning. On 1 October, a special train ride from Dharampur to Barog and back, with a delicious vegetarian lunch at the famous Barog Railway Station, was hosted by Om Sarup Dogra. Next day, tea was hosted by Aunty Fori and Aditya Nehru at their home in Kasauli. An impressive souvenir yearbook was published by Gita Bhatia and T-shirts, wrist watches, golf balls, watch straps, calendars and hand towels with 'Class of '54' and the School Crest inscribed, were presented to all.

We celebrated our Diamond Jubilee in 2014, and Blue Sapphire Jubilee in 2019 with equal enthusiasm, and are now eagerly looking forward to the big day: the Dodransbicentennial year at Founders' 2022.

**Gurdip Singh Kalyana**
Siwalik 1954 | 1948–1954
Pioneered Poultry and Seed Breeding in India | Panelist – World Food Congress, Iowa, USA 1976 | Founder President OSS 1979–1982 | Member, LSS Board of Governors 1998–2000

OS Sibling – Devinderpal Singh Kalyana | Siwalik 1954 | 1948–1954

OS Children – Daughter – Tandip (Singh) Kuckreja | Tanu | Himalaya
                  1983 | 1973–1983
                  Son – Sandip Singh | Himalaya 1986 | 1976–1986
                  Son – Shivneet Singh | Nilagiri 1986 | 1976–1986

# S–6

S-6 was my clothes-room ID that was inked onto my clothes at the beginning of my senior term at Sanawar. It was probably the only known ID I had. Prep School was different, with an ayah to keep track of the clothes we had, and those that were put for washing. Senior School was a dramatically different kettle of fish. If Prep School was Enid Blyton at her very best; Senior School was an adaptation of Charles Dickens' *Oliver Twist*. We were (always) hungry and poor.

Sanawar made a promise of squeezing out the very dregs of one's laziness and non-conformity. It delivered. We erased our individual identity and became one cohesive team on the soccer field of life. A British culture overrode our existing backgrounds and we learnt that 4 p.m. was tea-time. I have never had tea a few minutes off this time-mark. All my life. Of course, Chota Hazri; the beginning of the food parade at 6 a.m. was a delight, with cold margarine on bread and a cup of tea. Similarly, coffee and dog biscuits were most welcome after supper on cold and wintry nights. They were welcome even on summer nights.

My two-rupee pocket money had a life of ninety seconds. That's the time it took to dash down to Tuck Shop and boldly throw the money on the counter for a handsome bag of sweets. One paisa each. Or eat at Charlie's with your own money. Or store it for the next Sunday movie and bun samosa with free chutney, at Kas. If there was leftover change, Aam Papad or Churan were also bought. Churan came packaged in a small paperbag with a plastic toy. This could sometimes be exchanged for a fruit.

We had our own elaborate exchange rate. Bananas were the cheapest. Sometimes they were cut in half and served at meal times. Half a banana didn't get you anything. A full orange got you two bananas. And so on. The smaller mangoes were served, one each. Big mangoes were cleanly chopped in two. So every student got half each. It was generous, for it could have been quartered. Cake and custard were treats and thus, very highly valued on the exchange board. But, 'used' PT shoes for a pocketful of bhuttas from the villagers was even better. And when the PT shoes were not yours, the deal worked best.

So did the string from the hockey stick, that didn't belong to you. It was valued very highly, indeed. It was used for making a yoyo. The wooden part came from thread wheels that the darzi threw away.

Living amongst the beautiful pine trees was lovely. The needles of the pine were chewed upon and the juice sucked out. The unopened pinecone had a nut within. The bark was used to fashion boats and float them down the Nile that existed in the nallahs behind the dorms. Every Sunday, these nallahs smelled of sweet shampoo and we dreamt of a Hamam. Back then, Hamam was the only soap going around. Cantharidine hair oil worked wonders, on hair as well as cricket bats. And toothpaste came handy, for Home Day hidings.

Yes, life was simple. We simply didn't know any other way to exist.

Letter-writing was a sacred date with our parents, conducted under the watchful eye of the most easily-available teacher that day, during the last period on Saturday. We had to write or else we wouldn't get pocket money. It was a thoughtful way to tell us how to master the art of letter writing. Most of us became great letter writers because of it.

Saturday nights were fun. Lights-out was thirty minutes later and that time was utilized in playing 'torches'. This was Catching Cook with a torch beam. If the beam fell on you; you were caught. It was a simple game.

Sundays were the most enjoyable. Summer Sunday mornings meant the ice-cream being brought out, outside the dining hall. Some had the money to buy a slice at 0.50 p, while others just watched you lick it down. Both kinds enjoyed the experience thoroughly. After this, you could begin the Sunday outing to Kas.

The luggage room was a nice place that you could go to upon special request. That was where our home luggage was stored. We could open our trunks and smell our homes.

The teachers were nice. They hailed from all over the country and you could find your favourite native quite easily.

Oops, I have to stop. I am writing this under my blanket. It's lights-out and my torch is growing dim. Weak batteries can be exchanged too!

**Aditya Raj Kapoor**
Mickey | Siwalik 1972 | 1963–1969

# My Term as Head Boy

The special orders issued at the end of last year announced my appointment as the Head Boy for the year 1970. I was delighted to hear the news. Although earlier I wasn't sure whether it would be good for me to become the Head Boy and shoulder so many responsibilities, I was glad to hear the news. This was my chance to do what I could to improve Sanawar and show my worth. So I took up the challenge ahead of me. My duty was to look after, with the help of my team of prefects, the general discipline and goings-on at the school.

Aware of all the difficulties I would have to encounter in order to improve Sanawar, I decided to remain resolute in my decision. I was prepared to sacrifice everything for the sake of Sanawar.

The year started well and apart from a few problems here and there, everything was going on fine. Later, I did have some difficulties but with the help of some sincere friends and, of course, by God's grace, I overcame them and again, everything was smooth. I made a few changes and introduced a few new things in the hope of improving discipline as well as the outlook towards the life of boys in Sanawar. A great number of them were successful. But nothing was more successful than the 'Sanawar Cleaning Society' that was started by my team of prefects and myself. All those late for meals, parade etc. and for other similar violations would join this society and on the following Sunday, under the supervision of the Prefect on Duty, would go around cleaning various parts of Sanawar. As no one likes to ruin a Sunday, everyone did their best not to have to join the society and this greatly improved the discipline. This also helped in keeping Sanawar tidy.

We also revived the 'Prefect on Duty' system, which had almost become extinct. The prefect on duty had to, for that particular day, take charge of nearly everything. It was his duty to see that all bugles were sounded at the proper timings, everything went on smoothly at Assembly and at the pictures, and to take charge of a few other things.

Discipline can be achieved in various ways. Our team of prefects had decided that the discipline we push for should be a permanent and inner one, and not just temporary and outward. We can call ourselves disciplined only when we realize that we must do something because it is our duty and not because of the fear of punishment. The best way of improving discipline and the general behaviour is by setting a personal example. The prefects must themselves follow what they wanted to impress upon others. We avoided corporal punishment as far as possible, but there were occasions when we had to come down hard. At times, it was felt necessary.

A funny notion among boys is that headship affects one's studies. I don't really agree with this idea. I think a Head Boy can manage his duties and at the same time, not neglect his studies. One must study as well as do other activities and duties, but each thing should be done at the appropriate time. Cramming books is not education. Only bookworms, who prefer to remain excused from games throughout the year and prefer to study while others are doing athletics or playing games, will feel that

headship affects studies. But I don't think Sanawar is the right place for such people. However, I am prepared to accept that there may have been a few instances when it might have affected my studies, but then I made up for my deficiencies later. The amount lost, however, is no patch on what one gains by holding this position.

I feel I am lucky to have been appointed to this prestigious position as only a few get this opportunity. I made the best of it and gained whatever education I could from it. It has taught me to shoulder responsibilities and to face and overcome various types of problems. To be fully dutiful, one has to labour hard but it is worth working for. If at the end of the year, I feel there has been an improvement, I shall have achieved my purpose and done my duty well.

**Rakesh Bhan**
Head Boy 1970
Old Sanawarian (Siwalik 1970)

**Source and Acknowledgement:** *The Sanawarian* (December 1970)

# Six Weeks in the U.K.

Great Expectations. Don't think I'm talking about the novel by Charles Dickens but about the expectations we all had before going to the United Kingdom. Our expectations, which were a result of what we had heard about the UK from other people were soon shattered, when we saw the life there firsthand on our exciting trip.

The weather at Heathrow was quite chilly when we got off the Thai International DC-10. But a great surprise awaited us. The driver of the airport bus was a Sikh (Sardarji) who welcomed us cheerfully in his loud Punjabi voice. We weren't shocked, though we had all heard about the British streets being infiltrated by Indians.

What one usually hears about British domestic life makes one think that heaven is no better while India with its crying millions seems like the opposite thing. So to get a real idea about British life, we each spent about two weeks with different families at different places. I stayed in the county of Devon, and Mr. and Mrs. Cannon with whom I stayed really ensured a wonderful time. I did quite a lot of sightseeing etc. But from the very first day of my stay I noticed how different life was there. I think the word to describe it is – 'detached' or rather a total lack of interdependence. This was something that all the members of our trip afterwards unanimously agreed on. Anyway, after spending two weeks with the families, we all realized that just as Britain is well-developed scientifically, India is far more developed psychologically in its social or community life.

But observing the ways of living was one aspect of the trip. Another was sightseeing and we all saw many different places. The place where I stayed for those two weeks had picturesque countryside views to offer us and in those days, I just wished that I was a poet and could write about the countryside like Wordsworth. Jonathan Cannon, the boy with whom I stayed, was very interested in Cathedral architecture, with the result that I learnt so much about cathedrals, churches, abbeys, priories, etc. that I might as well have been converted to Christianity.

Anyway, after these two weeks, we all met at the Atlantic College in South Wales and each of us was overflowing with stories about our experiences. Nixi seemed the most unfortunate one since the only thing she had done was to go on a 200 miles-long cycling trip. And Guri—oh, she was just beaming with excitement to tell everybody how she had filled the House she had stayed in with Indian food, which she had cooked 'herself' and 'food' wasn't exactly the term she used at the time. Dalal had spent his two weeks with a girl and we all had to listen to his fairytales.

The next week, we all did some social and community work which was arranged for us by Mr Andrew Maclehose, who was the person in-charge for the trip in Britain. This social work varied from making gardens, taking interviews to cleaning dustbins and beaches. Some of us did social work with some problem children; after spending one week working with them, we came to the conclusion that the problem children in India are 'morally' far better than their British counterparts.

Atlantic College organizes a course, every year, called 'The Theory of Knowledge' which explains the logic behind knowledge and we participated in this course very actively. The course consisted of a whole lot of lectures on different subjects and group investigations etc. but one thing which struck us was the different methods of teaching there. One way to describe it in brief would be to say that there is 'active participation' by the students in the class and after very lecture, there was a discussion so that every student can express their views. Another thing which was different from Sanawar was the amount of reference work every student did. But I must say that they had a lot of free time to go to the library and work there, and after every lecture, all of us were always supplied with a bibliography.

The social life of Atlantic College is very different from ours. There is free mixing between boys and girls. The College has students from forty different countries so instead of having House shows, they have Nationals' Evenings and during our period of stay there, we all had an Indian Nationals' evening. Payal and Gagandeep successfully performed Indian classical dances. Gautam, Nakai and I did a Bhangra. Thank God those people did not know what real Bhangra is like. Praneet wore a colourful Rajasthani dress which gained her a lot of boyfriends (good for her). Guri sang some latest Punjabi hits energetically, and Mira really cooperated with every item very willingly. All this time, Mandy was busy taking photographs—although she hasn't thought of blackmailing us as yet. In brief, the girls were a big hit. I must tell you that they had a lot of trusted friends when they left Atlantic College, who even *cried* for them.

One thing about Atlantic College which I'll never forget is how one day, Mr B. Singh told me in a grief-stricken voice to get him some edible food from the local restaurant as he had got tired of the Atlantic College 'English' food. He looked so disturbed that I wouldn't have been surprised if he had burst out crying.

The last highlight of the college, I must say was their discotheque. I don't want to say much about it but one thing I can say is that if the Atlantic College students came to the Sanawarian Social, they'll term us and the social, prehistoric or primitive of the two.

At the end of the theory of knowledge course, we left the college and went on a two-day-long sightseeing trip. On the way, when Kabir went on and on narrating his exhaustive accounts of cars, motorbikes and other vehicles on the road, Kunal complained that he had got so fed up that he wanted to commit suicide.

Our last day was spent shopping in London. We came face to face with Britain's inflation. On this last day, the girls led such a shopping campaign in London's Oxford Circus that we boys most certainly thought that the United Kingdom was going to be denuded of all marketable commodities.

We all left London on 15 August, except for Kunal, who stayed on for an extra week. We bid a tearful goodbye (especially to Ann Richardson and Mr Maclehose, who had looked after us really well) to the foreign land, and so to cheer us all up, Ramyad sang a very melodious Indian wedding song.

P.S. Ramyad's songs were very popular in Atlantic College.

**Jatinder Pal Singh U-VI**
Old Sanawarian (Himalaya 1979)

**Source and Acknowledgement:** *The Sanawarian* **(December 1978)**

# It Began One Sunny Sunday

One Sunday morning, Deepa was sitting on her bed, contemplating her life when she heard a loud voice. 'So, girls, ready to walk down to the cricket field? Match begins in forty-five minutes, and we can't be late.' It was the prefect, making sure everyone was up and moving on that Sunday morning. This prefect was nothing like Parul, the prefect in her previous school.

'Yuck! Do we have to?' she moaned along with the others. The prefect ignored them, as usual. The girls with boyfriends had already prettied up and started walking across campus. Prettying up meant flowing hair, fruit-flavored shiny lip gloss, freshly plucked eyebrows, skirts rolled up well above the knees and stockings rolled down to the ankles.

Sona, Bindu, Gurpreet and Deepa had braided their hair. They looked anything but pretty; their skirts stopped well below their knees, and their stockings were pulled up to almost touch the skirts, no tweezer had ever touched their brow and basic Palmolive Vaseline was as much makeup as any of them could handle as they made their way out to the cricket field. The walk down was pleasant enough, across the hill and then down. Sona, reading their minds said, 'You know, the further down we go, the further up we have to come back.'

'We know, Sona. We are made to do this almost every other weekend. Who wants to go and see a bunch of boys play cricket of all things. Soccer would be interesting, but no one comes to play soccer, do they?' piped in Bindu. 'And soccer players are so good-looking! Not like these cricket players in their long white pants.'

'They are all usually the same people, Bindu, they just look different because their hairy legs show,' said Gurpreet. 'What do good-looking boys matter anyway? They never look at us.'

'But we can look at them,' Deepa said with a sigh.

Boys from both schools were warming up in the dusty field. The covered pavilion was packed with teachers and seniors. The nice thing about not wanting to see or be seen was that there were many spots along the hillside that they could sit and catch an occasional glimpse of the match, but mostly they could just laze leaning on rocks, crushing dried pine needles into little bits between their fingers.

Their school team was batting. The visiting team had taken their positions to field. After an hour of some average bowling and hitting, the home team hit a big one—a six! It came flying right in the girls' direction.

'Oh my god, it's coming right at us!' Gurpreet exclaimed as they watched the ball arc high in the air to begin its slow descent directly above them like a dead bird descending to earth, but they were too fascinated to move. When they finally looked away, and scurried out of the ball's path, Deepa looked up to see the most attractive boy she had ever seen, dusty and sweaty, running to get the ball. The ball fell right into their pile of broken pine needles and disappeared out of sight.

'Excuse me, have you seen the ball?' the boy asked breathlessly. All four of them were silent, boys never spoke to them. But they had to quickly tell him where the ball was or they would be accused of helping the home team score so they all pointed at the pine needle mountain in unison. The boy grabbed the ball out of the pile and looked at them quizzically.

Then he looked right at Deepa and said, 'See you around,' before he ran back to the pitch.

\* \* \*

And she did. Deepa met the boy again on a trip to Simla to visit her grandparents. One evening, Deepa, her sister Diya and her cousin Dev who was also visiting, left their grandparents at the ridge and went over to Baljee's for an early dinner before going to a play at Gaiety Theatre. After dinner, they stood outside the theatre with a crowd of people not unlike them, waiting for the doors to open. Deepa felt an excitement she couldn't explain or describe. She found out soon after the play began. One of the cast members in a prominent role—with a magnificent singing voice—was the young man from the cricket field. They had seats in the middle of the auditorium, but Deepa felt his eyes were only on her. She was unnerved by the sheer proximity of this person she thought she would never see again, and she was confused, though she couldn't really understand why. His name was Yash, she didn't notice his last name.

They waited outside as the crowd dwindled. And then there he was, with a group of cast members, beaming after the standing ovation. Dev walked over to some of the cast and shook their hands, congratulating them. Eventually, he reached Yash. Deepa was close behind him, watching his every move. She would have been too shy to engage with the cast members on her own. Diya was right next to her, also shaking hands with the actors and sometimes reaching out and hugging some of them. Yash was one of the people she hugged. He bent down and returned the hug. That was when he saw her over Diya's shoulder. He immediately exclaimed: 'Aha, pine needle girl!'

Deepa couldn't believe it. 'Her name is Deepa,' Dev chimed in. 'And you are Yash? Excellent performance. Well done. Where are you off to next? Are you touring all summer?'

Deepa remained silent, staring at the two young men chat. How comfortably they could talk to each other after having just met! Even her little sister was meting out hugs and little niceties without any effort whatsoever. These things didn't come so easily to her. She stood awkwardly as Dev continued talking to Yash before she finally nudged him.

'I've got Yash's number. He's from Bombay but spends time in Delhi with his grandparents. I'll arrange an ice cream date at Nirula's when you girls are back in Delhi. How's that?' Dev said.

'Sounds good, guys. Got to run. See you around, Deepa,' said Yash.

\* \* \*

And she did, yet again. Not only did Deepa see him again, but years later, her mother also arranged her marriage with him. The man she was to marry was the same Yash, the boy who expected everyone to look at him when he walked into a room. The boy who acted in plays that travelled to different cities and who sang the lyrics of Broadway musicals as if he'd seen the shows on Broadway. The boy who had said 'see you around' to everyone without meaning a word of it as if he had known that it was an American expression that simply meant 'bye'. It was the same Yash who came to Deepa's school to play cricket against the boys and who made all the girls swoon, both when he was dusty and grimy on the cricket field and when he was cleaned up with his school blazer on, accepting the winner's cup on behalf of his team.

This was the Yash she was going to marry. He wasn't the boy he had been and he hadn't turned into the man many such boys became when they grew up—not very different from what they were as boys. Boy Yash would not have agreed to marry Deepa. They were not from the same teenage social standing and while people change and grow up and mature, that teen hierarchy lasts forever. Something had changed for him, something significant, something that affected his image and how he wanted others to see him.

Yash had wandered through Deepa's head for years. Even while she dated other men, looking for that elusive one who was husband material, she had thought about him and their chance encounters. She didn't believe in destiny or serendipity or even feng shui, so she never thought they would meet and be arranged to marry. But his young visage walked through her dreams, casually, nonchalantly, in that way he had of sauntering across the cricket field for a water break.

**Priya Hajela**
Harpriya B. Singh | Himalaya 1985 | 1979–1985
Author, *Ladies' Tailor*, (HarperCollins Publishers India, 2022)

**This is an excerpt from a work-in-progress novel titled *Related***

OS Siblings – Sister – Aman B. Singh | Himalaya 1989 | 1980–1985

# Mistakes That Make Us

Each one of us, a speck in the universe, is also the universe. Our birth, parents, ancestors and genes, direct our lives and are directed by us. The phenotype, the exposure, the ambience, especially during the formative years, is the game changer.

There are and have been billions of people in the world, yet less than 15,000 have had the opportunity to be associated with Sanawar, in its 175 years of existence. I feel truly blessed that circumstances aligned to create an opportunity for me to spend some years at The Lawrence School, Sanawar. I was to join in August 1981. That April, Mrs and Mr Parel (Lily and MJ) came to Manali for Annual Camps. They gave me an opportunity to accompany the group in climbing Mangal Kot. It opened another facet of learning and growth and honed my skills for the game of life.

Lady Honoria and Sir Henry Lawrence's philanthropic vision lives on through the stalwarts – the torchbearers – who oversaw the growth of each pupil by thoughtful, sometimes imperceptible actions that had a profound bearing.

Life is full of trial, error and learning. Most of us do what is expected of us and don't live our life on our terms. We feel ecstatic when others praise us and despondent when someone finds fault. However, with time, we must learn to stand our own ground and be equanimous. And the hilltop proved to be the ideal incubator, in that sense.

Forty years ago, in March 1982, I was escorted back home with Bansiji, the office peon, for being caught cheating in L-V. I was fudging in Mrs Lily Parel's geography final exam, referring to the chit I had carried. I wanted to get full marks! On being caught, Heady called me to his office, asked me to leave immediately for home (Manali), explain to my parents what I had done and then come back. We travelled by bus, and on reaching, I broke the news to my parents. They drove me back immediately. I missed only one exam. They met Heady, who expressed his disappointment, 'Vineet is not learning to be a good citizen of the country'. And that made me decide to never cheat again in life. No matter what the stakes, the temptation, the ease or the peer pressure. There are some life-directing moments in a person's life; experiences which make a 'man' of you. And this, definitely, was one of mine.

My Housemaster, Dr H.P.S. Dhillon (aka UD) was also my English teacher. He had helped me settle in the dorm when I had joined in L-V. I still remember him cheering me on to complete the Hodson run. In one monthly assessment, he insisted on rewarding me a 'B6C', which resulted in me missing out on a 'Distinction' and signing the Honours Book for that academic year. He stood his ground and maintained that I did not deserve a distinction in that assessment. He did not care about the points at stake for the House. Later, on several occasions in my life, I have observed myself standing up for principles even if it resulted in an apparent 'loss' to me or someone I care about.

For an Upper Sixer, it was customary to have an aide-de-camp. When I was appointed school prefect, Ish Joshi took charge of waking me up for my Chota Hazri, making my bed and running other daily chores. On reflection, it saddens me to think that young, impressionable minds were tasked in this manner which could have scarred some for life.

One night, past lights-out, some of us decided to taste the 'forbidden fruit', i.e. Butter Chicken at Gyani's. On the way down to Sukhi Jodi, rehearsing the local dialect and accent '. . . *roti toh khani hi khani, chicken bhi khana* . . .', was abruptly halted by a pair of approaching headlights. We scrambled to cling onto the khud side. It was Heady's Jeep! 'Who's there?'

Something came over me. Being a school prefect, I decided that a lot was at stake and continued to hide, abandoning the others. I saw them climb up, be questioned and herded off in the Jeep. 'Chacun pour soi'—everyone is entitled to make their own choices in life. Returning on foot all by myself, I met Massey near Hospi and shammed having a splitting headache to cover my tracks. The others, in the meanwhile, were not picked up by Heady, but by Kripi, his driver, and dropped off near the Green Gate. They started on their way back to Moti Corner, were spotted by Abu and put on morning drill, till further orders. All in one night. So many forces at play. Though I'd read Gandhi by then, I hadn't really internalized his value system. Being dishonest in order to save my own backside, came easy to me. But something changed that night. I saw that my friends had stood up for me. They were willing to put their own interest on the line and look out for me. They had my back. I learnt what it takes to be a trustworthy friend.

Achievement in Sanawar, more often than not, was the result of a collective effort, where each individual gave his best to add to the House points tally. However, sometimes it so happened that an individual outshone the others, contributing disproportionately beyond the average. Nevertheless, protocol was always respected and it would be the House Captain who would go up to receive the trophy/cup on behalf of the entire House. We were assembled in Barne Hall. Himalaya House won the Study Cup. I, being an Honours Book signator, yielded to the prodding around me and marched up to receive it from Mrs Pheroza Das. Sharmaji captured the moment, in black and white, for posterity. Not a word was spoken of this, ever, but as I was walking back down the aisle, I realized that I had got carried away and erred. Jonathan Charles Karoki Lewis, our House Captain should have received it, in fact, along with the Girls' House Captain, Namrata Khungar. This was yet another lesson for life. Just the other day, I caught myself musing over this very incident as I watched our daughter Anshee, a key contributor, applauding her House Captain receiving the swimming trophy. Never make the same mistake twice, there are plenty of new ones . . .

Sanawar has gifted me integrity, etiquette, lessons for life, memories and the most dependable friends who are there till the last bugle's call. Life on the hilltop made me responsible, accountable and I believe, a person who rises to the occasion and can be trusted.

The legacy lingers on and calls out to Never Give In.

**Vineet Khanna**
Himalaya 1985 | 1981–1985
Teacher

# The School Colours

On 28 June 1853, Sanawar was granted its first stand of Colours by Governor General Lord Dalhousie in fulfilment of an intention he had expressed to the founder, following his first visit and inspection of the asylum in September 1851. The stand consisted of two flags, each of heavy-duty double silk. The Asylum Colour was a flag of plain yellow with the Union flag 'canton' (in the upper left quarter); in the centre of the flag were the words 'Lawrence Asylum Sanawar', embroidered in gold thread, encircled by a wreath of oak leaves entwined with the heraldic emblems of England, Scotland and Ireland (The Rose, Thistle and Shamrock, respectively). This centrepiece was surmounted by a Lion rampant 'or' (gold). The embroidery is said to have been done entirely by Lady Lawrence during the winter of 1852. The second was the Union flag, or 'Union Jack', granted by vice-regal assent. These two Colours were thereafter carried on all ceremonial occasions and Sunday morning Church Parades for the next seventy years.

On 13 March 1922, having been granted royal approval for a change of title from 'Lawrence Military Asylum' to 'The Lawrence Royal Military School', Sanawar was presented with a new school Colour by HRH the Prince of Wales at a Drumhead Service and ceremony held in Dehra Dun. The new Colour, again with the Union flag shown 'canton', had as its centrepiece the full Lawrence family Coat of Arms, encircled by the new school title in gold thread, and the whole surmounted by the Imperial Crown on a creamy white silk background. The Colour was the gift of Sir Alexander Waldemar Lawrence, fourth Baronet and grandson of the founder. The old Colour, now much faded and worn, was laid to rest in the Chapel. At the same ceremony, the school was presented with a new Union flag, to replace the old 'Queen's' Colour granted by Lord Dalhousie in 1853. These two new Colours were again carried on all ceremonial occasions and Sunday morning Church Parades until July 1937, when, owing to their fragile condition, the practice of carrying them on Sunday morning Church Parades ceased.

It is not known how or when the College of Arms first became involved in matters concerning the school Colour but on 8 July 1938, in a letter to the Director General, India Store Department, it was observed by the Garter Principal King of Arms and Inspector of Regimental Colours that the flag presented to Sanawar in 1922 did not conform to the regulations for the composition and design of unit or Regimental (school) Colours. Furthermore, the gift, although no doubt given in perfectly good faith, was in direct contravention of long-established heraldic protocols and principles. He pointed out that the flag displayed the full armorial bearings of the Lawrence family, and arms granted on the authority of the sovereign by Letters Patent cannot represent two or more different persons or entities. The school should have its own arms, he decreed. He accordingly proposed a standard with a centrepiece or roundel comprising 'a ragged cross gules (in red) bearing an eastern crown or (gold) . . .' on a white background, around which the title of the unit (school) was to be inscribed in gold lettering on a circular crimson band. This roundel was to be encircled by a wreath of oak leaves entwined with the heraldic emblems of England, Scotland and Ireland and additionally, a blue fir (deodar) representing the Himalayan setting. The complete emblem, surmounted by the Imperial crown, was to be set on a blue background, as required by the school's royal status. Royal regiments and schools always have blue facings.

Accordingly, on Founders' Day, 13 September 1940, a new, officially approved 'Regimental' Colour, as described above and pictured left, was duly presented to the school by the Governor-General Lord Linlithgow at a Drumhead Service held on Peacestead. The 'old', much-loved 1922 Colour was ceremoniously marched off the field and laid to rest in the Chapel. Many were disappointed that the new flag displayed very little of the Lawrence family escutcheon which, after so many years, had become the cherished emblem, symbol and badge of the school. Worse still, the words of the motto, long since adopted by the school, and which had inspired many generations of Sanawarians, were also omitted. So was the name Sanawar. Head Boy and Flag Bearer Bob James, who received the Colour from the Viceroy wrote many years later, 'I simply didn't like it. It was nothing like the old one and never meant as much to me'. He spoke for many Sanawarians (and staff) who felt the same way. Notwithstanding, this new, 'officially' approved school Colour was dutifully trooped on the King's Birthday and Founders' Day parades for the next five years.

Sometime after Founders' Day in October 1946 and before the King's Birthday Parade in June 1947, the central roundel applique was carefully unpicked and removed from the 1940 flag and replaced with the full, embroidered coat of arms of the Lawrence family. Close inspection reveals slight differences in the workmanship of the embroidery and adjustment of the crest and scroll to fit into the available space. It is not clear whether this change to the school Colour was officially approved or if it was, by whom. It is known that there had been lengthy correspondence on the matter between the school, the Adjutant General's Branch in Delhi and the Garter King of Arms in London since 1943, but the letters appear to have been lost. Certainly, special dispensation from the College of Arms would have been needed for such a radical change of policy and protocol. However, whether it was approved or not, this modified Colour was dutifully and proudly carried on the King's Birthday Parade in June 1947 and again on the Founders' Day Centenary Parade and memorial service, the following October. After Independence, this same Colour continued to be paraded until 1957 when it was finally laid to rest and replaced with the present Lawrence School Flag. The 1940 flag, along with the tattered remnants of its two predecessors, is today encased in glass and on display in the school Museum (Parker Hall).

The centrepiece, or 'roundel' applique, that was removed from the controversial 1940 'Regimental' Colour in 1946/47, was evidently given as a memento to Mr E.G. Carter. He was the officiating school secretary at the time and would no doubt have been closely and personally involved in the exchange of correspondence between the school, the Adjutant General's Branch and the College of Arms. Mr Carter, many years later, bequeathed the roundel to his son, Dr Timothy Carter, who in turn presented it to the school museum on behalf of the Class of 1953, at their sixtieth reunion in October 2013. The embroidered roundel remains on display behind glass in Parker Hall, with a plaque that reads, ' THE CENTREPIECE (ROUNDEL) OF THE REGIMENTAL COLOURS PRESENTED TO THE SCHOOL, ON FOUNDER'S DAY 1940, BY H.E. THE VICEROY LORD LINLITHGOW. THE SAME WAS BEQUEATHED BY MR E.G. CARTER, HEADMASTER 1947-56, TO HIS SON DR TIMOTHY CARTER, WHO PRESENTED IT TO THE SCHOOL, ON BEHALF OF THE CLASS OF 1953, AT THEIR 60TH REUNION ON 2ND OCTOBER, 2013'.

**D.V. Boddington**
LRMS Sanawar 1942–1947
October 2015

**Sources and Acknowledgements:**

- *The Lawrence Military Asylum: A Brief Account of the last 10 years*, compiled by the Rev. William J. Parker et al. (LMA Press, Sanawar, 1858).
- Extract from the Annual Report on the Lawrence Royal Military School, Sanawar for the year ending 31 March 1922 to the Chief of the General Staff, Army Headquarters, Simla, India by The Reverend G.D. Barne OBE, MA, Principal.
- LRMS ORDERS by The Reverend E.A. Evans, MA, No. 311 dated 8 July 1937.
- Letter dated 6 July 1938 from the Inspector of Regimental Colours, College of Arms, London to the Director General India Store Department and Adjutant General's Branch, AG11 (India). Former School archives.
- H. 'Bob' James and Peter Fuller, 'The New School Colour', *Old Sanawarian Association Magazine*, May 1991.

# Barne on Peacestead

This happened in 1965. I remember that night so well, when five of us decided to do something really adventurous in an attempt to liven up our mundane routine. To explore the realm of the dangerous and exciting . . . to tap into the paranormal . . .

We were aware that we would be breaking rules. The coven – though we weren't twelve in count – huddled in the Lower Dorm Common Room. A 70x56cm chart paper, with all alphabets and numbers from zero to nine written on it with a Camlin sketchpen, was to serve as our makeshift Ouija board. The exhilaration and anticipation in the room was palpable, as we took turns to put our index finger on the coin. Our guest for tonight's talk show was none other than The Rt. Rev. George Dunsford Barne. Oh God! The finger moved . . . our hair stood up in *salaami-shastr* . . .

Anita, catching her breath, asked, 'Are you here, Sir?'

The coin moved to 'Yes'.

As Pam prepared herself to ask the next question, we heard a voice outside.

Oh God! It was Mrs Kemp, the authoritarian Siwalik Housemistress. Disaster! Was this the end? Would we be expelled? You can imagine our dilemma. In that moment of panic, we forgot to send The Bishop 'back to the pavilion'. All of a sudden, the 'talking board' seemed to have acquired a life of its own, falling off the table. The holy spirit must have floated around as the door turned on its hinges and there she stood . . . grim-faced and seething with frenzied rage.

'I see that you have been calling spirits?' We had lost at our voices. Finally, I managed a 'Ma'am, we are very sorry.'

'How dare you dabble in such a dangerous transgression?'

More silence . . . 'Tomorrow, you will write a letter to your parents telling them exactly what you did, apologize for it, and promise that you'll never do it again.' Saying that, she left in a huff, as we mumbled our apologies.

The hapless Ouija board lay dead on the floor. We looked around to see where the hell George was. After all, we hadn't bid him farewell.

Hope he's not soul-stirring within the periphery of Peacestead . . .

So, so sorry, Sir . . .

**(Bhuvnesh Kumari) Jyoti Lall**
Bhuvi | Siwalik 1968 | 1963–1968
Owner – Playhouse Nursery School, Agra

OS Children – Daughter – Divya Lall | Jojo | Nilagiri 2001 | 1994–2001

# Terrorized by Mathematics

Those of us who were in Mr Idris's class for maths or had the pleasure of being taught by the very scary Mr Kohli, would remember how terrorizing maths was in school. So, on a freezing cold March 1982 evening, the day before our maths 10th boards, I witnessed the funniest episode ever. In fact, I still find it hilarious while retelling the story now, some forty years later. There were ten of us in our batch in Nilagiri House girls' dorm. Our beds were facing each other across the central aisle. Rohini Vij, affectionately called Vijjo, had her bed next to mine. We were all fervently cramming before the most horrid exam, tucked sitting up under our heavy, bulky quilts. As the evening wore on and it got late, a lot of us were dozing off, waking up, cramming a little more and eventually falling asleep with the book open in our laps. But not Vijjo. She was so terrified of maths that she wouldn't allow herself to sleep at all. However, it was getting increasingly difficult for her to keep awake as well. As we were in close proximity to one another, one sort of knew what the other was doing. So, here's the firsthand account of what happened that evening.

Now, Vijjo is resourceful and could think outside the box. So, in the silence of a very studious dorm, we saw Vijjo emerge from under her quilt, put aside her maths book and walk towards the loos. This piqued our interest as we knew Vijjo darling had been dreading this night the most. A few minutes passed in silence before the soft clangs of a metal bucket were heard, and then Vijjo came back, carrying a bucket full of water and a serious look on her face. Without looking around, she tenderly placed the bucket between her bed and mine, adjusting it close to the edge of her bed and then proceeded to stroke the outside rim with such loving affection as if her life depended on it. The rest of us were still perplexed as to why Vijjo needed a full bucket of water, so close by. As we watched, or rather peeked, pretending to be engrossed in maths revision, Vijjo got into her bed, smoothed the quilt over herself, brought the maths textbook onto her lap and then tucked her arms under the covers, proceeding to study maths with an exasperated look.

Time passed slowly as we watched silently, our gaze intently on her and she, oblivious to us watching. After fifteen minutes, that seemed like forty-five, we saw Vijjo sway slightly with sleep, as maths definitely bored her. The next instance, we saw Vijjo, bent from her waist, straight down towards or rather plunged into the bucket of water without taking her arms out from under the quilt or bothering to get up. This was followed by a loud splash as her face was submerged in the bucket and she rose from there like a phoenix, ready to battle again. Drenched . . . water dripping everywhere . . . and no towel in sight.

There was a moment's pause before the scene in front of us truly sunk in. We exploded in raucous laughter, waking everyone up. Mrs Sidhu, our matron, came out of her room and the prefects descended upon us ominously to see what was happening. I don't remember well what followed, but Vijjo, bending from her waist to reach the bucket, without taking her arms out of the quilt, is still the funniest sight I have seen in my life. This is how terrorizing maths was back in 1982!

P.S. Vijjo passed the maths boards. It's a different story how she learned maths and passed the exam, though. She had memorized the whole textbook by heart, page numbers and all.

**Anuradha (Varma) Bhatt**
Verms | Nilagiri 1984 | 1977–1984

OS Sibling – Brother – Alok Varma | Loki | Nilagiri 1986 | 1977–1983

# Forty Boys and Twenty Girls

India gained her independence on 15 August 1947 and on 4 October 1947, the then Governor-General Lord Mountbatten presided over the school's Centenary. Thereafter began the exodus of around 700 pupils, from the school that had served the children of the British soldiers for a hundred years.

When I joined in March 1948, I was among the first Indians (forty boys and twenty girls) to participate in and witness Sanawar transform to become one of India's leading public schools. We wore old, patched and darned military uniforms. The Mess food was spartan—cold porridge, ice-cold fried eggs, chilled bread, washed down with boiling hot tea for breakfast. Lunch was a plate of mashed potatoes, boiled fatty meat with a brown sauce and boiled vegetables. Pudding was for pampered newcomers only. Dinner was boiled dal, bread and some indeterminate vegetables. Rations came from the Army Supply Depot in Kasauli.

We were housed in the upper and lower dorms of Wavell Court. The transition was really tough, initially, and improvement ever so slow. I still remember the cry of delight when we found chapatis and chicken curry on our plates. We started getting half a day off from classes on Indian festivals, but had to make up with extra classes on the following Wednesdays. Discipline was strict and duly inculcated in us through a free use of canes on the naughty, and the privilege of getting an extra one if no 'thank you' was forthcoming. We were to speak English, think in English and even dream in English. So new boys provided tremendous entertainment. Jagbir Singh, in L-III, was heard telling another boy, 'If we went, then we went, if no went then no went, I am wenting to the Tuck Shop'.

The chief guest for Founders' Day was our first Defence Minister Baldev Singh and I remember Mrs Kemp giggling as my beret fell off while doing 'Eyes Right' at the march past. After Founders', the countdown to Home Day (18 December 1948) began. We would be back in our home clothes and would see some teary-eyed teachers. A few faint hearts readily forgave all the caning. Sanawar stood deserted but for the Union Jack that continued to flutter on the Chapel, every Sunday.

In 1949, the Lawrence Royal Military School, was handed over by the Ministry of Defence to the Ministry of Education in the corridors of Delhi, and became The Lawrence School. A letter from India's first C-in-C, Gen. Kodandera Madappa Cariappa to Mr Carter was displayed in Barne Hall. For us kids, the significance was lost, initially, but soon, change became visible—the withdrawal of the army havildar for PT, the closing of the practice of arms drill, the bell-tolling in the morning and evening instead of the bugle, etc. A limited version of Houses was reintroduced and children were divided into Blue and Yellow Houses, which, in 1950, became Nilagiri and Himalaya, respectively. The student strength started rising steadily. Education Minister Maulana Abdul Kalam Azad, when he came as the Founders' chief guest, exhorted us to prepare to serve the nation as the future now rested on our tiny shoulders. The Indian tricolour replaced the Union Jack atop the Chapel.

1950 was significant for me as I was among the first recipients of the first GOI Merit Scholarships that resulted in a double promotion, from U-III to U-IV. Also, my twelve-year heart missed a mighty beat as I fell in love with my classmate, the day she joined the class. The strength of BD crossed 100 as Gen. Cariappa removed his two children from Doon School, and brought Nanda and Nalini to join us instead. The Korean War had broken out, while the Communists had launched direct action in Telengana. The newspapers were full of these accounts. Mr Carter started holding weekly meetings with the Senior School to educate us on the world outside. An incipient interest was aroused that gradually became a genuine interest in international affairs and, in 1962, led to my joining the Indian Foreign Service—the first Sanawarian to do so.

The high standards set and implemented for the students were gradually impressing young and old alike in different parts of India, and with the passage of time, the student as well as faculty began to take on a national character. Gen. Cariappa was the chief guest at Founders' 1950.

In 1951, I was in L-V (called Junior Cambridge then) when first President Dr Rajendra Prasad was invited to be the chief guest at Founders'. Yet again, we were reminded of the national-interest tasks we were being prepared for. One of my favourite hymns I can still recall was, 'O Father in Heaven who lovest all, help Thy children when they call, that they may bring if need arise, no maimed or worthless sacrifice'.

I did not return in 1952 as after matriculation, I joined college.

What did Sanawar teach me in those formative years? To stand up in life on one's own feet, oppose the wrong and do the right . . . And Never Give In!

**Prithvi Raj Sood**
Ratty | Nilagiri 1953 | 1948 – 1951
Indian Foreign Service | Ambassador to several countries

# My Term as the Head Girl

'Tania Talwar, Head Girl' 'Hey! who's that?' 'Dimple, ya!?' 'Good heavens! how unexpected!' 'Congratulations', 'Best of luck'! When I myself heard of this, I was more shocked than anyone else, I think. At the same time, I was filled with a strange feeling—one of pride and fear, success and enthusiasm, but all along, there was a dark and sinister shadow in my mind, the possibility of being a failure.

Before coming to school, I was on top of the world. The idea of a cubicle to myself and attending all the various parties was most appealing. When I reached school, I received a severe shock.

The very fact that the discipline of the whole girls' school depended upon me was quite a load on my shoulders. The prefects who were new to their jobs often forgot some of their duties and this led to quite a few tiffs between them and me! It was eventually righted and we came to a clear understanding.

Even though I tried my very best to ring all the bells on time, there were quite a few times when they were rung late. I remember one instance clearly. It was in the first term. The timetable had changed that week and I hadn't realized, so I had the supper bell rung ten minutes late. The result was that the whole school double marched up to Parker Hall. I bit my tongue quite a few times that evening! But luck was on my side and we reached the hall just in time. There were other such instances when I wasn't so lucky.

There were days when my heart swelled with pride, when I was gay and light-hearted, when I wanted to sing till my throat went hoarse, but there were also streams of tears when I thought I had been grossly misunderstood, and felt miserable and sick at heart. But I soon came to realize that the girls were not really bad at heart. They were a little boisterous at first and thought I was a stick in the mud, but later, most of them realized that whatever I did was invariably in their interest. I only hope I have helped to make Sanawar better than it was and there are not many black marks against me.

My pride knew no bounds when I was introduced as Head Girl to Mr Pasricha, our new headmaster, and Mrs Pasricha. The fact that I was the first Head Girl at the beginning of this new era made me feel quite important.

Before ending, I would like to thank all the staff for all they have done for me, and also for providing such wonderful and unforgettable days. I would also like to wish the future Head Boy and Head Girl (I wonder who!) the very best of luck.

**Tania Talwar**
Head Girl 1970
Old Sanawarian (Vindhya 1970)

**Source and Acknowledgement:** *The Sanawarian* **(December, 1970)**

# CDH Knives, PD Girls, a Tree and a Play

A question: can a gaggle of twelve-year-old girls with blunt CDH kitchen knives get into deep trouble? And what if I said their intentions were good, but their approach probably as blunt as those knives?

The year was 1979 and our last in PD (we would eventually graduate as the '86 batch). Christmas was around the corner and winter vacations fast approaching. A group of us girls were intent on closing the year in style and giving the Girls' Prep School dorms a celebratory send-off. We planned a Christmas play and a gift (a milk and chocolate powder mix bought with our own pocket money and wrapped in paper) for every attendee. There was just one thing missing: a Christmas tree to pull it all together.

But of course, that was no problem. The beautiful pine trees cascading down every hillside looked like ours for the taking. So, the only problem was deciding when and how we would get the said tree.

The first part of the plan entailed each of us sneaking out a knife from CDH without being caught. The second was to identify a tree that was majestic, but easy enough to cut down, carry up, and thereafter hide in the dorm. And the third, to decide the date and time to start cutting the identified tree, so that it would be on hand just in time for the big reveal on our special day.

And so we spent a few precious Saturday evenings down the khud, first identifying, and then proceeding to cut the chosen tree. The blunt CDH knives were the start of our problems. But a gaggle of well-meaning, naive (or rebellious, as we thought of ourselves) girls can't be stopped. The tree was finally cut, carried up and hidden (near the boiler room, I think, with clear instructions to the boiler man that this was not wood for heating our baths). But a tree that size just can't be hidden for long. And our (mis)deed was reported to the PD headmistress, Mrs Kapila.

We were summoned to her office, given a sermon on the importance of trees (my first on the ecosystem and sustainability), that ended with us being banned from performing our play. We were aghast—our

645

intentions were good and Mrs Kapila, oh so bad! We were furious and then, very sad. Our hard work and plans dashed over a stupid tree that we couldn't see helping us either now or in the future—oxygen and clean air be damned!

But then, a few days later, in true Mrs Kapila style, she called us back into her office for another talk, and with amazing grace, withdrew her prescribed punishment and told us we were welcome to perform. And perform we did, with Mrs Kapila sitting up front and centre. She ended the evening detailing to the rest of the dorm our misdeed – but I seem to remember a hint of pride in her voice – because our intent was selfless and aimed to bring joy and smiles to all in the dorm.

Disclaimer: It's been thirty-plus years since this incident. Memories fade, so apologies to those who might remember it differently. The intent here also remains the same—bringing joy and smiles to all.

**Priya (Sarma) Mathur**
Siwalik 1986 | 1976–1985
Senior Sustainability Manager – Unilever (N. Africa, Middle East, Turkey, Russia, Ukraine and Belarus) | 'Top 10 Marketing Game Changers 2020'

by Campaign Magazine UAE for launching the UAE Chapter of the Unstereotype Alliance with UN Women

OS Parent – Mother – Grp. Capt. (Retd.) Kanta Sarma | Vindhya 1956 | 1951–1953

OS Siblings –Brother – Samar Vijay Sarma | Siwalik 1987 | 1980–1985
              Sister – Tanya Sarma | Bugsy | Siwalik 1995 | 1989–1995

# Dancing in the Air

Sanawar, a legendary institution where I was fortunate to have learnt some of the most treasured lessons in life, also gave me the 'Never Give In' spirit which has aided me to overcome every challenge that has come my way. These inspirational words, sung over and over again from the tender age of seven, and all through the teens, work their magic from time to time, forever rekindling fond memories of school.

An enchanting, steadfast bond bestowed upon each of us by our wonderful alma mater as we stepped out into the wider world—not just an everlasting connection with one another, but a plethora of experiences, tales, stories and cherished memories attached to Sanawar remain unfaded and forever magical.

One such memory is, and will always, remain close to my heart. It was my first Socials – a big deal, rather a deal of tremendous magnitude – with the excitement building up, rattling nerves, blushing cheeks with faces flushed and sweltering palms, we girls lined up on one side of Barne Hall, whilst the boys lined up on the other. Each one of us looked our best, rather breathtaking. Whispers in the air and teasing nudges were glaringly obvious all around—'He's looking at you . . . no, no, he's looking at you'. The hall seemed flooded with coy faces. All of a sudden, a hush fell . . . the trail of excitement seemed to have met its deadend.

Someone announced over the PA system, from the 'control room' up in the balcony: 'Can the Head Boy please set the ball rolling?' The next instant, I saw this slender, six-foot tall fellow making his way towards us. He stopped right in front of me, 'Can I have the first dance with you, please,' he said softly, as he stretched out his hand. A quick glance to my left and right and a little nudge from the girl next to me later, I went sort of numb. It seemed surreal. 'He's the Head Boy,' a nervous little-voice said from within me, as though warning me to not refuse him. As he led me to the centre of the hall, my heart seemed to skip every other beat, leaving me feeling timorous and abashed. The music began. I tried to glance up . . .

and up . . . and up, to look him in the eye. He was taller than the tallest of the boys. I was tiny in height . . . inches, rather a foot (or more) shorter, in comparison. There was no way my hand would ever reach his towering shoulders.

Before I could decide on my next move, I found myself being gently lifted off the floor. The fellow swayed with the music, holding me firmly in his arms. There was a sudden uproar of loud, shrieking voices, coupled with unreserved laughter. The hall echoed with feisty clapping from all corners. Before long, the dance floor was jammed up with girls and boys, throwing all caution to the wind. Finally, I found my feet on the ground once again. The Head Boy smiled and thanked me, escorting me back to my friends.

I don't recall getting any sleep that night, but the five-minute daunting experience that left me all quivery and embarrassed back then, changed into the sweetest everlasting memory I made in school.

**Sangeeta (Ahluwalia) Walia**
Ahlu | Himalaya 1980 | 1969–1979
Early Years Special Needs Coordinator for nine years | Published first book in 2017, *My Autistic Angel – The Ultimate Teacher*

OS Siblings – Sister – Kavita Ahluwalia | Himalaya 1976 | 1968–1976
Brother – Jitendra Ahluwalia | Himalaya 1970–1981

# Desserted on Sundae

Shortly after the Central Dining Hall (CDH) started in 1979, a few of us preppers were taken on a tour of the state-of-the-art kitchen. It was the first time most of us were seeing a commercial kitchen and it looked space-age. A sea of stainless steel and the whistling sound of steam greeted us. All around was gigantic food preparation and cooking equipment. The deep freezers and chillers were so large that one could walk into them. Huge lights in one corner bedazzled us. These, we were told assuredly, were heat lamps to keep cooked food warm. We were sure that it would easily be one of the best equipped and most hygienic school kitchens in the country. We felt our days of watery daals, soggy cabbage, leathery chapatis and solidified custard were well over, and finally, we had a kitchen that would cater to our tastes.

However, the food continued to be quite plain, though meeting our basic nutritional needs. We were always hungry (the myth that hunger helps in student character-building was still alive) and dreamt of raiding the kitchen or enjoying a midnight feast.

Ensuring adequate food for hundreds of hungry kids is an enormous task. This responsibility fell on Maj. Menon, the catering in-charge who should be considered one of the unsung heroes of our school. After years of overseeing food for army kitchens and creating ration packs for hardened soldiers during his days in the army supply corps, his experience at CDH must have made him realize that Napoleon Bonaparte's apocryphal comment, 'an army marches on its stomach' also applies to boarding school children.

The army of cooks that he commandeered were not known for their culinary skills, nor did they try to refine them, knowing that diners would come irrespective. One could often make out the quality of food about to be served without even seeing it. All one had to do was to decode the look on the brave Major's face while marching into CDH. Most days, he looked anxious and stressed, biting his lips or clasping his hands behind his back.

650

We knew the food would be bland and tasteless. A few times a month, he had a look of bewilderment, probably wondering why the marching up masses have never protested against what was provided to them for subsistence. We knew the food would again be very unpleasant and greasy. And the food was simply inedible on days when we detected fear on his face. He literally seemed ready for flight, and we would observe that he would even be ducking away from Mucchoo, afraid of being confronted (yes, it wasn't just us kids, but even the teachers would dodge Mucchoo at times).

The kitchen did attempt some refinements with modest success, like incorporating chicken stew, fried rice, sautéed vegetables, baked beans and classic spaghetti to the menu. A half-decent sweet dish (our name for desserts) was a pipe dream and each preparation, whether it was vermicelli, custard, fruit cream, tea cakes or bread and butter pudding, was an outrage for the taste buds. But it was the ice creams that always bemused me. How could one get it so wrong?

Even at Sanawar, it gets rather hot during the summer months and cooling off with ice cream or a swim in the pool was always a welcome respite. It must have been during one of the summers in the early '80s when it was announced that on the coming Sunday, ice cream would be served. Many of us visualized an ice-cream van pull up outside the school gate, which we could attack and then indulge in all those delicious flavours with fancy names.

The mood was still cheerful when we were told that it would be ice cream from CDH. After all, how wrong could one go following a recipe that basically comprises of milk, cream, sugar and some vanilla or strawberry extract? It was a sweltering day and at the appointed hour, we reached CDH for what we thought was special ice cream.

At first, I was not sure if what I was handed out was sorbet or ice cream. A tentative bite confirmed it was ice cream. But it had ice shards that mercilessly struck the roof of my mouth. I braved on and took a few more bites in the hope of tasting some creamy goodness. But it melted very quickly and turned gooey. This was not your regular ice cream, and definitely not with natural ingredients using full-fat milk from pasture-fed cows as I was wishing. I was about to discard it when on the cup, I read our school motto. The cups had abstract designs in the four House colors with our abiding motto emblazoned across it.

I was in a dilemma to throw or not to throw. Somehow, I summoned my courage and continued to tuck into it. I told myself that most sophisticated foods are an acquired taste. And so it might be the case with this unique ice cream. The last few bites were salty and even had a musty odour. But surprisingly, I relished it. We taste with our brains; perhaps by then, it had been conditioned into accepting anything from CDH as palatable.

I was back next Sunday and an even larger number of Sanawarians turned up to sate their summer craving. Many flavours were attempted, most of which could not be comprehended, but I did catch whiffs of what seemed like Odomos, muddy chocolate, minty banana and synthetic cinnamon (probably an attempt at vanilla). But one continued to encounter the icy shards and their mind-numbing effect.

Just as one got used to the taste and texture of the ice cream, an unexpected rumour spread that on the following Sunday, ice cream would be served in cones. My Sunday stopovers for ice cream immediately ended. I feared the ice cream cones might be 'doggie' biscuits by another name and shape. No human taste receptors could have withstood it unless one was suffering from pica.

Mercifully, it was nothing but a rumour and soon, it was time for summer holidays.

**Jugraj Singh**
Jogi | Siwalik 1986 | 1976–1986

Parent – Mother – Mrs. Harkirat Kaur | Matron GD | 1978–1982

OS Siblings – Brother – Mukhraj Singh | Mokhi | Siwalik 1987 | 1978–1987
Sister – Preeti Singh | Siwalik 1988 | 1979–1988

# Chronicles of the 60s

Maybe I should start feeling old, but somehow, that is yet to happen.

I still remember the motherly plump ayah in the Prep School dorm, refusing to respond because I didn't call her 'ayah ji'. The outwardly strict matron inspecting your tiny box and checking everything, including your underwear. We resented it but she looked at every need of the many children under her care.

Time now to move to Senior School. You felt big and responsible, and then realized that you were the smallest there. Reminds me of the homesickness, the bullying, the '*dhupping*'; haunches, invisible-chair, legs-up-hands-down, hockey sticks, caning, the 'run down' to Barnes Field, and of course, sitting all alone on your locker the whole of your weekly prized holiday. Punishments freely dispensed by the prefects. And oh! Having all your tuck forcibly distributed even to those who weren't really that close to you. 'Grab chaps, Grub!'

Early morning PT and punctuality being drilled into you by the ever watchful Jagga. I recall his announcement one morning during PT, when he'd caught some boys hiding, sharing Charlie's goodies in the bogs. His demeanour and voice had that disgust and open disbelief that they didn't even know that was not a place to eat anything. And that it was his responsibility to teach them even such basics.

Yes, we survived it all and emerged unscathed. We imbibed the part about being good and learned that it was important not to get caught when you weren't.

The beautiful view from all corners of the hillside; the thrill of having the whole place to yourself; of running on those little, slippery paths or making your own path up or down the khud. The excitement of being out of bounds. The pinecone collecting, way below Barnes, past the little village and the road, was it one, two or three humps? Lugging them up and sometimes, getting a little help from a friend who was equally loaded. Of selling your old shoes for—was it eighteen or twenty bhuttas? The Home Day hidings and the bonfire.

Of 25 paisa for an ice-cream cone. Of saving your meagre pocket money for the Home Day walk to Kalka station. Of taking the forbidden Monkey Point shortcut, getting lost, somehow reaching the road, exhausted. Hailing the first bus and finding Mr Kemp sitting on the front seat.

In L-III, one day, I was called to Heady's office. There was the initial trepidation then defiance, 'I haven't done anything, Sir'. I was confronted with, 'I am told that you are not happy in school? What is the matter? Is it the prefects or the bullying or the teachers?' Yet there was something reassuring about the way it had been said. Everyone knew and asked, and I was just as confused as all of them—why me?

The Hospital bread and soup or milk. The running around and mischief when you were well enough but couldn't be discharged because you either had measles or chicken pox or something else? Of having your pyjamas taken away till you promised to be a good boy, and the stern sister believed you.

Unconsciously, picking up cuss words till they almost became part of your everyday speech and having some senior chide you to never use them, also routinely.

Through all the fun and hobbies, games, treks and camps, classes and prep, were the undercurrents of the Cock House and the frustration that Siwalik had not made it for many years.

I played chess with Mr Bhalerao and Mr Jalota. They were surprised when I refused the senior bunk. Probably Jagga was too, but he never said it.

Athletics. My 400m record was broken in a few years. However, my 200m record, I believe, is still standing unbroken.

Discipline. Yes, that's what comes through most strongly and probably because of that, the fellowship, the closeness, that feeling of being one family could be built.

Yeah, those were the days. Once remembered, memories go on and on. Life can be difficult but Sanawar, true to its motto, taught us—Never Give In.

**Dr Arjun Rastogi**
Mark Anthony | Siwalik 1969 | 1961–1969
Consultant Physician

OS Sibling – Brother – Abhaya Rastogi | Siwalik 1972 | 1963–1967

# Fragrance – The Root of Evil

Of the many memorable, and some forgettable tales, from my twelve years in the hallowed environs of Sanawar, there is one worthy of mention, from 1976.

My good friend, KD (Vijay Kadan) and I were tasked by Dutt (Sanjay) to deliver a fancy perfume to Rajiv Khanna (Head Boy) up in Nilagiri House, prior to their House party on a particular Saturday. The mandate was fairly straightforward: hand it over (without wearing a drop) and retrieve the precious bottle, come Sunday morning.

With our weekend itinerary disturbed, we decided to recover lost ground by getting our pound of flesh. Two lads from Haryana, for the very first time, presented the finer fads of life. Taking matters into our own hands, one Jaat intellectualized, 'Let's convert this opportunity into our long-term gain'. The washout remained clueless. The genius went on detailing the plan. I understood. Daka (junior) was the most generous consumer of Ponds Cold Cream in the dorms. While KD stood guard, I skimmed the top shelf of the locker and pocketed the 'big' bottle. We set out on our mission, taking a detour behind Gaskel Hall. Spattering the cold cream on the stone wall, we wiped clean the insides with a makeshift pine-needle scrub. Turning our attention to the magical bottle, we undid the stopper—our first encounter with fragrance (I can still recollect the scent). We emptied our newly discovered aphrodisiac into Daka's – now ours – Ponds bottle. Haryana was well on its way to accomplish whatever Khanna, Dutt and some others had in mind – our very own ticket – from Birdwood to behind Art Room, via 'Leisure'.

However, we had overlooked one terminally disastrous outcome. '*Radix malorum est cupiditas*', a Latin Biblical quote that says, 'Greed is the root of Evil'. On barely sighting any contents in the perfume bottle, Khanna felt swindled and bamboozled. To rub salt into his wound, he heard one of the two pipsqueaks proposing that they'll be back early next morning, to get the bottle. He somehow managed to keep his shirt on, but still barked, '. . . may as well take this back to Dutt and save yourselves a trip'.

Needless to say, Haryana had a long Saturday night, which did not end well. What followed were strong-arm tactics, open threats and coercion. Two home pals from Haryana had been pitted against each other. None came out smelling good.

As they say, all's well that ends well . . . We two were never again assigned even a remotely sensitive mission. And, most importantly, the four of us are extremely close today.

**Naveen Vasisht**
Neeks | Siwalik 1979 | 1967–1979

OS Siblings – Brother – Praveen Vasisht | Peeks | Siwalik 1976 | 1965–1976
           Sister – Alka Vasisht | Fuzzy | Siwalik 1980 | 1968–1980

# The Imperial Challenge Shield

The Imperial Challenge Shield (Junior) Competition evolved from the highly prestigious and fiercely contested Earl Robert Trophy inaugurated in 1907. Since 1910, the competition was conducted annually under the auspices of the National Rifle Association, with the object of encouraging every boy of British birth, between the ages of twelve and nineteen years, to learn how to use a rifle. The competition was initially sponsored and supported by Lt. Col. Raymond Fennell of the South African Defence Force, and it was out of his generous gifts and endowments that prizes were provided annually and the administrative expenses of the competition defrayed. All school and college cadet corps throughout the British Empire participated. The competition was described in London papers as the largest sporting event to be taking place in the world at the time. In 1925, 23,000 competitors took part, and in 1938, the number rose to 28,000, in 1,302 competing teams.

The Lawrence Royal Military School, Sanawar won the coveted shield for two consecutive years in 1925 and 1926 with the highest individual scores and, in doing so, demolished an Empire record long held by the Australian and New Zealand Schools Cadet Corps. In both years, the Chief Instructor WOI (RSM) G.E. Foster IUL was awarded a bronze medal as instructor of the best team and a silver medal as premier instructor, Junior Division in the Empire. G.E. (George) Foster was himself an Old Sanawarian (1899–1904). The school was honoured with personal congratulations from The Right Honourable Secretary of State for India H.E. The Viceroy and H.E. The Commander-in-Chief (India). (See extract from LRMS Orders of 14 April 1926, appended below).

In recognition of this achievement, a full-size bronze replica of the shield was presented to the school in May 1927 by the National Rifle Association. For many years thereafter, it served as the official school trophy for inter-House shooting competitions and remains to this day on display in the school Museum.

In 1938, Sanawar won the Imperial Challenge Shield for a third time with an average score of 98.332, taking third place among the best hundred units in the Empire. In addition to winning the shield, there were several silver and bronze medals awarded to individuals in all eight of the school teams. Norman Kells, the Head Boy (1938), achieved the highest possible score of 100. Moreover, he was awarded silver medal as the highest individual scorer in the Empire for three successive years. The school was again honoured with personal congratulations from the Founder of the Imperial Challenge Shields Competitions, Hon. Colonel R.W. Ffennell of the South African Defence Force. (See extract from LRMS Orders of 12 April 1938, also appended below).

Competition for the shield ceased during the war years and resumed in 1948 under the name 'Commonwealth Challenge (Rifle) Shield'. An Australian school cadet team was the first to win the trophy under its new name.

## Appendix:

### LRMS ORDERS
### BY
### Rev. G.D. BARNE, MA, CIE, OBE, VD, PRINCIPAL
### SANAWAR, 14 April 1926

### No. 292 SPECIAL ORDER

The following Letter has been received from the Military Secretary to His Excellency the Viceroy:

'His Excellency the Viceroy has just received the results of the 1925 Imperial Challenge Shield Competitions of the National Rifle Association. He is delighted to see that the Lawrence Royal Military School Cadets have won the Junior Imperial Challenge Shield which was open to the whole of the British Empire, and he congratulates you and the Cadets most heartily.

This is, I understand, the first time that either of the Imperial Shields has been won by India, and His Excellency considers that the greatest credit is due to Regimental Sergeant Major Foster and to all who helped him to attain the success.

His Excellency is pleased to note that R.S.M. Foster's labours have been recognized by the grant of a Silver Medal to him from the NRA.

He wishes the School all success in future not only in NRA meetings, but also in all other various walks of life.'

LRMS ORDERS
BY
Captain W. H. G. REED, M.A., I. M. S, OFFICIATING
PRINCIPAL
SANAWAR, 12 April 1938

## No. 185 SPECIAL ORDER (NOTICES)

The following letter has been received from the Founder of the Imperial Challenge Shields Competitions (Hon. Colonel R. W. Ffennell of the South African Defence Force):

'I am writing to congratulate your School on winning the Junior Imperial Challenge Shield, with the very fine total score of 98.3 points.

I am delighted also to see that your School has taken third place among the best hundred units in the Empire.

I should like to add my special congratulations to the Chief Instructor, WO1 (R.S.M) E. Greenough on the very encouraging results obtained.

Your School has a splendid record in these competitions. With all good wishes.

Yours sincerely
Raymond W. Ffennell'

**D.V. Boddington**
LRMS Sanawar 1942–1947
May 2001

**Sources and References:**
- LRMS ORDERS No. 23, SPECIAL ORDER dated 27 January 1926.
- LRMS ORDERS No. 292, SPECIAL ORDER dated 14 April 1926.
- LRMS ORDERS No. 350, SHOOTING dated 12 May 1930.
- LRMS PART II ORDERS – NOTICES dated 12 April 1938.

# Four Years That Shaped My Life

When Sanawar was thrown open to Indians, my father, an espouser of boarding schools, thought it the perfect opportunity to pack all his kids off to the same school. The only hills we had visited before were the Murree hills in Pakistan, near our pre-Partition home in Rawalpindi.

We were soon rattling off in a train to Kalka station, from where my father, with three children in tow, took an army jeep up to school. Far more twisty than the hill roads we had known, neither I, nor my brother, Pickles, nor sister, Bubbles, escaped feeling terribly carsick on the drive. No doubt a feeling that many Sanawarians must have encountered on their first drive up. But hey it was worth it, wouldn't you say?

For us, it was the beginning of a very significant experience. The first sight of the big, gray buildings of Sanawar, looked so imposing and also promising adventure, all at once. That was in 1949, when there were about a hundred kids in school. Uniforms were given on arrival. Being army kids, we related at once to the Khaki woollen battle dress and felt terribly chuffed to get into shiny brogues, like officers. I took great pride in keeping those shoes shining and must admit that the passion stays with me till this day. In fact, my wife never lets me forget that on retiring from the army, even before we found a cook, I had employed my old syce, Sant Lal, to shine my shoes daily.

It took no time at all to settle into school life. And the best thing about our school was sports. I loved all sport and Sanawar opened opportunities to participate in all sport. Cricket was my favourite and I was thrilled to be in the Colts' team and the Senior Team at the same time. Armed with cricket gear, we would be full of zest as we ran down from the dormitory all the way to Barnes. But those walks up the hill, after play, with the same cricket gear to haul, were tough. Sanawar had an enviable cricket tradition and we were regaled with plenty of old stories. During the 1945 war, Denis Compton, one of England's greatest cricketers and a footballer, was posted in the Army PT school in Kasauli, as a sergeant. He would come and play cricket and football against the school team.

No memory of school comes without a memory of your friends. Gurkir Pal Singh Somal and I boxed in the second lowest weight, and I won my smallest and most coveted cup. Gurkir and I were such good friends that the referee had to stop our bout and warn us to start boxing and stop dancing. We played cricket together after school, too, for the NDA Team. Vijay Ratan Chowdhry, my greatest friend, and I, applied to the same selection board.

Mr Carter, the principal, encouraged us to be sporty. Unfortunately, school was not just all sports. I nearly always failed in English dictation and Mr Cowell, our senior master, tried his best to improve my spelling by keeping me in detention once a week. Cowell found another reason to give me a caning—laughing in Chapel, because Raj Sircar sat down on a sharp stone during the service.

Mr Cowell's mother was our Housemistress and had put me in-charge of lighting the lantern after lights-out. In those days, every dormitory had a lantern, which was the night light. For this task, I would get a box of matches every week. Since I did not ask for a matchbox after the first week,

Copyright © Birinder Malhans | Vindhya | 1955

she concluded that either I was not lighting the lantern or the boy in-charge before me was a smoker. One night, Dileshwar Preet Singh Rarewala and some of his friends decided to run away from school. They put out the lantern and I, seeing it turned off, lit it again. Many years later, when I met Biri, he told me he was fed up with me re-lighting that old lantern each time he put it out.

It was even more difficult to run around in the Hospi. Mrs Page, our nurse, had devised a unique way to keep her patients in bed. She'd take away our pyjamas and that ensured we remained rooted in bed.

Some of us were shy and didn't have the courage to chat up girls. But we noticed girls (and a few lady teachers, too) staring at Mr Salim Khan. He was a cricketer who had played for the famous Holkar cricket team and, hence, he was like a god to us cricketers. To the girls, he was just so very good-looking.

Sports also remind one of those age-old rivalries between Sanawar and BCS. We used to go up to Simla to play cricket, hockey and football. We'd always trudge up in the old army truck; a team of boys perched uncomfortably atop a pile of baggage, with Mr Kemp in-charge. What was pleasant about those journeys was the packed lunch of roast chicken that was handed out to us. By the way, the old rivalry still continues at the Delhi Golf Club, where we play an annual match. (I am sorry to say we let it slip away from us the last time, leaving BCS the winners, but we will be out to get our revenge the next time around).

My batch finished school in 1954. I wasn't there for the last years because I was preparing to join the army.

Another sport at which Sanawar excelled was the field of horsemanship. Even though there was no riding in school, we produced some of the best polo players and show jumpers in India. In this, the 61st Cavalry helped us. I can boast of being one of the first Sanawarians to join the 61st Cavalry and I was followed by many others, including my brother, Pickles. And after I commanded the regiment in 1976, the next six commandants were from Sanawar, including Col. Raj Kalaan, whose sons followed him to Sanawar. The latest Sanawarian carrying that flag is Navjit Singh Sandhu from the batch of 1991, I believe.

Talking of Sanawar and horses, I named my best horse Sanawar. And my wife always says it was because of Sanawar, the horse, that she agreed to marry me. So see what an influence Sanawar turned out to be!

**Col. Harinder Singh Sodhi (Retd.)**
Billy | Himalaya 1954 | 1949–1952
Best Cadet (Gold medallist) NDA 1957 | First Sanawarian in the 61st Cavalry (1958) | Commanded the President's Bodyguard | Arjuna Awardee – Equestrian | 5-goal Polo player for twenty-five years

OS Siblings – Brother – Col. R.S. Sodhi | Pickles | Himalaya 1952| 1949–1952
           Sister – Pamela Sodhi | Himalaya 1952 | 1949–1952

# You Can, but You May Not

Life takes many turns: for me, at eleven, it chose the path to Sanawar. I took quite a while to adjust to life in a boarding school. However, while sitting down to pen my memories, I realize that Sanawar shaped me into who I am today—disciplined, frugal, thoughtful, considerate . . .

So many memories spring to mind.

Running up to Parker Hall in shorts for a cup of hot tea and bread or a dog biscuit, to warm up before PT; going to our beautiful Chapel for the daily Assembly, which invariably ended with 'words of wisdom' from a teacher; summer camps, which we all looked forward to because we could lose our inhibitions and live in the moment; walking to the station to catch the train to Simla, for cold coffee, while listening to music on the 'juke-box'; throwing water on each other in the stream; being taken to Kas to see a movie; saving our pocket money for a bun samosa . . .

Watching the House shows was fun. Being rather shy and introverted, I never volunteered for any part. Hence, when a few of us were asked to read a passage in Hindi, I was quite surprised when my diction landed me a role in the Hindi play, one year.

Going through the graveyard to Doom's Pond aka Lover's Pond, to collect frogs that we would dissect during Biology, was always eerie. We inevitably got spooked by imaginary ghosts as the wind rustled through the pines.

Diwali night used to be magical. There would be a huge bonfire in the centre of Peacestead, while boys and girls played together, throwing crackers at each other. I remember calmly pulling a *phool-jari* out of my hair, one year.

Founders' was exciting. The school would be abuzz with parents. I looked forward to Tattoo and PT at night, followed by the NCC parade in the hot sun, the next day.

The sixth formers' farewell party was always one of the highlights of the school year. With great eagerness and enthusiasm, we would wait for the chance to dress up in saris . . .

My Housemistress Mrs Kemp was strict. Once, when I got caught with 'washed hair' on a weekday (Sunday was hairwash day) she grounded me from watching the weekly movie. Yet, she was also kind and caring. She would invite us to her home on weekends, where, while we drank tea and ate goodies, she taught us how to play mahjong.

Part of the legacy I carry are two phrases which I continue to use— 'Elbows off the table'; and 'You can, but you may not'.

**Anumeha (Rai) Manilal**
Siwalik 1969 | 1964–1969

# Do Not Let Me Down in Maths

I was eleven years old when I joined Sanawar. A photo of me curled up on the berth of the small train to Dharampur jogs my memory. Is that not, probably, the best rail journey in the world? From the very first trip that journey has fascinated me as indeed, did the school. Yes, the school! Isn't it a beautiful place? As a small boy, I was sure that I had reached fable land.

Fable land or not, it was definitely very different from the world I came from. For instance, nearly all the staff and students were white. Surely, this could not be a little corner of England? Very quickly, I was told that I was one of the first batch of Indians joining Sanawar. After all, it was 1949.

I was in Yellow House. Don't laugh, that is perfectly accurate. BD had only sixty to seventy boys then and we were conveniently divided into Yellows and Blues. I cannot remember how many were in GD, but there were some very pretty ones. In all, there were not enough in both BD and GD to fill up Parker Hall, which was our Dining Hall. I also remember that many of the buildings were uninhabited, thus starting many rumours (facts?) about ghosts. I am sure the present generation does not believe in this nonsense. Neither did I. I was just afraid of them.

This state of affairs did not last long. The following year, Yellows and Blues were rechristened to Himalaya and Nilagiri, which later became Siwalik and Vindhya. I am told it remains so today. I mean the Houses, though, not the population.

I was a terrific student at school. Yes, good at everything. At least that is what I have told my wife and children. The fact that my name is not on any of the numerous boards to prove it, is a mere detail. Chicky Evans, my Housemaster, would have agreed. I am still trying to remember why he caned me once. Probably to make a man out of me. It was also to teach me important things like how to sleep on one's stomach for a few days. There is also a bit of physics that he taught us that I can still remember. So, all was not bad. However, he was not as good as Mr Cousins whose teaching of history was a revelation. It was all in rhyme. So, you never forgot. Even now I regale to my dinner guests how I can remember the sequence of the Kings of England, especially as they were very short on names, sticking to names like George, Edward, etc. This is particularly useful to me now that I live in England. They are very surprised that an Indian should know more about their history than they do. So am I, but then remember how I joined an English school? So what else is expected of me?

I am not going to bore you with my five years in Sanawar. I expect they are like all of yours. I do, however, remember when I left school to join the NDA, my maths teacher, Mrs Carter (wife of the then headmaster) gave me a priceless bit of advice. She said, 'Vinoood, now that you are leaving us to join the outside world, remember whatever you do, do not let me down in maths'. No, Mrs C, I did not. After all, I became a gunner in the army for 12 years, and despite the 1965 war, lived to tell the tale. Yearning for more interesting things to do, I moved on to a career in computers. This may not seem like anything out of the ordinary to you, but remember I went into computers in 1969, when it was very much in its infancy.

London has been home for the last thirty or so years. Now that I have retired, I have the luxury to do what I want to do. I am still deciding what that is. Where's the hurry?

I do however look back to fond memories and many of these are from my schooldays in Sanawar. That's saying something. I even managed to persuade my two children to go from London to Sanawar for a term in the 80s, so that they could see for themselves. I hope they found it rewarding as well.

For me, the most important legacy of Sanawar is that I made some very close friends, and I still cannot get rid of them. I guess they too learnt the school motto well.

**Vinod Raj Kumar**
Himalaya 1953 | 1949–1953

# A Bouquet of Memories

I was in Sanawar for ten years. A few random thoughts and enthralling memories come to mind, as if it happened just yesterday . . .

We had just moved from Prep School to the big, bad world of Senior School, and without wasting any time, I started talking to this girl I liked. After a few 'dates', we met one evening on short-back, next to a lamp post . . . As we were about to say goodbye, I mustered up the courage to give her a peck on her cheek, which startled her so much that her head jerked back and hit the lamp post, making a loud cracking sound. The sound of that maiden kiss still rings in my ears. Rumour has it that she still wears that bump of my affection on her head.

Mr Abraham (Abu), our English teacher, was a great storyteller and a hopeless romantic (God bless his soul). It was during one such period of 'Cowboys and Indians' (native Americans, for the politically correct), when he saw one of the lady teachers he had a crush on, walking outside the class . . . He, the eternal cowboy, instinctively got on his horse and rode out of the class to rescue the damsel in distress. She was neither impressed nor amused.

Mr Mukherji (Mukho, God bless his soul) was a dapper, immaculately dressed and very organized teacher of physics. His classroom was the perfect setup to test all sorts of hypothesis, including the Archimedes' displacement theory: water tension, air pressure, weight of water, what psi can a human blow, etc. We loved practicals (as opposed to theory) and would eagerly await his instructions. All was well till we got to the last experiment. Gathered around the main table, we saw a long, clear tube draped over two hooks forming a U-shape, half-filled with liquid. Mukho challenged us claiming that no matter how hard we tried, we would be unable to blow the liquid out of the tube. The entire class, in a queue, gave it a go. It was my turn . . . I took a deep breath and blew with all my might, and sure enough, all the water 'flew' out; unfortunately, all over Mukho and a few of us, who in trying to jump out of range, knocked over a few beakers and pipettes. Mayhem ensued! This is where Newton stepped in with his third law (yes, yes . . . every action has an equal and opposite reaction). I did not see anything (so still remain in doubt about whether nothing moves faster than light), but felt the sting of an open palm making contact with my cheek, followed by a loud clap sound. I was made to stay back and clean up the mess. Inference: Archimedes and Newton are related.

Copyright © Jasmine Chauhan | Himalaya | 2019

During the twenty 'extra days' (to study for our Boards), we were huddled around the *angithi* in the U-VI dorms, wishing our parents had bought us warmer nightsuits. Someone suggested we play 'would you rather', a game where you choose between two ridiculous scenarios). Just then, a moth landed on the angithi, posing a live 'would you rather' question: eat a samosa or eat the moth and get 5 rupees. Ravneet (Mothy) was finally paid the promised sum on our twenty-fifth year reunion.

We had a foreign lady for our math teacher (I forget her name), who had just started her lesson and Bulldy, now rechristened Teddy Bear by the Dilli (OS 1984) dames, kept interrupting her. Being a good, front-row student, I could see her colour slowly change from pale white to deep red. At the next interruption, I was witness to the old adage 'hell hath no fury like that of a woman scorned' and in a flash, the duster went flying in the direction of Ashish, striking him above his eye—guess he did not get a duck in math. We now had two red faces in class. Needless to say, the rest of the class was overjoyed (sorry, Teddy Bear).

One fine Friday morning in U-VI, I hatched a plan to get away from Morning Assembly and classes till lunch. The plan was rather ingenuous and unsophisticated. During Assembly in Chapel that day, at the start of the Sanskrit prayer '*Om etadatnam shudnam pratiaksham brahma*', I would faint, a few would grab hold of me and, hopefully, be allowed to take me to Hospi. Simple! Now being prefects, we were seated in the nave, i.e., the central part of the Chapel around the altar, with the whole school looking on. As planned, I 'fainted' at the sound of 'OM' and not surprisingly, no one broke my fall . . . I barely avoided hitting the floor hard; thank you, Danny, Mr Dhani Ram, God bless his soul, for the gym training. There is a loud gasp and hushed whispers fill the Chapel. The 'saviours' finally take their cue together and are trying to revive me, when one teacher stops them, asks everyone to step back, and proceeds to unzip my trousers to help me get some air. Another gasp, this time from me. I did make a feeble attempt to discourage him, but to no avail. Finally, the chosen ones were permitted to carry me out into the light . . . and on to another glorious day of sunshine and laughter at 'the best school of all' . . .

**Hanut Ewari**
Nilagiri 1984 | 1975–1984

OS Siblings – Sister – Feroz (Ewari) Gujral | Nilagiri 1982 | 1976–1982
Sister – Anisha Ewari | Nilagiri 1987 | 1979–1987

# The Midnight Feast

Prep School, Form II, November 1974. Two weeks from Home Day, Tandip, Chitra and I decided to have a midnight feast. We were inspired by Enid Blyton's Mallory Towers and The Naughtiest Girl at School series.

Having decided, our secret meetings commenced in all earnestness. A venue needed to be chosen. Considering the fact that we were locked in every night, it was really the easiest decision—the dorm. The designated picnic spot marked was the passage between our bathing area and the Press Room. It had a row of hooks on one side, to hang our dressing-gowns and toilet bags. The floor had a coir mat, on which we often polished our PT shoes. I might add that this wasn't the sunniest of spots—but it was cozy and private enough.

Arranging the food was the greater challenge. No tuck was allowed in the dorm. It was all kept in the tuck cupboard in the dining hall downstairs. Furthermore, as it was the end of term, not much remained anyway. Nevertheless, we had just enough to get by—Tandip had a packet of ginger biscuits; Chitra had a box of homemade sweets (her aunt from Kotgarh had come visiting only a fortnight back); while I had a tin of mixed fruit jam. Party on . . .

First, the tuck had to be smuggled up to the dorm. Luckily, in November, we wore those long navy blue overcoats, with seemingly never-ending pockets. I remember transporting the huge biscuit packet. Chitra sneaked in with the sweets box, the next evening. The last consignment, mixed fruit jam, arrived two days later. It was Thursday evening. We were on schedule. The remaining forty-eight hours, between now and Saturday midnight, were critical. The booty had to be carefully hidden, away from the watchful locker inspections every evening by our matron, Mrs Kohli, as well as from the other girls (especially the Nilagirians) who would be quick to tattle us to Mary ayahji—the bichu-buti-wielding dragon.

After what seemed like an eternity, Saturday night was finally upon us. While going over the preparations one last time, we suddenly realized that we had no tin opener. Disaster! We just had to find a way out . . .

What we did have was a candle. Tandip had brought it from home for some obscure reason. And we even had matches!

Since bedtime was at 8.00 p.m., we decided to keep hourly watches until midnight. First watch was Tandip's, then Chitra, and finally me. But out of excitement, we all stayed awake till 10.30 p.m. and then . . . I simply don't remember anything!

I was shaken awake by Tandip. It was 12.30! We had overslept. We hopped out of our beds—it was bitterly cold. Three tiny girls sneaked into the dark passage. We lit our candle quickly. Brought out the tuck. Suppressing our giggles, we munched on a few dry biscuits. We dared not talk or make a noise, in case we got caught. Then, a bit cold and sleepy but very pleased with ourselves, we adjourned the adventurous feast.

It was done!

The secrecy, the planning, the daring act of smuggling tuck . . . we felt that we had lived in the pages of Enid Blyton's adventures for a while.

The story would have ended here, if it hadn't been for my younger brother. Totally inspired by us, he announced on Home Day of the next term: 'Last night, I also had a midnight feast, just like you.'

I asked him how many of his friends were there.

He said, like a typical Prepper, 'Oh, nobody. Just me.'

**Kirandip (Sandhu) Grewal**
KD | Himalaya 1983 | 1974–1983
Social Worker generating livelihood in rural Punjab by promoting traditional crafts, particularly weaving of Bridal Durrees and the Khes.

OS Parent – Gurbirinder S. Sandhu| Yellow 1951 | 1947–1951

OS Sibling – Karandeep S. Sandhu | KD | Himalaya 1987 | 1977–1987

OS Spouse – Ranbir Singh | Big Pixie | Vindhya 1979 | 1970–1979

OS Children –  Son – Ranjeet S. Grewal | Vindhya 2009 | 2007–2009
                Daughter – Indrani Grewal | Vindhya 2014 | 2007–2014

# Half on Ten

We, my twin sister Sonia and I, went to Sanawar in March 1953, much against our wishes. In retrospect, I feel it could not have been a better decision on the part of our parents to send us to the 'best school of all'.

It was a difficult adjustment – from a convent day school, where history was 'The War of the Roses' and Henry VII and Henry VIII, to a school that taught only Indian History – for us who came from a convent school with only girls to a co-ed school; from homecooked food and time to ourselves, to school food and no time to idle and daydream. In time, we did adjust and began to love the school, and of course, cried buckets when we left.

The discipline and the value system that was inculcated in us by our teachers, Mrs Carter, Mrs Kemp, Miss Chatterjee, Mr Vyas, Mr Saleem Khan, Mrs Coombes and Mr Rathin Mitra, to name a few, is the kind that has stood the test of time, and can be handed down to generations to stand them in good stead. We used to idolize our teachers and it was a great honour for us to have them write a few words in our autograph book. Mr Vyas wrote in mine: 'Those, who joy would win, must share it, happiness was born a twin'. I have never forgotten those lines and still have my autograph book.

Mr Gore was our maths teacher in 1954, after Mrs Carter left. He used to give us a test every Saturday, comprising of two sums, and on Monday morning, each of us had to stand and read our marks aloud. I used to dread Mondays as I always got 0.25, 0.50, or 0.75 on 10, not even 1. Both my sums would be wrong, so I don't know what I got that fraction of a mark for? Armed with my test-book, I went to Mrs Coombes, once, who was the Senior Mistress. I begged her to let me drop maths as a subject, but she looked at my book and said, 'Don't despair, Rena—maybe the 0.75 will turn to 1, and then to 2 and then to 5, and maybe 10 one day'. I was so dejected. Next Monday, I asked Mr Gore if he would kindly give me 0/10 instead of the 0.25 or 0.50. And anyway, what was the fraction for, since both my sums were wrong? He answered, 'Rena, I feel so sorry for you, because your work is so neat.' Finally, after two or three weeks of zeroes, I was allowed to drop maths and took up shorthand and typing instead. Since there was no teacher for this, I had to teach myself.

Many memories come crowding in. The happiest times were when our parents came up for the weekend and took us to Alasia for a meal. Then there was Charlie, who came thrice a week, with his goodies of samosas, gulab jamuns, pink and chocolate burfis. 'Leisure' was another of our favourite haunts on holidays. We, as prefects, were allowed to go there but it was out of bounds for the rest. There was always much excitement and bonding at annual events like the school picnic at Dagroo and Founders' Day in October. A trip to Kasauli, or even Garkhal, was heaven.

I was the only one from our class who went back to Sanawar to teach for a year in 1959, after doing my teachers' training at St. Bedes, Simla. It was great fun to be at par with all the teachers who had taught me—to not be in awe of them but be friends instead. That year, Mr Thomas from Lovedale was the Guest of Honour at Founders'. He was planning to leave Lovedale and move to Chennai, to start his own school. When someone asked him why he was leaving at the peak of his career, his answer was – 'I would like to leave when people ask "why", and not "when"'. I have never forgotten that.

All in all, happy memories of happy times passed in the cool and crisp environment of Sanawar.

**Rena (Thadani) Chandiramani**
Siwalik 1954 | 1953–1954

OS Siblings – Sister – Sonia (Thadani) Pandhi | Siwalik 1954 | 1953–1954
Brother – Anil Thadani | Siwalik 1962 | 1957–1962

OS Children – Son – Sunil Chandiramani | Siwalik 1973 | 1970–1973

# Treasured Moments

It is just not one story that resonates; there are a million . . .

So here's a selection of abridged and censored incidents that transpired between 1978 and 1984. It's been nearly four decades. However, the memories are still vivid—seems like only yesterday that we were on that hilltop . . .

Jaya fighting with monkeys to save that last piece of palang-tod from being snatched away – she chased them almost all the way across Peacestead.

Sneaking out of the dorms (was done!) at 1.00 a.m., with hockey sticks as weapons in case of an attack, for a picnic by the indoor swimming pool.

Stealing a baby white mouse from the Bio lab and hiding it in our pockets—till we realized that it wasn't a baby but a pregnant mother, who had three babies in Jaya's red blazer pocket during a Maths class.

Standing 'chowkidar' while one of us dated the heartthrob of the moment.

Rashmi giving Heady a lecture (when he found her in bed in U-VI, bunking PT), on how morning exercise, day after day, was not really beneficial and occasional breaks were recommended.

Shefali (straight from Bombay, with no ability to speak Hindi) being asked by Mr Dwivedi what Gandhi's contribution to 'Samachar' was. Her response, after a longish pause (and give *Doordarshan* credit here) was, '*Samachar samapt hua*'.

Zehra and Jaya directing a song sequence during prep – playing Jackie Shroff on a motorcycle – singing 'Ding Dong' (was it?).

Heady catching us on top of the CDH rooftop while he was surveying its construction—punishment drill?

Jaya, with Lacho in tow, rushing back to the dorms after dinner, convinced there was a leopard/hyena chasing them. We never found one . . .

Tying a string to Rashmi's finger at night, when one of us was having nightmares so that she would wake up if we tugged at it. No such luck. Her arm woke up but Rashmi slept on . . .

Behraji favouring Rashmi during Camps by giving her extra milk powder.

Nikka introducing Siwalik L-VI to 'peddle-pushers' and 'Top10' songs (D-I-S-C-O!) on arrival from Muscat.

During a measles outbreak, all of us rubbing ourselves with a hanky from the Hospital in the hope that we would be admitted to the isolation ward together.

Breaking bounds to go to the graveyard behind Moti's Corner, and one of us getting cut with a sharp blade of grass. Mona convinced us that ghosts would be coming to get us that night.

Copyright © Rathin Mitra | ART MASTER | 1950–1953

Sitting and chatting on Peacestead, waiting for a rain shower to pass— it lasted 3 days!

The unending queue for the loos; the three-minute baths; climbing every roof we could; box-room visits; Socials and House parties; Sports days and Hodson runs (*uff!*); that extra piece of chicken or paneer at lunch; camps and rucksacks that bit into our shoulder blades; Tattoo and blankets followed by cocoa; Chota with salties and sweeties; walks down for tutorials; House plays and musicals; needlework and music classes . . . too many memories to count.

Each as precious as the friendships that have lasted all these years . . . Sanawar!

**Rashmi (Sinha) Bhowmik**
Siwalik 1984 | 1978–1984

OS Sibling – Brother – Atul Sinha | Tulla | Siwalik 1982| 1977–1982

OS Children – Daughter – Ragini Bhowmik | Siwalik 2011 | 2007 – 2011

**Lakshmi (Mahey) Laroia**
Lacho | Siwalik 1984 | 1978–1984

# Naked on Bachloi Pass

For those of us who spent our full adolescence in Sanawar, the crucial point is how many of our formative experiences we can trace back to individual incidents. Some of them are stark and universal. Like the first time we were naked in public (which leaves most people too shocked to speak). Or the very first meal away from home, when the homesickness really hits. Others are situational, like when we were lined up to 'own up' to something someone did. Only the miscreant could speak and you were not allowed to tattle. Tattling is the cardinal sin at Sanawar. It's the worst thing any junior can do. Cruelty is probably the senior equivalent—but at that age, as a seventeen-year-old, one is too unthinking to have genuine empathy. So, let's settle on tattling to be the one and only cardinal sin.

There are not that many tattling stories to tell. Within the first term, every 'new guy' becomes aware of the rules. Stick with the team, no matter what. On the other side, if you made everyone suffer by not owning up, you were going to get your deserved share of ostracism (and true character revelation).

This is a story of an U-IV hike in April 1985. The destination was Bachloi Pass. We took the normal bus route to Simla from Dharampur and thereafter to Rampur Bushahr. After staying overnight at the PWD Rest House and a breakfast of paranthas, we took the unusual decision of crossing a wooden bridge to get across the Sutlej, and then, not finding the path to lead where we thought it should, we proceeded to climb a near-sheer hillside up to another path.

That begun a series of mishaps which made this the worst hike I have ever undertaken. After two days, the net result was that twenty thirteen-year-olds decided that this master could not be trusted and that they must rebel and return to Sanawar using their pocket money. Somehow, Mr AKB got wind of this plan and halfway up to Sarahan, he took the unprecedented and since-unequalled step of making us strip naked and standing in an ice-cold stream by way of punishment.

679

Try and visualize the sight. Twenty-five bare-torsoed boys wearing towels and waiting to stand alone naked in front of the rest. This was supposed to be our exorcism, instead it was the opposite. It confirmed to us the unfitness of this man who deserved ignominy for his supervision of not-unruly children, who should wake up the next day to find us all gone.

Needless to say, he got wind of this, too (The gentle boy in question did not survive this betrayal. He was gone the next year). We were to be individually summoned to his room that night and confess as to who the ringleaders of this mutiny were. It was one of those moments when the resolve of young rascals was going to be tested. That evening was spent in panicked discussions about what we should do. Obviously, we were sandwiched between a telephone booth and a local bus. In hindsight, I will never be able to believe that fifteen thirteen-year-olds decided to stand up to Mr AKB and tell him that they didn't care for his authority. That they would not stand to be treated like this. From my recollection and after checking with multiple sources, most of us had stuck together and told him to stuff it. Once we had decided to do that, it didn't matter who chose to tattle; we were prepared for the consequences.

That is a standard I've rarely risen to in the rest of my young life. This act of defiance was probably one of the greatest lessons of my time in Sanawar—the mettle from the Vindhya House U-IV batch of 1985. It is the kind of behaviour that fifty-year-old adults in the year 2021 would be hard-pressed to demonstrate in these morality-challenged times.

**Abhijit Dutta**
Sambo | Vindhya 1990 | 1981–1990

OS Parent – Father – Amar Nath Dutta | Vindhya 1960 | 1956–1960

OS Sibling – Brother – Abhishek Dutta | Chut Sambo | Vindhya 1995 | 1987–1995

# Nostalgic Nuggets

One fine morning of March 1960, I woke up and heard my father discussing a school in Simla hills with my mother and sister. In order to keep my tantrums under control, I was told that we would soon be going for a holiday to Kasauli. I had never been for a holiday to a hillstation, hence I was very excited and started talking about hill houses etc. with the staff at my father's Hospital.

The first day we drove to Kasauli, we stayed at a Major General's House, just before entering Kasauli. It had snowed a few days back and it was a cold, wet day. The next day, I was taken to Sanawar and admitted to Prep School. The holiday suddenly came to an end! Coming from a small city (village) Rohtak, everything looked so different here. For me, it was a whole new world. I was crying the whole evening I was dropped off, but thanks to the other students and matrons, I received all the help I needed to settle down.

I was in Prep School for three years, till 1962, and it prepared me well to shift to Senior School. Prep School laid the foundation for sports, hobbies, music classes and the stage show. My first experience on the big stage of Barne Hall was in October 1960 and till the end of my stay of nine years, I performed on that big stage every year. Stage performance and music became my most loved hobbies. I fondly remember my teachers, Ms Rudra, Ms Kaveri, Ms Cherian, Ms Suri, Ms Pamela and Ms Sinclair, our matron. A big thanks to them for my grooming at Prep School.

In 1963 came the big change of shifting to Senior School. That protective umbrella of Prep School disappeared. The dormitories were full of action with seniors and prefects shouting orders. I could make out that I was now in an Army School. The first term was a nightmare, something close to *The Jurassic Park*, but I managed to pull through. Home sickness was also very strong . . . especially when the prefect said, 'See me tonight'.

In mid-term 1964, some fresh admissions took place and I was shocked to see a new face wearing a stylish cap and walking outside the gym, opposite Himalaya dorms. I said hi to him and asked in alarm, 'How dare you wear this cap?' This was my first meeting with him, knowing little that we would be friends for life, God bless him.

From 1967 onwards, life in Sanawar become very interesting . . . I had the first-time experiences of camping at Tara Devi and staying in tents; air travel to Srinagar, where we stayed in the Army cantonment; and my first trip to Nanital. A big thanks to my teacher Dr D.C. Gupta who organized these trips. He was also the director of our House shows and included me in all the performances.

The year 1968–69 were the best years of my nine at school. I was now a senior, hence had a lot of freedom to move about and boss over the juniors. I would get a quick okay to go to Kausali or my House in Dharampur, from my Housemaster, Mr B. Singh, the most dreaded teacher of all. But I was the blue-eyed boy of his wife's and got a caning from him only once.

After having practised and struggled for seven years I, at last, managed to get to the first row of bandies' chairs from the last row of the junior standing bandies. I led the Bugle band for the Tattoo and was the main drummer for Brass band.

The big break for me in the form of a key role on stage came when the school headmaster decided to stage *Heer Ranjha* for Founders' 1968. After days of practice in the Music Room, the competition got very intense for the lead role of Ranjha. The selection, to be done by [the] headmaster himself, was between three candidates—my Siwalik buddy Rocky, Anil Auluck and myself. Each of us were also made to sing lines of the opera, first as Ranjha and then as Heer's father and Heer's uncle. I secured the role of Ranjha. The opera had the largest number of participants. This was the first time that I got the opportunity to interact and spend time with Major Som Dutt. He ordered a special diet for me for ten days before the show, and gave me special lozenges to keep my vocal cords protected.

I very fondly remember all my teachers—Mr B. Singh, Mr Atma Ram, Mr Bhalerao and his smoky Art Room cabin, Dr D.C. Gupta, Mr Massey and Mr Jagdish Ram.

Most of 1969 was a little slow, as the ISC exams were scheduled in December 1969. A special mention of my dear friend, Sati, is deserved, who helped me a lot with my art.

We bid a tearful goodbye to Sanawar, our friends and teachers in December 1969.

Thank you Sanawar for having given me such a good foundation and exposure.

**Rakesh Khosla**
Khosu | Himalaya 1969 | 1960–1969

# Hobson's Choice

I joined School in 1969. In Form I. Coming to Senior School (L-III) in 1971, I took up band as a hobby, beginning with the five notes of the bugle and later, progressing to the trumpet. In the following term, I made it to Bugle band and three years later, to the Brass band. In my final year, I was appointed the Drum Major for the Founders' Trooping of Colours parade. In 1974, when in U-IV, I was designated as the School Bugler, a rather celebrated appointment, but one with its share of responsibilities. The duties entailed sounding the reveille for Rouser at 0545 hours, Morning Inspection at 0740, fall-ins for breakfast (0745), lunch (1315) and supper (1945), and finally, the decree for lights-out at 2100 hrs. A full day's job.

The School Bugler, needless to say, had to be on the dot. The bugle was hung on the wall outside the Vindhya House dormitory, by the door flanking the BD pavement. It had to be sounded facing the Dining Hall, so as to be audible to one and all. Being in Himalaya House, I needed the extra two minutes to be able to run across from behind Himalaya to Siwalik and up the flight of stairs to Vindhya. Invariably, when I got there, the bugle would either be hidden away, and if not, would be stuffed with pairs of dirty socks or be chock-full of Pond's talcum powder. One day, I found a banana stuck in the internal tubing. Hence, I would, without exception, reach Vindhya House well in time so as to circumvent the miscreants' preferred prank of the day. The schedule for sounding the bugle (mentioned above), was detailed on the Weekly School Orders. However, as I learnt on the very first day of my new employment, it was customary for the School Bugler to await the Head Boy's affirmation, particularly for sounding the call at fall-in for meals.

Joginder Bikram (Jogi), a Nilagirian, was the Head Boy. He, therefore, walked the extra distance for all meals. One fateful day, at the fall-in for lunch, I was in position with my bugle in hand, waiting for the routine nod from Jogi. From the corner of my eye, I saw Jogi emerging from the shadows of the Gaskell Hall corridor, crossing the water tank, where we

Himalayans played 'kick-the-can'. At that very moment, Ashoke Joon who was the House Captain of Vindhya, came out and instructed me to not sound the bugle for another five minutes or so. Some crisis had erupted in the Vindhya senior dorms, which necessitated his immediate attention. Saying that, he disappeared inside the dorm. Jogi was, by now, at the Ropes. I was in a classic Catch-22, literally caught between the devil and the deep sea. At Jogi's signal, I would have to sound the bugle . . . and invite Joon's ire. Hobson's Choice, indeed!

Copyright © Rathin Mitra | ART MASTER | 1950–1953

I had to decide . . . and decide NOW. Instinct got the better of me and I hid behind the door, out of Jogi's sight. Jogi was bewildered. He could swear he'd seen me a few seconds back. Or was it just his mind playing tricks on him? He wasn't sure anymore . . . Two Nilagirians, Henna and Butalia, incidentally my classmates, were dispatched to Himalaya House to fetch me. The hungry were getting restless and noisier with every passing minute. I, from behind the door, was trying to catch Joon's attention. No such luck. He was busy thrashing two surds from L-V. Just then, there was a gentle pat on my left shoulder. I turned around, and nearly brushed my nose against the Moustache. 'Hyeee lad?' followed by a tender dhapp . . . Before I could find my voice and construct what to say in my mind, another dhapp . . . 'Lad, get on with it!' I marched two steps forward, firmly closed my lips, pulled my tummy in, and blew with all my might . . . playing the entire piece in the high, fifth note.

To little avail, though . . . While BD strolled in to savour the once-a-week favourite kadhi chawal, I, standing alongside Jogi, got a mouthful from Mucchoo. I had no appetite. Immediately after lunch, it was a long, petrifying walk up the Tuck Shop slope for a rendezvous with Jogi, that lasted a good forty-five minutes. And that still wasn't the end of this nightmare. Falling-in to march up to Birdwood for Evening Prep, Joon, perched on the BD pavement parapet, called out to me, 'Oye Surdie, see me tonight!'

**Maj. Gen. Kulpreet Singh (Retd.)**
Kulu | Himalaya 1979 | 1969–1979
Colonel of Regiment – 3 Cavalry and 10 Armoured | Military Information Officer – UN Mission, Sierra Leone | Head – Military Training (Neeraj Chopra, Javelin Gold Medalist, Tokyo Olympics 2020) | Mentor – Defence Services Staff College, Wellington

OSS PRESIDENT 2019–21

# The Nine-Year Journey

People often speak of a parallel universe. Sanawar was exactly that and more . . .

In 1989, I left St. John's, Chandigarh, an all-boys day school to join Sanawar in Form-II. Some memories are as fresh as the morning dew. My mother was strict, ambitious, articulate and forthright due to her army upbringing. She had a frugal yet fulfilling childhood, which in many ways, was similar, and yet a little different to my father's. My paternal grandfather did wear the olive greens, but had a different take on parenting. My mother, being an Elocution teacher at St. John's, ensured that I learnt well. Together with my father, a young, strapping Sikh corporate professional working at a Swedish MNC—they did their best for their firstborn, me. I was sporty, mischievous, outdoorsy and as energetic as a terrier, beaming with enthusiasm (perhaps a bit too much for my mother to handle), making me a perfect fit for boarding school life.

While growing up, I'd often be reprimanded and whacked. By the time I got to standard III, I was a certified kindergarten commando. I guess destiny was scripting my entry to Form-II. One fateful afternoon, on a hot summer day, after a sweltering walk back from my school bus on the dusty route home, I was met by my mother. She was holding a piece of paper. Her poker-faced expression scared me as she didn't utter a word. I readied myself to receive the customary two thunderclap slaps, with both her bony hands. She did not oblige, making me wonder at the enormity of my mystery blunder. It was mortifyingly confusing. She finally divulged, 'Baba, Sanawar has accepted. You leave in ten days'. My reaction was priceless. If walls had ears, they would've gone deaf. With uncontrolled excitement, I jumped with my knees touching my chest. My *jooda* bobbed so fiercely that the *patka* flew off, 'Yes! Yes! Yes!' It was most certainly the best news I'd received in my entire life.

And thus began the journey. Reality dawned once my parents departed. Surrounded by fifty-odd kids in the Prep School lower dorms (Vindhya and Siwalik), I was overwhelmed by a range of emotions. To begin with, the sheer diversity was overawing. Kids from all parts of the country had converged on the hilltop (sadly, over time, the Delhi, Calcutta and Bombay school parties have faded away, and today, it's Punjab all the way).

Women always leave the deepest impact on one's life, and in my case, they were Mrs Ram Singh and Sunehro Ayaji—the Sachin–Sehwag duo who made my innings meaningful, epitomizing the essence of 'home away from home', and 'the art of living'. Within the shortest possible time, friendships and relationships (for life) were built, stitched within the fabric of the House one belonged to (Vindhya, in my case). Deeper bonds burgeoned with hikes and Annual Camps. Playing sport defined my character and as I honed my abilities, more and more doors opened up.

Sneaking daal, rotis, bread, eggs from CDH and getting busted; Trump cards, Raja-Mantri-Chor-Sipahi, dots-and-boxes, tipi-tipi-tap, *pitthu*, kick-the-can, and Rescue, added joy de vivre to everyday life. It was quintessentially a dream ride of unabashed fun and new experiences, that sometimes included doing stupid things to attract the attention of the opposite sex.

BD was an altogether other world—a fresh flock of sheep for the eagerly waiting wolves with sharp fangs. Real survival instincts kicked in and new skill sets were quickly acquired—a crash course for a boy to become a young man. I learnt fairly quickly that 'tuck' was the currency that made the world go around; 'sliming' or 'tattling' was a career-ending move; and to be recognized in sport was the pinnacle of success. Not only did you earn that all-important point for your House—the 'inclusion' was sufficient to keep the 'wolves' at bay. And, in case you were exceptional, Mr Williams (cricket), Mr Sukhwinder Singh (hockey), Mr Chauhan (gymnastics) or Mr Sequeira (soccer) were forever hunting to strengthen their respective bench. Exciting beyond imagination, because sport is nearly all that I did back then.

The '90s was a special era for us to grow up (or try to grow up) in. Insta, Facebook and WhatsApp have, in my humble view, robbed today's kids of their childhoods. Maybe what's needed is, as a teacher famously said, 'put the slap to the face; fingers stay and the hand come back'.

Ah! What wonderful, wondrous years and how lucky were we to truly live life, back in the day . . . on the hilltop . . .

**Pratap Singh Bajwa**
Prapster | Vindhya 1998 | 1989–1998

OS Sibling – Sister – Kariba Bajwa | Vindhya 2000 | 1995–2000

# Treasured Memories

I joined school in 1964. I had heard and read such fun stories about boarding life. For the first three weeks, however, I cried myself to sleep every night. I was homesick; the routine was tough; the food was 'different'; the bed was cold and there was a sea of new faces—nothing seemed familiar or comforting.

All that changed soon . . . I learnt to take one day at a time and the hectic routine kept me on my toes. Along the way, I made new friends and learnt to adapt and remain cheerful; thoughts of home receded to the background.

The day would begin with our matron, Ms Ling, ringing the rouser bell loudly for what seemed like forever, until we dragged ourselves out of bed. The hurry and scurry for the day would start: PT, classes, hobbies, games, prep . . . everything worked with clockwork precision. There was no time to stand and stare. Before you knew it, the day was over and you reached the dorms exhausted and ready for a good night's sleep.

Every day would bring a new learning, whether it was making your own bed; polishing your shoes; keeping the locker tidy; throwing waste in the dustbins; sharing your tuck—you just learnt to obey. Habits formed at school have stayed for a lifetime.

The first term was always a longer one, but there was lots to look forward to: the House shows were such fun and one waited for them eagerly. Someone would always surprise you with their acting or singing talent. 'Camps' were another welcome break from routine. I still remember busloads of excited girls singing at the top of their voices while heading towards Gaura or Kandaghat. The following two to three days were the most adventurous in our young lives. A campfire on the last day would mark the end of those happy 'Camping Days'.

A Walking Out Pass to Kasauli was also special. We would start saving our pocket money of Rs. 2 per week well in advance, so as to buy bunsums, sticky toffee and double bubblegum. A good amount of time was spent calculating and recalculating how best to optimize your Rs. 2—our first informal lesson in budgeting. Another treat in the summers was ice cream. It meant a trip to BD, Vindhya House, to get that 'much-awaited' vanilla ice cream. Mrs Sehgal was in-charge. Needless to say, one was perpetually hungry in School. Charlie and his snacks were always welcome!

Our teachers were the best ever. They were our heroes and role models. They instilled in us values of honesty, integrity, hard work, loyalty and compassion, and made us what we are today. One can never thank them enough. Major Som Dutt, Mr B. Singh, Mr Kemp, Mr Gore, Dr Gupta, Mr Mukherjee, Mr Jagdish Ram, Ms Chuck, Mrs Mountford are some of the names that come to mind.

I can never forget the spectacular sunsets one saw from behind the Art Room. The beautiful hilltop Sanawar will always remain a home away from home.

**Mandeep (Sidhu) Grewal**
Mandy | Himalaya 1969 | 1964–1969
Teacher | Army Wives' Welfare Association

OS Siblings – Brother – Devinder S Sidhu | Vindhya 1967 | 1961–1967
                 Sister – Jagdeep Sidhu | Himalaya 1972 | 1967–1972

OS Children –  Son – Vikramjit S Grewal | Vindhya 1994 | 1987–1994
                 Daughter – Amrita Grewal | Vindhya 1997 | 1992–1997

# The School Memorials

1.  In the Sanctuary, Chancel and Choir:

   1.1.  Marble tablet. 'To The Memory Of The Revd. William John Parker, first principal of The Lawrence Military Asylum, who was selected by the Founders Sir Henry and Lady Lawrence; to carry out their benevolent design. He took charge of the asylum in 1847, when it contained but few children, and lived to see nearly 500 within its walls. The buildings in which they live, and the Church in which they worship, were designed and erected by him. Faithfully and devotedly he performed the duty entrusted to him; and after more than fifteen years of unbroken labour and responsibility, be was attacked by paralysis, while performing Divine Service with his flock on Sunday 28th December 1862, and died January 1st 1863, in his 51st year. This monument is erected by the Government of India, in grateful acknowledgment of his services to soldiers' children.'

   1.2.  Marble tablet. 'Sacred to the Memory of The Revd. John Cole. For 20 years, 1864–1884, Chaplain and Principal of The Lawrence Military Asylum, Sanawar who died at Isle Brewers, Somerset, on Nov. 30 1906, Aged 76. "Blessed are the dead which die in the Lord". This tablet is erected in loving remembrance by some of the Old Sanawar boys and girls.'

   1.3.  Marble tablet. 'To the glory of God and sacred to the Memory of The Reverend Alfred Herbert Hildesley 3rd principal who from April 1st 1884 to 1912 devoted his life, holding nothing back, to the boys and girls of British soldiers at the Lawrence Military Asylum Sanawar serving their best interest of body, mind and spirit. He loved this mountain home and had a great care for its beauty. He was a Master of Arts of the University of Cambridge (St. John's College), graduating as 16th Junior Optime in the

Mathematical Tripos in 1879, and a Fellow of the Punjab University. He was awarded the Kaiser-1-Hind Gold Medal for Public service. Vicar of Wyton, Huntingdonshire From 1912 to 1935 Born 1857-died 1939. This memorial is erected by Old Sanawarians and other friends, 1943.'

2.  In the North Aisle:

2.1.  Marble tablet, Virgin and Child. 'To the Glory of God and in affectionate memory of Elizabeth Softly. Born Jan. 25th 1879. Died June 24th 1929. Kindliness and understanding personified she was a real mother to all.'

2.2.  Brass plaque. 'In memory of Grace Davin, 1 January 1892, R.I.P.'

3.  Baptistry (North Aisle)

3.1.  Marble tablet. 'In Affectionate Memory of the Lady Honoria Lawrence, the beloved wife of the founder who died in the Lord at Mount Abo in Rajpootana. January 15$^{th}$ 1854 aged 45 years. She was a true friend to the soldier, and a worthy help-meet to her husband in all his benevolent designs, and especially in establishing this institution.'

3.2.  Bust of the Founder. 'Sacred to the memory of Sir H M Lawrence, K.C.B. Founder of this institution Born June 28th 1805. Died July 1857.'

3.3.  Marble tablet. 'In Memory of Letitia Catherine Infant daughter of Henry Montgomery and Honoria Lawrence who was born Novr. 1840 and died August 1$^{st}$ 1841. She was buried at Subathu. Also In Memory of A H Lawrence Eldest son of Sir H M Lawrence KCB. who was born September 6$^{th}$ 1838 and died August 27$^{th}$ 1864. He was buried at Simla.'

3.4.  Stained glass Window. 'The stained glass window in the baptistry is dedicated to the memory of Lady Honoria Lawrence, wife of the founder. It was put up in 1854 by Mr. Parker, 1$^{st}$ Principal, and the boys of the Lawrence Military Asylum.'

3.5.  Marble tablet. 'Sacred To the memory of Sir Henry Montgomery Lawrence K.C.B Brigadier General Chief Commissioner in Oudh. He commanded the Garrison of Lucknow at the outbreak of the Sepoy Mutiny of 1857; was wounded by a shell on the 2nd and died on the 4th day of July 1857. Aged 52 years Full of peace and Christian hope. This institution which he originated, and to which he contributed 87000 rupees, is his best monument. This tablet is erected by a few friends and the officers and children of this asylum to express the reverence & affection which they have for his memory. In his last hours he committed this asylum to the fostering care of the government which he had so long and faithfully served; and the trust has been generously accepted. Commending his soul to the mercy of God in Christ he thus bestowed his body; 'Let me be buried with the soldiers. Let nothing be put on my grave but the text Daniel IX vs IX : 'To the Lord our God belong mercies and forgiveness tho' we have rebelled against him' and 'HERE LIES HENRY LAWRENCE WHO TRIED TO DO HIS DUTY'.

4.  On the West Wall (either side of door):

4.1.  Stained glass window with Brass plaque. 'To the Glory of God and in memory of Sgt. and Mrs Keeling for 20 years on the staff of the Henry Lawrence School for children of British soldiers. A task in which they displayed great love and affection. This window is dedicated by Sanawarians, past and present, to the Greater Glory of God and in loving memory of Elizabeth Sarah Keeling, a member of the asylum staff from 1890–1908. Thy praise shall sanctify our rest.'

4.2.  Stained glass window with Brass plaque. 'This window is dedicated by Sanawarians, Past and Present, To the Greater Glory of God and in loving memory of Philip Keeling, A member of the Asylum Staff from 1889–1914. "Thine for ever".'

5.  In the South Aisle:

5.1.  Brass plaque. Reading, 'To the Glory of God and in memory of Frederick Sydney Cousins, Lieutenant I.U.L. Chief Clerk and Steward 1885–1914. Born 7 July 1858. Died 6 February 1925. Erected by those who were privileged to know his kindness, courtesy and rectitude. Well done, thou good and faithful servant.'

5.2.  Brass plaque. 'In loving memory of Ian Forrest Sgt. Pilot R.A.F. Killed in action in Italy on the night of 10th–11th November 1944 Aged 25 years and four months. Greater love hath no man than this, that a man lay down his own life for his friends.'

5.3.  Brass plaque. 'In loving memory of Hugh Hannan Stanley, Corporal 1st Bn. Royal Irish Rifles, who was killed in France on the 10th March 1915, while gallantly cutting the German wire entanglements at Neuve Chapelle. Aged 24 years. This tablet is erected by his mother and father to a brave and devoted son and is placed by them in the Chapel of his Old School and home. Thy will be done.'

5.4.  Brass plaque. 'To the Glory of God and in ever loving and sacred memory of my only son Charles Robert Trowadale. 2nd Lieutenant, Kings Royal Rifles, who died of wounds on the 3rd October 1918, whilst serving in France. This tablet is erected by his mother in the little Church where he first learnt to know God and to sing his praises. All things work together for good to them that love God.'

5.5.  Tablet. 'Sacred to the memory of Edward Miller Cowell, Esquire. Formerly a merchant of Calcutta, who died 30th April 1859 at Great Malvern, Worcestershire, England. This Tablet has, been placed in the Church in grateful acknowledgment of a Benefaction bequeathed by him to the Lawrence Military Asylum Sanawar.'

5.6.  Tablet. 'To the Glory of God and in memory of C.F. Oliver who for nearly 27 years faithfully did his duty in this Asylum. He won the respect of his colleagues and the affection of his pupils.'

5.7.  Marble (white tablet). 'To the memory of Major Thomas Henry Hill, CIE An inmate of this institution from 1849 to 1857. Born Feby. 14th 1844. Died Feby. 19th 1930.'

5.8.  Stained glass window. 'To the Glory of God and in affectionate memory of Cecil Hugh Line who in Sanawar as a boy, as a Student of the Training Class and finally as a master endeared himself to all. He enlisted with the first Sanawar contingent in June 1915 and died in the service of the Empire in Mesopotamia on the 14th July 1917, aged 25 years. This window is erected by Sanawarians Past and Present.'

5.9.  Tablet. 'In Affectionate Memory of James Tilley Chief Clerk of the L.R.M.S. 1914 to 1929. He transmuted the base metal of everyday life into the gold of a priceless service.'

5.10.  Wooden Boards (interim Memorial)

'Lawrence Royal Military School Roll of Honour. 1939-1945 H.B. Blaker Capt. I.A.M.C., K. Hughes R.A.F., N. Boon R.A.F., F.W. Johnson R.A.F., A. Bond F/Lt. R.A.F., L. Kells F/O. R.A.F., P. Busby R.A.F., A. Kelly, I.E., I. Capenhurst, Northants, J. Kelly Cpl. Yorks and Lancs, C. Cook, D. McConnel R.A.F., L. Cooper M.M., J. Middleton R.A., C. Crossley Sgt. S. Lancs, L. Norkett, G. Davenport-Jones R.A.F., H. Pearce, G. Drummond D.C.L.I., J.W. Phillips D.F.M. R.A.F., A. Edwards R.A.F., A. Roberts R.C.S., J. Edwards R.A.F., P. Ross, H. Fallows, N. Rowe Norfolk Regt., E. Fletcher R.A.0.C., E.A. Richardson N.Z.F., I. Forrest R.A.F., G. Stone D.F.M. R.A.F., G. C. Fremantle, A.J. Stripp, D.F.C, R.A.F., L. Frost R.A., C. Taylor R.A.F., E. Fuller D.F.M. R.A.F., O. Thorpe, H. Hodson, N. Tilsley R.A.C., C.H. Howie Maj-Genl., D. West R.E., A. Howie., N. Lord I.M.N.S., A. Reeks U.S.N.'

**Editor's note:** This provisional monument comprising two dark stained and polished hardwood boards inscribed with gold lettering, was erected on the wall of the south aisle in 1945, pending provision of a more permanent monument at a suitable site in the Chapel grounds. See para 6.3 below.

5.11.  Stained glass window (behind the altar of the Side Chapel).

'In beautiful memory of Elgar Seymour Hunt and of his children, Gloria and Theo Hunt. Dedicated at a special memorial service conducted by the Rt. Rev. H. Packenham-Walsh in June 1934.'

6.  The South Transept and Chapel Grounds.

6.1.  South Portal and Porch (Plaque). 'This Ante-Porch and Bell-Turret were erected in memory of the Founder by Col. Herbert Edwardes, C.B., H.E.I.C.S. AD 1858.'

**Editor's note:** This beautiful porch was commissioned by Colonel Herbert Benjamin Edwardes and dedicated to the memory of his friend and exemplar Henry Montgomery Lawrence. It was designed and built by the Reverend William J. Parker in 1858. His monogram is carved just below the bell tower.

6.2. World War I Memorial (Cenotaph). 'To the greater Glory of God and in proud memory of OLD SANAWARIANS who fell in the Great War, 1914-1918.

Ashcroft J. Pte. North Staffords, Berry L. Bdm. Midd'x Regt., Bloodworth F. Rfn. K.R.R.C., Bloodworth P. Cpl. S&T. Corps., Bruce A. J. Br. R.H.A., Byrne J. Sgt. R. lr. Rgt., Charlton L. Tpt. R F.A., Cross E.M.F. S.M. R.C.S., Cullen F.J. Telegraphs, Edge S. Pte. Royal Irish Regt., Gibbons E. Telegraphs, Hickie C.S. 2Lt. R.F.C., Houlding H. Cpl. Royal Irish Regt., Line C.H. Cpl. R.C.S., Malachowski von H, Cpl. Royal Irish Regt., McGregor R. Lt. S. Lancs Regt., Morris A. S/Sgt. S&T Corps, Nicholas D.J. Gunr. R.F.A., Oldall E.T. Cpl. R.M. Fus., Pitcher A. Cpl. R.I. Fus., Richards R.E. Cpl. 7th Hussars, Taylor W. Pte. D.W. Regt., Trowsdale C. Lt. K.R.R.C., White E. Tpt. R.F.A., Wren C. M.M. R.F.A., Wright G. Pte. R. Irish Regt.'

6.3. World War II, Sino-Indian and Indo-Pakistan War Memorial (Slate Tablets) is a recessed stone arch let in to the retaining wall adjacent to the World War I Memorial in the Chapel grounds. The monument is comprised of three dark slate tablets surmounted by the Lawrence School emblem and plaque:

'IN THE PROUD MEMORY OF OLD SANAWARIANS WHO FELL IN WAR KILLED IN ACTION 1939-45'

Here in two columns, inscribed on two of the three tablets erected in the recess, are the LRMS Old Sanawarians listed in para 5.10 above, although not in the same order and with some details omitted.

'KILLED IN ACTION-1962
CAPT YR PALTA, VrC SIKH REGT
CAPT CP SINGH GRENADIERS

KILLED IN ACTION-1971
LIEUT A KHETARPAL, PVC ARMOURED
MAJ VR CHOUDHRY, MVC ENGINEERS
MAJ DS PANNU, VrC SIKH REGT'

'At The Going Down Of The Sun & In The Morning
we will Remember Them'

**D.V. Boddington**
LRMS Sanawar 1942–1947
December 2001

**Sources and Referencess:**

- *The Sanawarian Magazine*, December 1918.
- LRMS Part I Orders No. 652 dated 7 November 1924.
- Pamphlet 'The School Memorials', November 1936.

# Achhe Aur Nek Insaan

My father visited Sanawar in 1950 to admit me and my younger brother, Col. Aman Singh Yadav (HBD '57) and his first impression of the school was, 'This is a family living on a lush green hilltop, with the aim of bringing up their children and making them *"achhe aur nek insaan"*.' We joined in 1951.

It was my third day in school. English being a huge handicap, I would just follow what the others were doing. It was the day of kit change. Not understanding what to do, I must have done something awfully wrong for Mrs Cowell, the Himalaya House matron to start shouting at me loudly. Trembling and not knowing what she was saying or asking, I managed to say, 'My name is Vijai Singh Yadav and my father's name is Capt. Puran Singh'. (those were the only two sentences I knew in English). I noticed that her anger turned into an affectionate smile that was followed by a long, tight hug.

I was perpetually on drill, including for not wishing the then Headmaster, Mr S.C. Cowell on his birthday. The next year, I knocked on his door at the stroke of midnight to wish him. I still remember that he hugged me. He was, in fact, a little teary-eyed.

Lady teachers were addressed as 'Miss'. Mrs Kemp objected to being called Miss. Thereafter (since 1952), all lady teachers, notwithstanding their marital status, were addressed as Ma'am.

Miss Dhamija joined in 1952. She was the one who suggested that students and staff alike must stand while *Vande Mataram* was played during the morning Assembly on every Friday, as it deserved the same respect as the national anthem. She encouraged the incorporation of Indian traditions and culture in our everyday life. On Founders', two plays in Hindi were staged, *Meri Fees Vapas Karo* by Mr Vyas (our Hindi teacher) and *Raja Harish Chandra* by Miss Dhamija, assisted by four of her students who grew up to be Admiral Vishnu Bhagwat, Dr G.S. Purewal, Mr Ramesh Pratap and Air Cmde. V.S. Yadav. Both plays were roaring successes.

In 1951, all punishments, if any, were carried out solely by the Head Boy, D. Macintosh. There was no drill or any caning, and his only method of punishment was a mild knock on the head. I still recall his uniform was unique and distinct from the rest of the students.

In 1952, Dishelshwar Rarewala was the school prefect and the hockey captain. Before the YPS Patiala match, the team was collecting their kit from his bunk while he was away to meet Mr Curzon, the hockey coach. They ended up making a mess of his bunk. He got so angry that he beat up the entire team, including his close friend, Swarenjeet Dhillon, and the Head Boy, Raj Sircar.

In 1952, the number of houses increased from two (Himalaya and Nilagiri) to four (adding Vindhya and Siwalik). The four Housemasters began selecting students for their respective House. I was Mr Evans' (Himalaya Housemaster) second choice, after Raj Sircar, who went on to become Head Boy. When asked why he had chosen me, Mr Evans replied, 'He will win the Cock House for Himalaya in the next two years.' In 1954, Himalaya House did win the Cock House. In the same year, the final soccer match between Himalaya and Nilagiri was the talk of the town. Nilagiri had seven players from the School XI, while Himalaya had just one (me). We were expected to lose by a minimum of six goals. Himalaya won by a solitary goal scored by Angrish.

Mr Cowell and his dog Wendy always came to see us off at the Dharampur Railway Station. A majority of us travelled by the school party. As the toy train chugged out of the platform, it was very touching to see Mr Cowell and Wendy cry.

In 2016, our class celebrated our Golden Jubilee. At the Founders' Parade, a fly-past was organized by the Indian Air Force. Three fighter aircrafts did a low run over Peacestead. Air Commodore Kiyani, Principal, Lawrence College, Ghora Gali, Murrie, Pakistan, was a special invitee. On learning that I was from IAF and celebrating our fiftieth, he invited our class to extend its celebrations by visiting Ghora Gali. We gladly agreed.

We were treated like state dignitaries. Warmly received at the Wagah Border by the principal, the Commanding Officer of the Rangers and the President of the Lahore Chapter, we dined at the Lahore Club. Next day, we visited Nanak Sahib (the birthplace of Guru Nanak) and Punja Sahib. At school, we were received by the HOD and the Head Boy. The reception at the Islamabad Club was attended by all the Gallians, with a few travelling all the way from Karachi. On our way back from Murree to

Lahore, the Gallians at Gujranwala had organized a massive reception. We were deeply touched by this gesture.

**Air Commodore Vijai Singh Yadav**
VS | Himalaya 1956 | 1951–1955

OS Sibling – Brother – Col. Aman Singh Yadav | Himalaya 1957 | 1951–1956

OS Children –  Son – Grp. Capt. Monish Yadav | Himalaya 1986 | 1979–1984
Son – Anuj Yadav | Himalaya 1989 | 1982–1985
Daughter-in-Law – Suhasini Yadav | Shinu | Himalaya 19991 | 1983–1991

OS Grandchild – Grandson – Tarun Yadav | Himalaya 2014 | 2011–2012

# Omelette with On-EE-Yun or Without

Sanawar bestowed us with stomachs of wrought iron. Anyone who could endure those meals could eat basically anything. The only probable reason for why breakfast was savagely gobbled up was because it broke our twelve-hour fast. Frankly, it was just about tolerable, repeatedly consisting of that tasteless, near-frozen lump referred to as porridge (it's taken me ages to get over that trauma and I have only recently been able to include oats in my diet); the chilled, greasy, fried (though without a trace of oil) egg that needed a JCB tractor to be peeled off the plate and the dot of butter (was that a joke?). All of these were guzzled up with the help of as many slices of the school bakery bread that one could possibly grab. In comparison, lunch was gold-standard—rich, balanced, refined; an aesthetic culinary art consisting of everything from chicken, mutton, keema to chole, rajma . . . and the weekly serving of Odomos-flavoured ice-cream.

Supper, by far, was the most unappetizing. Every single day. Seriously, what were they thinking? The dal reminded one of Linda Blair's vomit in *The Exorcist* (1973); the chapati could give Walter Morrison's frisbee a run for its money; the 'Vegetable of the Evening', unfailingly, was either *baingan*, *lauki* or tinda, and they all strangely managed to retain the reek and tang of their raw avatars. The only saving grace was Wednesday nights' 'English' spread consisting of kidney beans, not-so-creamy mashed potatoes, mutton cutlets and bread pudding. And then, in U-VI, there were the Friday nights, but solely for the 'August Eighteen' – the School Appointments – who attended the weekly official Heady's meetings, supposedly to discuss strategy and pave the way for a better tomorrow for everyone . . . Hogwash! We gluttons, the seven girls included, went with a singular agenda to stuff ourselves with the mouth-watering, delectable presentations of that night – ranging from sausage and ham pizza, mutton *shammi kebab*, chicken quiche, egg pie, lemon tarts – God bless Pheroza Ma'am and her skillfully trained assistant, Lala. Once the food arrived, we failed to catch most of Heady's key instructions.

The inedible, hard-to-swallow grub, dished out on most mornings, days and nights, led to many an innovative deprivation-combating methods. I'm not sure what the girls did, but one of every three boys exited the CDH with chapatis neatly tucked in the folds of his battle-jacket. In the summer, it was the pocket of his shorts. Within the twenty minutes available before inspection, and away from the hungry and roving eyes of the prefect, the stone-cold chapati was destroyed using one of the following: Pachranga achar (from Panipat), Moga mixed fruit jam, Kissan baked beans, luncheon meat, mackerel, sardines, tuna or other such delicacies. In exceedingly desperate times, one had to make do with Ferradol-wraps.

Moving to L-VI and U-VI had their distinct advantage, which was an enhanced sense of privacy, thanks to a makeshift bunk with blankets stapled together and hung three sides; two for corner bunks). Some of us considerably augmented our culinary skills using necessary appliances, but the worthy title holder of Chef de Cuisine during our time was Masa Chuba Jamir from Kohima, Nagaland. On most nights (except Wednesdays and Fridays—his weekly offs), Masa would, quite literally, cook up a storm—omelette, scrambled eggs, sunny-side-ups, noodles (in those pre-Maggi days), with butter toast and coffee with condensed milk. He was also a proficient catapult-hunter and was largely instrumental in depleting the avian count on the hilltop. To do justice to his cooking skills, he owned the most amazing paraphernalia one could imagine – hot plates, electric heaters, immersion rods, frying pans, plates, bowls, spoons, forks, plastic mugs and even a chopping board (a modified exam clipboard) – the works! One night, stirring up yet another gastronomic charm, the Chef de Cuisine confirmed a pending order, 'Ganche, you want omelette with on-ee-yun (read, onion) or without on-ee-yun?' Before Gancha could clarify his preference, a flash of lightning struck the L-VI dorms. Mucchoo, on his daily night-round, announced his arrival by tearing open Chuba's bunk 'curtain'.

For a fleeting moment, he thought he'd entered Nankoo's CDH Kitchen, but with Masa Chuba there. In his four decades of inspecting the dorms, he had never seen so many pots, pans and gadgets in one place. He just stood, momentarily gobsmacked, but quickly regained his sanity and barked, 'Hyeee, someone get me a blanket!'; 'Hyeee, WAIT, you nincompoop', and pulled off one of the bunk covers. Masa was subjected to a rather rigorous cross-examination, upon which he was made to declare every one of his movable assets. All worldly possessions were seized, dumped on the blanket and later, sealed and confiscated. To add insult to injury, Masa was himself made to carry his 'kitchen' bundle-wrapped, all the way to Tiger's Den. Henry Ford's famous words were playing in a loop, in his head: 'Failure is only the opportunity to begin again more intelligently'.

The next night, Masa was still reflecting on the way forward . . . the small immersion rod that missed last night's action was boiling water for a mood-lifting mug of Nescafé.

Never Give In!

**Pankaj Sapru**
Himalaya 1983 | 1976–1983
Senior Management – Petroleum Downstream sector | Travel & Street Photographer | Member – OSS Executive Committee 2019–21 | Vice President – OSS 2021–23

OS Sibling – Brother – Dhiraj Sapru | Himalaya 1985 | 1977–1985

# Divine Intervention

Some events in one's life remain etched in memory in spite of the passage of time. The incident narrated below occurred almost seven decades ago, but I have a vivid recollection of it as if it happened yesterday.

At the age of six and a half years, I had joined the Lawrence School Sanawar in 1953, in the Upper KG class of the Preparatory (Prep) Department. In those days, the first four classes or standards (LKG, UKG, Forms I and II) were conducted in the Prep Department, after which you transitioned into the Senior School.

Sanawar focused on the all-round development of its students; besides the academic curriculum, there were compulsory sports, hobbies, hikes and outdoors, military drill and physical training, to name some of the important facets. A lot of stress was also laid on inculcating a strong sense of discipline in the children, and all transgressions were suitably dealt with by awarding commensurate punishment, the highest on the scale being caning by [the] headmaster himself!

This incident occurred in the beginning of the 1955 term when I was in Form II. One morning during classes, the peon came to our classroom and handed over a slip of paper to our class teacher, Mrs Kate. She took a quick glance and then read out three names, saying that we were required to report to [the] headmaster, Mr E.G. Carter, for having been reported for indiscipline. It took me a few seconds to realize that she had called out my name too, as part of this dubious list. Two of the three were the certified 'mischievous' types, always up to some prank or the other, but I was as law abiding as they come—at least till then. So I was surprised to have made the list. Moreover, I wondered, what possible act of disobedience could an eight-year-old commit that would warrant an audience with none other than [the] headmaster himself?

While we were being ushered out, an equally surprised Mrs Kate asked me 'What have you been up to, Ardamanjit'? All I could say was 'I don't know Ma'am'. Being my Housemistress, she knew me well, and young as we were, we thought of her as a surrogate mother. She knew that I wasn't a 'rogue' and that perhaps I had got clubbed with the others for some reason not of my making. But she was helpless in preventing my punishment and sent me with the others, and I could see her looking tenderly at me as we were led out.

As we made our way to [the] headmaster's office (a short walk away) with the peon in tow, the thought which kept coming into my mind was 'why me?'. But then, God works in mysterious ways. We entered [the] headmaster's office to see Mr Carter hunched over his desk reading some document, with his dog lounging beside his chair. The dog's name was Raja, and he indeed had a very majestic look. Everyone knew of [the] headmaster's fondness for his dog, who was always by his side.

Being my first 'visit' here, I quickly measured the insides, noticing a wooden rack with six canes lined up. I was familiar with the catchphrase 'Six of the Best' – the severest punishment meted out to an erring student – referring to a whack with each of these six 'beauties' on the bottom of the hapless victim. Those with lesser 'crimes' got away with one whack. We stood quietly in front of him, quivering at the thought of what was sure to follow—'thwacks' with his cane.

After a couple of minutes, Mr Carter pushed his file aside, stood up and with a stern look, said, 'You boys have been up to mischief and have been reported to me for punishment. You know very well that I have zero tolerance for indiscipline'. He then picked up the closest cane, beckoned the first boy, asked him to bend and swung a clean whack. It made a swishing sound and the hapless lad let out a loud shriek. This ritual was repeated for the second boy.

It was now my turn. I had a forlorn look about me and my eyes begged for mercy, not that it would have any effect on this most strict disciplinarian made of the old mould. I had this sudden urge to pee. Before I could ask his permission to go, he waved his left hand asking me to step forward. Intuitively, I took a step backward instead. In a loud voice, he said, 'Step forward, young man'. My gaze was fixed on his right hand which held the cane in a firm grip. I paused just a bit and reluctantly moved towards him. And then, something unbelievable happened. His dog Raja got up from his place, moved and sat down on the side of his table, thereby blocking my path. Mr Carter frowned and hesitated, caught unawares by this development. He appeared undecided on his next move. Divine intervention? Almost on cue, he put the cane back in the rack and said, 'Raja doesn't want you to be caned, so I'll spare you. But stay out of trouble now.' We were then led out of the office.

I couldn't believe my luck. There is an old saying related to boxing, 'Saved by the gong'; to paraphrase that, I was 'saved by the dog'! Miracles do happen!

**Maj. Gen. Ardaman Jit Singh Sandhu**
Abdo | Vindhya 1962 | 1953–1962

# Sanawar – My Heartbeat

Draws you in like a magnet, doesn't it? Just the name 'Sanawar'? It drew me towards itself even before I ever stepped onto its hallowed grounds. When my elder brother, Rana, was admitted there in 1955, I, two years younger to him at age five, threw a right royal fit because I felt I was being cheated. I wanted to go, too. I lay down on the road in front of the car that was taking him up from Jalandhar, arms flailing, eyes streaming and lungs screaming, 'I want to go too! I want to go too!'

There was that mystery around it even before you got there. Two years later, March 1957, I made it!

And what a ride it's been ever since . . . and continues to be! Because it never leaves you and what it makes of you!

Even today, when I take off on my cross-country bike rides at age seventy-one, it is that spirit of 'Never Give In' that does it for me. Call it courage or an iron will or even a devil-may-care attitude, Sanawar ingrained in me a spirit of independence, fearlessness and firm resolve.

I had to negotiate and overcome many an obstacle during my years post college, because I was blessed with a different 'take' on life and what I wanted to make of it. I trod the less-beaten track to take the road less travelled, but I made it through with what are, to me, flying colours, and there is no denying the fact that it was the ten formative years I spent in Sanawar that egged me on, come what may!

So where does one begin?

I remember my first day up there in the Prep School like it was yesterday. I was seven years old and my mom and I had taken a bus from Chandigarh up to Garkhal. From Garkhal, we had to walk up to the school, with a porter carrying my steel trunk on his head.

Onto that vast pavement outside the Prep School dorms then, with my teary-eyed mom sitting on the low boundary wall, watching me run up and down the staircase connecting the two dorms. I was fascinated by it all: the

708

sense of space, the huge, double-storeyed dorms, the smell of the pines in the air, the sound of my feet thumping on the wooden stairs!

Thus began my love affair with Sanawar!

Etched in my memory is the dormitory at Prep School with its endless rows of beds along both sides, covered neatly in orange-coloured bedcovers. Beds on which we lay 'attention' every afternoon before games and hobbies, with Ms Muthhu's Hawkeye on us. Beds that we learnt to make ourselves: an art that comes in handy to this day!

On Sundays we gossiped, shared tales, played the clown or passed the time chipping bark off the pine trees that grew in such profusion around us, to carve out little boats with our tiny penknives. Or we would played Cops and Robbers in that vast expanse: down to the playfield and below, up to Moti's Corner to the north, behind the bathhouse and up towards Bleak House and then down to the classrooms and Hospital southward, past a little playground adjacent to Dr & Mrs Sakhuja's residence.

Boy, were we being primed from when the word 'go' was first spoken, to remain physically fit!

From there, we went onto Senior School, or BD (Boys' Department) as it was known then!

There were these prefects with their towering physiques and personalities who ladled out 'See me tonight' at the drop of a hat: for 'falling in' late at the call of the bugle; for marching out of step; for badly polished brogues—an endless list of dos and don'ts that instilled in us a sense of discipline that serves us well to this day.

Amongst our seniors, there were ace gymnasts, athletes, boxers, actors and singers, and they became our heroes—as did we when we stepped into their shoes, for those who followed us. Unknown to us then, Sanawar was becoming—and eventually became—a home away from home for all of us. A home we came to cherish and love deeply.

Who can forget the cool spring air up on the Hilltop that one craved every year towards the end of the much-too-long winter break? I, for one, could never wait to get back! And those hikes and treks to Gurkha Fort and Ozark with our seniors, who drove us on relentlessly till we got to our destination . . . Camping for the night beside a stream under an open sky, unafraid! The arduous trek to Churi Chandani/Chaur Peak when we were the seniors, egging everyone along with shouts of 'Never Give In', those who had fallen behind and were raising their hands in surrender!

Or puffing up Tilley's Hill on the mighty Hodson Run, gasping for breath but keeping the legs pumping, knowing that at the last bend, before the Arch, there would be girls screaming their lungs out to get you to breast that tape before anyone else did!

And, finally, the highs of 'My Fair Lady' and 'Lemon Tree' in our final year, 1966!

Thank you, thank you, Sanawar! For all this and more, and most of all for those wonderful teachers we had the privilege of being nurtured and mentored by. The list is long, but no teacher is forgotten!

And our Sanawarian girls! Stalwarts in their own right! Upright, confident and graceful! We were lucky to have them around when growing up. It promoted in us a healthy attitude towards the 'superior' sex!

Our days in Sanawar finally came to an end. On that last, 'break-up night', as I delivered my farewell speech, I burst into uncontrollable tears in the middle of it. It was an emotional moment and I gave into it! Little did I know then that I was not going anywhere! That Sanawar was not going anywhere!

Because it stays with you, inside of you. Wherever you may go, whatever you choose to do, Sanawar, with its 'Never Give In' spirit never leaves you!

And lucky we are that it doesn't . . .

**Amar Talwar**
Amroo | Vindhya 1966 | 1957–1966
Living life on his terms | Actor | Photographer | Generous Philanthropist | Devoted tree-planter/carer

OS Siblings – Brother – Rana Talwar | Vindhya 1964 | 1955–1964
                Sister – Tania (Dimple) Talwar | Vindhya 1970 | 1964–1970

OS Children – Son – Manoj Talwar | Vindhya 1999 | 1993–1999

# A Gentleman's Journey

When my dad left for Congo, I was sent to Sanawar. Mom, along with my sister, moved to Kasauli to join me in school later. Vindhya House awaited me. Initiation into boarding life was a challenge after the pampering care of my parents—a *sahayak* to help make my bed, pack my schoolbag and walk me to school; playing and sometimes fighting with my sister; a dog, pigeons and poultry for pets. All left behind.

The routine at Sanawar was different, to put it mildly. Rouser by a bugle call, fondly referred to as 'Charlie Charlie Get Out Of Bed, Charlie Charlie Give me Some Bread'; a cup of tea and a doggy biscuit; PT, bath (with Rulda timing the water); inspection (to check for polished shoes and tidied lockers); day's orders by the Head Boy; 'eyes left' at the War Memorial; Assembly, classes, lunch, 20 minutes of rest, games or hobbies. Evenings were spent energetically polishing the toe of drill shoes (the extra smart ones even polished the heels). Water, cotton, a candle, a spoon and some spit—if one could see a mirror image of one's teeth on the toe, things were fine. Wetting the beret and setting it over the eye. Did it sit right? Two fingers above the eyebrow. This was followed by Evening Prep (marched up again), dinner, and lights-out at 9 p.m. (preceded by BBC news). Prefects, in the meanwhile, were busy inspecting almost everything they could.

I soon adapted to this battalion life and the all-important House spirit; stopped shedding tears from homesickness; took to the running, swimming, somersaulting, boxing and studying—living for the House to win the coveted Cock House.

On the appointed day for the Parade, the squads lined up on Peacestead—uniforms spic-and-span, shoes shining, haircut to the tee, sideburns aligned with the eyebrows and ears, nails cut and cleaned, wearing spats/sashes/red hackles. The band, in vibrant colours and with glittering instruments, set the pace, the embankment lined with an array of colours as guests watched the march past. Stepping in tune, we timed our feet with the beat of the drum, eyes aimed at the podium, marching past the Chief Guest. The band followed with the Drum Major leading, twirling the drumstick, tossing it up in the air for two-and-a-half turns to catch it, to a thundering applause.

I learnt that an eye for detail could make all the difference—to any organization, community, or nation. I learnt that a nation without character, without pride or a sense of belonging in the hearts of its citizens, cannot prosper.

Major Som Dutt, our headmaster, was a larger-than-life personality and a great leader, who had a lasting influence on my impressionable mind. Humble in his approach, soft-spoken, appropriately dressed for each occasion, well-read, and at the same time also 'firm' in his decisions. A keen sportsman, he encouraged us to play games in the right spirit of sportsmanship, be it cricket, soccer or boxing, in addition to angling and trekking. His boxing lessons for us were great, 'You must learn how to dance', he would often say, 'Glide across the ring with grace and agility'. But what struck me most was his view about bullies and tattling. He invariably told us never to tattle and to always stand up to bullies who, he said, were cowards. All in all, he made us all 'Men of Honour' and 'Gentlemen'.

A memorable drive was to Chail in Heady's 'Black Zephyr'. Ashwini Marwah (Puffy) and I were invited to play cricket as part of Gen. Harbaksh Singh's team against Raja Patiala's Captain Amarinder, who has served as the Chief Minister of Punjab, and was then the ADC. An Australian was the umpire. As I ran up to bowl to Amarinder, the umpire stopped me, handed me an apple, taking away the ball with a wry smile and a wink. He said 'bowl'. I delivered a full-toss, much to the batsman's delight, and saw him smash it into thin air. The umpire then took out the 'real' ball from his pocket and the crowd broke into laughter. 1967 saw Kunjpura Sainik School and BCS visit Sanawar. A personal record of sorts, which I believe remains unbroken till date—was of my five wickets for twenty-three runs against Kunjpura and six wickets for seven runs against BCS. The stadium resonated with cries of 'Cats of Venus, Dogs of Mars' as we showed the Cottonians stars in broad daylight!

Mr Jagdish Ram Acharya (fondly called Jagga), was an overpowering personality, well-respected and invariably dressed in immaculate white. Maninderjeet Singh (Manny), a Vindhyan, decided to skip boxing class. As he walked in late, Jagga asked why. Prompt came the reply, 'Sir, I have hydrophobia of the leg'. Jagga, looking concerned, replied, 'OK my boy, you can take rest'.

Upinder Fotedar (Siwalik) decided to ask Jagga for a cricket bat on a Sunday morning. We, the younger lot, were busy at the gym as Fotedar walked up and asked, 'May I have a bat, Sir?' *Thwack!* Came the sound of slap. And, Jagga shouted, 'Wish me first, Fool!' Fotedar got his bat after a meek 'Good morning, Sir'. During Mass PT rehearsals at Peacestead, Jagga stood on the steps looking down at us as we lined up. Suddenly, we heard his loud sonorous voice, 'You there, the gurl with a funny name(name withheld). Stop scraping the ground with your foot like a goat.'

Mr B. Singh, another iconic figure, taught us history and other aspects of gentlemanly conduct. He was known for his wit, sense of humour and acting prowess, displayed at the Amateur Dramatics Society play every year. History class could get a bit boring, listening to what Mahmud of Ghazni or Lord Clive did. Mr B. Singh would react, 'Ah ah ah, there you go again, yawning like a chimpanzee, physically fully grown, mentally yet to be born . . . WAKE UP!' Fond of his evening tippler, rumour has it that he was walking back from Kas one evening. Measly (I'm forgetting his real name) was following him. Noticing that he was a bit tipsy, Measly sneaked up close, kicked him and ran off. He got to the dorm, quickly changed into his nightsuit and tucked into bed. Soon enough, Mr B. Singh arrived and he was heard shouting in anger, 'where is Measly?' then seeing him curled up in his bed, he yanked Measly out and gave him a solid thrashing, explaining in his soft voice, 'My dear lad . . . I was only half drunk.'

Nappi, our barber, was by then an old man with a creased forehead; he was busy the year round, his forefinger being the measure for the permitted length of hair as his scissors clicked away to clip anything that protruded beyond that bony boundary.

Ahhhh . . . memories . . .

**Pradeep Sharma**
Chesty | Vindhya 1967 | 1961–1967

# Letter Writing

The last class at the end of the week was reserved for letter writing. It was mandatory for all Prep School students to write home to their parents that they were doing well and enjoying the happy and healthy life at school.

A sample letter was normally written on the blackboard, which was assiduously copied by the KG students and even by some from the higher classes.

One Saturday, when the three of us, Pradeep, Amrit and I, entered the letter-writing class, we saw our teacher Mrs Blossom Lyall already seated at her table, with the sample letter clearly visible on the blackboard. Mrs Lyall was a kind, motherly, middle-aged lady with a large heart and mercurial temper.

Pradeep, an army doctor's son, had joined Sanawar a few months back. He was very helpful and friendly with us, his peers, but alert and cautious with his seniors and teachers. He generally looked nervous and fidgety. He had just learnt that his father had been posted to Ambala. He now wanted to write to his father about all the gifts he wanted before the approaching Diwali.

As we settled down, Mrs Lyall told us she was doing important work, replying to our parents' letters, so she did not want to be disturbed. Even thereafter, she had to warn Pradeep on two occasions not to whisper loudly or look into others' letters. Soon, the class was quiet as we were quickly trying to finish our letters to our parents, before the final bell was sounded.

Suddenly, I found Pradeep craning over me from behind and pointing to the last sentence in my letter, about to say something, when a sharp and loud, 'Pradeep, SIT DOWN' from Ma'am was accompanied by a whizzing sound and a thud of Pradeep falling to the ground.

There was pandemonium all over the class; before we could gather our senses, the final bell rang. There was confusion all around. Pradeep slowly picked himself up off the floor, watching out for Ma'am. But Ma'am was not at her table! She was now at the back of the class, comforting the

last boy behind Pradeep's desk! He was the unintended recipient of the projectile (ink bottle), after the deft dive to the floor by the intended target. The contents of the entire bottle were all over him and his letter, leaving him inconsolable.

While the rest of the boys and girls were talking excitedly about what had really occurred, Pradeep quietly walked out of the door, unscathed and unnoticed, leaving the turmoil behind him.

**Debabratamaya Mitra**
Debu | Siwalik 1964 | 1956–1964

# The School Grapevine

It was 1974 and my wife was expecting our third child. We had two daughters and as it always happens in most middle-class Indian families, the hopes and expectations were that this time around, it would be a boy.

How universally shared this hope and expectation was in the school, was brought home to me when Jai Singh Pathania, the then Head Boy of the school, who would become a lifelong friend and supporter, came up to me one morning and stammered, 'Sir, you are going to have a son. I had a dream last night. I saw an old holy man giving some mangoes to Mrs Dhillon. I have heard my mother tell other ladies that fruit being given to an expectant mother in a dream means that she is going to have a son.'

I was so deeply touched that I replied impulsively, 'God bless you, Jai—if it is a boy, we'll name him after you.'

The news of my son's birth came to me ten minutes short of the end of evening prep. I took five minutes to get the deputy headmaster's permission to go down and then I rushed home to pack my bag. I was still in the process of packing, when the bell rang. In the next few minutes, the little House was swarming with dozens of children, all calling out excitedly, 'Give our love to chut Jai Singh. Sir, give our love to chut Jai Singh.'

How the news spread in so short a time, that too while the children were at prep, has remained, till this day, one of the most enduring mysteries of my life. But it is a great tribute to the strength and beauty of the Sanawar grapevine.

This strength has, thankfully, remained undiminished over the years. In May 2010, my daughter, who teaches in Sanawar, was to have her second child. The children in Sanawar, with their usual interest and concern, had asked her what she would name her child. She said if it was a girl, she would be called Ismat and if it was a boy, he would be named Rehaan. It was a boy. He was born in Chandigarh at 8.47 in the morning, but because my younger daughter, who also teaches in Sanawar, was in school, I was only able to give her the news a few hours later. The bell rang for milk break and children swarmed in from all directions, crowding around her, jostling and pushing to catch her attention and the discordant babble of voices had one repeated refrain, 'Give our love to little Rehaan—Ma'am, give our love to little Rehaan.'

I sat still when I heard this, my heart and mind overwhelmed by the complexity of my emotions. In this world, so seething with change that one is often left confused and perplexed, I was reassured by the continuity of the strength and beauty of the grapevine in my old school.

**Dr Harishpal S. Dhillon**
UD | Nilagiri 1957 | 1949–1957
STAFF 1971–1986 | HOD English | Housemaster | Headmaster 1995–1999 | Headmaster YPS Patiala 1986–1995 | YPS Mohali 1999–2010

OS Sibling – Sister – Yogindra (Dhillon) | Nilagiri 1956 | 1951–1956

OS Children –  Daughter – Priya Dhillon | Himalaya 1988 | 1979–1988
          Daughter – Naina Dhillon | Himalaya 1988 | 1979–1988
          Son – Jai Singh Dhillon | Nilagiri 1991 | 1982–1989

OS Grandchildren – Granddaughter – Mannat Tipnis | Himalaya 2013 | 2006–2013
          Grandson – Abhay Tipnis | Himalaya 2017 | 2009–2011
          Granddaughter – Inaaya Kumar | Himalaya | 2018–To Date
          Grandson – Rehaan Kumar | Himalaya | 2020–To Date

**Source and Acknowledgements:**
Published as a Middle in *The Tribune* on 11 December 2006 and reproduced in *Of Cabbages and Kings – A Book of Middles*, (New Delhi: Picus Books, Hay House Publishers India, 2014).

# The Night of the Nighties

In 1976, our batch and our immediate seniors went on Annual Camps to Manali. We were tented up along the hill by the Mountaineering Institute, the Boys' and Girls' tents in adjoining sections. On the last night of camp, the customary bonfire – dinner along with some inspired singing – was planned. However, as the boys and girls normally remained segregated in two corners, Mr and Mrs Longman devised a plan so as to liven up another lackluster evening.

Mrs Longman was to ensure that all the girls arrived at the bonfire earlier than the boys and took up the best seats. Meanwhile, Mr Longman began executing his dastardly plot. He rounded up a team of around ten trusted boys from our batch and directed us to the now-empty girls' tents, while they were blissfully enjoying the best of the warm seats. We were instructed to rummage through their belongings and find nighties, or any dresses that we could fit into. Given that time was of the essence, we feverishly 'hunted' with due abandon. A tornado had hit the tent with clothes strewn all over the place.

Some of us had to try really hard to take to those ill-fitting dresses, while the nighties-finders comfortably slipped through. When all of us were ready, including Mr Longman, who was wearing his wife's nightie, we waited for our cue. Mrs Longman then announced that the boys were going to perform a special fancy dress dance. The music was turned up and we all ran about, prancing around the bonfire (none of us could actually dance). Initially, Mr Longman attracted all the attention and the accompanying screams of delight, until it dawned on the girls that the boys were wearing their clothes. Howls of laughter were drowned out by shrieks of shock and exclamations, 'Hey! That's my nightie . . . How dare you?!'

What would have been an inoffensive prank (and a good laugh) in the UK, was objectionable and distasteful in conservative India. The girls felt their privacy had been invaded and were clearly distraught. A suitably chastened Mr Longman had to issue an apology.

**Tarun Sawney**
Taru | Vindhya 1979 | 1971–1978

Mother – Josephine Winifred Sawney | Jo | 1970–1978 | Teacher – English and Piano

OS Siblings – Brother – Ravi Sawney | Mad | Vindhya 1976 | 1971–1976
Brother – Sunil Sawney | Tommy | Vindhya 1981 | 1970–1978

# Batch of '75: Abiding Bonds

My story has to do with how we have evolved as a caring and wonderfully integrated group of friends, from the time we were dressed in shorts and patched-up cardigans to an almost grandmotherly/fatherly set of adults with memories of living together stacked within. Obviously, we've all come a long way, and there will be many more years to enjoy together. But if the markers of universal and long-lasting relationships can be encapsulated at all, I'd attempt to do so in the following few questions:

1. Do we reach out to each other's families to know how our children, spouses, and grandchildren are doing?
2. Are we celebrating our successes, exchanging joy, and being there for one another in times of need?
3. Are we willingly making plans to meet up, especially when someone comes visiting our neighbourhood? Do we readily drop our routine to make way to greet old buddies?
4. Are we happy to spend a longish weekend away from it all, to enjoy all the khup and laugh at past memories? Do the non-Sanawarians amongst us also readily partake in these walkdowns and relate to the good old stories recounted many a times before?
5. Are we truly in a state of no malice, holding no grudge against one another? A non-judgemental group of each other's 'earliest and most loyal' friends?

We, the batch of 1975, are an excellent example of all this and more. We were the first batch to finish our higher secondary in early April, having stayed through the winter preparatory months, experiencing the thick blanket of snow on the pines and deodars; to see our mirror hills of Kasauli with the majestic Monkey Point in white splendour. We enjoyed our meals together, took the time to walk with our colleagues, discuss the upcoming exams and ruminate on the life that post-school days were about to spring

720

on us. In a way, it all seemed like a dream from which we were about to be released into an aspect of life that we really knew very little of. What would college be like? What would the ramifications of being without our friends, teachers and support staff be? What were the results of our exams going to be like? And yet, we lived through those intense days in a bubble, not knowing what life had in store. In retrospect, these weeks of utter bonding, helping one another out, rustling up large batches of espresso coffee and enjoying the crackle of amazing pinecone fires must have laid the foundation for what has come to pass today.

As is wont to happen with school friends, we scattered like the autumn leaves and pine-needles that our existence was so used to. A few stayed in touch, more because we happened to be in the same city, while others pushed on, onto new adventures that opened out before them.

We began to rediscover ourselves and started reaching out, perhaps after twelve to fifteen years, as our babies became schoolbound, while our careers were established. Smaller groups gave way to larger ones, with our homes being opened to each other and the best whiskies being generously poured. Along the way, unfortunately, we lost a couple of our brethren.

However, their families today are an integral part of the 1975 family. Every batch has its share of people, but I truly believe that ours is a group that genuinely cares for one another. Many of our children and spouses are not averse to joining in the fun and to be able to share our lives together. We are solid, we are a prism of all the House colours, and we embody a glowing spirit of bonhomie and kindred spirit and that's what makes our 'inclusive' batch an envy for the others.

And so our tales of inclusivity, our love for one another and the feeling that we are truly children of a shared Sanawarian heritage, keep our flags flying—and in good shape, at that.

**Vivek Ahluwalia**
Alu | Vindhya 1975 | 1965–1975

# Stoned Cows

We had gone camping in 1976 to Renuka Lake. On one shore of the lake, there was an old temple that housed a few sadhus and their cows. The backyard had a fenced-off garden patch, where the sadhus grew Ganja (marijuana). Befriending the sadhus made sense. We would come to the temple frequently.

One day, while there, we noticed the cows stretching their necks to get to the 'plant'. As they could not reach them, I broke a healthy bunch and offered it to two cows.

Shortly after, we returned for another round and noticed one of the cows walking weirdly on her slim legs. She would take a step forward, sway, take another step, lose her balance and fall on her side. A little ahead was the second cow, lying on her side, trying hard to get up but to no avail. I guess I had fed them a bit too much.

The next day, one of the sadhus confronted us as the cows would not stand still while being milked. They were also mad that we had contaminated their milk supply. We got scared, gave them some money and fled the scene. That was the first and last time I saw a stoned cow . . . or two.

**Harjaspreet Singh Gill**
Clay | Siwalik 1979 | 1969–1977
Lives in Seattle USA | Passionate about golf, music, dance, real estate development and software engineering

# The (L)Only Dame

I'm standing outside a classroom, from which emerges an explosion of noise. Nervous does not even begin to describe how I feel—it's my first day of school, my first class – physics – with my new classmates. I'm in L-VI C, having just joined Sanawar, in my new (old) uniform and textbooks that have seen better days tucked under my arm. I wonder what to expect.

I step into the room cautiously . . . The noise comes to a sudden halt. Total silence and what feels like a hundred pairs of eyes boring into me. It's a bright room, rows of benches, with boys of various sizes and shapes arranged across them. A quick glance around and I realize that there are no other girls in this class. I can't stand the stares any longer, and quickly slip into the first bench.

Behind me, I hear the murmurs starting up, slowly building back up to their previous level. The teacher walks in, a young woman, and introduces herself. She is new too, and I feel a burst of sympathy, as the boys take her measure. Poor Miss Jerath, she doesn't stand a chance. A gentle and mild-mannered scholar, she has no idea of how to discipline this riotous bunch. She focuses on me, but every question I answer is met with a chorus of feedback from the back benches. I resort to silence. She doesn't have that alternative and soldiers on.

Next class is chemistry with Nimitz. He seems to exude a natural authority, and the boys behave better. The relentless ragging slows to a trickle, and I can actually breathe. Lab practicals follow the lesson. We are supposed to conduct them in pairs, and the teacher announces who the partners will be. My partner, Mayadas, approaches me, looking equal parts terrified and delighted. Behind him, a chorus of calls: 'Aiiiin . . . aiiin . . .'

The pattern continues. I'm not just a new 'chick', I'm the only 'dame' . . . and the boys seem to regard me as an alien species. I'm sure some of these young men are decent chaps, and a few even smile or address me with a comment: Kaul, Sapru, Sud . . . I get to know their names. But there's a core group, formed around the nucleus of an obnoxious chap called Khara.

They take great joy in being as rude as possible. This is my first experience of co-education, and it doesn't give me much hope for the male half of the species.

After a couple of weeks, I'm desperate. Each class is emotional torture. I go to see Mr B. Singh. I've heard a lot about how strict he is, and I'm very nervous. 'Sir, I want to change my section,' I blurt out. 'Why?,' he asks, as his mobile eyebrows climb up his forehead. 'Well, Sir . . . you see, I'm the only girl in the class'. What an inadequate statement to explain my quandary. For a moment, he looks at me. Did I imagine a twitch of a smile and the famous moustache quivering? I can see that he is thinking over it and I'm desperate to explain my plight, but can't quite find the words. But I don't really need to. The wise one grasps the situation, no explanation needed. He's an expert, and knows what these boys are capable of. 'Lass, you can join D Section, and continue taking economics with C.'

Overwhelmed with relief, I run out of his office. Tomorrow will be a new day!

Sure enough, it is . . .

**Geetika Gupta**
Himalaya 1983 | 1981–1983
Educator and Learner

# Taught Us How to Play the Game . . .

Sanawar had some unforgettable teachers, who made Kipling's words come true. They believed in strictness, but also in fair play. The ones that stand out include: Mr E.G. Carter, the principal, was a disciplinarian of standing, and due to his overall discerning eye, the school did very well, compared to other public schools of the country.

The Maharaja of Patiala was Head of Patiala and East Punjab States Union (PEPSU) and a prominent visitor and patron of the school, which was situated in his territory. He was also a distinguished guest at the Sanawar for Founders' one year. Since the Maharaja was so impressed with the school, he decided to send both his sons for admission to K.G. here. Giving due consideration to his status, it was suggested that the princes would initially be put up in their parents' rooms for a week or ten days, whereby the official caretakers, attendants and pets could say goodbye and, thereafter, the boys could move to the PD dormitories. This suggestion was rejected by the Maharaja and he approached the Ministry of Education to send a suitable directive to the school. The ministry, however, referred the matter to the Board of Governors of the school, who stated that Pandit Nehru's three nephews, Gen. Cariappa's two children and scores of other dignitaries' children lived in dormitories. The Board then left the last word with the principal, who insisted that all children in the school were equal and would be treated the same. Boy was that some discipline. It is another matter that the two princes consequently did not join Sanawar. Similarly, there was to be no exception to there being only boarders and no day scholars, even children of serving teachers and the principal.

Mr S.C. Cowell, senior master, Boys School, too, was all for discipline and his task was difficult, as enforcement at the grassroots level included observance by one and all, of the early morning wake-up bell or bugle, especially in the winter; House inspection before cook-House bugle and House-wise lining up outside the dining hall, when the rats in the stomach

726

were taking their toll; marching up to Chapel for morning prayers, later replaced by Assembly in Barne Hall.

At Assembly, Mr. Cowell would stand close to the singers and pull at the seam of the gray uniform shorts of off-singers, thereby signalling to keep mum and let there be silent lip movement; checking in the evening that everyone was out on the playing fields, Upper Barnes, Lower Barnes or the gym, and not loitering in the dormitories, just as each one of us had to be out for morning PT; to fall-in House-wise, or sometime class-wise, to march up to Birdwood for prep, where prefects ensured seriousness in completion of homework; and lights-out with the last bugle, subsequently replaced by a bell. And Mr Cowell had the entire Boys' Department going like clockwork. It would appear that Mr Cowell's passion for this disciplined regime, his devotion to his old, but mentally and physically fit mother, and his love for his equally old dog, Wendy (well, a bitch, actually, but never with too many pups), forced him to remain a 'faithful' bachelor.

Mrs Carter, Senior Mistress GD and wife of the principal, kept the Girls' Department ever on their toes and was, perhaps, the moving spirit behind the superb plays and skits performed on many occasions, especially at Founders'. She took maths for Senior School and advanced maths for the Sixth Form appearing for the Senior Cambridge Exams. One day, she was five minutes late to arrive in class. In she walked, with the morning paper

*Statesman* in her right hand and showed the front page to the class, asking them to tell her if they could find an error. Well, the top bold headline read, 'Ship now sails at 23.7 knots per hour'. A couple of us guessed that the use of 'per hour' was, perhaps, superfluous. Mrs Carter explained, 'You must know that knots means sea-miles per hour and here is the most famous English National daily misleading the intelligentsia of the country'. Such was her penchant for correct English.

Mr K.C. Kemp was initially the Housemaster for Blues, and taught chemistry. He taught his from 'First Principles' and also practiced a similar approach in all his dealings. But his pet issue was English pronunciation, particularly as in the class of seventeen students (boys and girls), some were little more than beginners in English speaking. On many occasions, we started the class with a lesson in chemistry, then there were several breaks, while Mr Kemp corrected pronunciation of a certain word and, when the bell rang at the end of the period, we did not remember whether we had finished a class in chemistry or English. He liked his orders followed and demonstrated it with his pet dog, who performed many tricks, including pipe-smoking, on his command.

Mrs Coombes had no equals when it came to forthrightness. She was an 'all-rounder' in teaching, but geography was her pet subject and she taught it from the lowest to the highest classes. Her son, James, was also in my class and he was decidedly very good at geography, as if it were in his blood. I was good at studies and had earned a double-promotion and managed, thereafter, to do well and remain within the first three positions. But James, acknowledged by all of us as excellent in geography, was not even once given a first in this subject and I recollect that finally, it was I who got the annual award for geography. So on one occasion, we talked to Mrs Coombes informally and asked why James had not got the geography prize. She said she couldn't possibly give her own son the prize, however good he may be . . . his head would swell.

All these staff members and all of the others who taught us also doubled up to train us on the sports field and I was proud to be taken into the Spartan Club for excellence in football, hockey and athletics. Our teachers truly taught us 'how to play the game . . .'

**Om Sarup Dogra**
Siwalik 1954 | 1949–1954
Indian Railways | Mention in Despatches

# Dennis Compton on
# Big Plain (Barnes) – June 1945

## A True Story

In early 1945, while completing his National Service at the Signal Training Centre Mhow in Madhya Pradesh, Dennis Compton (at that time a young Middlesex county cricketer), came on a course to the Army School of Physical Training at Kasauli. While he was there, he played for the Kasauli Garrison Cricket Team. We played them away on 10 June at Kasauli and again on 17 June at home on Barnes. We drew the game at Kasauli, but it was generally mooted that Compton had deliberately 'held back' his play. He had come in at No.5 and was not out at 68.

On the return match the following Sunday, Kasauli elected to bat first and as one of the openers, Compton let loose and slogged our bowlers all around the pitch. That day, the 'fags' were kept busy retrieving balls from way down the khud-sides as never before. He was eventually taken LBW in an unguarded, flippant moment at around 98. We lost the game that day, but thanks to a couple of fine half centuries from our middle-order batsmen—only by 20 or so runs.

The bowler who took Compton's wicket was a Nicholson lad called 'Chillip' Nugent—and needless to say, for the next year or so, we never heard the end of it.

**Derek Boddington**
Roberts 1942–47

With grateful acknowledgements for corroborative data from Dave Williams (Hodson).

# The March of Time

There is little that I can recall of 7 March 1954, the day I joined Sanawar, other than the excitement of studying in a school with my elder brother. Prep School was one happy family with lots of naughty children for company and Ms Groulie, the matron of Upper Dorm as our foster mother. Given our fairly busy schedule and the fact that all our needs were taken care of, I did not miss home. It was only in the silence of the night that I would occasionally weep till sleep which got the better of me. The high point of my life in PD was that I won the 'most well-behaved child', even though I visited Heady's office (for canes – six of the best) with a group of boys caught having a midnight feast. I was lucky to spend a fair amount of time in the Hospital because that meant no classes and being pampered by the senior girls with whom Preppers shared the ward. In those happy and carefree days, the one thing I did not like was the sight of the staircase leading to the classrooms.

The transition from PD to BD was made without any fear. In a flash, I felt like a big boy not wanting to be seen being hugged by my mother. Life in BD was exciting, with lots of competitive sports and outdoor activities like trekking, exploring the khud-side and bhutta (corn)/*khurmanee* (apricot) raids in Sanawara village. A Sunday hike to Gurkha Fort without the supervision of a teacher was planned and undertaken at the drop of a hat. Children were safe in those days and our mentors had confidence in us to always do the right thing. I stumbled through my academics. I could not come to grips with the numericals and equations, and so, disliked studies. The fallout was that I mastered the technique of feigning illness before the weekly tests.

The brighter side was sports! I did well at sports, participating in school teams in various age groups, culminating in me attaining captaincy of one of the best school cricket teams. In athletics, I broke the 800m and 1500m records, set twelve years prior by the legendary Ranjit Bhatia (V '52). Ranjit represented India at the 1960 Rome Olympics in 5000m and the Marathon. I had the honour of being inducted into the prestigious Spartan Club of Sanawar.

I was appointed the School Prefect of Vindhya House in 1964, a decision that still remains a mystery to me! If I led the House successfully, it was because of the co-operation of my classmates and friends, who always stood by me. Following the principles of justice, I did not shy away from admonishing my contemporaries for their wrongdoings. This never affected our friendship. My greatest failing was that I could not stop my Vindhyan classmates from going to GD en masse at night, just for a laugh and some biscuits. In hindsight, I think it was good that I failed, because boys will be boys, and Sanawar was not for grooming holy cows only. The 'crime' was uncovered only a few months before our final exams. Three of my classmates, who were prefects, were demoted to lower classes while the rest suffered other restrictions.

If I were to look back and select the best of the many qualities of character that we imbibed in Sanawar, it would be a sense of justice, a quality which I attribute to Major Som Dutt, [the] headmaster. He was the epitome of a classic headmaster—a strict disciplinarian, absolutely fair and a person worth emulation.

Passing out of Sanawar, I graduated from Government College, Chandigarh and joined the army, a career I was most suited for because of my Sanawar lifestyle. The 'Sword of Honour' (for the best all-round Gentlemen Cadet) and the Gold Medal (for standing First in the order of merit) I was awarded at the Officers' Training School are both attributable to my grooming at Sanawar. I was commissioned into the Armoured Corps (Central India Horse) and went on to command 51 Armed Regiment. I was fortunate to see action during the 1971 Operations on the Western Front (it was here that I lost my elder brother Maj. Devinderjit in battle. For his act of gallantry, he was awarded the Vir Chakra). I served in the army for twenty-nine years and retired as a Colonel. I must say that what saw me through my army service were my qualities of self-discipline, justice and fair play, sincerity and last but not the least, fearlessness—all of which were imbibed in Sanawar. Our high standard of physical fitness can only be attributed to Mr Jagdish Ram (Jagga)—a true titan. I still pursue my interest of trekking and must be among the oldest—at the age of 72—to walk to Everest Base Camp, Kalapathar.

I was extremely fortunate to be called upon, in 1998, to serve as the Bursar in Sanawar. I considered this as an *Act of God*, resigned from the

Army and drove up to the Hill Top. I was Bursar for four-and-a-half years (Jan 1999 to July 2003). These were interesting times, to say the least. I served with two Headmasters, Mrs Soloman (Offg. HM) and Mr Andrew Gray. Both these educationists had very different views and manners of implementation. I had to walk a fine balance between the 'Old & the New' and learnt a new art of walking on the edge!

Some interesting initiatives I took included formally identifying the boundaries of Sanawar. I wonder how many of you know that Long Back is within the land area of Sanawar; a 100-yard shooting range exists below the Dhobi Ghat or that Moti's Corner is an encroachment on the School land? Water harvesting and a water recycling system were also put in place at school. I re-established our connect with institutions important to Sanawar – the Army establishments in Subathu, Kasauli and Western Command in Chandimandir – playing a vital role in the sustenance of everyday life in Sanawar.

I thank my parents who, despite numerous difficulties, were able to afford my education in Sanawar, where I built lifelong friendships. These are people who are, to this day, a source of strength in moments when I want to give up . . . but in the spirit of a true Sanawarian, I will NEVER GIVE IN!

**Col. Nirmaljit S. Pannu**
NJS | Vindhya 1964 | 1954–1964
Sword of Honour – Gentlemen Cadet Officers' Training Academy; Gold medal – 1st in Order of Merit – Officers' Training Academy
School Bursar 1999–2003

OS Sibling – Brother – Maj DS Pannu VrC (Posthumous) |Vindhya
                    1957 | 1952–1957
                    Brother – H S Pannu | Vindhya 1966 | 1956–1966

OS Children – Daughter – Amrita Pannu | Vindhya 1992 | 1989–1992
                    Daughter – Avneet Pannu | Vindhya 2001 | 1995–2001

# George Dunsford Barne

I am deeply conscious of the task and privilege given me to write an article on George Barne for *The Sanawarian* on the 125th anniversary of the founding of the school now known as The Lawrence School, Sanawar, to which many hundred boys and girls owe so much, and apologize for its obvious inadequacy. The loyalty and love for this great school was engendered by the great principals of the past whose capacity for organization had to be equalled by their humanity and devotion to the sons and daughters of serving personnel of the British forces stationed in India. The establishment had to hold a balance between the educational standards laid down by the Educational Department of the Punjab Government and the requirements acceptable to the War Office in Great Britain as a military establishment administered by Army Headquarters under the Commander-in-Chief.

It was a military school, stark in its Spartan-like toughness and Christian in its ethics with the Chapel and daily worship as its focal centre. Only men of tremendous calibre could hope to meet the challenge of those days, and among such men, George Barne stands out preeminently as a pioneer of the changing traditions on the educational scene during the post-war years of 1914–1938. During the twenty-odd years of his principalship, the school developed from the old army school idea of a Military Asylum (by its very connotation, an anchorage and haven from the vagaries of the Barrack Room life of Kipling's day and avoiding the insalubrious hot summers with the attendant epidemics so rife in India during those days) into a school named the Lawrence Royal Military School, acknowledged as a Royal School of the Empire by Charter, recognized by the Universities of Cambridge and London as a school having potential scholarship material, and considered by the War Office as a school worthy of recognition and increasing financial support.

It was during the Principalship of George Barne that the school came of age with a ceremony in Dehra Dun at the foothills of the Himalayas. What preceded this event and its consequence is written into the lives and accomplishments of the scholars who were fortunate to come within the sphere of influence of this great man and the lieutenants he chose to be the executives of his own hopes and aspirations for his boys and girls. Why was it that into whatever field of endeavour Sanawarians felt called, they brought a dedication and a loyalty often unmatched by their contemporaries? Surely, it belonged to the standards set by the principal and his staff, whose utter devotion to the children under their care brought out the very best in their own characters. They did their best and accepted nothing but the best. One remembers the sonorous voice of the Boss, 'Pace! Pace! Pace!' at many an inter-school match. Shirking and cowardice in any form was an anathema, and love for the school and all it stood for, remained indelibly printed upon the characters of Old Sanawarians. Of course, it was tough – terribly tough – and it is no small wonder that the supreme achievement was to be elected a member of the Spartan Club; the inner lining of each blazer was blood red! What imagination, what inspiration this great man instilled into all who came under his dignified yet gracious personality! A man worthy of hero worship. George Barne was appointed Principal of the Lawrence Military Asylum in about 1911, inheriting from his predecessor a school in which, I feel sure, he saw rare and infinite possibilities. With his background of Clifton College, Bristol, and Oriel College, Oxford, together with a Chaplaincy to the Forces, it was not long before his own tremendous personality began to exert a profound influence on those with whom he came in contact. With Mr. William Gaskell as Headmaster of the Boys' School, and Miss Ada Parker as Headmistress of the Girls' School, he had two admirable leaders in the field of education; and seldom did he interfere with the children except on the question of ethics.

We were soon to learn the priorities he placed on a high standard of personal integrity and discipline, on personal cleanliness and smartness, and the idea that keeping the children really busy and employed meant less boredom and less mischief. The Chapel was the central hub of the school and often did we have to stay back a wee while to hear a homily discounting the waywardness of youth. To the 'fag' in the Lower School, he was the 'Boss', and his presence struck terror into the hearts of us smaller fry. If I remember right, his humanity and power as a leader first struck me when the First World War broke out, and the first contingent comprising members of the staff, some boys and some members of the Government Training College for Teachers – then part of the school establishment –

volunteered to go overseas to fight. I remember how the school lined the road at 'Chota Dharampur' to say farewell to a battalion of the Seventh Hampshire Regiment (who had given us an amusing and exhilarating Variety Show a few nights previously) as they marched down on their way to Kalka and the front!

I remember at Evensong on Ascension Day, a year or so later, when during his address in Chapel, a telegram was handed to him saying that William Taylor, the Head Boy who had joined that contingent, had died; his ashen face and drooped shoulders showed how he felt that loss. He loved the children – they were his – for he had none of his own, and when death or serious illness struck in later years, he was always emotionally moved. The first benefit he bestowed upon the school was the innovation of electricity instead of gas for lighting purposes. His love for games, especially cricket, soon became apparent. He himself was a born 'gamester', having played Golf for Oxford and Cambridge against Harvard and Yale in America in 1902, and also, I believe, represented England against America in the Walker Cup. He was an 'Authentie' in cricket at Oxford, and would certainly have got his 'Blue' as a fast bowler but for the intervention of Dr W. G. Grace of immortal fame, who insisted that his younger brother E. M. Grace should be capped that year. He was a 'Corinthian' Soccer player, a member of the famous Amateur Soccer Club in England, and he was no mean hockey player either. No wonder that the boys and girls, too, held him in such high esteem. He regularly captained the staff side against the boys on Wednesday and Saturday afternoons in all sports, and later, when a proper sports ground was constructed for the girls near the old cemetery (later converted into a Park by the Revd. Agard Evans), he played both hockey and lacrosse with the girls, captaining the staff side made up of mistresses. Later, tennis was to become one of the Girls' sports and he had 'Wimbledon' court built, where the girls played against visiting schools like Auckland House, Simla.

He divided the school year into four sports' seasons. In the Spring, the boys and girls played hockey; from May to July, the boys played cricket and the girls tennis; August to early September, the school trained for athletics; and the rest of the year, the boys played soccer and the girls lacrosse. It is to be remembered that all this took years to evolve, for suitable playing fields had to be built and gradually, the organized games came in, and while all this was going on, the normal military training, combined with a good brass band, was kept as the initial priority. His selection of staff capable of organizing and coaching all these facets of a school year showed his remarkable talent for selectivity of the right type of men. His appointment of Sgt. Major George Foster of the North Staffordshire Regiment, an Old Sanawarian, as Chief Instructor, was a masterpiece of vision for this soldier who was to become a legend in military training in all its ramifications. He was a magnificent rifle shot, musketry instructor, a long-distance runner of repute, and a magnetic personality, who, for many years, built up the discipline, comradeship and a sense of achievement in keeping with the school motto 'Never Give In'.

The inculcation of rivalry between each company of boys was enhanced by the naming of each company after one of the Indian Mutiny heroes. Lawrence, Roberts, Herbert, Edwards, Nicholson and Hodson. The Inter-House competitions in every sport including small-bore and ·303 rifle shooting, swimming and boxing, challenged each boy (and girl) to do the best for the honour of the House. From these contests, 'colours' were awarded to those selected to represent the school against other schools like Bishop Cotton School, Simla, or the La Martiniere College, Lucknow. Going further afield in later years, a team of boxers under the able coaching and influence of Sgt. Hawkes, the gymnastics instructor, the School won the All-India Boxing Contest in Mussoorie, and the Boys' School won the Imperial Challenge Shield for small-bore shooting open to all the schools in the British Empire, two years in succession. All this needed so much planning and foresight, and here George Barne had the invaluable help for many years of Sgt. Jim Tilley, the first bursar of the school, whose cheerful personality, integrity and marvellous organizing ability made him the principal's right-hand man in all extracurricular activities. Jim Tilley's wife, an Old Sanawarian, has become a legend in her own lifetime, for she coached all games in the Girls' School with remarkable success, and it was because of her enthusiasm and selfless devotion to the girls, that the standards reached were so high. Subsequently, she has been the rallying point of all reunions of Old Sanawarians in the United Kingdom, and the Central Box Office for information of scattered Sanawarians throughout the world.

On the scholastic side, George Barne inherited two great Heads in 'Billy' Gaskell and 'Governess' Ada Parker. Here again, the principal set the seal of his tremendous vision. Some girls on the completion of their High School Certificate, went on to St. Bede's College, Simla, to be trained as school teachers, while others who wanted to be nurses spent a time of probation in the school hospital and then were fully trained at the Marylebone Infirmary in London. The widening scope of education led to his attempting to finding vocations for his boys outside the normal acceptance into branches of the services and the medical faculty in India. Soon boys were channelled through the agency of the War Office into the technical trades of the army and were sent to Chepstow, while others went

into the Royal Air Force at Halton in England. In 1923, he brought in the examinations for Junior School Certificates set by Cambridge University for external students, and in 1924, he brought in the teaching of science. Thus, the school came into line with the general trend of education elsewhere in the world. Graduate teachers from England were added to the staff. Since the old school building was inadequate for all this expansion, something decisive had to be done. The Government transferred the Teachers' Training College to Ghora Gali in the Murree Hills, and with its going, sufficient land became available for a completely new building.

George Barne used his influence, which over several years, had been growing among the military authorities at General Headquarters in Simla, to put before Sir William Birdwood, the then Commander-in-Chief, the idea of a new school complex, bringing in science laboratories and an Art School. Sir William, I believe, had been at Clifton College with George Barne, and this may have (sheer conjecture, of course), tilted the scales. However, before long, Birdwood School rose in all its magnificence, and all the landscaping from the school War Memorial outside the school Chapel up to the top of that spur of Sanawar, revealed both beauty of concept and utility in dimension. George Barne was a keen gardener, and here he found an outlet to his planning with two artillery guns pointing over the valley to Kasauli, and the hillside, a blaze of dahlias, cosmos and several annuals. October in Sanawar was a month of glory, both of sky and scenery and horticulture, and I know this left a lasting impression on its pupils. In 1920, the school entered a new phase of recognition when a contingent of boys, including the school band, went by train to Debra Dun to receive from the hands of the Prince of Wales, later Edward VIII, a new set of school colours made by the descendants of the founder, Sir Henry Lawrence, to replace the old colours presented to the school by, I believe, Lord Dalhousie, when he was Viceroy of India. Both these Colours were later hung in the school Chapel with due ceremony, and annually afterwards, the Trooping of the Colour Parade carried out according to King's Regulations with all its dignity and military precision by the Boys' School under the command of the Head Boy. Attendant upon the ceremonial parades held on the King's Birthday, Empire Day and Founders' Day, the principal invited the viceroy or the commander-in-chief or some other dignitary to take the salute. It was at the parade in Dehra Dun that the name of the school was changed from the Lawrence Military Asylum to the Lawrence Royal Military School.

Another event in the School year which led to the solidarity and affection which united Old Sanawarians to the 'School on the Hill' and to one another, was the inauguration by George Barne of Founders' week. It was a week in early October when Old Sanawarians returned for a week's holiday and residence to be reunited with their contemporaries and try their skill at games with the present generation. Added to this were such features as school plays, inter-House athletics for both boys and girls, and most wonderful of all, Founders' Day, on the Thursday. The ceremonial parade, Chapel, the prize-giving and a most wonderful dinner and dance, at which the school band played. Such things cannot be forgotten.

During the early period of his principalship, George Barne realized the inadequacy of the Hospital to cater to so many children and the absence of a Medical Officer on the spot. This was overcome by the position of the Vice Principal being inaugurated and this position was filled by a qualified member of the Indian Medical Service. An adequate operating theatre was added to the Hospital, and an infection ward. Both these additions proved of inestimable value in the years that lay ahead. Then later, a creche was built for servicemen's babies left motherless, and under the capable supervision of Mrs Cowell, this early part of a child's life was catered to, so that a child could enter the school at a few weeks old and leave at eighteen years of age, having completed that space of life so vital to its physical and spiritual education, in one situation. The principal's frequent visits to all these departments of the school enabled him to keep his finger on the pulse of so large a community. In 1933, our principal, the Reverend Canon George Barne, Commander of the Indian Empire, recipient of the Order of the British Empire, Master of Arts, was elected to succeed Bishop Durrant as Bishop of Lahore. At his consecration, he received among other gifts from Old Sanawarians throughout the world, his gold Pectoral Cross.

In all he did, his help mate and constant adviser was his gracious lady and wife, Mrs Barne, to whom all Sanawarians of his day must always owe a deep sense of gratitude, for the awesome Boss became, as the years went by, the *Grand Old Man*, loved and cherished by his boys and girls, admired and respected by those who were fortunate to become members of his staff. To me, personally, the words of Jesus were fulfilled so well in his life, for he sought always to serve his Master and another's good; and was rewarded by an appreciative government. 'But seek ye first the Kingdom of God and His righteousness, and all these things shall be added up to you.'

What Arnold was to Rugby, Barne was to Sanawar. His name will live for ever among those who were inspired by his personality, for he lived and died a great Christian gentleman.

**The Reverend F.E. Eccleston**
LMA and LRMS Sanawar, 1912–1923; 1926–1937

# Looking Back

I was seven and finally going to Sanawar, to reap the benefits of 'goodies' and 'tuck' that my older brother got when he came home or went back. I was travelling with the school party and I have a vivid memory of waiting excitedly for the train at the New Delhi railway station, where Mrs Joshi was to chaperone us to Sanawar.

I was amongst the youngest new students and was assigned the first bed next to the bathrooms on the ground floor of Honoria Court. Stories of the dorm being haunted by Lady Honoria's ghost were rampant. My first experience of the 'ghost' came in the middle of one cold night, while I was asleep. I awoke because I was cold, my blanket had been pulled off and I was unable to move at all. I was terrified and lay freezing and still as a statue all night. Next morning, Mary ayah arrived to discover that the girl from the next bed had walked to the bathroom half-asleep and on returning, had slept on top of me instead of her own bed. Since she was cold, she had pulled off my blanket. I remember the senior girls allaying my fears by telling me that ghosts were really afraid of girls with curly hair and would never dare come near me. I actually believed that!

For the most part, I was a happy camper through school. At the U-V year end, it was announced that I was to be the Head Girl the next year. I was as surprised as the others. The matron must have overlooked my cubicle one morning because I overslept, missed Chota Hazri and PT, and reached Parker Hall at the tail end of breakfast. I remember being embarrassed and really tense about the consequences of my lapse. To my amazement, the teachers were really understanding. I was not reprimanded but was told nicely that as a Head Girl, I needed to be more responsible and careful than the others. That experience has stayed with me through life.

I led the girls NCC troop at Founders' where Mr Jagdish Ram's main concern was whether my mop of unruly curls would fit into the NCC cap.

Camp at Kandaghat and the trek to Simla; begging people on the street in Kas to watch the movie we wanted to watch because the owner would only run it if he collected Rs 50; picnics at Eagles' Nest and Lover's Pond—they were all memorable experiences. We complained about many things in school only to appreciate them later in life. And cried like crazy when leaving school. Sigh, I could go on and on . . .

There are many instances and teachings from our Sanawar days that have moulded us into thinking the way we do and making us who we are. So many decisions and actions in my life are the consequences of the events I experienced in school.

More than half our batch attended the 2014 Founders' for our fiftieth year Golden Jubilee class reunion. I was overwhelmed to see them all, many after decades. Some had not changed much, while most had completely transformed. It was great just meeting them but I do wish we had had more time to catch up on news of our families and where our lives had led us. I was sad, and deeply missed class fellows who are no more with us.

**Amita (Sobti) Kumar**
Himalaya 1964 | 1956–1964

OS Siblings – Brother – Arun Sobti | Himalaya 1961 | 1954–1961
                 Sister – Anita Sobti | Himalaya 1966 | 1958–1966

# Letter to My Parents

Dear (deceased) Mother and Father,

Sixty-eight years ago, you admitted me to Sanawar. We walked up from Garkhal, with a coolie carrying my trunk.

At the top of Tilley's hill, on the left of the broad road, were the first, barrack-style buildings. In the veranda of one such room was a small school, with poor children sitting on the floor, reciting after a teacher. I quickly gathered: these were the children of the staff of my new school. Father, your words to me have stayed with me ever since. You said, 'Son, you are going to a big school, on a scholarship, so that one day the whole of India can have schools like yours.' Such wonderful words. I had a mission.

At the bakery, we were given a guest room. You had prepared me well. I was not afraid and was enchanted by the pretty school. We walked along the narrow road of Short Back, with a stunning view of snowclad mountains in the distance and lush bamboos along the path. There were bright flowers in carefully maintained flower beds at Prep School. There were high, dense trees, sprinkling sunlight on us on this cool morning. We arrived at the funny-looking round School Office, on a little hill of flowers! This was a wonderful place!

There was paperwork to do. There was a meeting with Mrs Kemp, acting Head of Prep, very pretty, sharply dressed in a pinstriped suit, severe. There was a medical examination at the charming little Hospital. Dad, you whispered to me not to admit to the doctor that I sometimes still wet my bed at night. My schooling in the ways of the world thus started.

On the way back, I crossed and my eyes met with Passi and Champa, going through the same motions with their parents—fellow soldiers, lifelong companions.

But when you left, I soon realised I was not so well-prepared. I found myself alone, in a dormitory of twenty other boisterous kids, and an unkind, un-pretty matron. The uphill journey had started. I learned to cope, copying the others. I managed to dress, tie my shoelaces, do my buttons, eat with a knife and fork, make friends, avoid enemies. Those Prep School friends remained precious to me for the next nine years and another fifty, thereafter. But the hardest of all, in that first term, was to learn to navigate the primitive toilets, a shuddering memory.

In class, I was more at ease, but others, from Hindi-speaking homes, took some time to find their feet. The teachers were kindly but distant. And class was short, only till lunch time. For the rest of the day, you were on your own, with the other children, no grown-ups, no introductions, nobody to explain things to you, no encouragement, no mother, no father.

And so, painfully, with our little six- or seven-year-old minds, we bungled through that first term. Per force, we became little independent persons. We learned to fly on our own, or most of us did. This is because quite a few faces did not show up from one term to the next. There were fallen soldiers. Oh, Happy Master, where are you?

Once I had learned to read and write, I was not so lonely. There were enjoyable storybooks to fill free time. But most importantly, there were weekly letters to you, dear parents. My letters were perfunctory, simple letters, at first, dictated by our teachers. But they were a lifeline back to the warmth of home, to individuality and recognition. Thank you, Father, for your faithful, regular letters back. It was the force that kept me going.

And as I grew older, classes became more interesting: I learned about the sun and the moon, circles and triangles, gases and prisms, microscopes and telescopes, planets and Sputniks . . . Each day explained another wondrous thing.

And that was only till lunchtime. After lunch and a siesta, the rest of the day in Sanawar, you were free to play and loiter around these lovely hills, for nine long years. There was compulsory sport, but also plenty of free time with your mates for hobbies, music, books, treasure hunts, pinecone collection, hikes, walks, cocoa bonfires in the evenings. And on weekends, there were films, plays and music in Barne Hall.

And that was how the amazing school that is Sanawar took over, shaped and moulded us, educated us, made us into the smart Sanawarians we became. But what I have come to realize is this: the original strength, the strength to make the most of what Sanawar had to give us, came from you, from home, what you had already given me, before Sanawar. It was with that strength, with that inner light, that I was able to go, with the others, from Rouser to lights-out, from Prep School to Senior School, from Lower III to Sixth Form, from short pants to flannels and blazer.

Like many of us kids, my most happy memories of Sanawar are the two times you came to Founders'. How thrilled I was to share my school life with you. How proud and lovely you looked, in the bright October light! At the Fiftieth Anniversary Founders' in 2014, watching the parade, I could not hold back my tears when the band played the final salute to the Chief Guest.

I have worked it out now: those tears were for you, dear Mother and Father. You were the Chief Guests for me. How I wished the band had played and played for you.

**Dr Harbans Rajpal Singh Nagpal**
Naggy | Nilagiri 1964 | 1956–1964
Psychiatrist and Doctor at the Embassy of India, Paris

# The A.D.S.

The much talked-about A.D.S. Play was staged on 8 October at 2.00 p.m. in Barne Hall. Fifteen minutes before time, the Hall was packed to capacity. People did not mind the fifteen minutes' wait before the start because Max Geiger and his band entertained the audience with some fine music.

At 2.00 p.m. sharp, the curtain lifted to show us a room, poorly furnished (if furnished at all) and very badly kept—inappropriately called the Assistant Master's Common Room at Hilary Hall. I don't think a staff common room at Hilary Hall was a necessity, because we found that there were only two members of staff, excluding the Head.

After some time, Mr Tassel (Virendra Vyas), a young man just back from the wars, introduces us to Rainbow, the school porter (Saleem Khan). The next person to appear is Mr Billings (Bhupinder Singh), who is back for the opening of term. He greets Mr Tassel warmly. They talk about old times. From the conversation, we come to know that Mr Tassel prides himself on being a lady-charmer, while Mr Billings is a staunch hater of women but does not mind the pretty ones, as is evident from his collection of pictures. Mr Pond (Trevor Kemp), the school Head, suddenly comes out of nowhere to tell the other staff that he has just had a letter from the Ministry telling him that another school by the name of St. Swithins is going to share their premises, as its own buildings are in shambles. At once, they arrive at a conclusion satisfactory to all three. Near the end of the act, we are introduced to the staff of St. Swithins, which unfortunately turns out to be a girls' school. They are Miss Whitchurch (Audrey Kemp) the principal, Miss Gossage (Jessie Thun) and Miss Harper (Piki Bedi). Once again, I must say that St. Swithins also seems to be short of staff.

At once, the guests make themselves conformable and begin using the Hilary Hall premises as if they were their own. This act of the girls is not liked by the boys of Hilary Hall, who in later scenes, show their disgust. At the same time, Miss Harper and Mr Tassel develop an attraction for each other. Finally, after providing us an hour's fun, the act comes to an end.

In the second act, we are shown how some boys of Hilary Hall play mean tricks on the girls but escape all punishment as Mr Pond thinks that the girls deserved what they got, while the main culprit Hopcroft Minor, is actually rewarded with five 'bob' by Mr Billings who highly approves of the joke. Later in the scene, we make acquaintance of the Pecks (A. Bhalerao and D. Gidwani) who have a daughter in St. Swithins, and the Sowters (S. Cowell and E. Paranjoti) who have a son at Hilary Hall. At this point, we are shown some childish tricks by which the staff of the two schools think they will be able to stop the parents from knowing that boys and girls are staying together. Their tricks are indeed jolly amusing and the audience reacts to them with loud guffaws. After another hour, during which most of us had stomachaches from laughing, we finally come to the end of another most enjoyable act.

With great impatience, we wait for the third act to begin. As the curtain goes up, we find that the Sowters and the Pecks have both decided to withdraw their children from the schools. It is indeed very distressing as well as amusing to see the staff of both the schools trying to make the parents change their minds. I may add that I was apt to feel sorry for them as they tried their hardest to thwart the parents' plans. The parents, however, have faithful allies in two children, Barbara Cahoun (Sheila Sinclair) and Hopcroft Minor, who make it their business to see that the parents finally succeed in withdrawing their children from the school. Near the end of the act, Mr Pond gets another letter from the Ministry saying that another school is coming to stay at Hilary Hall. At this juncture, the combined staff really show their lack of sense when they start barricading the Common Room as if that were the only building in Hilary Hall. The curtain then drops and we are left clutching our sides, raising the roof with our loud laughter.

The A.D.S. really deserve our sincere congratulations, for the play really provided top-class entertainment (and excellent potrayals of the people they were acting as) for over three hours, which was only possible after a lot of hard work put in by the staff of the school. I am sure that everyone is wishing that these plays become an annual event in our Founders' celebrations; one thing, however, is certain, the boys will always look forward to the next A.D.S. play. Well done, the A.D.S.!

**Bhupinder Pal Singh U-V**
Old Sanawarian [Vindhya 1956]

**Source and Acknowledgement:** *The Sanawarian* (December 1955)

# Pocket Money – Sixty Years Ago

We even had a special bugle call for it. Militarily, it was called the 'pay parade' and we fell-in as the drill book demanded, but not before raucous voices echoed the bugle call with tuneless 'Pocket money today, boys—pocket money today!' There was no need for a roll-call. No Sanawar boy missed this parade. 'Whatcha going to spend yours on?' This from the corner of a mouth cut short by a curt 'Stop talking in the ranks', from authority. This was a parade, after all.

A regimental number was called by the sergeant instructor Housemaster. 'No. Ninety-six!' I sprang to attention and rapped out 'Sir!' turned right, stepped out of the ranks and marched to the table in front of the company. Saluted. The Sgt. instructor handed me four annas. It was war time. There was no metal coin. Four annas was represented by four pieces of cardboard bearing the school crest and the value. The export of Indian currency was banned. I counted them to see that there were four and not three. The SI counted them to see that there were four and not five. Saluted. Turned left and rejoined the ranks. Waited till the parade was dismissed.

Then I joined the other plutocrats seated on the pavement wall. The subject was common. How to spend this wealth? Two annas were bespoke. One for the collection plate in Chapel on Sunday, one for a postage stamp for the compulsory letter home every week. Four minus two left two, approximately. 'Chucks?' 'No, Man; don't get enough for an anna!' (Chucks were sweets) Deep meditation. Then enlightenment. 'Monkey nuts?' 'Hmm! Yes, but isn't there anything else?' 'What?' 'Sao!' (We really called it something else, rather rude and to do with parrots). Decision. One would buy monkey nuts, the other would buy sao and then share-out. 'Let's go to the shop'; 'No, let's wait for Ramrick to come round with his box and we can dive in when he's not looking'. Agreed.

Ramrick was an institution. Charlie has taken his place but with all sorts of refinements. And so Ramrick would arrive. His box would be opened on the veranda of Gaskell and would immediately become the centre of attraction for all Sanawar boys with two annas to spend and no dignity to go with it. An anna worth of monkey nuts would fill a newspaper cone, an anna worth of sao would fill a smaller cone. One hand would dispense the goodies, the other hand would fend off prying fingers, sometimes successfully. Then came the division of the spoils. Newspaper cones were fragile, needs must that the monkey nuts be transferred to the uniform slouch hat. Seated on the pavement wall, hat between knees, nut for nut counted, equal halves. You can bet your bottom dollar if there was one over, it was broken in two. Panic – SM Foster approaching – spring to attention, hat on head. Salute. 'What's in the hat?' 'Nothing, Sir!' It was conical on the wearer's head, both of them. 'Nothing?' and with a wry smile on his face, the SM lifted the hat and showered the wearer with monkey nuts. 'Don't make a mess with the shells,' he added and walked away laughing. Didn't he do the same when he was a Sanawar boy?

The cone of sao was reclining uneasily in the 'bosom' of the second boy. The nuts were consumed with relish, nut for nut—a little goes a long way, as the boy said when he put one nut on the giraffe's tongue. Shells were deposited in the bosom of the first boy, to be offered later to Kishnoo in the BD kitchen as fuel, receiving one cooked spud in return. Everything had a value.

Sao represented a more difficult division. No two coils were alike but piled on top of each other, the coils would present a fair means of division, the height being the deciding factor. It was time-consuming and the holder of the sao saw another boy approaching. Here comes that 'darb' Smithy, he's a pukka 'splung'. Translated: 'Here comes that Lower School fellow, he's a voracious eater.' 'Go chase yourself down the khud, Smithy! You're getting none of this.' 'Alright! but don't come and ask me for any skinnyjibs after dinner. Smith was a past master at collecting bits of bread, raw onion, a discarded dry chilli and even some potato, and making a mixture of the same in a wash basin, to be consumed under his bed after prep.

So that repast came to an end. All that was left was the Boss's deep voice asking us to 'rend our hearts and our garments' when the plate came round for collection at Church Parade Service on Sunday. One anna would be deposited reverently. Came the hour of compulsory letter-writing. The 'darbs' letters were identical—'Dear Mother, Please send me a parcel. I am well, hope you are the same, your loving son . . .' The postage stamp on the envelop read 'One Anna'.

**William H. 'Bill' Colledge (Bilkul)**
Old Sanawarian (Roberts 1917–1927)

**Source and Acknowledgement:** *The Sanawarian*, 1976

# Class of 2021

No matter how idyllic you remember your time at Sanawar being; no matter how rose-tinted your glasses, there is every chance that your happiness is contingent, at least to some degree, on your tenure as a Sixth Former. (I speak only for the boys, of course.) In my time, that would mean specifically the U-VI year, so for the rest of the world, twelfth grade. So much of what made life as a junior on the hilltop bearable was daydreaming of the time you'd be having when it was your turn, finally, at the top of the hierarchy. Every time a bit of tuck was taken away from you; a 'favour' extracted; a bed allotted too close to the pans, you promised yourself it would be different when your time came. When it was your turn at the top of the chain of pain.

Among other notable ways in which the 'Corona' class of 2021 (and, as things stand, the class of 2022 as well) has been so abjectly short-changed: it never got to enjoy its final year where it truly matters, which is in school itself.

No prefect-ship. No wearing trousers, even in summer. No tutorials with Heady and the Housemasters, finally being treated as an adult-in-waiting and not merely a child.

The members of those unfortunate classes won't know what it is like to not have to carry the kitbags down to games. They'll never have experienced the utter freedom of Birdwood, which you only know when you walk down it in your last year. Before, of course, you're dodging between the arches, hoping not to catch the eye of some moron who forgot his books; wants to impress a girl; has had a bad day. That is the lot of the junior, after all; you carry the weight of your seniors' days.

In my time, in the distant 1980s—a century, a millennium ago—negotiating the school day, yours and everyone else's, could be like a minefield. You only knew you'd made it to the other side when you got to U-VI.

Yet the poor class of 2021 spent its final year, the golden one that its memories should be made of, at home, crouched miserably in front of a computer screen.

The class of 2022 fared a bit better. They were actually in school, apparently, but with only the other Boards class for company, their final year spent mugging in masked solitude. What good is a kingdom, when you have no subjects? Imagine the echoing silence of Birdwood, with only the purposeful tread of Boards-bound students alleviating the hush, as they walk from class to prep to dinner. It would be like going to school during the hols; and who in the whole wide world ever wanted to do that?

There is a lesson in this, of course. There always is. You don't always get what you want or think you deserve. But to be served the moral of the story like this, and so early on—that is hard indeed.

When Partition happened, my father's elder brother was in his final year of school in Lahore. He, like his younger siblings, had to finish the school year in an 'Indian' school. He was lucky; a few of his classmates were with him; he wasn't the only import stuck there for the few months it would take till they took their Senior Cambridge examinations. My father and his younger brother were comparatively luckier. They had a few years in their new school, time enough to bed in, make friends in that new place, think of it as their own.

But my Taiaji; I wonder how he felt. Clearly, he didn't hate the school he finished from. He sent his own sons there (bitter rival; ugly town; name begins with D and rhymes with 'goon'). But all his stories were of the place he had left behind. He was an intelligent, self-reflective man. He knew his own loss paled in comparison to the deeper fissures that traumatic time had opened in the world, cracks that still live on in our own lives.

Still—the teams he had played on; the prizes he thought he would win (he was an outstanding student and athlete); the honours he had earned and would have enjoyed if Partition hadn't intervened.

And finally, the memories he had made.

That old school in Pakistan made a huge effort to reach out to their Indian alumni over the years, having them over for Founders' celebrations and the like. Prize distributions were organized. Taiaji was very proud of the various certificates he came back with, the records of which enterprising masters had tenaciously dug out of the old archives. Among them were prizes he was almost certainly never given while he was still in Lahore. To get them as a grey-bearded adult; to complete the circle he had begun decades earlier, as a boy; to hear young boys and grown men cheering as his name was read out and a scroll presented and a medal hung around his neck: what a thrill that must have been.

We all want to be recognized for the things we've done. We all want to be remembered. To leave a mark on our shared hilltop, sure, but this is a life lesson as well.

I wonder if there is some way the class of 2021 (and 2022) can be feted. At the other end of all this, if time allows; a weekend, or even a whole week, for the class to gather. To be given a drink by Heady, because they are finally adults. To run their final Hodsons. To present a show of some sort, if at all possible, in Barne Hall. To compete for a PT and Gym Cup, and box with their peers.

Surely, their names belong in Gaskell Hall as well.

And for all those who were spear-carriers in school (and the vast majority are, no matter what they remember afterwards), the chance to walk down the crowded cloisters of Birdwood in trousers, knowing there isn't a single, solitary thing anyone can do to you.

I'd go uphill for that.

**Avtar Singh**
Chajju | Siwalik 1990 | 1986–1990

Author, *The Beauty of These Present Things* (2000), *Necropolis* (2014) | Founding Editor, *Time Out Delhi* | Managing Editor, *The Indian Quarterly*

# Tubelight

Every Old Sanawarian claims that his was the golden period on the hilltop . . . especially the days in the Senior Dorm. But only those beyond redemption—i.e., eighty-five souls housed in an L-shaped structure atop the Green Berets', were the chosen ones. The Vindhya House Boys' Dorms was an incubator; an experiment that was crucial for humanity. These supreme beings were classified into two broad categories: 'Duffer' and 'Brain', while sub-categories of 'wannabe Brain' and varying mutations of 'Duffer' also existed. The Punjab and Himachal strains were predominant, while those from Delhi, Calcutta and Mumbai, made up the numbers.

It was the pre-Google era and there was Chelpark ink in our pens. A good pen had the power to uplift a D3D to B6B. The Brains scaled greater heights of A8B and beyond, while the Wannabes had spurts of C7B or C6C, thanks to some Brain pasting his answers on the cloud, for which one had to have his windows open. And for the much-proclaimed well-rounded development, we rigorously trained to become proficient in the art of landing unidentified objects on Banda's roof.

The beds and lockers aligned in one straight line left little scope for creativity. However, gazing at thin metal strings hanging freely from the false-ceiling, on which thick white tubelights were attached, encouraged a lot more free-thinking. All the tubelights in the dorm were switched on or off with one single switch.

This was the moment everyone waited for . . . the buzz under the counterpanes would commence . . . the black market did brisk business—immersion rods and coffee powder exchanged hands, sneaked chapatis and pickle, jam, condensed milk or whatever was available, were sold and bought at a price. If one was caught, he was put on morning drill. However, hungry bellies knew no fear. The men housed in the corner bunks were always on the lookout though, new surveillance techniques and 'detectives' were deployed, and finally, drones were invented. The new SOP warranted all to lay down their slippers (which were either brown or blue) outside the prefect's bunk at lights-out. The moment the SONAR detected any movement, the drone would be launched, landing on the perpetrator's nut. A piece of the pie or a few mouthfuls from the mug had to be apportioned to the prefect. This Tom-and-Jerry game continued; skills were continually enhanced and then countered; drones acquired more accuracy, mastering artificial intelligence networks and chartering default flight paths.

Till the day the damn drone went rogue, and instead of continuing on its low trajectory, decided to reach for the skies, thereby destroying all that came in its way. A loud crash was heard . . . something had broken. A second later, another crash followed . . . then pin-drop silence . . . one could sense the panic, chaos, and fear . . . till someone piped up, 'Oye, the tubelight is . . .' Silence! The prefect instructed, 'take out your torches, clear all the glass.' One counterpane was forfeited and in the still of the night, all evidence buried . . . down the khud.

New sunrise. New challenges. New warriors. 'Oye, who broke the tubelight?'; 'Don't know, ya'; 'I never saw it'; 'Which one?' The diktat was issued: 'We need a new tubelight . . . before tonight's inspection.' The crack-team was selected: two Duffers that nobody would suspect, Jack and Geom-box. Geom-box asked, 'Oye, can't we sign a loss-slip?' and received two tight slaps. 'Idiot, there are no tubelights in Tuck Shop.' Heads joined, thoughts crystallized and a plan emerged . . . nobody could know . . .

Jack and Geom ate only one chapati each for lunch. There was ice cream that day—the ultimate sacrifice. Minutes before the bell could ring, the two sneaked out from the side-door (by the food counter). They had precisely seven minutes before the rest would start heading down.

Birdwood corridor. Geography Class. Geom stood guard. Jack climbed onto the desk and eased out the tubelight. No one was in sight. They ran towards the covered passage near Heady's House, tubelight in '*bagal-shastr*' position, held with care—not too tight. Halfway across the BD Quad, a sense of accomplishment overtook them . . . nearly home.

Just then, two heads appeared on the horizon; on the Himalaya House Junior dorms footway. Jack and Geom froze in their tracks. Thinking on their feet, they resumed the walk . . . slow, easy, casual . . . the tube-light shifted to the left hand, but still protruding out, over their heads like an antenna. Mr K.J. Parel and Mr Onkar Singh were in the middle of a conversation on the ramp outside Gaskell Hall. Their paths crossed. 'Good afternoon, Sir.' 'Good afternoon!' Keep walking . . . almost crossing them . . . crossed . . . a few more steps . . . 'OYE!' KJ had spotted the protrusion. 'What's that?' 'What, Sir?' 'That, in your hand.' 'Ohh, (Jack managed a smile) tube . . . tubelight, Sir'; 'I can see that, but why do you have it?' 'Ooh, we are taking it to the dorms, Sir' 'From where?' 'From Birdwood, Sir'. Still zapped, he asked, 'Why would you do that?' Silence ensued . . . Jack and Geom looked at each other, and knew the game was over.

'Sir, we broke one, Sir . . . and are now replacing it.' He finally got it, grinned and advised, 'Wait here . . . for Mr B. Singh.' They sat on the parapet with the tubelight on their lap, as the entire BD walked past. At least a hundred idiots, of varying sizes and shapes, asked the same question. Well, the mission had been compromised. Morning Drill for the rest of the term, it had to be. The quartermaster replaced the tubelight. The drones were decommissioned. However, the code of brotherhood remained intact.

Jack and Geom-box had earned their stripes . . .

**Vikas Kohli**
Jack | Vindhya 1987 | 1981–1987

OS Sibling – Brother – Vivek Kohli | Jack | Vindhya 1989 | 1987–1989

OS Children – Daughter – Ada Kohli | Vindhya 2018 | 2011–2018
                    Son – Arjun Kohli | Vindhya 2019 | 2011–2017

# The Definitive Vocabulary

5.45 a.m. The rouser bell rings for Nilgarians and the bugle for the others. 'Oi Rouser' someone's *razai* is pulled off. 'Oi, sleepy chap, get up!' And so, begins a typical day at Sanawar.

Dehydrated bread with a trace of butter at Chota Hazri. PT over. Inspection: 'Your shoes are not shining . . . See me tonight'. Bad start to the day.

'*Baiye Dekh* (Eyes left)' marching past the Memorial onto Birdwood. 'Do it properly, sloppy guys' Coming up the Golden Staircase, we see the school flag being hoisted by the prefect on duty.

First School (otherwise called class). Someone cracks a cheap 'Want to know? Let's have it out' Prompt retort, 'Meet me behind Gaskie, you'll get a thramming . . . gassy guy, acting like a pumpy'.

Breakfast Fall-in. Lumpy porridge and chilled fried eggs. 'Your butter for my cutlet?'

Back to Birdwood. Those planning to 'bunk school' are cautioned not to get 'gagged.' DLTGH (Days Left to go Home) is updated. Teams are decided for the Kalka walking-down school party via the rabbit shortcut. Milk Break; 'grabbo' for 'Doggies' (Khattas or Mitthas—dames call them Salties and Sweeties). Run down to Gaskie to check the Boxing 'Weighing and Measuring' at Hospi, scheduled for the afternoon.

Danny's roll-call in Gaskie: 'All the missing ones, stand up.' Sniggers interrupted, 'Hyeeee lad, I'll give you a kick and you'll fly across Monkey Point . . . misguided humorists.' Mucchoo's not happy with someone's hair and drags him by the ear to 'Naapi'. Casanovas are on the lookout for a junior, 'Oi, keep guard behind the Art Room.' Linseed oil on cricket bats and hockey sticks, along with jabs with a compass.

'Open the windows, let the climate enter!'

Tincture Iodine, the wonder-drug. 'Rescue' was played on Sundays, much to the chagrin of the House matron, thanks to the plenty of torn shirts and shorts. Bagzzed was critical. Tapping (someone while dancing) was evil. Turned down by a girl . . . 'Oi, got a kela?' Physical exercise had many asanas—invisible chair (holding Solo's Psycho book), UD's 'keep rolling', while Murga, legs-up-hands-down, jumping haunches were also part of the course.

Post-afternoon activities, off to 'Charlie'—samosa, gulabs, palang-tod, stick-toff . . . 'Oi, who's giving a treat at Tuck Shop?' Baked beans, luncheon meat, cream crackers . . .

Assessment Meeting concludes: Distinctions (handful), Commendations (few more), Satisfactory (majority), Housie's (fluctuating) and Heady's (usual suspects with a few surprises). 'Oi, you got Heady's? Hahahahha.' 'Shut up, fool.'

Evening Prep, 'Oi, I'm going to piddle . . . coming?' 'No, yesterday you went to Kas and didn't get me a bunsum. Heights, Yaar'.

Dinner on Wednesdays was special: mutton cutlets. Post-dinner dating around the School Office or at the House show rehearsals. Latecomers to the dorms would explain 'She's going around with me'. And would be promptly asked, 'Oi, Surdie, does she know?' The not-so-confident ones would not approach the 'chick' directly but through her best friend, 'Ask her if she wants to go steady'. And later, 'what did she say?'

Night Inspection. Sidey announces: 'Oi, Unda has said no more 'bhutta raids . . . He has the names of the guys who went down last Saturday, so watch out. Also, too many of you are sneaking chapatis in your battle-dress jackets.' Next night: 'Oi, no more whipping coffee with your 6-inchie in the tin mugs. Your immersion rods are confiscated NOW.'

09.30 p.m.: 'Lights-Out, Oi.' The *pinnis*, *chapatis* and *Panchranga* come out . . .

Never Give In!

**Col Dhyan Mayadas (Retd.)**
Bull | Nilagiri 1983 | 1979–1983
Served in the Indian Army for twenty-seven years | Presently with an MNC in Mumbai, India

# Our Quest for Grub

School breakfast meant milk, porridge, toast, butter, cutlets/eggs and tea. Lunch and dinner were sad, except the kadhi-chawal served on alternate Thursdays for lunch and the 'smashed' potatoes, boiled eggs, rajma and bread served every Friday for supper.

A solution was found. The 'Punjab' boys, on return to school, carried pure desi ghee, an assortment of achaars, *gudhh* or powdered *shakkar* and shared them with all at the dining table. Stiff, dry chapatis were coated with ghee; the tasteless daal and subzi were given the much-desired 'tadhka'. A dozen or more chapatis were smuggled into the dorms, rolled in napkins and eaten post the 'official' lights-out at 8.50 p.m., stuffed with shakkar, along with hot coffee (made with an electric mini-immersion rod in a large plastic mug).

A prescription from Dr Sakhuja, the RMO, for 'tasty' accompaniments, viz. Ferradol and Waterbury's Compound, helped. These could not be bought over-the-counter at Tuck Shop and needed to be listed on our monthly Tuck Shop slip signed by the Housemaster. The entire contents (of the bottle) would be devoured within minutes of breaking the seal. Kisan fruit squashes, mainly orange and lemon, could be bought (if one had some extra money) and consumed in its concentrated form directly from the bottle because no one had the patience to mix the squash with water in mugs. Nestlé Milkmaid Condensed Milk, was sucked out from the tin by piercing two holes, one to sip and the other for air inflow to accelerate decantation. Buying 40–50-paisa coupons from the Tuck Shop before 12 noon, for an ice cream cone or cup was a regular feature every Sunday.

Once or twice a year, particularly on Rakhi, I received a parcel of delicious milkcake from home. It was a tradition that the one who got the parcel, or Goody Goodies when parents came visiting, would get almost nothing. The whole stuff was snatched and eaten by friends and other Housemates. The local Himachal boys like Naveen Chouhan, the Stokes, Sirkecks and Singha boys, whose families owned apple orchards, suffered similar consequences. During season, their staff brought over crates of fruit that were opened and kept near the fireplace, at the head of the dorm. It was a free-for-all—anybody could pick up an apple or two, whenever he felt like it.

One Sunday in a month, we were allowed to go to Kasauli. We would take a shortcut at the Garkhal Gurudwara, break at Alasia Hotel, to relax and feel like kings, royally spending our one-rupee pocket money there. Otherwise, 12 annas got one a morning-show ticket (for a wooden seat in the front four rows) at the Army's Defence Cinema; and 4 annas to buy the all-time favourite delicacy of every Sanawarian, the bun samosa, topped with lots of sweet imli chutney. One Sunday, *Son Of India* was being screened. Since we rarely saw a Hindi movie, the manager was requested to screen it for the morning show, in lieu of the English one. He agreed, provided we collected at least a hundred boys to make up for a decent collection. We immediately took the lead in spreading the word around. Everyone enjoyed the movie.

Having met success on our first attempt, this formula became quite a routine. On another Sunday, almost the entire Girls' School, under the supervision of Miss Pamela Doherty (later Mrs Mountford), came to spend the day at Kasauli. They came in the School Bus and not on foot like us. That day, a Meena Kumari-starrer *Main Bhi Ladki Hoon* was on during the matinee show. On popular demand, we succeeded in convincing the manager. The boys were made to sit in the Third Class (12 annas) comprising the front four rows, while the last four were accommodated in the Second Class with the girls. I was one of the unfortunate four. 'Unfortunate' because we sat in a most uncomfortable position, almost upright, not daring to touch the chair armrest, for the fear of accidentally touching the girl sitting next to us. A 'popular' girl, with a huge fan-following, sat to my left. Such was the discomfort, we did not enjoy the movie at all.

The craving for stick-jaws, tandoori chicken, seekh kababs and other such delicacies remained unsatiated. Money would be given to 'friends' in the School teams, to bring back 'indulgences' on their return from Simla, Dehradun or Patiala. They however, lasted only a few seconds. Great team work.

In 1967, Mr Hardeep Sikund was appointed Siwalik Housemaster. He was very cool and casual in his approach, and did not bother whether we took his permission to go to Kasauli. Taking liberty, we often walked to Garkhal, hired a bicycle, rode to Dharampur for samosas and pakoras at a roadside tea-stall near the picturesque Dharampur Railway Station, and then cycled back via the bridle path, pushing the bicycle up across the graveyard till Moti's Corner, and finally 'flying' down to Garkhal . . . back in time for the Evening Prep. Word soon got around, 'Siwalikans were breaking bounds . . . and not getting caught'. So the Vindhyans, too, made an attempt, and got caught by their Housemaster Mr M.V. Gore.

In our final year (1969), the Brigadier at Kasauli (whose son was a Siwalikan, three years our junior), invited the Sixth Formers for Dussehra celebrations at Dagshai Cantonment. A military truck picked us up, accompanied by Mr B. Singh, Mr Jagdish Ram, Mr Hardeep Sikund, Mr Vijay Jalota, Miss Rudra and some others. We witnessed the Gurkha Regiment's official 'Bali' ceremony (sacrificial beheading of a bull to please the gods). Oh My God! We then moved to a tent where the Jawans were seated on durries, and rum, from kettles, was being poured in their aluminium mugs. While our school staff got busy holding their brimming glasses and dancing to popular army songs like 'Nainitalo . . . Nainitalo', we gulped down heavily diluted quantities of rum, not taking the slightest chance of getting tipsy. We then joined the officers in their dining tent. A full roast goat was placed on a huge tray, and we carved out the our 'choicest cuts' with a *khukri*.

On Home Day, BD boys were allowed to walk down to Kalka, to join staff-escorted school parties. Till 1965, we were allowed to leave school after breakfast, and reach Kalka by lunch. With time on hand, we resorted to naughty hooliganism—whacking books and magazines from the A.H. Wheeler stall; eating at the local stalls as well as the Railway Restaurant, and then quietly slipping out one by one, paying only a partial amount. Thereafter, we were allowed to start the walk down only after lunch. So we would run down to Jabli, hitch a lift to Dhalli, and get down near the Koti tunnel, at the famous 'Meat Ka Achaar' roadside shop. Apart from eating, we would buy a few varieties to take home. From there, it was an easy downhill walk on the motorable road to Kalka.

**Ravinder Raizada**
Chini | Siwalik 1969 | 1959–1969

OS Sibling – Ramakant Raizada | Kant | Siwalik 1968 | 1958–1968

# Scarface

The Vindhya House show in 1975 was a complete disaster—with the exception of one impromptu skit that salvaged the honour of the House and also gave the students the only real entertainment that evening; of course, to the utter consternation of staff who demanded that all references to this skit be stricken from school records.

Here's what happened: after a disorganized mock fashion show, a so-so Indian classical dance performance, a completely off-tune song sequence, came the Hindi play *Anju Didi*. Scene one and two pass off reasonably well, when all of a sudden, the rotation of the stage gets stuck. Banda (Mr Katoch) panics. Abu (Mr Abraham), the presiding teacher sitting in the front row, but not associated with Vindhya House at that time, walks up from the side steps to take stock of the situation. He promptly asks three helpers – Fadda (the man with fifty-two nicknames), Bajja and Chhota Curly – to bring down the curtains and do something to keep the audience entertained, while he got the rotation of the stage fixed.

Now these three twerps were always up to no good and started salivating at the thought of creating khup and thus come up with an impromptu skit. Bajja covers Fadda's head with a towel and informs the audience that the person covered with the towel is *so ugly* that anybody who takes a peek at his face will collapse and die. To demonstrate its veracity, he invites Chhota Curly to take a look; and sure enough, Curly collapses (pretending to be dead)! Bajja then challenges Abu to sneak a peek if he had the guts! Not one to cower down and just to play along with these U-III buffoons, Abu jaunts back up to the stage . . . and as soon as he takes a peek under the towel, it's Fadda that looks at Abu's face and collapses instead! Abu just stands there with a frozen sneer while the audience is in laughing splits . . . Priceless!

You can probably imagine the thrashing we got afterwards—knuckles and murga in the Quad, and everything in between!

**Sanjeet S. Bajwa**
Bajja | Vindhya 1982 | 1973–1977
Chief Procurement Officer | Head of Manufacturing Market Sector, British Petroleum | Corporate Vice President, Covanta | Vice President, Siemens | Group Commercial Management, Honeywell | MIM, The American Graduate School of International Management | MBA and BSc, San Diego State University

OS Sibling – Sister – Madhvi (Bajwa) Zingde | Mini | Vindhya 1979 | 1974–1977

# Presentation of the New Colours – 13 March 1922

A detachment of 100 boys with the necessary staff (Company Sergeant Major G.H. Foster, Sergeant Instructor A.R. Hawkes and Sergeant Instructor A.K Baker), under Major The Reverend G.D. Barne, OBE, MA (Principal), represented the school at the Presentation of New Colours by His Royal Highness The Prince of Wales in Dehra Dun on 13 March 1922. Assistant Surgeon G. Aling went with the detachment in medical charge.

The full ceremonial as laid down by army regulations was carried out.

The old Colours were presented to the school by the Earl of Dalhousie in 1853 and have been carried continuously ever since that date. The new King's Colour was presented by the Army Department and the new school Colour by Sir Alexander Lawrence, Bart., grandson of the founder, in memory of his father the late Sir Henry Waldemar Lawrence, Bart. A full account of the presentation appeared in the papers. It will however be sufficient for the purpose of this report merely to quote the Prince's speech and the Principal's reply on behalf of the school.

His Royal Highness said, 'I should feel proud to belong to a college, which was founded by the brave Sir Henry Lawrence, which was built and started by the gallant Major Hodson and to which my father gave the name of Royal in recognition of the services of its old boys during the Great War. To boys belonging to this college, I need not explain the meaning of Colours. All soldiers' sons take pride in Colours, such as their fathers have served under. Your old Colours will now hang in your Chapel, to remind you of the record of your old boys. Your new Colours I entrust to your keeping. Cover them with glory and honour; may they be an inspiration to you to serve your King and country as faithfully as John and Henry Lawrence did in the hour of need.'

The principal replied as follows: 'Your Royal Highness, it is my privilege as principal of the Lawrence Royal Military School and also on behalf of Old Sanawarians scattered throughout the Empire to express to you our most dutiful and grateful thanks for the high honour which you have done the school in presenting these new Colours this morning. Today is indeed a red letter day in our annals. It will be our endeavour to carry these Colours fearlessly and without reproach, always bearing in mind their sacred symbolism and continuously inspired by the gracious words Your Royal Highness has addressed to us.'

**D.V. Boddington**
LRMS Sanawar 1942–1947
May 2005

Extract from the Annual Report on the Lawrence Royal Military School, Sanawar for the year ending 31 March 1922 to the Chief of the General Staff, Army Headquarters, Simla, India by The Reverend G.D. Barne OBE, MA, Principal.

# The Coming Back

The train drew to a halt and he got out quickly, eager to escape the crowd. He walked a few steps. The strap of his heavy suitcase cut into his hand and he put it down to change hands. As he did so, he looked around. Yes, by coincidence, it was the same platform. Fourteen years and it was still the same platform. He had stood at the end of it and watched the train move out, waving to all those familiar faces; some loved, others taken for granted, most of whom he knew he would never see again. He had been young then and the tears had come coursing down his cheeks, dimming those faces, the last glimpse of which he wanted so desperately to fix in his mind. Then, from one of the last carriages, had come a loud and unmistakeable voice: 'God bless, Harry'. And he had quickly wiped the tears away to see Thicky's face—the bald head, the thick-rimmed glasses and the tobacco-stained teeth flashing in what had become for him the most beautiful smile in the world. He had stood there waving till the small red light had been swallowed by the darkness and then he had turned towards the platform on which his train stood waiting. Now he picked up his suitcase in his right hand and walked towards the waiting room.

The bus climbed up the Kalka–Dharampur road and he peered anxiously out of his window, trying to recognize landmarks. But it was of no use. Once or twice, he did feel that he remembered a tree or a hamlet they passed through, but he couldn't be sure that it wasn't the memory of similar trees or similar hamlets on another road. But then he had hardly ever been on this road before. The school parties had always travelled by train between Kalka and Dharampur, and fourteen years is a long time.

Was he doing the right thing going back? Sanawar through all the ups and downs of his life, through all the miseries and misfortunes, had come to symbolize security, comfort and the memories of school and all that it meant, had been his one sole anchor to sanity. Those agonizing days in the Hospital, the pain both physical and psychological, when he had lost his leg—he wondered if he would have got through it all if he had not implicitly believed in the old school motto, 'Never Give In'. And much later, on a cold, bleak night in the stillness of another Hospital, when he had walked down the darkened corridor with the still warm body of his son in his arms, was it not Sanawar that had made him rise above his own grief and turn quietly at the main door to thank the staff – the doctors, the night-duty sister, and the sweeper – for all that they had done for his son during his brief four hours' stay in the Hospital?

And now, he was going back. He wondered if Sanawar would be what he had treasured it in his heart and mind for being, or if he would find it to be something completely different and his own picture of it had been only the work of time, distance and too vivid an imagination.

The bus took the turn towards Kassuli and Sanawar. In heartwarming flashes of recognition, he saw to the left the bridle path going up to Sanawar and then to the right, the place where the railway track went under the road and a little later, a glimpse of the tiny, almost doll-like Dharampur station. Lots of people got into the bus at Dharampur till it was packed like a tin of sardines; it was hot and there was a strong smell of stale sweat and crude tobacco. He kept his face glued to the open window, glad for the fresh air. After what seemed like an eternity, the bus reached Garkhal and he got out. He got a coolie for his suitcase and began the climb to Sanawar. At the first bend, he looked up at the hillside expectantly—but no, there was no sign of the laughing rock. Disappointed, he wondered what could have happened to it. Then he turned the bend and there was the old hilltop. He stopped for a moment, overcome by emotion, his eyes moving greedily over the hill.

Birdwood, the Chapel, Mr Cowell's House, Upper Barnes, Garden City, the Dhobi Ghats—he took it all in. As he began walking slowly up the hill again, memories came chasing each other into his mind. Incidents that he had completely forgotten now came back: Dhami and he hiding under their beds so that they would not have to kiss the matron goodnight; Anjon Mehra trying to set fire to Honoria Court with toilet paper; Dopey and him being caned for raiding one of the fruit trees below Barnes (Mr Cowell knew how to cane!); Mr Carter teaching Browning's 'Home Thoughts From Abroad' and telling Amarjeet Singh Grewal, 'It is not Italee, my dear boy, but Italy'; the clip-clopping of Miss Chatterji's heels down the corridor so that there was no need to keep someone on watch for her coming and, of course, her pansies; Bhupi, the first time he was teaching their class, giving all of them a shock by asking: 'Have you understood?'; Saleem's strong tobacco perfume which reached them a minute before he did and warned them to put away their comics; Bhalerao's favourite comment on a just finished painting, 'Oh it is lovely', pause, 'but on the contrary, it is all out of proportion'; Thicky's brown corduroys, old and faded but still swishing against each other as he walked vigorously down to his office. On and on the memories went.

So many of the old staff had left: Mr Carter and Mr Cowell had left while he was at school, then Saleem, Mr Vyas, Mr Rawat, Major Som Dutt, and even Thicky had gone the previous December. A lump formed in his throat and he wondered what Sanawar would be like now that all these people had left. Then suddenly, on the last bend, he became aware of the sharp pungent smell in the air. What was it? Oh, of course! It was the smell of pine. There was the school gate and besides it, a new wooden board proclaiming a little too obviously (and rather unnecessarily, he thought) that this was The Lawrence School, Sanawar; Founded A.D. 1847. Up Sergeant Tilley's Hill and past the gate to the House where the Tilleys' had lived, and which had originally given the slope its name. Through the Green Gate, past Suji Fort—Thicky's House. In the earlier days, when there had been only Blues and Yellows, and Thicky had been the Housemaster for Blues, they had often assembled outside Suji Fort to set out on those memorable moonlight walks to the cemetery. But all that was in the past. Thicky had gone. He wondered who lived in Suji Fort now. Independence Garden, Warriors' Grove, Leisure and finally, the Quad. A group of boys strolled past obviously on their way back from the Tuck Shop. They stared at him, and one more polite than the others, said, 'Good morning, sir,' and then the others followed his lead.

'Good morning. Can you tell me where Mr Bhupinder Singh stays?'

'There, sir, below those steps.' Mr Cowell's House.

'Thank you', he said and went down those steps. He had been told to contact Bhupi for his room and for his timetable. Would Bhupi recognize him? Doubtful. It had been so long ago and he had changed so much. But then Bhupi knew he was coming and would be looking out for him. He knocked at the door and after a while, a lady came to answer it. This must be Mrs Bhupinder Singh. He had heard that the highly eligible bachelor had got married, at last. Often, over the years, while thinking of Sanawar, he had wondered what Mrs Bhupinder Singh would be like. Well here she was.

'Please come in,' she said, 'Do sit down.'

'Is Mr Bhupinder Singh at home?'

'No. He's down at the match.'

'I am the new English Teacher. I had to see Mr Bhupinder Singh.'

'Have a cup of tea. I'll send someone down to call him.'

'No, thank you. I'll go down. What match is it?'

'It is a cricket match against Bishop Cotton's School from Simla.'

He could see she was relieved that she wouldn't have to sit and make polite conversation with a stranger.

'I'll send someone to show you the way.'

'No, it's alright. I know the way. I'm an Old Sanawarian.' He paid the coolie and leaving his suitcase with Mrs Bhupinder Singh, went towards Jacob's Ladder.

He stood at the top for a moment, looking down towards Barnes. Without his glasses, he couldn't see very clearly and the figures on the field were just blurry dots. But he knew the scene—every detail of it. And as he stood there, quite distinctly on the breeze, the cheering came floating up to him: 'S-A-N-A-W-A-R, That's the way we spell it, That's the way we yell it, Sanaaaaaa . . .'

He knew then that it was alright. Slowly, as he walked down those steps, a feeling of warmth and reassurance returned to him. Sanawar, in essence, would always remain the same. There would be changes, of course, many changes. That was only natural; for without the ability to change, to adapt to the changing world around it, Sanawar would never have remained so vitally alive. But Sanawar changed only when change was necessary—never merely for the sake of change. Because of this, Sanawar was not merely a thing of stone and mortar, of trees and flowers—it was a living, breathing entity with a spirit and a soul of its own, and this spirit, this soul would always breathe to anyone who cared to listen. Everything else could change but not this. No matter who came and who went, Sanawar was Sanawar, and would always remain so.

**Dr Harishpal S. Dhillon**
Staff | Headmaster 1995–1999
Old Sanawarian (Nilagiri 1957)

**Source and Acknowledgement:** *The Sanawarian* (December 1971)

# Friends for Life

The impossible happened. For thirty years, I have not been ill. Then suddenly, as if by a thief in the night, my health was stolen and I was struck with pneumonia. Not only that, but my heart was affected. Suddenly, at the young age of ninety-one (all but a few days) with the world as my oyster and my ambitions as wild as making it to the top of Tilley's Hill; the danger of dying had filled me with renewed energy. I am pleased to tell you that I have made it to the top of Tilley's Hill and I am well again, puffing a little, but well enough. I shall just have to take it easy over the next twenty years or so.

The last time I had pneumonia was when I was thirteen. It was in the summer of 1933 and I was admitted to the school hospital. I was given M&B tablets. That was the only medication there was in those days, a panacea for all ills, somewhat like penicillin, the antibiotic, today. You either got over your illness or died. In fact, I never knew anyone to die from any illness in the seven years I was at school. It was mere coincidence that the school doctor's name was Capt. Butcher of the Royal Army Military Corps. He had a weakness for cutting people up and even removed my brother's tonsils instead of mine. He operated on me for hernia and I have an embarrassing scar in an intimate place that's so ugly that I have to explain it as a war wound to the few who have been privileged to see it. Capt. Butcher's successor was Capt. Savage.

There were no deaths, as I have said, from illness, but two boys did die on a monsoon weekend. They attempted to cross a stream that had swollen with the heavy rains and become a raging torrent. They were swept away and their broken bodies and limbs were found downstream.

I am going to be ninety-one on 30 September. My old school friend, Jock Howie, will be ninety-two, two days before I turn ninety-one. He sent me a birthday card of a cricket scene and reminded me that in 1936, when he was in the cricket First XI, they lost so badly to BCS that the whole team was flogged. The following year, he was Captain of our team and I had won my cap as opening bat. He reminded me that I made a duck in both innings against BCS. I was out to two identical balls from the same bowler and caught in slips by the same fielder. Jock saved me from getting flogged. He scored 61 and we beat BCS. Whenever he ribs me about my performance, which is boringly frequent, I let him know that his saving me from a flogging is the only reason I have remained friends with him for over eighty years.

The great thing about Sanawar is that it is not just a school. It is a magical place where friendships are forged with bonds as strong as family ties.

**George Browne**
Havelock 1937 | 1930–1937

# The School That 'Probably Won'
# The Battle of Basantar

If the proverbial Battle of Waterloo was won in the playfields of Eton, then the Battle of Basantar was 'probably won' in the playfields of The Lawrence School, Sanawar in Himachal Pradesh. The school popularly called 'Sanawar', referring to its location, is one of the oldest co-ed residential schools, set up as The Lawrence Asylum in 1847 to train and educate orphaned wards of British Other Ranks (BORs) residing in India. The asylum was conceptualized to train the boys to become future soldiers in British Regiments. Thereafter, the school's role and size grew with its annual contribution of soldiers, seen in action on many battlefields across the Empire.

In 1853, the school was presented with The King's Colour and became one of only six schools and colleges ever to be honoured as such in the British Empire. An honour shared with Eton, Shrewsbury, Cheltenham, the Duke of York's Royal Military School, and the Royal Military College, Sandhurst. The military honour changed the school's title to the 'Lawrence Royal Military Asylum' in 1858. The military orientation of the school saw several contingents of boys enlisting directly and marching onto the battlefields of WWI. Towards the end of the war, in 1920, it was re-designated as 'Lawrence Royal Military School' and in 1922, the Prince of Wales presented the school with new Colours. On 3 October 1941, a BBC Radio broadcast cited more than two hundred Sanawarians serving in the Second World War.

Post Independence, the school passed into the hands of the Ministry of Education and Indians enrolled in the school for the first time; many of them later went on to serve as officers in the tri-services. 1962 saw two Sanawarians killed in action; Captains C.P. Singh and Y.R. Palta, VrC (Posthumous). Thereafter, the school's military contribution remained exemplary in 1965, 1971, and all C.I. ops where its alumni continue to serve to the present day.

Of all the battles fought in 1971, the study of Shakargarh sector, particularly Basantar, brings to fore my thesis that Basantar was 'probably won' in the playfields of Sanawar. There is no attempt to downplay the contribution of any other school, nor the sacrifices of every soldier who fought the war. However, it is interesting to note that all three of the nation's highest war-time gallantry awards were earned by Sanawarians in this sector, vis. 2/Lt. Arun Khetarpal, PVC (Posthumous); Maj. Vijay Rattan Chowdhary, MVC (Posthumous); Maj. Amarjit Singh Bal, MVC and Maj. Malvinder Singh Shergill, VrC; while Maj. Kamaljit Singh and Capt. Brijinder Singh were mentioned in despatches. The six gallantry awards earned by Sanawarians fighting in one sector makes me say that the war was 'probably won' by Sanawarians.

At twenty-one, Arun Khetarpal became a legend as the youngest recipient of the PVC. The school honoured him by renaming a playfield as Khetarpal Stadium, where graduating students march past each year during the trooping of the school's flag. Recently, the school instituted a bravery award, named in honour of him and unveiled a full-size statue that overlooks Khetarpal Stadium. When *Fauji India Magazine* announced that it would be covering stories on the Battle of Basantar, I grabbed the opportunity to write about Arun Khetarpal, an alumni I look up to. I searched through my albums to find a picture of the war memorial arch in Sanawar, where we marched past and saluted before the names of all our fallen. The names of 2/Lt. Arun Khetarpal, PVC; Maj. Vijay Rattan Chowdhary, MVC and Maj. Devinderjit Singh Pannu, VrC glared at my screen, while I wondered at the odds of any of them serving near each other. A search of their citations unveiled a startling fact that both Arun and Vijay fought in the Battle of Basantar and died, a day apart from each other. An intuitive feeling about another Sanawarian, Maj. (Later Lt. Gen.) Malvinder Singh Shergill, whom I had heard about, made me look up his VrC citation, to find that he won it in the Shakargarh sector, too.

With considerable effort, I contacted Lt. Gen. M.S. 'Binny' Shergill, VrC to inquire about his war-time location in Shakargarh and asked him how far he was from Arun, to which he replied 'we were in the same area, in the sense that Arun's tanks were a little distance away from ours'. Then in an absolutely excited tone, I revealed to him my discovery that three Sanawarians served in the same area and won all three gallantry awards PVC, MVC and VrC; and that their story must be told.

'Oh, so you are drawing the Sanawarian connect, then let me tell you that there were seven of us there,' he exclaimed. Maj. Kamaljit Singh of Himalaya House was commanding 'A' Squadron with me in the 7th Light Cavalry, he was mentioned in despatches. Maj. Amarjit Singh Bal, from Siwalik House, was commanding a squadron of the 17th (Poona) Horse and got his MVC along with 2/Lt. Arun Khetarpal, PVC (Posthumous) who was from Nilagiri House and a squadron troop leader with him. Then there was Capt. Brijendra Singh of Himalaya House, who was the second in command of a squadron from The Scinde Horse, he was mentioned in despatches. We lost my good friend and classmate Maj. Vijay Rattan Chowdhry who was killed in action, very close to where Arun's tanks were, and he got his MVC for his role in mine clearance throughout the war. It was his team's efforts that enabled Arun's tanks to get across. And Maj. Vijay Nair of Vindhya House, was commanding a squadron of Skinner's Horse.

While we are at it, let me tell you about another classmate of mine; Maj. Devinderjit Singh Pannu, who was commanding a Company of the 5th Battalion, The Sikh Regiment, at a post in Pt. 303, in the Chhamb sector. He was wounded, yet refused to evacuate and kept on defending against the enemy. He bled to his death and was later conferred the Vir Chakra. That is Sanawar for us. His post is still in Pakistan occupied territory, so I got a memorial constructed for him in Akhnoor, while I was commanding 10 Infantry Division, where I laid a wreath in his honour.

'Since you ask, let me tell you more facts, my class of 1957 had a unique history, whereby two of my batchmates had joined the Air Force and died in aircrashes. Our first battle casualty was 2/Lt. C.P. Singh, killed in the 1962 operations, whose name is mentioned in the school's memorial. Another had joined the Navy. By the way, let me tell you, in the autumn of 1961, the entire polo team of the IMA were Sanawarians and all four of us made it to the national team, representing the country for a very long time. We were the ones who started polo and equestrian sports in the army, even though none of us had ridden horses at Sanawar. Lastly, we had the unique honour of being five Sanawarians commanding five different armoured brigades at the same time. We were brigadiers: Kamaljit Singh, Vijay Nair, Amarjit Bal, Joginder Pal Singh (16 Cav.) and my self, all Sanawar batch of 1957.'

Gen. Shergill then wished me good luck, said that he was a lifetime subscriber of this magazine and looked forward to seeing what we wrote about Basantar. I was surprised to hear this lesser-known fact that either destiny or happenstance brought seven Sanawarians together in the same sector during the 1971 war, yet nobody has ever mentioned this fact. All of them were recognized for their contribution towards the war effort, and their individual citations mention traits such as conspicuous gallantry, indomitable fighting spirit, tenacity of purpose, exceptional devotion to duty, extraordinary bravery, inspiring leadership, supreme sacrifice, professional skill and leadership of a high order. These characteristics, are often mentioned in many citations for awards, yet, when a reader contextualises the background of these officers, it reiterates the school motto 'Never Give In' in a way that Sir Henry Newbolt's famous poem 'Vitai Lampada' comes to life: the river of death has brimmed its banks . . . But the voice of a schoolboy rallies the ranks, 'Play up! Play up! And play the game!'

Thereafter, I wanted to draw in some civilian perspective and contacted Mr Mukesh Khetarpal, brother of 2/Lt. Arun Khetarpal, PVC (Posthumous) to know what he had to say about his heroic brother. Mukesh was a year younger than Arun and both of them attended Sanawar. They belonged to a third-generation army family wherein their great grandfather had fought in the Sikh Wars; grandfather had fought WWI (Mediterranean); father had fought in WWII in Indonesia and other regions. In fact, their father Brig. M.L. Khetarpal, AVSM had served in the same sector 'Shakargarh' during the 1965 war. Mukesh introduced his thoughts on Arun by saying that 'what happened in the battle is well-recorded, but the question I ask is what if there was a replay of events, would he have done the same thing in the same way? And, I think he wouldn't have been any different, after all we are three to four generations in the army. In Sanawar, we learnt to stand up for our team in every sport we played. We learnt to give an arm and a leg for them and live up to the school motto "Never Give In"!'

The telephonic interview that followed went as follows:

**Me:** Why didn't your brother bail out of his burning tank when he was ordered to do so?

**Mukesh:** What is recorded and told was that Arun realized that his infantry brigade couldn't stand up to the enemy armour unless his tanks were operational. So, he couldn't have walked out of the situation, because then a lot of lives would have been sacrificed, and he knew his vulnerable position with his burning tank and the fire spreading. But, by then, looking at our family and school, he would never have done anything to let them down. That's something any Sanawarian would have done; they don't walk away—it's the done thing!

**Me:** Did he have such tendencies as a child?

**Mukesh:** If you see the recent movie *Neerja*, the lady's bravery is somewhat similar to my brother's. The idea that they displayed extraordinary courage since childhood may be overplaying it, but given his background and from where he came, he just had to do it. That's how I see it, you know.

**Me:** So how did your family deal with the aftermath?

**Mukesh:** We were a small family, just the four of us: my mother, father, Arun and myself. You see, when someone dies at an early age, before his time, then it *is* painful for you. Life was never the same for my parents, who lived to their ripe old age into their eighties. It was painful and difficult to get over that!

**Me:** What has been his impact, on your life, even after forty-five years?

**Mukesh:** Even today, almost on an everyday basis, youngsters who were born after '71, call up. Many of them have no connection with the military, yet they want to know about him. Those who are in the armed forces hold him in high regard. Even in the NDA and IMA, they have some sort of memorial for him. Yet, civilians are also connected, especially through the Internet. I always wonder why would somebody want to create a website in his honour and why twenty–thirty-year-olds visit it so often. It only means that a lot of you people agree with Arun and draw inspiration from him. This connection is a good thing. The NCERT has introduced his battle story in their school curriculum and I think that's the right thing to do. 'Cause if you can inspire youngsters by building the right moral fibre before they give in to other things, they can go a long way.

Listen, I am sixty-four years old, but Arun is twenty-one years young!

**Me:** How do people sympathize with your family?

**Mukesh:** For our family, the loss is irreparable, but as a family, we can only say that it was destined. We can't do much about it! The fact that you are choosing to write about this battle, forty-five years later, means enough.

For your information, Arun's tank is placed in Ahmedanagar as a case study for all to see. J.P. Dutta, just a few months ago, said that its too old a story to make a movie; so another Sanawarian, Apoorva Lakhia has expressed interest in making a full-line feature film.

**Me:** A personal and final question, why didn't you join the army after Arun and all your forebears?

**Mukesh:** We came from a time when the father decided what careers the children would choose. The reality is that my father was an engineer in the army's Bombay Engineer Group. So he decided that one of his sons would join the army and the other would become an engineer. Actually, Arun was more intelligent; he was supposed to be the engineer, while I was not as good as him, so I would join the army. Unfortunately, he appeared in the IIT and NDA exams and qualified for the NDA only. So my father told him 'you had a chance, now go join the NDA'. Then he came to me and said, 'now you go join IIT'. That's how I graduated from IIT Delhi, a few years later.

After speaking to Mr Khetarpal, I spoke to Mr Aminder Singh Bal, son of Brigadier Amarjit Singh Bal, MVC and an extract of our telephonic conversation is as follows:

> My father spoke about his friends and time at Sanawar very often and proudly. I think the school had quite an impact on him. He did talk about the war while we were growing up, to sort of influence me, but not towards the end of his life; he didn't talk much about it. We heard so much about it from the Regiment, from the army, from what has been written about it, that now it tends to clutter the mind, becoming difficult to ascertain what I know from him and what I have picked up from others. He was a private person who never really spoke much; he carried his gallantry award very lightly, never showed off. Although extremely proud of it, he didn't speak about it unless spoken to. He was extremely humble, in fact, far too humble for his own good.
>
> Now Arun was a hero in the Regiment and in the army. I had an opportunity to meet his family in the past, but since I was born after '71,

I grew up seeing him in the Mess, in the offices and all over the place. Indeed, he was quite a hero! Whenever I asked my father about their role in the war or about Arun, I had to really probe him to answer my queries about the battle that they had fought. People used to call my father the 'modern Gandhi' since he was not really made for the modern world. Just that, I think, was one of his best traits and everyone remembers him as a gentleman and as a soldier, rather than anything else.

Father was a very God-fearing person, although [despite being born] a Sikh, he wasn't really religious or spiritual. I guess he was more a good human being. He never took to spiritualism, in the sense that he was a very secular person who believed in the teachings of all religions. He picked up all that was best in them and tried to imbibe it in his life. In the fauj, most of the Paltans have a Sarva Dharma Sthal (place of worship for all religions) and he made it a point that when I came back from boarding school, in those two to three months, we would go to every temple, gurudwara, mosque . . . so he was a believer in that.

He was extremely proud of being Indian and I recall at that time, if we spoke about anything in the world, he would tell us that there is so much in India, why should I go anywhere else? 'India is so diverse, it is beautiful, it has got everything, it has got opportunities and so much more . . . yet you youngsters are always thinking about the West and trying to get too Westernised.' He was extremely Indian and very proud of being one. That's all I can say for now, why don't you come down to Delhi and spend some time with us? We can see what else you want to explore about his time.

In closing of my analysis of how Basantar was 'probably won' in the playfields of Sanawar, one has to reflect on the school's system. The battlefield action by Old Sanawarians in Basantar, highlight the role Sanawar played and how its values motivated the men to do the 'done thing'. Public schools in the British era were designed to inculcate loyalty, with the idea being that 'if a boy could be made loyal to his House, then he would become loyal to his school and thereafter he would be loyal to the King'. Strict discipline, orientation towards sports, and the judicious use of religion to create followers of ethical living, rather than blind faith, marked the character of any graduate from such schools. Sanawar was no different. It has further evolved from its military ethos, to make its mark in other fields such as the civil services, business, films, journalism, amongst others.

Yet, every graduate carries forward the original legacy and traits that live on through the culture and practice of traditions that are followed in the school. Thereby, there lives a Khetarpal, a Chowdhary, a Pannu in each one of them. Just trivia: all four Houses of the school were represented in the Battle of Basantar, thus truly representing the entire school.

## Post Script

Lt. Gen. Kamaljit Singh contacted me after the article was published to inform that his 'A' Squadron 2ic Capt. (later Col.) Vijay Rosha was also a Sanawarian and both of them were mentioned in despatches. 'Vijay got a very clean wound because the splinter went in without touching the bone of his right arm, although a lot of blood was oozing. He was wincing in pain so I gave him a morphine injection and evacuated him to the RAP. Then the second Sanawarian was Capt. (later Col.) RIS "Bobby" Verdi, who was 2Ic to Maj. (later Lt. Gen.) M.S. "Binny" Shergill.'

I researched this input to find that three Sanawarians consecutively commanded 7th Light Cavalry in order: Kamaljit Singh; M.S. Shergill and V.S. Rosha. In addition, it was found that Capt. (Later Lt. Gen.) B.S. Takhar, was the adjutant and third Sanawarian in 17 Horse (Poona) during the 1971 war, along with Brigadier Amarjit Singh Bal, MVC and 2/Lt. Arun Khetarpal, PVC, whose story was told in the first publication. The current known figures for Sanawarians in Basantar stand revised to ten, and the author looks forward to finding more alumni who served.

**Sagat Shaunik**

Nilagiri 2009 | 2007–2009
Senior Consultant – Deloitte | Military History Researcher and Published Author

OS Parents – Father – Gautam Shaunik | Himalaya 1979 | 1975–1979

**Sources and Acknowledgements:**

- *Fauji India: The United Voice of Veterans and Sainiks*, Vol. 2(9), 2016, pp. 60–63.
- *Untold Battlefield Tales*, Fauji Foundation of India, 2019, pp. 181–189.